A PEOPLE & A NATION

A HISTORY OF THE UNITED STATES

Third Edition

Volume II: Since 1865

Mary Beth Norton
Cornell University

David M. Katzman
University of Kansas

Paul D. Escott
Wake Forest University

Howard P. Chudacoff
Brown University

Thomas G. Paterson
University of Connecticut

William M. Tuttle, Jr.
University of Kansas

HOUGHTON MIFFLIN COMPANY   BOSTON
Dallas   Geneva, Illinois   Palo Alto   Princeton, New Jersey

Mary Beth Norton

Now the Mary Donlon Alger Professor of American History at Cornell University, Mary Beth Norton was born in Ann Arbor, Michigan. She received her B.A. from the University of Michigan (1964) and her Ph.D. from Harvard University (1969). Her dissertation won the Allan Nevins Prize the following year. She has written *The British Americans* (1972) and *Liberty's Daughters* (1980), and she has edited *To Toil the Livelong Day: America's Women at Work, 1790–1980* (with Carol Groneman, 1987), *Women of America* (with Carol Berkin, 1979) and *Major Problems in American Women's History* (1989). Her many articles have appeared in such journals as the *William and Mary Quarterly, Signs,* and the *American Historical Review*. Mary Beth has served on the National Council on the Humanities, and she has been president of the Berkshire Conference of Women Historians and Vice President for Research of the American Historical Association. She has advised many colleges on curriculum development in the areas of women's history and gender studies. She is also one of the organizers of the new International Federation for Research in Women's History. Her scholarship has received assistance from the Shelby Cullom Davis Center, Charles Warren Center, National Endowment for the Humanities, American Antiquarian Society, and Rockefeller Foundation. Siena College, Marymount Manhattan College, and DePauw University have recognized her with honorary degrees.

David M. Katzman

Born in New York City and a graduate of Queens College (B.A., 1963) and the University of Michigan (Ph.D., 1969), David M. Katzman is now a professor of history at the University of Kansas. Known for his work in labor, black, and social history, David has written *Before the Ghetto: Black Detroit in the Nineteenth Century* (1973) and *Seven Days a Week: Women and Domestic Service in Industrializing America* (1978), which won the Philip Taft Labor History Prize. With William M. Tuttle, Jr., he has edited *Plain Folk* (1981). He has contributed to *Three Generations in Twentieth-Century America: Family, Community, and the Nation* (2nd edition, 1981), has written articles for the *Dictionary of American Biography,* and has served as associate editor and editor of *American Studies*. The Guggenheim Foundation, National Endowment for the Humanities, and Ford Foundation have awarded him research assistance. He has been Visiting Professor of Modern History at University College, Dublin, Ireland, and Visiting Professor of Economic and Social History, University of Birmingham, England. David has served as an elected member on the Professional Committee of the American Historical Association. His many activities also include the regional selection panel for the Harry S. Truman Scholarships. At the University of Kansas he has been Director of the Honors Program.

Paul D. Escott

Born and raised in the Midwest (St. Louis, Missouri), Paul D. Escott studied in New England and the South. His interest in southern history and the Civil War/Reconstruction era probably began with southern parents, but it became conscious at Harvard College (B.A., 1969) and matured at Duke University (Ph.D., 1974). Now a professor of history at Wake Forest University, Paul taught for many years at the University of North Carolina, Charlotte. He has written *After Secession: Jefferson Davis and the Failure of Confederate Nationalism* (1978), *Slavery Remembered: A Record of Twentieth-Century Slave Narratives* (1979), *Many Excellent People: Power and Privilege in North Carolina, 1850–1900* (1985), and *Land of the South* (1989, with James Clay, Douglass Orr, and Alfred Stuart). Fellowships from the Rockefeller Foundation, American Philosophical Society, and Whitney M. Young, Jr., Memorial Foundation have aided his research and writing. He has co-edited *Race, Class, and Politics in Southern History* (1989, with Jeffrey J. Crow and Charles L. Flynn, Jr.), and has also collaborated with David Goldfield on two edited works: *Major Problems in the History of the American South* (1990) and *The South for Non-Southerners* (1990). Paul's articles have appeared in *Civil War History* and *Journal of Southern History,* among many others. He has also contributed to Robert W. Twyman and David C. Roller, eds., *The Encyclopedia of Southern History* (1980) and W. Buck Yearns, ed., *The Governors of the Confederacy* (1984).

Howard P. Chudacoff

A professor of history at Brown University, Howard P. Chudacoff was born in Omaha, Nebraska, and earned his degrees from the University of Chicago (A.B., 1965; Ph.D., 1969). Howard has written *Mobile Americans: Residential and Social Mobility in Omaha, 1880–1920* (1972), *The Evolution of American Urban Society* (3rd edition, 1987, with Judith Smith), and *How Old Are You? Age Consciousness in American Culture* (1989). The National Endowment for the Humanities, Ford Foundation, and Rockefeller Foundation have assisted his research. His many articles on topics in urban and social history have appeared in such journals as the *Journal of Family History, Reviews in American History,* and *Journal of American History.* He contributed "Success and Security: The Meaning of Social Mobility in America" to Stanley I. Kutler and Stanley N. Katz, eds., *The Promise of American History* (1982). In this country and in Europe Howard has lectured on many subjects, among them the American family and social mobility. At Brown University, where he has taught since 1970, Howard has co-chaired the American Civilization Program, served on the executive boards of both the Urban Studies Program and the Population Studies and Training Center, and chaired the department of history.

Thomas G. Paterson

Born in Oregon City, Oregon, and graduated from the University of New Hampshire (B.A., 1963) and the University of California, Berkeley (Ph.D., 1968), Thomas G. Paterson is now professor of history at the University of Connecticut. He has written *Meeting the Communist Threat* (1988), *On Every Front* (1979), *Soviet-American Confrontation* (1973), and *American Foreign Policy* (3rd edition, 1988, with J. Garry Clifford and Kenneth J. Hagan). Tom has edited and contributed to *Kennedy's Quest for Victory* (1989) and *Major Problems in American Foreign Policy* (3rd edition, 1989). His many articles have appeared in such journals as the *American Historical Review, Journal of American History,* and *Diplomatic History.* He has served on the editorial boards of the latter two journals. The National Endowment for the Humanities and Institute for the Study of World Politics, among others, have assisted his research and writing. He has been president of the Society for Historians of American Foreign Relations, has directed National Endowment for the Humanities Summer Seminars for College Teachers, and has been a member of the Board of Trustees of Stonehill College. Active in the profession, he has served on committees of the Organization of American Historians and the American Historical Association. Tom has lectured widely in the United States on history of foreign relations topics, as well as in the Soviet Union, Puerto Rico, China, Canada, and New Zealand.

William M. Tuttle, Jr.

A native of Detroit, Michigan, William M. Tuttle, Jr., received his B.A. from Denison University (1959) and his Ph.D. from the University of Wisconsin (1967) before becoming a professor of history at the University of Kansas. Bill has written the award-winning *Race Riot: Chicago in the Red Summer of 1919* (1970) and has edited *W.E.B. Du Bois* (1973) and *Plain Folk* (1982, with David Katzman). His many articles have appeared in such journals as the *Journal of American History, Agricultural History, Journal of Negro History, American Studies, Labor History,* and *Technology and Culture.* His scholarly work has been assisted by the American Council of Learned Societies, Institute of Southern History at Johns Hopkins University, Charles Warren Center at Harvard University, Guggenheim Foundation, and Stanford Humanities Center. From 1986 to 1989 he held a grant from the National Endowment for the Humanities to study the importance of the Second World War in the lives of America's home-front children. As a historical consultant, Bill has helped prepare several public television documentaries and docudramas, including *The Killing Floor,* which appeared on PBS's "American Playhouse." Bill was elected to the Nominating Board of the Organization of American Historians. He has also been active in local politics, having served as a party precinct committeeman for the past ten years.

About the Cover

Disc with Horses (jack-knife carving) by Bernard Schmitz, Sr., 1981. Red Lake Falls, Minnesota. Balsa wood, painted pine, and leather. Courtesy: University of Minnesota Art Museum, Minneapolis, Minnesota, from the exhibition, *Circles of Tradition: Folk Arts in Minnesota*. Photo: Eric Mortenson.

Cover photograph researched by Rose Corbett Gordon/Corbett Gordon Associates.

Text photographs researched by Pembroke Herbert/Picture Research Consultants.

Photo on page 620: Frances B. Johnston, "Physics. The Screw as applied to the cheese press," plate from an album of Hampton Institute. 1899–1900. Platinum print, 7½ × 9½″. Collection, The Museum of Modern Art, New York. Gift of Lincoln Kirstein.

Printed in the U.S.A.

Library of Congress Catalog Card Number: 89-080952
ISBN: 0-395-43309-6
  BCDEFGHIJ-VH-9543210

Brief Contents

Contents

23 ▶ AMERICA AT WAR, 1914–1920   663

24 ▶ THE NEW ERA OF THE 1920s   695

25 ▶ THE GREAT DEPRESSION AND THE NEW DEAL, 1929–1941   727

Maps and Charts

Preface

In preparing for the third edition, the authors of *A People and a Nation* met in Boston with Houghton Mifflin editors and art researchers. In several sessions we re-evaluated and discussed every aspect of the book—themes, organization, emphases, coverage, interpretation, scholarship, writing style, and illustrations. In these planning meetings, we analyzed many instructors' reports and profited from their advice. Our goals for this edition were to improve the organization of the book, delineate themes even more sharply, clarify specific passages, and incorporate the best of recent scholarship. Our basic approach to American history as the story of all the people remains the same, and in the third edition we have preserved and strengthened those characteristics of the second edition that students and faculty have found so attractive.

As teachers and students we are always recreating our past, restructuring our memory, rediscovering the personalities and events that have shaped us, inspired us, and bedeviled us. This book is our rediscovery of America's past—its people and the nation they founded and have sustained. This history is sometimes comforting, sometimes disturbing. As with our own personal experiences, it is both triumphant and tragic, filled with injury as well as healing. As a mirror on our lives, it is necessarily revealing—blemishes and all. As memory, it is the way we identify ourselves.

We draw on recent research, authoritative works, and our own teaching experience to offer a comprehensive book that tells the whole story of American history. Politics, government, diplomacy, wars, and economic patterns have been at the core of writing on American history for generations. Into this traditional fabric we weave social history in order to discuss both the public and private spheres of Americans. We investigate the everyday life of the American people, that of the majority of Americans—women—and that of minorities. We explore the many ways Americans have identified and still identify themselves: gender, race, class, ethnicity,

▶ **Characteristics of the Book**

religion, work, sexual preference, geographic region, politics.

From the ordinary to the exceptional—the factory worker, the slave, the office secretary, the local merchant, the small farmer, the plantation owner, the ward politician, the president's wife, the film celebrity, the scientist, the army general—Americans have personal stories that have intersected with the public policies of their governments. Whether victors or victims, all have been actors in their own right, with feelings, ideas, and aspirations that have fortified them in good times and bad. All are part of the American story; all speak in *A People and a Nation* through excerpts from letters, diaries, oral histories, and other historical materials that we have integrated into this narrative history.

Several questions guided us in this third edition. On the official, or public, side of American history, we emphasize Americans' expectations of their governments and the practices of those local, state, and federal institutions. We look not only at politics but also at the culture of politics. We identify the mood and mentality of an era, searching for what Americans thought about themselves and their public officials. In our discussion of foreign relations, we ask why negotiations failed to prevent wars, why the United States became an expansionist, interventionist, global power, and how the domestic setting influenced diplomacy and vice versa.

▶ **Major Themes**

In the social and economic areas, we emphasize patterns of change in the population, geographic and social mobility, and people's adaptation to new environments. We study the often friction-ridden interactions of people of different color, social class, national origin, religious affiliation, sectional identity, and gender, and the efforts made, often in reform movements, to reduce tensions. As well, we focus on the effects of technological development on the economy, the worker and the workplace, and lifestyles.

In the private, everyday life of the family and the home, we pay particular attention to gender roles, childbearing and childrearing, and diet and dress. We ask how Americans have entertained themselves, as participants or spectators, through sports, music, the graphic arts, reading, theater, film, radio, and television. Throughout American history, of course, this private sphere of American life and public policy have interacted and influenced one another.

Students and instructors have commended the book for its discussion of these many topics in clear, concrete language, and they have commented on how enjoyable the book is to read. We have appreciated hearing, too, that we challenged them to think about the meaning of American history, not just to memorize it; to confront one's own interpretations and at the same time to respect the views of others; and to show how the historian's mind works to ask questions and to tease conclusions out of vast amounts of information. We especially welcome these responses because they tell us that we have met our goal: to convey the excitement and fascination we feel as teacher-scholars in recreating and understanding the past.

For this third edition, literally hundreds of changes—major and minor—have been made throughout the book. Among the major changes, the third edition is one chapter

▌**Changes in the Third Edition** shorter than the second edition as a result of the merger of two chapters that covered the Hoover and Roosevelt periods. Now the Great

Depression and the New Deal are presented in one chapter, 1929–1941. In addition, half of the stories that open chapters are new, and throughout we have provided new examples to illustrate themes.

A number of other revisions deserve special mention. Mary Beth Norton, who had primary responsibility for Chapters 1–7, has introduced new material on the Spanish and French colonies and on the soldiers who fought in colonial wars and the American Revolution. She has also revised the discussion of African migration and slavery and of early political parties. David M. Katzman, who had primary responsibility for Chapters 8–9 and 11–12, has expanded the coverage of the War of 1812, agriculture's adjustment to a market-oriented economy, city and country life, public disorder, Indian removal, abolitionism, and Jacksonian politics. He has reworked the discussion of reform to link it more closely to social and economic changes, religion, and politics. He has also introduced new ma-

terial on how people experienced the market economy, public space, the growing gender divisions in work, asylums, single women, and Hispanics in Texas and California. Paul D. Escott, who had primary responsibilty for Chapters 10 and 13–15, has expanded the treatment of the spread of market relations among southern yeomen and the influence of slavery on national life and, in the chapter on Reconstruction, of black activism in the South, splits among Republicans in Congress, and Supreme Court cases.

Howard P. Chudacoff, who had primary responsibility for Chapters 16–21 and 24, has added new material on Indians and the cultural conflict between their subsistence societies and the market-oriented economy; post–Civil War land policy; child labor; eating habits; and women's history. He has expanded the discussion of immigration and family life, urban reform, the new consumer society, and the origins of feminism. Chapter 20 especially has been reworked to develop the theme of inclusion versus exclusion in politics. Thomas G. Paterson, who had primary responsibility for Chapters 22–23, 26, 29, and 31, and the foreign relations parts of 33 and 34, has sharpened the discussion of expansionism and imperialism and expanded the treatment of the origins of the First World War in Europe and the clash of "systems" before the Second World War. He has added new material on the everyday lives of soldiers, Eisenhower's domestic policies and views on race relations, and the grassroots nature of the civil rights movement. He has also reworked treatment of the world economy, termination policy toward Indians, and the Vietnam War—protest, lessons, and veterans. Paterson served as the coordinating author for *A People and a Nation* and also prepared the Appendix.

William M. Tuttle, Jr., who had primary responsibility for Chapters 25, 27–28, 30, and 32–34, has combined coverage of the Great Depression and the New Deal into one chapter. He has expanded discussion of the Second World War experience of soldiers, McCarthyism, women in higher education, the baby boom, and the 1970s economy. He also reworked treatment of the War on Poverty, the 1968 election, and the fragmentation of the Democratic party. New material on Asian-Americans appears in Chapter 33, and the foreign policy of Jimmy Carter has been relocated there. Finally, Chapter 34 on the Reagan years and the beginnings of the Bush administration has been thoroughly revised; besides carrying the story to the end of the 1980s, the last chapter includes new discussion of Reagan's popularity, AIDS, the Iran-contra scandal, feminization of poverty, and drugs.

We have also revised the "Important Events" lists and moved them toward the front of each chapter. The end-of-chapter bibliographies have been revised to reflect recent scholarship. The Appendix now includes the Articles of Confederation as well as updated information. New illustrations—many of them in color—have been introduced, and new maps have been added and other maps revised.

To make the book as useful as possible for students and instructors, several learning and teaching aids are available, including a *Study Guide* and *MicroGuide* (a computerized study guide), an *Instructor's Manual,* a *Test Items* file, *Diploma III* (test generator and class management software), and *Map Transparencies.* The *Study Guide,* which was prepared by George Warren and Cynthia Ricketson of Central Piedmont Community College, includes an introductory chapter on study techniques for history students, learning objectives and a thematic guide for each chapter in the text, exercises on evaluating and using information and on finding the main idea in passages from the text, map exercises where appropriate, new sections on organizing information for some chapters, and test questions (multiple choice and essay) on the content of each chapter. An answer key tells students not only which response is correct but also why each of the other choices is wrong. The *Study Guide* is available as *MicroGuide,* a computerized, tutorial version that also gives students feedback on incorrect as well as correct answers.

The *Instructor's Manual* contains chapter outlines, suggestions for lectures and discussion, and lists of audio-visual resources. The *Test Items* file, also by Professor Warren, offers more than 1,500 new multiple-choice and essay questions and more than 700 identification terms. The test items are available to adopters for IBM and Macintosh computers. In addition, there is a set of 93 full-color *Map Transparencies* available on adoption.

Study and Teaching Aids

Acknowledgments

Many instructors have read and criticized the several drafts of our manuscript. Their suggestions have made this a better book. We heartily thank:

John K. Alexander, *University of Cincinnati*
Sara Alpern, *Texas A & M University*
Dee Andrews, *California State University, Hayward*
Robert Asher, *University of Connecticut*
Edward L. Ayers, *University of Virginia*
Len Bailes, *El Paso Community College*
Delmar L. Beene, *Glendale Community College*
Michael Bellesiles, *Emory University*
Sidney R. Bland, *James Madison University*
Frederick J. Blue, *Youngstown State University*
Bill Cecil-Fronsman, *Washburn University*
William F. Cheek, *San Diego State University*
Michael S. Coray, *University of Nevada, Reno*
Donald T. Critchlow, *University of Notre Dame*
Bruce Dierenfield, *Canisius College*
Charles E. Dickson, *Clark State Community College*
Richard W. Etulain, *University of New Mexico*
Owen E. Farley, Jr., *Pensacola Junior College*
Lacy K. Ford, Jr., *University of South Carolina*
Donald E. Green, *Central State University*
L. Ray Gunn, *University of Utah*
Joseph M. Hawes, *Memphis State University*
Gary R. Hess, *Bowling Green State University*
Joseph P. Hobbs, *North Carolina State University*
Alan M. Kraut, *American University*
Monroe H. Little, Jr., *Indiana University, Purdue University at Indianapolis*
Cathy Matson, *University of Tennessee, Knoxville*
Michael N. McConnell, *University of Alabama, Birmingham*
Melissa L. Meyer, *University of Minnesota*
J. Bruce Nelson, *Dartmouth College*
Allan B. Spetter, *Wright State University*
Kathleen Xidis, *Johnson County Community College*
Charles A. Zappia, *San Diego Mesa College*

We also thank the following for their contributions to this third edition: Daniel H. Usner, Jr., Sharyn Brooks Katzman, Theodore A. Wilson, Eric Foner, Phillip Paludan, Nancy Fisher Chudacoff, Elizabeth Mahan, Ellen C. Garber, Kathryn N. Kretschmer, Samuel Watkins Tuttle, David Thelen, and Ronald Schlundt. We owe our special thanks to the many people at Houghton Mifflin who always set high standards, gave this book excellent guidance and care, and have become our friends.

Thomas G. Paterson

Saturday, May 16, was a beautiful spring day in 1868. Sunlight and balmy weather bathed the nation's capital, but few people paused to relax or enjoy their surroundings. Washington was tense with excitement. Professional gamblers had flooded into the city, outnumbered perhaps only by the reporters who leaped upon every rumor or scrap of information. As the morning passed, a crowd gathered around the Senate chamber. Foreign dignitaries filled the diplomatic box, and spectators packed the Senate galleries. Outside the chamber thousands milled about, choking the hallways and spilling onto the terraces and streets.

15

RECONSTRUCTION BY TRIAL AND ERROR, 1865–1877

Precisely at noon the chief justice of the United States entered the Senate. Managers and counsel stood ready. Soon two senators who were seriously ill slowly made their way into the chamber, bringing the number of senators present to the full complement of fifty-four. All principals in this solemn drama were present before the High Court of Impeachment except the accused: Andrew Johnson, president of the United States. Johnson, who never appeared to defend himself in person, waited anxiously at the White House as Chief Justice Salmon Chase ordered the calling of the roll. To each senator he put the questions, "How say you? Is the respondent, Andrew Johnson, President of the United States, guilty or not guilty of a high misdemeanor, as charged in this article?" Thirty-five senators answered, "Guilty"; nineteen, "Not guilty." The thirty-five votes for conviction were one short of the required two-thirds majority. The United States had come within one vote of removing the president from office.

How had this extraordinary event come about? What had brought the executive and legislative branches of government into such severe conflict? An unprecedented problem—the reconstruction of the Union—furnished the occasion; deepening differences over the proper policy to pursue had led to the confrontation. By 1868 president and Congress had reached a point of bitter antagonism; some congressmen were charging that the president was siding with traitors.

In 1865, at the end of the war, such an event seemed most unlikely. Although he was a southerner from Tennessee, Johnson had built his career upon criticizing the wealthy planters and championing the South's small farmers. When an assassin's

The Shackle Broken by the Genius of Freedom (detail of Hon. Robert B. Elliott of South Carolina delivering his great speech on civil rights in the House of Representatives, January 6, 1874). Color lithograph published by E. Sachs & Company, Baltimore, 1874. *Chicago Historical Society.*

bullet thrust him into the presidency, many former slaveowners shared the worries of a North Carolina lady who wrote, "Think of Andy Johnson [as] the president! What will become of us—'the aristocrats of the South' as we are termed?" Northern Radicals who sounded out the new president on his views also felt confident that he would deal sternly with the South. When one of them suggested the exile or execution of ten or twelve leading rebels to set an example, Johnson had vigorously replied, "How are you going to pick out so small a number? Robbery is a crime; rape is a crime; *treason* is a crime; and *crime* must be punished."

Moreover, fundamental change was already under way in the South. During his army's last campaign, General William T. Sherman had issued Special Field Order No. 15, which set aside for Negro settlement the Sea Islands and all abandoned coastal lands thirty miles to the interior, from Charleston to the Saint John's River in northern Florida. Black refugees quickly poured into these lands; by the middle of 1865, forty thousand freed people were living in their new homes. One former slaveowner who visited his old plantation in Beaufort, South Carolina, received friendly and courteous treatment, but his ex-slaves "firmly and respectfully" informed him that "we own this land now. Put it out of your head that it will ever be yours again."

Before the end of 1865, however, these signs of change were reversed. Although Jefferson Davis was imprisoned for two years, no Confederate leaders were executed, and southern aristocrats soon came to view Andrew Johnson not as their enemy but as their friend and protector. Johnson pardoned rebel leaders liberally, allowed them to take high offices, and ordered government officials to reclaim the freedmen's land and give it back to the original owners. One man in South Carolina expressed blacks' dismay: "Why do you take away our lands? You take them from us who have always been true, always true to the Government! You give them to our all-time enemies! That is not right!"

The unexpected outcome of Johnson's program led Congress to examine his policies and design new plans for Reconstruction. Out of negotiations in Congress and clashes between the president and the legislators, there emerged first one, and then two, new plans for Reconstruction. Before the process was over, the nation had adopted the Fourteenth and Fifteenth Amendments and impeached its president.

Racism did not disappear. During the war the federal government had been reluctant to give even black troops fair treatment, and in Congress northern Democrats continued to oppose equality. Republicans were often divided among themselves, but a mixture of idealism and party purposes drove them forward. Ultimately, fear of losing the peace proved decisive with northern voters. The United State enfranchised the freedmen and gave them a role in reconstructing the South.

Blacks benefited from greater control over their personal lives and took the risks of voting and participating in politics. But they knew that the success of Reconstruction also depended on the determination and support of the North. Southern opposition to Reconstruction grew steadily. By 1869 a secret terrorist organization known as the Ku Klux Klan had added large-scale violence to southern whites' repertoire of resistance. Despite federal efforts to protect them, black people were intimidated at the polls, robbed of their earnings, beaten, or murdered. Prosecution of Klansmen rarely succeeded, and Republicans lost their offices in an increasing number of southern states. By the early 1870s the failure of Reconstruction was apparent. Republican leaders and northern voters had to decide how far they would persist in their efforts to reform the South.

As the 1870s advanced, other issues drew attention away from Reconstruction. Industrial growth accelerated, creating new opportunities and raising new problems. Interest in territorial expansion revived. Political corruption became a nationwide scandal and bribery a way of doing business. North Carolina's Jonathan Worth, an old-line Whig who had opposed secession as strongly as he now fought Reconstruction, deplored the atmosphere of greed. "Money has become the God of this country," he wrote in disgust, "and men, otherwise good men, are almost compelled to worship at her shrine." Eventually these other forces triumphed; politics moved on to new concerns; and the courts turned their attention away from civil rights. Even northern Republicans gave up on racial reforms in 1877.

Thus the nation stumbled, by trial and error, toward a policy that attempted to reconstruct the South. Congress insisted on equality before the law for black people and gave black men the right to vote. It took the unprecedented step of impeaching the president. But more far-reaching measures to advance black freedom never had much support in

Chapter 15: Reconstruction by Trial and Error, 1865–1877

1865	Johnson begins Reconstruction
	Confederate leaders regain power
	Black codes
	Congress refuses to seat southern
	    representatives
	Thirteenth Amendment ratified
		1871	Enforcement Act of 1871
			Ku Klux Klan Act
			Treaty with England settles
			    Alabama claims

1866	Civil Rights Act
	Congress approves Fourteenth
	    Amendment
	Freedmen's Bureau renewed
	Most southern states reject
	    Fourteenth Amendment
	Ex parte Milligan
		1872	Amnesty Act
			Liberal Republicans organize
			Debtors urge government to keep
			    greenbacks in circulation
			Grant re-elected

1867	Military Reconstruction Act;
	    Tenure of Office Act
	Purchase of Alaska
	Constitutional conventions called
	    in southern states
		1873	*Slaughter-House* cases
			Panic of 1873

		1874	Grant vetoes increase in paper money Democrats win House

1868	House impeaches Johnson; Senate
	    acquits him
	Most southern states readmitted
	Fourteenth Amendment ratified
	Ulysses S. Grant elected president
		1875	Several Grant appointees indicted
			    for corruption
			Civil Rights Act
			Congress requires that after 1878
			    greenbacks be convertible into
			    gold

1869	Congress approves Fifteenth Amendment (ratified in 1870)	**1876**	*U.S.* v. *Cruikshank; U.S.* v. *Reese* Presidential election disputed
1870	Enforcement Act	**1877**	Congress elects Hayes Black Exodusters migrate to Kansas

Congress, and when suffrage alone proved insufficient to remake the South, the nation soon lost interest. Reconstruction proclaimed anew the American principle of human equality but failed to secure it in reality.

Equality: The Unresolved Issue

For America's former slaves, Reconstruction had one paramount meaning: a chance to explore freedom. A southern white woman admitted in her diary that the black people "showed a natural and exultant joy at being free." Former slaves remembered rejoicing and singing far into the night after federal troops reached their plantations. The slaves on one Texas plantation jumped up and down and clapped their hands as one man shouted, "We is free—no more whippings and beatings."

A few blacks gave in to the natural desire to do what had been impossible before. One grandmother who had long resented her treatment "dropped her hoe" and ran to confront the mistress. "I'm free!" she yelled at her. "Yes, I'm free! Ain't got to work for you no more! You can't put me in your pocket [sell me] now!" Another man recalled that he and others "started on the move" and

Equality: The Unresolved Issue

To escape the plantation and seek new opportunities, many blacks migrated to southern cities. In Jacksonville, Florida, some found work on the docks. *Library of Congress.*

left the plantation, either to search for family members or oftentimes just to exercise their new-found freedom of movement. As he traveled, one man sang about being free as a frog, " 'cause a frog had freedom to get on a log and jump off when he pleases."

Most freedmen reacted more cautiously and shrewdly, taking care to test the boundaries of their new condition. "After the war was over," explained one man, "we was afraid to move. Just like tarpins or turtles after emancipation. Just stick our heads out to see how the land lay." As slaves they had learned to expect hostility from white people, and they did not presume it would instantly disappear. Life in freedom, they knew, might still be a matter of what was allowed, not what was right. "You got to say master?" asked a freedman in Georgia. "Naw," answered his fellows, but "they said it all the same. They said it for a long time."

One sign of this shrewd caution was the way freedmen evaluated potential employers. "Most all the niggers that had good owners stayed with 'em, but the others left. Some of 'em come back and some didn't," explained one man. If a white person

had been relatively considerate to blacks in bondage, blacks reasoned that he might prove a desirable employer in freedom. Other blacks left their plantation all at once, for, as one put it, "that master am sure mean and if we doesn't have to stay we shouldn't, not with that master."

In addition to a fair employer, the freedmen wanted opportunity through education and especially through land of their own. Land represented

Blacks' Desire for Land

their chance to farm for themselves, to have an independent life. It represented compensation for their generations of travail in bondage. A northern observer noted that freedmen made "plain, straight-forward" inquiries as they settled the land set aside for them by Sherman. They wanted to be sure the land "would be theirs after they had improved it." Not just in the Sea Island region but everywhere, blacks young and old thirsted for homes of their own. One white southerner noted with surprise in her diary that

Uncle Lewis, the pious, the honored, the venerated, gets his poor old head turned with false notions of freedom and independence, runs off to the Yankees with a pack of lies against his mistress, and sets up a claim to part of her land!

Lewis simply wanted a new beginning. Like other freedmen, he hoped to leave slavery behind.

No one could say how much of a chance the whites, who were in power, would give to blacks. During the war the federal government had refused at first to arm black volunteers. Many whites agreed with Corporal Felix Brannigan of the Seventy-fourth New York Regiment. "We don't want to fight side and side with the nigger," he said. "We think we are a too superior race for that." In September 1862, Abraham Lincoln said, "If we were to arm [the Negroes], I fear that in a few weeks the arms would be in the hands of the rebels."

Necessity forced a change in policy; because the war was going badly, the administration authorized black enlistments. By spring 1863, black troops were proving their value. One general reported that his "colored regiments" possessed "remarkable aptitude for military training," and another observer said, "They fight like fiends." Lincoln came to see "the colored population" as "the great *available* and yet *unavailed of* force for restoring the Union," and recruitment proceeded rapidly.

Black leaders hoped that military service would secure equal rights for their people. Once the black soldier had fought for the Union, wrote Frederick Douglass, "there is no power on earth which can deny that he has earned the right of citizenship in the United States." If black soldiers turned the tide, asked another man, "Would the nation refuse us our rights . . . ? Would it refuse us our vote?"

Wartime experience seemed to prove that it would. Despite their valor, black soldiers faced persistent discrimination. In Ohio, for example, a mob shouting "Kill the nigger" attacked an off-duty soldier; on duty, blacks did most of the "fatigue duty," or heavy labor. Moreover, black soldiers were expected to accept inferior pay as they risked their lives. The government paid white privates $13 per month plus a clothing allowance of $3.50. Black troops earned $10 per month less $3 deducted for clothing. Blacks resented this injustice so deeply that in protest two regiments refused to accept any pay, and eventually Congress remedied the discrimination. Still, that was only a small victory over prejudice.

The general attitude of northerners on racial questions was mixed. Abolitionists and many Re-publicans helped black Americans fight for equal rights, and they won some victories. In 1864 the federal courts accepted black testimony, and New York City desegregated its streetcars. The District of Columbia did the same in 1865, the year the Thirteenth Amendment won ratification. One state, Massachusetts, enacted a comprehensive public accommodations law. Nevertheless, there were many signs of resistance to racial equality. The Democratic party fought hard against equality, charging that Republicans favored race-mixing and were undermining the status of the white worker. Voters in three states—Connecticut, Minnesota, and Wisconsin—rejected black suffrage in 1865.

The fact that the racial attitudes of northerners seemed mixed and uncertain was significant, for the history of emancipation in the British Caribbean indicated that, if equality were to be won, the North would have to take a strong and determined stand. In 1833 Great Britain had abolished slavery in its possessions, providing slaveowners with £20 million in compensation and requiring all former agricultural slaves to work the land for six more years as apprentices. Despite such generosity to the slaveowners, the transition to free labor had not been easy.

Everywhere in the British Caribbean planters fought tenaciously to maintain control over their laborers. Retaining control of local government, the planters fashioned laws, taxes, and administrative decisions with an eye to keeping freedmen on the plantations. With equal determination, the former slaves attempted to move onto small plots of land and raise food crops instead of sugar. They wanted independence and were not interested in raising export crops for the world market. The British, even abolitionists, however, judged the success of emancipation by the volume of production for the market. Their concern for the freedmen soon faded, and before long the authorities assisted planters further by allowing the importation of indentured "coolie" labor from India.

In the United States, some of the same tendencies had appeared on the Sea Islands long before the war ended. The planters had fled and therefore were not present to try to control their former slaves. The freedmen, however, showed a strong desire to leave the plantations and establish small, self-sufficient farms of their own. Northern soldiers, officials, and missionaries of both races brought education and aid to the freedmen but also wanted them to grow cotton. They disapproved of charity and emphasized the values of competitive capitalism. "The danger to the Negro," wrote one worker in the Sea Islands, was "too high wages." Indeed it would be "most unwise and injurious," declared another worker, to give former slaves free land.

"The Yankees preach nothing but cotton, cotton!" complained one Sea Island black. "We wants land," wrote another, "this very land that is rich with the sweat of we face and the blood of we back." Asking only for a chance to buy land, this man complained that "they make the lots too big, and cut we out." Indeed, the government did sell thousands of acres in the Sea Islands for nonpayment of taxes, but 90 percent of the land went to wealthy investors from the North. Even after blacks pooled their earnings, they were able to buy less than 2,000 of the 16,749 acres sold in March 1863. Thus even from their northern supporters, the former slaves had received only partial support. How much opportunity would freedom bring? That was a major question to be answered during Reconstruction, and the answer depended on the evolution of policy in Washington.

Johnson's Reconstruction Plan

Through 1865 the formation of Reconstruction policy rested solely with Andrew Johnson, for shortly before he became president Congress recessed and did not reconvene until December. In the nearly eight months that intervened, Johnson devised his own plan and put it into operation. He decided to form new state governments in the South by using his power to grant pardons.

Johnson had a few precedents to follow in Lincoln's wartime plans for Reconstruction. In December 1863 Lincoln had proposed a "10-percent" plan for a government being organized in captured portions of Louisiana. According **Lincoln's Reconstruction Plan** to this plan, a state government could be established as soon as 10 percent of those who had voted in

1860 took an oath of future loyalty. Only high-ranking Confederate officials would be denied a chance to take the oath, and Lincoln urged that at least a few well-qualified blacks be given the ballot. Radicals bristled, however, at such a mild plan, and a majority of Congress (in the Wade-Davis bill, which Lincoln pocket-vetoed) favored stiffer requirements and stronger proof of loyalty.

Later, in 1865, Lincoln suggested but then abandoned more lenient terms. At Hampton Roads, where he raised questions about the extent of emancipation (see page 418), Lincoln discussed compensation and restoration to the Union, with full rights, of the very state governments that had tried to leave it. Then in April he considered allowing the Virginia legislature to convene in order to withdraw its support from the Confederate war effort. Faced with strong opposition in his cabinet, however, Lincoln reversed himself, denying that he had intended to confer legitimacy on a rebel government. At the time of his death, Lincoln had given general approval to a plan drafted by Secretary of War Stanton that would have imposed military authority and the appointment of provisional governors as steps toward the creation of new state governments. Beyond these general outlines, it is impossible to say what Lincoln would have done had he survived.

Johnson began with the plan Stanton had drafted for consideration by the cabinet. At a cabinet meeting on May 9, 1865, Johnson's advisers split evenly on the question of voting rights for freedmen in the South. Johnson said that he favored black suffrage, but only if the southern states adopted it voluntarily. A champion of states' rights, he regarded this decision as too important to be taken out of the hands of the states.

Such conservatism had an enduring effect on Johnson's policies, but at first it appeared that his old enmity toward the planters might produce a plan for radical changes in class relations among whites. As he appointed provisional governors in the South, Johnson also proposed rules that would keep the wealthy planter class out of power. He required every southern voter to swear an oath of loyalty as a condition of gaining amnesty or pardon. Some southern whites, however, would face special difficulties in regaining their rights.

Johnson barred certain classes of southerners from taking the oath and gaining amnesty. Former federal officials who had violated their oaths to support the United States and had aided the Confederacy could not take the oath. Nor could graduates of West Point or Annapolis who had resigned their commissions to fight for the South. The same was true for high-ranking Confederate officers and Confederate political leaders. To this list Johnson added another important group: all southerners who aided the rebellion and whose taxable property was worth more than $20,000. Such individuals had to apply personally to the president for pardon and restoration of political rights; otherwise, they risked legal penalties, which included confiscation of their land.

Thus it appeared that the leadership class of the Old South would be removed from power, for virtually all the rich and powerful whites of prewar days needed Johnson's special pardon. Many observers in both South and North sensed that the president meant to take his revenge on the haughty aristocrats whom he had always denounced and to raise up a new leadership of deserving yeomen.

Johnson's provisional governors began the Reconstruction process by calling constitutional conventions. The delegates chosen for these conventions had to draft new constitutions eliminating slavery and invalidating secession. After ratification of these constitutions, new governments could be elected, and the states would be restored to the Union with full congressional representation. But no southerners could participate in this process who had not taken the oath of amnesty or who had been ineligible to vote on the day the state seceded. Thus freedmen could not participate in the conventions. It was theoretically possible for the white delegates to enfranchise them, but unlikely.

If Johnson intended to end the power of the old elite, his plan did not work out as he hoped. The old white leadership proved resilient and influential; prominent Confederates (a few with pardons, but many without) won elections and turned up in various appointive offices. Then, surprisingly, Johnson helped to subvert his own plan. He started pardoning aristocrats and chief rebels, who should not have been in office. By the fall of 1865 the clerks at the pardon office were straining under the burden, and additional staff had to be hired to churn out the necessary documents. These pardons, plus the return of planters' abandoned lands, put the old elite back in power.

Combative and inflexible, President Andrew Johnson contributed greatly to the failure of his own reconstruction program. *Brady photograph, National Portrait Gallery, Smithsonian Institution, Washington, D.C.*

Why did Johnson issue so many pardons? Perhaps vanity betrayed his judgment. Scores of gentlemen of the type who had previously scorned him now waited on him for an appointment. Too long a lonely outsider, Johnson may have succumbed to the attention and flattery of the pardon seekers. Whether he did or not, he clearly had allowed himself too little time. It took months for the constitution making and elections to run their course; by the time the process was complete and Confederate leaders had emerged in powerful positions, the reconvening of Congress was near. Johnson faced a choice between admitting failure and scrapping his entire effort or swallowing hard and supporting what had resulted. The choice was not difficult for someone who believed in white supremacy and wanted southern support in the next election. Johnson decided to stand behind his new governments and declare Reconstruction completed. Thus in December 1865 many Confederate congressmen traveled to Washington to claim seats in the United States Congress, and Alexander Stephens, vice president of the Confederacy, returned to the capital as senator-elect.

Many northerners frowned on the election of such prominent rebels, and other results of Johnson's program also sparked negative comment in the North. Some of the state conventions were slow to repudiate secession; others only grudgingly admitted that slavery was dead. Two refused to take any action to repudiate the large Confederate debt. Even Johnson admitted that these acts showed "something like defiance, which is all out of place at this time." Furthermore, to define the status of freedmen, some legislatures merely revised large sections of the slave codes by substituting the word *freedmen* for *slave,* and new laws written from scratch were also very restrictive. According to the new black codes, former slaves who were supposed to be free were compelled to carry passes, observe a curfew, live in housing provided by a landowner, and give up hope of entering many desirable occupations. Stiff vagrancy laws and restrictive labor contracts bound supposedly free laborers to the plantation, and "anti-enticement" laws punished anyone who tried to lure these workers to other employment. Finally, observers noted that the practice in state-supported institutions, such as schools and orphanages, was to exclude blacks altogether. It seemed to northerners that the South was intent on returning black people to a position of servility.

Black Codes

Thus it was not surprising that a majority of northern congressmen decided to take a close look at the results of Johnson's plan. On reconvening, they voted not to admit the newly elected southern representatives, whose credentials were subject under the Constitution to congressional scrutiny. The House and Senate established an important joint committee to examine Johnson's policies and advise on new ones. Reconstruction entered a second phase, one in which Congress would play a strong role.

The Congressional Reconstruction Plan

Northern congressmen disagreed on what to do, but they did not doubt their right to play a role in Reconstruction. The Constitution mentioned neither secession nor reunion, but it did assign a great many major responsibilities to Congress. Among them was the injunction to guarantee to each state a republican government. Under this provision, the legislators thought, they could devise policies for Reconstruction, just as Johnson had used his power to pardon for the same purpose.

They soon found that other constitutional questions had a direct bearing on the policies they followed. What, for example, had rebellion done to the relationship between southern states and the Union? Lincoln had always insisted that the Union remained unbroken, but not even Andrew Johnson accepted the southern view that the wartime state governments of the South could merely re-enter the nation. Johnson argued that the Union had endured, though individuals had erred—thus the use of his power to grant or withhold pardons. In contrast, congressmen who favored vigorous Reconstruction measures tended to argue that war *had* broken the Union. The southern states had committed legal suicide and reverted to the status of territories, they argued, or the South was a conquered nation subject to the victor's will. Moderate congressmen held that the states had forfeited their rights through rebellion and had thus come under congressional supervision.

These diverse theories mirrored the diversity of Congress itself. Northern legislators fell into four major categories: Democrats, conservative Republicans, moderate Republicans, and other Republicans called Radicals. No one of these groups had decisive power. In terms of ideology the majority of congressmen were conservative. In terms of partisan politics the Republican party had a majority; but there was considerable distance between conservative Republicans, who desired a limited federal role in Reconstruction and were fairly happy with Johnson's actions, and the Radicals. The Radicals, led by Thaddeus Stevens, Charles Sumner, and George Julian, were a minority within their party, but they had the advantage of a clearly defined goal. They believed that it was essential to democratize the South, establish public education, and ensure the rights of freedmen. They favored black suffrage, often supported land confiscation and redistribution, and were willing to exclude the South from the Union for several years if necessary to achieve their goals. Between the conservative Republicans and the Radicals lay the moderates, who held the balance of power.

The Radicals

One overwhelming political reality faced all the groups in Congress: the 1866 elections were approaching in the fall. Since Congress had questioned Johnson's program, its members had to develop some modification or alternative program before the elections. The northern public expected the legislators to develop a new Reconstruction plan, and as politicians they knew better than to go before their constituents empty-handed. Thus they had to forge a majority coalition composed either of Democrats and Republicans or of various elements of the Republican party. The kind of coalition that formed would determine the kind of plan that Congress developed.

Ironically, Johnson and the Democrats eliminated the possibility of a conservative coalition. The president and the Democrats in Congress refused to cooperate with conservative or moderate Republicans. They insisted, despite evidence of widespread northern concern, that Reconstruction was over, that the new state governments were legitimate, and that southern representatives should be admitted to Congress. These unrealistic, intransigent positions threw away the Democrats' potential influence and blasted any possibility of bipartisan compromise. Republicans found themselves all lumped together by Democrats; to form a new program, conservative Republicans had to work with the Radicals. Thus bargaining over changes in the Johnson program went on almost entirely within the Republican party. This development and subsequent events enhanced the influence of the Radicals. In 1865, however, Republican congressmen were reluctant to break with the president; he was, for better or worse, the titular head of their party, so they made one last effort to work with him.

Early in 1866 many lawmakers thought a compromise had been reached. Under its terms Johnson would agree to two modifications of his program. Under one bill the life **Congress** of the Freedmen's Bureau, which **Struggles** Congress established in March **for a** 1865 to feed the hungry, negotiate **Compromise** labor contracts, and start schools, would be extended; second, a civil rights bill would be passed to counteract the black codes. This bill, drawn up by a conservative Republican, was designed to force southern courts to practice equality before the law by giving federal judges the power to move cases in which blacks were treated unfairly from state courts into federal courts. Its provisions applied to discrimination by private persons as well as by government officials. As the first major bill to enforce the Thirteenth Amendment's abolition of slavery, it was a significant piece of legislation, and it became very important in the twentieth century (see page 944).

But in spring 1866, Johnson destroyed the compromise by vetoing both bills (they were later repassed). Denouncing any change in his program, the president condemned Congress's action. In inflammatory language he questioned the legitimacy of congressional involvement in policymaking and revealed his own racism. Because the civil rights bill defined United States citizens as native-born persons who were taxed, Johnson pronounced it discriminatory toward "large numbers of intelligent, worthy, and patriotic foreigners . . . in favor of the negro." The bill, he said, would "operate in favor of the colored and against the white race."

All hope of working with the president was now gone. But Republican congressmen sensed that their constituents remained dissatisfied with the results of Reconstruction. Newspapers reported the daily violations of blacks' rights in the South and carried troubling accounts of anti-black violence—notably in Memphis and New Orleans, where police aided brutal riots against black citizens. Such violence convinced Republicans, and the northern public, that more needed to be done. The Republican lawmakers therefore pushed on, and from bargaining among their various factions there emerged a plan. It took the form of a proposed amendment to the Constitution—the fourteenth—and it represented a compromise between radical and conservative elements of the party. The Fourteenth Amendment was Congress's alternative to Johnson's program of Reconstruction.

Of four points in the amendment, there was nearly universal agreement on one: the Confederate debt was declared null and void, the war debt of the United States guaranteed. **Fourteenth** Northerners uniformly rejected **Amendment** the notion of paying taxes to reimburse those who had financed a rebellion, and business groups agreed on the necessity of upholding the credit of the United States government. There was also fairly general support for altering the personnel of southern governments. In language that harkened back to Johnson's proclamations on amnesty or pardon, the Fourteenth Amendment prohibited political power

Police joined rioters in New Orleans to shoot down and kill thirty-four blacks and three white Republicans. At this time President Johnson was insisting that Reconstruction was over. *The Historic New Orleans Collection.*

for prominent Confederates. Only at the discretion of Congress, by a two-thirds vote of each house, could these political penalties be removed.

The section of the Fourteenth Amendment that would have by far the greatest legal significance in later years was the first (see the Appendix). On its face, this section was an effort to strike down the black codes and guarantee basic rights to freedmen. It conferred citizenship on freedmen and prohibited states from abridging their constitutional "privileges and immunities." Similarly, the amendment barred any state from taking a person's life, liberty, or property "without due process of law" and from denying "equal protection of the laws." These clauses were phrased broadly enough to become powerful guarantees in the twentieth century of black Americans' civil rights—indeed, of the rights of all citizens. They also took on added meaning with court rulings that corporations were legally "persons" (see page 504).

The second section of the amendment, which dealt with representation, revealed the compromises and political motives that had produced the document. Northerners, in Congress and out, disagreed about whether black citizens should have the right to vote. Commenting on the ambivalence of northern opinion, a citizen of Indiana wrote that there was strong feeling in favor of "humane and liberal laws for the government and protection of the colored population." But he admitted to a southern relative that there was prejudice, too. "Although there is a great deal [of] profession among us for the relief of the darkey yet I think much of it is far from being cincere. I guess we want to compell you to do right by them while we are not willing ourselves to do so."

Republican congressmen shied away from confronting this ambivalence, but political reality required them to do something. Under the Constitution, representation was based on population. During slavery each black slave had counted as three-fifths of a person for purposes of congressional representation. Republicans feared that emancipation, which made every former slave five-fifths of a person, might increase the South's power in Congress. If it did, and if blacks were not allowed to vote, the former secessionists would gain seats in Congress.

What a strange result that would seem to most northerners. They had never planned to reward the South for rebellion, and Republicans in Congress were determined not to hand over power to their political enemies. So they offered the South a choice. According to the second section of the Fourteenth Amendment, states did not have to give black men the right to vote. But if they did not do so, their representation would be reduced proportionally (this clause has never been invoked, despite the clear intent of the amendment). If they did enfranchise black men, their representation would be increased proportionally—but Republicans would be able to appeal to the new black voters. This compromise protected northern interests and gave Republicans a chance to compete if freedmen gained the ballot.

The Fourteenth Amendment dealt with the voting rights of black men but ignored female citizens, black and white. For this reason it provoked a strong reaction from the women's rights movement. Advocates of equal rights for women had worked with abolitionists for decades, often subordinating their cause to that of the slaves. During the drafting of the Fourteenth Amendment, however, female activists demanded to be heard. When legislators defined them as nonvoting citizens, prominent women's leaders such as Elizabeth Cady

Chapter 15: Reconstruction by Trial and Error, 1865–1877

Stanton and Susan B. Anthony decided that it was time to end their alliance with abolitionists. Thus the independent women's rights movement grew.

In 1866, however, the major question in Reconstruction politics was how the public would respond to the amendment. Would the northern public support Congress's plan or the president's? Johnson did his best to block the Fourteenth Amendment and to convince northerners to reject it. Condemning Congress for its refusal to seat southern representatives, the president urged state legislatures in the South to vote against ratification. Every southern legislature except Tennessee's rejected the amendment by a large margin. It did best in Alabama, where it failed by a vote of 69 to 8 in the assembly and 27 to 2 in the senate. In three states the amendment received no support at all.

Southern Rejection of the Fourteenth Amendment

To present his case to northerners, Johnson arranged a National Union convention to publicize his program. The chief executive also took to the stump himself. In an age when active personal campaigning was rare for a president, Johnson boarded a special train for a "swing around the circle" that carried his message far into the Midwest and then back to Washington. In cities such as Cleveland and St. Louis, Johnson criticized the Republicans in a ranting, undignified style. But increasingly audiences rejected his views and hooted and jeered at him.

The election of 1866 was a resounding victory for Republicans in Congress. Men whom Johnson had denounced won re-election by large margins, and the Republican majority increased as some new candidates defeated incumbent Democrats. Everywhere Radical and moderate Republicans gained strength. The section of the country that had won the war had spoken clearly: Johnson's policies, people feared, were giving the advantage to rebels and traitors. Thus Republican congressional leaders received a mandate to continue with their Reconstruction plan.

But, thanks largely to Johnson, that plan had reached an impasse. All but one of the southern governments created by the president had turned their backs on the Fourteenth Amendment, determined to resist. Nothing could be accomplished as long as those governments existed and as long as the southern electorate was constituted as it was. The newly elected northern Republicans were not going to ignore their constituents' wishes and surrender to the South. To break the deadlock, Republicans had little choice but to form new governments in the South and enfranchise the freedmen. They therefore decided to do both. The unavoidable logic of the situation had forced the majority toward the Radical plan.

The Radicals hoped Congress would do much more. Thaddeus Stevens, for example, argued that economic opportunity was essential to the freedmen. "If we do not furnish them with homesteads from forfeited and rebel property, and hedge them around with protective laws; if we leave them to the legislation of their late masters, we had better left them in bondage," Stevens declared. To provide that opportunity, Stevens drew up a plan for extensive confiscation and redistribution of land. Significantly, only one-tenth of the land affected by his plan was earmarked for freedmen, in 40-acre plots. All the rest was to be sold to generate money for veterans' pensions, compensation to loyal citizens for damaged property, and payment of the federal debt. By these means Stevens hoped to win support for a basically unpopular measure. But he failed, and in general the Radicals were not able to command the support of the majority of the public. Northerners of that era were accustomed to a limited role for government, and the business community staunchly opposed any interference in private property.

As a result, the Military Reconstruction Act that was passed in 1867 incorporated only a small part of the Radical program. The act called for new governments in the South and a return to military authority until they were set up. It barred from political office the Confederate leaders listed in the Fourteenth Amendment. It guaranteed freedmen the right to vote in elections for state constitutional conventions and for subsequent state governments. In addition, each southern state was required to ratify the Fourteenth Amendment; to ratify its new constitution; and to submit its new constitution to Congress for approval. Thus black people gained an opportunity to fight for a better life through the political process, but the only weapon put into their hands was the ballot. The law required no redistribution of land and guaranteed no basic changes in southern social structure. It also permitted an early return to the Union.

Military Reconstruction Act of 1867

The confrontation between Congress and Andrew Johnson culminated in the president's impeachment. Here the Senate conducts his trial, which ended in acquittal by a margin of one vote. *Library of Congress; colored by Karla Cinquanta.*

Congress's role as the architect of Reconstruction was not quite over, for its quarrels with Andrew Johnson grew more bitter. To restrict Johnson's influence and safeguard its plan, Congress passed a number of controversial laws. First it set the date for its own reconvening—an unprecedented act, for the president traditionally summoned the legislature to Washington. Then it limited Johnson's power over the army by requiring the president to issue military orders through the General of the Army, Ulysses S. Grant, who could not be sent from Washington without the Senate's consent. Finally, Congress passed the Tenure of Office Act, which gave the Senate power to interfere with changes in the president's cabinet. Designed to protect Secretary of War Stanton, who sympathized with the Radicals, this law violated the tradition that a president controlled his own cabinet.

Johnson took several belligerent steps of his own. He issued orders to military commanders in the South limiting their powers and increasing the powers of the civil governments he had created in 1865. Then he removed any officers who conscientiously enforced Congress's new law, preferring commanders who allowed disqualified Confederates to vote. Finally, in August 1867 he tried to remove Secretary of War Stanton. With that attempt the confrontation reached its climax.

Twice before, the House Judiciary Committee had considered impeachment, rejecting the idea once and then recommending it by only a 5-to-4 vote. The recommendation had been decisively defeated by the House. After Johnson's last action, however, a third attempt to impeach the president carried easily.

Impeachment of President Johnson

In 1868, the angry House was so determined to indict Johnson that it voted before drawing up specific charges. The indictment concentrated on Johnson's violation of the Tenure of Office Act, though modern scholars regard his systematic efforts to impede enforcement of the Military Reconstruction Act as a far more serious offense.

Johnson's trial in the Senate lasted more than three months. The prosecution, led by such Radicals as Thaddeus Stevens and Benjamin Butler, argued that Johnson was guilty of "high crimes and misdemeanors." But they also advanced the novel idea that impeachment was a political matter, not a judicial trial of guilt or innocence. The Senate ultimately rejected such reasoning, which would have

Chapter 15: Reconstruction by Trial and Error, 1865–1877

This lithograph celebrates the passage of the Fifteenth Amendment, which was important but fell short of an outright guarantee of the right to vote. *Library of Congress.*

transformed impeachment into a political weapon against any chief executive who disagreed with Congress. Although a majority of senators voted to convict Johnson, the prosecution fell one vote short of the necessary two-thirds majority. Johnson remained in office for the few months left in his term, and his acquittal established the precedent that only serious misdeeds merited removal from office.

In 1869, in an effort to write democratic principles and colorblindness into the Constitution, the Radicals succeeded in presenting the Fifteenth Amendment for ratification. This measure forbade states to deny the right to vote "on account of race, color, or previous condition of servitude." The wording fell short of an outright guarantee of the right to vote because many northern states denied the suffrage to women and certain groups of men—Chinese immigrants, illiterates, those too poor to pay taxes. Ironically, the votes of four uncooperative southern states—compelled by Congress to approve the amendment as an added

> **Fifteenth Amendment**

condition to rejoining the Union—proved necessary to impose even this language on parts of the North. Although several states outside the South refused to ratify, the Fifteenth Amendment became law in 1870.

Reconstruction Politics in the South

From the start, Reconstruction encountered the resistance of white southerners. Their opposition to change appeared in the black codes and other policies of the Johnson governments as well as in private attitudes. Many whites set their faces against emancipation, and—as was true in the British Caribbean—the former planter class proved especially unbending. In 1866 a Georgia newspaper frankly declared, "Most of the

> **White Resistance**

Thomas Nast, in this 1868 cartoon, pictured the combination of forces—southern opposition and northern racism and indifference—that threatened the success of Reconstruction. *Library of Congress.*

used guardianship and apprentice laws to bind black families to the plantation.

Whites also blocked blacks from acquiring land. A few planters divided up plots among their slaves, but most condemned the idea of making blacks landowners. One planter in South Carolina refused to sell as little as an acre and a half to each family. Even a Georgian whose family was known for its concern for the slaves was outraged that two property owners planned to "rent their lands to the Negroes!" Such action was "injurious to the best interest of the community." The son of a free black landowner in Virginia who sold nearly two hundred acres to former slaves explained, "White folks wasn't lettin' Negroes have nothing." These realities severely limited for blacks the rewards of a supposedly free labor system.

Adamant resistance by propertied whites soon manifested itself in other ways, including violence. In one North Carolina town a local magistrate clubbed a black man on a public street, and bands of "Regulators" terrorized blacks in parts of that state and Kentucky. Such incidents were predictable in a society in which many planters believed, as a South Carolinian put it, that blacks "can't be governed except with the whip."

After President Johnson encouraged the South to resist congressional Reconstruction, many white conservatives worked hard to capture the new state governments. Elsewhere, large numbers of whites boycotted the polls in an attempt to defeat Congress's plans. Since the new constitutions had to be approved by a majority of registered voters, registered whites could defeat them by sitting out the elections. This tactic was tried in North Carolina and succeeded in Alabama, forcing Congress to base ratification on a majority of those voting.

Very few black men stayed away from the polls. Enthusiastically and hopefully they seized the opportunity to participate in politics, voting solidly Republican. Most agreed with one man who felt that he should "stick to the end with the party that freed me." Illiteracy did not prohibit blacks (or uneducated whites) from making intelligent choices. Although William Henry could read only "a little," he testified that he and his friends had no difficulty selecting the Republican ballot. "We stood around and watched," he explained. "We saw D. Sledge vote; he owned half the country. We knowed he voted Democratic so we voted the other ticket so it would be Republican."

white citizens believe that the institution of slavery was right, and . . . they will believe that the condition, which comes nearest to slavery, that can now be established will be the best." Unwillingness to accept black freedom would have been a major problem in any circumstances; Andrew Johnson's encouragement of southern whites actively to resist Congress only intensified the problem.

Fearing the end of their control over slaves, some planters attempted to postpone freedom by denying or misrepresenting events. Former slaves reported that their owners "didn't tell them it was freedom" or "wouldn't let [them] go." Agents of the Freedmen's Bureau agreed. One agent in Georgia concluded, "I find the old system of slavery working with even more rigor than formerly at a few miles distant from any point where U.S. troops are stationed." To hold onto their workers some landowners claimed control over black children and

Zeal for voting spread through the entire black community. Women, who could not vote, encouraged their husbands and sons, and preachers exhorted their congregations to use the franchise. Such community spirit helped to counter white pressure tactics, and the freedmen's enthusiasm showed their hunger for equal rights.

With a large black turnout, and with prominent Confederates barred from politics under the Fourteenth Amendment, a new southern Republican party came to power in the constitutional conventions. Among Republican delegates were some blacks (265 out of the total of just over 1,000 delegates throughout the South), northerners who had moved to the South, and native southern whites who favored change. Together these Republicans brought the South's fundamental law into line with progressive reforms that had been adopted in the rest of the nation. The new constitutions were more democratic. They eliminated property qualifications for voting and holding office, and they made elective state and local offices that had been appointive. They provided for public schools and institutions to care for the mentally ill, the blind, the deaf, the destitute, and the orphaned, and they ended imprisonment for debt and barbarous punishments such as branding.

The conventions also broadened women's rights in possession of property and divorce. Usually, the main goal was not to make women equal with men but to provide relief to thousands of suffering debtors. In families left poverty-stricken by the war and weighed down by debt, the husband had usually contracted the debts. Thus, giving women legal control over their own property provided some protection to their families. There were some delegates, however, whose goal was to elevate women. Blacks in particular called for laws to provide for women's suffrage, but they were ignored by their white colleagues.

Under these new constitutions the southern states elected new governments. Again the Republican party triumphed, bringing new men into positions of power. The ranks of state legislators in 1868 included some black southerners for the first time in history. Congress's second plan for Reconstruction was well under way. It remained to be seen what these new governments would do and how much change they would bring to society.

> **Triumph of Republican Governments**

There was one possibility of radical change through these new governments. That possibility depended on the disfranchisement of substantial numbers of Confederate leaders. If the Republican regimes used their new power to exclude many whites from politics as punishment for rebellion, they would have a solid electoral majority based on black voters and their white allies. Land reform and the assurance of racial equality would be possible. But none of the Republican governments did this, or even gave it serious consideration.

Why did the new legislators shut the door on the possibility of deep and thoroughgoing reform? First, they appreciated the realities of power and the depth of racial enmity. In most states whites were the majority of the population, and former slaveowners controlled the best land and other sources of economic power. James Lynch, a leading black politician from Mississippi, candidly explained why Negroes shunned "the folly of" disfranchisement. Unlike northerners who "can leave when it becomes too uncomfortable," former slaves "must be in friendly relations with the great body of the whites in the state. Otherwise . . . peace can be maintained only by a standing army." Despised and lacking in economic or social power, southern Republicans saw mere acceptance and legitimacy as ambitious goals.

Second, blacks believed in the principle of universal suffrage and the Christian goal of reconciliation. Far from being vindictive toward the race that had enslaved them, they treated leading rebels with generosity and appealed to white southerners to adopt a spirit of fairness and cooperation. Henry McNeil Turner, like other Negro ministers, urged black Georgians to "love whites . . . soon their prejudice would melt away, and with God for our father, we will all be brothers." (Years later Turner criticized his own naiveté, saying that in the constitutional convention his motto had been "Anything to please the white folks.") Therefore southern Republicans quickly (in some cases immediately) restored the voting rights of former Confederates, as Congress steadily released more individuals from the penalties of the Fourteenth Amendment.

Thus the South's Republican party committed itself to a strategy of winning white support. To put the matter another way, the Republican party condemned itself to defeat if white voters would not cooperate. In just a few years Republicans were reduced to the embarrassment of making futile appeals to whites while ignoring the claims of their strongest supporters, blacks.

But for a time both Republicans and their opponents, who called themselves Conservatives or Democrats, moved to the center and appealed for support from a broad range of groups. Some propertied whites accepted congressional Reconstruction as a reality and declared that they would try to compete under the new rules. As these Democrats angled for some black votes, Republicans sought to attract more white voters. Both parties found an area of agreement in economic policies.

The Reconstruction governments devoted themselves to stimulating industry. This policy reflected northern ideals, but it also sprang from a growing southern interest in industrialization. Confederates had learned how vital industry was, and many postwar southerners were eager to build up the manufacturing capacity of their region. Accordingly, Reconstruction legislatures designed many tempting inducements to investment. Loans, subsidies, and exemptions from taxation for periods up to ten years helped to bring new industries into the region. The southern railroad system was rebuilt and expanded, coal and iron mining laid the basis for Birmingham's steel plants, and the number of manufacturing establishments nearly doubled between 1860 and 1880. This emphasis on big business interests, however, produced higher state debts and taxes, took money from schools and other programs, and multiplied possibilities for corruption. It also locked Republicans into a conservative strategy. They were appealing to elite whites who never responded, and the alternate possibility of making a strong, class-based appeal to poorer whites was lost.

▶ **Industrial-ization**

Policies appealing to black voters never went beyond equality before the law. In fact, the whites who controlled the southern Republican party were reluctant to allow blacks a share of offices proportionate to their electoral strength. Black leaders, aware of their weakness, did not push for revolutionary economic or social change. In every southern state blacks led efforts to establish public schools, but most did not press for integrated facilities. Having a school to attend was the most important thing at the time, for the Johnson governments had excluded

▶ **Other Republican Policies**

blacks from schools and other state-supported institutions. As a result, virtually every public school organized during Reconstruction was racially segregated, and these separate schools established a precedent for segregation. By the 1870s segregation was becoming a common, but not universal, practice in theaters, trains, and other public accommodations in the South.

A few black politicians did fight for civil rights and integration. Most were mulattos from cities such as New Orleans or Mobile, where large populations of light-skinned free blacks had existed before the war. Their experience in such communities had made them sensitive to issues of status, and they spoke out for open and equal public accommodations. Laws requiring equal accommodations won passage throughout the Deep South, but they often went unenforced or required the injured party to bring legal action for enforcement.

Economic progress was uppermost in the minds of most freed people and black representatives from agricultural districts. Land, above all else, had the potential to benefit the former slave, but few black state legislators promoted confiscation. Some hoped that high taxes on large landowners would force portions of these estates onto the market (small farmers' lands were protected by homestead exemptions). And in fact, much land fell into state hands for nonpayment of taxes and was offered for sale in small lots. But most freedmen had too little cash to bid against investors or speculators, and few gained land in this way. South Carolina established a land commission, but its purpose was to assist in the purchase of land. Any widespread redistribution of land had to arise from Congress, which never supported such action.

Within a few years, as centrists in both parties met with failure, the other side of white reaction to congressional Reconstruction began to dominate. Some conservatives had always favored fierce opposition to Reconstruction through pressure and racist propaganda. They put economic and social pressure on blacks: one black Republican complained that "my neighbors will not employ me, nor sell me a farthing's worth of anything." Charging that the South had been turned over to ignorant blacks, conservatives deplored "black domination." The cry of "Negro rule" now became constant.

Such attacks were gross distortions. Blacks participated in politics but did not dominate or control events. They were a minority in eight out of ten

Chapter 15: Reconstruction by Trial and Error, 1865–1877

One notable success in Reconstruction efforts to stimulate industry was Birmingham, Alabama. Here workers cast iron into blocks called pigs. *Birmingham Public Library.*

state conventions (transplanted northerners were a minority in nine out of ten). Of the state legislatures, only in the lower house in South Carolina did blacks ever constitute a majority; generally their numbers among officials were far inferior to their proportion in the population. Sixteen blacks won seats in Congress before Reconstruction was over, but none was ever elected governor, and only eighteen served in a high state office such as lieutenant governor, treasurer, superintendent of education, or secretary of state. Freedmen were participating in government, to be sure, but there was no justification for racist denunciations of "Ethiopian minstrelsy, Ham radicalism in all its glory."

Conservatives also stepped up their propaganda against the allies of black Republicans. "Carpetbagger" was a derisive name for whites who had come

> **Carpet-baggers and Scalawags**

from the North. It suggested an evil and greedy northern politician, recently arrived with a carpetbag into which he planned to stuff ill-gotten gains before fleeing. The stranger's carpetbag, a popular travel bag whose frame was covered with heavy carpet material, was presumably deep enough to hold loot

stolen from southern treasuries and filched from hapless, trusting former slaves. Immigrants from the North, who held the largest share of Republican offices, were all tarred with this brush.

In fact most northerners who settled in the South had arrived before Congress gave blacks the right to vote. They had come seeking business opportunities or a warmer climate, and most never entered politics. Those who did generally wanted to democratize the South and to introduce northern ways, such as industry, public education, and the spirit of enterprise. Hard times and ostracism by white southerners made many of these men dependent on officeholding for a living, a fact that increased Republican factionalism and damaged the party. Although carpetbaggers supported black suffrage and educational opportunities, most opposed social equality and integration.

Conservatives invented the term "scalawag" to stigmatize and discredit any native white southerner who cooperated with the Republicans. A substantial number of southerners did so, including some wealthy and prominent men. Most scalawags, however, were representatives of the yeoman class, men from mountain areas and small farming districts—average white southerners who saw that

Reconstruction Politics in the South

Throughout the South, black people welcomed the opportunity to participate in democratic governments. Here a convention of blacks assembles in Washington, D.C., to discuss Reconstruction problems.

they could benefit from the education and opportunities promoted by Republicans. Banding together with freedmen, they pursued common class interests and hoped to make headway against the power of long-dominant planters. Cooperation even convinced a few scalawags that "there is but little if any difference in the talents of the two races" and that all should have "an equal start."

Yet this black-white coalition was usually vulnerable to the issue of race, and scalawags shied away from support for racial equality. Republican tax policies also cut into upcountry, yeoman support, because reliance on the property tax hit some small landholders hard. In addition, poll taxes (whose proceeds were often earmarked for education) endangered the independence of other small farmers, forcing them toward participation in the market in order to obtain cash.

Taxation was a major problem for the Reconstruction governments. Financially the Republicans, despite their achievements, were doomed to be unpopular. Republicans wanted to continue prewar services, repair war's destruction, stimulate industry, and support important new ventures such as public schools. But the Civil War had destroyed much of the South's tax base. One category of valuable property—slaves—was entirely gone. Hundreds of thousands of citizens had lost much of the rest of their real and personal property—money, livestock, fences, and buildings—to the war. Thus an increase in taxes was necessary even to maintain traditional services, and new ventures required even higher taxes. Eventually and inevitably, Republican tax policies aroused much opposition.

Corruption was another powerful charge levied against the Republicans. Unfortunately, it was true. Many carpetbaggers and black politicians sold their votes, taking part in what scholars recognize was a nationwide surge of corruption (see page 545). Although white Democrats often shared in the guilt, and despite the efforts of some Republicans to stop it, Democrats convinced many voters that scandal was the inevitable result of a foolish Reconstruction program based on blacks and carpetbaggers.

All these problems damaged the Republicans, but in many southern states the deathblow came through violence: the murders, whippings, and intimidation of terrorist groups who **Ku Klux** most often used the name Ku Klux **Klan** Klan. Terrorism against blacks occurred throughout Reconstruction, but after 1867 white violence became more

Chapter 15: Reconstruction by Trial and Error, 1865–1877

organized and purposeful. The Ku Klux Klan rode to frustrate Reconstruction and keep the freedmen in subjection. Nighttime visits, whippings, beatings, and murder became common, and in some areas virtually open warfare developed despite the authorities' efforts to keep the peace.

Although the Klan persecuted blacks who stood up for their rights as laborers or people, its main purpose was political. Lawless nightriders made active Republicans the target of their attacks. Prominent white Republicans and black leaders were killed in several states. After blacks who worked for a South Carolina scalawag started voting, terrorists visited the plantation and "whipped every nigger man they could lay their hands on." Klansmen also attacked Union League Clubs (Republican organizations that mobilized the black vote) and schoolteachers who were aiding the freedmen.

Klan violence was not spontaneous; certain social forces gave direction to racism. In North Carolina, for example, Alamance and Caswell counties were the sites of the worst Klan violence. They were in the Piedmont, where slim Republican majorities rested on cooperation between black voters and whites of the yeoman class, particularly yeomen whose Unionism or discontent with the Confederacy had turned them against local Democratic officials. Together these black and white Republicans had ousted officials long entrenched in power. But the Republican majority was a small one, and it would fail if either whites or blacks faltered in their support.

In Alamance and Caswell counties the wealthy and powerful men who had lost their accustomed political control organized a campaign of terror. They brought it into being and used it for their purposes. They were the secret organization's county officers and local chieftains; they recruited members and planned atrocities. They used the Klan to regain political power: by whipping up racism or frightening enough Republicans, the Ku Klux Klan could split the Republican coalition and restore a Democratic majority.

Klan violence injured Republicans across the South. No fewer than one-tenth of black leaders who had been delegates to the 1867–1868 constitutional conventions were attacked, seven fatally. In one judicial district of North Carolina the Ku Klux Klan was responsible for twelve murders, over seven hundred beatings, and other acts of violence including rape and arson. A single attack on Ala-

The Ku Klux Klan aimed to terrorize and intimidate its victims by violence and other methods. Mysterious regalia, such as the pointed hood (which was held up by a stick inside) contributed to a menacing atmosphere. The miniature coffin, typically left on a Republican's doorstep, conveyed a more direct threat. *KKK hood: Old Court House Museum, Vicksburg, Miss. Photo by Bob Pickett; KKK coffin: Collection of State Historical Museum, Mississippi Department of Archives and History. Photo by Gib Ford.*

bama Republicans at the town of Eutaw left four blacks dead and fifty-four wounded. In South Carolina five hundred masked Klansmen lynched eight black prisoners at the Union County jail, and nearby in York County the Klan committed "at least eleven murders and hundreds of whippings." According to historian Eric Foner, the Klan "made it virtually impossible for Republicans to campaign or

Reconstruction Politics in the South

vote in large parts of Georgia." Clearly, "violence had a profound effect on Reconstruction politics."

Thus a combination of difficult fiscal problems, Republican mistakes, racial hostility, and terror brought down the Republican regimes, and in most southern states so-called Radical Reconstruction was over after only a few years. The most lasting failure of Reconstruction governments, however, was not political; it was social. The new governments failed to alter the South's social structure or its distribution of wealth and power. Exploited as slaves, freedmen remained vulnerable to exploitation during Reconstruction. Without land of their own, they were dependent on white landowners, who could use their economic power to compromise blacks' political freedom. Armed only with the ballot, southern blacks had little chance to effect major changes.

> **Failure of Recon-struction**

To reform the southern social order, Congress would have had to redistribute land, but never did a majority of congressmen favor such a plan. Radical Republicans like Albion Tourgée condemned Congress's timidity. Turning the freedman out on his own without protection, said Tourgée, constituted "cheap philanthropy." Indeed, freedmen who had to live with the consequences of Reconstruction considered it a failure. The North should have "fixed some way for us," said former slaves, but instead it "threw all the Negroes on the world without any way of getting along."

Freedom had come, but blacks knew they "still had to depend on the southern white man for work, food, and clothing," and it was clear that most whites were hostile. Unless Congress exercised careful supervision over the South, the situation of the freedmen was sure to deteriorate. Whenever the North lost interest, Reconstruction would collapse.

The Social and Economic Meaning of Freedom

Black southerners entered upon life after slavery hopefully, determinedly, but not naively. They had too much experience with white people to assume that all would be easy. As one man in Texas advised his son, even before the war was over, "Our forever was going to be spent living among the Southerners, after they got licked." Expecting to meet with hostility, black people tried to gain as much as they could from their new circumstances. Often the most valued changes were personal ones—alterations in location, employer, or surroundings that could make an enormous difference to individuals or families.

One of the first decisions that many made was whether to leave the old plantation or remain. This meant making a judgment about where the chances of liberty and progress would be greatest. Former slaves drew upon their experiences in bondage to assess the whites with whom they had to deal. "Most all the Negroes that had good owners stayed with them," said one man, "but the others left." Not surprisingly, cruel slaveholders usually saw their former chattels walk off en masse. "And let me tell you," added one man who abandoned a harsh planter, "we sure cussed ole master out before we left there."

On new farms or old, the newly freed men and women reached out for valuable things in life that had been denied them. One of these was education. Whatever their age, blacks hungered for the knowledge in books that had been permitted only to whites. With freedom they started schools and filled classrooms both day and night. On "log seats" or "a dirt floor," many freedmen studied their letters in old almanacs, discarded dictionaries, or whatever was available. Young children brought infants to school with them, and adults attended at night or after "the crops were laid by." Many a teacher had "to make herself heard over three other classes reciting in concert" in a small room, but the scholars kept coming. The desire to escape slavery's ignorance was so great that many blacks paid tuition, typically $1.00 or $1.50 a month, despite their poverty. These seemingly small amounts constituted one-tenth of many people's agricultural wage and added up to more than $1 million by 1870.

> **Education for Blacks**

The federal government and northern reformers of both races assisted this search for education. In its brief life the Freedmen's Bureau founded over four thousand schools, and idealistic men and women from the North established others and staffed them ably. The Yankee schoolmarm—dedicated, selfless, and religious—became an

Chapter 15: Reconstruction by Trial and Error, 1865–1877

Freed from slavery, blacks of all ages filled the schools to seek the educations that had been denied to them in bondage. *William Gladstone Collection.*

agent of progress in many southern communities. Thus, with the aid of religious and charitable organizations throughout the North, blacks began the nation's first assault on the problems created by slavery. The results included the beginnings of a public school system in each southern state and the enrollment of over 600,000 blacks in elementary school by 1877.

Blacks and their white allies also realized that higher education was essential—colleges and universities to train teachers and equip ministers and professionals for leadership. The American Missionary Association founded seven colleges, including Fisk and Atlanta universities, between 1866 and 1869. The Freedmen's Bureau helped to establish Howard University in Washington, D.C., and northern religious groups such as Methodists, Baptists, and Congregationalists supported dozens of seminaries, colleges, and teachers' colleges. By the late 1870s black churches had joined in the effort, founding numerous colleges despite their smaller

financial resources. Although some of the new institutions did not survive, they brought knowledge to those who would educate others and laid a foundation for progress.

Even in Reconstruction, blacks were choosing many highly educated individuals as leaders. Many blacks who won public office during Reconstruction came from the prewar elite of free people of color. This group had benefited from its association with wealthy whites, who were often blood relatives. Some planters had given their mulatto children outstanding educations. Francis Cardozo, who served in South Carolina's constitutional convention and was later that state's secretary of the treasury and secretary of state, had attended universities in Scotland and England. P. B. S. Pinchback, who became lieutenant governor of Louisiana, was the son of a planter who had sent him to school in Cincinnati at age nine. The two black senators from Mississippi, Blanche K. Bruce and Hiram Revels, were both privileged in their educations. Bruce was the son of a planter who had provided tutoring on his plantation; Revels was the son of free North Carolina mulattos who had sent him to Knox College in Illinois. These men and many self-educated former slaves brought experience as artisans, businessmen, lawyers, teachers, and preachers to political office.

While elected officials wrestled with the political tasks of Reconstruction, millions of former slaves concentrated on improving life at home, on their farms, and in their neighborhoods. A major goal of black men and women was to gain some living space for themselves and their families. Surrounded by an unfriendly white population, they sought to insulate themselves from white interference and to strengthen the bonds of their own community. Throughout the South they devoted themselves to reuniting their families, moving away from the slave quarters, and founding black churches. Given the eventual failure of Reconstruction, the practical gains that blacks made in their daily lives often proved the most enduring.

The search for long-lost family members was awe inspiring. With only shreds of information to guide them, thousands of black people embarked on odysseys in search of a husband, wife, child, or parent. By relying on the black community for help and information, many succeeded in their quest, sometimes almost miraculously. Others walked through several states and never found loved ones.

Reunification of Black Families

Husbands and wives who had belonged to different masters established homes together for the first time, and parents asserted the right to raise their own children. Saying "You took her away from me and didn' pay no mind to my cryin', so now I'm takin' her back home," one mother reclaimed a child whom the mistress had been raising in her own house. Another woman bristled when her old master claimed a right to whip her children, promptly informing him that "he warn't goin' to brush none of her chilluns no more." One girl recalled that her mistress had struck her soon after freedom. As if to clarify the new ground rules, this girl "grabbed her leg and would have broke her neck." The freedmen were too much at risk to act recklessly, but as one man put it, they were tired of punishment, and "they sure didn't take no more foolishment off of white folks."

Many black people wanted to minimize all contact with whites. "There is a prejudice against us . . . that will take years to get over," Reverend Garrison Frazier told General Sherman in January 1865. To avoid contact with intrusive whites, who were used to supervising and controlling them, blacks abandoned the slave quarters and fanned out into distant corners of the land they worked. Some moved away to build new homes in the woods. "After the war my stepfather come," recalled Annie Young, "and got my mother and we moved out in the piney woods." Others described moving "across the creek to [themselves]" or building a "saplin house . . . back in the woods" or "'way off in the woods." Some rural dwellers established small all-black settlements that still can be found today along the backroads of the South.

Even once-privileged slaves shared this desire for independence and social separation. One man turned down the master's offer of the overseer's house as a residence and moved instead to a shack in "Freetown." He also declined to let the former owner grind his grain for free, because it "make him feel like a free man to pay for things just like anyone else." One couple, a carriage driver and trusted house servant during slavery, passed up the fine cooking of the "big house" so that they could move "in the colored settlement."

The other side of this movement away from whites was closer communion within the black community. Freed from the restrictions and regulations of slavery, blacks could build their own institutions as they saw fit. The secret church of slavery now came out into the open; in countless communities throughout the South, "some of the niggers started a brush arbor." A brush arbor was merely "a sort of . . . shelter with leaves for a roof," but the freedmen worshiped in it enthusiastically. "Preachin' and shouting sometimes lasted all day," ex-slaves recalled, for there were "glorious times then" when black people could worship together in freedom. Within a few years independent black branches of the Methodist and Baptist churches had attracted the great majority of black Christians in the South.

Founding of Black Churches

The desire to gain as much independence as possible carried over into the freedmen's economic arrangements. Since most former slaves lacked money to buy land, they preferred the next best thing—renting the land they worked. But many whites would not consider renting land to blacks; there was strong social pressure against it. Because few blacks had the means to rent a farm, other alternatives had to be tried.

Northerners and officials of the Freedmen's Bureau favored contracts between owners and laborers. To northerners who believed in "free soil, free labor, free men," contracts and wages seemed the key to progress. For a few years the Freedmen's Bureau helped to draw up and enforce such contracts, but they proved unpopular with both blacks and whites. Owners often filled the contracts with detailed requirements that reminded blacks of their circumscribed lives under slavery. Disputes frequently arose over efficiency, lost time, and other matters. Besides, cash was not readily available in the early years of Reconstruction; times were hard and the failure of Confederate banks had left the South with a shortage of credit facilities.

Black farmers and white landowners therefore turned to a system of sharecropping: black families worked for part of the crop while living on the landowner's property. The land-

Rise of the Share- cropping System

lord or a merchant "furnished" food and supplies needed before the harvest, and the sharecropper, landowner, and furnishing merchant all received payment from the crop. Republican laws gave laborers a first lien, or legal first claim, on the crop, increasing their feeling of ownership. Naturally, landowners tried to set the laborers' share at a low level, but blacks had some bargaining power. By holding out and refusing to make contracts at the end of the year, sharecroppers succeeded in lowering the owners' share to around one-half during Reconstruction.

The sharecropping system originated as a desirable compromise. It eased landowners' problems with cash and credit; blacks accepted it because it gave them a reasonable amount of freedom from daily supervision. Instead of working under a white overseer as in slavery, they were able to farm a plot of land on their own in family groups. Sharecropping later proved to be a disaster, both for blacks and for the South. Unscrupulous owners in a discriminatory society had many opportunities to cheat sharecroppers. Owners and merchants frequently paid less for blacks' cotton than they paid for whites'. Greedy men could overcharge or ma-

nipulate records so that the sharecropper always stayed in debt. The problem, however, was even more fundamental than that.

Southern farmers were concentrating on cotton, a crop with a bright past and a dim future. During the Civil War, India, Brazil, and Egypt had begun to

Overdepen- dence on Cotton

supply cotton to Britain, and not until 1878 did the South recover its prewar share of British cotton purchases. This temporary loss of markets reduced per capita income, as did a decline in the amount of labor invested by the average southern farmer. Part of the exploitation of slavery had been the sending of black women and children into the fields. In freedom these people like their white counterparts stayed at home when possible. Black families valued human dignity more highly than the levels of production that had been achieved under the lash.

But even as southerners grew more cotton, matching and eventually surpassing prewar totals, their reward diminished. Cotton prices began a long decline whose causes merely coincided with the Civil War. From 1820 to 1860 world demand for cotton had grown at a rate of 5 percent per year, but from 1866 to 1895 the rate of growth was only 1.3 percent per year. By 1860 the English textile industry, world leader in production, had penetrated all the major new markets, and from that point on increases in demand were slight. As a result, when southern farmers planted more cotton they tended to depress the price.

In these circumstances overspecialization in cotton was a mistake, but for most southern farmers there was no alternative. Landowners required sharecroppers to grow the prime cash crop, whose salability was sure. Because of the shortage of banks and credit in the South, white farmers often had to borrow from a local merchant, who insisted on cotton production to secure his loan. Thus southern agriculture slipped deeper and deeper into depression. Black sharecroppers struggled under a growing burden of debt that reduced their independence and bound them to landowners almost as oppressively as slavery had bound them to their masters. Many white farmers became debtors too and gradually lost their land. These were serious problems, but few people in the North were paying attention.

The Social and Economic Meaning of Freedom

The End of Reconstruction

The North's commitment to racial equality had never been total, and by the early 1870s it was evident that even the North's partial commitment was weakening. New issues were capturing people's attention, and soon voters began to look for reconciliation with southern whites. In the South, Democrats won control of one state after another, and they threatened to defeat Republicans in the North as well. Before long the situation had returned to "normal" in the eyes of southern whites.

The Supreme Court, after first re-establishing its power, participated in the northern retreat from Reconstruction. During the Civil War the Court had been cautious and reluctant to assert itself. Reaction to the *Dred Scott* decision had been so violent, and the Union's wartime emergency so great, that the Court had refrained from blocking or interfering with government actions. The justices, for example, had breathed a collective sigh of relief when legal technicalities prevented them from reviewing the case of Clement Vallandigham, who had been convicted of aiding the enemy by a military court when regular civil courts were open (see page 425).

But in 1866 a similar case, *Ex parte Milligan,* reached the Court through proper channels. Lambdin P. Milligan of Indiana had participated in a plot to free Confederate prisoners of war and overthrow state governments; for these acts a military court had sentenced Milligan, a civilian, to death. Milligan challenged the authority of the military tribunal, claiming that he had a right to a civil trial. In sweeping language the Supreme Court declared that military trials were illegal when civil courts were open and functioning, thus indicating that it intended to reassert itself as a major force in national affairs. This decision could have led to a direct clash with Congress, which in 1867 established military districts and military courts in the initial phase of its Reconstruction program. But Congress altered part of the Court's jurisdiction; it was constitutionally empowered to do so but had never taken such action before (and has not taken it since). By altering the Court's jurisdiction, Congress protected its Reconstruction policy and avoided a confrontation.

In the 1870s, interpretations by the Supreme Court drastically narrowed the meaning and effectiveness of the Fourteenth Amendment. In 1873 the

Supreme Court Decisions on Reconstruction

Court decided *Bradwell* v. *Illinois,* a case in which Myra Bradwell, a female attorney, had been denied the right to practice law in Illinois on account of her gender. Pointing to the Fourteenth Amendment, Bradwell's attorneys contended that the state had unconstitutionally abridged her "privileges and immunities" as a citizen. The Supreme Court rejected her claim, alluding to women's traditional role in the home.

The next day, in the *Slaughter-House* cases, the Court made its restrictive reading of the Fourteenth Amendment even more clear. The *Slaughter-House* cases had begun in 1869, when the Louisiana legislature granted one company a monopoly on the slaughtering of livestock in New Orleans. Rival butchers in the city promptly sued. Their attorney, former Supreme Court Justice John A. Campbell, pointed out that Louisiana had discriminated, violating the rights of some of its citizens to favor others. More fundamentally, Campbell argued that the Fourteenth Amendment had revolutionized the constitutional system by bringing individual rights under federal protection. Campbell thus expressed an original and central goal of the Republican party: to nationalize civil rights and guard them from state interference. Over the years his argument would win acceptance, offering shelter from government regulation to corporate "persons" in the nineteenth century and providing protection for blacks and other minorities in the twentieth.

But in the *Slaughter-House* decision, the Supreme Court dealt a stunning blow to the scope and vitality of the Fourteenth Amendment and to the hopes of blacks. Refusing to accept Campbell's argument, it interpreted the "privileges and immunities" of citizens so narrowly that it reduced them almost to trivialities. Although the Fourteenth Amendment clearly protected citizens' rights, the Court declared that state citizenship and national citizenship were separate. National citizenship involved only such things as the right to travel freely from state to state and to use the navigable waters of the nation, and only these narrow rights were protected by the Fourteenth Amendment. With this interpretation, the words "No state shall make or enforce any law which shall abridge the privileges or immunities of citizens of the United States" disappeared, for decades, as a meaningful or effective part of the Constitution.

The Supreme Court also concluded that the butchers who sued had not been deprived of their rights or property in violation of the "due process" clause of the amendment. Thus the justices dismissed Campbell's central contention: that the Fourteenth Amendment guaranteed the great basic rights of the Bill of Rights against state action. In so doing, the Court limited severely the amendment's potential for securing and protecting the rights of black citizens.

In 1876 the Court weakened the Reconstruction-era amendments even further by emasculating the enforcement clause of the Fourteenth Amendment and revealing deficiencies inherent in the Fifteenth Amendment. In *United States* v. *Cruikshank* the Court dealt with Louisiana whites who were indicted for attacking a meeting of blacks and conspiring to deprive them of their rights. The justices ruled that the Fourteenth Amendment did not empower the federal government to redress the misdeeds of private individuals against other citizens; only flagrant discrimination by the states was covered. In *United States* v. *Reese* the Court noted that the Fifteenth Amendment did not guarantee a citizen's right to vote but merely listed certain impermissible grounds for denying suffrage. Thus a path lay open for southern states to disfranchise blacks for supposedly nonracial reasons—lack of education, lack of property, or lack of descent from a grandfather qualified to vote before the Military Reconstruction Act. (So-called grandfather clauses became a way of including illiterate whites in the electorate yet excluding blacks, because the grandfathers of most blacks had been slaves before Reconstruction and unable to vote.)

The retreat from Reconstruction continued steadily in politics as well. In 1868 Ulysses S. Grant, running as a Republican, defeated Horatio Seymour, a Democrat of New York,

Election of 1868 in a presidential campaign that revived sectional divisions. Although he was not a Radical, Grant realized that Congress's program represented the wishes of northerners, and he supported a platform that praised congressional Reconstruction and endorsed Negro suffrage in the South. (The platform stopped short of endorsing black suffrage in the North.) The Democrats went in the opposite direction; their platform vigorously denounced Reconstruction. By associating themselves with rebellion and with Johnson's repudiated program, the Democrats went down to defeat in all but eight states, though the popular vote was fairly close.

In office Grant sometimes called out federal troops to stop violence or enforce acts of Congress, but only when he had to. He hoped to avoid confrontation with the South, to erase the image of dictatorship that his military background summoned up. In fact, neither he nor Johnson imposed anything approaching a military occupation on the South. Rapid demobilization reduced a federal army of more than 1 million to 57,000 within a year of the surrender at Appomattox. Thereafter the number of troops in the South continued to fall, until in 1874 there were only 4,082 in the southern states outside Texas. Throughout Reconstruction, the strongest federal units were in Texas and the West, fighting Indians, not white southerners.

In 1870 and 1871 the violent campaigns of the Ku Klux Klan moved Congress to pass two Enforcement Acts and an anti-Klan law. These laws, for the first time, made acts by *individuals* against the civil and political rights of others a federal offense. They permitted martial law and suspension of the writ of habeas corpus to combat murders, beatings, and threats by the Klan. Federal troops and prosecutors used them vigorously but with only partial success. Out of hundreds of indictments, a few dozen Klansmen were convicted, more confessed, and many others (roughly two thousand in South Carolina alone) fled their states to avoid prosecution. A conspiracy of silence frustrated some prosecutions: frightened witnesses were unwilling to testify and juries unwilling to convict. After the passage of anti-Klan legislation, the Klan disbanded officially and went underground. Paramilitary organizations known as Rifle Clubs and Red Shirts often took the Klan's place.

Klan terrorism tested Republicans' resolve to change things in the South in an especially clear-cut way. Yet even on this issue there were ominous signs that the North's commitment to racial justice was fading. Some conservative but influential Republicans opposed the anti-Klan laws, basing their opposition on the charge that the laws infringed on states' rights. It was striking that some Republicans were echoing an old and standard line of the Democrats. This opposition foreshadowed a more general revolt within Republican ranks in 1872.

Disenchanted with Reconstruction, in 1872 a group calling itself the Liberal Republicans bolted the party and nominated Horace Greeley, the well-

Liberal Republicans Revolt

known editor of the *New York Tribune,* for president. The Liberal Republicans were a varied group, including civil service reformers, foes of corruption, and advocates of a lower tariff. Normally such disparate elements would not cooperate with each other, but they were united by two popular, widespread attitudes: distaste for federal intervention in the South and a desire to let market forces and the "best men" determine events in the South. The Democrats also gave their nomination to Greeley in 1872. The combination was not enough to defeat Grant, but it reinforced his desire to avoid confrontation with white southerners. Grant continued to use troops sparingly and in 1875 refused a desperate request from the governor of Mississippi.

The Liberal Republican challenge reflected growing dissatisfaction with Grant's administration. Strong-willed but politically naive, Grant made a series of poor appointments. His secretary of war, his private secretary, and officials in the Treasury and Navy departments were all involved in bribery or tax-cheating scandals. Instead of exposing the corruption, Grant defended some of the culprits. As the clamor against dishonesty in government grew, Grant's popularity and his party's popularity declined. In the 1874 elections Democrats recaptured the House of Representatives.

Congress's resolve on southern issues weakened steadily. By joint resolution it had removed the political disabilities of the Fourteenth Amendment from many former Confederates.

Amnesty Act

In 1872 it adopted a sweeping Amnesty Act, which pardoned most of the remaining rebels and left only five hundred excluded from political participation. A Civil Rights Act passed in 1875 purported to guarantee black people equal accommodations in public places, such as inns and theaters, but it was weak and contained no effective provisions for enforcement. (The law was later struck down by the Supreme Court; see page 490.)

Democrats regained power in the South rather quickly, winning four states before 1872 and a total of eight by the start of 1876 (see map). As they did so, northern Republicans worried about their opponents' stress on the failure and scandals of Reconstruction governments. Many Republicans sensed that their constituents were tiring of the same old issues.

In fact, new concerns were catching the public's eye. Industrialization and immigration had surged forward, hastening the changes in national life. Only eight years after the war, industrial production had increased by an impressive 75 percent. For the first time, nonagricultural workers outnumbered farmers, and only Britain had a greater industrial output. Government financial policies had done much to bring this rapid growth about. Soon after the war Congress had shifted some of the government's tax revenues to pay off the interest-bearing war debt. The debt fell from $2.33 billion in 1866 to only $587 million in 1893, and every dollar repaid was a dollar injected into the economy for potential reinvestment. Thus approximately 1 percent of the gross national product was pumped back into the economy from 1866 to 1872 and only slightly less than that during the rest of the 1870s. Low taxes on investment and high tariffs on manufactured goods also aided industrialists. With such help the northern economy quickly recovered its prewar rate of growth.

In the same period 3 million new immigrants had entered the country, most of them joining the labor force of industrial cities in the North and West. As the number of immigrants began to rise again, there was a corresponding revival of ingrained suspicions and hostilities among native-born Americans. The Mormon question too—how Utah's growing Mormon community, which practiced polygamy, could be reconciled to American law—became prominent.

Then the Panic of 1873 occurred, which ushered in over five years of continuing economic contraction. The panic threw 3 million people out of work and focused attention on economic and monetary problems. The clash between labor and capital became the major issue of the day, and class attitudes diverged, especially in the larger cities. Debtors and the unemployed sought easy-money policies to spur economic expansion. Businessmen, disturbed by the strikes and industrial violence that accompanied the panic, became increasingly concerned about the defense of property.

The monetary issue aroused strong controversy. Civil War greenbacks had the potential to expand the money supply and lift prices if they were kept in circulation. In 1872, Democratic farmers and debtors had urged such a policy, but they were overruled by

Greenbacks Versus Sound Money

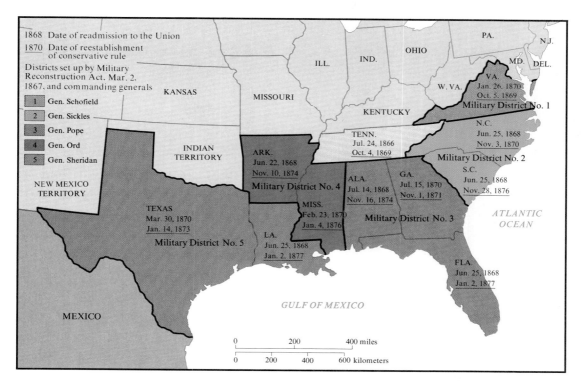

The Reconstruction

"sound money" men. Now hard times swelled the ranks of "greenbackers"—voters who favored greenbacks and easy money. In 1874, Congress voted to increase the number of greenbacks in circulation, but Grant vetoed the bill in deference to the opinions of financial leaders. The next year sound-money interests prevailed in Congress, winning passage of a law requiring that after 1878 greenbacks be convertible into gold. The law limited the inflationary impact of the greenbacks and aided creditors, not debtors such as hard-pressed farmers.

In international affairs there was renewed pressure for, and controversy about, expansion. Secretary of State William H. Seward accomplished a major addition of territory to the national domain in 1867. Through negotiation with the Russian government, he arranged the purchase of Alaska for $7.2 million dollars. Opponents ridiculed Seward's venture, calling Alaska Frigidia, the Polar Bear Garden, and Walrussia. But Seward convinced important congressmen of Alaska's economic potential, and other lawmakers favored the dawning of friendship with Russia. In the same year the United States took control of the Midway Islands, a

thousand miles from Hawaii; they were scarcely mentioned again until the Second World War. In 1870 President Grant tried to annex the Dominican Republic, but Senator Charles Sumner blocked the attempt. Seward and his successor, Hamilton Fish, used diplomacy to arrange a financial settlement of claims against Britain for permitting the sale of the *Alabama* and other Confederate cruisers (see page 427).

By 1876 it was obvious to most political observers that the North was no longer willing to pursue the goals of Reconstruction. The results of a disputed presidential election confirmed this fact. Samuel J. Tilden, Democratic governor of New York, ran strongly in the South and took a commanding lead in both the popular vote and the electoral college over Rutherford B. Hayes, the Republican nominee. Tilden won 184 electoral votes and needed only one more for a majority. Nineteen votes from Louisiana, South Carolina, and Florida were disputed; both Democrats and Republicans claimed to have won in those states despite fraud on the part of their opponents. One vote

Election of 1876

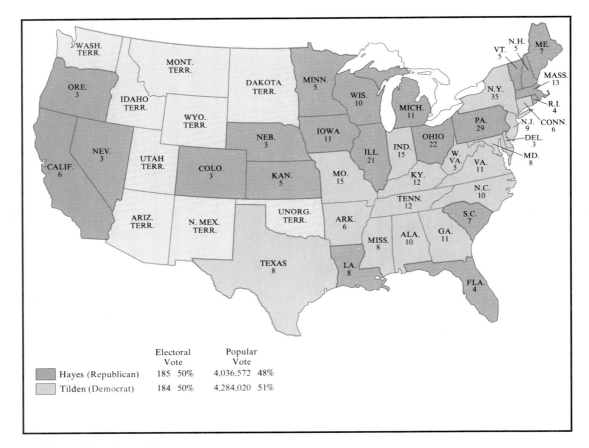

Presidential Election, 1876

Electoral Vote / Popular Vote

- Hayes (Republican) — 185 50% / 4,036,572 48%
- Tilden (Democrat) — 184 50% / 4,284,020 51%

from Oregon was undecided due to a technicality (see map).

To resolve this unprecedented situation, on which the Constitution gave no guidance, Congress established a fifteen-member electoral commission. In the interest of impartiality, membership on the commission was to be balanced between Democrats and Republicans. But one independent Republican, Supreme Court Justice David Davis, refused appointment in order to accept his election as a senator. A regular Republican took his place, and the Republican party prevailed 8 to 7 on every decision, a strict party vote. Hayes would become the winner if Congress accepted the commission's findings.

Congressional acceptance, however, was not certain. Democrats controlled the House and had the power to filibuster to block action on the vote. Many citizens worried that the nation had entered a major constitutional crisis and was slipping once

again into civil war. The crisis was resolved when Democrats acquiesced in the election of Hayes. Scholars have found that negotiations went on between some of Hayes's supporters and southerners who were interested in federal aid to railroads, internal improvements, federal patronage, and removal of troops from southern states. But the most recent studies suggest that these negotiations did not have a deciding effect on the outcome. Neither party was well enough organized to implement and enforce a bargain between the sections. Northern and southern Democrats decided they could not win and failed to contest the election. Thus Hayes became president, and southerners looked forward to the withdrawal of federal troops from the South. Reconstruction was unmistakably over.

Southern Democrats rejoiced, but black Americans grieved over the betrayal of their hopes for equality. Tens of thousands of blacks pondered leaving the South, where freedom was no longer

Chapter 15: Reconstruction by Trial and Error, 1865–1877

Exodusters, southern blacks dismayed by the failure of Reconstruction, left the South by the thousands for Kansas or states farther west in the late 1870s. This photo shows one of the leaders of the movement to Kansas, Benjamin "Pap" Singleton. *Kansas State Historical Society.*

> **Black Exodusters**

a real possibility. "[We asked] whether it was possible we could stay under a people who had held us in bondage," said Henry Adams, who led a migration to Kansas. "[We] appealed to the President . . . and to Congress . . . to protect us in our rights and privileges," but "in 1877 we lost all hopes." Thereafter many southern blacks "wanted to go to a territory by ourselves." In South Carolina, Louisiana, Mississippi, and other southern states, thousands gathered up their possessions and migrated to Kansas. They were known as Exodusters, disappointed people still searching for their share in the American dream. Even in Kansas they met disillusionment, as the welcome extended by the state's governor soon gave way to hostile public reactions.

Thus the nation ended over fifteen years of bloody civil war and controversial reconstruction without establishing full freedom for black Americans. Their status would continue to be a major issue. A host of other issues would arise from industrialization. How would the country develop its immense resources in a growing and increasingly interconnected national economy? How would farmers, industrial workers, immigrants, and capitalists fit into the new social system? Industrialization promised not just a higher standard of living but also a different lifestyle in both urban and rural areas. Moreover, it increased the nation's power and laid the foundation for an enlarged American role in international affairs. Again Americans turned their thoughts to expansion and the conquest of new frontiers. As the United States entered its second hundred years of existence, it confronted these serious challenges. The experiences of the 1860s and 1870s suggested that the solutions, if any, might be neither clear nor complete.

Suggestions for Further Reading

National Policy, Politics, and Constitutional Law

Richard H. Abbott, *The Republican Party and the South, 1855–1877* (1986); Herman Belz, *Emancipation and Equal*

Rights (1978); Herman Belz, *A New Birth of Freedom* (1976); Herman Belz, *Reconstructing the Union* (1969); Michael Les Benedict, *A Compromise of Principle: Congressional Republicans and Reconstruction, 1863–1869* (1974); Michael Les Benedict, *The Impeachment and Trial of Andrew Johnson* (1973); David W. Bowen, *Andrew Johnson and the Negro* (1989); Charles S. Campbell, *The Transformation of American Foreign Relations, 1865–1900* (1976); Adrian Cook, *The Alabama Claims* (1975); Michael Kent Curtis, *No State Shall Abridge* (1987); David Donald, *Charles Sumner and the Rights of Man* (1970); Harold M. Hyman, *A More Perfect Union* (1973); Ronald J. Jensen, *The Alaska Purchase and Russian-American Relations* (1975); William S. McFeely, *Grant* (1981); William S. McFeely, *Yankee Stepfather: General O. O. Howard and the Freedmen* (1968); Eric L. McKitrick, *Andrew Johnson and Reconstruction* (1966); James M. McPherson, *The Abolitionist Legacy* (1975); Kenneth M. Stampp, *The Era of Reconstruction* (1965); Mark W. Summers, *Railroads, Reconstruction, and the Gospel of Prosperity* (1984); Glyndon C. Van Deusen, *William Henry Seward* (1967).

The Freed Slaves

Roberta Sue Alexander, *North Carolina Faces the Freedmen* (1985); Ira Berlin, ed., *Freedom: A Documentary History of Emancipation, 1861–1867* (1984); Edmund L. Drago, *Black Politicians and Reconstruction in Georgia* (1982); Paul D. Escott, *Slavery Remembered* (1979); Eric Foner, "Reconstruction and the Crisis of Free Labor," in Eric Foner, ed., *Politics and Ideology in the Age of the Civil War* (1980); Peter Kolchin, *First Freedom* (1972); Leon Litwack, *Been in the Storm So Long* (1979); Howard Rabinowitz, ed., *Southern Black Leaders in Reconstruction* (1982); C. Peter Ripley, *Slaves and Freedmen in Civil War Louisiana* (1976); Willie Lee Rose, *Rehearsal for Reconstruction* (1964); Emma Lou Thornbrough, ed., *Black Reconstructionists* (1972); Okon Uya, *From Slavery to Public Service* (1971); Clarence Walker, *A Rock in a Weary Land* (1982).

Politics and Reconstruction in the South

Richard N. Current, *Those Terrible Carpetbaggers* (1988); Jonathan Daniels, *Prince of Carpetbaggers* (1958); W. E. B. Du Bois, *Black Reconstruction* (1935); Paul D. Escott, *Many Excellent People: Power and Privilege in North Carolina, 1850–1900* (1985); W. McKee Evans, *Ballots and Fence Rails: Reconstruction on the Lower Cape Fear* (1966); Eric Foner, *Reconstruction: America's Unfinished Revolution, 1863–1877* (1988); Eric Foner, *Nothing but Freedom* (1983); William C. Harris, *William Woods Holden, Firebrand of North Carolina Politics* (1988); William C. Harris, *The Day of the Carpetbagger* (1979); Thomas Holt, *Black over White: Negro Political Leadership in South Carolina During Reconstruction* (1977); Robert Manson Myers, ed., *The Children of Pride* (1972); Elizabeth Studley Nathans, *Losing the Peace* (1968); Lillian A. Pereyra, *James Lusk Alcorn* (1966); Michael Perman, *The Road to Redemption* (1984); Michael Perman, *Reunion Without Compromise* (1973); Lawrence N.

Powell, "The Politics of Livelihood," in J. Morgan Kousser and James M. McPherson, eds., *Region, Race and Reconstruction* (1982); Lawrence N. Powell, *New Masters* (1980); George C. Rable, *But There Was No Peace* (1984); James Roark, *Masters Without Slaves* (1977); James Sefton, *The United States Army and Reconstruction, 1865–1877* (1967); Mark W. Summers, *Railroads, Reconstruction, and the Gospel of Prosperity* (1984); J. Mills Thornton III, "Fiscal Policy and the Failure of Radical Reconstruction," in J. Morgan Kousser and James M. McPherson, eds., *Region, Race and Reconstruction* (1982); Albion W. Tourgée, *A Fool's Errand* (1979); Allen Trelease, *White Terror* (1967); Ted Tunnell, *Carpetbagger from Vermont* (1989); Ted Tunnell, *Crucible of Reconstruction* (1984); Michael Wayne, *The Reshaping of Plantation Society* (1983); Sarah Woolfolk Wiggins, *The Scalawag in Alabama Politics, 1865–1881* (1977).

Women, Family, and Social History

Ellen Carol Dubois, *Feminism and Suffrage* (1978); Herbert G. Gutman, *The Black Family in Slavery and Freedom, 1750–1925* (1976); Elizabeth Jacoway, *Yankee Missionaries in the South* (1979); Jacqueline Jones, *Labor of Love, Labor of Sorrow* (1985); Jacqueline Jones, *Soldiers of Light and Love* (1980); Robert C. Kenzer, *Kinship and Neighborhood in a Southern Community* (1987); Rebecca Scott, "The Battle over the Child," *Prologue,* 10, no. 2 (Summer 1978), 101–113.

The End of Reconstruction

Michael Les Benedict, "Southern Democrats in the Crisis of 1876–1877," *Journal of Southern History,* LXVI, no. 4 (November 1980), 489–524; William Gillette, *Retreat from Reconstruction, 1869–1879* (1980); William Gillette, *The Right to Vote* (1969); Keith Ian Polakoff, *The Politics of Inertia* (1973); John G. Sproat, *"The Best Men": Liberal Reformers in the Gilded Age* (1968); C. Vann Woodward, *Reunion and Reaction* (1951).

Reconstruction's Legacy for the South

Robert G. Athearn, *In Search of Canaan* (1978); Norman L. Crockett, *The Black Towns* (1979); Stephen J. DeCanio, *Agriculture in the Postbellum South* (1974); Steven Hahn, *The Roots of Southern Populism* (1983); Susan Previant Lee and Peter Passell, *A New Economic View of American History* (1979); Jay R. Mandle, *The Roots of Black Poverty* (1978); Nell Irvin Painter, *Exodusters* (1976); Howard Rabinowitz, *Race Relations in the Urban South, 1865–1890* (1978); Roger L. Ransom and Richard Sutch, *One Kind of Freedom* (1977); Laurence Shore, *Southern Capitalists* (1986); Peter Wallenstein, *From Slave South to New South* (1987); Jonathan M. Wiener, *Social Origins of the New South* (1978); Joel Williamson, *After Slavery* (1966); C. Vann Woodward, *Origins of the New South* (1951).

They called themselves Dine', which meant "The People." The Spanish had named them *Apaches de Nabahu,* or "Strangers of the Cultivated Fields." White Americans called them *Navahos.* Whatever their name, they were a civilization who lived in what would become northern Arizona and New Mexico and who devoted their lives to achieving *k'e*—a universal harmony of love, peace, and cooperation. *K'e* was symbolized by motherhood, by the birthing and raising of children and by everything that was life giving. To the Navahos, said one observer, "the earth is called mother, the sheep herd is called mother, corn is called mother, and the sacred mountain soil bundle is called mother." They tried to achieve *k'e* by living in unity with the land and all other objects of nature.

White people did not understand Navaho beliefs. When they moved into territory inhabited by Navahos and other Native American peoples, they wanted more than they needed simply to survive. They wanted to dig into the earth to remove tons of minerals, cut down forests for lumber to build cities, and plow the earth's surface to grow crops to sell at distant markets. The Indians did not understand why white people urged them to adopt these practices and improve their lives by creating material wealth. When told he must become a commercial farmer and grow crops for profit, a member of the Comanche tribe (which like the Navahos believed in the order of the natural environment) replied, "The earth is my mother. Do you give me an iron plow to wound my mother's breast? Shall I take a scythe and cut my mother's hair?" And when confronted with native resistance to their wishes, whites responded with brutal violence.

The withering of Indian subsistence cultures, coercive government policies, and the triumph of market economies exemplifies what happened when white Americans transformed the western frontier in the late nineteenth century. Settlement of the West proceeded at a furious pace. Between 1870 and 1890 the population living between the Mississippi River and the Pacific Ocean swelled from 7 million to nearly 17 million. Frontiers vanished in the South as well. Shortly after Reconstruction ended, cotton production reached pre–Civil War levels, and people were taking

16

THE TRANSFORMATION OF THE WEST AND SOUTH, 1877–1892

Cañon de la Rio Las Animas by William Henry Jackson. His camera captured a train snaking along the Denver & Rio Grande Line in Colorado's San Juan Mountains. Jackson added the color for lithographic printing by the Detroit Publishing Company, in which he held an interest. *Colorado Historical Society (neg. #2883).*

advantage of new opportunities afforded by the region's abundant natural resources to sell and to profit.

By 1890 farms, ranches, mines, towns, and cities could be found in almost every region of what was to become the continental United States. That year, the superintendent of the census acknowledged that

> up to and including 1880, the country had a frontier of settlement, but at present the unsettled area has been so broken into by isolated bodies of settlement that there can hardly be said to be a frontier line. In the discussion of its extent and its westward movement, etc., it can not therefore, any longer have a place in the census reports.

What had happened on the frontier and what effect did its disappearance have on the nation?

In popular thought, the frontier represented the birthplace of American self-confidence and individualism. Conquering the continent's vast wilderness and bringing forth food and raw materials from it, not to mention building cities within a single generation, filled white Americans with a sense of power and a faith that anyone eager and persistent enough could succeed. That self-confidence, however, was easily transformed into the arrogant belief that Americans were somehow special, and individualism often exerted itself at the expense of racial minorities and people without property.

Most Americans rarely thought about conserving resources because there always seemed to be more territory to exploit and bring into the market economy. The fading of the frontier, though of great symbolic importance, had little direct impact on people's behavior, because vast stretches of land remained unsettled. Millions of people continued to stream into the West, and more land in the South fell under cultivation. Compared with undeveloped regions in Siberia, South America, Africa, and Canada, the American West and South were relatively tame. American settlers who failed in one region usually did not perish; they moved on and tried again somewhere else. Although life in the West was less romantic and comfortable than settlers might have hoped, and the unreconstructed South failed to fulfill its potential, the western and southern frontiers gave Americans the feeling that they would always have a second chance. The belief in an infinity of second chances left its imprint on the American character.

The Transformation of Native American Cultures

Historians have sometimes defined the American frontier as "the edge of the unused," implying that the frontier faded when open land began to be used for farming or the building of cities. The definition is misleading when applied to the American West because Native Americans were using the land long before white Americans migrated there. Neither passive nor impotent in the face of nature, western Indians had been shaping their environment for centuries. Nevertheless, in the late nineteenth century almost all Indian economic systems failed. Why and how did these declines happen?

Numerous western tribes differed in culture—some were nomadic, others more settled—but the economies of all were based to some extent on four activities: crop raising; livestock raising; hunting, fishing, and gathering; and raiding. Corn was the most common crop; sheep and horses were the livestock; and buffalo were the objects of hunts. Tribes raided each other for food, hides, and slaves. They also warred with, killed, and displaced each other over hunting grounds and in defense of property. The goal of all these activities was subsistence, the maintenance of life at its most basic level. Indians tried to balance their economic systems to achieve subsistence. Thus when a buffalo hunt failed, a tribe could still feed itself on crops being grown; when crops failed, a tribe could still hunt buffalo and steal food from another tribe. Indians also traded with each other and with whites, mainly to obtain necessities such as horses and furs.

Subsistence Cultures

For Indians on the Plains, whether they were nomads such as the Lakotas or village dwellers such as the Pawnees, much of everyday life focused on the buffalo. For centuries they had cooked and preserved buffalo meat; fashioned hides into clothing, shoes, and blankets; used sinew for thread and bowstrings; carved tools from bones; and made horns into implements. Pawnees and other tribes also depended heavily on horses, for transportation and hunting and as symbols of wealth. To provide food for their herds of horses, these Indians often

1862	Homestead Act
	Morrill Land Grant Act
1869	First transcontinental railroad, the Union Pacific, completed
1874	Barbed-wire fence patented
1876	Custer's Last Stand (Battle of Little Big Horn)
1878	Timber and Stone Act
1880	George Manypenny, *Our Indian Wards*
1881	Helen Hunt Jackson, *A Century of Dishonor*
1882–83	Transcontinental routes of Santa Fe, Southern Pacific, and Northern Pacific completed
1883	*Civil Rights Cases*
	Standardization of national time zones
1887	Dawes Severalty Act
	Hatch Act
1889	Statehood granted to North Dakota, South Dakota, Washington, and Montana
1890	Wounded Knee massacre
	Census Bureau announces closing of the frontier
	Statehood granted to Wyoming and Idaho
	Establishment of Yosemite National Park
1896	*Plessy* v. *Ferguson*
	Development of Rural Free Delivery
	Statehood granted to Vermont
1899	*Cummins* v. *County Board of Education*

set fire to tall-grass prairies. The fires burned away dead growth, enabling the sun to warm the earth and facilitating the growth of grass in the spring so the horses could feed all summer.

In the Southwest, Native Americans placed great value on sheep, goats, and horses. Old Man Hat, a Navaho, advised, "The herd is money. . . . You know that you have some good clothing; the sheep gave you that. And you've just eaten different kinds of food; the sheep gave that food to you. Everything comes from the sheep." He did not mean "money" in a business sense, however. To the Navahos, the herds were means to achieving security. Like many Native Americans, the Navahos emphasized generosity and distrusted private property and wealth. Within the family, sharing was expected; outside the family, gifts and reciprocity governed personal relations.

This world of subsistence and ecological balance began to dissolve when whites entered the West

to plow the soil and extract minerals. Perceiving buffalo as well as Indians as hindrances to their ambitions on the Plains, whites endeavored to remove both. As one army officer advised, "Kill every buffalo you can. Every buffalo dead is an Indian gone." To help remove the buffalo, railroads sponsored hunts for eastern sportsmen, who rode on slow-moving trains and shot at the bulky targets. Some hunters collected $1 to $3 offered by tanneries for hides; others did not even stop to pick up their kill. By the 1880s only a few hundred remained of the estimated 13 million buffalo that had existed in 1850. As the buffalo herds dwindled, Pawnees and other Plains tribes had to hunt farther from their villages. As a result they clashed with rival tribes over scarce buffalo and left their own settlements vulnerable to raids by hostile tribes seeking food. The scarcity of buffalo further upset the subsistence system by leaving Indians less

> **Slaughter of Buffalo**

A Sioux Indian camp in South Dakota, 1891. The Sioux led a nomadic life, carrying out their subsistence economy in harmony with the natural environment. When they packed up and moved on, they left the landscape almost undisturbed. This photograph shows the temporary situation characteristic of their camps. *Library of Congress.*

food to supplement their diets if their crops failed or were stolen.

Government policy reinforced efforts to remove Indians from the path of white ambitions. Like the British before them (see pages 25–26), American government officials considered Indian tribes to be separate nations with whom they could make treaties that ensured peace and defined the boundaries of native and white lands. But the treaties seldom promised the Indians any future land rights; rather, whites assumed that eventually they could settle wherever they wished. As white settlers pressed into Indian territories in the West, treaties made one week were violated the next. Some tribes acquiesced; others resisted with attacks on settlements, herds, and troops. Whites responded with murders of individuals and massacres of entire villages. At Sand Creek, Colorado, in 1864 United States troops murdered about 150 Cheyennes, mostly women and children.

By the 1870s, federal officials and humanitarians, seeking peaceful means of dealing with western tribes, began emphasizing policies that in some ways would treat Native Americans similarly to blacks and immigrants. Instead of being considered foreign nations, Indian tribes were to be "civilized" and "uplifted" through education. White missionaries and teachers, with government encouragement, would attempt to inculcate in Indians the values of the white mobility ethic: hard work, ambition, thrift, and materialism. To achieve this transformation, however, Indians would have to abandon their traditional cultures.

From the 1860s to the 1880s, the federal government tried to force Indians onto reservations, where, it was thought, they could best be civilized.

Reservation Policy
Reservations usually consisted of the areas of a tribe's previous territory that were least desirable to whites (see map, page 478). In assigning Indians to specific territories, the government promised protection from white encroachment and agreed to provide food, clothing, and other necessities.

This painting from about 1895 shows a buffalo hunt of a Crow Indian tribe. In addition to mounted hunters, three cowboys are depicted in the upper left corner, suggesting that whites and Native Americans may have combined on some hunts. *Museum of the American Indian, Heye Foundation.*

Buffalo kills and reservation policy were means to the establishment of a market economy that, more than any other feature of Anglo-American culture, undermined Native American subsistence systems. In the early years of contact between Indians and whites, trade had been beneficial to both and had taken place on a nearly equal basis. Tribes obtained clothing, guns, tools, and other manufactured items in return for wool, hides, and sometimes military service. Gradually, however, whites' needs and economic power grew disproportionate to the needs and power of Indians. The balance shifted. Indians became more dependent as whites increasingly dictated what was to be traded, what the terms were, and how Indians were to use what they received. Navahos, for example, were encouraged to sell their wool and handmade blankets, but in doing so they paid less attention to crop raising and were forced to buy food because the market economy lured them away from subsistence

agriculture. White traders persuaded Navaho weavers to produce heavy rugs suitable for eastern customers and to use different dyes and yarn and adopt new designs and colors to help sales. Soon many tribespeople were selling their land and labor to whites as well as their products, making it easier to force them onto reservations.

Reservation policy had troublesome consequences. First, Indians had no say over their own affairs on reservations. Supreme Court decisions in 1884 and 1886 denied Indians the right to become United States citizens, leaving them unprotected by the Fourteenth and Fifteenth Amendments, which had given blacks rights of citizenship. Second, it was impossible to protect reservations from white farmers, miners, and herders, who continually sought even remote Indian lands for their own purposes. Third, the government disregarded variations among tribes, even concentrating tribes habitually at war with each other on the same reservation. Rather than acting as civilizing communities, reservations became more like antebellum slave quarters.

Not all tribes easily succumbed to market forces and reservation restrictions. Pawnees, for example, resisted heavy trading as well as the liquor that white traders used to addict many Indians and tempt them into disadvantageous deals. Even as they became dependent upon whites, some tribes tried to preserve their traditional cultures. Navahos traded for food in order to restore their subsistence way of life, and Pawnees agreed to leave their Nebraska homelands for a reservation in the hope that they could hunt buffalo and grow corn as they once had done.

Indian Resistance

Native Americans also actively defended their homelands against white intrusion and violence in a series of bloody conflicts and revolts. The most famous battle occurred on June 25, 1876, when 2,500 Dakota Sioux, led by Chiefs Rain-in-the-Face, Sitting Bull, and Crazy Horse, annihilated white troops led by the rash Colonel George A. Custer near the Little Big Horn River in southern Montana. There were other Indian victories, but shortages of supplies and relentless pursuit by white troops eventually overwhelmed armed Indian resistance.

These conditions kindled new efforts to reform Indian policy in the 1880s. Publication of reform treatises such as George Manypenny's *Our Indian Wards* (1880) and Helen Hunt Jackson's *A Century of Dishonor* (1881) plus unfavorable comparison with Canada's management of Indian affairs aroused the American conscience. In Canada, tribespeople had been given the rights of British subjects and were defended against whites by the Royal Mounted Police. Canadian officials were more tolerant of tribal customs and proceeded more slowly than Americans in efforts to acculturate Indians. A high rate of intermarriage between Indians and Canadian whites also aided relations in Canada.

In the United States, the two most important Indian reform organizations were the Women's National Indian Association (WNIA) and the Indian Rights Association (IRA). The WNIA, a social feminist group that sought to extend women's domestic virtues to the public sphere rather than seek political rights, urged gradual assimilation of Indians. The IRA sup-

Reform of Indian Policy

ported citizenship and landholding by individuals. Most reform groups believed Indians were culturally, not racially, inferior to whites and assumed Indians could succeed economically only if they adopted middle-class values of cleanliness, diligence, monogamy, and education.

The reformers especially deplored Indians' sexual division of labor. Women seemed to do all the work—tending crops, raising children, cooking, curing hides, making tools and clothes—and seemed to be servile to men, who did the hunting but otherwise were idle. Groups such as WNIA and IRA wanted Indian men to bear more responsibilities and become like the heads of white middle-class households. While reformers urged that Indian women be treated more respectfully by their menfolk, the effect of their reforms would have been—and sometimes was—reduced economic independence of Indian women.

Prodded by reformers, Congress in 1887 reversed its reservation policy and passed the Dawes Severalty Act, which dissolved community-owned tribal lands and granted land allotments to individual families. The act also awarded citizenship to all who accepted allotments and authorized the government to sell unallotted land and to set aside proceeds for the education of Indians. These provisions applied to most western tribes, the exception being Pueblo peoples who had retained land rights granted to them by the Spanish.

Dawes Severalty Act

United States Indian policy, as carried out by the Indian Bureau of the Interior Department, now took on three main features. First and foremost, land was distributed to individual families in the belief that they would acquire white people's wants and values by learning how to manage their own property. Second, bureau officials believed that Indians would lose their "barbaric" habits more quickly if their children were removed and educated in boarding schools away from the old reservations. Third, officials tried to suppress what they believed were dangerous religious ceremonies by providing money for white church groups to establish religious schools among the Indians and teach them to become good Christians. Implementation of the Dawes Act did not end violence, however. In 1890, the government sent the Seventh Cavalry, Custer's old regiment, to apprehend some Sioux who were believed to be

Chapter 16: The Transformation of the West and South, 1877–1892

The Carlisle School in Pennsylvania was founded by the United States government in 1879 to teach Indians to behave and dress like whites. This view shows Tom Torleno, a Navaho, before he entered the Carlisle School and how he looked after three years at the school. *Smithsonian Institution.*

armed for revolt. During an encounter at Wounded Knee Creek in South Dakota, the troops trained newly acquired cannon on the Indians and massacred two hundred sick and hungry men, women, and children in the snow.

In one crucial respect, the Dawes Act effectively accomplished what whites wanted and Indians feared: it reduced Indian control over land. In spite of some protection against such practices, eager speculators induced Indians, inexperienced in commercial dealings, to part with their newly acquired property. Between 1887 and the 1930s, Indian landholdings dwindled from 138 million acres to 52 million. Land-grabbing whites were particularly cruel to the Chippewas of the northern plains. In 1906, Senator Moses E. Clapp of Minnesota attached a rider to an Indian appropriations bill declaring that mixed-blood adults on the White Earth reservation were "competent" enough to sell their land without having to observe the twenty-five-year waiting period stipulated in the Dawes Act. When the bill became law, white speculators duped many Chippewas, declared "mixed-bloods" by white experts on the basis of fraudulent evidence, into signing away their land in return for counterfeit money and worthless merchandise. More than half their original holdings passed from their control, and economic ruin overtook the tribe.

The Dawes Act had other drawbacks as well. The boarding-school program affected thousands of children, but most returned to their reservations rather than submit to assimilation into white society. Efforts to suppress religious observances only forced them under cover. By the end of the century, Native Americans became what historian Richard White has labeled "a population without control over resources, sustained in its poverty by payments controlled by the larger society, and subject to increasing pressure to lose their group identity and disappear."

The western tribes were overcome by political and ecological crises. Decline of buffalo herds, poverty caused by enemy raids that carried away their crops, disease, and military force combined to

The Transformation of Native American Cultures

> **Decline of Western Tribes**

bring subsistence culture to the point where the Indians were willing to yield their lands to market-oriented whites. Believing themselves to be superior in every way, whites were determined to turn Indians into "virtuous" farmers by making them appreciate the value of private property, educating them in American ideals, and forcefully eradicating their "backward" cultural practices, languages, lifestyles, and religions.

Whites used brutal means to accomplish these goals, but white military superiority was not the only factor contributing to defeat of the western tribes. Indian economic systems had started to break down before the military defeats occurred. Although Native Americans tried to retain their culture by both adapting and yielding to all the various pressures, the West was won at their expense, and they remain casualties of an aggressive age.

The Exploitation of Natural Resources

Unlike the Indians, who controlled the natural environment to meet subsistence needs, white migrants to the Plains and West were driven by a get-rich-quick mentality. To them the vast stretches of unsettled territory were areas full of resources awaiting discovery and promising profits. The extraction and marketing of these resources not only advanced settlement and opened new markets but also primed the revolutions in transportation, agriculture, and industry that swept the United States in the late nineteenth century. At the same time, the exploitation of nature's wealth gave rise to a spirit of carelessness toward the environment, reinforced the sexual division of labor, and fed habits of racial oppression.

In the years just before the Civil War, eager prospectors began to comb remote forests and mountains looking for gold, silver, iron, coal, timber, oil, and copper. The mining frontier advanced rapidly, drawing thousands of people to California, Nevada, Idaho, Montana, and Col-

> **Mining and Lumbering**

orado. Prospectors tended to be restless optimists, willing to tramp mountains and deserts, searching for a telltale glint of precious metal. They shot game for food and financed their explorations by convincing merchants to advance credit for equipment in return for a share of the lode yet to be discovered. When their credit ran out, unlucky prospectors took jobs and saved up for another search for riches.

The ultimate goal was to sell large amounts of minerals, but extracting substances from the ground involved high expenses for excavation and transportation. Thus individual prospectors who did discover veins of metal seldom mined them. Instead they sold their claims to mining syndicates, lived it up on their new wealth, and then set off on another quest. The mining companies had ample capital to bring in engineers, heavy machinery, railroad lines, and work crews. Although discoveries of gold and silver first drew attention to the West and its resources, mining companies usually moved into the Rocky Mountain states to exploit less romantic but equally lucrative bonanzas of lead, zinc, tin, quartz, and copper.

Lumber production—another large-scale extractive industry—required vast amounts of forest land. As lumber companies moved into the Northwest, they grabbed millions of acres by exploiting the Timber and Stone Act (1878). This measure, passed by Congress to stimulate settlement in California, Nevada, Oregon, and Washington, allowed private citizens to buy at the low price of $2.50 per acre 160-acre plots "unfit for cultivation" and "valuable chiefly for timber." Taking advantage of the act, lumber companies hired seamen from waterfront boarding houses to register claims to timberland and turn them over to the companies. By 1900, claimants had bought over 3.5 million acres under Timber and Stone Act provisions, but most of that land belonged to corporations.

While lumbermen were acquiring timberlands in the Northwest, oilmen were beginning to sink wells in the Southwest. In 1900 most of the nation's petroleum came from the Appalachians and Midwest, but promising developments were under way in southern California and eastern Texas. Although most oil and kerosene were still used for lubrication and lighting, discoveries in the Southwest were to become a vital new source of fuel in the twentieth century.

Two women stand on a hill overlooking Helena, Montana, a typical mining town of the 1870s. In spite of their small numbers, women exerted a settling influence on frontier towns. *Montana Historical Society, Helena.*

Much of the natural-resource frontier was a man's world. In 1880, white men outnumbered white women by more than two to one in Colorado, Nevada, and Arizona. Yet many western communities had substantial numbers of women. Most women who went to the mining frontier did so for the same reasons as men: to find a fortune. But their independence on the mining frontier as elsewhere was limited. They usually accompanied a husband or father and seldom prospected themselves. Even so, many women realized their own opportunities in the towns, where they provided cooking, laundering, and, in some cases, sexual services for the miners. In some families the woman became the main breadwinner when her husband failed to strike it rich. As one wife recalled, "I began at once to figure in my mind how many men I could cook for, if there should be no better way of making money." While they pur-

> **Frontier Society**

sued new opportunities and freedoms, women also helped to bolster family and community life by campaigning against vice.

Many of the mining and lumber communities contained small numbers of Chinese, Mexicans, Indians, and blacks. Most Chinese migrated to work on American railroads, but some were employed in the camps to do cooking and cleaning. Blacks also held such jobs. Mexicans and Indians often had been the original settlers of land coveted by whites, and some stayed to resist white intruders. Each of these minority groups encountered white prejudice, especially as whites tried to reserve for themselves the riches that the mines and forests might yield. California imposed a tax on foreign miners and denied blacks, Indians, and Chinese the right to testify or submit evidence in court. Just as land treaties with Indians were frequently broken, any claims that Mexicans might have had to land sought by white miners were often ignored or stolen.

The Exploitation of Natural Resources

Blacks and Chinese who worked in mining camps often suffered abuse and violence, such as the attack on Chinese laborers by white miners in Rock Springs, Wyoming, in 1885. Not all harassment came from whites, however; in California, for example, Mexican bandits preyed on the Chinese even more than on the Anglos. Nonwhites defended themselves as well as they could against intimidation, but their most common tactic was to pack up and seek jobs and homes in another town or mining camp.

Development of the nation's oil, mineral, and timber resources raised serious questions about what belonged to all the people, as represented by

Use of Public Lands

the federal government, and what belonged to private interests whose motive was profit. Two factors worked at cross-purposes. First, much of the undeveloped territory west of the Mississippi was public domain, and some people believed that the federal government, as owner, should receive some return from the exploitation of it. But the government, lacking both motivation and the means to dig mines, sink wells, and cut forests, sold the land to private interests who would take the initiative.

The developers of natural resources were seldom interested in landowning. They wanted trees, not forest land that would become useless once the trees had been cut down. They wanted oil, not the scrubby plain that would be worthless if—as often happened—wells were dug but no oil was found. To avoid purchase costs, oilmen and iron miners often leased property from private owners or from the government and paid royalties on the minerals extracted. Some lumbermen simply cut trees on public lands without paying a cent and used trickery to buy land cheaply under the Timber and Stone Act. Even when Congress and the U.S. Land Office tried to prevent fraud by passing new legislation and sending out more investigators, many communities resisted in fear that such crackdowns would slow local economic growth.

Questions about natural resources caught Americans between the desire for progress and the fear of spoiling the land. By the late 1870s and early 1880s, people concerned about the natural landscape began to coalesce into a conservation movement. A leading figure was western naturalist John Muir, who helped establish Yosemite National Park in 1890. The next year, under pressure from Muir

and others, Congress authorized President Benjamin Harrison to create on public land forest reserves protected from cutting by private interests. Such policies met with strong objections. Lumber companies, lumber dealers, and railroads were joined in their opposition by private householders accustomed to cutting timber freely for fuel and building material. Public opinion on conservation also split along sectional lines. Most supporters came from eastern states, where resources had become less plentiful; opposition was loudest in the West, where people were still eager to take advantage of nature's bounty.

Development of the mining and forest frontiers, plus the farms and cities that followed, brought western territories to the threshold of statehood. In

Admission of New States

1889, Republicans seeking to solidify their control of Congress pushed through an omnibus bill granting statehood to North Dakota, South Dakota, Washington, and Montana. Wyoming and Idaho were admitted in 1890. Congress denied statehood to Utah until 1896, when the Mormons, who were a majority of the territory's population and controlled its government, agreed to abandon polygamy.

The mining towns and lumber camps in these states spiced American folk culture and fostered a go-getter optimism that distinguished the American spirit. The lawlessness and hedonism of places like Deadwood, in Dakota Territory, and Tombstone, in Arizona Territory, gave the West notoriety and romance. Legends grew up about inhabitants of these towns whose lives both typified and magnified western experience. One such character was Martha Jane Canary, known as Calamity Jane, who in the 1870s worked in eastern Wyoming and western Dakota as a scout and wagon driver. Skilled with a rifle and dressed in men's clothes, Calamity Jane acquired a reputation for wild behavior that fiction writers later glorified. Yet according to an army captain who employed her, Jane was "eccentric and wayward rather than bad and had adopted male attire more to aid her in getting a living than for any improper purpose."

Arizona mining towns, with their free-flowing cash and loose law enforcement, attracted numerous gamblers, thieves, and opportunists whose names came to stand for the Wild West. Near Tombstone, the infamous Clanton family and their partner John Ringgold (known as Johnny Ringo)

The mining boom often created towns so fast that there was no time to remove rubble. This photograph of Leadville, near the gold and silver mines at the head of the Arkansas River, shows how the community grew up around a settler's cabin, which remained in the middle of the main street. *Colorado Historical Society.*

engaged in smuggling and cattle rustling. Inside the town, the Earp brothers—Wyatt, Jim, Morgan, Virgil, and Warren—and their friends William Barclay ("Bat") Masterson and John Henry ("Doc") Holliday operated on both sides of the law as gunmen, gamblers, and politicians. A feud between Clanton and Earp factions climaxed on October 26, 1881, in a shootout at the OK Corral, where three Clantons were killed and Virgil and Morgan Earp were seriously wounded.

Characters like Wild Bill Hickok, Poker Alice, and Bedrock Tom became western folk heroes, and fiction writers like Mark Twain and Bret Harte captured for posterity the flavor of mining life. But violence and eccentricity were far from common. Most miners and lumbermen worked seventy hours a week and had no time, energy, or money for drinking, gambling, or gunfights. Women worked as long or longer as teachers, cooks, laundresses, storekeepers, and housewives; only a few were sharpshooters or dance-hall queens. For most westerners, life was a matter of adapting and surviving.

The Age of Railroad Expansion

On May 10, 1869, the whole country knew what was happening at Promontory Point in the mountains of Utah. There, the Central Pacific Railroad, built 689 miles eastward from Sacramento, California, met the Union Pacific Railroad, built 1,086 miles westward from Omaha, Nebraska, to form the nation's first transcontinental rail route. Work crews of six hundred Irish, Chinese, Mexicans, and white and black Americans participated in the completion ceremony. A gold railroad spike was used to commemorate the event, but the last spike was actually made of steel because it was wired to a telegraph line and when pounded would signal to the world that the railroad had been completed. Governor Leland Stanford of California was given the honor of driving that final spike. As the crowd hushed, he drew back his silver hammer, swung—and missed

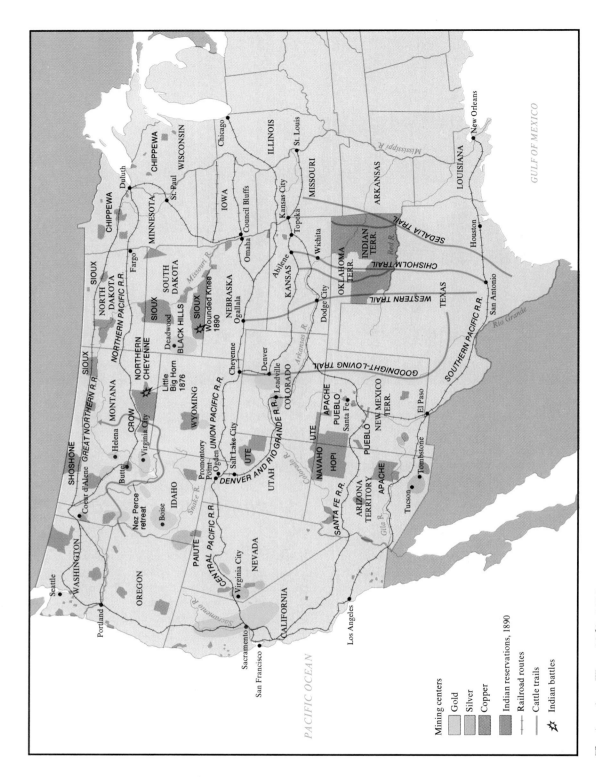

The American West, 1860–1890

Mining centers
Gold
Silver
Copper
Indian reservations, 1890
Railroad routes
Cattle trails
Indian battles

CHIPPEWA
CHIPPEWA
WISCONSIN
Duluth
St. Paul
MINNESOTA
Chicago
ILLINOIS
St. Louis
GULF OF MEXICO
New Orleans
LOUISIANA
ARKANSAS
MISSOURI
Kansas City
Council Bluffs
IOWA
Fargo
NORTH DAKOTA
SIOUX
SIOUX
SOUTH DAKOTA
Missouri R.
Omaha
Topeka
Wichita
INDIAN TERR.
Red R.
SEDALIA TRAIL
Houston
NORTHERN PACIFIC R.R.
Deadwood
BLACK HILLS
Wounded Knee 1890
SIOUX
NEBRASKA
Ogallala
Abilene
KANSAS
CHISHOLM TRAIL
OKLAHOMA TERR.
TEXAS
San Antonio
SOUTHERN PACIFIC R.R.
Rio Grande
SHOSHONE
GREAT NORTHERN R.R.
SIOUX
NORTHERN CHEYENNE
Little Big Horn 1876
Cheyenne
Denver
Dodge City
WESTERN TRAIL
Arkansas R.
GOODNIGHT-LOVING TRAIL
El Paso
MONTANA
CROW
Virginia City
Helena
Butte
WYOMING
UNION PACIFIC R.R.
Leadville
COLORADO
APACHE
PUEBLO
Santa Fe
NEW MEXICO TERR.
Coeur d'Alene
Nez Perce retreat
IDAHO
Boise
Snake R.
Promontory Point
Ogden
Salt Lake City
UTE
DENVER AND RIO GRANDE R.R.
UTAH
UTE
NAVAHO
HOPI
Colorado R.
PUEBLO
APACHE
ARIZONA TERRITORY
Tombstone
Tucson
Gila R.
SANTA FE R.R.
PAIUTE
NEVADA
Virginia City
CENTRAL PACIFIC R.R.
OREGON
WASHINGTON
Seattle
Portland
Sacramento R.
CALIFORNIA
San Francisco
Sacramento
Los Angeles
PACIFIC OCEAN
Mississippi R.

Employing Chinese laborers, western railroads accomplished great feats of engineering, clearing the terrain and building grades for track. *California State Railroad Society Library.*

the spike. The telegrapher sent the message anyway, and across the nation church bells rang and shouting multitudes celebrated.

The discovery and development of natural riches provided the base on which the nation's economy expanded. But raw wealth would have been of limited use without the means of carrying it to factories, marketplaces, and ports. Railroads filled this need, spreading a web of tracks across the country and refashioning the economy in the process.

Between 1865 and 1890, total track in the United States grew from 35,000 to 200,000 miles (see map). By 1910 the nation had one-third of all railroad track in the world. The Central Pacific imported seven thousand Chinese to build its tracks, and the Union Pacific used Irish construction gangs. Workers were housed in shacks and tents that could be dismantled, loaded on flatcars, and relocated at intervals of sixty or seventy miles. At one time, the Union Pacific needed forty railcars to supply its crews with rails, ties, bridge materials, and food.

The economic consequences of railroads were immense. After 1880, when durable steel rails began to replace iron rails, railroads helped to boost

Effects of Railroad Construction

the nation's steel industry to international leadership. Moreover, railroad expansion spawned a number of related industries, including coal production, passenger and freight car manufacture, and depot construction.

Railroads also altered Americans' conceptions of time and space and spurred a movement for standardization. First, by overcoming barriers of distance, railroads in effect transformed space into time. Instead of using geographical distance to measure the separation between places, it became easier to use the amount of time it took to travel from one place to the other. Second, railroad scheduling necessitated nationwide agreement on time. Before railroads, each locale had had its own time. Community church bells and steeple clocks had struck twelve when the sun was overhead, and

Cities such as Fargo, North Dakota, pictured above, became important centers for western railroads. Tracks of the Northern Pacific cut diagonally across this lithograph, advertising to potential settlers Fargo's advantages as a transportation center. The tiny inset in the lower right corner, showing what Fargo looked like just eight years previously, emphasizes the city's phenomenal growth. *The Phelps Stokes Print Collection, The New York Public Library.*

people had set clocks and watches accordingly. But because the sun was not overhead at exactly the same moment everywhere, there were variations in time from place to place. For example, clocks in Boston differed from those in New York by almost twelve minutes. To achieve some regularity, railroads created their own time zones. By 1880 there still were nearly fifty different standards, but in 1883 railroads finally agreed—without consulting anyone in government—to establish four standard time zones for the whole country. Most communities adjusted their clocks (though Chicago held out briefly), and railroad time became national time.

Third, railroad construction brought about technological and organizational reforms. By the late 1880s, almost all lines had adopted standard-gauge rails so their tracks could connect with one another. Westinghouse air brakes, automatic car couplers, standardized handholds on freight cars, and other devices made rail transportation safer and more efficient. The need for gradings, tunnels, and bridges spurred the growth of the American engineering profession. Organizational advances included systems for coordinating complex pas-

senger and freight schedules and the adoption of uniform freight-classification systems.

From other perspectives, however, the effects of railroads were less favorable. For example, the high cost of construction and equipment demanded that new railroads begin operation as soon as possible in order to generate revenues to repay debts and maintain investors' confidence. As a result, many miles of track were laid hastily, without regard for safety or durability.

Railroads nevertheless became extremely influential and acquired a uniquely American function. In Europe railroads were usually built to link established market centers and to improve or replace existing routes of traffic. In the United States, however, railroads often created the very communities they were meant to serve and carried traffic that had never before existed. Particularly in the West and South, railroads accelerated the growth of regional centers such as Omaha, Kansas City, Cheyenne, Los Angeles, Portland, Seattle, Atlanta, and Nashville.

Railroads accomplished these feats with the help of some of the largest government subsidies in American history. Railroad executives argued that

Chapter 16: The Transformation of the West and South, 1877–1892

Government Subsidy of Railroads

their activities benefited the public and that the government should aid them by giving them land from the public domain. Congress was sympathetic. In order to encourage construction, the government granted over 180 million acres, mostly to interstate routes chartered between 1850 and 1871. These grants usually consisted of a right of way plus alternate sections of land in a strip twenty to eighty miles wide along the right of way. Railroad corporations financed construction by using the land as security for bonds or by selling it for cash.

States and localities heaped further subsidies on new routes. State land was frequently offered to railroads by legislators, many of whom were handsomely bribed by executives and investors eager for the advantages railroads could bring. Total state grants amounted to about 50 million acres. Counties, cities, and towns also assisted railroads, usually by offering loans or by purchasing railroad bonds or stocks.

Government subsidies had mixed effects. Although capitalists argued against government interference, they nevertheless accepted government aid and pressured governments into meeting their needs. The Southern Pacific, for example, threatened to by-pass Los Angeles unless the city came up with a bonus and built a depot. Without public help, few railroads could have prospered sufficiently to attract private investment, yet public aid was not always salutary. During the 1880s, the policy of assistance haunted communities whose zeal for railroads had prompted them to commit too much to lines that were never built or that defaulted on loans. Some laborers and farmers fought subsidies, arguing that companies like the Southern Pacific would become too powerful. Many communities, however, boomed because they had linked their fortunes to the iron horse. Moreover, railroads drew farmers deeper into the market economy.

Farming the Plains

In an 1880 article, *Harper's New Monthly Magazine* marveled at the success of Oliver Dalrymple's farm in Dakota Territory's Red River valley. "You are in a sea of wheat," the writer rhapsodized. "The railroad train rolls through an ocean of grain. . . . We encounter a squadron of war chariots . . . doing the work of human hands. . . . There are 25 of them in this one brigade of the grand army of 115, under the marksmanship of this Dakota farmer." Dalrymple's farm exemplified two important achievements of the late nineteenth century: the taming of wide, windswept prairies so that the land would yield crops to benefit humankind; and the transformation of agriculture into big business by means of mechanization, long-distance transportation, and scientific cultivation.

These achievements did not come easily. The climate and landscape of the Plains presented formidable challenges, and overcoming them did not guarantee success or provide security. Agricultural development of the West turned the United States into the world's breadbasket, but it also scarred the lives of hundreds of thousands of men and women who made that development possible.

Migration to the Plains

Settlement of the Plains and the West involved the greatest migration in American history. Between 1870 and 1900, more acres were settled and put under cultivation than in the previous 250 years. Between 1860 and 1910, the number of farms tripled, from 2 million to over 6 million. During the 1870s and 1880s, hundreds of thousands of people streamed into states like Kansas, Nebraska, Texas, and California.

Most, though not all, migrants came from the eastern states or Europe. Several western states opened immigration bureaus in the East and in Europe to lure settlers westward. Land-grant railroads were especially aggressive, advertising cheap land, arranging credit terms, offering reduced fares, and promising instant success. Railroad agents—often former immigrants—traveled to Europe to recruit prospective settlers and greeted newcomers at eastern ports. In California, fruit and vegetable growers imported laborers from Japan and Mexico to work in the fields and canneries.

Most migrants went west because opportunities there seemed to promise a better life. Between 1870 and 1910 the nation's population rose from 40 million to 92 million, and total urban population swelled by over 400 percent. Railroad expansion made remote farming regions more accessible, and the construction of grain elevators eased problems of shipping and storage. As a result of population

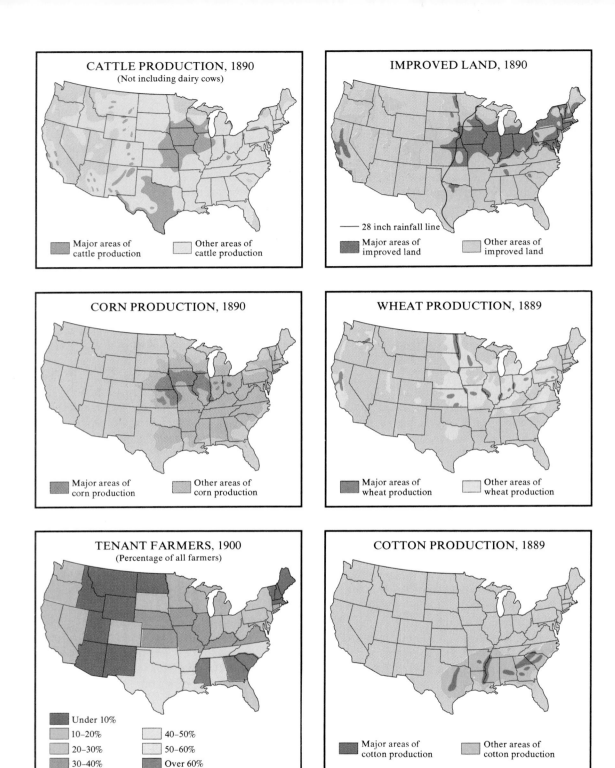

Agricultural Regions, 1889 and 1900 *Source: From Charles A. Paullin,* Atlas of the Historical Geography of the United States. *Used by permission of Carnegie Institution of Washington.*

growth, the demand for farm products grew rapidly, and developments in transportation and storage made the possibilities for commercial farming, growing crops for profit, more favorable than ever.

Life on the Plains, however, was much harder than the advertisements suggested. Migrants often encountered scarcities of essentials they had once taken for granted. The open prairies contained little lumber for housing and fuel. Pioneer families were forced to build houses of sod and to burn manure for heat. Water was as scarce as timber. Few families were lucky or wealthy enough to buy land near a stream that did not dry up in summer and freeze in winter. Machinery for drilling wells was scarce until the 1880s, and even then it was very expensive, so that many wells were dug by hand.

> **Hardships of Life on the Plains**

Even more formidable than the terrain of the Plains was the climate. The expanse between the Missouri River and the Rocky Mountains divides climatologically along a line running from Minnesota southwest through Oklahoma, then south, bisecting Texas. East of this line, annual rainfall averages about 28 inches, enough for most crops (see map). West of the line, life-giving rain was never certain; farmers, heartened by adequate water one year, gagged on dust and broke their plows on hardened limestone soil the next.

Weather seldom followed predictable cycles on either side of the line. In summer, weeks of torrid heat and parching winds would suddenly give way to violent storms that washed away crops and property. Winter blizzards piled up mountainous snowdrifts that halted all outdoor movement. In March and April, melting snow swelled streams, and flood waters threatened millions of acres. In the fall, a week without rain could turn dry grasslands into tinder, and the slightest spark could ignite a raging prairie fire.

Even when the climate was favorable, nature could be cruel. Weather that was good for crops was also good for breeding insects. Worms and flying pests ravaged corn and wheat. In the 1870s and 1880s swarms of grasshoppers virtually ate up entire farms. Heralded only by the rising din of buzzing wings, a cloud of insects a mile long would smother the land and devour everything in sight: plants, seeds, tree bark, and clothes. As one farmer lamented, the "hoppers left behind nothing but the mortgage."

Settlers of the Plains also had to contend with social isolation. In Europe farmers lived together in a village and traveled each day to their nearby fields. This pattern was rare in the American West. Instead, various peculiarities of land division compelled American rural dwellers to live apart from each other. The Homestead Act of 1862 and other measures adopted to encourage western settlement offered free or cheap plots to people who would live on and improve their property. Because most homesteads and other plots acquired by small farmers were rectangular—usually encompassing 160 acres—at most four families could live near each other, but only if they congregated around the shared four-corner boundary intersection. In practice, farmers usually lived back from their boundary lines, and at least a half-mile separated farmhouses. Often land adjacent to farmhouses was unoccupied, making neighbors even more distant.

> **Social Isolation**

Many observers wrote about the loneliness and monotony of life on the Plains. Men might find escape by working outdoors and taking occasional trips to sell crops or buy supplies. Women were more isolated, confined by domestic chores to the household, where, as one writer remarked, they were "not much better than slaves. It is a weary, monotonous round of cooking and washing and mending and as a result the insane asylum is 1/3d filled with wives of farmers."

The letters that Ed Donnell, a young Nebraska homesteader, wrote to his family reveal how time and circumstances could dull optimism. In the fall of 1885, Donnell wrote to his mother in Missouri: "I like Nebr first rate. . . . I have saw a pretty tuff time a part of the time since I have been out here, but I started out to get a home and I was determined to win or die in the attempt. . . . Have got a good crop of corn, a floor in my house and got it ceiled overhead." Already, though, Donnell was lonely. He went on: "There is lots of other bachelors here but I am the only one I know who doesn't have kinfolks living handy. . . . You wanted to know when I was going to get married. Just as quick as I can get money ahead to get a cow." A year and a half later, Donnell's dreams were dissolving, and he was beginning to look for a second chance elsewhere. As he explained to his brother, "The rats eat my sod stable down. . . . I may sell out this summer, land is going up so fast. . . . If I sell I am going west and

Three generations of a homesteading family overflow their primitive sod home on the Oklahoma frontier. This photograph reveals how dry and vacant the scrub Plains were, yet it also suggests a quiet confidence among the people who lived there. *University of Oklahoma Western History Collection.*

grow up with the country." By fall, things had worsened, and Donnell wrote his parents, "We have been having wet weather for 3 weeks. . . . My health has been so poor this summer and the wind and the sun hurts my head so. I think if I can sell I will . . . move to town for I can get $40 a month working in a grist mill and I would not be exposed to the weather." Donnell's doubts and hardships, shared by thousands of other people, fed the cityward migration of farm folk that characterized late-nineteenth-century urban growth (see pages 529–530).

Farm families survived by depending on their resolve and by organizing churches and clubs where they could socialize a few times a month.

> **Mail-Order Companies and Rural Free Delivery**

By the early 1900s, two external developments had combined to bring rural settlers into closer contact with modern consumer society (though people in sparsely settled regions west of the 28-inch rainfall line remained isolated for several more decades). First, starting in the 1870s and 1880s,

mail-order houses—Montgomery Ward and Sears Roebuck—expanded and made new industrial products available to almost everyone. Emphasizing personal attention to customers, Ward's and Sears Roebuck were outlets for sociability as well as material goods. Letters from customers to Mr. Ward often reported family news and sought advice on everything from gifts to childcare. A man from Washington State wrote, "As you advertise everything for sale that a person wants, I thought I would write you, as I am in need of a wife, and see what you could do for me." Another wrote: "I suppose you wonder why we haven't ordered anything from you since the fall. The cow kicked my arm and broke it and besides my wife was sick, and there was the doctor bill. But now, thank God, that is paid, and we are all well again, and we have a fine new baby boy, and please send plush bonnet number 29d8077."

Second, during the 1890s, scores of rural communities petitioned Congress for extension of the postal service, and in 1896 the government made Rural Free Delivery (RFD) widely available. Farm-

TIME AND COST OF FARMING AN ACRE OF LAND BY HAND AND BY MACHINE, 1890

Crop	Hours Required		Labor Cost	
	Hand	Machine	Hand	Machine
Wheat	61	3	$3.65	$ .66
Corn	39	15	$3.62	$1.51
Oats	66	7	$3.73	$1.07
Loose hay	21	4	$1.75	$ .42

Source: Ray Allan Billington, Westward Expansion: A History of the American Frontier, *2nd ed. (New York: Macmillan, 1960), p. 697.*

ers would no longer lack news and information; they could receive letters, newspapers, advertisements, and catalogues at home nearly every day. In 1913 the postal service inaugurated parcel post, which enabled people to receive packages, such as orders from Ward's and Sears, more easily. By 1920, rural families had access to industrializing society through the mails.

In the years following the Civil War, the extension of the farming frontier, the growth of national and international markets for food, and the expansion of railroad routes, which made possible the shipment of goods from farm to market, brought about an agricultural revolution. But that transformation would not have been possible, nor would the Plains have been conquered, without the expanded use of machinery. When the Civil War drew men away from farms in the upper Mississippi River valley, the female and male laborers who remained behind began using reapers and other implements extensively to meet the demand for grain and to take advantage of high prices. After the war, continued demand and high prices encouraged farmers to depend more on machines, and inventors worked to develop new implements for farm use. Seeders, combines, binders, mowers, and rotary plows were introduced to the Plains and California in the 1870s and 1880s.

Mechanization of Agriculture

For centuries the acreage of grain a farmer could plant had been limited by the amount that could be harvested by hand. Machines—driven first by animals, then by steam—increased productivity beyond imagination. Before mechanization, a farmer working alone could harvest about 7.5 acres of wheat. Using an automatic binder that cut and tied bundles of grain, the same farmer could harvest 135 acres. Machines dramatically reduced the time and cost of farming various other crops as well (see table).

During this period, Congress and scientists were making efforts to improve existing crops and develop new ones. The 1862 Morrill Land Grant Act (see page 412) gave each state public lands to sell in order to finance agricultural and industrial colleges. Although the act discriminated against western states by granting 30,000 acres for each senator and representative (New York thus received about 1 million acres, Kansas only 90,000), it did promote the establishment of educational institutions that aided agricultural development. (A second Morrill Act in 1890 aided more schools, including a number of public black colleges.) The Hatch Act of 1887 provided for agricultural experiment stations in every state, further encouraging the advancement of farming technology.

Legislative and Scientific Aid to Farmers

Meanwhile, scientific advances were enabling farmers to use the soil more efficiently. Agricultural researchers developed the technique of dry farming, a system of plowing and harrowing that prevented precious moisture from evaporating. Botanists perfected varieties of "hard" wheat whose

This lithograph advertises the advantages of mechanized farming, portraying how one crew of workers could use steam engines to set a new one-day world's record in threshing. *Department of Special Collections, F. Hal Higgins Library of Agricultural Technology, University of California.*

seeds could withstand northern winters, and millers invented an efficient process for grinding those tougher wheat kernels into flour. Agriculturists also adapted new varieties of alfalfa from Mongolia, corn from North Africa, and rice from Asia. Californian Luther Burbank developed a wide range of new plants by crossbreeding. Tuskegee Institute's chemist George Washington Carver created hundreds of new products from peanuts, soybeans, sweet potatoes, and cotton wastes and taught methods of soil improvement. Scientists developed means of combating plant and animal diseases. Although turbulent times for farmers lay just ahead, development of the agricultural hinterland by settlement, science, and technology made America "the garden of the world."

The Ranching Frontier

While commercial farming was spreading, one of the West's most romantic industries, cattle ranch-

ing, was evolving. Early in the nineteenth century, huge herds of cattle, originally introduced by the Spanish and developed by Mexican ranchers, roamed southern Texas and bred with cattle brought by American settlers. The resulting longhorn breed multiplied and became valuable by the 1860s, when the East's as well as the West's growing population increased demand for food and railroads made the transportation of beef more feasible. By 1870, drovers were herding thousands of Texas cattle northward to Kansas, Missouri, and Wyoming (see map, page 478). On these long drives, mounted cowboys (as many as 25 percent of whom were blacks) supervised the herds, which fed on open grassland along the way. At the northern terminus—usually Abilene, Dodge City, or Cheyenne—the cattle were either sold as stock for northern ranches or loaded onto trains and sent eastward to Chicago and St. Louis for slaughter and distribution.

The long drive gave rise to its own romantic lore, but it was not very efficient. In trekking 1,500 miles, the cattle became sinewy and tough. Herds traveling through Indian lands and farmers' fields were sometimes shot at and later prohibited from such trespass by state laws. The ranchers' only solution was to eliminate long drives by raising herds nearer to railroad routes.

When ranchers discovered that crossing sturdy Texas longhorns with heavier Hereford and Angus breeds produced cattle better able to survive northern winters, cattle raising spread across the Great Plains. Between 1860 and 1880 the cattle population of Kansas, Nebraska, Colorado, Wyoming, Montana, and Dakota increased from 130,000 to 4.5 million.

Cattle raisers needed vast stretches of land where their herds could graze, and they wanted to incur as little expense as possible in using such land. Thus they often bought a few acres bordering streams and turned their herds loose on adjacent public domain that no one wanted to own because it lacked water access. By this method, called open-range ranching, a cattle raiser could control thousands of acres by owning only a hundred or so.

▶ **Open-Range Ranching**

Neighboring ranchers often formed associations and allowed their herds to graze together. An owner distinguished his or her cattle from someone else's by burning a special mark, or brand, into the hide of every animal. Each ranch had its own brand—an improvised shorthand for labeling movable property. Twice each year, cowboy crews rounded up the cattle in order to brand new calves in the spring and to drive mature animals to market in the fall.

Roundups provided easterners with colorful images of western life: bellowing cattle, mounted rope-swinging cowboys, the smell of singed hides and smoky campfires. But roundups and open-range ranching were short-lived because they were too successful. Opportunities for profit first provided new fortunes for Civil War veterans in Texas and other states. By the early 1880s, the profitability of beef raising had lured scores of investors to the industry. As one publication explained:

> A good sized steer when it is fit for the butcher market will bring from $45.00 to $60.00. The same animal at its birth was worth but $5.00. He has run on the plains and cropped the grass from the public domain for four or five years, and now, with scarcely any expense to its owner, is worth $40.00 more than when he started on his pilgrimage.

National and international demand for beef kept rising, and ranchers and capital flowed into the Plains. Soon cattle began to overrun the range.

Meanwhile, sheepherders from California and New Mexico moved into the cattle ranges. Ranchers complained that sheep ruined grassland by eating down to the roots and that cattle refused to graze where sheep had been because the "woolly critters" left a repulsive odor. Armed conflict occasionally erupted between cowboys and sheepherders who resorted to violence rather than settle disputes in court, where the judge would discover that both were using the land illegally. More important than these disputes was the fact that the farming frontier was advancing into the West, from the Missouri to the Pacific.

Fearing depletion of the prairie and loss of control, ranchers began to fence in their pastures with newly invented barbed wire—even though they had no legal title to the land. Fences eliminated the open range and often provoked disputes between competing ranchers, between cattle raisers and sheep raisers, and between ranchers and farmers who claimed use of the same land. In 1885, President Grover Cleveland ordered the removal of illegal fences on public lands and Indian reservations. Enforcement was slow, but the order signaled that free use of public domain was ending.

Open-range ranching made beef a staple of the American diet and created a few fortunes, but its extralegal features could not survive the rush of history. By 1890, big businesses were taking over the cattle industry and applying scientific methods of breeding and feeding. Most ranchers owned or leased the land they used, though some illegal fencing continued. The cowboy became just another corporate wage earner, though the myth of his freedom and individualism grew rather than faded.

The South After Reconstruction

While the West was being transformed in various ways, the South developed its own kinds of resource exploitation and market economies. In 1880, four times as many farmers lived in the South as on the Plains. Ravaged by the Civil War, which had killed one-third of all draft animals and destroyed half of the region's farm equipment, south-

The ranching frontier quickly turned into a commercial enterprise when cowboys herded scores of long-horns to places like this Montana stockyard, from which the cattle were then loaded onto eastbound trains. *Montana Historical Society.*

ern agriculture recovered slowly. Rather than diversify, farmers concentrated on cotton growing even more heavily than before the war. High prices for seed and implements, declining prices for crops, taxes, and, most of all, debt trapped many white families in poverty. Conditions were even worse for blacks, who had to endure brutal racial prejudice along with economic hardship.

To achieve sectional independence, some southern leaders tried to promote industrialization. Their efforts partially succeeded, but by the early 1900s many southern industries were mere subsidiaries of northern firms. Moreover, southern planters, shippers, and manufacturers depended heavily on northern banks to finance their operations. Equally important, low wages and stunted opportunities prevented inflows of people—laborers, farmers, businesspeople, and professionals—who would have brought along inflows of capital. Thus

although in some ways the South grew as rapidly as the North, it remained an isolated region, poorly integrated into the national economy.

During and after Reconstruction, a significant shift in the nature of agriculture swept through the South. Between 1860 and 1880, the total number of farms in southern states more than doubled, from 450,000 to 1.1 million. The number of landowners, however, did not increase, and the size of the average farm actually decreased—from 347 to 156 acres. The result was that a larger proportion of southern farmers rented, rather than owned, their farms. Southern agriculture was dominated by landlords rather than by laborlords (slave owners), and the system was characterized by sharecropping and tenant farming (see page 000). Over one-third of the farmers counted in 1880 were sharecroppers and tenants, and the proportion increased to two-thirds by 1920.

Sharecropping and tenant farming entangled millions of southerners in a web of humiliation. At its center was the crop lien, which worked in the following way. Currency was scarce, and most farmers were too poor ever to have cash on hand. Forced to borrow in order to buy necessities, they could offer as collateral only what they could grow. Thus a farmer in need of supplies would deal with a nearby "furnishing merchant," who would exchange supplies for a certain portion, or lien, of the farmer's forthcoming crop. In the fall, after the crop was harvested and brought to market, the merchant collected his debt. But all too often the farmer's debt exceeded his crop's value, and the merchant frequently took advantage of the customer's powerlessness by inflating prices. Thus the farmer owed the merchant, received no cash for the crop, and still needed food and supplies. His only choice was to commit the next year's crop to the merchant and sink deeper into debt.

Crop-Lien System

Prices charged to credit customers averaged 30 to 40 percent higher than prices charged to cash customers. Credit customers also had to pay interest ranging from 33 to 200 percent on the advances they received. Suppose, for example, that a farmer needed a 20-cent bag of seed or a 20-cent piece of cloth and had no cash. The furnishing merchant would extend credit for the purchase but would also boost the price to 28 cents. At year's end that 28-cent loan would have accumulated interest, raising the farmer's debt to, say, 42 cents—more than double the item's original cost. The farmer, having pledged more than his crop's worth against scores of such debts, fell behind in payments and never recovered. If he fell too far behind, he could be evicted. As one writer remarked about the crop-lien system, "When one of these mortgages has been recorded against the Southern farmer, he had usually passed into a state of helpless peonage."

The lien system caused hardship in former plantation areas where tenants and sharecroppers, blacks and whites, grew cotton for the same markets that had existed before the Civil War. But in the southern backcountry, which in the antebellum era had contained small farms, relatively few slaves, and diversified agriculture, problems of crop liens were compounded by other economic changes.

New spending habits of backcountry farmers reflected the most important of these changes. In 1884, Jephta Dickson of Jackson County in the northern Georgia hills bought $53.37 worth of flour, meal, peas, meat, corn, and syrup from one merchant and $2.53 worth of potatoes, peas, and sugar from another. Such expenditures would have been rare in the upcountry before the Civil War, when most farmers grew almost all the food they needed. But after the war, yeoman farmers like Jephta Dickson shifted from semisubsistence agriculture to more commercialized farming, and in the South that meant cotton raising. They made this change for two reasons: debts that they had incurred during the war and Reconstruction forced them to grow a crop that would bring in cash, and railroad expansion enabled them to transport cotton to markets more easily than before. As backcountry yeomen put more acres under cotton cultivation, they raised less of what they needed on a day-to-day basis and were forced more frequently into positions where they were at the mercy of merchants. In this respect, their economies resembled those of western Indians.

At the same time, backcountry farmers suffered from new laws that essentially closed the southern range. This change also resulted from the commercialization of agriculture. Before the 1870s southern farmers, like open-range ranchers in the West, had always been able to let their livestock roam freely on other people's land in search of food and water. By custom, farmers who wished to protect their crops from foraging animals were supposed to build fences around those crops. But as commercial agriculture invaded the backcountry, large landowners and merchants induced county and state legislative bodies to require farmers to fence in their animals rather than their crops. Such laws hurt poor farmers who had very little land, because the laws prevented them from letting their animals feed on an open range and caused them to use more of their precious land for pasture. The laws were consistent with the concept of individual responsibility for private property, but they undermined traditional cooperative customs that yeomen cherished. As one farmer asserted, "God makes the grass . . . and corn in the valleys grow, so let's not try to deprive our poor neighbors from receiving his blessing." Increasingly, yeoman farmers developed antagonisms toward merchants, large land-

Closing the Southern Range

owners, and other supporters of commercialized agriculture. Their disaffection would find political expression that eventually coalesced into populism (see Chapter 20).

Poor whites of the rural South not only faced economic threat from loss of the open range; they also feared that newly enfranchised blacks could undermine whatever political and social superiority (real and imagined) the poor whites held. Wealthy white landowners and merchants fanned these fears, using racism to keep poor whites and blacks divided and to prevent protests over economic distress from threatening their power.

The majority of the nation's black people lived in the South, worked in agriculture, and found that under freedom they faced the same disadvantages they had faced under slavery. As

Condition of Blacks in the prewar era, blacks adapted to racial bias by creating and controlling their own social institutions: churches, schools, and family networks. The abolition of slavery had altered their legal status, but it had not improved their opportunities relative to those of whites. In 1880, 90 percent of all southern blacks depended for a living on farming or personal and domestic service—the same occupations they had held as slaves.

Pushed into sharecropping and burdened with crop liens, blacks also had to contend with new forms of social and political oppression. With slavery dead, white supremacists fashioned new ways to keep blacks in a position of inferiority. Southern leaders, embittered by northern interference in race relations during Reconstruction and eager to reassert their authority after the withdrawal of federal troops (see page 462), instituted racist measures to discourage blacks from voting and to legally segregate them from whites.

The end of Reconstruction had not stopped blacks from voting. Although threats and intimidation against them increased, blacks still formed the backbone of the Republican party and some still won elective offices. In North Carolina, for example, forty-three black men were elected to the state house and eleven to the state senate between 1877 and 1890. White politicians, however, began to seek ways to reduce the "Negro vote" by establishing restrictions that appeared neutral but would actually bar blacks from the polls. Beginning with Georgia in 1877, southern states levied taxes of $1 to $2 on all citizens wishing to vote. These poll taxes were prohibitive to most black voters, who were so deeply in debt to furnishing merchants and landlords that they never had cash for any purpose. Other schemes disfranchised black voters who could not read. For example, voters might be required to deposit ballots for different candidates in different ballot boxes. In order to do so correctly, voters had to be able to read instructions. These measures also disqualified many poor whites, but their main objective was to curtail voting by blacks.

Racial discrimination also stiffened in social affairs. Alongside slavery, a widespread informal system of separation had governed race relations in the antebellum South. After the Civil War, this system was formalized in law. In a series of cases during the 1870s, the Supreme Court opened the door to discrimination by ruling that the Fourteenth Amendment protected citizens' rights only against infringement by state governments. The federal government, according to the Court, had no authority over what individuals or organizations did. If blacks wanted protection under the law, the Court said, they must seek it from the states, which under the Tenth Amendment retained all powers not specifically assigned to Congress.

Spread of Jim Crow Laws

The climax to these rulings came in 1883, when in the *Civil Rights Cases* the Court struck down the 1875 Civil Rights Act, which had prohibited segregation in public facilities such as streetcars, hotels, theaters, and parks. Again the Court declared that the federal government could not regulate the behavior of private individuals in matters of race relations. Subsequent lower-court cases in the 1880s established the principle that blacks could be restricted to "separate-but-equal" facilities. The Supreme Court upheld the separate-but-equal doctrine in *Plessy* v. *Ferguson* (1896) and officially applied it to schools in *Cummins* v. *County Board of Education* (1899).

Thereafter, segregation laws—known as Jim Crow laws—piled up throughout the South, confronting black people with daily reminders of their inferior status. State and local laws restricted blacks to the rear of streetcars, separate drinking and toilet facilities, and separate sections of hospitals, asylums, and cemeteries. A Birmingham, Alabama, ordinance required that the races be "distinctly separated . . . by well defined physical barriers" in "any room, hall, theatre, picture house, auditorium,

Racial segregation, already a long-established practice in the South, became further institutionalized in the late nineteenth century. Whites in New Orleans, for example, could enjoy balls, restaurants, and theater; blacks, even when they could afford such entertainment as the theater, had to accept confinement to separate and inferior galleries. *Historic New Orleans Collection.*

yard, court, ballpark, or other indoor or outdoor place." Local laws defined certain districts or blocks as all-black or all-white. Mobile, Alabama, passed a curfew requiring blacks to be off the streets by 10 P.M, and Atlanta required separate Bibles for black witnesses swearing before court. Thus for thousands of black southerners race relations deteriorated after emancipation, and they would not improve markedly until the 1960s, when a turbulent civil rights movement overturned many of the old restrictions (see Chapter 33).

In industry, breezes of change were being stimulated by new manufacturing initiatives, but there too a distinctively southern quality prevailed. Two of the South's leading industries in the late nineteenth century relied on traditional staple crops, cotton and tobacco. In the 1870s, textile mills began to appear in the Cotton

Industrialization of the South

Belt. Powered by the region's abundant rivers and streams, manned cheaply by poor whites eager to escape crop liens, and aided by low taxes, such mills grew rapidly. By 1900 the South had four hundred mills with a total of over 4 million spindles, and twenty years later the region was replacing New England in textile-manufacturing supremacy. Proximity to raw materials and cheap labor also aided the tobacco industry, and the invention in 1880 of a cigarette-making machine immensely enhanced the marketability of tobacco.

Cigarettes were manufactured in cities by black and white workers; textile mills were concentrated in small towns and developed their own exploitative labor system. Financed mostly by local investors, mills employed women and children from nearby poor white families and paid 50 cents a day for twelve or more hours of work. Such wages were barely half of what northern workers received.

Textile mills, such as this one in Greensboro, North Carolina, represented the growing industrialization of the New South around 1900. Here, low-paid millworkers are shown feeding cotton into machines. *Library of Congress.*

Many companies built villages around their mills and controlled housing, stores, schools, and churches. Criticism of the company was forbidden, and attempts at union organization were squelched. Mill families soon found that factory jobs changed their status very little. The company store replaced the furnishing merchant, and the mill owner replaced the landlord.

Several other industries were launched in the South, mainly under sponsorship of northern or European capitalists. Between 1890 and 1900, northern lumber syndicates moved into the pine forests of the Gulf states, boosting production by 500 percent. During the 1880s, northern investors developed southern iron and steel manufacturing, much of which centered in the boom city of Birmingham. Coal mining and railroad construction also expanded rapidly, but New York and London financiers dominated the boards of directors of most southern companies. Moreover, the South lacked technological innovators, such as those in

the machine-tool industry who had enabled northern industries to compete with other industrializing nations. Southern industries had to wait until techniques were developed elsewhere and then try to make use of them.

Regardless of outside influence, industrialization prompted southern boosters to herald the emergence of a New South ready to compete economically with other sections. Henry Grady, editor of the *Atlanta Constitution* and the most articulate voice of southern progress, proclaimed, "We have sowed towns and cities in the place of theories, and put business in place of politics. We have challenged your spinners in Massachusetts and your iron-makers in Pennsylvania. . . . We have fallen in love with work." Yet in 1900 the South remained as rural as it had been in 1860. Staple-crop agriculture supported its economy, and white supremacy permeated its social and political relations, keeping blacks out of industrial jobs and away from the polls. Furthermore, the South attracted few immigrants because of its low wages and thus enjoyed little of their energizing influence. In 1910 only about 2 percent of the southern population was foreign-born. A New South would emerge, but not until after a world war and a massive black exodus had jostled old habits and attitudes.

As the continent filled in and the West and South were transformed, white Americans exhibited their best and worst characteristics. The development of the West was accomplished with courage and creativity that amazed the rest of the world. The optimistic conquerors, however, displayed a waste-fulness, violence, and greed that tarnished the American image by overwhelming the culture of the land's original inhabitants and sacrificing environmental balance for market profits. In the South recovery and growth kindled new optimism, but careless exploitation exhausted the soil and left poor farmers as downtrodden as ever. In an age of expansion, blacks saw their rights and opportunities narrowing. Industrialization failed to lessen the dominance of southern staple-crop agriculture, and by 1900 the South was more dependent economically on the North than it had been before the Civil War. In the West and the South the appeal of commercial exchange drew natives and newcomers away from their subsistence ways of life and into the marketplace. The raw materials and agricultural products of both sections improved living standards and contributed to industrial progress, but not without human and environmental costs.

Suggestions for Further Reading

The Western Frontier

Ray A. Billington and Martin Ridge, *Westward Expansion*, 5th ed. (1982); Odie B. Faulk, *Tombstone: Myth and Reality* (1972); William S. Greever, *Bonanza West: Western Mining Rushes* (1963); Robert V. Hine, *The American West*, 2nd ed. (1984); Julie Roy Jeffrey, *Frontier Women* (1979); Patricia Limerick, *The Legacy of Conquest: The Unbroken Past of the American West* (1987); Frederick Merk, *History of the Westward Movement* (1978); Ruth Moynihan, *Rebel for Rights: Abigail Scott Duniway* (1983); Rodman W. Paul, *The Far West and the Great Plains in Transition, 1859–1900* (1988); Rodman W. Paul and Richard W. Etulain, *The Frontier and the American West* (1977); Richard Slotkin, *The Fatal Environment: The Myth of the Frontier in the Age of Industriali-*

zation (1985); Henry Nash Smith, *Virgin Land: The American West as Symbol and Myth* (1950); Roberta B. Sol-lid, *Calamity Jane* (1958); Kent Ladd Steckmesser, *The Western Hero in History and Legend* (1965).

Railroads

Alfred D. Chandler, ed., *Railroads: The Nation's First Big Business* (1965); Robert W. Fogel, *Railroads and Economic Growth* (1964); Edward C. Kirkland, *Men, Cities, and Transportation* (1948); George R. Taylor and Irene Neu, *The American Railroad Network* (1956); Alan Trachtenberg, *The Incorporation of America* (1982); O. O. Winther, *The Transportation Frontier* (1964).

Indians

Ralph K. Andrist, *The Long Death: The Last Days of the Plains Indians* (1964); Norris Hundley, Jr., ed., *The American Indian* (1974); Francis Paul Prucha, *The Great Father: The United States Government and the American Indians* (1984); Edward H. Spicer, *Cycles of Conquest: The Impact of Spain, Mexico, and the United States on the Indians of the Southwest* (1962); Robert M. Utley, *The Indian Frontier of the American West, 1846–1890* (1984); Robert M. Utley, *Frontier Regulars: The United States Army and the Indian* (1973); Wilcomb E. Washburn, *Red Man's Land/White Man's Law* (1971); Richard White, *The Roots of Dependency* (1983).

Ranching and Settlement of the Plains

Lewis Atherton, *The Cattle Kings* (1961); Allan G. Bogue, *From Prairie to Corn Belt* (1963); Everett Dick, *The Sod-House Frontier* (1937); Gilbert C. Fite, *The Farmer's Frontier* (1963); Joe B. Frantz and Julian Choate, Jr., *The American Cowboy* (1955); Walter Prescott Webb, *The Great Plains* (1931).

The New South

Orville Vernon Burton and Robert C. McMath, Jr., eds., *Toward a New South?: Post–Civil War Southern Communities* (1982); Thomas D. Clark and Albert D. Kirwan, *The South Since Appomattox* (1967); Paul Gaston, *The New South Creed* (1970); Dewey Grantham, Jr., *The Democratic South* (1963); Steven Hahn, *The Roots of Southern Populism: Yeoman Farmers and the Transformation of the Georgia Upcountry, 1850–1890* (1983); Stanley P. Hirshson, *Farewell to the Bloody Shirt: Northern Republicans and the Southern Negro* (1962); J. Morgan Kousser, *The Shaping of Southern Politics* (1974); Melton A. McLaurin, *Paternalism and Protest: Southern Cotton Mill Workers and Organized Labor* (1971); Howard N. Rabinowitz, *Race Relations in the Urban South, 1865–1890* (1978); Theodore Saloutos, *Farmer Movements in the South, 1865–1933* (1960); C. Vann Woodward, *The Strange Career of Jim Crow* (1966); C. Vann Woodward, *Origins of the New South,* rev. ed. (1951); Gavin Wright, *Old South, New South* (1986).

Conrad Carl tried to appear calm, but he was understandably nervous. It was spring 1882, and Carl, who for nearly thirty years had been a tailor who did piecework in his New York City tenement apartment, was appearing before a group of United States senators in Washington, D.C. The Committee on Education and Labor was conducting an investigation into the causes of recent labor unrest, and Senator James L. Pugh, a former Confederate congressman from Alabama, was asking Carl to explain changing work conditions in the tailoring business.

Admitting that his testimony would probably cost him his job, Carl nevertheless answered candidly. When he first began tailoring, Carl explained, he and his wife and children had pieced together garments by hand. The pace of their work was relaxed, yet he was able to save a few dollars each year. Then, said Carl, "in 1854 or 1855, . . . the sewing machine was invented and introduced, and it stitched very nicely, nicer than the tailor could do; and the bosses said: 'We want you to use the sewing machine; you have to buy one.'"

17

THE MACHINE AGE, 1877–1920

Carl and his fellow tailors used their meager savings to buy machines, hoping they could earn more by producing more. But employers cut wages instead of raising them. The tailors "found that we could earn no more than we could without the machine; but the money for the machine was gone now, and we found that the machine was only for the profit of the bosses; that they got their work quicker, and it was done nicer." Moreover, Carl, now old and discouraged, had seen that mechanization had other troubling effects on workers and those around them. "The machine," he said, "makes too much noise and the neighbors want to sleep, and we have to stop sewing earlier, so we have to work faster. We work now in excitement— in a hurry. It is hunting; it is not work at all; it is a hunt."

Conrad Carl's testimony to the Senate committee was one worker's view of the industrialization that was relentlessly overtaking American society. The forces prevailing in the new order were both inspiring and ominous. The factory and the machine broke down manufacturing into minute, routinized tasks and organized work according to the dictates of the clock. Corporations merged and amassed frightening power in the quest for produc-

The Big Blow—The Bessemer Process (detail) by Aaron Bohrod. Oil on canvas. *Private Collection.*

tivity and profits. Defenders of the new system devised new social and economic theories to justify it, while critics tried to counteract what they thought were abuses of power. Workers, who had long thought of themselves as valued producers, were caught in the changing modes of production and fought to avoid becoming slaves to machines.

Industrialization was and is a complex process whose chief feature is the production of goods by machine rather than by hand. Associated with industrialization in America were the following characteristics:

1. Involvement of an increasing proportion of the work force in manufacturing
2. Concentration of production in large, intricately organized factories
3. Accelerated technological innovation, emphasizing new inventions and applied science
4. Expanded markets, no longer merely local and regional in scope
5. Growth of a nationwide transportation network based on the railroad, and an accompanying communications network based on the telegraph and telephone
6. Increased accumulation of capital for investment in the expansion of production
7. Growth of large enterprises and specialization in all forms of economic activity
8. Rapid increase in population
9. Steady increase in the size and predominance of cities

In 1860 about one-fourth of the American labor force worked in manufacturing and transportation; over one-half did so in 1920. The number of people gainfully employed rose from 17.4 million in 1880 to 41.6 million in 1920. In 1870 Western Union handled over 9 million telegraph messages on 112,000 miles of wire; by 1900 it processed over 63 million messages on 933,000 miles of wire. Between 1879 and 1920 the value of exports increased twelvefold. By the dawn of the twentieth century, the United States was not only the world's largest producer of raw materials and food, but the most productive industrial nation as well.

Accelerated migration from farms and mass immigration from abroad swelled the industrial work force (see Chapter 18); but machines, more than people, boosted American productivity. Only by using machines could manufacturers lower production costs and significantly raise each worker's output. Mechanization relied on the use of standardized parts and brought about more specialization on factory assembly lines.

A spirit of nationalism infused American industrialization. Many industrialists believed that productivity was the key to national welfare. Thus John D. Rockefeller linked his business activities to a nationalistic mission, explaining, "I wanted to participate in the work of making our country great. I had an ambition to build." Yet the accomplishments of industrial expansion, like expansion into natural resources and agricultural frontiers, involved waste and greed. The vigor and creativity that marked the half-century after the end of the Civil War gave rise to both constructive and destructive forces.

These trends weighed most heavily on the industrial work force. Economic growth furnished jobs and income to millions of families who had left American farms and European villages in search of a better existence. But industry's emphasis on productivity and profitability often kept wages at or below subsistence levels and harnessed workers to monotonous routines. Fearful that American industrialism might create a class of helpless proletarians who had lost control over their economic livelihoods, laborers fought to retain independent work habits and to be paid a living wage. Although the period was not a triumphant one for labor, it did contain a strong undercurrent of worker activism in reforms, cooperatives, and unions, as workers tried to reconcile new economic realities with the desire to live a life of comfort and dignity.

Technology and the Quest for Wealth

In 1876, Thomas A. Edison and his associates moved into a long wooden shed in Menlo Park, New Jersey, where Edison intended to turn out "a minor invention every ten days and a big thing every six months or so." Here was the brash American spirit adapting itself to a new age. If Americans wanted new products, they had to organize and work purposefully to bring about progress. Edison envisioned his Menlo Park laboratory as an invention factory, where creative people would pool

1873–78	Hard times	**1894**	Pullman strike
1877	Widespread railroad strikes		Henry Demarest Lloyd, *Wealth Against Commonwealth*
1879	Henry George, *Progress and Poverty*	**1895**	*U.S.* v. *E. C. Knight Co.*
	Edison perfects the incandescent light bulb	**1896**	*Holden* v. *Hardy*
1882	Formation of the Standard Oil trust	**1901**	U.S. Steel Corporation founded
1884–85	Hard times	**1902**	Reorganization of E. I. du Pont de Nemours and Company
1886	Haymarket riot	**1903**	Ford Motor Company founded
	American Federation of Labor founded	**1905**	*Lochner* v. *New York*
			Industrial Workers of the World founded
1888	Edward Bellamy, *Looking Backward*	**1908**	*Muller* v. *Oregon*
1890	Sherman Anti-Trust Act		First Ford Model T built
1892	Homestead Steel strike	**1911**	Triangle Shirtwaist fire
1893–97	Hard times	**1913**	First moving assembly line begins operation at Ford

their ideas and skills to fashion marketable products. Such efforts were part of a process that enlivened American industrialization at the end of the nineteenth century.

The years between 1865 and 1900 were a time of invention and innovation. Important devices like the steam engine, dynamo (generator), and sewing machine, which had existed in Europe and the United States since the early or mid-nineteenth century, were adapted more fully to the needs of industry and agriculture. Moreover, late-nineteenth-century inventions and refinements in electricity, internal combustion, and industrial chemistry laid the technical foundations for twentieth-century industrial development. The patent system, created by the Constitution to "promote the Progress of science and useful Arts," testified to an outburst of American inventiveness. Between 1790 and 1860 the U.S. Patent Office had granted a total of 36,000 patents. In 1897 alone, however, it granted 22,000 patents, and in the seventy years after 1860 it granted 1.5 million.

Thomas Edison, one of the world's pioneers in the electrical industry, came close to fulfilling the goal he set at Menlo Park. He patented over a thousand inventions, many of which used electrical power to transmit light, sound, and images. Perhaps the biggest of his "big thing" projects began in 1878 when he formed the Edison Electric Light Company and embarked on a search for a cheap, efficient means of indoor lighting. Gas, candles, and oil lamps had become impractical for lighting streets and large buildings. So Edison turned to light made by an electric current flowing between two carbon rods. His major contribution, reached after tedious trial-and-error work, was perfection of an incandescent bulb, which used a filament in a vacuum. At the same time he worked out a system of power production and distribution—an improved dynamo and a parallel circuit of wires—that would provide cheap, convenient lighting to a large number of customers.

Birth of the Electrical Industry

Technology and the Quest for Wealth

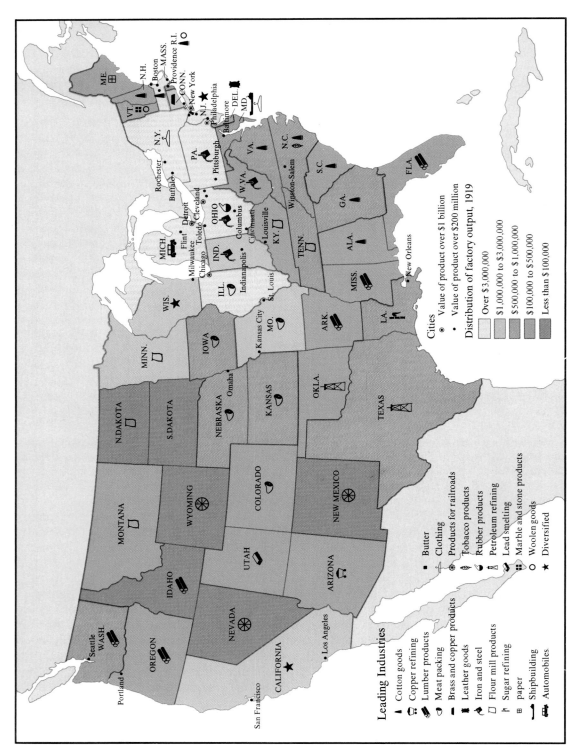

Industrial Production, 1919 *Source:* © *American Heritage Publishing Co., Inc., American Heritage Pictorial Atlas of United States History; data from U.S. Bureau of the Census,* Fourteenth Census of the United States, 1920. *Vol. IX: Manufacturing (Washington: U.S. Government Printing Office, 1921).*

Cities
⊚ Value of product over $1 billion
• Value of product over $200 million

Distribution of factory output, 1919
Over $3,000,000
$1,000,000 to $3,000,000
$500,000 to $1,000,000
$100,000 to $500,000
Less than $100,000

Leading Industries

Cotton goods
Copper refining
Lumber products
Meat packing
Brass and copper products
Leather goods
Iron and steel
Flour mill products
Sugar refining
paper
Shipbuilding
Automobiles

Butter
Clothing
Products for railroads
Tobacco products
Rubber products
Petroleum refining
Lead smelting
Marble and stone products
Woolen goods
Diversified

Thomas Alva Edison (1847–1931) at work in his laboratory around 1890. Edison developed countless inventions, including the incandescent light bulb, the phonograph, and early forms of motion picture reproduction. He also was a skilled publicist, capable of selling his ideas for commercial purposes. *Library of Congress.*

Aware that he had to make his ideas marketable, Edison acted as his own publicist. During the 1880 Christmas season he illuminated Menlo Park with forty incandescent bulbs, and in 1882 he built a power plant that would light eighty-five buildings in New York's Wall Street financial district. When this Pearl Street Station began service, a *New York Times* reporter marveled that working in his office at night "seemed almost like writing in daylight." The next year, New Yorkers celebrated Edison's achievement by staging a ballet complete with an electrically lighted model of the Brooklyn Bridge and ballerinas whose costumes were wired so they glowed.

Edison's system had a major limitation: it used direct current at low voltage and could thus send electric power only a mile or two. George Westinghouse, an inventor from Schenectady, New York, who at age twenty-three had become famous for

devising an air brake for railroad cars, solved the problem. Westinghouse used alternating current and transformers to reduce high-voltage power to lower voltage levels, thus making transmission over long distances cheaper.

Once Edison and Westinghouse had made their technological breakthroughs, others helped distribute their inventions to a wide market. Samuel Insull, Edison's private secretary, who later amassed a huge electric utility empire, deftly attracted investments and organized Edison power plants across the country. In the late 1880s and early 1890s financiers Henry Villard and J. P. Morgan consolidated patents in electric lighting and merged equipment-manufacturing companies into the General Electric Company. Equally important, General Electric and Westinghouse Electric established research laboratories that paid practical-minded scientists to find new uses for electricity. Under

Technology and the Quest for Wealth

talented scientist and organizer Willis M. Whitney, the General Electric lab pioneered in myriad developments ranging from vacuum tubes for radios to atomic theory.

A number of inventors worked independently and tried, sometimes successfully, sometimes not, to sell their handiwork to manufacturing companies. One such inventor was Granville T. Woods, a black electrical and mechanical engineer from Columbus, Ohio. Working in machine shops, first in Cincinnati and then in New York City, Woods patented thirty-five devices vital to electronics and communications. Among his inventions, most of which he sold to electric companies such as General Electric, were an automatic circuit breaker, an electric incubator, an electromagnetic brake, and various instruments to aid communications between railroad trains.

The era's most visionary manufacturer was Henry Ford. In the 1890s he worked as an electrical engineer in Detroit's Edison Company and in his spare time experimented with a gasoline-burning internal combustion engine to power a vehicle. George Selden, a lawyer from Rochester, New York, had been tinkering with internal combustion engines since the 1870s. But Ford applied his organizational genius to this invention and spawned a massive industry.

Like Edison, Ford had a scheme as well as a product. In 1909 he declared, "I am going to democratize the automobile. When I'm through everybody will be able to afford one, and about everyone will have one." The way to do so, according to Ford, was to produce millions of identical cars in exactly the same way. The key was mass production, and the watchword was flow. Adapting models from the meat-packing and metalworking industries, Ford managers and engineers set up assembly lines that drastically reduced the time and cost of producing cars. Instead of a single worker being responsible for numerous tasks, production was broken down so that each worker had responsibility for only one task, constantly repeated by using the same specialized machine. There was a continuous flow of these tasks as each component part was fashioned and the finished product was progressively assembled. When the Ford Motor Company began operation in 1903, there were only 8,000 autos on the streets of Detroit. In 1908, the

> **Mass Production of the Automobile**

first year the famous Model T was built, Ford sold 10,000 cars. By 1914, the year after the first moving assembly line was inaugurated, 248,000 Fords were sold. Many of them cost $490 apiece, only about one-fourth of what they would have cost a decade earlier.

Even $490 was beyond the means of many workers, who earned at best $2 a day. In 1914, however, Ford tried to spur productivity, prevent high turnover among his employees, and head off unionization by offering his workers combined wages and profit sharing of $5 a day. "This is neither charity nor wages," he explained, "but profit sharing and efficiency engineering." Moreover, rising automobile production made for more jobs, higher earnings, and higher profits in such related industries as oil, paint, rubber, and glass. The value of automobiles manufactured, only $6 million in 1900, reached $420 million by 1914. The Model T was indeed replacing the family horse.

The du Ponts did for the chemical industry what Edison and Ford did for the electrical and automobile industries. The du Pont family had been

> **Du Ponts and the Chemical Industry**

manufacturing gunpowder and other explosives in America since the early 1800s. In 1902 three du Pont cousins, Alfred, Coleman, and Pierre, took over the family company and began to broaden production. Branching out from explosives research in 1911, du Pont laboratories began to adapt the flammable substance cellulose to the eventual production of such materials as photographic film, rubber, lacquer, and textile fibers. The company also pioneered in systematic organization, devising efficient methods of management, accounting, and earnings investment.

Although the timing of mechanization varied from one industry to another, a host of machines and processes helped to alter the nation's economy and everyday life between 1865 and 1900. The telephone and typewriter revolutionized communications, making face-to-face conversations less important and facilitating business correspondence and recordkeeping. Sewing machines made mass-produced clothing available to almost everyone. Refrigeration changed American dietary habits by making it easier to preserve meat, fruit, vegetables, and dairy products. Streetcars, elevated railroads, and subways extended city limits and enabled people to live farther from their workplaces. Cash reg-

The assembly line at the Ford Motor plant shows how the process of production was broken down into simple, repetitive tasks—here, the fashioning of auto seats. Rather than building the entire product, specialized crews worked on individual parts that later were assembled into the whole automobile. *Ford Motor Company.*

isters and adding machines revamped accounting and created new clerical jobs.

All these inventions and more thrust the United States into the vanguard of industrial nations, but other effects were less positive. Industrial expansion created countless new jobs, but because most machines and inventions were labor-saving devices, fewer workers could produce more in less time—as Conrad Carl knew all too well. Mechanization not only destroyed time-honored crafts but subordinated men and women workers to rigid schedules and repetitive routines. The scramble for patents resulted in as much waste as technological advancement. Entrepreneurs spent huge sums hoping to profit from inventing something slightly different from what already existed, or they purchased patents on the remote chance that they might be profitable. Companies like Bell Telephone and individuals like George Selden clogged the courts with suits alleging patent infringement. To minimize uncertainty, manufacturers pooled patents and tried to monopolize new discoveries by confining research to their own labs. As in farming and mining, bigness and consolidation in industry engulfed the individual.

The Triumph of Industrialism

In the industrial sector, higher profits resulted from higher production at lower costs. As railroads and technological innovations made large-scale production more economical, sizable factories began to replace small ones. Between 1850 and 1900 the average amount of capital invested in a manufacturing firm increased from $700,000 to $1.9 million. Only large factories could afford to buy new machines and operate them at full capacity. And large factories could best take advantage of discount rates for shipping products in bulk and for buying raw

Huge machines dwarf workers in the Minneapolis General Electric Company's Main Street Station, symbolizing the way mechanization made many human skills outmoded by the end of the nineteenth century. *Minnesota Historical Society, Louis D. Sweet, photographer.*

materials in quantity. Economists call such advantages *economies of scale*.

Machines and large factories made such efficiencies possible, but profitability was as much a matter of organization as of mechanics. In other words, running a successful factory depended on how production was arranged as well as on the machines that were used. Thus by the 1890s, engineers and managers planned every work task to increase output economically and efficiently. Their efforts not only allowed standardization of tasks and quality in mass production but also reduced the skill level and independent judgment of workers involved in production.

> **New Emphasis on Efficiency**

Of the many people who espoused systems of efficient production, the most influential was Frederick W. Taylor. As foreman and engineer for the Midvale Steel Company in the 1880s, Taylor observed that the only way a company could lessen fixed costs and thus increase profits was to base production on scientific studies of "how quickly the various kinds of work . . . ought to be done." The "ought" was crucial because it signified the goal of producing more for a lower cost per unit—reducing labor costs by eliminating unnecessary workers. The "how quickly" meant that time and money were equivalent.

In 1898 Taylor took his stopwatch to the Bethlehem Steel Company to illustrate how his principles of scientific management worked. His experiments, he explained, involved identifying the "elementary operations of motions" used by specific workers, selecting better tools, and devising "a series of motions which can be made quickest and best." Applying the technique to the shoveling of ore, Taylor designed fifteen kinds of shovel and prescribed the proper motions for using each one. As a result he reduced a crew of 600 men to 140 and cut company costs in half. The remaining shovelers received higher wages, though their jobs became more tedious and stressful because of the new demands placed upon them.

Taylor's writings helped make time studies and scientific management a national obsession. Workers' skills became less valued, and managers increasingly controlled the pace and scale of output. Time, as much as quality, became the measure of acceptable work, and science rather than tradition determined the right ways of doing things. As integral features of the assembly line, where work was divided into specific time-determined tasks, employees had become another kind of interchangeable part.

At the same time, large manufacturers were adding new marketing techniques to their technological and organizational innovations. Meat processor

> **New Marketing Techniques**

Gustavus Swift used branch slaughterhouses and refrigeration to enlarge the market for fresh meat. James B. Duke, whose American Tobacco Company made cigarettes a big business, saturated communities with billboards and free samples and offered premium gifts to retailers for selling more cigarettes. Companies like International Harvester and Singer Sewing Machine set up systems for servicing their products and introduced financing schemes to permit customers to buy the machines more easily. In many instances marketing innovations enabled producers to sell directly to retailers, squeezing out wholesalers and eliminating the excess costs that wholesaling entailed.

The Corporate Consolidation Movement

Neither the wonders of industrial production nor the new techniques of market promotion masked unsettling factors in the American economy. Competition and the race for higher productivity and new markets had costs as well as benefits. New technology demanded that factories operate at near-capacity in order to produce goods most economically. But the more manufacturers produced, the more they had to sell. And in order to sell more, they had to reduce prices. In order to profit more, they expanded production further and often reduced wages. In order to expand, they had to borrow money. In order to repay the money, they had to produce and sell even more. This circular process strangled small firms that could not keep pace and thrust workers into conditions of constant uncertainty. The same cycle affected trade, banking, and transportation as well as manufacturing.

This environment encouraged rapid growth, but optimism could dissolve at the hint that debtors were unable to meet their obligations. In the final third of the nineteenth century, financial panics afflicted the economy at least once a decade, depressing wages and prices, destroying businesses, and putting workers out of jobs. Economic hard times that began in 1873, 1884, and 1893 each hovered over the nation for several years. Business leaders failed to agree on what caused the declines. Some blamed overproduction; others pointed to underconsumption; still others attributed downturns to lax credit and investment practices. Whatever the reason—and there were usually several— businesspeople began seeking ways to combat the uncertainty of the business cycle. In those years of boom and bust cycles, many corporate leaders turned to centralized and cooperative forms of economic power, notably corporations, pools, trusts, and holding companies.

Industrialists, unlike laborers, never questioned the capitalist system or lost faith in entrepreneurial leadership. Instead, they built on the corporate

> **Role of Corporations**

base that had supported economic growth since the early 1800s when states had passed incorporation laws to encourage commerce and industry (see page 259). Under such laws, almost anyone could start a company and raise money by selling stock to investors. Full responsibility for company administration was left in the hands of managers. Stockholders could share in profits yet avoid most losses because the laws limited their liability for company debts only to the extent of their own investment; the rest of their wealth was protected should the company fail. Corporations proved to be the best instruments for raising capital needed for industrial expansion, and by 1900 they were responsible for two-thirds of all goods manufactured in the United States. Moreover, in the

1880s and 1890s corporations received broad judicial protection when the Supreme Court ruled that they, like individuals, were protected by the Fourteenth Amendment. States could not deny corporations equal protection of the laws and could not deprive them of rights or property without due process of law.

As economic disorder and the urge for profits mounted, corporation managers began to seek stability in new and larger forms of economic concentration. Between the late 1880s

Pools, Trusts, and Holding Companies

and early 1900s, an epidemic of consolidation swept the United States, eventually resulting in the massive conglomerates that have dominated the American economy in the twentieth century. At first, such efforts were tentative and informal, consisting mainly of cooperative agreements among firms that made the same product or offered the same service. Through these arrangements, called *pools,* competing companies tried to control the market by agreeing how much each should produce and what prices should be charged. Used by railroads (to divide up traffic), steel producers, and whiskey distillers, pools depended on their members' honesty. Such "gentlemen's agreements" worked during good times when there was enough business for all; but during slow periods, the desire for profits often tempted pool members to evade their commitments by secretly reducing prices or selling more than the agreed quota. The Interstate Commerce Act of 1887 outlawed pools (see page 584), but by then their usefulness was already fading.

John D. Rockefeller disliked pools, calling them "ropes of sand." In 1879 one of his lawyers, Samuel Dodd, devised a more stable means of dominating the market. Since state laws prevented one corporation from holding stock in another corporation, Dodd adapted an old device called a *trust,* which in law existed as an arrangement whereby responsible individuals would manage the financial affairs of a person unwilling or unable to handle them alone. Dodd reasoned that stockholders of companies could be lured or forced into turning over control of their stock "in trust" to a board of trustees that could then supervise all operations under the name of one company. This device allowed Rockefeller to achieve *horizontal integration* in 1882 by combining the management of his Standard Oil Company of Ohio with that of other companies he bought up, thus strengthening his grip on the highly profitable petroleum industry.

In 1888 New Jersey adopted new incorporation laws allowing corporations chartered there to own property in other states and to own stock in other corporations (trusts provided for trusteeship but not ownership). This liberalization led to the creation of the *holding company,* which owned a partial or complete interest in other companies. Holding companies could in turn merge their constituent companies' assets (buildings, equipment, inventory, cash, and the like) as well as their management. Thus Rockefeller incorporated the holding company of Standard Oil of New Jersey, merging the assets of forty constituent companies. By 1898, Standard Oil refined 83.7 percent of all oil produced in the nation, commanded most pipelines, and had moved into natural-gas production and ownership of oil-producing properties.

Standard Oil's expansion into activities besides oil refining exemplified a new form of economic integration. In an effort to control the market, many companies took over several levels of production and distribution, including raw materials and transportation as well as manufacturing. The prime example of this *vertical integration* was Gustavus Swift's meat-processing operation. During the 1880s, Swift boldly invested in livestock, slaughterhouses, refrigerator cars, and marketing to assure the sale of his beef without unexpected inconvenience. The holding company aided this kind of consolidation, which fused a broad range of business activities into one entity under unified management.

Mergers became the answer to industry's search for order. Between 1889 and 1903, some three hundred combinations were formed, most of them trusts and holding companies. By far the most spectacular was the U.S. Steel Corporation, formed in 1901 and financed by J. P. Morgan. This new enterprise, made up of iron-ore properties, freight carriers, wire mills, plate and tubing companies, and other firms, was capitalized at over $1.4 billion. Other mammoth combinations included the Amalgamated Copper Company, American Sugar Refining Company, American Tobacco Company, and U.S. Rubber Company, each worth over $50 million.

The merger movement created a new species of businessmen, whose vocation was financial organizing rather than producing a particular good or

This cartoon from 1904 depicts the Standard Oil Trust as a greedy octopus whose sprawling tentacles are snaring Congress, state legislatures, and the taxpayer in their grasp and are reaching for the White House. *Library of Congress.*

Role of Financiers service. Shrewd operators sought opportunities for combination, formed corporations, and then persuaded producers to sell their firms to the new company. These financiers usually raised money by selling stock and borrowing from banks. Not wed to any one industry, their attention ranged widely. Thus W. H. Moore organized the American Tin Plate Company, Diamond Match Company, and National Biscuit Company. Elbert H. Gary aided consolidation of the barbed-wire industry and U.S. Steel. Investment bankers like J. P. Morgan and Jacob Schiff piloted the merger movement, inspiring awe with their financial power and organizational skills.

The growth of corporations in the late nineteenth century turned financial exchanges into centers of activity where investors bought and sold stocks and bonds feverishly. By the end of 1886, trading on the New York Stock Exchange had reached 1 million shares a day. By 1914 the number of industrial stocks traded had reached 511, compared with 145 in 1869. Investment could not have occurred without growth in the capital available for such purposes. Between 1870 and 1900 foreign investment in American companies rose from $1.5 billion to $3.5 billion. More important, personal savings and institutional investment mushroomed: assets of savings banks, concentrated in the Northeast and on the West Coast, rose by $900 million between 1875 and 1897 to a total of $2.2 billion. States gradually loosened regulations to enable banks to invest in railroads and industrial enterprises. Commercial banks, insurance companies, and corporations also invested heavily. As one journal proclaimed, "Nearly the whole country (including the typical widow and orphan) is interested in the stock market." This statement was a gross exaggeration, but it reflected what optimistic industrial capitalists wanted to believe.

The Gospel of Wealth

To corporate investors, growth was not only desirable; it was necessary. Profits depended on it, and profits meant everything. Pursuit of wealth had become a struggle for life. As Milton H. Smith of the

CRESTED BUTTE NUMBER

VOL. 1   APRIL 26, 1902   NO. 20

CAMP AND PLANT

PUBLISHED WEEKLY WITH ILLUSTRATIONS

SUBSCRIPTION PRICE ONE DOLLAR A YEAR

A publication by the Colorado Fuel and Iron Company tries to convey the image that company officials were concerned with the homes and working conditions of their employees. That concern, however, reflected the company's paternalism and could evaporate if workers should decide to unionize and pursue their own interests by going out on strike.

Louisville and Nashville Railroad put it, "Society, as created, was for the purpose of one man's getting what the other fellow has, if he can, and keep out of the penitentiary."

The merger movement that resulted in trusts and holding companies upset this philosophical underpinning. J. P. Morgan, whose steely eyes, full mustache, and bulky frame gave him the look that reinforced his image as a commanding figure among American capitalists, heralded the new order when he told a meeting of railroad directors, "The purpose of this meeting is to cause the members of this association to no longer take the law into their own hands . . . as has been too much the practice heretofore. This is not elsewhere customary in civilized communities, and no good reason exists why such a practice should continue among railroads." Business leaders turned to consolidation under new corporate forms to promote growth and to cut down competition. The monopolistic companies that resulted, however, found it necessary to justify their size and power to a public raised on the ideology of open competition.

Defenders of business thus eagerly embraced the doctrine of Social Darwinism, which seemed to justify aggression in human society. Developed by English philosopher Herbert Spencer and preached in the United States by Yale professor William Graham Sumner, Social Darwinism loosely adapted Charles Darwin's theory of the origin of species to the principles of laissez faire, the doctrine opposing government interference in economic affairs. Human society had evolved naturally, Social Darwinists reasoned, and any interference with existing institutions would only hamper progress and aid the weak. In a free society operating according to the principle of survival of the fittest, power would flow naturally to the most capable. The holding and acquisition of property were therefore sacred rights, and wealth was a mark of well-deserved power and responsibility. Civilization depended on this system, explained Sumner. "If we do not like the survival of the fittest," he wrote, "we have only one possible alternative, and that is survival of the unfittest." Many clergymen, journalists, and popular writers also proclaimed the doctrine of Social Darwinism, assuring the public that progress would result only from natural evolution.

> **Social Darwinism**

This philosophy required that people be left free to accumulate and dispose of wealth. In fact, however, new corporate forms, with their domination of production and finance, prevented most individuals who did not already have wealth from acquiring it. To compensate for this inconsistency, Social Darwinists reasoned that humanitarian elites could provide for the needs of those less fortunate or less capable. Thus captains of industry strongly believed that their wealth carried moral responsibilities. Steel baron Andrew Carnegie, who proclaimed his philanthropic activities the "Gospel of Wealth," believed that he and other powerful industrialists were trustees for society's wealth and that his duty was to fulfill that trust in humane ways. Over his lifetime, Carnegie gave away more than $350 million for libraries, education, peace, and the arts.

Such philanthropy, however, had limits. John D. Rockefeller once stated, "I believe it is my duty to make money and still more money and to use the money I make for the good of my fellow man according to the dictates of my conscience." This belief implied a right for men like Rockefeller and Carnegie to define what they believed was good and necessary for society. It meant that the wealthy could and should endow churches, hospitals, and schools, since such gifts promoted progress by raising the "moral culture" of all classes. But it also meant that government should not force the rich, through taxation or regulation, to become more humanitarian.

Paradoxically, business executives who exalted individual initiative and independence also pressed for government assistance. They denounced any measures that might aid unions or regulate factory conditions; such legislation, they said, thwarted natural economic laws. At the same time, though, they lobbied forcefully and successfully for subsidies, loans, and tax relief that would encourage business growth. Tariffs were by far the largest form of government assistance to industry. By putting high import duties on competing goods from abroad, such as kerosene, steel rails, worsted wools, and tin plate, Congress enabled American producers to keep the prices of their goods relatively high. Industrialists argued that tariff protection encouraged the development of new products and the founding of new enterprises. But tariffs also forced consumers to pay artificially high prices for many products.

Government Assistance to Business

Railroads and industrial firms also manipulated state and local governments to their own advantage. As reformer Henry Demarest Lloyd remarked in 1881, Standard Oil "has done everything with the Pennsylvania legislature except refine it." In the South, railroads and mining companies often leased prisoners to work as laborers. Such companies paid the states about ten cents per prisoner for a day's work, in preference to paying a free laborer a dollar a day. Although business executives believed that natural law would lead directly to economic progress, they were not above enlisting help to ensure that natural law would work profitably for them.

Whatever their inconsistencies, business leaders took great pride in the achievements of their era. Many accepted credit for the meteoric rise of the American standard of living—national wealth rose 550 percent between 1860 and 1900, and per capita income increased 150 percent—and they scoffed at charges that only the wealthy were benefiting. Carroll D. Wright, a pioneering social statistician, denied that the rich were getting richer and the poor poorer. "To the investigator," he testified, "the phrase should be, The rich are growing richer; many more people than formerly are growing rich; and the poor are better off."

This materialistic philosophy rested on a somewhat shaky foundation. Believers justified it by invoking natural economic law and the survival of the fittest. But mounting criticism forced them into the illogical position of defending such principles by emphasizing how fragile they were. Thus, they warned, government intervention in the business system—in the form of regulation, taxation, or aid to the poor—would stall or even reverse progress. Government interference in the form of tariffs and other aid, however, they considered to be quite another matter.

▼

Dissenting Voices

Writers who attacked trusts rarely challenged this reasoning; instead, they based their arguments on traditional American beliefs in independence and opportunity. In doing so, they argued within the same framework of values as did corporate leaders who defended the new economic system. While defenders insisted that trusts were the natural and efficient outcome of economic development, critics charged that trusts were unnatural because they were created by greed and inefficient because they stifled opportunity. Underlying such charges was an ardent fear of monopoly, the domination of an economic activity by one powerful company such as Standard Oil. As Charles Francis Adams, descendant of two presidents, put it, "In the minds of the great majority, and not without reason, the idea of any industrial combination is closely connected with that of monopoly, and monopoly with extortion." Those who feared monopoly believed that large corporations could exploit consumers by fixing prices, demean workers by cutting wages, destroy opportunity by eliminating small businesses, and threaten democracy by corrupting politicians—all of which was not only unnatural but immoral. To critics of trusts, ethics eclipsed economics.

Many believed there was a better way to achieve progress. By the mid-1880s, a number of young professors, troubled by the growing size of industrial and financial firms, began to challenge Social Darwinism and laissez faire. Some, like pioneering sociologist Lester Ward, attacked the application of evolutionary theory to social and economic relations. In *Dynamic Sociology* (1883), Ward argued that human control of nature, not natural law, accounted for the advance of civilization. To Ward, a system that guaranteed survival only to the fittest was wasteful and brutal; instead, he reasoned, cooperative activity, fostered by planning and government intervention, was the best means to unity and happiness. Economists Richard Ely, John R. Commons, and Edward Bemis agreed that natural forces should be harnessed for the public good. In 1885 they and others of like mind formed the American Economic Association and denounced the laissez-faire system for its "unsound morals." They preferred the positive assistance of the state, which was, Ely declared, "an educational and ethical agency whose positive aid is an indispensable condition of human progress." This sentiment provided a strong rationale for government action during the Progressive era in the early twentieth century (see Chapter 21).

While academics were recommending intervention into the natural economic order, others were proposing more utopian schemes for combating monopolies. Reformer Henry George, whose early life of poverty as a printer and writer had sensitized him to the exploitative power of large enterprises, declared that inequality stemmed from the ability of a few to profit from rising land values. Land values rose, George argued, without effort on the part of owners simply because a growing population increased demand for living and working space, especially in cities. To restore equality, George proposed to tax the "unearned increment"—the rise in land values caused by increased market demand rather than by owners' improvements—and to eliminate all other taxes. By confiscating undue profits, George insisted, this single tax would end monopolistic tendencies and ensure social progress. George's scheme, argued forcefully in his

Utopian Economic Schemes

book *Progress and Poverty* (1879), had great popular appeal and almost won him the mayoralty of New York City in 1886 on a Labor party ticket.

Unlike George, who approved of private ownership, novelist Edward Bellamy envisioned a socialist state where government would own and oversee the means of production and distribution and would unite all people under moral laws. Bellamy outlined his vision in *Looking Backward, 2000–1887,* published in 1888. The novel, which sold over 1 million copies within a few years, depicted Boston in the year 2000 as a peaceful community where all people belonged to an industrial army. Each person was paid not with money but with credits enabling him or her to obtain consumer goods and entertainment. By depicting this ordered utopian world, free of lawyers, politics, and class divisions, Bellamy tried to convince readers that a "principle of fraternal cooperation" could replace vicious competition and wasteful monopoly. He did not explain how this system, which he called Nationalism, could be implemented, but his ideas sparked the formation of Nationalist clubs around the country and vitalized popular appeals for civil service reform, social welfare measures, and government ownership of railroads and utilities.

Journalist and reformer Henry Demarest Lloyd arrived at a similar conclusion by a different route. His *Wealth Against Commonwealth* (1894) was an indictment of Standard Oil and its monopolistic supremacy. Using evidence loosely, Lloyd portrayed John D. Rockefeller as a ruthless ogre who trampled widows and invalids as well as competing oil refiners in his rush for profits. Lloyd warned that such unbridled aggression and resulting monopolistic power would lead only to public enslavement. As an alterative, he offered a cooperative commonwealth similar to Bellamy's. Government ownership and operation of the means of production, Lloyd explained, would create a society in which "the organization of processes have become so far developed that the profit-hunting Captains of Industry may be replaced by the public-serving Captains of Industry. . . . We are to have a private life of new beauty. . . . We are to be commoners, travelers to Altruria."

While George, Bellamy, Lloyd, and others grappled with ways to meet what they believed to be a moral crisis, public clamor against monopolies and trusts began to prod legislators into action.

Antitrust Legislation Before 1900, very few people advocated the kind of government ownership envisioned by Bellamy and Lloyd, but several state governments did take steps to prohibit monopolies and regulate big business. By the end of the century, fifteen states had constitutional provisions outlawing trusts, and twenty-seven had laws forbidding pools. Most were states in the agricultural South and West, responding to antimonopolistic pressure exerted by various farm organizations. But problems of definition and enforcement mounted. State attorneys general lacked staff and judicial support for a concerted attack on big business, and corporations always found ways to evade restrictions. Consequently, a need for national legislation became more pressing.

Throughout the 1880s both major parties moved gingerly toward such legislation, and in 1890 Congress passed the Sherman Anti-Trust Act. Introduced by Senator John Sherman of Ohio and rewritten by eastern conservatives in the Senate, the law made illegal "every contract, combination in the form of trust or otherwise, or conspiracy in the restraint of trade." People found guilty of violating the law faced fines and jail terms, and those wronged by illegal combinations could sue for triple damages. However, the law was purposely vague because that was the only way it could have been passed in Congress. It did not define clearly what a restraint of trade was. Moreover, it consigned interpretation of its provisions to the courts, which at that time were strong allies of business. As one corporate lawyer scoffed, "Legislators madly dashed to the work, threw ink upon paper, and called it a statute . . . and they asked the courts to enforce it—enforce a statute based upon doubt and guess and speculation and against the natural laws of trade and business."

Judges—particularly the majority of justices on the Supreme Court—blurred distinctions between reasonable and unreasonable restraints of trade. When in 1895 the United States government prosecuted the so-called Sugar Trust for owning 98 percent of the nation's sugar-refining capacity, eight of nine Supreme Court justices ruled that control of manufacturing did not necessarily mean control of trade (*U.S.* v. *E. C. Knight Co.*). According to the Court, the Constitution empowered Congress to regulate interstate commerce, but manufacturing, which in the case of the Knight Company took place entirely within the state of Pennsylvania, did not fall under congressional control. The Sugar Trust, said one justice, was trying to increase its profits from refining but was innocent of trying to restrain trade.

This interpretation left the antitrust act with only token power to combat industrial bigness. The law, passed to soothe public clamor, found little support among public officials, even those entrusted with enforcing it. Thus Attorney General Richard Olney was prompted to remark, "You will have observed that the Govt has been defeated in the Supreme Court on the trust question. I always supposed it would be & have taken the responsibility of not prosecuting under a law I believed to be no good." Between 1890 and 1900 the federal government prosecuted only eighteen cases under the act. The most successful of these were aimed at railroads directly involved in interstate commerce. Ironically, the Sherman Act did serve government officials as a tool for breaking up labor unions: courts that did not consider monopolistic production a restraint of trade willingly applied antitrust provisions to strikes that affected trade.

The antimonopoly spirit did not die; in fact, "trustbusting" accelerated between 1900 and the First World War. But the problems of enforcing the Sherman Act reflected the uneven distribution of power among American interest groups. Corporate enterprises had been the first to consolidate, and they controlled great resources of economic and political power. Other groups—farmers, laborers, intellectuals, humanitarians—had numbers and ideas but lacked power. Almost all members of these groups desired the material gains that technology and large-scale production were providing, but they increasingly feared that business was acquiring too much influence. How to rebalance economic power in American society became the pressing dilemma of industrialism.

Mechanization and the Changing Status of Labor

By 1880, when almost 5 million Americans worked in manufacturing, construction, and transportation, the status of labor had shifted dramatically from

Even as work became more routinized, laborers held onto traditional customs. In this photograph a cigar maker reads the newspaper to his fellow workers, according to tradition. *International Museum of Photography, George Eastman House.*

what it had been a generation earlier, when there were only 1.5 million workers in those industries. Most workers could no longer accurately be termed producers, as craftsmen and farmers had traditionally considered themselves. The enlarged working class consisted mainly of employees, people who worked only when someone else hired them, not when or how they pleased. Whereas producers were paid by consumers according to the quality of what they produced, employees were paid wages based on time spent on the job.

As mass production subdivided manufacturing into small tasks, workers spent their time repeating one specialized operation. One investigator who looked into the effects of specialization on a typical laborer found that he became

> a mere machine. . . . Take the proposition of a man operating a machine to nail on 40 to 60 cases of heels in a day. That is 2,400 pairs, 4,800 shoes in a day. One not accustomed to it would wonder how a man could pick up and lay down 4,800 shoes in a day, to say nothing of putting them . . . into a machine. . . . That is the driving method of the manufacture of shoes under these minute subdivisions.

No longer was it up to the worker to decide when to begin and end the workday, when to rest, and what tools and techniques to use. Especially as assembly-line production and the kinds of factory rules established by New England textile mills earlier in the century spread, employees lost their independence. As a Massachusetts factory worker complained in 1879, "During working hours the men are not allowed to speak to each other, though working close together, on pain of instant discharge. Men are hired to watch and patrol the shop." And workers were now surrounded by others who, like themselves, worked at the same rate for the same pay, regardless of the quality of their work.

Men and women affected by these changes did not accept them passively. Workers reacted to industrialization by struggling to retain independence and self-respect against employers' ever-increasing power. As new groups of people encountered the industrial system, they resisted in various ways. Artisans such as cigar makers, glass workers, and coopers, caught in the transition from

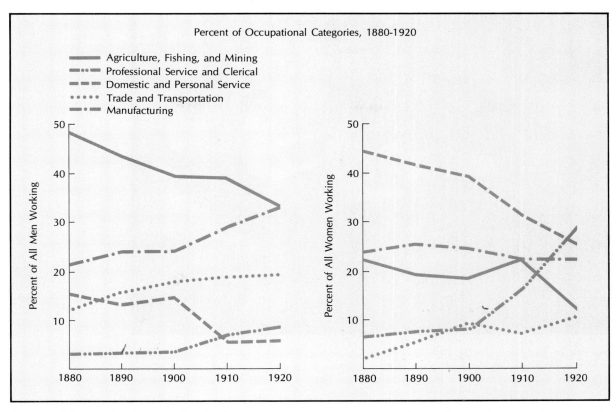

Percent of Occupational Categories, 1880–1920

Percent of Occupational Categories, 1880–1920 *Source: U.S. Bureau of the Census, Census of the United States, 1880, 1890, 1900, 1910, 1920 (Washington: U.S. Government Printing Office).*

hand labor to machine production, fought to preserve the pace and quality of their efforts and held on to such customs as appointing a fellow worker to read aloud while they worked. When immigrants went to work in factories, they often succeeded in getting their relatives and friends hired, thus maintaining the on-the-job family and village ties they had always known. Off the job, workers continued to get together for traditional leisure-time activities like social drinking and holiday celebrations.

Employers in turn took steps to establish standards that they thought would enhance efficiency and productivity. In order to make workers docile (like machines), they supported temperance and moral reform societies, dedicated to combating supposed drinking and debauchery on and off the job. Managers at Ford Motors required workers to meet the company's behavior code before they could earn the profit-sharing segment of the Five-Dollar-Day plan. Other employers established piece rates, paying workers only for the number of items they produced, to encourage maximum use

of machines. And they lowered wages, forcing people to work harder and longer just to maintain the same income.

As machines and assembly-line production reduced the need for skilled workers, employers cut wage costs by hiring more women and children.

▶ **Employment of Women**

Between 1880 and 1900, the numbers of employed women grew from 2.6 million to 8.6 million, and their occupational patterns underwent major changes (see figure). First, the proportion of women engaged in domestic and personal service jobs (maids, cooks, laundresses), traditionally the most common form of female employment, dropped dramatically as jobs opened in other economic sectors. Some new jobs were in manufacturing, usually menial positions in textile mills and food-processing plants that paid women as little as $1.56 a week for seventy hours of labor. The number of female factory hands tripled, but the proportion of women workers in these jobs remained about the same.

The rise of clerical occupations was one of the most important developments in employment for women at the beginning to the twentieth century. Employers readily hired women to operate typewriters and adding machines and paid them less than male employees. Note the male supervisors in this photograph. *Minnesota Historical Society.*

Second and more important, a major shift was occurring that set the trend among female workers for much of the twentieth century. Numbers and percentages of women in clerical jobs—clerks, typists, bookkeepers, salespersons—skyrocketed. These workers served new needs of retail marketing and corporate recordkeeping. From the late nineteenth century onward, the invention of the typewriter, cash register, adding machine, and other machines greatly simplified office and sales work. Firms could increase efficiency by hiring more clerks to operate machines and to replace expensive managers. An official of a sugar company observed in 1919 that "all the bookkeeping of this company . . . is done by three girls and three bookkeeping machines . . . one operator takes the place of three men."

By 1920 nearly half of all clerical workers were women; only 4 percent had been women in 1880. Previously, men had dominated office positions when the work demanded many different skills: accounting, drafting, recordkeeping, letter-writing, and others. New inventions such as the typewriter and adding machine intensified the division of

labor so that only narrow skills were needed for clerical jobs. Companies eagerly hired large numbers of women streaming into the labor market who had taken courses in typing and shorthand in school and who desired the better pay and conditions that these jobs offered over factory and domestic work. Employers did not have to invest much in training female employees and thus could train men for higher positions.

A similar trend affected sales clerks. Women were attracted to sales jobs because of the respectability, nice surroundings, and contact with affluent customers, but the division of labor removed responsibilities of billing and counting money (in department stores separate cashiers took in cash and made change) and thereby reduced the amount of training needed by sales clerks. Sex discrimination thus pervaded the clerical sector. The new jobs opened employment opportunities that gave women at least some possibilities for advancement to supervisory positions, but women posed no threat to men's managerial jobs.

Although most working children toiled on their parents' farms, the number in nonagricultural occu-

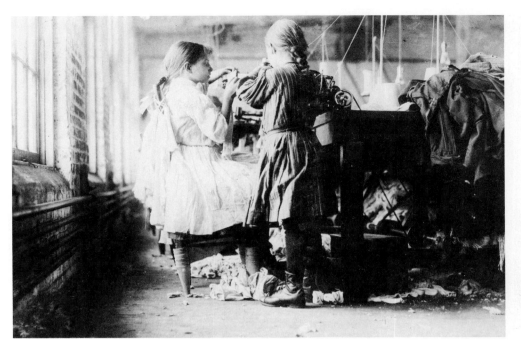

Families in need of extra income often sent children to work in textile mills and other factories, where numerous unskilled jobs existed. Children such as the textile workers above operated machines and did jobs such as sorting and carrying at wages that were a fraction of those paid to adults. *Library of Congress.*

pations tripled between 1870 and 1900. In 1890, over 18 percent of all children between ages ten and fifteen were gainfully employed. Many textile workers were below age sixteen. Mechanization created a number of light unskilled tasks (such as running errands and helping machine operators) that children could handle at a fraction of adult wages. Conditions were especially bad for child laborers in the South, where burgeoning textile mills needed unskilled workers. Mill owners induced poor white families, who otherwise might not have had any jobs or income, to bind their children over to the factories at miserably low wages.

Employment of Children

Several states, especially in the Northeast, had laws limiting the ages and hours of child labor, but such laws had little effectiveness. Since state statutes did not affect firms engaged in interstate commerce, most large companies fell outside state regulation. It was difficult to enforce age requirements, and many parents lied about their children's ages to help them get jobs to supplement the family income. In the South, mill operators staunchly defended their independence against state interference and insisted that parents should have full authority over the activities of family members. By 1900, state child-labor laws and further automation had reduced the number of children working in manufacturing, but many more worked in street trades—shining shoes and peddling newspapers—and as helpers in stores. Reformers turned to federal legislation as the remedy for child labor, an issue that became a major focus of the Progressive era (see Chapter 21).

Although working conditions loomed as the major issue laborers had to face, the problem of wages was often the immediate catalyst of worker unrest. Many employers believed in the "iron law of wages," which dictated that employees be paid according to the conditions of supply and demand. Ideally, this principle meant that workers would receive the highest possible wages that would not drive the employer out of business. In reality it meant that employers did not have to raise wages—and could even cut them—as long as there were people who would accept low pay. Employers justified the system with references to individual

On March 25, 1911, a fire at the Triangle Shirtwaist Company in New York City, in which 147 workers, nearly all women, died, provided gruesome evidence of what could happen as a result of the appalling conditions under which many people worked. The building in which the company was located was full of combustible materials, and many of the victims leaped to their death because doors to the stairways were locked. *Museum of the City of New York.*

freedom: a worker who did not like the wages being paid was free to quit and find a job elsewhere. Courts reinforced the principle, denying workers the right to organize and bargain collectively and instead saying that whatever wages an employee received should be the result of an individual deal between employee and employer. Wage earners saw things differently. They believed the wage system trapped and exploited them. As one Massachusetts worker testified in 1879, "The market is glutted, and we have seasons of dullness; advantage is taken of men's wants, and the pay is cut down; our tasks are increased, and if we remonstrate, we are told our places can be filled. I work harder now than when my pay was twice as high."

Even steady employment was insecure. Repetitive tasks using high-speed machinery dulled concentration, and the slightest mistake could cause serious injury. Industrial accidents rose steadily before 1920, killing or maiming hundreds of thousands of people each year. As late as 1913, after factory owners had installed safety

Industrial Accidents

devices, some 25,000 people died in industrial mishaps, and close to 1 million were injured. Each year sensational disasters, such as explosions, mine cave-ins, and fires, aroused public clamor for better safety regulations. The most notorious of these tragedies was the fire at New York City's Triangle Shirtwaist Company in 1911, which killed 146 workers, most of them women. Equally tragic, however, were the countless accidents that resulted in mangled limbs, infected cuts, chronic illness, and death. A railroad brakeman described his accident in 1888:

> It was four or five months before I "got it." I was making a coupling one afternoon. . . . Just before the two cars were come together, the one behind me left the track. . . . Hearing the racket, I sprang to one side, but my toe caught the top of the rail. I was pinned between the corners of the cars as they came together. I heard my ribs cave in like an old box smashed with an ax.

Families stricken by such accidents suffered acutely because disability insurance and pensions were almost nonexistent. Laissez-faire attitudes stifled protective legislation for workers, and employers would not take responsibility for employees' well-being. As one railroad manager told his workers, "The regular compensation of employees covers all risk or liability to accident. If an employee is disabled by sickness or any other cause, the right to claim compensation is not recognized." The only recourse for a stricken family was to sue and prove in court that the killed or injured worker did not realize the risks involved and had not caused the accident.

Reformers, including union leaders, in several states lobbied Congress to pass laws to ease working conditions, but the Supreme Court limited their impact by narrowly defining what jobs were dangerous and which workers needed protection. Initially, in *Holden* v. *Hardy* (1896), the Court upheld a law regulating the working hours of miners because their work was so dangerous that overly long hours would increase the threat of injury. In *Lochner* v. *New York* (1905), however, the Court struck down a law limiting bakery workers to a sixty-hour week and a ten-hour day. In response to the argument that a state had authority to protect workers' health and safety, the Court ruled that baking was not a dangerous enough occupation to justify restricting the right of workers to sell their labor freely. According to the Court, interference with the right of individuals to make contracts for their labor would violate the Fourteenth Amendment's guarantee that no state could "deprive any person of life, liberty, or property without due process of law."

Courts Restrict Labor Reform

Then, in *Muller* v. *Oregon* (1908), the Court used a different rationale and sociological evidence to uphold a law limiting working hours for women to ten a day. In this case, the Court set aside its *Lochner* argument. Labor legislation for women was necessary, the Court asserted, because a woman's health "becomes an object of public interest and care in order to preserve the strength and vigor of the race." As a result, women were barred from many occupations, such as printing and transportation, which required long or nighttime hours, and they thus were confined to the same menial jobs they had always held.

Throughout the nineteenth century, tensions rose and fell as workers confronted mechanization. Adjustments were made in different ways as different groups—rural migrants, foreign immigrants, women, and children—entered the industrial labor force. Some people bent to the demands of the factory, the machine, and the time clock. Some tried to blend old ways of working into the new system. Some never adjusted and wandered from place to place, from job to job. Others, however, turned to organized resistance.

In many ways, the year 1877 was a historical watershed. In July a series of strikes broke out among railroad workers who were protesting wage cuts. Violence spread across Pennsylvania and Ohio all the way to Chicago and St. Louis. Venting their anger against corporations rather than against individual employers, rioters attacked railroad property, derailing trains and burning rail yards. State militia companies, which were commanded and organized by employers, broke up picket lines and fired into threatening crowds. In several communities, factory workers, wives, and even local merchants aided the strikers, while railroads enlisted strikebreakers to replace union men. The worst violence occurred in Pittsburgh, where on July 21 militiamen from Philadelphia bayoneted and then fired on a crowd of rock-throwing demonstrators, killing ten and wounding many more. Infuriated, the mob drove the soldiers into a railroad roundhouse and set a series of fires that destroyed 39 buildings, 104 engines, and 1,245 freight and passenger cars. The next day, the troops shot their way out of the roundhouse and killed twenty more citizens before fleeing the city.

Strikes of 1877

After more than a month of unprecedented carnage that reached from Maryland to Illinois, Texas, and California, President Rutherford B. Hayes sent federal troops to restore order and end the strikes. His action marked the first significant use of troops to quell labor unrest.

The immediate cause of these strikes was the squeeze of hard times. In the economic slump that followed the Panic of 1873, railroad managers cut wages, increased workloads, and laid off workers, especially those who had joined a union. Such actions drove workers to strike and riot. Laborers in other industries who suffered the same conditions sympathized with the strikers, as did other members of their communities. A Pittsburgh militiaman, ordered out to break the 1877 strike by his fellow townsmen, recalled, "I talked to all the strikers I could get my hands on, and I could find but one spirit and one purpose among them—that they were justified in resorting to any means to break down the power of the corporations."

The Union Movement

Anxiety over the loss of independence and a desire for better wages, hours, and working conditions drove some workers into unions to protect their interests. The union movement had precedents but few successes. Craft unions of skilled workers in a particular trade dated from the early nineteenth century, but their emphasis on exclusive membership left them without broad power. The National Labor Union, which was founded in 1866 and claimed 640,000 members in 1868, died during the hard times of the 1870s. The only broad-based labor organization to survive that depression was the Knights of Labor. Founded in 1860 by Philadelphia garment cutters, the Knights opened their doors to other workers during the 1870s. In 1879, when the union still had fewer than 10,000 members, it elected Terence V. Powderly, a machinist, as grand master. Under his guidance, Knights membership mushroomed, peaking at 730,000 in 1886.

Arising at a time when the factory system was not yet firmly established, the Knights of Labor tried to avert the bleak future that they believed industrialism portended by building an alliance among all producers that would offer an alternative to industrial capitalism and the profit system. At that time, most labor organizations were trade unions, including only skilled workers in particular crafts. The Knights, however, recruited women, blacks, immigrants, and unskilled and semiskilled workers, who were excluded from craft unions. The Knights believed that all people could eliminate conflict between workers and employers by establishing a cooperative society in which laborers worked for themselves, not for those who possessed capital. The goal, argued Powderly, was to "eventually make every man his own master— every man his own employer. . . . There is no good reason why labor cannot, through cooperation, own and operate mines, factories, and railroads."

Technological and economic changes were making it impossible for each worker to be his or her own employer. But like many farmers, the Knights saw producer and consumer cooperatives as preferable alternatives to the forces of greed that surrounded them. They agreed with Edward Bellamy that a society in which all groups lived cooperatively was possible. This view was the source of the organization's strength and of its weakness. The cooperative idea, attractive in the abstract, did not give laborers much bargaining power with employers. It was too vague a concept, and employers held most of the economic leverage. Strikes were a means of seeking immediate goals, but Powderly and some other Knights leaders opposed strikes because they tended to divert progress away from the long-term goal of a cooperative society and because workers tended to lose strikes more often than win them.

But many Knights leaders plus the rank and file did engage in militant actions, such as demanding higher wages and union recognition from railroads in the Southwest in 1886. Railroad baron Jay Gould refused to negotiate with the Knights, and a strike began on March 1 in several Texas communities, spreading to Kansas, Missouri, and Arkansas. As violence increased, Powderly met with Gould and called off the strike, hoping to settle the conflict. But Gould again refused concessions, and violence broke out again. The Knights had no choice but to give in and end the strike. By mid–1886, as Powderly began to denounce radicalism and violence, and as the more militant craft unions broke away, membership in the Knights of Labor dwindled. The union survived in only a few small towns, where it made a brief attempt to unite with Populists in the 1890s. The special interests of craft unions overcame the Knights' general and often vague appeal, and dreams of labor unity faded.

As the hard times of the 1870s subsided and better conditions returned in the early 1880s, a number of labor groups, including the Knights of Labor, began to campaign for an eight-hour workday as a means of spreading jobs so as to reduce unemployment and prevent fatigue. This effort by laborers to regain control of their work gathered momentum in Chicago, where radical anarchists, who believed that all government authority was undesirable and that society operates best on the principle of voluntary cooperation, as well as various craft unions—perhaps as many as 100,000 workers in all—agitated for the cause. On

> **Knights of Labor**

> **Haymarket Riot**

This engraving of the Haymarket riot in Chicago in May of 1886 shows labor demonstrators pelting police with bricks and the officers threatening to retaliate. The day after this incident, a bomb exploded near a police brigade, and police fired into the surrounding crowd, killing seven men. *The Bettmann Archive.*

May 1, 1886, a day of mass strikes and the largest spontaneous labor demonstration in the country's history, Chicago police were mobilized to prevent disorder, especially among striking workers at the huge McCormick reaper factory. The day passed calmly, but two days later police stormed an area near the McCormick plant and broke up a battle between striking unionists and nonunion workers hired as strikebreakers. Police shot and killed two unionists and wounded several others. The next evening, labor groups rallied at Haymarket Square, near downtown Chicago, to protest police brutality. As a company of police officers approached the meeting, a bomb exploded near their front ranks, killing seven and injuring sixty-seven. Mass arrests of anarchists and unionists followed. Eventually eight men, all anarchists, were tried and convicted of the bombing, though there was no evidence of their guilt. Four were executed and one committed suicide in prison. The remaining three were pardoned in 1893 by Illinois governor John P. Altgeld, who believed they had been victims of the "malicious ferocity" of the courts.

Like the southwestern railroad strike, the Hay-market bombing drew public attention to the growing discontent of labor but also revived middle-class fear of radicalism. The fact that anarchists and socialists, many of them foreign-born, had participated in some of the agitation, created a sense of crisis, a feeling that forces of law and order had to act swiftly to prevent social turmoil. To protect their city, private Chicago donors helped to establish Fort Sheridan and the Great Lakes Naval Training Station. Elsewhere police forces and armories were strengthened. Employer associations of manufacturers in the same industry worked to counter labor militancy by agreeing to resist strikes and by purchasing strike insurance.

The newly formed American Federation of Labor was the major workers' organization to emerge after the 1886 upheavals. A combination of national craft unions, the AFL initially had about 140,000 members, most of whom were skilled native-born workers. As a federation, it allowed member unions autonomy in their own areas of interest but tried to develop a general policy that would suit the self-interest of all

American Federation of Labor

members. Since these unions were organized by craft (skill) rather than by workplace, they had little interest in including unskilled workers. Led by Samuel Gompers, pragmatic and opportunistic head of the Cigar Makers' Union, AFL unions avoided the idealistic rhetoric of worker solidarity to press for specific goals, such as higher wages, shorter hours, and the right to bargain collectively. As Gompers's associate Adolph Strasser explained, "We have no ultimate ends. We are going from day to day. We are fighting only for immediate objects—objects that can be realized in a few years." Thus the AFL, in contrast to the Knights of Labor, accepted industrialism and worked to achieve better conditions within the wage-and-hours system.

Under Gompers the AFL grew to over 1 million members by 1901 and 2.5 million by 1917, when it contained 111 national unions and 27,000 local unions. The national organization required that all constituent unions hire organizers to expand membership, and it collected dues for a fund to aid members on strike. The AFL avoided party politics, choosing instead to follow Gompers's dictum of supporting labor's friends and opposing its enemies regardless of party.

The AFL and the labor movement in general staggered in the early 1890s, when once again labor violence evoked public fears. In July 1892, Henry C. Frick, the stubborn president of Carnegie Steel Company, closed the plant in Homestead, Pennsylvania, when the AFL-affiliated Amalgamated Association of Iron and Steelworkers refused to accept pay cuts and went on strike. Shortly thereafter, angry workers attacked and routed three hundred Pinkerton guards hired by Frick to protect the plant. State militia were summoned, and after five months the strikers gave in. By then public opinion opposed the strike because a young anarchist—who was not a striker—had tried to assassinate Frick.

In 1894, workers at the Pullman Palace Car Company walked out in protest over exploitative policies at the company town near Chicago. The paternalistic company head **Pullman Strike** George Pullman tried to do everything for the twelve thousand residents of his so-called model town. His company owned and controlled all land and buildings, the school, bank, and water and gas systems. It paid wages, fixed rents, and employed spies to report on disgruntled employees. One laborer grumbled, "We are born in a Pullman house, fed from the Pullman shop, taught in the Pullman school, catechized in the Pullman church, and when we die we shall be buried in the Pullman cemetery and go to the Pullman hell."

One thing Pullman would not do was negotiate with workers. When the hard times that began in 1893 threatened his business, Pullman managed to maintain profits and pay dividends to stockholders by cutting wages 25 to 40 percent while holding firm on rents and prices in the model town. Workers, squeezed into debt and deprivation, sent a committee to Pullman in May 1894 to protest his policies. Pullman reacted by firing three members of the committee. Enraged workers, most of whom had joined the American Railway Union, called a strike. Pullman retaliated by closing the plant. When the American Railway Union, led by the charismatic young organizer Eugene V. Debs, voted to aid the strikers by boycotting all Pullman cars, Pullman stood firm and rejected arbitration. The railroad owners' association then enlisted the aid of U.S. Attorney General Richard Olney, who obtained a court injunction to prevent the union from "obstructing the railways and holding up the mails." President Grover Cleveland sent federal troops to Chicago, supposedly to protect the mails but in reality to crush the strike. Within a month the strike was over, and Debs was jailed for six months for contempt in defying the injunction. The Supreme Court upheld Debs's sentence on grounds that the federal government had the power to remove obstacles to interstate commerce.

After 1900, an increasing number of battles occurred between workers and employers in the mining industry. The fledgling United Mine Workers led several strikes in the coal fields of Pennsylvania, Colorado, and West Virginia between 1902 and 1922. Out of the western mining struggles emerged the Industrial Workers of the World (IWW), a radical labor organization founded in 1905 that fused the vision of worker solidarity with the tactics of strikes and sabotage. In contrast with the AFL, the IWW hoped to organize workers along industrial, not craft, lines. Using the rhetoric of class conflict— "The final aim is revolution," according to an IWW organizer—the "Wobblies," as they were called, believed that workers should seize the nation's industries and run them without interference from industrialists or politicians. Because of their anticapitalist goals and threatening tactics, the Wobblies attracted considerable attention in spite of their small numbers, and their activities influenced debates on labor reform during the Progressive era (see Chapter 21).

It must be emphasized that during the half-century following the Civil War, only a small fraction of American workers belonged to unions. In 1900 only about 1 million out of a total of 27.6 million workers were unionized. In 1920, total union membership had grown to 5 million—still only 13 percent of the work force. Unionization was strong among workers in building trades, transportation, communications, and to a lesser extent manufacturing. But organizers took no interest in large segments of the industrial labor force and intentionally excluded others.

Many unions, such as those of the AFL, were openly hostile toward women. Of the 6.3 million employed women in 1910, only 125,000 were in

Women and the Labor Movement

unions. Male unionists often explained the exclusion of women by saying that women should not be employed. According to one labor leader, "I believe that woman is not qualified for the conditions of wage labor. . . . The mental and physical makeup of woman is in revolt against wage service. She is competing with the man who is her father or husband or is to become her husband." Fear of competition was crucial. Because women were paid less than men, males worried that their own wages would be lowered if women joined them in the workplace. Moreover, men feared that the entry of women would transform many jobs from all-male to all-female, just as clerical jobs were changing. Male workers, accustomed to sex segregation in employment, could not recognize or accept the possibility of men and women working side by side. Yet female employees could organize and fight employers as strenuously as men could.

Since the early years of industrialization, female workers had formed their own unions. Some, such as the Collar Laundry Union of Troy, New York, organized in the 1860s, succeeded in carrying out strikes and achieving higher wages. The first inclusive women's labor federation was the Women's Trade Union League (WTUL), founded in 1903 and patterned after a similar union in England. The WTUL worked for protective legislation for female workers, sponsored educational activities, and campaigned for women's suffrage. In 1909 it joined

Rose Schneiderman, a cap-maker in New York City, was one of the most forceful and influential leaders of the Women's Trade Union League, founded in 1903. As a union organizer, she gave numerous speeches representing the cause of working-class women to upper- and middle-class reformers. *Robert F. Wagner Labor Archives, New York University.*

with the International Ladies Garment Workers Union in support of a massive strike against New York City sweatshops. Although the WTUL had forceful working-class leaders—notably Agnes Nestor, a glove maker, Rose Schneiderman, a cap maker, and Mary Anderson, a shoe worker—it was dominated by middle-class women who had humane but generally nonmilitant reasons for helping working women. In the early 1920s, the WTUL fought a constitutional amendment guaranteeing equal rights to women, arguing that women needed protection from exploitation more than they needed equality. Such reasoning fit the assertion of males who argued that women belonged in their own sphere at home, out of the work force and out of unions. As the WTUL gradually backed away from active union organization, it lost the support of working-class women, and by 1930 it had virtually dissolved.

> **Immigrants, Blacks, and the Labor Movement**

Organized labor also excluded most immigrant and black workers. Some trade unions welcomed skilled immigrants—foreign-born craftsmen were prominent leaders of several unions—but only the Knights of Labor and the IWW had firm policies of accepting immigrants and blacks. Blacks were among the organizers of the coal miners' union, and they had a presence in other unions involving trades in which blacks were a significant part of the work force: construction, barbers, dock workers. But often blacks could belong only to segregated local unions in the South, and the majority of northern AFL unions had exclusion policies as well. Resentments, already fueled by long-held prejudices, increased when blacks and immigrants worked as strikebreakers. It is likely that few strikebreakers understood the full effects of such employment when they were recruited to fill the jobs of striking workers; but even for those who did, the lure of employment was too great to resist.

The millions of men, women, and children who were not unionized tried in their own ways to cope with the pressures of the new machine age. Increasing numbers of workers, both native-born and immigrant, turned to fraternal societies. These organizations, which for small monthly or yearly contributions provided members with life insurance, sickness benefits, and funeral expenses, became widespread by the early twentieth century. For many workers, issues of wages and hours were meaningless; getting and holding a job was the first priority. Job instability and the seasonal nature of work seriously hindered organizing efforts. Few companies employed a full work force all year round; most employers hired workers during peak seasons and laid them off during slack periods. Thus employment rates often fluctuated wildly. The 1880 census showed that in some communities 30 percent or more of adult males had been unemployed at some time during the previous year.

For most American workers, then, the machine age had mixed results. Industrial wages rose between 1877 and 1914, boosting purchasing power and creating a mass market for standardized goods (see Chapter 19). Yet in 1900 most employees worked sixty hours a week at wages that averaged twenty cents an hour for skilled work and ten cents an hour for unskilled work. Moreover, as wages rose, living costs increased even faster. The industrial transformation had thrust the United States into international leadership in economic capability. But in factories as well as on farms, some people were beginning to question whether a system based on ever-greater profits was the best way for Americans to achieve the nation's democratic destiny.

Suggestions for Further Reading

General

Daniel J. Boorstin, *The Americans: The Democratic Experience* (1973); Thomas C. Cochran and William Miller, *The Age of Enterprise* (1942); Carl N. Degler, *The Age of the Economic Revolution* (1977); Ray Ginger, *The Age of Excess* (1965); Samuel P. Hays, *The Response to Industrialism* (1975).

Technology and Invention

Robert W. Bruce, *Bell: Alexander Graham Bell and the Conquest of Solitude* (1973); Roger Burlingame, *Henry Ford* (1957); George H. Daniels, *Science and Society in America* (1971); Sigfried Giedeon, *Mechanization Takes Command* (1948); Matthew Josephson, *Edison* (1959); Leo Marx, *The Machine in the Garden: Technology and the Pastoral Ideal* (1964); Elting E. Morison, *Men, Machines, and Modern Times* (1966); Allan Nevins and Frank E. Hill, *Ford*, 3 vols. (1954–1962); Nathan Rosenberg, *Technology and American Economic Growth* (1972); Harold I. Sharlin, *The Making of the Electrical Age* (1963); Peter Temin, *Steel in Nineteenth Century America* (1964); Frederick A. White, *American Industrial Research Laboratories* (1961).

Industrialism, Industrialists, and Corporate Growth

W. Eliot Brownlee, *Dynamics of Ascent: A History of the American Economy,* 2nd ed. (1979); Stuart Bruchey, *Growth of the Modern Economy* (1973); Alfred D. Chandler, *The Visible Hand: The Managerial Revolution in American Business* (1977); Alfred D. Chandler, *Pierre S. du Pont and the Making of the Modern Corporation* (1971); Alfred D. Chandler, *Strategy and Structure: Chapters in the History of American Industrial Enterprise* (1966); Thomas C. Cochran, *Business in American Life* (1972); Francis L. Eames, *The New York Stock Exchange* (1968); Rendigs Fels, *American Business Cycles, 1865–1897* (1959); David F. Hawkes, *John D.: The Founding Father of the Rockefellers* (1980); Robert

Higgs, *The Transformation of the American Economy, 1865–1914* (1971); Matthew Josephson, *The Robber Barons* (1934); Edward C. Kirkland, *Industry Comes of Age* (1961); Harold C. Livesay, *Andrew Carnegie and the Rise of Big Business* (1975); Daniel Nelson, *Managers and Workers: Origins of the New Factory System in the United States, 1800–1920* (1975); Allan Nevins, *Study in Power: John D. Rockefeller,* 2 vols. (1953); Glen Porter, *The Rise of Big Business* (1973); Joseph Wall, *Andrew Carnegie* (1970).

Attitudes Toward Industrialism

Sidney Fine, *Laissez Faire and the General Welfare State* (1956); Louis Galambos and Barbara Barron Spence, *The Public Image of Big Business in America* (1975); Richard Hofstadter, *Social Darwinism in American Thought,* rev. ed. (1955); T. Jackson Lears, *No Place of Grace: Antimodernism and the Transformation of American Culture* (1981); Henry Demarest Lloyd, *Wealth Against the Commonwealth* (1894); Robert McCloskey, *American Conservatism in the Age of Enterprise* (1951); John L. Thomas, *Alternative America: Henry George, Edward Bellamy, Henry Demarest Lloyd, and the Adversary Tradition* (1983).

Work and Labor Organization

Stanley Buder, *Pullman* (1967); Alan Dawley, *Class and Community* (1977); Melvin Dubofsky, *Industrialism and the American Worker* (1975); Melvin Dubofsky, *We Shall Be All: A History of the Industrial Workers of the World* (1969); Sarah Eisenstein, *Give Us Bread, Give Us Roses: Working Women's Consciousness in the United States, 1890 to the First World War* (1983); Leon Fink, *Workingmen's Democracy: The Knights of Labor and American Politics* (1982),

Philip S. Foner, *The Great Labor Uprising of 1877* (1977); Herbert G. Gutman, *Work, Culture and Society in Industrializing America* (1976); Tamara K. Hareven, *Family Time and Industrial Time: The Relationship Between the Family and Work in a New England Industrial Community* (1982); Stuart Bruce Kaufman, *Samuel Gompers and the Origins of the American Federation of Labor* (1973); Alice Kessler-Harris, *Out to Work: A History of Wage Earning Women in the United States* (1982); Susan Levine, *Labor's True Women: Carpet Weavers, Industrialization, and Labor Reform in the Gilded Age* (1984); Harold Livesay, *Samuel Gompers and Organized Labor in America* (1978); Milton Meltzer, *Bread and Roses: The Struggle of American Labor, 1865–1915* (1967); Stephen Meyer III, *The Five Dollar Day: Labor Management and Social Control in the Ford Motor Company, 1908–1921* (1981); David Montgomery, *The Fall of the House of Labor: The Workplace, the State, and American Labor Activism, 1865–1925* (1987); David Montgomery, *Workers' Control in America: Studies in the History of Work, Technology, and Labor Struggles* (1979); Daniel J. Walkowitz, *Worker City, Company Town* (1978); Barbara Mayer Wertheimer, *We Were There: The Story of Working Women in America* (1977); Leon J. Wolff, *Lockout: The Story of the Homestead Strike of 1892* (1965); Irwin Yellowitz, *Industrialization and the American Labor Movement* (1977).

For nearly thirty years, Frank Ventrone had successfully pursued his dream until one night his world literally shattered. In the 1880s, Ventrone had emigrated from Isernia, a town in southern Italy, to Providence, Rhode Island, a bustling city in industrializing America. By saving money and buying property, Ventrone became a prominent businessman in the city's fast-growing Italian immigrant community, many of whose residents had also come from Isernia. Ventrone's biggest success was a pasta business that furnished the community's staple food. But this business was also the source of his trouble.

In the summer of 1914, food prices were rising, and Ventrone followed the trend by increasing the price of his pasta. Angered by the threat to their already overburdened incomes, people of Providence's Italian section vented their frustration against Ventrone. On a warm August weekend, they marched through the neighborhood, broke windows in a block of property owned by Ventrone, entered his business establishment, and dumped his stock of macaroni into the street. When police arrived to quell the disturbance, rioters resisted with catcalls and violence, insisting that the matter was an internal one to be resolved by the community. The next Monday, Ventrone's agent met with community members and agreed to lower his prices. Ventrone had overstepped the bounds of ethnic loyalty and suffered as a result. "Signor Ventrone . . . owes everything to our colony," declared the neighborhood newspaper. "Our brave colony, when we all stand together, will be given justice."

The Providence "macaroni riot," with its various dimensions —the transfer of immigrant cultures from Old World to New, the mobility of some people from rags to respectability, the continued poverty of others amid economic uncertainty, the eruption of violence—was just one of millions of events that came to characterize life in an American city. A similar protest might have occurred in Italy, but the American context amplified the drama. By 1900, Providence was a rapidly growing city, and the United States was the most rapidly urbanizing nation in the Western world. The hopes, frustrations, and conflicts that urban growth generated seemed both dazzling and bewildering. Clanging trol-

18

THE FAME AND SHAME OF THE CITIES, 1877–1920

New York, February, 1911 (detail) by George Wesley Bellows. Oil on canvas. *National Gallery of Art, Washington, D.C., Collection of Mr. and Mrs. Paul Mellon.*

The paving of streets was vital to the progress of cities because increased transportation needs made old dirt pathways, which could become clogged with mud, inefficient. Before asphalt was widely available, many cities such as St. Louis, pictured above, undertook huge projects to lay bricks over major roadways. This photograph shows how cumbersome such projects must have been. *Missouri Historical Society, Swekosky Collection.*

leys, smoky air, crowded streets, a jumble of languages—these sensations and more contrasted with the slow, quiet pace of village and farm life. As cities grew, they became places of both opportunity and misery.

In the 1830s and 1840s, the nation's urban population started to grow much faster than its rural population (see pages 311–312). But not until the 1880s did the United States begin to become a truly urban nation. By 1920 the major milestone of urbanization had been passed: that year's census showed that, for the first time, a majority of Americans (51.4 percent) lived in cities. This new fact of national life was as significant as the disappearance of the frontier in 1890. The era of the yeoman farmer was over, and urban growth became another major theme, along with the development of natural resources (Chapter 16) and industrializa-

tion (Chapter 17), of American expansion in the late nineteenth and early twentieth centuries.

Cities served as marketplaces, bringing together the people, resources, and ideas that were responsible for many of the changes American society was experiencing. By 1900 a network of small, medium, and large cities spanned every section of the country. These cities attracted both exuberant admirers and sneering detractors. Some people relished the opportunities cities offered. As one editor wrote, it was "better [to] be the 1/1,000,000,000 of New York than the 1/1 of Aroostook County." Others found the crudeness of American cities disquieting. "Having seen it," British poet Rudyard Kipling wrote of Chicago, "I urgently desire never to see it again." But whatever people's personal impressions, the city had become central to American life. To a large extent, modern American society has been shaped

1867	First law passed regulating tenements (New York)	**1893**	World's Columbian Exposition (Chicago)
1880s	"New" immigrants from eastern and southern Europe begin to arrive in large numbers	**1898**	Race riot in Wilmington, North Carolina
1883	Brooklyn Bridge completed	**1900–10**	Peak years of immigration
1886	First settlement house opened	**1906**	Race riot in Atlanta, Georgia
1890s	Electric trolleys replace horse-driven mass transit	**1920**	Majority (51.4 percent) of Americans live in cities

by the ways people built their cities and adjusted to the new urban environment.

Transportation and Industrial Growth in the Modern City

In March 1912, a party of street-railway officials boarded a private trolley in downtown Boston. Traveling west to Worcester and Springfield in Massachusetts, then south to Hartford, New Britain, New Haven, Bridgeport, and Stamford in Connecticut, the car carried its passengers from one set of tracks to another. The 200-mile journey ended when the car rolled into New York City, having made the entire trip on a continuous route of streetcar tracks. With enough patience and enough nickels for $2.40 in fares and transfers, anyone could have made the same trip. The possibility of such a journey illustrates the extraordinary connection between mass transit and urban growth that occurred at the end of the nineteenth century.

By 1900, the modern American city was reaching maturity. The compact city of the early nineteenth century—where residences were mixed in among shops, factories, and warehouses

> **New Shape of the City**

—had burst open. From Boston to Los Angeles, developed areas sprawled outward several miles from the original central core. No longer did walking distance determine a city's size, and no longer did different social groups live physically close together: poor near rich, immigrant near native, black near white. Instead, cities divided into distinct districts: working-class neighborhoods, black ghettos, a ring of suburbs, business districts. Two forces were responsible for this new arrangement. One was centrifugal, propelling people and enterprises outward from the confines of the old walking city. The other was centripetal, drawing human and economic resources inward. Mass transportation powered the centrifugal force; economic change, the centripetal.

Mass transportation enabled people to move faster and farther. Before the 1870s, horse- and mule-drawn vehicles had been the major means of transport. But they were inefficient. They could carry relatively few riders, and purchasing, feeding, and cleaning up after the animals were costly chores. Once the technology was developed, entrepreneurs adopted better ways to transport people. Steam-powered commuter railroads had appeared in a few cities during the 1850s and 1860s, but not until the late 1870s did inventors begin to mechanize mass transit. The first power-driven devices were cable cars, carriages that traveled over tracks by clamping

> **Mechaniza- tion of Mass Transportation**

Sometimes the extension of mass transit preceded residential development. This trolley line in Oak Park, Illinois, a suburb of Chicago, was built in anticipation of the housing construction that eventually filled the lots on either side of the tracks. Photographed in 1903. *Oak Park Public Library.*

onto a moving underground wire. Cheaper than horse cars, cable cars could more easily haul passengers up and down steep hills. In the 1880s, cable-car lines operated in Chicago, San Francisco, and many other cities.

By the 1890s, however, electric-powered streetcars were replacing early forms of mass transit. Designed almost simultaneously by Charles J. Van Doeple in Montgomery, Alabama, and Frank Sprague in Richmond, Virginia, electric trolleys spread quickly to nearly every large city. Between 1890 and 1902, total mileage of electrified track in American cities grew from 1,300 to 22,000 miles. Meanwhile horse-railway track shrank. "The long-haired mule shall no longer adorn our streets," mused one observer.

In a few cities, trolley companies raised part of their track onto stilts, enabling vehicles to travel above jammed downtown districts without interference from other traffic. In Boston, New York, and Philadelphia, transit firms dug underground passages for their cars, also to avoid tie-ups and delays. Elevated railroads and subways were extremely expensive to construct. They thus appeared only in the few cities where companies could amass enough capital to build them and where there were enough riders to ensure profits.

Mass-transit lines launched millions of urban dwellers into outlying neighborhoods and created a commuting public. Those who could afford the fare—usually five cents a ride— could live outside the crowded, dirty central city but return there for work, shopping, and entertainment. Working-class families, whose incomes rarely topped a dollar a day, found the fare too high and could not benefit from the streetcars. But for the growing middle class, a home in a quiet, tree-lined neighborhood became a real possibility. Real-estate development boomed around the periphery of scores of cities. Between 1890 and 1920, for example, developers in the

Beginnings of Urban Sprawl

Chapter 18: The Fame and Shame of the Cities, 1877–1920

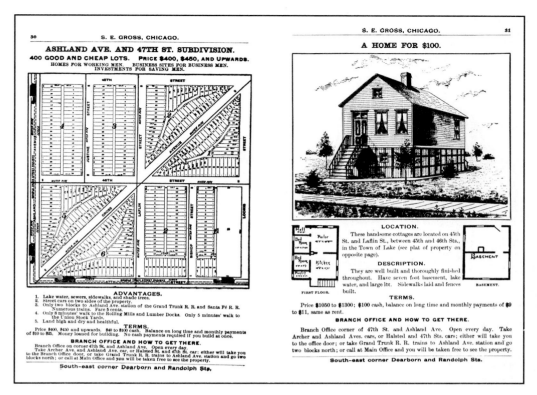

Not all land on the outskirts of cities was reserved for wealthy residents. Inexpensive homes such as this one were built in large numbers for successful working-class families. For just $100 down and monthly payments that were advertised as being as cheap as rent, a family could own a free-standing two-bedroom cottage in one of the newer subdivisions of Chicago. *Chicago Historical Society*.

Chicago area opened 800,000 new lots—enough to house at least three times the city's population in 1890. A home several miles from downtown was inconvenient, but benefits seemed to outweigh the costs. As one suburbanite wrote in 1902, "It may be a little more difficult for us to attend the opera, but the robin in my elm tree struck a higher note and a sweeter one yesterday than any *prima donna* ever reached."

Although urban sprawl was essentially unplanned, certain patterns emerged. Eager to capitalize on new commuting possibilities, thousands of small investors who bought land in anticipation of settlement paid little attention to the need for parks, traffic control, and public services. Construction of mass transit was guided by the profit motive and thus served the urban public unevenly. Streetcar lines serviced mainly those neighborhoods that promised the most riders—those whose fares, in other words, would provide increased dividends for stockholders.

Streetcars, elevateds, and subways altered commercial as well as residential patterns. As consumers moved outward, businesses followed. Secondary business centers sprouted at trolley-line intersections and elevated-railway stations. Branches of downtown department stores and banks joined groceries, theaters, drugstores, taverns, and specialty shops to create neighborhood shopping centers, the forerunners of today's shopping malls. Meanwhile, the urban core became the work zone, where offices, stores, warehouses, and factories loomed over streets clogged with traffic. Districts like Chicago's Loop and New York's Lower Manhattan consolidated practically every kind of business and cultural institution.

Cities also became the main arenas for industrial growth, generating and attracting concentrations of economic power. As centers of resources, labor, transportation, and communications, cities provided everything that factories

> **Urban-Industrial Development**

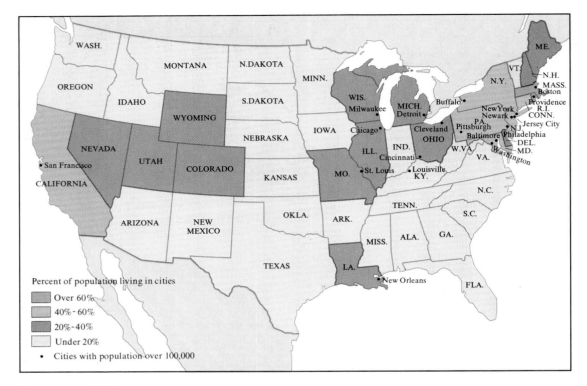

Urbanization, 1880

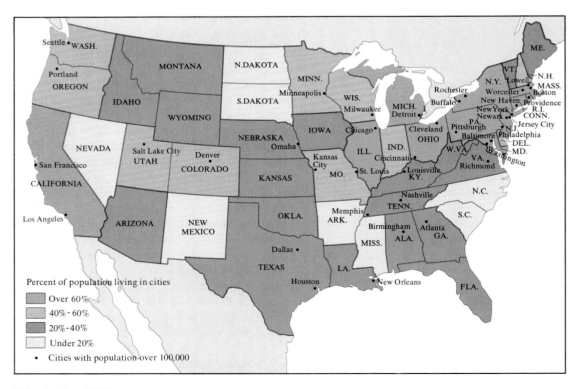

Urbanization, 1920

Chapter 18: The Fame and Shame of the Cities, 1877–1920

needed. Capital accumulated by the cities' commercial enterprises—gathering and distributing raw materials and finished goods—fed industrial investment once mass production became possible. And urban populations furnished consumers for myriad new products. Thus urban growth and industrialization wound together in a mutually beneficial spiral. The further industrialization advanced, the more opportunities it created for work and investment in cities. Increased opportunity drew more people to cities; as workers and as consumers, they in turn fueled further industrialization. By the end of the nineteenth century, urban firms were producing nine-tenths of America's industrial output.

Although most cities contained a variety of industrial activities, specialization in a single product became common. Some cities, such as New York, contained large numbers of workers employed in the mass production of clothing; the shoe industry was prominent in Philadelphia and Lynn, ready-made garments in New York City, and textiles in several New England cities. Major industries in other cities prepared products from surrounding agricultural regions: flour in Minneapolis, cottonseed oil in Memphis, beer in Milwaukee. Still others processed natural resources: gold and copper in Denver, fish and lumber in Seattle, coal and iron in Pittsburgh and Birmingham, oil in Houston and Los Angeles. These and other activities increased the magnetic attraction of cities.

Urban and industrial growth transformed the national economy and freed the United States from dependence on European capital and manufactured goods. Imports and foreign investments still flowed into the United States. But by the early 1900s, cities and their factories, stores, and banks were converting America from a debtor, agricultural nation into a major industrial, financial, and exporting power.

Peopling the Cities: Migrants and Immigrants

Economist Edmund J. James had good reason to assert in 1899 that the era he was living in was "not only the age of cities but the age of great cities."

The first contact with America that most immigrants had was on Ellis Island, just offshore of New York City. Upon debarking from their ships, the immigrants were herded into pens where they were registered and then into rooms where medical personnel examined them for disease. As the photograph suggests, the experience could be quite dehumanizing. *Brown Brothers.*

Between 1870 and 1920, the total number of people living in American cities exploded from 9.9 million to 54.3 million. During the same period, the number of cities with populations over 100,000 grew from fifteen to sixty-eight, and the number with more than 500,000 swelled from two to twelve (see maps). These figures are dramatic enough by themselves, but they also represent millions of stories of hope and frustration, adjustment and confusion, success and failure.

The population of a given place can grow in three ways: by extension of its borders to annex land and people; by natural increase, an excess of births over deaths; and by migra-

How Cities Grew tion, an excess of in-migrants over out-migrants. Between the 1860s and early 1900s, many cities annexed nearby suburbs, thereby increasing their populations. The most notable consolidation occurred in 1898 when New York City, which had previously consisted only of Manhattan and the Bronx, merged with Brooklyn, Staten Island, and part of Queens and grew overnight from 1.5 million to over 3 million people. The thirst for expansion was insatiable. As one observer remarked, "Those who locate near the city limits are bound to know that the time may come when [the city] will extend the limits and take them in." Moreover, suburbs often desired annexation because they needed the schools, water, fire protection, and sewer systems that cities had developed. Annexation also added vacant land where new city dwellers could live. Cities like Chicago, Minneapolis, and Cincinnati incorporated hundreds of undeveloped square miles into their borders in the 1880s, only to see them fill up in succeeding decades. Although annexation did increase urban populations, its major effect was to enlarge the physical size of cities.

Natural increase did not account for very much of any city's population growth. In the late nineteenth century, death rates declined in most regions of the country, but birthrates fell also (see the Appendix). In urban areas, birthrates decreased more rapidly than they did in rural areas, so that in cities there was not much gap annually between the numbers of people who were born and those who died.

Migration and immigration made by far the greatest contribution to urban population growth. In fact, migration to cities nearly matched the migration to the West that was occurring at the same time. Each year millions of people were on the move, many of them lured by the cities' promise of opportunity. Urban newcomers arrived from two major sources: the American countryside and Europe. Asia, Canada, and Latin America also supplied immigrants, but in smaller numbers.

In all sections of the country, a variety of factors dashed farmers' hopes and drove them off the land and toward the opportunities that cities seemed to offer. Rural populations of New York, Ohio, and Illinois declined during the 1880s as their urban populations burgeoned. Growth occurred not only in Cleveland, Detroit, and Chicago but also in scores of secondary cities like Toledo, Indianapolis, Salt Lake City, Birmingham, and San Diego. The thrill and bustle of city life beckoned especially to young people. A character in

> **Major Waves of Migration and Immigration**

George Fitch's play *The City* voiced the dreams of many youths when she exclaimed, "Who wants to smell new-mown hay, if he can breathe in gasoline on Fifth Avenue instead! Think of the theaters! The crowds! *Think* of being able to go out on the street and *see some one you didn't know by sight!*"

An even larger number of newcomers consisted of immigrants who had fled foreign farms, villages, and cities for American shores. Many did not intend to stay. They hoped instead to make enough money to return home and live in greater comfort and security. For every hundred foreigners who entered the country, around thirty left. Still, most of the 26 million immigrants who arrived between 1870 and 1920 stayed, and the great majority settled in cities, where they helped to shape modern American culture.

These immigrants to the United States were part of a global movement. In various parts of developed countries, two forces prompted people to emigrate. First, industrialization undercut local crafts such as weaving and shoemaking, making it more difficult for artisans to supplement their agricultural income with household production. Second, as in the United States, the growth of cities worldwide increased demand for agricultural goods, thereby encouraging large-scale commercial production, which in turn made small-scale farming less profitable. Population pressures and economic changes resulting from land redistribution and industrialization induced millions of small farmers and craftsmen to leave Europe and Asia for Canada, Australia, Brazil, Argentina, and other relatively unsettled places as well as the United States. Countless others migrated shorter distances, usually from a rural village or town to an industrial city. Migration always has been a key chapter in human history, but now the telegraph, railroad, and steamship made communications and travel cheaper, quicker, and safer.

The United States had been the destination of immigrants from northern and western Europe since the 1840s (see pages 324–328), but after 1880 similar economic and demographic changes propelled a second wave of mass immigration from new sources. Northern and western Europeans continued to arrive, but the new wave contained mainly people from eastern and southern Europe, plus smaller contingents from Canada, Mexico, and Japan (see map and

> **The New Immigration**

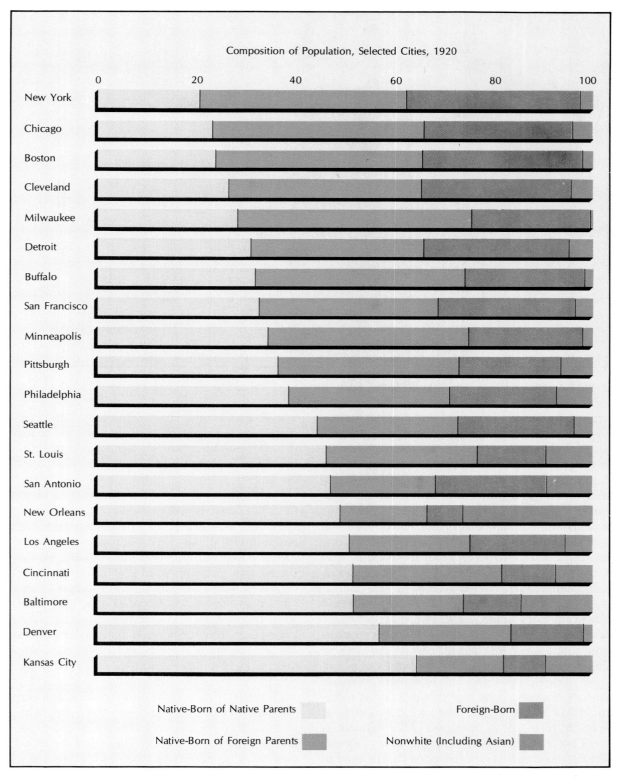

Composition of Population, Selected Cities, 1920

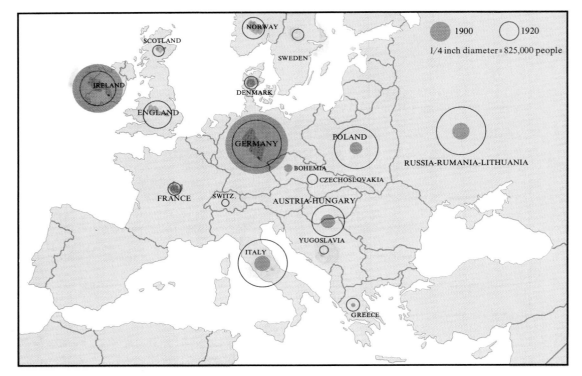

Sources of Foreign-Born Population, 1900 and 1920

figure). Two-thirds of the newcomers who arrived in the 1880s were from Germany, England, Ireland, and Scandinavia; between 1900 and 1909, however, two-thirds were from Italy, Austria-Hungary, and Russia. By 1910, arrivals from Mexico were beginning to outnumber arrivals from Ireland, and large numbers of Japanese had moved to the West Coast and Hawaii. Foreign-born blacks, chiefly from the West Indies, also increased in number, from forty thousand in 1910 to seventy-four thousand in 1920 (see the Appendix for nationalities of immigrants).

The immigrants varied widely in age, marital status, and other social characteristics, but certain traits can be identified. Generally, about two-thirds of newcomers, especially after 1900, were male, and about two-thirds were between the ages of fifteen and thirty-nine. Immigrants were not as illiterate as natives assumed; although there were disparities between particular groups, almost three-fourths of all immigrants could read and write at least in their native language. Also immigrants were not as rural as observers sometimes thought. Among those reporting occupations at the time of entry, half stated that they were unskilled laborers or domestic workers (maids, cooks, cleaners).

These occupations may have reflected the immigrants' expectations of how they would be employed in America, but they also suggest that many had lived in a city for at least a short time before emigrating.

Many Americans feared that the strange customs, Catholic and Jewish religions, illiteracy, and poverty of "new" immigrants made them less desirable and assimilable than "old" immigrants, whose languages and beliefs seemed less alien. This view received sober support from authorities like future president Woodrow Wilson, who wrote in his *History of the American People* (1902), "The immigrant newcomers of recent years are men of the lowest class from the South of Italy, and men of the meaner sort out of Hungary and Poland, men out of the ranks where there was neither skill nor energy, nor any initiative or quick intelligence."

In reality, however, old and new immigrants resembled each other more closely than many Americans wished to believe. The majority of both groups had lived in a world where their family was the focus of everything they did. Decisions of whether and when to emigrate had been made to match family needs, and family bonds and interests continued to prevail once immigrants reached the New World. Those leaving the homeland almost always knew where they wanted to go and how to get there because they received aid from relatives who had already immigrated. In many instances, workers helped kin obtain jobs, and at home family members pooled resources to maintain, if not improve, their standard of living. The bywords for all immigrants were "cooperate and survive."

Perhaps most important, all immigrants brought with them memories of their homelands and they adjusted to American life in light of those memories. In new surroundings

> **Immigrant Cultures**

where the language was a struggle, the workday followed the clock rather than the sun, and housing and employment were often uncertain, immigrants anchored their lives on what they knew best: their culture. Many immigrant neighborhoods consisted of enclaves of Italians from the same province, Japanese from the same island district, or Russian Jews from the same *shtetl* (village). In these transplanted communities, Old World customs persisted. People practiced religion as they always had, held traditional feasts and pageants, married within their group, and pursued old feuds with people from rival villages and provinces. As in eastern Europe, Jewish men grew long sidelocks, women wore wigs, and children attended afternoon religious training. Italians transplanted the system whereby a boss, or *padrone,* found jobs for unskilled workers by negotiating with an employer, and they recreated their Old World mutual benefit associations to help families with emergency aid as well as provide sickness and death benefits. Pasquale Cruci, an immigrant from Salerno, explained that he helped to found such an association in Bridgeport, Connecticut, because

> I felt that the Italian people of this city should have some security from death and accidents. The Italian people of this time didn't trust the big insurance companies because they thought they would get cheated. They felt that if some organization was Italian that it was all right.

Yet the very diversity of American cities forced immigrants to modify their attitudes and habits. Few newcomers could avoid contact with people different from themselves, and few could prevent such contacts from altering their traditional ways of life. Although many foreigners identified themselves by their village or region of birth, native-born Americans categorized them by nationality. People from County Cork and County Limerick were lumped together as Irish; those from Schleswig and Wurttemberg were Germans; those from Calabria and Campobasso were Italians. Mutual benefit and fraternal societies that aided the sick and paid burial expenses were recreated along village and provincial lines. For example, Japanese transferred their *ken* societies, which organized social celebrations and relief services, and Chinese from Canton brought *hui* institutions, which raised money to help members acquire businesses. But other immigrant institutions, such as newspapers and churches, found they had to appeal more broadly to the entire nationality in order to survive.

Mostly, there was a combination of Old World culture with New World realities. Although immigrants struggled to maintain native languages and to pass them down to younger generations, English was taught in the schools and needed on the job; it soon penetrated nearly every community. Foreigners cooked ethnic meals using American foods and fashioned American fabrics in European styles. When they were ill, Italians went to American physicians but still carried traditional amulets in their pockets to ward off evil spirits. Chinese expanded their traditional gambling games to include poker. Music especially revealed adaptations. Polka bands still entertained Polish social gatherings, but their repertoires expanded to blend American and Polish folk music and the bands, once dominated by violins, added accordions, clarinets, and trumpets to enable them to play more loudly. Mexican ballads acquired new themes that reflected adventures of border-crossing and hardships of labor in the United States. Eventually most immigrants grew accustomed to trusting American institutions. An Italian woman in Bridgeport, Connecticut, admitted

> that time [previously] they had all the societies that give you the money if you die, and that's . . . why all the women they were belonging to these societies. . . . Now they don't do this so much, they get the insurance from the Metropolitan and the other companies. . . . Now us Italian people we are more "Americanizata."

The influx of so many immigrants between 1870 and 1920 transformed the United States from a basically Protestant nation into a society of Protestants, Catholics, and Jews. Newcomers from Italy, Hun-

> **Influence on Religion**

Immigrant families showed inventiveness in their use of living quarters. While reformers such as Jacob Riis, who took this photograph, could see only clutter and unhealthfulness in the tenements, it is remarkable how the people themselves could adapt space to their needs. This family of garment makers carefully utilizes every inch of space for work, sleep, cooking, and storage. Note how the family also manages some semblances of decoration. *Museum of the City of New York.*

gary, and what would become Czechoslovakia, Yugoslavia, and Poland joined Irish and Germans to boost the proportion of Catholics in several cities. In places like Buffalo, Cleveland, Chicago, and Milwaukee, Catholic immigrants and their offspring approached a majority of the population. Catholic Mexicans constituted over half the population of El Paso. German and Russian immigrants gave New York one of the largest Jewish populations in the world.

Partly in response to Protestant charges that they could not retain Old World religious beliefs and still assimilate into American society, many Catholics and Jews tried to accommodate their faiths to the new environment. A number of Catholic and Jewish leaders, usually from older, more established immigrant groups, supported liberalizing trends such as use of English in sermons, the phasing-out of Old World rituals such as saints' feasts, and a preference for public over church

schools. As long as new immigrants continued to arrive, however, these tendencies met stiff opposition. Newcomers usually sought to retain familiar practices, whether the folk Catholicism of southern Italy or the orthodox Judaism of eastern Europe; they recoiled from reforms. Catholic immigrants continued to press for ethnically separate parishes in spite of church attempts to make American Catholicism more uniform. Bishops often had to accede to pressures for Polish rather than German-born priests to serve predominantly Polish congregations. Eastern European Jews, believing that Reform Judaism sacrificed too much to American ways, established the Conservative branch, which retained traditional ritual, though it did abolish the segregation of women in synagogues and eased English prayers into service.

In the 1880s, another group of migrants began to move into American cities. Thousands of rural blacks moved northward and westward, fleeing

Black Migration to the Cities

crop liens, violence, and political oppression and seeking better employment. Although numbers of black urban dwellers would grow much larger after 1915, thirty-two cities contained ten thousand or more blacks by 1900, and 79 percent of all blacks outside the South lived in cities. Black migrants resembled foreign immigrants in their rural backgrounds and economic motivations, but they differed in several important ways. Because few factories would employ blacks, most black workers found jobs in the service sector—cleaning, cooking, carting—rather than in the industrial trades. Also, because the majority of jobs in domestic and personal service were traditionally female jobs, black women outnumbered black men in cities such as New York, Baltimore, and New Orleans.

Each of the three major migrant groups that peopled American cities—native whites, foreigners, and native blacks—contributed to the making of modern American culture. Just as the cities grew because they centralized the varied economic functions of commerce, finance, and production, so too they nurtured rich cultural variety: American folk music and literature, Italian and Mexican cuisine, Irish comedy, Yiddish theater, African-American jazz and dance, and much more. Like their predecessors, newcomers in the late nineteenth century changed their environment as much as they were changed by it.

Living Conditions in the Inner City

Population growth created intense pressures on the public and private sectors of the city. Masses of people jammed inner-city districts, where they were known less for their cultural contributions than for the problems they bred. American cities seemed to harbor all the afflictions that plague modern society: poverty, disease, crime, decay, and other unpleasant conditions that develop when large numbers of people live close together. City dwellers were forced to adjust as best they could. Although technology, science, private enterprise,

and public authority failed to relieve all of these problems, some remarkable successes were achieved. In the late nineteenth century and early twentieth, construction of buildings, homes, streets, sewers, and schools proceeded at a furious pace. American cities set world standards for fire protection and water purification. Yet hardship and other ills awaited solution.

One of the most persistent shortcomings of American cities has been their failure to provide adequate housing to all who need it. The failure has roots in nineteenth-century urban

Housing Problems

development. In spite of massive construction in the 1880s and the early 1900s, population growth outpaced housing supplies. This condition especially affected working-class families who, because of low-paying jobs, had to rent their living quarters. As cities grew, landlords took advantage of shortages in low-cost rental housing by splitting up existing buildings to house more people, constructing multiple-unit tenements, and hiking rents. Low-income families adjusted to high costs and short supply by sharing space and expenses. Thus it became common in many big cities for a one-family apartment to be occupied by two or three families or by one family plus a number of paying boarders.

Such conditions created unprecedented crowding. In 1890, there were 702 people per acre in New York City's immigrant-packed Lower East Side, one of the highest population densities in the world. Low-rent districts had distinctive physical appearances: block after block of six- to eight-story barracks-like buildings in New York; dilapidated row houses in Baltimore and Philadelphia; converted slave quarters in Charleston and New Orleans; and crumbling two- and three-story frame houses in Boston, Chicago, and St. Louis. Everywhere crowding was acute.

Inside many buildings, living conditions were inhumane. The largest rooms were barely ten feet wide, and interior rooms either had no windows at all or opened onto narrow shafts that bred vermin and rotten odors. "You see," said an immigrant housekeeper describing one such shaft, "it's damp down there, and the families, they throw out garbage and dirty papers and the insides of chickens, and other unmentionable filth. . . . I just vomited when I first cleaned up the air shaft." Few buildings had indoor plumbing, and the only source of heat was dangerous, polluting coal-burning stoves.

Just as they utilized indoor space as efficiently as possible, tenement dwellers adapted what little outdoor space they had to their needs. In this cramped block of six-story tenements in New York, scores of families hang their wash in the spaces behind the buildings. Note that there is virtually no space between buildings, meaning that only the rooms in front and back, not those on the sides, were exposed to light and air. *Library of Congress.*

In several places housing problems aroused concerned citizens to mount reform campaigns. New York State took the lead in 1867, 1879, and 1901 by legislating light, ventilation, and safety codes for new tenement buildings. These and similar laws in other states could not remedy the ills of existing buildings, but they did impose minimal government regulations on landlords' property rights. A few reformers, such as Jacob Riis and Lawrence Veiller, advocated housing low-income families in model tenements, with more spacious, airier rooms and better facilities. Model tenements, however, required landlords and investors to accept lower profits—a sacrifice few were willing to make. Neither reformers nor public officials would consider government financing of better housing, fearing such a step would undermine private enterprise. Still, the codes and commissions that resulted from reform campaigns did

Housing Reform

strengthen the power of local government to regulate housing construction. Most important was the earnest concern for the lives of inner-city residents that reformers helped to cultivate. As Veiller urged, "We must stop people living in cellars before we concern ourselves with changes in methods of taxation. We must make it impossible for builders to build dark rooms in new houses before we urge the government to subsidize the building of houses. We must abolish privy vaults before we build model tenements."

Housing reforms had only limited success, but scientific and technological advances enabled city dwellers and the nation in general to live and work in greater comfort and safety. By the 1890s, most doctors had accepted the germ theory of disease. As a result, cities established more efficient systems of water purification and sewage disposal. Although disease and death rates remained higher in the city than in the countryside, and tuberculosis and other respiratory ills continued to plague inner-city districts, public health regulations helped to control such dread diseases as cholera, typhoid fever, and diphtheria. Street paving, modernized firefighting equipment, and electric streetlighting spread rapidly across urban America. Steel-frame construction, which supported a building by a metal skeleton rather than by masonry walls, made possible the construction of skyscrapers—and thus more efficient use of scarce, costly urban land. Electric elevators and steam-heating systems serviced these buildings. Streetcars and subways hastened the pace of urban travel, and steel-cable suspension bridges, developed by John A. Roebling and epitomized by the great Brooklyn Bridge (completed in 1883), linked metropolitan sections more closely.

None of those improvements, however, lightened the burden of poverty. The urban economy, though generally expanding, advanced erratically.

Urban Poverty Employment, especially for unskilled workers in manufacturing and construction, rose and fell with business cycles and changing seasons. Often, to make ends meet, more than one member of a working-class family had to work. But the wages other family members could earn were minuscule. Thus an ever-increasing number of families lived on the margins of survival, where an unlucky occurrence could plunge them into destitution.

Since colonial days, Americans have never agreed on how much responsibility the general public should assume for poor relief. In the late nineteenth and early twentieth centuries, many people held to traditional beliefs that anyone could escape poverty through hard work and clean living and that poverty was inevitable only because some people were weaker than others. Such reasoning bred fears that assistance to poor people would encourage paupers to depend on public relief rather than on self-reliance. As cases of poverty increased, this attitude hardened, and city governments discontinued direct grants of food, fuel, and clothing to needy families. Instead, cities either provided relief in return for work on public projects or sent special cases to state-run institutions such as almshouses, orphanages, and homes for the blind, deaf, and mentally ill.

Private philanthropic agencies also concerned themselves with helping only the "worthy poor,"

The new technology of steel-frame construction, in which a steel skeleton covered by a facade supported the structure, made it possible to erect much taller buildings than those that were supported solely by the outer masonry walls. "Skyscrapers" like the one above enabled cities to grow upward as well as outward. *Library of Congress.*

but their efforts to professionalize relief did foster some change in attitude. Between 1877 and 1892, philanthropists in ninety-two cities formed Charity Organization Societies, an attempt to put social welfare on a more scientific and systematic basis by merging disparate charity groups into a coordinated unit. Believing poverty to be caused by personal defects such as alcoholism and laziness, members of these organizations spent most of their time visiting poor families and encouraging them to be thriftier and more virtuous.

Living Conditions in the Inner City

Close observation of the poor caused some welfare workers to conclude that people's environments, rather than personal shortcomings, caused poverty—that is, they came to believe that the ills of poverty could be cured by improving housing, sanitation, and job opportunities rather than by admonishing the poor to be more moral. This new attitude, which had been gaining ground since the mid-nineteenth century, fueled drives for building codes, factory regulations, and public health measures. Most middle- and upper-class Americans nevertheless remained wedded to the beliefs that in a society of abundance only the unfit were poor and that relief of poverty should be tolerated but never encouraged. As one charity worker urged, relief "should be surrounded by circumstances that shall . . . repel every one . . . from accepting it."

Even more than crowding and pauperism, crime and disorder alarmed Americans and nurtured fears that urban growth, especially the growth of immigrant slums, threatened the nation. The more cities grew, it seemed, the more they shook with violence. While homicide rates in other urban-industrial nations like England and Germany declined, those in America rose alarmingly: 25 per million people in 1881; 107 per million in 1898. Pickpockets, swindlers, sneak thieves, and holdup men roamed every city. Some acquired as much notoriety as western desperadoes (see page 476). One infamous urban bank thief was Rufus Minor, alias Rufus Pine. Short, stocky, and bald, Minor looked more like a clerk than an outlaw, but one police chief labeled him "one of the smartest bank sneaks in America." A sometime associate of Billy "The Kid" Burke, he often grew a heavy beard before holding up a bank, then shaved afterward. Thus even when he was arrested, he often was released because he could not be identified as a participant in the robbery. Minor was implicated in bank robberies in New York City, Cleveland, Detroit, Brooklyn, Providence, Philadelphia, Albany, Boston, and Baltimore—all between 1878 and 1882.

Despite the fear of urban crime waves, it is possible that as a greater proportion of the population concentrated in cities, crime merely became more conspicuous and sensational rather than more prevalent. To be sure, urban wealth and the mingling of different kinds of people provided new opportunities for organized thievery, petty larceny,

Crime and Violence

vice, and violent grudge-settling. But how did such activities compare to the lawlessness and brutality of backwoods mining camps and southern plantations? Native whites were quick to blame Irish bank-robbery gangs, German pickpockets, and Italian Black Hand murderers for urban disorder, but there is little evidence that more immigrants than natives populated the rogues' gallery. One investigation of jails in 1900 concluded that "we have ourselves evolved as cruel and cunning criminals as any that Europe may have foisted upon us."

Whatever the extent of criminality, city life in this period certainly supported a thesis that there is a tradition of violence in the United States. Cities served as arenas for many of the era's worst riots. As laborers and employers tried to adjust to the uncertainties of industrialization, violence became, in the words of one observer, "a sort of natural and inevitable concomitant." Ethnic and racial minorities were often victims of the violent bigotry that was the underside of the American myth of equality. The cityward movement of black people roused white fears, and as the twentieth century dawned, a series of race riots spread across the nation: Wilmington, North Carolina, 1898; Atlanta, Georgia, 1906; Springfield, Illinois, 1908. In cities of the Southwest and Pacific Coast, Chinese and Mexican immigrants often felt the sting of intolerance. In addition, thousands of minor disruptions made cities scenes of constant turbulence.

Since early in the nineteenth century, city dwellers had increasingly depended on the police to protect life and property. But by the early 1900s, law enforcement had become complicated and controversial because different groups had different interpretations of the law and how it should be enforced. Disadvantaged groups —usually ethnic and racial minorities—could not escape arrest as easily as those with economic or political influence. Police officers would apply the law less harshly to members of their own ethnic group (police work was a route of mobility for several immigrant groups) or to people who bought exemptions through bribes.

Role of the Police

As the public's chief law-enforcement agency, the police were often caught between conflicting pressures for swift and severe action on the one hand and leniency on the other. When some people clamored for police crackdowns on drinking, gambling, and prostitution, others privately

◄   Chapter 18: The Fame and Shame of the Cities, 1877–1920

A professional police force, with officers wearing uniforms and badges and sometimes carrying weapons, became common in cities in the late nineteenth century. As the agents of law enforcement with powers to keep order and protect property, police often had to make difficult decisions concerning when to arrest someone for breaking a law or when to ignore unpopular laws that restricted personal liberty. *Brown Brothers.*

supported loose law enforcement so they could indulge in these so-called customer crimes. As American society became more diversified, especially in cities, and as different groups asserted different interests, achieving a balance between the idealistic intentions of criminal law and people's desire for individual freedom became increasingly difficult. It has remained so to this day.

The mounting problems of city life seemed to many Americans to demand greater government action. Thus city governments passed more laws and ordinances that regulated housing, provided poverty relief, and expanded police power. Yet public responsibility always ended at the boundaries of private property. Eventually some advances in housing construction, sanitation, and medical care did reach slum dwellers. But for most people,

the only hope was that their children would do better or that opportunities would be better somewhere else.

Promises of Mobility

Between the Civil War and the First World War, Baptist minister Russell Conwell delivered the same sermon more than six thousand times to untold millions across the United States. Titled "Acres of Diamonds," his immensely popular lecture affirmed the belief that any American could achieve success. People did not have to look very far for riches, Conwell preached; acres of diamonds lay at everyone's feet. Night after night, he would insist to his audience, "the opportunity to get rich, to attain unto great wealth, is here . . . within the reach of almost every man and woman who hears me speak tonight. . . . I say you ought to get rich, and it is your duty to get rich. . . . If you can honestly attain unto riches it is your Christian and Godly duty to do so." Success, then, was not only possible; it was a religious obligation.

How possible was it for people actually to improve their lot and fulfill that duty? The answer is a mixed story, with chapters of small successes but also accounts of dashed hopes, discrimination, and failure. Basically, there were three ways a person could get ahead: occupational advancement (and the higher income that accompanied it); acquisition of property (and the potential for greater wealth it represented); and migration to an area of better conditions and greater opportunity. These options were open chiefly to white men. Although many women worked, owned property, and migrated, their economic standing was usually defined by the men in their lives—husbands, fathers, or other kin. Women could improve their economic status by marrying men with wealth or potential, but other avenues were mostly closed. Laws restricted women's economic rights, for example, by limiting what they could inherit; educational institutions closed off the training of women in professions such as medicine and law; and prevailing assumptions assigned men higher aptitude for manual skills and business than women. Men and women who were African-American, American Indian, Mexican-American, or Asian-American had even fewer opportunities for success. Pinned to the bottom of society by prejudice, these groups were forced to accept their imposed station.

To large numbers of people, however, urban and industrial expansion of the late nineteenth century should have offered broad opportunity for occupational mobility. Thousands of small businesses were needed to supply goods and services to burgeoning urban populations. As corporations grew larger and centralized their operations, they required new managerial personnel. Although capital for a large business was hard to obtain, a person could open a saloon or small store for only $200 or $300. Knowledge of accounting or typing could qualify one for new white-collar jobs that sometimes paid better

Occupational Mobility

than manual labor. Thus nonmanual work and the higher social status that tended to accompany it were possible.

Such advancement occurred often. To be sure, only a very few traveled the rags-to-riches path that men like Andrew Carnegie and Henry Ford discovered. Studies of the era's wealthiest businessmen show that the vast majority started their careers with distinct advantages: American birth, Protestant religion, better-than-average education, and relatively affluent parents. Yet considerable movement occurred along the path from rags to moderate success as men climbed from manual to nonmanual jobs or saw their children do so. Thus personal successes like that of Meyer Grossman, a Russian immigrant to Omaha, Nebraska, who worked as a teamster before saving enough to open a successful furniture store, were common.

Rates of occupational mobility in American communities between 1870 and 1920 were slow but steady. In new, fast-growing cities such as Atlanta, Los Angeles, and Omaha, approximately one in five white manual workers rose to white-collar or owner's positions within ten years—provided they stayed in the city that long. In older northeastern cities like Boston and Newburyport, upward mobility averaged closer to one in six in ten years. Some people slipped from a higher to a lower rung of the occupational ladder, but rates of upward movement almost always doubled downward rates. Though patterns were far from consistent, immigrants generally experienced lower rates of upward mobility and higher rates of downward mobility than the native-born did. Still, regardless of birthplace, the chances for a white male to rise occupationally over the course of his career or to have a higher-status job than his father had were relatively good.

It must be remembered, however, that what constitutes a better job depends on one's definition of improvement. Many an immigrant artisan, such as a German carpenter or an Italian shoemaker, would have considered an accountant's job demeaning and unproductive. People with long traditions of pride in manual skills neither wanted nonmanual jobs nor encouraged their children to seek them. As one Italian tailor explained, "I learned the tailoring business in the old country. Over here, in America, I never have trouble finding a job because I know my business from the other side [Italy]. . . . I want that my oldest boy learn my trade because I

Changing one's place of residence has been one of the most universal experiences of urban dwellers throughout American history. By the end of the nineteenth century, moving companies like this one in Omaha, Nebraska, arose to assist families seeking to improve their living conditions in a new home. *Bekins Industries, Inc.*

tell him that you could always make at least enough for the family."

Business ownership, moreover, entailed risks. Rates of failure were high among shopkeepers, saloon owners, and other small proprietors in working-class neighborhoods because the low incomes of their customers made business uncertain. Thus many manual workers sought security rather than mobility, preferring a steady wage to the risks of ownership. A Sicilian who lived in Bridgeport, Connecticut, observed that "the people that come here they afraid to get in business because they don't know how that business goes. In Italy these people don't know much about these things because most of them work on farms or in [their] trade."

In addition to or instead of advancing occupationally, a person could achieve social mobility by acquiring property. But property was not easy to acquire in turn-of-the-century America. Banks and savings institutions were far stricter in their

▶ **Acquisition of Property**

lending practices than they would become after the 1930s, when the federal government began to insure real-estate financing. Mortgage loans carried relatively high interest rates and short repayment periods. Thus renting, even of single-family houses, was common, especially in big cities. A general rise in wage rates nevertheless enabled many families to amass savings, which could be used as down payments on property. Among working-class families who stayed in Newburyport for as long as ten years, a third to a half managed to accumulate some property; two-thirds did so within twenty years. Although ownership rates varied regionally—higher rates in western cities, lower in eastern cities—in 1900, 36.3 percent of urban American families owned their homes, the highest homeownership rate of any Western nation with the exception of the Scandinavian countries Denmark, Norway, and Sweden.

Each year millions of families tried to improve their living conditions by packing up and moving elsewhere. As early as 1847, a foreign visitor,

Residential Mobility

amazed by American transiency, wrote, "If God were suddenly to call the world to judgment He would surprise two-thirds of the American population on the road like ants." Americans have always followed the maxim that movement means improvement. This urge to move affected every region, every city. From Boston to San Francisco, from Minneapolis to San Antonio, no more than half the families residing in a city at any one time could be found there ten years later.

Some evidence shows that many people who left one place for another, particularly unskilled workers, did not improve their status; they simply floated from one low-paying job to another. Others, however, did find greener pastures. Studies of Boston, Omaha, Atlanta, and other cities have revealed that most men who rose occupationally had migrated from somewhere else. Thus while cities frustrated the hopes of some, they offered opportunities to others.

In addition to population movement between cities, extraordinary numbers of people moved from one residence within the same city. In American communities today, one in every five families moves in a given year. A hundred years ago, the proportion was closer to one in four, or even one in three. In Omaha between 1880 and 1920, for example, nearly 60 percent of those families who remained in the city for as long as fourteen years had lived at three or more addresses during that span of time. Population turnover affected almost every neighborhood, every ethnic and occupational group.

Rapid residential flux undermined the stability of even the most homogeneous neighborhoods. Rarely did a single nationality make up a clear majority in any large area, even when that area was known as Little Italy, Jewtown, Polonia, or Greektown. Even in heavily ethnic Chicago, a survey of one district found a kaleidoscope of immigrants packed tightly together:

Ethnic Neighborhoods and Ghettos

> Between Halsted Street and the river live about ten thousand Italians, Neapolitans, Sicilians, and Calabrians. . . . To the South on Twelfth Street are many Germans, and the side streets are given over almost entirely to Polish and Prussian Jews. Further south, three Jewish colonies merge into a huge Bohemian colony. . . . To the north-west are many Canadians . . . and to the north are many Irish.

Moreover, the families inhabiting a certain neighborhood at one point were not likely to be living there five or ten years later. Residential change dispersed immigrants from their original areas of settlement into many different neighborhoods. In New York, Boston, and other eastern ports, ethnically homogeneous districts did exist, and people tended to change residences within those districts rather than move away from them. Elsewhere, however, most immigrant families lived dispersed in ethnically mixed neighborhoods rather than in ghettos.

In most places an area's institutions and enterprises, more than the people who actually lived there, identified a district as an ethnic neighborhood. A certain part of town, familiar and accessible to a particular group, became the location of its churches, clubs, bakeries, markets, and other establishments. Some members of the group lived nearby; others lived farther away but could travel there on streetcars or on foot. Thus some of the secondary business centers that formed at the intersections of mass-transit routes became locations of ethnic business and social activity. A Bohemian Town, for example, received its nickname because it was the location of Swoboda's Bakery, Cermak's Drug Store, Cecha's Jewelry, Knezacek's Meats, St. Wenceslaus Church, and the Bohemian Benevolent Association. Such institutions gave a district an ethnic identity even though surrounding neighborhoods were mixed and unstable.

If the term *ghetto* is defined as a place of enforced residence from which escape is at best difficult, only nonwhites in this era had a true ghetto experience. Wherever Asians and Mexicans immigrated, they encountered discrimination in housing, employment, and other facets of public life. Although these groups often preferred to remain separate in Chinatowns and *barrios,* white Americans made every effort to keep them confined. In the 1880s the city of San Francisco, for example, tried to prohibit Chinese laundries from locating in most neighborhoods, and its school board tried to isolate Japanese and Chinese children in Chinatown schools. In the *barrios* of Los Angeles and San Antonio, Anglo teachers and administrators dominated the schools and were insensitive to the language needs of Hispanic students.

Prejudice and discrimination not only trapped blacks at the bottom of the occupational ladder but

By the beginning of the twentieth century, several cities were developing dense ghettos of African-American residents. This photograph of frame tenements in Washington, D.C., shows the poor housing that blacks were forced to occupy. Yet within these districts, blacks participated in an active street life and nurtured their own social, cultural, and economic institutions. *George Eastman House, International Museum of Photography.*

operated in housing markets to limit residential opportunities. Whites organized protective associations that pledged not to sell homes to blacks and occasionally used violence to scare away black families who did move into white neighborhoods. Such efforts seldom worked. Whites who lived on the edge of black neighborhoods often fled, leaving homes and apartments to be sold and rented to black occupants. In almost every city, totally black residential districts expanded while white native and ethnic neighborhoods dissolved. By 1920 in Chicago, Detroit, Cleveland, and other cities outside of the South, two-thirds or more of the total black population lived in only 10 percent of the residential area. Within these districts, blacks nurtured cultural institutions that helped them adjust to urban life: storefront churches, business and educational organizations, social clubs, and saloons. But the ghettos also bred frustration, the result of stunted opportunity and racial bigotry. Color, more than any other factor, made the urban

experiences of blacks different from those of whites.

All groups, however, including blacks, could and did move—if not from one part of the city to another, then from one city to another. Americans were always seeking greener pastures, and hope that things might be better somewhere else acted as a safety valve, relieving some of the tensions and frustrations that simmered inside the city. At times these emotions erupted into violence; more often, people simply left. A railroad ticket from one city to another cost a few dollars; there was little to lose by moving.

The possibilities for upward mobility, moreover, seemed to temper people's dissatisfaction. Although the gap between the very rich and the very poor widened, the expanding economies of American cities created more room in the middle of the socioeconomic scale. Few could hope to become another Rockefeller, and failed or blocked mobility frustrated others; but many did become respectable merchants, shopkeepers, foremen, clerks, and agents. If advancement was not possible in one generation, it could be possible in the next. Finally, if migration, occupational mobility, and the acquisition of property offered little hope of improvement or relief, there was still one sphere to which city dwellers could turn: politics.

The Rise of Urban Boss Politics

The sudden growth and mounting rivalry among social and economic interest groups that occurred in the late nineteenth century mired cities in a governmental swamp. Burgeoning populations, business expansion, and technological change created urgent needs for water, sewers, police and fire protection, schools, parks, and other services. Such needs strained governments beyond their capacities. Furthermore, city governments approached these needs in a disorganized fashion. Legislative and administrative functions were typically scattered among a mayor, city council, and independent boards that administered health regulations, public works, poverty relief, and other matters. Philadelphia at one time had thirty different boards plus a mayor and council to tend to the city's needs. State governments often imposed their will on city administrations, appointing board members and limiting local rights to levy taxes and borrow money.

Power thrives on confusion, and out of this governmental chaos arose the political machine. Unlike political parties, which ideally exist for higher purposes than merely electing their candidates to office, machines were organizations whose main goals were the rewards— whether money, influence, or prestige—of getting and keeping political power. In order to achieve such goals, a machine had to win popular support. Machine politicians routinely used bribery and graft to further their ends. But they could not have succeeded if they had not provided relief, security, and municipal services to large numbers of people. By doing so, machine politicians accomplished things that other agencies had been unable or unwilling to attempt.

Political Machines

Machines were also beneficiaries of new urban conditions. As cities grew larger and economically more complex, business leaders either vied to use government to advance their own interests or withdrew from local affairs to pursue their interests in interurban or interregional economic organizations. At the same time, hordes of newcomers, often unskilled and foreign-born, crowded into cities. As they acquired citizenship and voting rights, sometimes fraudulently with the help of political machines, the men of these groups became a substantial political force.

These circumstances bred a new kind of leader: the political boss. Conflicting interest groups needed brokers who could by-pass governmental stalemates, and urban newcomers had needs that required government attention. Bosses and machines established power bases among new urban voters and used politics to solve some important urban problems. Most bosses had immigrant backgrounds and had grown up in the inner city, so they knew the needs of their constituents firsthand. Machines made politics a full-time profession. According to George Washington Plunkett, a small-time boss in New York City who published his memoirs in 1905, "As a rule [the boss] has no business or occupation other than politics. He plays politics every day and night in the year and his headquarters bears the inscription, 'Never closed.'"

Bosses and machines were rarely as dictatorial or corrupt as critics charged. To be sure, fraud, bribery, and thievery tainted the system. Bosses such as Philadelphia's "Duke" Vare, Kansas City's Tom Pendergast, and New York's Richard Croker lived like kings, though their official incomes were slim. A few bosses had no permanent organization; rather, they were freelance opportunists who bargained for power, sometimes winning and sometimes losing. But from the 1880s onward, most machines evolved into highly organized political structures that wedded accomplishments for the city with personal gain for politicians.

The system rested on a popular base and was held together by loyalty and service. City machines were coalitions of smaller machines that derived power directly from neighborhoods, particularly inner-city neighborhoods inhabited by native and immigrant working classes. In return for votes, bosses provided jobs, built parks and bathhouses, distributed food to the needy, and helped when someone ran afoul of the law. Such personalized

Political bosses won friends and courted voters by offering benevolence and entertainment to working-class residents of ethnic neighborhoods. This ferry cruise, sponsored by Timothy D. "Big Tim" Sullivan of Tammany Hall, was one of many events that the boss provided for his constituents. *Brown Brothers.*

service cultivated mass attachment to the boss; never before had government or public leaders assumed such responsibility for people in need.

Bosses, moreover, were genuinely public people. They attended weddings and wakes, joined clubs, and held open house in saloons where neighborhood people could contact them personally. Each boss had his own style. Pittsburgh's Christopher Magee gave his city a zoo and hospital. Brooklyn's Hugh McLaughlin provided free burial services. Boston's James Michael Curley would approach a haggard old woman and tell her that "a woman should have three attributes. She should have beauty, intelligence, and money." Then he would press a silver dollar into her hand, adding "Now you have all three."

▶ **Techniques of Bossism**

In order to finance their largess and support their system, bosses exchanged favors for votes or money. Their power over local government enabled machines to control the letting of contracts, the granting of utility or streetcar franchises, and the distribution of city jobs. Recipients of city business and jobs were expected to repay the machine with a portion of their profits or salaries and to cast supporting votes on election day. Bosses called this process gratitude; critics called it graft. Machines constructed public buildings, sewer systems, mass-transit lines, and more that otherwise might not have been built; but bribes and kickbacks made such projects costly to taxpayers. Machines dispersed favors to illegal businesses as well as to legitimate ones. Payoffs from gambling, prostitution, and illegal liquor traffic became important sources of machine revenue.

Bosses held onto their power because they knew people's needs firsthand and because they tended to problems of everyday life. Martin Lomasney, boss of Boston's South End, explained, "There's got to be in every ward somebody that any bloke can come to—no matter what he's done—and get help. Help, you understand, none of your law and justice, but help." In an era when unemployment insurance and welfare were virtually unknown, machine politicians believed that government existed to aid people in need and to provide services.

The Rise of Urban Boss Politics

The boss system, however, was neither innocent nor fair. Jobs, Christmas turkeys, and funeral money were accompanied by bribery, thievery, and extortion. Bosses never distributed favors equitably. New immigrant groups such as Italians and Poles, and racial minorities like blacks and Latinos, received only token recognition, if any. Because machines emphasized personal and neighborhood issues, they effectively deflected working-class residents from workplace issues and may have prevented unions from growing more rapidly. Nevertheless, in an age of economic individualism, bosses were no more guilty of self-interest and discrimination than the respectable business leaders who exploited workers, spoiled the landscape, and manipulated government in pursuit of profits. Sometimes humane and sometimes criminal, bosses were brokers between various sectors of urban society and an uncertain world.

Civic Reform

While bosses were consolidating their power, others were attempting to destroy political machines and improve the quality of urban life. This urban reform effort, which paralleled its agrarian counterpart (see pages 590–593) and laid the foundation for national reforms of the Progressive era (see Chapter 21), shared the strengths and weaknesses of the American liberal tradition of government activism.

In 1885, Congregational minister Josiah Strong wrote, "The city is the nerve center of our civilization. It is also the storm center. . . . It has become a serious threat to our civilization." Strong's sentiments moved many middle- and upper-class Americans who feared that immigrant-based political machines menaced the republic and that unsavory alliances between bosses and businesses undermined municipal finances. Anxious over the poverty, crowding, and disorder that seemed to accompany population expansion, and convinced that urban services were making taxes too high, civic reformers organized to install more responsible leaders at the helm of urban administrations.

Urban reform partly derived from the industrial system's emphasis on eliminating waste and inefficiency. Business-minded reformers were persuaded that government could be made more efficient if it were run like a business. They believed that the only way to prevent civic decay was to elect officials who would hold down expenses and prevent corruption. Thus their major goals were to reduce city budgets, make employees work longer, and cut taxes.

In order to introduce sound business principles to government, civic reformers supported a number of structural changes, such as the city-manager and commission forms of government and nonpartisan, citywide election of officials. Each of these reforms was meant to remove politics from government and place decision making in the hands of experienced experts. Armed with such strategies, reformers believed they could centralize administration under their control and thereby undermine bosses' power bases in the wards and neighborhoods. They rarely realized, however, that bosses succeeded because they used government to meet people's needs. Reformers only noticed the waste and corruption that machines bred.

Structural Reforms in Government

A few reformers did move beyond structural changes to a genuine concern for social problems. Hazen S. Pingree, mayor of Detroit from 1889 to 1896; Samuel "Golden Rule" Jones, mayor of Toledo from 1897 to 1904; and Thomas L. Johnson, mayor of Cleveland from 1901 to 1909, worked to provide jobs for poor people, reduce charges by transit and utility companies, and establish greater governmental responsibility for the welfare of all citizens. Some supported public ownership of gas, electric, and telephone companies, a quasi-socialist reform that alienated their business allies. But Pingree, Jones, and Johnson were exceptions. Most civic reformers were narrow of vision. They achieved temporary success, but they could not match the bosses' political savvy and soon found themselves out of power.

Seeds of social reform nevertheless were beginning to sprout outside of politics. Convinced that laissez-faire ideology was not applicable in a complex urban-industrial world and driven by an urge to identify and address urban problems, a number of men and women—mostly young and middle-class—embarked on campaigns for social betterment. These urban social reformers operated within a variety of fields. Housing reform-

Social Reform

ers wanted local government to pass building codes to ensure safety in tenements. Protestant reformers influenced by the Social Gospel movement, which emphasized social responsibility as a means to salvation, built churches in slum neighborhoods and urged businesses to be socially responsible. Believing that service to fellow humans was a Christian duty, Social Gospel clergymen such as Washington Gladden of Columbus, Ohio, and Walter Rauchenbusch of Rochester, New York, worked to alleviate poverty and to make peace between employers and labor unions. Educational reformers such as William T. Harris of St. Louis saw public schools as a means of preparing immigrants and their children for citizenship by teaching them American values as well as the English language.

Perhaps the most ambitious and inspiring feature of the urban reform movement was the settlement house. Patterned after London's Toynbee Hall and mostly led by women, settlements were efforts by educated, middle-class young adults to bridge the gulf between classes by going to live in slum neighborhoods. The first American settlement house opened in New York City in 1886. Early settlement founders such as Jane Addams, Florence Kelley, and Graham Taylor wanted to improve the lives of slum dwellers by helping them to obtain education, appreciation of the arts, better jobs, and better housing. Settlement houses provided neighborhood residents with a wide array of activities, ranging from vocational classes to childcare for working mothers to ethnic art exhibits and pageants. Because of their efforts in areas such as the establishment of school nurses, the passing of building safety codes, construction of public playgrounds, and support for labor unions, settlement workers often became reform leaders in cities and in the nation. Although the neighborhood residents they served sometimes mistrusted them because they were outsiders to working-class and immigrant cultures, settlement workers made valuable contributions to inner-city life.

While settlement workers tried to revive neighborhoods, other reformers tried to beautify whole cities. Inspired by the World's Columbian Exposition of 1893, a dazzling world's fair held in a specially built White City on Chicago's South Side, architects and city planners worked to redesign the urban landscape. Their efforts have been labeled as the City Beautiful

Beautification Campaigns

movement. Led by architect Daniel Burnham, City Beautiful advocates built civic centers, parks, boulevards, and transportation systems that would make cities more attractive as well as economically efficient. "Make no little plans," Burnham urged city officials. "Make big plans; aim high in hope and work." This attitude spawned beautifying projects in Chicago, San Francisco, and Washington, D.C., in the early 1900s. Yet most big plans turned out to be only big dreams. Neither government nor the private sector could muster enough money to undertake major projects, and planners disagreed with each other and with social reformers over whether beautification would really solve urban problems.

Whether they concentrated on government, social services, or city design, urban reformers wanted to save cities, not abandon them. Men and women of the various reform movements believed that they could improve urban life by restoring feelings of service and cooperation among all citizens. They often failed to realize, however, that cities were places of great diversity and that different people had different views of what reform actually meant. Distributing city jobs on the basis of civil service exams rather than party loyalty meant progress to government reformers, but to working-class men it signified reduced employment opportunities. Moral reformers tried to prohibit the sale of alcoholic beverages to prevent working-class breadwinners from wasting their wages and ruining their health, but European immigrants saw such crusades as interference in their long-held wine- and beer-drinking customs. Planners saw new civic buildings and transportation systems as modern necessities, but such structures often replaced low-cost housing units and displaced the poor. Well-meaning humanitarians criticized immigrant mothers for the way they dressed, did housework, raised children, and went shopping without regard for the new pressures that the consumer economy created. Thus in early urban reform, idealism merged with naiveté and insensitivity.

It is important to note, however, that important decisions and accomplishments affecting urban life were made outside of the context of bossism and reform. Sanitation, garbage disposal, streetlighting, bridge and street building, and other such needs posed problems that required technical, not political or humanitarian, creativity. In addressing these issues, American ur-

Engineering Reforms

Consumer reform originated in many cities at the end of the nineteenth century. Various organizations of reform-minded women promoted campaigns for laws and agencies to inspect for adulterated milk and other tainted foods dangerous to health. Here, a group of middle-class women is teaching a class in home economics to immigrant children. *Museum of the City of New York.*

ban dwellers, and especially the engineering profession, developed systems and standards of worldwide effect.

Take, for example, the problems of refuse. Experts in 1900 estimated that every New Yorker generated annually some 160 pounds of garbage (food and bones), 1,200 pounds of ashes (from stoves and furnaces), and 100 pounds of rubbish (old shoes, furniture, and other items). Europeans of that era produced only about half of those amounts. At the same time, there were as many as three-and-a-half-million horses in American cities, and each one produced about 20 pounds of manure and a gallon of urine daily. Because city horses were worked so hard that they lived only a few years, each city also had to dispose of thousands of carcasses every year. (No wonder people heralded the automobile as the harbinger of cleaner streets!) In past eras, trash and excrement could be dismissed as nuisances; by the twentieth century they were threats to public health and safety, and citizens groups were raising loud protests against inadequate refuse collection and disposal.

Although most people agreed that government had ultimate responsibility, the problem raised difficult questions. Who should be responsible for waste removal, city workers or a private contractor hired by the city? Previously, cities dumped refuse on vacant land and in nearby rivers and lakes. What alternatives were there to these unsafe practices? Should trash be sorted so that some, such as metals, could be salvaged and others be recycled as fertilizer and landfill? How frequently should streets be cleaned and by whom?

To solve their problems, cities increasingly depended on engineers, who, next to teachers, had become the largest profession in the country by 1900. These individuals applied technical expertise in establishing systems for incinerating refuse, for dumping trash while still ensuring safe water supplies, for constructing sewers and transporting sewage, and for instituting regular streetcleaning

Chapter 18: The Fame and Shame of the Cities, 1877–1920

(including snow removal). Engineers also sponsored studies of local problems and advised officials on budgetary matters and contracts. They had similar influence in matters of streetlighting, parks, fire protection, and more. Engineers were not immune to political scandal, but they generally carried out their responsibilities without great publicity and left lasting marks on their communities without becoming involved in politics.

The Legacy of Urbanism

Much of what American society is today originated in the urbanization of the late nineteenth century. American cities may have been less orderly and beautiful than European cities, but they hummed with energy and excitement. When old-fashioned native inventiveness met the traditions of European, African, and Asian cultures, a new kind of society emerged. This society seldom functioned smoothly; in fact, there really was no coherent urban community, only a collection of subcommunities. Yet its jumble of social classes, ethnic and racial groups, political organizations, and other components left important legacies.

By the early 1900s, American cities had become so diverse that immigrant groups were straining to protect their cultures in a changing, bewildering world. Fearful and puzzled, native

> **Cultural Pluralism**

whites tried to Americanize and uplift immigrants, but the newcomers stubbornly clung to their rituals, languages, family and social organizations, and drinking and eating habits. Optimists had envisioned the American nation as a melting pot where various nationalities would blend to become a new, unified people. Instead, many ethnic groups proved to be unmeltable, and racial minorities got burned on the bottom of the pot.

As a result of immigration and urbanization, the United States became a culturally pluralistic society—not a melting pot but a salad bowl. As one immigrant priest told a social worker, "There is no such thing as an American." He meant the same thing literary critic Randolph Bourne meant when he dubbed the United States "a cosmopolitan federation of national colonies." This kind of reasoning produced hyphenated identifications:

This cartoon satirizes the urban apartment house of the future, which the artist predicted would become ever taller and more elaborate. Every amenity of city life can be found in this comical structure, including a park, theater, railroad depot, fire station, church, grocery, saloon, and more. Here was the epitome of urbanization all housed under one roof. *Judge 1884.*

people considered themselves Irish-American, Italo-American, Polish-American, and the like.

Pluralism and its attendant interest-group loyalties made politics an important institution. If America was not a melting pot, then different groups were competing with each other for power, wealth, and status. When lack of skills, education, capital, and influence closed paths to success, immigrants turned to politics to protect their interests and to open new opportunities. American cities became arenas in which different groups formed coalitions to achieve their goals. But such coalitions were fragile, and their membership shifted according to the issue in question.

Adherents of diverse cultural traditions battled over how much control government should exercise over people's lives (see page 595). The most

Cultural-	provocative issue concerned use
Political	of leisure time and celebration of
Alignments	Sunday, the Lord's day. In the Puri-

tan tradition, the native-born supported blue laws (see page 327)
designed to prevent desecration of the Sabbath by
prohibiting various commercial and recreational
activities. European immigrants, accustomed to
feasting and playing after church, fought the closing
of saloons and other restrictions on the only day
they had free for fun and relaxation. Thus in 1913,
when the New York legislature proposed a law
granting cities authority to end restrictions on Sunday baseball games and liquor sales, both sides argued vehemently. One rural Republican charged
that such a measure amounted to "amending
Moses' law," while a New York City Democrat of
Irish lineage retorted that "Moses was an organization Democrat" who wrote the commandment
"Don't covet your neighbor's rights." At about the
same time, the Illinois and Ohio legislatures split
over whether to legalize boxing, which small-town
Protestants opposed and urban Catholics and Jews
favored. Similar splits developed over public versus
parochial schools and prohibition versus free availability of liquor.

Such conflicts, fueled by hard times as well as the
ever-growing diversity of the American population,
illustrate why local politics and state politics were
so heated. Some people carried polarization to extremes and tried to suppress everything new and
allegedly un-American. In many communities during the depression of the 1890s, the American Protective Association attracted attention by attacking
"the diabolical works of the Catholic Church" and
demanding an end to immigration. Such sentiment
influenced national legislation. In 1882, Congress
bowed to pressure from West Coast nativists and
prohibited Chinese immigration for ten years. In
1902 a new law excluded the Chinese indefinitely;
not until 1943 was the ban lifted. Also, periodic
attempts were made to prevent foreign-born citizens from voting by imposing literacy tests on
them.

Efforts to enforce homogeneity generally failed,
however, because the country's cultural diversity
prevented domination by a single ethnic majority.
By 1920, immigrants and their offspring outnumbered natives in many cities, and the national economy depended on new workers and consumers.

These new Americans had transformed the United
States into an urban nation; they had given American culture its rich and varied texture; and they had
laid foundations for the liberalism that would characterize future American politics.

Suggestions for Further Reading

Urban Growth

Howard P. Chudacoff and Judith E. Smith, *The Evolution of American Urban Society*, 3rd ed. (1988); Kenneth T. Jackson, *The Crabgrass Frontier: The Suburbanization of the United States* (1985); Arthur M. Schlesinger, *The Rise of the City* (1933); Jon Teaford, *City and Suburb: The Political Fragmentation of Metropolitan America, 1850-1970* (1979); Sam Bass Warner, Jr., *The Urban Wilderness* (1982); Sam Bass Warner, Jr., *Streetcar Suburbs* (1962).

Immigration, Ethnicity, and Religion

Aaron I. Abell, *American Catholicism and Social Action* (1960); Josef J. Barton, *Peasants and Strangers: Italians, Rumanians, and Slovaks in an American City* (1975); John Bodnar, *The Transplanted* (1985); John Bodnar et al., *Lives of Their Own: Blacks, Italians, and Poles in Pittsburgh, 1900-1960* (1982); John W. Briggs, *An Italian Passage* (1978); Jack Chen, *The Chinese of America* (1980); Hasia Diner, *Erin's Daughters in America* (1983); John B. Duff, *The Irish in the United States* (1971); Elizabeth Ewen, *Immigrant Women in the Land of Dollars* (1985); Mario T. Garcia, *Desert Immigrants: The Mexicans of El Paso, 1880-1920* (1981); Nathan Glazer and Daniel P. Moynihan, *Beyond the Melting Pot*, rev. ed. (1970); Caroline Golab, *Immigrant Destinations* (1977); Milton Gordon, *Assimilation in American Life* (1964); Victor Greene, *For God and Country: The Rise of Polish and Lithuanian Ethnic Consciousness in America* (1975); Oscar Handlin, *The Uprooted*, 2nd ed. (1973); Marcus Lee Hansen, *The Immigrant in American History* (1940); John Higham, *Strangers in the Land: Patterns of American Nativism* (1955); Arthur William Hoglund, *Finnish Immigrants in America* (1960); Yusi Ichioka, *The Issei: The World of the First Japanese Immigrants, 1885–1924* (1988); Edward R. Kantowicz, *Polish-American Politics in Chicago* (1975); Harry Kitano, *Japanese Americans: The Evolution of a Subculture* (1969); Alan M. Kraut, *The Huddled Masses: The Immigrant in American Society, 1880-1921* (1982); Matt S. Maier and Felciano Rivera, *The Chicanos* (1972); Henry F. May, *Protestant Churches and Industrial America* (1949); Ewa Morawska, *For Bread with Butter: Life-Worlds of East Europeans in Johnstown, Pennsylvania, 1890–1940* (1986); Humbert S. Nelli, *The Italians of Chicago* (1970); Moses Rischin, *The Promised City: New York's Jews* (1962); Judith E.

Smith, *Family Connections* (1985); Werner Sollors, *Beyond Ethnicity* (1986); Stephan Thernstrom, ed., *Harvard Encyclopedia of American Ethnic Groups* (1980).

Urban Needs and Services

Robert H. Bremner, *From the Depths: The Discovery of Poverty* (1956); James H. Cassedy, *Charles V. Chapin and the Public Health Movement* (1962); Lawrence A. Cremin, *American Education: The Metropolitan Experience* (1988); Marvin Lazerson, *Origins of the Urban School* (1971); Martin V. Melosi, *Garbage in the Cities* (1981); Eric Monkkonen, *Police in Urban America* (1981); Thomas L. Philpott, *The Slum and the Ghetto* (1978); James F. Richardson, *The New York Police* (1970); Barbara Gutmann Rosencrantz, *Public Health and the State* (1972); Mel Scott, *American City Planning Since 1890* (1969); Christopher Tunnard and Henry Hope Reed, *American Skyline* (1955); David B. Tyack, *The One Best System: A History of American Urban Education* (1974).

Mobility and Race Relations

Howard P. Chudacoff, *Mobile Americans* (1972); Thomas C. Cox, *Blacks in Topeka, Kansas, 1865–1915* (1982); Clyde Griffen and Sally Griffen, *Natives and Newcomers* (1977); Jacqueline Jones, *Labor of Love, Labor of Sorrow: Black Women, Work and the Family from Slavery to the Present* (1985); David M. Katzman, *Before the Ghetto* (1973); Thomas Kessner, *The Golden Door* (1977); Kenneth L. Kusmer, *A Ghetto Takes Shape* (1976); Gilbert Osofsky, *Harlem: The Making of a Ghetto* (1966); Elizabeth H. Pleck, *Black Migration and Poverty: Boston, 1865–1900* (1979); Howard N. Rabinowitz, *Race Relations in the Urban South* (1978); Allan H. Spear, *Black Chicago* (1967); Stephan Thernstrom, *The Other Bostonians: Poverty and Progress in the American Metropolis* (1973); Olivier Zunz, *The Changing Face of Inequality: Urbanization, Industrial Development and Immigrants in Detroit, 1880–1920* (1982).

Boss Politics

John M. Allswang, *Bosses, Machines and Urban Voters* (1977); Blaine Brownell and Warren E. Stickle, eds., *Bosses and Reformers* (1973); Alexander B. Callow, Jr., ed., *The City Boss in America* (1976); Lyle Dorsett, *The Pendergast Machine* (1968); Zane L. Miller, *Boss Cox's Cincinnati* (1968); Bruce M. Stave and Sondra Stave, eds., *Urban Bosses, Machines, and Progressive Reformers* (1984).

Urban Reform

John D. Buenker, *Urban Liberalism and Progressive Reform* (1973); James B. Crooks, *Politics and Progress* (1968); Allen F. Davis, *American Heroine: The Life and Legend of Jane Addams* (1973); Allen F. Davis, *Spearheads for Reform* (1967); Michael Ebner and Eugene Tobin, eds., *The Age of Urban Reform* (1977); Melvin Holli, *Reform in Detroit* (1969); C. H. Hopkins, *The Rise of the Social Gospel in American Protestantism* (1940); Roy M. Lubove, *The Progressives and the Slums* (1962); Martin J. Schiesl, *The Politics of Efficiency: Municipal Administration and Reform in America* (1977).

When the police arrested her in November 1904, she called herself "Caroline Hobart," but that was not her real name. She was the wife of a prominent New Jersey lawyer, and she was too embarrassed to tell the truth because she had been caught shoplifting several pins from the jewelry counter of a fashionable New York City shop. "Caroline Hobart" was not alone. Each year thousands of otherwise law-abiding middle-class women were caught stealing candy, buttons, gloves, scarves, jewelry, and ribbons from department stores and shops. These upstanding citizens presumably could afford to buy such items, yet they broke the law. Theft certainly was not the major activity of middle-class women, and men were arrested more often than women for all kinds of crime. But the context of shoplifting provides insights into important changes in American society at the end of the nineteenth century and beginning of the twentieth.

Like millions of American women in this period, "Caroline Hobart" had a vital job. She was a shopper. The term should not be taken lightly. Technological change and rising levels of industrial production had made the family a consumer rather than a producer of goods. Women, as managers of the home, assumed the role of making decisions about what their family would consume, and shopping became the process by which these vital decisions were implemented. At the same time, department stores became major arenas in which the material cornucopia of the new industrialism was presented. Store managers of places like Wanamaker's in Philadelphia, Lord and Taylor in New York, and Marshall Field in Chicago made a science out of displaying merchandise to tempt potential buyers. Glass cases, mirrors, brightly colored decorations, rest rooms, and other features were used to appeal especially to female shoppers. Like church work, shopping became a public activity—in contrast to the private world of the home—for women, and it was not long before middle-class women engaged in shopping for their own enjoyment as well as for buying necessities.

The success of department stores, however, created a dilemma. Amid the spectacle of materialism, some women surrendered to temptation and stole. Store managers were so concerned with

19

EVERYDAY LIFE AND CULTURE, 1877–1920

their commercial image that they often chose not to prosecute customers caught shoplifting. The manager of the store from which "Caroline Hobart" stole tried to withdraw the charges, explaining to the judge that Mrs. Hobart "has been suffering from severe illness for three years. We believe that in this instance she committed the theft under stress of some sudden mental defection." But other merchants and judges, including the judge in Hobart's case, favored prosecution. To explain the thefts, doctors, lawyers, and merchants claimed these women suffered from a particular female illness called *kleptomania*. This disease, which supposedly had origins in the female reproductive system, was defined as the inability to resist impulses for material things. In this regard, of course, women were no different from men, whose impulses led them to strip the environment and seize the belongings of Indians and other less-powerful people as well as steal consumer goods and money. But the experts did not think this way. They presumed that female weakness, and not campaigns to tempt shoppers to acquire more than they had intended to buy, caused the crime.

The invention of kleptomania not only reflects contemporary negative attitudes about women but also represents an unanticipated consequence of the shifting focus from production to consumption. During the half-century between the end of Reconstruction and the end of the First World War, the nation's farms and factories were producing so much that Americans could afford to reorient their attitudes toward material wants. What had once been accessible only to a few was becoming available to many; what had formerly been dreams were becoming necessities. No trend affected everyday life more decisively than this one. As Americans tried to adapt to new values of consumption and its attendant conflicts, they raised questions about their goals and values that have not been resolved to this day.

At the dawn of this new era, most Americans were still relatively isolated. In 1880, seven out of ten people lived on farms and in small towns. Life in such places was shaped by the dictates of nature and traditional institutions of family and church. In the fields and in the household, people worked from sunup to sundown—though they could usually control the pace of their work and the number of breaks they took. Most foods and clothes were made at home or nearby. Houses were heated by

wood- or coal-burning stoves and lit by oil lamps; most had no bathroom, only basins and tubs indoors and outhouses in the back yard. Families burned what little trash they had, fed their garbage to animals, and poured waste water outside. Besides getting together at church, people mingled at the general store and at such special occasions as fairs, circuses, political rallies, and evangelical revivals. Fatigue and pitch-darkness restricted nighttime activities. People normally went to bed at 9 or 10 P.M. and rose at 4 or 5 A.M.

But lifestyles changed rapidly. As the nation's population became increasingly urban, a new society of street corners, saloons, shops, and commercial amusements replaced the village church and general store. People tended to spend more time with their peers—members of the same age group—and less with their families. The rapid spread of railroad, postal, telephone, and electrical service drew even isolated communities into the orbit of a consumer-oriented society. American ingenuity combined with technology, mass production, and mass marketing to fashion and advertise myriad goods that had not previously existed or had been the exclusive property of the wealthy. This new material well-being, brought about by the advent of such products as ready-made clothes, canned foods, and home appliances, had a dual effect. It enabled Americans of differing status to join communities of consumers—communities defined not by place or class but by common possession. It also accentuated differences between those who could afford such goods and services and those who could not, and it created new allurements that got people like "Caroline Hobart" into trouble.

Standards of Living

If the affluence of a society can be measured by how quickly the society converts luxuries into commonplace articles of everyday life, the United States was indeed becoming affluent in the years between 1880 and 1920. In 1880, for example, smokers rolled their own cigarettes; only wealthy women could afford silk stockings; only residents of Florida, Texas, and California could enjoy fresh oranges; the sweets people ate were made at home;

1859	Founding of Great Atlantic Tea Company (A&P)
1867	Alger, *Ragged Dick*
1869	Alcott, *Little Women*
1876	National League of Professional Baseball Clubs founded Twain, *Tom Sawyer*
1880s	Spread of chain-pull toilets in U.S. Acceptance of germ theory of disease Mass production of tin cans begins
1881	First federal trademark law
1883	Pulitzer buys *New York World*
1884	Twain, *Huckleberry Finn*
1885	Invention of the safety bicycle
1889	Edison invents the motion-picture camera and viewing device
1895	Hearst buys *New York Journal*
1896	Frank Merriwell series begins
1900s	Rise in popularity of vaudeville
1903	First baseball World Series
1905	Intercollegiate Athletic Association formed
1915	*Birth of a Nation,* film directed by D. W. Griffith

and few people ever bought soap. By 1899, manufactured and perishable products were becoming increasingly common. That year Americans bought 2 billion machine-produced cigarettes (an average of 27 per person) and 151,000 pairs of silk stockings, consumed oranges at the rate of 100 crates for every 1,000 people, and spent an average of $1.08 per person on store-bought candy and pastries and 63 cents on soap. By 1921 the transformation was even more advanced. Americans smoked 43 billion cigarettes that year (403 per person), ate 248 crates of oranges per 1,000 people, bought 217 million pairs of silk stockings, and spent $1.66 per person on confectionery goods and $1.40 on soap. How did people afford these goods? How did changes in standards of living come about?

What people can afford depends on their resources and incomes. Data for the period from 1880 to 1920 are incomplete, but there is no doubt that incomes rose. The rapidly expanding economy spawned massive fortunes and created a new industrial elite. The writer of "The Coming Billionaire," an article published in *Forum* magazine in 1891, estimated

Rising Personal Income

that there were already 120 Americans worth at least $10 million. By 1920, when income-tax figures made possible the first accurate tabulations of income distribution, the richest 5 percent of the population was receiving almost one-fourth of all income in the country. Returns on investments were even more skewed; the same top 5 percent received almost half of all interest payments and 85 percent of all stock and bond dividends.

But incomes also rose among the middle classes. For example, the average pay for clerical workers rose 36 percent between 1890 and 1910 (see table, page 557). After the turn of the century, employees of the federal executive branch were averaging $1,072 a year, and college professors $1,100—not handsome sums but much more than manual workers received. With these incomes, the middle class, whose numbers were increasing as a result of new job opportunities, could afford relatively comfortable housing. A six- or seven-room house cost around $3,000 to buy or build and $15 to $20 per month to rent.

Wages for industrial workers increased as well, though they varied widely and income figures were deceiving. On average, annual wages of factory

A newly married middle-class couple displays all their wedding gifts, a cornucopia of products readily available in the new consumer age. New mass production and marketing techniques made such materialism possible. *Missouri Historical Society.*

workers rose from $486 in 1890 to $630 in 1910, about 35 percent. Hourly rates in industries with large female work forces, such as shoe and paper manufacturing, were lower than in industries with predominantly male employees, such as coal mining and iron production. Also, regional variations were wide. Nevertheless, wages for all moved upward (see table). Income for farm laborers followed the same trend, though wages remained relatively low because generally those workers received room and board along with their pay.

Income scales for industrial and farm workers, however, omit a vital aspect of living standards. Wage increases mean little if living costs rise as fast as or faster than wages, and that **Cost of** is what happened. According to **Living** one economic index, the weekly cost of living for a typical wage earner's family of four rose over 47 percent between 1889 and 1913. In other words, a quantity of food and other items that may have cost $6.78 in 1889 increased, after a slight dip in the mid-1890s, to $10.00 by 1913 (see table for specific food prices). Very rarely did the income for a particular working-class occupation rise at the same rate as the cost of living.

How then could working-class Americans afford the new goods and services that the industrial age offered? Many could not. The daughter of a textile worker, recalling her school days described how "some of the kids would bring bars of chocolate, others an orange. . . . I suppose they were richer than a family like ours. My father used to buy a bag of candy and a bag of peanuts every payday. . . . And that's all we'd have until the next payday. If we asked for something my mother would say, 'Well, we're too poor. We can't afford to buy that.' " Another woman explained how her family coped with high prices and low wages: "My mother made our clothes. People then wore old clothes. My mother would rip them out and make them over."

Still, a working-class family could raise its income and partake at least partially in the consumer society by sending children and women into the labor market. In a household where the father made $600 a year, the wages of other family mem-

AMERICAN LIVING STANDARDS, 1880–1920

	1880	1890	1900	1910	1920
Income and earnings:					
Annual income:					
Clerical worker		$848		$1,156	
Public school teacher		$256		$492	
Industrial worker		$486		$630	
Farm laborer		$233		$336	
Hourly wage:					
Soft-coal miner		$0.18[a]		$0.21	
Iron worker		$0.17[a]		$0.23	
Shoe worker		$0.14[a]		$0.19	
Paper worker		$0.12[a]		$0.17	
Labor statistics					
Number of people in labor force	17.4 million	28.5 million			41.7 million
Average workweek, manufacturing		60 hours		51 hours	47.4 hours
Food costs					
10 pounds potatoes		$0.16		$0.17	
1 dozen eggs		$0.21		$0.34	
1 pound bacon		$0.12½		$0.25	
Demographic data					
Life expectancy at birth:					
Women			48.3 years		54.6 years
Men			46.3 years		53.6 years
Death rate per 1,000 people			172		130
Birthrate per 1,000 people	39.8		32.3		27.7
Other					
Number of students in public high schools		203,000			2.3 million
Advertising expenditures	$20 million		$95 million		$500 million
Telephones per 100 people		0.3[b]	2.1[c]		12.6[d]

[a] 1892 [b] 1891 [c] 1901 [d] 1921

Supplements to Family Income bers might lift total income to $800 or $900. Many families also rented household space to boarders and lodgers, a practice that could yield up to $200 a year. These means of increasing family income enabled people to spend more and save more. Between 1889 and 1901, working-class families markedly increased expenditures for such items as life insurance, amuse-

ments, alcoholic beverages, and union dues. Thus workers were able to improve their living standards, but not without sacrifices in their family and home life.

The work people did was part of a highly developed money economy. Between 1890 and 1920, the American labor force grew from 28 million workers to 42 million. These figures, however, are somewhat misleading. In general, they represent a

As the new consumerism enveloped American society, department stores became the main arenas in which shopping skills were performed. Their abundance, shining through huge glass windows and piled in tempting displays, attracted shoppers from working-class as well as middle-class families. *Joseph J. Pennell Collection, Kansas Collection, University of Kansas Libraries.*

change in the nature of work rather than an increase in the number of available jobs relative to the number of people who could work. In the rural society that the United States was in the nineteenth century, women and children had tasks that were important to the family's daily existence—cooking, cleaning, planting, and harvesting. Their jobs were often hard to define, and they seldom appeared in employment figures because they earned no wages. But as the nation industrialized and the agricultural sector's share of national income and population declined, wage and salaried employment became more common. Jobs in industry and commerce were easier to define and easier to count. It is probable, then, that the proportion of Americans who were working was not increasing markedly—most Americans, male and female, had always worked. What was new was the increase in paid employment, which also made purchases of consumer goods and services more affordable.

Scientific developments eased some of life's struggles, and their impact on living standards increased after 1900. Advances in medical care and improved living conditions sharply reduced death rates and extended the life span. Between 1900 and 1920, life expectancy rose six years and the death rate dropped by 24 percent (see table, page 557). During the same period there were spectacular declines in death rates from typhoid, diphtheria, influenza (except for a harsh epidemic in 1918 and 1919), tuberculosis, and intestinal ailments—diseases that had been the scourge of earlier generations. There were, however, significantly more deaths from cancer, diabetes, and heart disease. Americans also found more ways to kill: although the suicide rate remained about the same, homicides and automobile deaths increased dramatically between 1900 and 1920.

> **Higher Life Expectancy**

Not only were amenities and luxuries more readily available in the early 1900s than they had been a half-century earlier, but the means to upward mobility seemed more accessible as well. The spread of public education—particularly high schools—

helped equip young people to achieve a standard of living higher than their parents'. Between 1890 and 1922 the number of students enrolled in public high schools grew dramatically (see table). More than ever before, education was becoming the key to success. The creation of new white-collar occupations in growing service industries helped to stem the downward mobility that resulted when mechanization pushed skilled workers out of their crafts. Yet the inequality that had pervaded earlier eras remained. Race, sex, religion, and ethnicity still determined one's access to power.

Material abundance and consumerism, moreover, seemed to make places, things, and experiences too similar. Some people mourned for the individualistic, self-reliant (and partly mythical) past, when Americans had to pay more attention to summer heat and winter cold, when they had to make things for themselves. Critics charged that the new society was creating products and demands that were unnecessary and even harmful. But it was too late to turn back. Americans had set their course toward a consumer-oriented future that promised prosperity and comfort.

The Quest for Convenience

One of the most representative agents of the revolution in American lifestyles at the end of the nineteenth century was the toilet. The chain-pull, washdown water closet, invented in England around 1870, was adopted in the United States in the 1880s. Shortly after 1900 the flush toilet was developed, and thanks to the mass production of enamel-coated fixtures, it soon became common in American homes and buildings.

The indoor toilet, suddenly cheap and easy to install, brought about a shift in habits and attitudes. In the past, people had believed there was no danger in disposing of human waste on or below the ground; only luxury hotels and estates had private bathrooms. By the 1890s, however, acceptance of the germ theory of disease had raised fears about human pollution as a source of infection and water contamination. Much more rapidly than Europeans did, Americans combined a desire for cleanliness with an urge for convenience, and water closets

By the end of the nineteenth century, a great variety of canned foods became common to the diet of millions of urban dwellers. Often advertising in women's magazines, some food processors made recipe books available to consumers who bought their products. *Collection of Campbell Soup Company. Photo courtesy of Sally Fox.*

became common, especially in middle-class urban houses. Bodily functions took on an unpleasant image, and the home bathroom became a place of utmost privacy. Also, the toilet and the private bathtub gave Americans new ways to use—and waste—water. Advancements in plumbing were part of a broader change that accompanied mass production and consumerism: the democratization of convenience.

The tin can also altered lifestyles. Before the mid-nineteenth century, Americans ate most foods only in season. Drying, smoking, and salting could preserve meat for a short time, but the availability of fresh meat, like that of fresh milk, was very limited; there was no way to prevent spoilage. Around 1810, a French inventor developed the cooking-and-sealing process of canning, and in the 1850s, an

Processed and Preserved Foods

American named Gail Borden developed a means of condensing and preserving milk. Canned goods and condensed milk became more common during the 1860s, but supplies remained low because cans had to be made by hand. By 1880, however, inventors had fashioned stamping and soldering machines that mass-produced cans from tin plate. Early commercial canning methods were not always safe, and some housewives shunned canned goods as an insult to their skills and functions as cooks. But other people, such as cowboys on the trail, readily consumed canned oysters, tomatoes, milk, and other items as alternatives to previously monotonous diets. Also, housewives did do their own preserving of meats, fruits, and vegetables, "putting up" foods in glass jars, which proved more sanitary than tin cans.

Other trends and inventions helped make it possible for Americans to vary their daily diets. Growing urban populations created the demand that encouraged fruit and vegetable farmers to raise more produce. Railroad refrigerator cars enabled growers and meatpackers to ship perishables greater distances and to preserve them for longer periods. By the 1890s, northern city dwellers could enjoy southern and western strawberries, grapes, and tomatoes for up to six months of the year. Increased use of iceboxes enabled middle-class families to store perishables. An easy means of producing ice commercially was invented in the 1870s, and by 1900 the nation had over two thousand commercial ice plants, most of which made home deliveries. In the 1870s, John H. Kellogg, manager of the Western Health Reform Institute in Battle Creek, Michigan, began serving patients new health foods, including peanut butter and wheat flakes. A few years later his brother, Will K. Kellogg, invented Corn Flakes, and Charles W. Post invented Grape Nuts, revolutionizing breakfast food. Just before the First World War, scientists discovered the dietetic value of vitamins A and B (vitamins C and D were discovered after the war). Growing numbers of published cookbooks and the opening of new cooking schools reflected heightened interest in food and its possibilities for health and enjoyment.

Even the working class had a more diversified diet. The lowest-income people still ate what their counterparts in previous eras had eaten: cheap foods, heavy with starches and carbohydrates. Southern textile workers, for example, ate corn mush and fatback (the strip of meat from a hog's back) almost every day. Poor urban families seldom could afford meat. Nevertheless, many could buy previously unavailable fruits, vegetables, and dairy products to achieve more varied fare. Workers had to spend a high percentage of their income—almost half the main breadwinner's wages—on food, but they never suffered the severe malnutrition that plagued other developing nations.

Just as tin cans and iceboxes made many foods widely available, the sewing machine brought about a revolution in clothing. In the eighteenth century, almost all the clothes

▶ **Ready-made Clothing** Americans wore were made at home, and a person's social status was apparent by what he or she wore. Then in the 1850s the sewing machine, invented in Europe but refined by Americans Elias Howe, Jr., and Isaac M. Singer, came into use for clothing and shoe manufacture. Demand for uniforms during the Civil War boosted the ready-made clothing business, and by 1890 annual retail sales of mass-produced garments reached $1.5 billion. Through mass production, manufacturers could turn out good-quality garments at relatively low cost and develop standard sizes to fit different body shapes. By the turn of the century, only the poorest families could not buy "ready-to-wear" clothes, and tailors and seamstresses, once the originators of fashion, had been relegated to repair work. The development and easy purchase of dress patterns simplified the remaining home production of clothing and gave even those who could not afford ready-made clothes access to stylish fashions.

Mass-produced clothing and dress patterns enabled a large segment of the population to become concerned with style. Restrictive Victorian fashions still dominated women's clothing, but some of the most burdensome features were beginning to be abandoned. Women's dress styles began to place greater emphasis on comfort. Designers used less fabric; by the 1920s a dress required three yards of material instead of ten. Long sleeves and skirt hemlines receded, and high-boned collars disappeared. Petite was still the ideal, however: the most desirable waist measurement was 18 to 20 inches. Corsets were big sellers at 79 cents apiece, and reformers complained that women often tried to squeeze into dresses, gloves, and shoes that were a size too small. In the early 1900s, long hair tied at the back of the neck was the most popular style. But by the First World War, when many women worked in hospitals and factories, shorter, more manageable styles had become acceptable.

Men's clothes too became more lightweight and more stylish. Before 1900, among the middle and affluent working classes, a man would have had no more than two suits for year-round wear, one for Sundays and special occasions and one for everyday use. After 1900, however, manufacturers began to produce garments from fabrics of different weights. Men began wearing soft felt hats rather than stiff derbies. Soft collars and cuffs replaced stiff ones, and plain dark-blue serge gave way to softer shades and more intricate weaves. Workingmen's clothes did not change markedly: laborers still needed the most durable, least expensive overalls, shirts, and shoes. But even for those of modest means, clothing was becoming something to be bought rather than to be made and remade at home. It too had become a feature of mass consumerism.

Department stores and chain stores helped to create and serve this new consumers' world. The great boom occurred between 1865 and 1900,

Department and Chain Stores

when companies like Macy's, Wanamaker's, Jordan Marsh, and Marshall Field became fixtures of metropolitan America. With their open displays of clothing, housewares, and furniture—all available in large quantities to anyone who had the purchase price—department stores effected a merchandising revolution. Not only did they offer wide variety; they added home deliveries, liberal exchange policies, and charge accounts. The Great Atlantic Tea Company, founded in 1859, became the first chain-store system. Renamed the Great Atlantic and Pacific Tea Company in 1869 and known more familiarly as A&P, the firm's stores sold groceries on a cash-and-carry basis. By buying in volume, the chain could sell to the public at low prices. By 1915 there were 1,712 A&P stores, and 12,000 more were built in the next ten years. Other chains, such as Woolworth's, grew rapidly during the same period.

Family Life

Although the overwhelming majority of Americans continued to live their lives within a family, this

While American women had always sewn their own clothes, by the end of the nineteenth century the availability of sewing machines and standard dress patterns made the process much easier than ever before. The front of this trade card shows a group of women sewing clothes; the reverse side of the card advertised the patterns of the dresses they are wearing. *Collection of Sally Fox.*

most basic of social institutions underwent considerable strain during the industrial era. As American society became more affluent and complex, it generated new institutions—schools, social clubs, political organizations, and others—that competed with the family to provide nurture, education, companionship, and security. Many popular and scholarly writers warned that rising divorce rates, growing separation between home and work, the entrance of large numbers of women into the work force, and loss of parental control over children spelled peril for home and family. Yet the family retained its fundamental usefulness as a cushion in a hard, uncertain world.

These photographs show two dramatic shifts in American culture between 1880 and 1920. The photo on the left presents a large, three-generation (extended) family dressed in the heavy, dark fabrics common in the years just after the Civil War. On the right, a smaller, two-generation (nuclear) family is dressed in more lightweight colorful garments that became common in the early twentieth century. *Left: Library of Congress; right: The Bettmann Archive.*

Throughout modern Western history, most people have lived in two overlapping kinds of basic units: household and family. A *household* is a resi-

> **Family and Household Structures**

dential unit, a group of related or unrelated people who live in the same abode. A *family* is a group of people related by kinship, some of whom typically live together. The distinction between household and family is important in describing how Americans lived in the late nineteenth and early twentieth centuries, because the two institutions followed different patterns.

At the most elementary level, Americans between 1877 and 1920 grouped themselves in traditional ways. As in the past, the vast majority (75 to 80 percent) of households consisted of *nuclear families*—usually a married couple with or without children. About 15 to 20 percent of households consisted of *extended families*—usually a married couple with or without children plus a combination of one or more relatives such as grandparents, grandchildren, aunts, uncles, in-laws, or cousins. About 5 percent of households consisted of people

who lived alone. Despite slight variations among ethnic, racial, or socioeconomic groups, the prevailing pattern held relatively constant.

Several factors explain this pattern. Because the United States was a nation of immigrants who tended to be young, the country had a very young population. In 1880 the median age was under twenty-one, and by 1920 it was still only twenty-five. (Presently it is almost thirty-one.) Moreover, fewer people than now lived to old age. In 1900 the death rate among people aged forty-five to sixty-four was over twice what it is currently. As a result, there were relatively few old people: in 1900 only 4 percent of the population was sixty-five or older, compared with nearly 15 percent currently. Thus few families could form extended three-generation households. Fewer children than today knew their grandparents, and the experience of being a grandparent was rarer. Upward social mobility and migration separated many families, and the ideal of a home of one's own encouraged nuclear household organization.

The relative size of nuclear families did change over time, however. In the nineteenth century al-

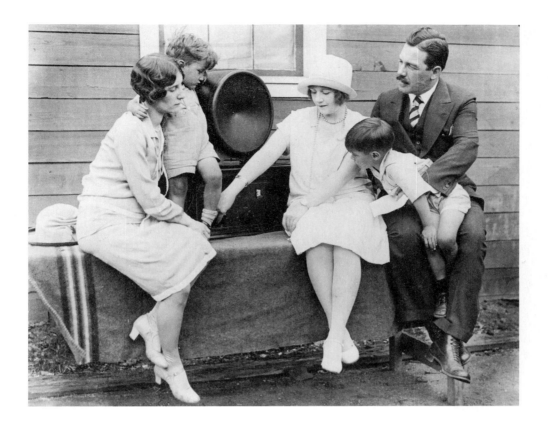

most all of Europe and North America experienced a decline in birthrates. In the United States the decline began early in the 1800s and accelerated toward the end of the century. In 1880 the birthrate was 39.8 live births per 1,000 people; by 1900 it had dropped to 32.3, by 1920 to 27.7. Several reasons can be offered to explain this decline. First, the United States was becoming an urban nation, and birthrates in cities generally are lower than in rural areas. On farms, where children could work at home or in the fields at an early age, each child born contributed a new set of hands to the family work force. In the wage-based urban economy, children could not contribute significantly to the family income for many years, and a new child simply represented another mouth to feed. Second, as diet and medical care improved, infant mortality fell and families did not have to have many children just to ensure that some would survive. Third, it appears that decisions to limit family size—by abstaining from sex during the wife's fertile period or by using other forms of contraception and abortion—resulted from growing con-

> **Declining Birthrates**

sciousness that people could improve the quality of life for themselves and their children if their families were smaller than their ancestors' families.

Although fertility among blacks, immigrants, and rural dwellers was consistently higher than among white native urban dwellers, birthrates of all groups fell. As a result, families with six or eight children became less common; three or four became more usual. Thus the nuclear family tended to reach its maximum size and then decline in size faster than in earlier eras.

In spite of the predominance of the nuclear family, the household typically expanded and contracted over the lifetime of a given family. First, family size fluctuated as children were born and later left home. Male and female children, especially in working-class families, often left home before they were twenty years old, usually to work. Second, the process of leaving home made for huge numbers of young people—and some older people—who lived as boarders and lodgers, especially in cities. Middle- and working-class families commonly took in boarders to help pay the rent or

> **Boarding**

to occupy unused rooms vacated by grown children. Immigrants often lodged newly arrived relatives and fellow villagers until they could establish themselves. Historians have estimated that at the end of the nineteenth century there was a 50 percent chance that a city dweller had lived either as a boarder or with boarders at some point during his or her lifetime.

Housing reformers charged that boarding caused overcrowding and loss of privacy. Yet for those who boarded, the practice was highly useful. As one immigrant woman recalled:

> We had four boarders and I had to cook for them. When I first came here I didn't want to do this because everybody want to have their own house. Well, I change my mind because everybody was doing this thing. That time some of the people that came from the other side didn't have no place to stay and we took some of the people in the house that we knew. . . . This is the way that everybody used to do it that time.

Boarding gave a household flexibility, bringing in extra income. For immigrants and young people who had left home, it was a transitional stage, providing them with a quasi-family environment until they set up their own households.

Some households included extended family members who lived as quasi-boarders. Especially in communities where economic hardship or rapid growth made housing expensive or scarce, newlyweds tended to live with the husband's or wife's parents until they could afford their own place. Often a family would take in a widowed parent or an unmarried sibling who would otherwise have had to live alone. For immigrants and migrants, the family served as a refuge in a strange new place. Having moved from the Old World to the New or from one region to another, they sought out relatives who had preceded them. A Russian Jewish woman prepared for emigration by writing to relatives in New York. "When I came off the ship," she recalled, "an uncle of mine was supposed to pick me up. . . . But I didn't live with this uncle because I had my mother's sister so I stayed with her."

Kinship had important functions, especially for immigrants and others in need. At a time when welfare and service agencies were rare, the family continued to be the institution to

Importance of Kinship which people could turn. Even when relatives did not live together, they often lived nearby

and could help each other with childcare, meals, shopping, advice, and consolation. Family members also obtained jobs for each other. Factory foremen usually had responsibility for hiring, and they often recruited new workers recommended by their employees. According to one new arrival, "After two days my brother took me to the shop he was working in and his boss saw me and he gave me the job." A woman who worked in an optical factory recalled, "My uncle was foreman there. . . . That was my first job. I worked there with my mother. . . . My sister worked there a while too."

Obligations of kinship, however, were not always welcome or even helpful. Immigrant families often put pressure on last-born children to stay at home and care for aging parents, a practice that stifled opportunities for education, marriage, and economic independence. As an aging Italian-American father confessed, "One of our daughters is an old maid [and] causes plenty of troubles. . . . It may be my fault because I always wished her to remain at home and not to marry for she was of great financial help." Tensions also developed when one relative felt another was not helping out enough. One woman, for example, complained that her brother-in-law "resented the fact that I saved my money in a bank instead of handing it over to him." Kinship, for better or worse, nevertheless provided people a means of coping with the many stresses caused by an urban industrial society. Social and economic change did not dissolve family ties.

While the family remained resilient and adaptable, subtle but momentous changes began to occur in individual life patterns. Before the twentieth century, stages of life were less

Stages of Life distinct than they are today, and generations blended into each other with relatively little separation. Childhood, for instance, was regarded as a period in which young people prepared for adulthood by gradually assuming more adult roles and responsibilities. The subdivisions of youth—toddlers, schoolchildren, adolescents, and the like—were not nearly as clear-cut as they are today. Because few people lived past age sixty-five or left work voluntarily and because homes for the elderly were rare, old people were not treated as separately as in later periods. Married couples had relatively large numbers of children born over a longer time span than is common among twentieth-century couples, so active parenthood occupied most of their adult lives. And older children, who often cared for younger sisters and brothers, might begin parenting even before reaching adulthood.

By the turn of the century, demographic and social changes had altered these patterns. Decreasing birthrates reduced the period of parental responsibility, so more middle-aged couples experienced a stage when all their children had grown up and left home. Longer life expectancy and a tendency among employers, especially in manufacturing, to force the retirement of aged workers further isolated the old from the young. At the same time, work became more specialized and education in graded schools more formalized—especially after states passed compulsory-school-attendance laws in the 1870s and 1880s. Childhood and adolescence therefore became more distinct from adulthood. As a result of these and other trends (including the lower birthrate, which gave people fewer sisters and brothers to relate to), Americans became more age- and peer-conscious. People's roles in school, in the family, on the job, and in the community came to be defined by age as much as by any other characteristic.

Thus by the early 1900s, family life and its functions were both changing and holding firm. New institutions were assuming tasks formerly performed by the family. Schools were making education more of a community responsibility. Employment agencies, personnel offices, labor unions, and legislatures were taking responsibility for employee recruitment and job security. Age-based peer groups were exerting greater influence over people's values and activities. In addition, migration and a soaring divorce rate seemed to be splitting families apart: 19,633 divorces were granted in the United States in 1880; by 1920, that number had grown to 167,105. Yet in the face of these changes, the family remained a resilient institution. Households and families adjusted by expanding and contracting to meet temporary needs, and kinship remained a dependable though not always appreciated institution. At the time, popular and scholarly writers were predicting the decline of the family just as they are today. But for the majority of people, family life was vital. "As I grew up, living conditions were a bit crowded," one woman reminisced, "but no one minded because we were a family . . . thankful we all lived together."

Better diets and improved living conditions increased life expectancy so that the numbers and proportions of older people in the American population grew. As a result, even though generations became more separated from each other, children were more likely than those of previous generations to have more of their grandparents alive to dote on them, as this photograph from Horton, Kansas, in 1907 reveals. *Jules A. Bourquin Collection, Kansas Collection, University of Kansas Libraries.*

The New Leisure and Mass Culture

On December 2, 1889, as hundreds of workers paraded through Worcester, Massachusetts, in support of shorter working hours, a group of carpenters hoisted a banner that proclaimed, "Eight Hours for Work, Eight Hours for Rest, Eight Hours for What We Will." That last phrase, "for What We Will," was significant, for it marked recognition of a special segment of everyday life that belonged to the

Played on empty lots and fields throughout the country, baseball was truly the "national sport." Although it was played in the open air on a green field reminiscent of the pastoral countryside, baseball also included specialization (in the various positions), standardization (in its rules), and quantification (in its statistics and records) that made it suited to the modern, industrial age. *Library of Congress.*

individual. Increasingly, leisure activities filled this time segment, among working classes as well as middle and upper classes.

American inventors and tinkerers had always tried to create labor-saving devices, but not until the late 1800s did technological development become truly time-saving. Mech-

▶ **Increase in Leisure Time**

anization and assembly-line production helped to cut the average workweek for manufacturing workers from sixty-six hours in 1860 to sixty in 1890 and forty-seven in 1920. These reductions not only meant shorter workdays but also freer weekends. White-collar workers spent eight to ten hours a day on the job and often worked only half a day or not at all on weekends. Mechanization helped to expand free time on farms. To be sure, thousands still spent twelve- or fourteen-hour shifts in steel mills and sweatshops and had no time or energy for leisure. Nevertheless, more Americans began to partake of a variety of diversions, and for the first time a substantial segment of the economy began providing for—and profiting from—leisure. By the early 1900s, many Americans were enmeshed in the business of play.

After the Civil War, amusement became an organized activity like production and consumption. The vanguard of this trend was sports. Formerly a fashionable indulgence of the genteel class, organized sports quickly became the most popular pastime of all classes, attracting huge numbers of participants and spectators. Even those who could

not play or watch became involved by reading about sports in the newspapers.

The first and most popular organized sport was baseball. Evolving out of older bat, ball, and base-circling games, baseball was formalized in 1845

▶ **Baseball**

when a group of wealthy New Yorkers organized the Knickerbocker Club and codified rules of play. By 1860 there were at least fifty baseball clubs, and pick-up games were played on city lots and rural fields across the nation. In 1869 a professional club, the Cincinnati Red Stockings, went on a national tour, and several other clubs quickly followed suit. The National League of Professional Baseball Clubs, founded in 1876, gave the sport a stable, businesslike structure. By the 1880s, professional baseball was a big business. In 1887, over 51,000 people paid to watch a championship series between St. Louis and Detroit. In 1903, the National League and competing American League (formed in 1901) began a World Series between their championship teams, further entrenching baseball as the national pastime. The Boston Red Socks beat the Pittsburgh Pirates in that first series.

Baseball appealed mostly to men. But croquet, which also swept the nation after the Civil War, attracted both sexes. Across the country, middle- and upper-class people held cro-

▶ **Croquet and Cycling**

quet parties and even rigged wickets with candles for night games. In an era when the removal of work from the home had separated men's from women's spheres, croquet increased opportunities for social contact between the sexes.

Bicycling achieved a popularity rivaling that of baseball—especially after 1888, when the cumbersome velocipede, with its huge front wheel and tall seat, gave way to the safety bicycle with pneumatic tires and wheels of identical size. By 1900 Americans owned over 10 million bicycles, and cycling clubs such as the League of American Wheelmen were pressing state and local governments to build more paved roads. One journal boasted that cycling cured dyspepsia, headaches, insomnia, and sciatica and gave "a vigorous tone to the whole system." Like croquet, bicycling brought men and women together. Especially on the bicycle-built-for-two, it provided a combination of courtship and exercise. Moreover, the bicycle played an influential role in freeing women from the constraints of Victorian fashions. In order to ride bikes, even the dropped-frame female models, women had to wear divided skirts and simple undergarments. Gradually freer styles of cycling costumes began to have an influence on everyday fashions. As the 1900 census declared, "Few articles . . . have created so great a revolution in social conditions as the bicycle."

Tennis and golf won enthusiasts of both sexes from the 1880s onward but remained pastimes of the wealthy. Played mostly at private clubs, these sports lacked baseball's team competition and cycling's informality.

Football

American football also began as a sport for people of high social rank. At first mainly an intercollegiate sport, football attracted mostly players and spectators wealthy enough to have access to higher education. By the end of the century, however, football was attracting a broader class of supporters. The 1893 Princeton-Yale game drew fifty thousand spectators, and informal football games were being played in yards and playgrounds throughout the country.

At the same time, college football was becoming a national scandal because of its violence and use of "tramp athletes," nonstudents whom colleges hired to play on their teams. Critics charged that football mirrored the worst features of American society. An editor of *The Nation* complained in 1890 that "the spirit of the American Youth, as of the American man, is to win, to 'get there,' by fair means or foul; and the lack of moral scruple which pervades the struggles of the business world meets with temptations equally irresistible in the miniature contests of the football field." The scandals climaxed in 1905, when 18 football players died from game-related injuries and over 150 were seriously injured. President Theodore Roosevelt, a strong advocate of athletics, convened a White House conference to discuss ways of eliminating brutality and foul play. The conference founded the Intercollegiate Athletic Association (renamed the National College Athletic Association in 1910) to police college sports. In 1906 the association altered the rules of football to make it less violent and more open. New rules outlawed "flying wedge" rushes, extended the distance to be gained by the first down from 5 to 10 yards, legalized the forward pass, and tightened player eligibility requirements.

As more women attended college, they began to pursue other forms of physical activity besides croquet, horseback riding, and bicycling. Believing that to succeed intellectually they needed to be active and healthy, college women participated in a variety of sports, such as rowing, track, and swimming. Eventually basketball became the most popular sport among college women. Invented in 1891 as a winter sport for men, basketball was given women's rules (that limited dribbling and running and encouraged passing) by Senda Berenson of Smith College in the 1890s, and intercollegiate games became common.

The rise of American show business paralleled the rise of sports and similarly became a mode of leisure created by and for common people. Circuses—traveling shows of acrobats and animals—had existed since the 1820s. But after the Civil War, railroads enabled circuses to reach more of the country, and the popularity of the big show increased enormously.

Circuses

Circuses offered two main attractions: so-called freaks of nature, both human and animal, and the temptation and conquest of death. More important was the sheer astonishment aroused by the trapeze artists, lion tamers, high-wire artists, acrobats, and clowns. Writer Hamlin Garland captured the circus's effect on a thousand towns and villages:

From the time the "advance man" flung his highly colored posters over the fence till the coming of the glorious day, we thought of little else. . . . It was our brief season of imaginative life. In one day—in a part of one day—we gained a thousand new conceptions of the world and of human nature. It was the embodiment of all that was skillful and beautiful in human action. . . . It gave us something to talk about.

Several branches of American show business matured with the growth of cities. Popular drama, musical comedy, and vaudeville all gave Americans

Popular Drama and Musical Comedy

a chance to escape from the harsh realities of urban-industrial life into melodrama, adventure, and comedy. Plots were simple, the heroes and villains instantly recognizable. For urbanized people increasingly distant from the frontier, popular plays brought to life the mythical Wild West and Old South through stories of Davy Crockett, Buffalo Bill, and Civil War romances. Virtue, honor, and justice always triumphed in melodramas such as *Uncle Tom's Cabin* and *The Old Homestead,* reinforcing the popular belief that even in an uncertain and disillusioning world, goodness would nevertheless prevail.

Musical comedies raised audiences' spirits with song, humor, and dance. American musical comedy grew out of the lavishly costumed operettas popular in Europe. By introducing American themes (often involving ethnic groups), folksy humor, and catchy tunes and dances, these shows launched the nation's most popular songs and entertainers. George M. Cohan, born into an Irish family of vaudeville entertainers, became the master of American musical comedy after the turn of the century. Drawing on urbanism, patriotism, and traditional values in songs like "Yankee Doodle Boy" and "You're a Grand Old Flag," Cohan helped to reinforce national morale during the First World War. Comic opera too became a fad, the talented, beautiful, dignified Lillian Russell its most admired performer. The first American comic operas were weak imitations of European musicals, but by the early 1900s composers like Victor Herbert were writing for American audiences. Shortly thereafter Jerome Kern began to write more sophisticated musicals, and American musical comedy came into its own.

The French term *vaudeville* first referred to light drama with musical interludes, but in the United States vaudeville became a unique entertainment

Vaudeville

form. Originally staged by saloonkeepers to attract customers, vaudeville variety shows were developed by skilled promoters who used the term to lend respectability to a once-disreputable entertainment. Vaudeville was probably the most popular entertainment in early-twentieth-century America because its variety made it attractive to mass audiences. Shows included magic and animal acts, juggling, stunts, comedy (especially ethnic humor), and song and dance. Around 1900, the number of vaudeville theaters and troupes skyrocketed. Fostered by sharp promoters who did for entertainment what Edison and Ford did for technology, vaudeville quickly became big business. The most famous promoter, Florenz Ziegfeld, brilliantly packaged popular entertainment in a stylish format—the Ziegfeld Follies—and gave the nation a new model of femininity, the Ziegfeld Girl, whose graceful dancing and alluring costumes were meant to suggest a haunting sensuality.

Show business provided new economic opportunities for women, blacks, and immigrants, but also indulged in stereotyping and exploitation. Lillian Russell, vaudeville singer and comedienne Fanny Brice, and burlesque queen Eva Tanguay attracted intensely loyal fans, commanded handsome fees, and won respect for their genuine talents. In contrast to the demure Victorian female, they conveyed pluck and creativity. There was something both shocking and refreshingly confident about Eva Tanguay when she sang earthy songs like "I Want Someone to Go Wild with Me," "It's All Been Done Before But Not the Way I Do It," and her theme song "I Don't Care." But lesser female performers were often exploited by male promoters and theater owners, many of whom wanted only to titillate the public with the sight of scantily clad women.

Before the 1890s, the chief form of commercial entertainment open to black performers was the minstrel show. By century's end, however, minstrel

Blacks and Immigrants in Vaudeville

shows had given way to more sophisticated musicals, and blacks had begun to break into vaudeville. As stage sets shifted from the plantation to the city, music shifted from folk tunes to ragtime. Pandering to the prejudice of white audiences, composers and performers of both races ridiculed blacks. The popularity of songs like "He's Just a Little Nigger, But He's Mine All Mine," and "You May Be a Hawaiian on Old Broadway, But You're Just Another Nigger to Me" confirms that blacks on the stage suffered in the same way they did elsewhere in society. Even

Lavish musical reviews and vaudeville shows became a very popular form of American entertainment. Filled with song, dance, and comedy, these performances reflected the new scale and organization of the American economy and culture. *Culver Pictures.*

Burt Williams, a highly paid black comedian and dancer who was one of the era's most talented performers, achieved his tormented success mainly by playing the stereotypical roles of darky and dandy.

Much of the uniqueness of American mass entertainment came from its ethnic flavor. Indeed, immigrants were the core of American show business. Vaudeville particularly drew on and embellished ethnic humor, exaggerating dialects and other national traits. Skits and songs reinforced ethnic stereotypes and made fun of ethnic groups, but such distortions were more self-conscious and sympathetic than those directed at blacks. Ethnic humor often focused on difficulties faced by immigrants. A typical scene involving Italians, for example, would revolve around a character's uncertain grasp of English, which caused him to confuse *mayor* with *mare, diploma* with *the plumber,* and *pallbearer* with *polar bear.* Such scenes allowed audiences to laugh at the human condition and reminded them that, deep down, all people—

at least white people—were the same. Blacks, however, were never assumed to share the same hopes and frustrations as whites.

Shortly after 1900, live entertainment began to yield to an even more accessible form of amusement: moving pictures. Perfected by Thomas Edison in the late 1880s, movies began as slot-machine peepshows in penny arcades and billiard parlors. Eventually images were projected onto a screen so large that audiences could view them, and a new medium was born. At first, the subject matter of films was unimportant; it was enough merely to awe viewers with moving pictures of speeding trains, galloping horses, and writhing belly dancers.

Movies

Producers soon discovered, however, that a film could tell a story—and tell it with flair. By 1910 motion pictures had become an art form, thanks to creative directors like D. W. Griffith. Griffith's most famous work, *The Birth of a Nation* (1915), an epic

The New Leisure and Mass Culture

By the end of the nineteenth century, recreation of all sorts became a value of, and attainable by, almost all classes for the first time in American history. Note the free-spirited relaxation of these bathers on a Coney Island beach; their poses contrast markedly with the stiff formality of people on city streets and the serious concentration of people at work. *Library of Congress.*

film about the Civil War and Reconstruction, fanned racial prejudice by depicting blacks as threatening white moral values; its exaltation of the Ku Klux Klan also helped to revive the hooded empire. The film also provoked an organized black protest against it, led by the infant National Association for the Advancement of Colored People (see page 621). But the film's innovative techniques—close-ups, fade-outs, and battle scenes—gave viewers heightened drama and excitement. From the beginning, movies were popular among all classes (admission usually cost a nickel), and audiences idolized such film stars as Mary Pickford, Lillian Gish, and Charlie Chaplin with a passion no stage performer ever enjoyed.

The still camera, modernized by inventor George Eastman, enabled ordinary people to make their own photographic images; and the phonograph, another of Edison's inventions, brought musical performances to the home. The spread of movies, photography, and phonograph records meant that access to live performances no longer

limited people's exposure to art and entertainment. Technology dissolved the uniqueness of experience and made it possible to mass-produce sound and images. Entertainment became a consumer good more widely available than ever before.

To some extent, new amusements and pastimes had a homogenizing influence, bringing together disparate ethnic and social groups into a common experience. Parks, ball fields, vaudeville shows, and movies were designed for and appealed to everyone; they were nonsectarian and apolitical. Yet various groups adopted leisure institutions in their own way. Even though promoters and entrepreneurs were responsible for the spread of amusements, consumers often used them to reinforce their own cultural habits. For example, in some communities working-class immigrant groups used parks and amusement parks as locations for traditional family and ethnic gatherings. Much to the dismay of reformers who hoped that recreation would help assimilate newcomers and teach them habits of restraint, immigrants used picnics and

Chapter 19: Everyday Life and Culture, 1877–1920

Fourth of July celebrations as occasions for boisterous drinking and sometimes violent behavior. Young working-class men and women resisted parents' and reformers' warnings and frequented urban dance halls, where they explored new forms of peer association and sexual morality. Many early movies intentionally had working-class characters and settings (Charlie Chaplin's films, for instance), reflecting the tastes of their audiences. Thus as Americans learned to play, their leisure—like their work and politics—was shaped by pluralistic forces.

The Transformation of Mass Communications

With so many new things to do and buy, how did Americans decide what they wanted? Two new types of communication influenced consumer tastes and mass opinion. Modern advertising molded people's needs and consumption patterns, and popular journalism spread mass culture throughout the country.

A society of scarcity does not need advertising. When demand exceeds the supply of goods and services, producers have no trouble selling what they market. But in a society of abundance such as industrial America, supply frequently outstrips demand, making necessary a means of creating or increasing demand. Advertising had existed in the United States long before the late nineteenth century, but it took on a new scale and function just before 1900. In 1865 about $9.5 million was spent on advertising; by 1900 the sum had reached $95 million, and by 1919 nearly $500 million.

Advertising

The American salesperson's function has traditionally been to respond to a particular need and to convince a customer that a certain product—an insurance policy, an article of clothing, a home appliance—is uniquely suited to fill that need. Advertisers, on the other hand, aim to *invent* a demand by convincing whole groups that everyone in that group should buy a specific product—a brand of cigarettes, a particular cosmetic, a certain company's canned foods. Indeed, the growth in the late nineteenth century of large companies that

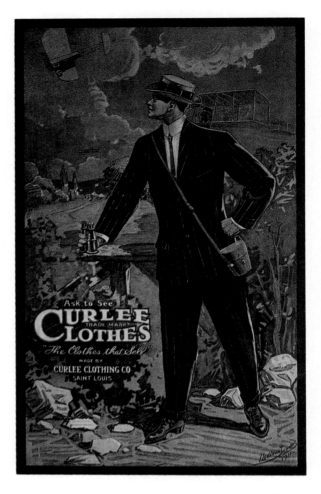

Advertisers made great efforts to entice buyers by linking their products with the potential consumers' dreams and aspirations. Here a manufacturer of men's clothing shows one of its suits being worn by a sporty, sophisticated man who also is connected suggestively with the new wonder of the early twentieth century, the airplane. *Missouri Historical Society.*

mass-produced consumer goods gave advertisers the task of creating "consumption communities"—bodies of consumers loyal to a particular brand name.

In 1881, Congress passed a federal trademark law enabling producers to register and protect brand names. Thousands of companies eventually did so, creating such well-known products as Hires Root Beer, Carter's Little Liver Pills, Uneeda Biscuits, and Grape Nuts. Advertising agencies—a new service industry pioneered by N. W. Ayer & Son of Philadelphia—offered expert advice to companies that wished to cultivate brand loyalty. By the turn of the century, advertising techniques had been perfected to such an extent that French composer Jacques Offenbach observed, "Decidedly the American advertising men play upon the human mind as a musician plays on his piano."

The major vehicle for advertising was the newspaper. Around the mid-nineteenth century, publishers began to pursue greater revenues from advertising by selling more ad space, especially to big urban department stores. In 1879 Wanamaker's placed the first full-page ad, and at about the same time newspapers began to allow advertisers to print pictures of products. Such attention-getting techniques transformed advertising into news. More than ever before, people read newspapers to find out what was for sale as well as what was happening.

Just as advertising became news, news became a form of advertising, or at least of publicity. Canny publishers made people crave news just as they craved amusements and consumer goods. City life and the increase in leisure time seemed to nurture a fascination with the sensational, and from the 1880s onward popular newspapers increasingly whetted and catered to that appetite.

Joseph Pulitzer, a Hungarian immigrant who bought the *New York World* in 1883, pioneered journalism as a branch of mass culture. Believing that newspapers should be "dedicated to the cause of the people rather than to that of the purse potentates," Pulitzer filled the *World* with stories of disasters, crimes, and scandals. Sensational headlines, set in large bold type like that used for advertisements, screamed from every page. Pulitzer's journalists not only reported news but sought it out—and sometimes even created it. *World* reporter Nellie Bly (real name Elizabeth Cochrane) faked her way into an insane asylum and wrote a sensational exposé of the sordid conditions she found. Other reporters staged stunts and sought out heart-rending human-interest stories. Pulitzer also popularized the comics, and the yellow ink they were printed in gave his emphasis on the sensational the nickname "yellow journalism."

> **Yellow Journalism**

Pulitzer's strategy was immensely successful. In one year he increased the *World*'s daily circulation from 20,000 to 100,000, and by the late 1890s it had reached 1 million. Soon other publishers, such as William Randolph Hearst, who bought the *New York Journal* in 1895 and started an empire of mass-circulation newspapers, adopted Pulitzer's techniques. Yellow journalism became a nationwide phenomenon, enhancing interest in bizarre aspects of the human condition and kindling sentiments for reform.

Pulitzer and his rivals fanned popular interest even further by emphasizing sports and women's news. Newspapers had always reported on sporting events, but yellow-journalism papers gave such stories far greater prominence by printing separate, expanded sports sections. Such sections did more than anything else to promote sports as a leisure-time attraction. Sports news became a new addiction, recreating a particular game's drama through narrative and statistics. At the same time they expanded sports news, mostly for male readers, newspapers were adding more women's news. A special section devoted to household tips, fashion, decorum, and club news captured the interest of female readers. Like crime and disaster stories, sports and women's sections helped to make news a mass commodity.

By the early twentieth century, communications media, like the mass consumption of goods, were becoming commonplace. Alongside newspapers, mass-circulation magazines were overshadowing expensive elitist journals of earlier eras. Publications like *McClure's, Saturday Evening Post,* and *Ladies' Home Journal* offered human-interest stories, muckraking exposés (see pages 608–609), titillating fiction, and eye-catching ads to a growing mass market. Benefiting from extensive advertising, heavy use of photographs, and colorful covers, these magazines not only had much higher sales than their predecessors but also contained many more pages. Like magazines, which were aided by the steam-driven high-speed rotary printing press—an important technological innovation—the total number of books published more than quadrupled between 1880 and 1917. This rising popular consumption of news and books reflected growing literacy. Between 1870 and 1920, the proportion of Americans aged ten or over who could not read or write fell from 20 percent to 6 percent.

Other forms of communication were also expanding. In 1891 there were 0.3 telephones per 100 people in the United States; by 1901 the number had grown to 2.1, and by 1921 it had swelled to 12.6. In 1900 Americans used 4 billion postage

A newsstand beneath an elevated railway station displays a large variety of popular magazines and newspapers. By the early 1900s these publications were read by millions daily—for their advertisements as well as for their news and sports. *Ford Archives, The Henry Ford Museum.*

stamps; in 1922 they used 14.3 billion. Little wonder, then, that the term *community* took on new dimensions, as people used the media, the mail, and the telephone to extend their horizons far beyond their place of residence. More than ever before, people in different parts of the country knew about and discussed the same news event, whether it was a sensational murder, a sex scandal, or the fortunes of a particular entertainer or athlete. America was becoming a mass society.

Popular Literature

The same society that celebrated the machine also idolized Tarzan the Ape Man. American culture has long focused one eye on an increasingly complex technological future while casting the other at a sentimentalized, simpler past. These two dispositions shaped the popular mind between 1877 and 1920. When modern wonders like telephones, high-speed printing presses, phonographs, and cameras made information and entertainment more accessible, people demanded diversions that reaffirmed traditional values of optimism, individualism, and freedom. Thus in 1914, just when they were beginning to appreciate automobiles, movies, and electricity, Americans made Edgar Rice Burroughs's *Tarzan of the Apes* a best seller.

Popular fiction writers in tune with the times concentrated on the sensational. Such efforts were not exactly new; since the 1840s, low-priced, paperbound adventure novels had **Dime** circulated widely among the lit- **Novels** erate public. After the Civil War such books, called dime novels, became the most widely read variety of American literature, especially among youths. As one man recalled, "I read them at every chance; so did every normal boy of my acquaintance. . . . We swapped them on the basis of two old volumes for every new one; we maintained a clandestine circulating library system which had its branch offices in every stable-loft in our part of town." The principal publisher of dime novels was the firm Beadle and Adams, which issued over thirteen hundred titles before it went out of business in 1897. Popular magazines like *Tip Top Weekly,* which serialized adventure stories, also attracted hundreds of thousands of readers.

These publications offered three types of stories. The first evoked the Wild West for a population that was seeing the frontier fade into the past. Intertwining fact and fiction, writers like Zane Grey wove adventure stories around famous folk heroes like Buffalo Bill Cody, the Lone Ranger, and Wild Bill Hickok. During the 1880s, however, many authors, recognizing the lure and growing impact of city life, began to give their tales urban settings and themes. Detective thrillers became the leading type of popular urban fiction, and hard-nosed, wily characters like Old Cap Collins and Nick Carter captivated readers of various ages. Just before the end of the century, science fiction and character heroes came to the fore. Influenced by marvels of new scientific discoveries, such works as the Tom Swift series described spaceships, gravity nullifiers, and other inventions that surpassed even Edison's inventive imagination.

One popular writer, Horatio Alger, moved beyond the fantasies of dime novels and offered readers a formula for contending with new social and economic forces. A failed Unitarian clergyman, Alger began writing boys' stories in the 1860s, producing 130 titles over the next three decades. As Alger's titles attest, each story emphasizes the virtues of self-reliance and hard work: *Work and Win, Do and Dare, Struggling Upward, Rise from the Ranks.*

Moral Messages of Popular Fiction

Alger's heroes begin their lives in poverty and call on ambition, honesty, courage, thrift, and luck to overcome obstacles and achieve success. But his message was more than an exhortation to morality and frugality. The moral of Alger's stories was that success came to those who were not only virtuous but alert enough to capitalize on a lucky break. Thus Ragged Dick, the hero of Alger's first novel, is clean, honest, and polite, but his opportunity to escape poverty arrives when he rescues the drowning child of a banker. The hero of *Bound to Rise* ministers to a lonely old man who repays him with a bundle of real-estate deeds. Thus while the main theme emphasized virtue as the means to overcome poverty, Alger also made his characters models of American resourcefulness.

A few years before Alger's death in 1899, one of America's most popular character heroes, Frank Merriwell, was created by Gilbert Patten (using the pen name of Burt Standish), a writer of hack fiction since his teens. Frank Merriwell's adventures had a common theme that accorded with the way many Americans liked to think of themselves and their nation: Merriwell attempted and accomplished the impossible. Merriwell's name symbolized American virtues: according to Patten, "I took the three qualities I most wanted him to represent—frank and merry in nature, well in body and mind—and made the name Frank Merriwell."

In a series of fast-paced adventures, Merriwell provided youthful readers with one of the first character models in popular fiction. Whether performing amazing athletic feats or daring rescues, he was a picture of refinement and valor who taught by example, not by preaching. In one story, Frank knocks down a thug hired to break his arm before a big game. Graciously, Frank helps him to his feet and befriends him. The thug exclaims, "Gee, I don't know w'y it is, but jes' bein' wid youse makes me want ter do de square t'ing." Patten wrote 208 Merriwell novels, with titles such as *Frank Merriwell's Trip West, Frank Merriwell at Yale, Frank Merriwell's Air Voyage,* and *Frank Merriwell on Wall Street.*

Young women found escape and inspiration in sentimental tales about growing up and about animals. One of the most widely read was Louisa May Alcott's *Little Women,* published in two parts in 1868 and 1869. This novel, which eventually sold over 2 million copies, recreated the domestic delights and moral trials of four girls based on Alcott and her sisters. A generation later, Gene Stratton-Porter's romantic novels about animals, like *Freckles* (1904) and *Laddie* (1913), became best sellers. Others in the same vein were Margaret Sidney's *Five Little Peppers* (1880), Anna Sewell's *Black Beauty* (1890), Kate Douglas Wiggins's *Rebecca of Sunnybrook Farm* (1903), and Lucy M. Montgomery's *Anne of Green Gables* (1908).

Popular literature for adults also oozed sentimentality. The best-selling titles of the late nineteenth century included Marie Corelli's *Thelma* (1887) and Charles Majors's *When Knighthood Was in Flower* (1898)—both romances about chivalry and honor—and *Ben Hur* (1880), General Lew Wallace's powerful religious melodrama set in the Roman Empire. Not since *Uncle Tom's Cabin* did a book capture as much attention as *Ben Hur,* which sold 2 million copies by 1933. Self-help and inspiration, both perennial themes in American popular literature, also burgeoned. The style pioneered by *Poor Richard's Almanac* and *McGuffey's Readers* was developed in such works as Andrew Carnegie's *Gospel of Wealth* (1901) and Russell Conwell's published sermon "Acres of Diamonds" (see pages 539–540).

While some popular writers focused on escapism, others tried to introduce realism into romance. During the 1870s and 1880s, a number of "local-color" writers began producing works that depicted the people and environment of a particular region more realistically.

> **Local Colorists**

This movement was centered in the South, whose writers felt compelled to rebuild the region's national image. Joel Chandler Harris, who created the popular Uncle Remus stories; Mary Noailles Murfree, who located her tales in Appalachia; and George Washington Cable, who captured the aura of exotic New Orleans, all produced authentic characters and dialects. Regional writers of the Far West and Midwest included Bret Harte, who spun tales about the California mining experience; Edward Eggleston, who recreated the life of his native southern Indiana; and Constance Fenimore Woolson, who wrote about lumbering and fur-trading districts of the Great Lakes. Each of these writers used authentic manners and ways of speech to depict a romantic, rustic past.

One local colorist, Mark Twain (the pen name of Samuel Clemens), moved beyond romance and adventure and in doing so won recognition from both intellectuals and the masses. A westerner who had grown up in Hannibal, Missouri, Twain worked as a river pilot on the Mississippi and traveled through mining towns of the Far West. Though he wrote several works about Europe, such as *Innocents Abroad* (1869) and *A Connecticut Yankee at King Arthur's Court* (1889), he was best

> **Literary Classics**

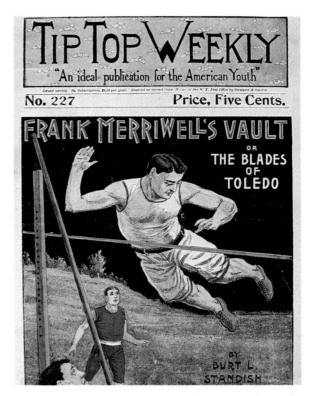

Frank Merriwell, the fictional hero of hundreds of sports and adventure stories, was a popular character model for young men. In this story, Frank accomplishes a heroic feat to win an important track meet for his school team and at the same time teaches a lesson in loyalty and morality. *Bettmann Archive.*

known for his books about the American West: *Tom Sawyer* (1876), *Life on the Mississippi* (1883), and *Huckleberry Finn* (1884). These antisentimental novels were realistic portrayals of western life and of human weakness. Twain was sensitive to both the comic and the tragic sides of life, and his writing reflected the dynamic energy and materialism of his era. He once wrote that "my books are mainly autobiographies," and his most famous character, Huck Finn, seemed to represent the daring, hypocrisy, and amiability of both Twain and his nation.

A number of Twain's contemporaries shunned the falseness of escape writing and focused instead on the moral tests that life holds. Realists like William Dean Howells, Edith Wharton, and Henry James wrote chiefly about upper-class Americans (James usually wrote about Americans in Europe), but other realists examined the lives of ordinary folk and in so doing opened new literary vistas. These writers, sometimes called naturalists, often viewed life in terms of the survival of the fittest; they portrayed ruthless struggles for survival and power in frank detail. Among the naturalists were Stephen Crane, whose *Maggie: A Girl of the Streets* (1893) shocked readers with its candid description of slum life and sexual immorality; Kate Chopin, who in her novel *The Awakening* (1899) addressed sensitive topics of sexuality and divorce; Hamlin Garland, whose *Main Traveled Roads* (1891) portrayed a depressing side of rural America; Frank Norris, whose *McTeague* (1899) graphically exposed the brutality of human greed; Jack London, whose stories of the West and Northwest described violence among humans and animals; and Theodore Dreiser, whose *Sister Carrie* (1900) depicted the seamy side of urban life in shocking detail.

The escapism of popular fiction and the realism of serious fiction, though seemingly at odds, offered similar commentaries on American society of the early twentieth century. It was no coincidence that Frank Merriwell replaced Horatio Alger's heroes in popular fiction around 1900: by then Americans knew that it took more than honesty, energy, and a timely rescue to become rich. Numberless little-noticed revolutions had transformed the world that Alger and others had known. The obstacles to success were not simple, and making one's way in the world required technological skills, organizational know-how, and a lot of capital. More sophisticated and more familiar with the possibilities offered by a consumer-oriented society, readers craved more from their heroes, such as prowess in the new mass cult of sports (Merriwell), conquest of science (Tom Swift), or abilities to commune with nature (Gene Stratton-Porter's characters).

Meanwhile serious authors, striving to recreate realistically what they saw around them, examined the flaws of progress. Whereas virtue still triumphed in popular and juvenile literature, naturalist writers saw that the new demands that an industrial age placed on individuals threatened traditional American values of family, practicality, and moral restraint.

Industrialization and urbanization wrought important changes in people's daily lives. Technological and scientific innovations, mass production, and mass communications affected habits of work, play, family and social relationships, diet, and dress in ways still apparent today. But the benefits of change were not spread evenly, and the costs to those excluded from the new consumerism could be high. Just how—and whether—the political system would adjust to the challenges of these changes would pose perplexing questions for national, state, and local governments in both the Gilded Age of the late nineteenth century and the Progressive era of the early twentieth century.

Suggestions for Further Reading

Living Standards and New Conveniences

Susan Porter Benson, *Counter Cultures: Saleswomen, Managers, and Customers in American Department Stores, 1890–1940* (1986); Daniel J. Boorstin, *The Americans: The Democratic Experience* (1973); T. J. Jackson Lears and Richard W. Fox, eds., *The Culture of Consumption* (1983); Godfrey M. Lebhar, *Chain Stores in America* (1962); Harvey A. Levenstein, *Revolution at the Table: The Transformation of the American Diet* (1988); Clarence D. Long, *Wages and Earnings in the United States, 1860–1890* (1960); H. Pasadermadjian, *The Department Store* (1954); Peter R. Shergold, *Working Class Life: The "American Standard" in Comparative Perspective, 1899–1913* (1982); Gwendolyn Wright, *Building the Dream: A Social History of Housing in America* (1983); Lawrence Wright, *Clean and Decent* (1960).

Family and Individual Life Cycles

W. Andrew Achenbaum, *Old Age in the New Land* (1979); John E. Bodnar et al., *Lives of Their Own: Blacks, Italians, and Poles in Pittsburgh, 1900–1960* (1982); Howard P. Chudacoff, *How Old Are You? Age in American Culture* (1989); Carl N. Degler, *At Odds: Women and the Family in America* (1980); David H. Fischer, *Growing Old in America* (1977); Michael Gordon, ed., *The American Family in Social-Historical Perspective*, 3rd ed. (1983); Carole Haber, *Beyond Sixty-five: Dilemmas of Old Age in America's Past* (1983); Tamara K. Hareven, *Family Time and Industrial Time: The Relationship Between the Family and Work in a New England Industrial Community* (1981); Tamara K. Hareven, ed., *Transitions: The Family and Life Course in Historical Perspective* (1978); Joseph Kett, *Rites of Passage: Adolescence in America* (1979); Ellen K. Rothman, *Hands and Hearts: A History of Courtship in America* (1986).

Mass Entertainment and Leisure

Robert Clyde Allen, *Vaudeville and Film, 1895–1915: A Study in Media Interaction* (1977); Gunther Barth, *City People* (1980); Foster R. Dulles, *America Learns to Play* (1966); Roland Gelatt, *The Fabulous Phonograph* (1965); Allen Guttmann, *A Whole New Ball Game: An Interpretation of American Sports* (1988); John F. Kasson, *Amusing the Million: Coney Island at the Turn of the Century* (1978); Donald J. Mrozek, *Sport and American Mentality, 1880–1910* (1983); Joseph A. Musselman, *Music in the Cultured Generation: A Social History of Music in America, 1870–1900* (1971); Beaumont Newhall, *The History of Photography,* rev. ed. (1964); Kathy Peiss, *Cheap Amusements: Working Women and Leisure in Turn-of-the-Century New York* (1986); Benjamin G. Rader, *American Sports* (1983); Roy Rosenzweig, *Eight Hours for What We Will! Workers and Leisure in an Industrial City, 1870–1920* (1983); Harold Seymour, *Baseball,* 2 vols. (1960–1971); Robert Sklar, *Movie-Made America* (1976); Sigmund Spaeth, *History of Popular Music* (1948); Robert C. Toll, *On with the Show: The First Century of Show Business in America* (1976); David Q. Voigt, *American Baseball,* 2 vols. (1966–1970).

Advertising and Journalism

Stephen Fox, *The Mirror Makers: A History of American Advertising and Its Creators* (1984); George Juergens, *Joseph Pulitzer and the New York World* (1966); Frank L. Mott, *American Journalism,* 3rd ed. (1962); Frank L. Mott, *A History of American Magazines,* 5 vols. (1930–1968); Daniel Pope, *The Making of Modern Advertising* (1983); W. A. Swanberg, *Citizen Hearst* (1961); Bernard A. Weisberger, *The American Newspaperman* (1961).

Popular Literature

Katharine Anthony, *Louisa May Alcott* (1938); John G. Cawelti, *Apostles of Success in America* (1965); John L. Cutler, *Patten and His Merriwell Saga* (1934); Theodore P. Greene, *America's Heroes: The Changing Models of Success in American Magazines* (1970); Frank L. Mott, *Golden Multitudes: The Story of Best Sellers in the United States* (1947); Edmund L. Pearson, *Dime Novels* (1929); Moses Rischin, ed., *The American Gospel of Success* (1965); Henry Nash Smith, *Mark Twain* (1962); John W. Tebbel, *From Rags to Riches: Horatio Alger, Jr., and the American Dream* (1963); Dixon Wector, *Sam Clemens of Hannibal* (1952); Irvin G. Wyllie, *The Self-Made Man in America* (1954).

The platform written by the newly organized People's party that met in Omaha, Nebraska, in July 1892 bristled with discontent. Claiming to speak "in the name and on behalf of the people of this country," the platform's preamble charged that the nation had been "brought to the verge of moral, political, and material ruin. Corruption dominates the ballot-box, the legislatures, the Congress, and touches even . . . the bench." More importantly, corruption fostered greed and inequality that threatened to split American society. "The fruits of the toil of millions," the platform charged, "are boldly stolen to build up colossal fortunes for a few. . . . From the same prolific womb of governmental injustice we breed the two great classes—tramps and millionaires." To a modern reader such rhetoric may seem like the ranting of extremists, yet to millions of Americans in the late nineteenth century these words rang true.

Transformation of the nation by the commercialization of agriculture, industrialization, and urbanization (see Chapters 16, 17, and 18) generated forces that upset time-honored customs and values. Most members of the People's party, called Populists, were farmers who believed that new, large-scale modes of production threatened their rights to equality and freedom. Like labor unions and socialists, Populists protested that the economic system was creating irresponsible concentrations of power and wealth that crushed small producers and dominated government. Thus they gathered in Omaha to preserve a sense of cooperation and justice against the greed of market competition and the despotism of big business.

In some ways the Populists were right. Corruption and greed tugged at the fabric of democracy, and the era's venality prompted novelists Mark Twain and Charles Dudley Warner to dub the 1870s and 1880s the Gilded Age. Officeholders used their positions to amass personal fortunes and dispense patronage appointments to their supporters. Congress, though split by powerful partisan and regional rivalries, did grapple with important issues, such as railroad regulation, tariffs, and currency, and legislated some reforms; but many of its accomplishments were either weak compromises or favors to special interests. Meanwhile, the

20

GILDED AGE POLITICS, 1877–1900

Electioneering in a Country Town, 1913 (detail) by E. L. Henry. Oil on canvas. *Private Collection.*

Campaign pins from presidential elections in the Gilded Age depict Winfield Hancock, the Democratic candidate who lost to James Garfield in 1880, thumbing his nose at James G. Blaine, the Republican candidate who lost to Grover Cleveland in 1884. *Museum of American Political Life, University of Hartford. Photo by Sally Anderson-Bruce.*

grants—could not vote and therefore could not even attempt to use the supposed tools of democracy to redress their grievances. These qualities—special interests, corruption, exclusion—were part of a delicate equilibrium consisting of a stable party system and a regional balance of power.

Then in the 1890s, two developments shattered the equilibrium: the climax of rural discontent that accompanied the transformation of the West and South; and a deep economic depression that bared flaws in the industrial system. Amid these crises, a presidential campaign in 1896 stirred Americans as they had not been stirred for a generation. A new party arose; old parties split; sectional unities dissolved; and questions about the nation's future congealed around a single election. The nation emerged from the turbulent 1890s with new political alignments, just as it had developed new economic configurations. These alignments prepared the way for the new century and for reforms designed to overcome injustices that the People's party had listed in its Omaha platform.

The Nature of Politics

Historian Henry Adams, grandson and great-grandson of presidents, wrote that in American political history, the period between 1870 and 1895 "was poor in purpose and barren in results." The inveterate Adams was only partially right, for he overlooked important characteristics, especially the spirited competition between major parties and the emotional commitments that Americans, even those who could not vote, made to politics.

At no other time in the nation's history was public interest in elections higher. Consistently, 80 to 90 percent of eligible voters (white and black males in the North, mostly white males in the South) cast ballots in local and national elections. (Fewer than 50 percent typically do so today.) Even among those who could not vote, politics was the prime form of mass entertainment, outdistancing baseball, vaudeville, and circuses. Voting was only the last stage in a process that included rallies, parades, picnics, and speeches, all of which were as much public amusement as civic responsibility. As one observer re-

Party Allegiances

judiciary became active in determining public policy. By defending vested rights of property against state and federal interference, courts supported big business. The presidency was filled by a series of honest, respectable men who seldom took initiative; but when they did, they often found themselves beaten back by Congress and the courts.

During the 1870s and 1880s, several major themes characterized politics. The influence of powerful special interests emerged as the most prominent theme. Manufacturers, railroad managers, creditors, and wealthy men in general directed political affairs, so much so that humorist Ambrose Bierce caustically defined "politics" as "A strife of interests masquerading as a contest of principles. The conduct of public affairs for private advantage." Domination by special interests also infused politics with corruption. Vote fraud, bribery, and unfair advantage roused reformers and defined several major legislative issues. Exclusion was another theme of politics, because the majority of Americans—including women, southern blacks, Indians, illiterate whites, and unnaturalized immi-

1873	Coinage of silver dollars ends
1873–78	Economic hard times
1876	Hayes elected president *U.S.* v. *Reese*
1877	*Munn* v. *Illinois*
1878	Bland-Allison Act Anthony women's suffrage amendment defeated in Congress
1880	Garfield elected president
1881	Garfield assassinated; Arthur assumes the presidency
1883	Pendleton Civil Service Act
1884–85	Depression
1884	Cleveland elected president
1886	*Wabash* case
1887	Collapse of farm prices Interstate Commerce Act
1888	Harrison elected president
1890	McKinley Tariff Sherman Silver Purchase Act "Billion-Dollar Congress" "Mississippi Plan"

1892	Populist convention in Omaha Cleveland elected president
1893	Repeal of the Sherman Silver Purchase Act
1893–97	Depression
1894	Wilson-Gorman Tariff Pullman strike; Debs arrested and turns to socialism Coxey's march
1895	Cleveland deals with bankers to save the gold reserve
1896	McKinley elected president
1897	Dingley Tariff *Maximum Freight Rate* case
1898	Louisiana enacts first grandfather clause
1900	Gold Standard Act McKinley re-elected

marked, "What the theatre is to the French, or the bull fight . . . to the Spanish . . . [election campaigns] and the ballot box are to *our* people."

Politics was a personal as well as a community activity. In an era before advertising, polls, and mass media influenced choices, people formed strong loyalties to individual politicians, loyalties that often overlooked crassness and corruption. James G. Blaine, congressman and senator from Maine, twice secretary of state, and frequent presidential aspirant, typified this appeal. His followers named him the "Plumed Knight," composed songs in his honor, paraded for him, and sat mesmerized

by his long speeches, while disregarding his corrupt alliances with businesses and railroads, his animosity for laborers and farmers, and his ignorance of economic issues.

Allegiances to parties and candidates on the national level were usually so evenly distributed that no major faction or party gained lasting control. Between 1877 and 1897, Republicans held the presidency for three terms, Democrats for two. The same party controlled the presidency and both houses of Congress for only three two-year spans: Republicans twice, Democrats once. In the 1880s and early 1890s, elections were extremely close,

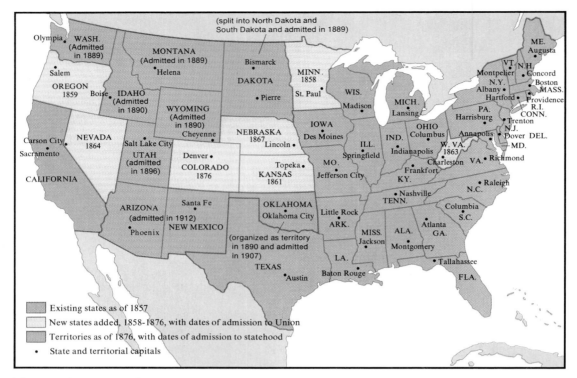

The following labels appear on the map:

Olympia, WASH. (Admitted in 1889), Salem, OREGON 1859, Boise, IDAHO (Admitted in 1890), Carson City, Sacramento, NEVADA 1864, Salt Lake City, UTAH (admitted in 1896), CALIFORNIA, ARIZONA (admitted in 1912), Phoenix, NEW MEXICO, Santa Fe, MONTANA (Admitted in 1889), Helena, WYOMING (Admitted in 1890), Cheyenne, Denver, COLORADO 1876, (split into North Dakota and South Dakota and admitted in 1889), Bismarck, DAKOTA, Pierre, NEBRASKA 1867, Lincoln, KANSAS 1861, Topeka, OKLAHOMA (organized as territory in 1890 and admitted in 1907), Oklahoma City, TEXAS, Austin, MINN. 1858, St. Paul, WIS., Madison, IOWA, Des Moines, MO., Jefferson City, ARK., Little Rock, LA., Baton Rouge, MICH., Lansing, ILL., Springfield, IND., Indianapolis, KY., Frankfort, TENN., Nashville, MISS., Jackson, ALA., Montgomery, GA., Atlanta, FLA., Tallahassee, OHIO, Columbus, W. VA. 1863, Charleston, VA., Richmond, N.C., Raleigh, S.C., Columbia, PA., Harrisburg, N.Y., Albany, Annapolis, MD., DEL., Dover, N.J., Trenton, CONN., Hartford, R.I., Providence, MASS., Boston, VT., Montpelier, N.H., Concord, ME., Augusta

Existing states as of 1857
New states added, 1858–1876, with dates of admission to Union
Territories as of 1876, with dates of admission to statehood
• State and territorial capitals

The United States, 1876–1912

especially on the national level. The outcome of presidential elections often hinged on a small number of "doubtful" states—Connecticut, New York, New Jersey, Ohio, Indiana, and Illinois. Parties tried to win advantages with voters by nominating presidential and vice-presidential candidates from these states (and also by perpetrating vote frauds on their candidates' behalf). Balance persisted despite the admission of six territories to statehood during this period (see map).

Republicans and Democrats competed avidly for office, but internal quarrels split both parties. Among Republicans, factional feuds and personal rivalries often took precedence over national concerns. On one side stood the "Stalwarts," led by New York's pompous Senator Roscoe Conkling. A physical-fitness devotee and former boxer who once was dubbed "the finest torso in public life," Conkling sought party influence and government jobs for his supporters. On the other side stood the "Half Breeds," led by James G. Blaine. Blaine pursued influence as much as Conkling did but attempted to disguise his aims by court-

> **Party Factions**

ing support from independents. On the sidelines were the more idealistic liberals, or "Mugwumps" (an Indian term meaning "undisciplined chiefs"), who, like Senator Carl Schurz of Missouri, disliked the political roguishness that tainted their party and believed that only righteous, dedicated men like themselves should govern. Meanwhile, Democrats tended to separate into white-supremacy southerners, immigrant-stock urban machine members, and business interests favoring low tariffs. Like Republicans, Democrats eagerly pursued the spoils of office.

At the state level, one party usually dominated, and within that party one or two men usually dictated political affairs. Often that state "boss" was a senator because his election by the state legislature (senators were not popularly elected until the Seventeenth Amendment to the Constitution was ratified in 1913) signified his power over the legislature and because he provided a direct link to federal patronage jobs. Senators also parlayed their state power into major national influence. Their ranks included Blaine of Maine, Conkling and Thomas C. Platt of New York, Nelson W. Aldridge of

Rhode Island, Calvin S. Brice and Mark A. Hanna of Ohio, Matthew S. Quay of Pennsylvania, and William Mahone of Virginia. Some were Republicans, some Democrats; but party affiliation seemed merely a route to power, and the private interests of business found alliances among these leaders regardless of party.

National Issues

In Congress, however, parties split over longstanding political and economic issues, such as sectional controversies, patronage, railroad regulation, tariffs, and currency. Long after Reconstruction ended, Americans were haunted by conflicts and disruptions that had followed the Civil War. Republicans capitalized on war memories by "waving the bloody shirt" when they faced Democratic challenges. As one Republican orator harangued in 1876, "Every man that tried to destroy this nation was a Democrat. . . . Soldiers, every scar you have on your heroic bodies was given you by a Democrat." In the South voters also waved the bloody shirt, calling all Republicans traitors. Use of such emotional appeals persisted well into the 1880s.

Politicians were not the only ones who attempted to profit by keeping the war alive. In the 1880s and 1890s, the Grand Army of the Republic, an organization of Union Army veterans numbering over 400,000, allied with the Republican party and pressured Congress into legislating generous pensions for former soldiers and their widows. Many pensions were deserved. Union soldiers had been poorly paid, and thousands of women had been widowed. But for many veterans, the war's emotional wake provided opportunity to profit at the public's expense. By the 1890s the federal government was spending $157 million annually for soldiers' pensions, one of the largest welfare commitments it had ever made. No Confederate veterans received any of the largess, though several southern states did fund small pensions and built old-age homes for ex-soldiers.

Few politicians could afford to oppose Civil War pensions, but a number of reformers attempted to dismantle the spoils system. The practice of award-

▶ **Civil Service Reform**

ing government jobs to party workers, regardless of their qualifications, had taken root in antebellum years and flourished after the Civil War. As building construction, the postal service, the diplomatic corps, and other government activities expanded, so did the number of jobs on public payrolls. Between 1865 and 1891 federal government positions tripled, from 53,000 to 166,000. Elected officials scrambled to control new appointments as a means of cementing support for themselves and their parties. In return for the comparatively short hours and high pay of government jobs, appointees pledged their votes and a portion of their earnings.

A system so susceptible to corruption vexed a growing number of independents, who began advocating appointments and promotions based on merit rather than on connections. The movement grew during the 1870s, when scandals in the Grant administration bared defects of the spoils system. It reached full flower in 1881 with formation of the National Civil Service Reform League, led by George W. Curtis, editor of *Harper's Weekly*, and E. L. Godkin, editor of the *Nation*. The same year, Charles Guiteau, a frustrated and demented jobseeker, assassinated President James Garfield, and the murder hastened the drive for civil service reform.

Late in 1882 Congress passed the Pendleton Civil Service Act, and President Chester Arthur signed it early in 1883. The law outlawed political contributions by officeholders and created the Civil Service Commission to oversee competitive examinations for government positions. The act, however, gave the commission jurisdiction over only about 10 percent of federal jobs—though the president could expand the list.

In the 1880s railroads, still a young industry, provided an example of how economic development caused political problems at both the state and the national levels. As the nation's rail network expanded, so did competition. In their quest for customers, railroad lines reduced rates to outmaneuver rivals, but rate wars soon cut into profits and wild vacillations of rates angered shippers and farmers.

Ironically, while rates generally were falling, complaints about excessively high rates were rising. Railroads often boosted rates as high as possible on noncompetitive routes to compensate for

Before passage of the Pendleton Act of 1883, many government positions were filled by patronage; hat in hand, job seekers beseeched the president to find a place for them. Here a member of Congress presents constituents for office in return for their past political support. *Library of Congress.*

unprofitably low rates on competitive routes, making pricing disproportionate to distance. Charges on short-distance shipments served by only one line could be far higher than those on long-distance shipments served by competing lines. Railroads also gave reduced rates to large shippers and offered free passenger passes to important customers and politicians.

During the 1870s, such favoritism stirred farmers, shippers, and reform politicians to demand that government regulate railroad practices, especially

Railroad Regulation

rates. Most early attempts at regulation occurred at the state level. By 1880, fourteen states had established commissions to limit the freight and storage charges of state-chartered lines. Railroads bitterly fought these measures, arguing that rights of private property superseded public authority. This belief in the sacred freedom to acquire and use property without government restraint prevented the ultimate step—public ownership of railroads—but did not halt regulation. In 1877 the Supreme Court upheld the principle of rate regulation in *Munn* v. *Illinois*, saying that rail-

roads were private property acting in the public interest and therefore must submit to regulation for the "common good."

State agencies, however, could not control large, interstate lines, a limitation affirmed by the Supreme Court in the *Wabash* case of 1886, in which the Court declared that only Congress could limit rates involving interstate commerce. Reformers demanded federal regulation. Congress responded in 1887 by passing the Interstate Commerce Act. The act prohibited pools, rebates (see page 504), and long haul–short haul rate discrimination, and it directed that "all charges . . . shall be reasonable and fair." It also created the Interstate Commerce Commission (ICC) and gave the ICC power to investigate railroads, issue "cease-and-desist" orders against illegal practices, and seek court aid to enforce compliance. However, the legislation proved to be only a flimsy roadblock to business interests: lack of provisions for enforcement left railroads room for evasion, and federal judges chipped away at ICC powers. In the *Maximum Freight Rate* case of 1897, the Supreme Court ruled that the ICC did not have power to set rates, and in the *Alabama Midlands* case the same year the Court overturned prohibitions against long haul–short haul discrimination. Still, the principle of government regulation, though weakened, remained.

Initially, Congress had created and raised tariff rates to protect American manufactured goods and some agricultural products from European competition. But tariffs quickly became a

Tariff Policy

tool by which special interests could protect and enhance profits. By the 1880s there were separate tariffs on over four thousand items, and resulting revenues were producing an embarrassing surplus in the federal Treasury. Although a few economists and farmers argued for free trade, most politicians still claimed that high tariffs were necessary to support industry and preserve jobs.

The Republican party, claiming responsibility for economic growth, put protective tariffs at the core of its policies. Democrats complained that tariffs made prices artificially high, benefiting interests, such as woolen manufacturers, whose products were protected while hurting farmers whose crops were not protected and consumers who had to buy manufactured goods. For example, a yard of flannel might have cost ten cents to produce abroad and ship to the United States, but a tariff of eight cents was added to the price, making the total cost to consumers eighteen cents. A manufacturer of a similar yard of flannel in the United States could charge seventeen cents, thereby underselling foreign competition while still pocketing a large profit at the consumer's expense, especially since only about three cents of the seventeen was used to pay laborers. Although Democrats generally saw the need for some protection of manufactured goods and raw materials, they favored lower tariff rates to encourage foreign trade and reduce the treasury surplus.

Privileged interests and their congressional allies fought off objections and maintained control over tariff policy. The McKinley Tariff of 1890 boosted already-high rates by another 4 percent. When in 1894 House Democrats supported by President Grover Cleveland passed a bill to reduce tariff rates, Senate Republicans, aided by southern Democrats eager to protect their region's infant industries, added some six hundred amendments restoring most cuts (Wilson-Gorman Tariff). In 1897 a new tariff bill, the Dingley Act, raised rates further, though it expanded reciprocity provisions. Introduced in the McKinley Tariff of 1890 and designed to encourage new foreign trade and discourage foreign retaliation against high American duties, reciprocity gave the president authority to remove items from the free list if their countries of origin placed unreasonable tariffs on American goods. Attacks against the tariff had little success, but they did make tariffs the symbol of privileged business, which became the focus of Progressive reformers after 1900 (see Chapter 21).

The currency controversy was even more tangled than the tariff issue. It involved opposing reactions to the fall in prices caused by increased industrial and agricultural production after the Civil War (see pages 460–461). Farmers, most of whom were debtors, suffered because they had to pay fixed mortgage and interest payments while prices for their crops were dropping. Correctly perceiving that an insufficient money supply made debts more expensive relative to other costs, farmers favored schemes like the coinage of silver to increase the amount of currency in circulation. Creditors, on the other hand, believed that overproduction had caused prices to decline. They favored a more stable, limited money supply backed only by gold as a means of maintaining the

Monetary Policy

During the 1880s and 1890s the kind and content of money dominated political debates. These pins of "Gold Bugs" and "Silver Bugs," the names given to supporters of the gold standard and the silver standard for American currency, were common to the age and reflected the dedication that supporters of each side had to their cause. *Museum of American Political Life, University of Hartford. Photo by Sally Anderson-Bruce.*

confidence of investors in the American economy.

But the issue involved more than economics. The quantity and quality of money symbolized a series of conflicts—social, regional, and emotional. Creditor-debtor conflict translated into haves versus have-nots. The debate also aroused a sectional cleavage: western silver-mining areas and agricultural regions of the South and West against the more conservative industrial Northeast. Finally, the issue carried moral, almost religious, overtones. Gold, the traditional basis of money, was a durable yet malleable metal. Those qualities plus its beauty and rarity gave it a magical potency and made it seem a God-given symbol of value. But others considered the gold standard for currency too limiting for the machine age; prosperity, they felt, demanded new attitudes.

By the early 1870s, the currency controversy was a matter of gold versus silver. Up to that time the government had coined both silver and gold dollars. A silver dollar weighed sixteen times more than a gold dollar, meaning that gold was officially worth sixteen times as much as silver. Gold discoveries after 1848, however, had increased the supply and lowered gold's market price relative to that of silver. Because silver came to be worth more than one-sixteenth the value of gold, silver producers preferred to sell their metal on the open market rather than to the government. Silver dollars disappeared from circulation—owners hoarded them rather than spend them—and in 1873 Congress officially stopped coining silver dollars. At about the same time, European nations also stopped buying silver. Thus the United States and many of its trading partners adopted the gold standard, meaning that their currency was backed chiefly by gold.

Within a few years, new mines in the American West began to flood the market with silver, and its price dropped. Gold once again was worth more than sixteen times what silver was worth. It became profitable to spend silver dollars, and it would have been worthwhile to sell silver to the government in return for gold, but the government was no longer buying silver. Debtors, who were suffering from the economic hard times of the mid-1870s in addition to falling prices, and who saw silver as a means of expanding the currency supply, joined with silver producers to denounce the "Crime of '73" and press for the resumption of coinage at the old sixteen-to-one ratio.

Congress, split into silver and gold factions, tried to neutralize the issue with compromise legislation: the Bland-Allison Act of 1878, which required the Treasury to buy between $2 million and $4 million worth of silver each month; and the Sherman Silver Purchase Act of 1890, which fixed the monthly purchase of silver in weight (4.5 million ounces) rather than in dollars. But neither act satisfied the different interest groups. The Sherman Act, passed partially in response to economic decline in the mid-1880s, failed to expand the money supply: as the price of silver dropped, the government, required only to buy a certain weight of silver, could spend less to purchase the stipulated number of ounces. Thus the money supply was not increased as substantially as hoped, and debtors had more reason to believe

the government favored privileged interests. Not until after a depression in the 1890s and an emotion-filled presidential election would the money issue subside.

While debates over tariffs and money raged, supporters of women's suffrage began to pressure Congress and state legislatures more fervently than ever before. The fortunes of this reform reflected the interaction of the issue of exclusion with political equilibrium. In 1878 Susan B. Anthony, the staunch fighter for human rights who had been rebuffed by the courts when she tried to vote in 1872, convinced Senator A. A. Sargent of California, a proponent of women's suffrage, to introduce a constitutional amendment stating that "the right of citizens of the United States to vote shall not be denied or abridged by the United States or by any state on account of sex." The bill was killed by a Senate committee, but supporters, such as the National Woman Suffrage Association (NWSA), got it reintroduced many times over the next eighteen years. On the few occasions when the bill reached the Senate floor, it was voted down by senators who expressed fears that suffrage would interfere with women's family responsibilities and ruin female virtue.

> **Women's Suffrage**

While NWSA and others fought for the vote on the national level, the American Woman Suffrage Association worked for constitutional amendments at the state level. (The two suffrage groups joined in 1890 to form the National American Woman Suffrage Association.) Between 1870 and 1910, there were seventeen referenda in eleven states (all but three of which were west of the Mississippi River) to legalize women's suffrage. These attempts seldom succeeded, but they attracted attention to newly formed women's clubs and trained a corps of female leaders in organizing and public speaking. Women did attain partial victories: by 1890 nineteen states allowed women to vote on school issues, and three granted suffrage on tax and bond issues. But broader rights would have to await a later generation.

Throughout the Gilded Age, legislators did address some basic issues, but they focused chiefly on protection of private property and stability of the investment climate—solid criteria for economic progress. The needs of debtors, farmers, laborers, women, racial minorities, and others who believed themselves disadvantaged found increased expression; but the formal political institutions of Congress and state legislatures excluded their interests while catering to the interests of those who already had social and economic privileges.

The Presidency in Eclipse

American presidents in the years between 1877 and 1900 contrasted sharply with forceful predecessors like Andrew Jackson and Abraham Lincoln. Operating under the cloud of Andrew Johnson's impeachment, Grant's scandals, and questions over the legitimacy of the election of 1876 (see Chapter 15), these presidents had to proceed gingerly in attempting to restore the authority of their office. Proper, honorable, and honest, Presidents Rutherford Hayes (1877–1881), James Garfield (1881), Chester Arthur (1881–1885), Grover Cleveland (1885–1889, 1893–1897), Benjamin Harrison (1889–1893), and William McKinley (1897–1901) won public respect but seldom provoked strong positive or negative emotions. Like other politicians, they used symbols. Hayes served lemonade at the White House to emphasize that, unlike his predecessor Ulysses Grant, he was no hard drinker. McKinley put aside his cigar in public so photographers would not catch him setting a bad example for youth. But none of the era's presidents was an inspiring personality, nor could any dominate the factional chieftains of his party. Each president made a few initiatives in domestic policy and utilized the veto to combat Congress, but the major presidential actions were in foreign policy (see Chapter 22).

Rutherford B. Hayes had been a Union general and an Ohio congressman and governor before his disputed election to the presidency (see pages 461–462), an event that prompted opponents to label him "Rutherfraud B. Hayes." Once in office, he avoided such controversial issues as the tariff and sectional rivalry. He did, however, exercise some presidential power, though mainly in support of privileged business interests. Thus he took a conservative position on currency by supporting the gold standard, and in 1877 he ordered out troops to quell the railroad strikes. Hayes pleased civil service advo-

Hayes, Garfield, and Arthur

James A. Garfield, pictured on this trade card, was a Civil War hero from Ohio who won a narrow electoral victory in 1880 to become the nation's seventeenth president. His death at the hand of an assassin in 1881 spurred efforts to establish civil service as a means of appointing federal employees. *Museum of American Political Life, University of Hartford. Photo by Sally Anderson-Bruce.*

cates by appointing reformer Carl Schurz to the cabinet and battling New York's patronage king, Senator Roscoe Conkling. (He fired Conkling's protégé, Chester Arthur, from the post of New York customs house collector.) But Hayes demanded that his own appointees contribute to Republican coffers for the 1878 elections. He was not a beloved leader. As one reformer wrote, "I have little or no patience with Mr. Hayes. He is a victim of . . . good intentions and his contributions to the pavement of the road to the infernal regions are vast and nefarious."

When Hayes declined to run for re-election in 1880, Republicans selected another Ohio congressman and Civil War hero, James A. Garfield. A husky, serious, and cautious man, Garfield defeated Democrat Winfield Scott Hancock, also a Civil War hero, by just 40,000 votes out of over 9 million. By carrying the pivotal states of New York and Indiana, however, Garfield won in the electoral college by a comfortable margin, 214 to 155. Garfield spent most of his brief presidency trying to secure an independent position among party potentates. He had ambitions for reducing the tariff and developing American economic interests in Latin America, but he had to spend most of his time dealing with hordes of office-seekers. "Once or twice," he complained, "I felt like crying out in the agony of my soul against the greed for office and its consumption of my time." He pleased civil service reformers by rebuffing Conkling's patronage demands, but Garfield's chance to make lasting contributions ended in July 1881 when Charles Guiteau shot him in a Washington railroad station. Not seriously wounded at first, Garfield lingered for seventy-nine days while doctors tried vainly to remove a bullet lodged in his back. His condition steadily deteriorated, and he succumbed to infection, dying September 19.

Garfield's vice president and successor was New York politician Chester A. Arthur, the spoilsman Hayes had fired in 1878. Arthur had been nominated for vice president only to help Republicans carry New York State; his elevation to the presidency made reformers shudder, yet he became a dignified and temperate executive. Arthur signed the Pendleton Act, urged Congress to modify outdated tariff rates, and spoke in favor of federal regulation of railroads. Using the veto as a means to influence Congress, Arthur killed a number of bills that excessively benefited privileged interests. But his ideas for reducing the tariff and building up the navy were frustrated by party politics within Congress. Arthur hoped to run for re-election in 1884, but he lost the nomination to James G. Blaine on the fourth ballot at the Republican national convention.

The 1884 presidential campaign magnified the era's political banalities. To run against Blaine, Democrats named New York's Governor Grover Cleveland, a rotund and righteous bachelor whose respectable reputation was tainted by his having once fathered an illegitimate son—a fact he admitted openly during the campaign. Each party focused on the sordid side of the opposition. Disapproval of Blaine was so strong that a number of Mugwump Republicans deserted their party for Cleveland. On election day Cleveland beat Blaine by only 23,000 popular votes; his tiny margin of

1,149 votes in New York gave him that state's 36 electoral votes, enough for a 219-to-182-vote victory in the electoral college. Cleveland may have won New York because in the campaign's last week a local Protestant minister publicly equated Democrats with "rum, Romanism, and rebellion" (drinking, Catholicism, and the Civil War). Democrats eagerly publicized the slur among New York's large Irish-Catholic population, urging voters to protest by turning out for Cleveland.

Cleveland, the first Democratic president since James Buchanan (1857–1861), complained like his Republican predecessors of the "cursed constant grind" of his office and the "want of rest." He did, however, exert more vigorous leadership. Cleveland used the veto extensively against outrageous pension bills— in fact, he vetoed two-thirds of all the bills Congress passed—and he expanded the civil service. His most forceful action was his unsuccessful campaign for tariff reform. Worried about the growing Treasury surplus, Cleveland urged Congress to cut duties on raw materials and manufactured goods. When advisers warned him that his stand might weaken his chances for re-election, the president retorted, "What is the use of being elected or re-elected, unless you stand for something?" Cleveland's firmness did not prevail, though. The Mills tariff bill of 1888, passed by the House in response to Cleveland's wishes, was killed by the Senate. Although Democrats renominated Cleveland for the presidency in 1888, protectionists in the party convinced Cleveland to temper his attacks on high tariffs.

Republicans in 1888 nominated Benjamin Harrison, an intelligent but chilly former senator from Indiana and grandson of President William Henry Harrison (1841). The campaign was less savage than the 1884 campaign had been, but it was far from clean. Some shrewd Republicans manipulated the British minister in Washington into stating that Cleveland's re-election would be good for England. Irish Democrats took offense, as intended, and Cleveland's campaign was weakened. Perhaps more helpful to Harrison was the bribery and multiple voting that helped him to win Indiana by 2,300 votes and New York by 14,000. (Democrats also indulged in bribery and vote fraud, but Republicans were more successful at it.) Those crucial states assured Harrison's victory; although Cleveland out-

> **Cleveland and Harrison**

This handkerchief from the presidential campaign of 1892 depicts Democrat candidate Grover Cleveland as a just and patriotic statesman. He remains the only president to have served two nonconsecutive terms, 1885–1889 and 1893–1897. *Museum of American Political Life, University of Hartford. Photo by Sally Anderson-Bruce.*

polled Harrison by 90,000 popular votes, Harrison carried the electoral vote by 233 to 168. After the election, Harrison told Matthew Quay, the Republican national chairman, "Providence has given us the victory." Quay later quipped to a friend, "Think of the man. He ought to know that Providence hadn't a damned thing to do with it. . . . [He] would never learn how close a number of men were compelled to approach the gates of the penitentiary to make him president."

Harrison was the first president since 1875 whose party had majorities in both houses of Congress, but he had little control over legislators, and he easily alienated supporters. "Harrison can make a speech to ten thousand men," mused an associate, "and every man of them will go away his friend. Let him meet the same ten thousand in private, and every one will go away his enemy." Harrison professed support for civil service and appointed Theodore Roosevelt a civil service commissioner,

but the president's lackluster character prompted the reform-minded and impatient Roosevelt to call him a "cold-blooded, narrow-minded, prejudiced, obstinate, timid, old psalm-singing Indianapolis politician." Harrison also signed the Dependents' Pension Act, which provided disability pensions to all Union veterans of the Civil War and granted aid to veterans' widows, if dependent upon their own labor for support, and their minor children. The bill doubled the number of pensioners, from 490,000 to 966,000. By 1911, the nation had spent over four billion dollars on Civil War pensions, a sum that vastly exceeded the war's entire cost. Politics had provided for another special interest.

As a result of the Pension Act and other grants and appropriations, the federal budget surpassed one billion dollars in 1890 for the first time in the nation's history. Democrats labeled the "Billion-Dollar Congress" as the fault of spendthrift Republicans, and voters responded by unseating seventy-eight Republicans in the congressional elections of 1890. Democrats, seeking to capitalize, nominated Cleveland to run against Harrison again in 1892. This time Cleveland attracted heavy contributions from business and beat Harrison by 380,000 popular votes (3 percent of the total) and by 277 to 145 electoral votes.

In office once more, Cleveland took bolder steps to meet problems of currency, tariffs, and labor unrest. But his actions reflected a narrow orientation toward the interests of business and bespoke political weakness. In order to protect the nation's gold reserve, which was shrinking during the Panic of 1893, Cleveland enlisted aid from bankers, who in 1895 bailed out the nation on terms highly favorable to themselves. During the election campaign Cleveland had promised sweeping tariff reform, but he made little effort to line up support for such reform in the Senate, where protectionists undercut all efforts to reduce rates. And when 120,000 boycotting railroad workers paralyzed western trade in the Pullman strike of 1894 (see page 518), Cleveland bowed to requests for federal troops from railroad managers and Attorney General Richard Olney. Throughout Cleveland's second term, events—particularly economic downturn and Populist ferment—seemed too much for the president. Cleveland's party abandoned him in 1896.

Stirrings of Agrarian Unrest

While the government labored to sustain order and prosperity, critical debates about the nature of democracy were occurring outside the political system, where inequities in the new agricultural and industrial order were creating the first rumblings of a mass movement that was to shake American society. The agrarian revolt—a complex mixture of strident rhetoric, nostalgic dreams, desires for economic security, and hard-headed egalitarianism—began when farmers' alliances formed in Texas in the late 1870s, then spread across the Cotton Belt and Plains in the 1880s. The movement caught on chiefly in areas where farm tenancy, crop liens, furnishing merchants (see page 489), railroads, banks, weather, and insects threatened the ambitions and economic well-being of hopeful farmers. Once under way, it inspired visions of a truly cooperative, democratic society.

Agricultural expansion in the West and South exposed millions of people to the hardships of rural life (see Chapter 16). Uncertainties might have been more bearable if rewards had been more promising, but such was not the case for farmers of small and middle-size landholdings. As growers put more land under cultivation, as mechanization boosted productivity, and as foreign competition increased, supplies exceeded national and worldwide demand for agricultural products. Consequently, prices for staple crops dropped steadily. A bushel of wheat that sold for $1.45 in 1866 brought only 80 cents in the mid-1880s and 49 cents by the mid-1890s. Meanwhile, transportation, storage, and commission fees remained high relative to other prices. Costly seed, fertilizer, manufactured goods, taxes, and mortgage interest combined with social isolation to trap many farm families in disadvantageous and sometimes desperate circumstances. In order to buy necessities and pay bills, farmers had to produce more. But the spiral only wound more tightly, because the more farmers produced, the lower prices dropped.

Even before the full impact of these developments was felt, small farmers had begun to organize to relieve mounting distress. With aid from

Grange Movement

Oliver H. Kelley of the Department of Agriculture, farmers founded a network of local organizations called Granges in almost every state during the late 1860s and early 1870s. By 1875 the Grange had nearly twenty thousand local branches and over 1 million members. Strongest in the Midwest and South, Granges served chiefly as social organizations, sponsoring meetings and educational events to help relieve the loneliness of farm life. Family-oriented and open to all, local Granges made specific provisions for women's participation.

As membership flourished, Granges moved beyond social functions into economic and political action. At its 1874 convention, the national Grange proposed to avoid high retail prices by forming local cooperatives to buy equipment and supplies directly from manufacturers. Granges also encouraged the formation of sales cooperatives, whereby farmers would pool their grain and dairy products and then divide the profits. In a few instances, Grangers operated implements factories and insurance companies. Most enterprises failed, however, because farmers lacked cash for cooperative buying and because ruthless competition from large manufacturers and dealers undercut them. In politics, Grangers used their numbers to some advantage, electing sympathetic legislators and pressing for laws to regulate transportation and storage rates.

Despite their progressive, even radical, efforts, Granges declined in the late 1870s. A requirement that cooperatives run on a cash-only basis excluded large numbers of farmers who rarely had any cash. Efforts to regulate business and transportation withered when corporations won court support against "Granger laws." Politically, Granges disavowed third parties but could not overcome the power of business interests within the two major parties. Finally, the Grange's promotion of thrift and hard work hardly helped families already overburdened with both virtues. Thus, after a brief assertion of influence, the Grange reverted to an organization of farmers' social clubs.

Rural activism then shifted to Farmers' Alliances, two networks of organizations—one in the Plains and one in the South—that by 1890 constituted a genuine mass movement. The first

▶ **Farmers' Alliances** Alliances sprang up in Texas, where hard-pressed small farmers rallied against crop liens, furnishing merchants, and railroads in particular, and against "money power" in general. Adopting an effective system of traveling lecturers to recruit members, Alliance leaders extended the movement to other southern states. By 1889 the Southern Alliance boasted over 3 million members, including the powerful Colored Farmers' National Alliance, which claimed over 1 million black members. A similar movement flourished in the Plains, where by the late 1880s 2 million members were organized in Kansas, Nebraska, and the Dakotas.

Alliance members pushed the Grange concept of cooperation to new limits by sponsoring organizational rallies, educational meetings, and cooperative buying and selling agreements. Seeing themselves as laborers battling capitalists in a new age, some Alliance members advocated unity with the Knights of Labor and other workers' groups in the campaign against unfair privilege. As one Alliance organizer proclaimed, "We extend to the Knights of Labor our hearty sympathies in their

THE NEW UNCLE SAM
How the Farmers' Alliance propose to have the Government run when they get the power.

The Farmers' Alliance movement organized agrarian unrest into a cogent list of reforms. This cartoon shows how alliance members hoped to protect their mortgages and crops with a series of economic proposals that would make the currency system more flexible. *Library of Congress.*

manly struggle against monopolistic oppression and . . . we propose to stand by the Knights."

Beyond urging democratic cooperation, the Alliance movement proposed a scheme to alleviate the most serious rural problems: lack of cash and lack of credit. The subtreasury

▶ **Subtreasury Plan** plan, adapted from French and Russian precedents, called for the federal government to construct warehouses in every major agricultural county. At harvest time, farmers could store crops in these subtreasuries while awaiting higher prices, and the government would loan farmers Treasury notes amounting to 80 percent of the market price the stored crops would bring. Farmers could use these Treasury notes as legal tender to pay debts and make purchases. Once stored crops were sold, farmers would pay back the loans plus small interest and storage fees.

The subtreasury scheme was meant to replace the crop-lien system and to give farmers greater control over their financial affairs by freeing them from dependence upon exploitive storage operators and purchasers. No longer would merchants be able to take advantage of farmers at harvest time, when market gluts depressed prices. No longer would farmers have to mortgage crops (through crop liens) at high interest. No longer would they lack cash to buy supplies. And by issuing Treasury notes, the government would be injecting money into the economy and encouraging the kind of inflation that would raise crop prices without raising the costs of supplies and rents. If the government subsidized business, reasoned Alliance members, why should it not help farmers earn a decent living too?

Implementation of their plans confronted Alliance members with questions of political participation. If the various Alliance groups in the North and South had been able to unite, they would have made a formidable political force; but sectional differences and personality clashes thwarted early attempts at merger. At a meeting in St. Louis in 1889, white southerners, fearing reprisals from landowners and objecting to participation by blacks, rejected proposals that would have ended secrecy in Alliance activities and white-only membership rules. Northerners too shied away from amalgamation, fearing they would be dominated by the more experienced southern leaders. Differences on issues also prevented unity. Northern farmers, who were mostly Republicans, wanted protective tariffs to keep out foreign grain; white southerners, mostly Democrats, wanted low tariffs to keep the costs of foreign manufactured goods low. Both Alliances did favor governmental control of transportation and communications, liberal credit policies, equitable taxation, prohibition of landownership by foreign investors, and currency reform.

Growing membership and rising confidence drew Alliances more deeply into politics. By 1890, farmers had elected a number of officeholders sympathetic to their programs— especially in the South, where Alliance members controlled four governorships, eight state legislatures, forty-four seats in the U.S. House of Repre-

Rise of Populism

sentatives, and three seats in the U.S. Senate. In the Midwest, Alliance candidates often ran on independent third-party tickets and achieved some success in Kansas, Nebraska, and the Dakotas. Campaigns included spirited rallies and parades that resounded with songs and orations; their banners proclaimed, "We Are All Mortgaged But Our Votes." During the summer of 1890, the Kansas Alliance held a "convention of the people" and nominated candidates who swept the fall elections. Formation of this People's party, whose members were called Populists (from *populus,* the Latin word for "people"), gave a name to the political activism by Alliances.

Election results in 1890 energized new efforts to unite all Alliance groups into a single Populist party. A meeting in May 1891 of northern and southern Alliances in Cincinnati failed when southerners chose to remain Democrats rather than risk joining a third party. But by early 1892, southern Alliance members were ready for independent action. Meeting with northern counterparts in St. Louis, they issued a call for a People's party convention in Omaha on July 4 to draft a platform and nominate a presidential candidate.

The new party's platform was one of the most comprehensive reform documents in American history. Declaring in its preamble that "wealth belongs to him that creates it," the Omaha platform presented a host of proposals generated by rural unrest. Most planks addressed three central issues: transportation, land, and money. Frustrated with weak state and federal regulation, Populists demanded government ownership of railroad and telegraph lines. They urged the federal government to reclaim all land owned for speculative purposes by railroads and foreigners. The monetary plank called for a flexible currency system based on free and unlimited coinage of silver that would increase the money supply and enable farmers to pay debts more easily. Other planks advocated a graduated income tax, postal savings banks, direct election of United States senators, and shorter hours for workers. As its presidential candidate, the party nominated James B. Weaver of Iowa, a former Union general and supporter of a liberally increased money supply.

The Populist campaign featured colorful personalities and vivid rhetoric. The Kansas plains rumbled with the speeches of "Sockless Jerry" Simpson, an unschooled but canny rural reformer, and of Mary Ellen Lease, a fiery orator who urged farmers to "raise less corn and more hell." The South produced equally forceful but less flamboyant leaders, such as Charles W. Macune of Texas, Thomas Watson of Georgia, and Leonidas Polk of North Carolina. Minnesota's Ignatius Donnelly, pseudoscientist and writer of apocalyptic novels, became chief ideologue of the northern Plains and was responsible for the thunderous language in the Omaha platform. Finally, the campaign had opportunists, like James Hogg, the three-hundred-pound governor of Texas, and one-eyed Senator "Pitchfork Ben" Tillman of South Carolina, who were not genuine Populists but used the rising agrarian fervor for their own political ends.

Although Weaver lost badly in 1892, he garnered over 1 million popular votes (8 percent of the total), winning majorities in four states and 22 electoral votes. Not since 1856 had a third party won so many votes in its first national effort. The party's central dilemma—whether to stand by its ideals at all costs or compromise those ideals in order to gain power—still loomed ahead (see pages 598–599). But in the early 1890s, rural dwellers in the South and West foresaw a promising future. The Alliance movement had kindled an emotional faith. Although Populists were not perfectly democratic—their mistrust of blacks and foreigners gave them a reactionary vein—they sought change in order to fulfill their version of American ideals. Amid hardship and desperation, millions of people had begun to believe that they could overcome corporate power with a cooperative democracy in which government would ensure equal opportunity. A banner hanging above the stage at the Omaha convention summed up the movement's spirit: "We do not ask for sympathy or pity. We ask for justice."

The Depression of the 1890s

Early in 1893, shortly before Grover Cleveland became president for the second time, a relatively minor but ominous economic event occurred: the Philadelphia and Reading Railroad, once a thriving and profitable line, went bankrupt. Like other rail-

Mary E. Lease (1850–1933) was a fiery and controversial speaker for the Farmers' Alliance and Populist party in Kansas. Tall and intense, she had a deep, almost hypnotic voice that made her an effective publicist for the farmers' cause. She was one of the founders of the Populist party and gave a seconding speech to the presidential nomination of James B. Weaver at the party convention in 1892. *Library of Congress.*

roads, the Philadelphia and Reading had borrowed heavily to lay track and build stations and bridges. But overexpansion cut into revenues. Profits dwindled, and the company was unable to pay its debts.

The same problem nagged manufacturers. For example, output at McCormick farm machinery factories was nine times greater in 1893 than it had been in 1879, but revenues had only tripled. To compensate, the company tried to boost profits by buying more machines and squeezing more work out of fewer laborers. This strategy, however, only enlarged the debt and increased unemployment, and it pushed unemployed workers into the same plight as their employers: they could not pay their creditors.

Banks suffered too. As primary lending agents, their problems compounded when customers defaulted. Failure of the National Cordage Company in May 1893 set off a chain reaction of business and bank closings. During the first four months of 1893, 28 banks failed. By June the number reached 128. In 1894 one adviser warned President Cleveland, "We are on the eve of a very dark night." He was right; between 1893 and 1897, the nation suffered the worst economic depression it had yet experienced.

Personal hardship arrived in the wake of business failures. Although records are sketchy, it appears that about 2.5 million people, or nearly 20 percent of the labor force, were jobless for a significant time during the depression. Falling demand caused the cost of living to drop between 1892 and 1895, but that decline in the cost of living was more than offset by layoffs and wage cuts. Many people could not afford basic necessities. New York police estimated that twenty thousand homeless and jobless people roamed the city's streets. Surveying the depression's impact on Boston, Henry Adams wrote, "Men died like flies under the strain, and Boston grew suddenly old, haggard, and thin."

As the depression deepened, currency problems reached a critical stage. The Sherman Silver Purchase Act of 1890 had committed the government to buy 4.5 million ounces of silver

Currency Problems each month (see page 586). Payment was to be in gold, at the ratio of one ounce of gold for every sixteen ounces of silver. But the western mining boom made silver more plentiful, and its value relative to gold fell. Thus every month the government exchanged gold, whose worth remained fairly constant, for less-valuable silver. Fearful that the dollar, which was based on Treasury holdings in silver and gold, was losing value, merchants at home and abroad began to cash in paper money and securities for gold. As a result, the nation's gold reserve dwindled, falling below $100 million in April 1893.

The $100-million level was psychologically significant. If business leaders believed that the country's gold reserve was disappearing, they would lose confidence in its economic stability and refrain from investing. For example, British capitalists owned some $4 billion in American stocks and bonds. If the dollar were to depreciate too much, they would stop investing in American economic growth. Yet the lower the gold reserve dropped, the more people rushed to redeem their money and securities—to get their gold before it disappeared. Panic spread, causing further bankruptcies and unemployment.

President Cleveland, promising to protect the gold reserve, called a special session of Congress to repeal the Sherman Silver Purchase Act. But although repeal passed in October 1893, the run on the Treasury continued through 1894. By early 1895 gold reserves had fallen to $41 million. In desperation, Cleveland accepted an offer of 3.5 million ounces of gold in return for $62 million worth of federal bonds from a banking syndicate led by J. P. Morgan. When bankers resold the bonds to the public, they profited handsomely at the nation's expense. Cleveland claimed that the gold reserves had been saved, but discontented farmers, workers, silver miners, and even some members of Cleveland's own party saw only humiliation in the president's openly dealing with big businessmen to bail the country out of trouble. "When Judas betrayed Christ," charged South Carolina's Senator "Pitchfork Ben" Tillman, "his heart was not blacker than this scoundrel, Cleveland, in betraying the [Democratic party]."

No one knew what the president really was enduring. At about the time that Cleveland called Congress into special session, doctors discovered a malignant tumor on his palate. The cancer required immediate removal. Fearful that public knowledge of his illness would hasten the run on gold, and intent on preventing Vice President Adlai E. Stevenson, a silver supporter, from gaining influence, Cleveland kept his condition a secret. He announced that he was going sailing, and doctors removed his cancerous upper left jaw while the yacht floated up the East River from New York City. Outfitted with a rubber jaw, Cleveland resumed a full schedule five days later, hiding terrible pain to dispel rumors that he was seriously ill. He eventually recovered, but those who knew about his operation believed it had sapped his vitality.

The deal between Cleveland and Morgan did not end the depression. After slight improvement in 1895, the economy plunged again. Farm income, on the decline since 1887, continued to slide; factories closed; banks that remained open restricted withdrawals and refused to honor checks. The tight money supply and reduced immigration depressed housing construction, drying up an important source of jobs. Each night police stations in almost every city filled with vagrants who had no other place to stay.

In the final years of the century, new gold discoveries in Alaska, good harvests, and industrial growth brought better times and, as in previous hard times, the depression finally

Effect of New Economic Structures ran its course. But the depression of the 1890s had hastened the crumbling of an old system and the emergence of a new one. The processes of industrial development and technological change had been under way for some time. Since the 1850s, railroads had been at the center of American economic development, opening new markets, boosting steel production, spawning banking. But organizational features of the new business system—consolidation and a trend toward bigness—were just beginning to solidify when the depression hit.

The national economy had reached the point of interdependence, at which the fortunes of a business in one part of the country or the world had repercussions elsewhere. By the 1890s many companies had expanded too rapidly; when contraction occurred, their reckless investments inevitably crumbled and they pulled other industries down with them. In the first half of 1893, for example, thirty-two steel companies failed. In all, five hundred banks and sixteen thousand businesses toppled into bankruptcy that year. European economies also slumped, and more than ever before the fortunes of one country affected those of other countries.

To complicate matters, American farmers had to contend not only with fluctuating transportation rates and falling crop prices at home, but also with Canadian and Russian wheat growers, Argentine cattle ranchers, Indian and Egyptian cotton producers, and Australian wool producers. When farmers fell into debt and lost purchasing power, their depressed condition in turn affected the economic health of railroads, farm-implements manufacturers, banks, and other businesses. The downward spiral reversed late in 1897, but the depression left deep scars.

Depression-Era Protests

The depression bared problems in the industrial system. For half a century technological and organizational changes had been widening the gap between employers and employees. By the 1890s workers' protests against exploitation threatened economic and political upheaval. In 1894, when the American economy plunged, there were over thirteen hundred strikes and countless riots. Violence reached an alarming pitch, and radical rhetoric escalated. Contrary to the fears of business leaders, all protesters were not anarchists or communists from Europe come to sabotage American democracy. The disaffected included thousands of men and women who believed that in a democracy their voices should be heard.

The era of protest began with the disruptive railroad strikes of 1877 (see page 515). The vehemence of those strikes and the support they drew from working-class people prompted defenders of American prosperity to fear that the United States would repeat what had happened in France six years earlier, when a popular uprising briefly overturned the government and introduced communist principles. Such anxieties were heightened by the Southwest railroad strike of 1885, the Haymarket riot of 1886, a general strike in New Orleans in 1891, and a prolonged strike at the Homestead Steel plant in 1892. In the West, too, miners were becoming embittered; in 1892 violence broke out at a silver mine in Coeur d'Alene, Idaho. Angered by wage cuts and a lockout, strikers seized the mines and battled federal troops sent to subdue them. Such actions caused some business owners to believe that force was the only effective response to radicalism allegedly promoted by socialists and anarchists.

Socialists were involved in these and other incidents, but their numbers were small, consisting of several parties such as the Socialist Labor party, led

Socialism by Daniel DeLeon, a fiery West Indian-born lawyer and lecturer. Socialists generally agreed with Karl Marx, the father of communism, that whoever controlled the means of production held power to determine how well people lived. Marx had written that under industrial capitalism workers become divorced from the means of production and profits are generated by paying workers less than the value of their labor. In the process, mechanization and the division of labor demean labor. Thus, Marx contended, capitalists and laborers are in inherent conflict as they fight to control whether workers will receive the true value of their labor. Marx believed that only by abolishing the return to capital— profits—could work receive its true value. This was

Eugene V. Debs (1855–1926) was the country's leading socialist at the turn of the century. His forceful oratorical skill and keen intellect not only attracted large audiences but also prompted the Socialist party to nominate him for president five times. *Brown Brothers.*

possible, of course, only if workers owned the means of production. Marx predicted that workers throughout the world would become so discontented that they would revolt and seize factories, farms, banks, and transportation lines. The societies resulting from this revolution would end exploitation and establish a new order of social justice and equality. Marx's vision appealed to some workers because it promised them independence and abundance, and it appealed to intellectuals because it promised an end to class conflict and crude materialism.

American socialism suffered from internal disagreements and lack of strong leadership. DeLeon and other leaders failed to attract the mass of unskilled workers, even though many immigrants had been exposed to socialism before they left Europe. American socialists often focused on ideals while neglecting the everyday needs of workers, and they could not counteract arguments by clergy and busi-

ness leaders who preached mobility, self-improvement, and consumerism. As well, the process of social mobility undermined socialist aims. Workers hoped that they or their children would improve themselves through education or the acquisition of property or by becoming their own boss; thus most workers sought individual improvement rather than the betterment of all workers.

Events in 1894 triggered changes within the socialist movement. That year the government's quashing of the Pullman strike and of the newly formed American Railway Union created a new, inspiring socialist leader. Eugene V. Debs, the railway union president, had become a socialist while serving a six-month prison term for defying an injunction against the strike. Once released, the bald, forceful Indianan became the leading spokesman for American socialism, combining visionary Marxism with Jeffersonian and Populist antimonopolism. Though never good at organizing, Debs captivated huge audiences with passionate eloquence and indignant attacks on the free enterprise system. "Many of you think you are competing," he would lecture. "Against whom? Against Rockefeller? About as I would if I had a wheelbarrow and competed with the Santa Fe [railroad] from here to Kansas City." Debs's major accomplishments would occur later, but by 1900 the group soon to be called the Socialist Party of America was beginning to unite around him.

In 1894, however, it was not the tall, animated Debs but a short, quiet businessman from Massillon, Ohio, who captured public attention. His

> **Coxey's Army**

name was Jacob S. Coxey, and like Debs he had a vision. Coxey had become convinced that, to help debtors, the government should issue paper money unbacked by gold—purposeful inflation, in other words. As the depression spread, Coxey recommended a federal public works program financed by an issue of $500 million of this "legal tender" paper money to relieve unemployment and revive consumer spending. He planned to publicize his scheme by leading a march from Massillon to Washington, D.C., gathering a "commonweal army" of unemployed workers along the way. Coxey was so enthusiastic about his project that he christened his newborn son Legal Tender and proposed that his eighteen-year-old daughter, wearing a red-white-and-blue gown, lead the procession on a white horse.

About two hundred strong, Coxey's army left Massillon on March 24, 1894. Moving across Ohio and into Pennsylvania, they received food, housing, and recruits from depressed industrial towns and rural villages. Many participants succumbed to boredom or the weather and dropped out of the march, but elsewhere in the country similar armies organized and began the trek toward Washington.

Coxey's troops, including women and children, entered the capital on April 30. The next day (May Day, a date that made police nervous because of its traditional association with socialist demonstrations), the citizen army of five hundred people marched to the Capitol, armed with "war clubs of peace." When Coxey and a few others vaulted the wall surrounding the Capitol grounds, mounted police moved in and routed the crowd. Coxey tried to speak from the Capitol steps, but police dragged him away. As arrests and clubbings continued, Coxey's dreams of a demonstration of 400,000 jobless

workers dissolved. Like the strikes, the people's first march on Washington had yielded to police muscle.

Coxey's march was an expression of frustration by people who were seeking relief from uncertainty. Unlike socialists, who wished to alter the economic system, Coxey commonwealers merely wanted more jobs and better living standards. Today, in an age of union contracts, regulation of business, and government-sponsored job relief in times of high unemployment, their goals do not appear radical. Yet the brutal reactions of officials reveal how threatening the dissenters, from Coxey to Debs, must have seemed to the defenders of special interests.

Populists and the Silver Crusade

Populists too were part of the protest activism. Although they did not experience the government suppression experienced by unions and Coxey's army, Populists suffered problems that surfaced just when their political goals seemed attainable. In 1892 their presidential candidate had received over 1 million votes, and as late as 1894 Populist candidates were making good showings in local and state elections in the West and South. Like previous third parties, Populists were underfinanced and underorganized. They had strong and colorful candidates but not enough of them to wrest control from the major parties. Many voters were reluctant to break old loyalties, and Populists had trouble luring supporters away from the Republicans and Democrats. Moreover, the two major parties fought to destroy Populist voting strength, especially in the South.

By the 1890s, the threat of biracial political dissent posed by the farmers' Alliances prompted southern white Democrats to take urgent action.

> **Curtailment of Black Voting**

During the 1880s southern legislatures had enacted several measures to curtail black voting, including poll taxes and literacy tests (see pages 490–491). Not satisfied that these measures would thwart a coalition of black and white voters in the Populist party and fearful that northern Republicans might revive federal supervision of elections, southern states tried more directly to prevent all blacks from voting.

Disfranchisement was accomplished in clever and devious ways. In 1876 the Supreme Court had affirmed that the Fifteenth Amendment prohibited states from denying the vote to people "on account of race, color, or previous condition of servitude." But, said the Court, Congress had no control over state elections beyond provisions set by the Fifteenth Amendment (*U.S.* v. *Reese*). Subsequently, state legislatures found ways to exclude black voters without ever mentioning race, color, or previous condition of servitude. In 1890, a state constitutional convention established the "Mississippi Plan," which required all voters to pay a poll tax eight months before an election, to keep and present the receipt at election time, and to prove that they could read and interpret the state constitution. Registration officials applied much stiffer standards to blacks than to whites, even declaring black college graduates ineligible on grounds of illiteracy. In 1898 Louisiana enacted the first grandfather clause, which established literacy and property qualifications for voting but exempted sons and grandsons of those eligible to vote before 1867. The law effectively excluded blacks from voting because few could meet the qualifications and none had been able to vote before 1867. Other southern states initiated similar measures.

These and other restrictions proved effective. In South Carolina, for example, 70 percent of eligible blacks had voted in the presidential election of 1880; by 1896 the rate had dropped to 11 percent. By the early 1900s, blacks had effectively lost political rights in every southern state except Tennessee. Disfranchisement affected poor whites also, because many of them could not meet poll tax, property, and literacy requirements. Thus by 1892 in Mississippi, the total number of eligible voters had shrunk from 257,000 to 77,000.

To a large extent, white fears were unjustified, for fundamental factors impeded the acceptance of blacks by white Populists. To be sure, some Populists sought a coalition of distressed black and white farmers. Tom Watson, Georgia's most prominent Populist, noted that "the crushing burdens which now oppress both races in the South will cause each to . . . see a similarity of cause and a similarity of remedy." But even poor white farmers could not put aside their racism. Many came from families

that had supported the Ku Klux Klan during Reconstruction; some had once owned slaves, and they considered blacks to be a permanently inferior people who would never be able to act for themselves. They seemed to take comfort in the belief that there would always be people worse off than they were. Thus Populists seldom addressed the needs of black farmers and used white-supremacist rhetoric to avoid charges that they encouraged racial mingling.

On the national level, the Populist crusade against "money power" settled on the issue of silver. Many people saw silver as a simple solution to the nation's complex ills. To them, free silver meant the end of special privileges for the rich and the return of government to the people. William H. Harvey, author of the immensely popular *Coin's Financial School* (1894), preached that by coining silver "you increase the value of all property by adding to the number of money units in the land. You make it possible for the debtor to pay his debts; business to start anew, and revivify all the industries of the country, which must remain paralyzed so long as silver as well as all other property is measured by a gold standard."

> **Free Silver**

Using this reasoning, Populists adopted free coinage of silver as their political battle cry. But as the elections of 1896 approached, they faced the dilemma of what strategy to use to translate their few previous electoral victories into larger success. Would they lose their identity by joining with sympathetic factions of the major parties, or would they remain independent as a third party and settle for at best minor successes? Except in the Rocky Mountain states, where free coinage of silver had strong support, Republicans were unlikely allies. Although Republican politicians could be as moralistic as Populist politicians, their anti-inflationist conservatism, support for the gold standard, and big-business orientation stood for everything Populists opposed. In the North and West, alliance with Democrats was more plausible. In many areas the Democratic party retained vestiges of antimonopoly ideology as well as some sympathy for a looser currency system, although gold Democrats like President Cleveland and Senator David Hill of New York did exert powerful opposition. Populists believed they also had links with traditionally Democratic urban workers, who, they assumed, suffered from the same oppression that stifled farmers. In

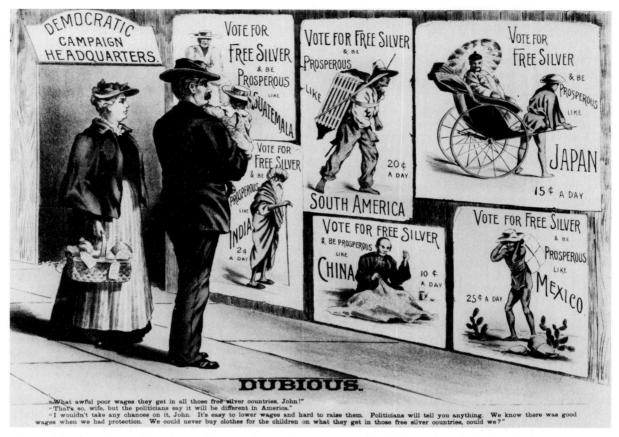

"What awful poor wages they get in all those free silver countries, John!"
"That's so, wife, but the politicians say it will be different in America."
"I wouldn't take any chances on it, John. It's easy to lower wages and hard to raise them. Politicians will tell you anything. We know there was good wages when we had protection. We could never buy clothes for the children on what they get in those free silver countries, could we?"

Critics of the free silver policy advocated by Populists and Democrats in the 1896 presidential election tried to convince voters that such a policy would result in poverty and low wages. The message of this broadside is that free silver would make Americans as downtrodden as peasants of the most backward countries. *Smithsonian Institution.*

the South, fusion with Democrats seemed less likely, since there the party was the very power structure against which Populists had revolted in the late 1880s. Regardless of their options, Populists had made certain that the political campaign of 1896 would be like none before it.

The Election of 1896

The presidential election of 1896 brought the nation's political turbulence to a climax. Each party was divided. Republicans, under the direction of Marcus Alonzo Hanna, a prosperous Ohio industrialist, had only minor problems. Since early

McKinley and Bryan

in 1895, Hanna had been maneuvering to win the nomination for Ohio's governor, William McKinley. By the time the party convened in St. Louis in 1896, Hanna had corralled enough delegates to succeed. "He had advertised McKinley," quipped Theodore Roosevelt, "as if he were a patent medicine." The Republicans' only distress occurred when the party adopted a moderate platform supporting gold, rejecting a prosilver stance proposed by Senator Henry M. Teller of Colorado. Teller, who had been among the party's founders forty years earlier, walked out of the convention in tears, taking a small group of silver Republicans with him.

At the Democratic convention, silver delegates paraded through the Chicago Amphitheatre wearing silver badges and waving silver banners. Observing their tumultuous demonstrations, one eastern delegate wrote, "For the first time I can

William Jennings Bryan (1860–1925) poses for a photograph taken in 1896 when he first ran for president at the age of thirty-six. Bryan was an emotional speaker who turned agrarian unrest and the issue of free silver into a moral crusade. *Library of Congress.*

committee, Bryan helped write a platform calling for free coinage of silver.

When the committee presented the platform to the full convention, Bryan rose to speak on its behalf. In the heat and humidity of the Chicago summer, Bryan's now-famous closing words ignited the delegates:

> Having behind us the producing masses of this nation and the world, supported by the commercial interests, the laboring interests, and the toilers everywhere, we will answer their [the wealthy classes'] demand for a gold standard by saying to them: You shall not press down upon the brow of labor this crown of thorns, you shall not crucify mankind upon a cross of gold.

The speech could not have been more timely; indeed, Bryan planned it to be so. Friends who had been pushing Bryan for the presidential nomination now had no trouble enlisting support. It took five ballots to win the nomination, but finally the magnetism of the "Boy Orator" proved irresistible. In bowing to the silverite will of southerners and westerners and repudiating Cleveland's policies in its platform, the party became more attractive to discontented farmers. But like the Republicans, it too drove away a dissenting minority wing. A group of gold Democrats withdrew and nominated their own candidate.

Bryan's nomination presented the Populist party with a dilemma. Should Populists join Democrats in support of Bryan, or should they nominate their own candidate? Tom Watson of Georgia, expressing southern sentiment against fusion with Democrats, warned that "the Democratic idea of fusion [is] that we play Jonah while they play whale." But others reasoned that supporting a different candidate would split the anti-McKinley vote and allow the Republicans to win. In the end the convention compromised, first naming Watson as vice-presidential nominee to preserve party identity (Democrats had nominated Maine shipping magnate Arthur Sewall for vice president) and then nominating Bryan for president.

The campaign, in the words of journalist William Allen White, "took the form of religious frenzy. . . . Far into the night, the voices rose—women's voices, children's voices, the voices of old men, of youths and of maidens, rose on the ebbing prairie breezes, as the crusaders of the revolution rode home, praising the people's will as though it were

understand the scenes of the French Revolution!" "All the silverites need is a Moses," remarked a *New York World* reporter. They found one in William Jennings Bryan.

Bryan arrived at the Democratic national convention in Chicago in July 1896 as a member of a contested Nebraska delegation. A former congressman whose support for free coinage of silver had annoyed President Cleveland, he was only thirty-six years old, avidly religious, and highly distressed by what the depression had done to midwestern farmers. The convention, as expected, chose to seat Bryan and his colleagues instead of a competing faction that supported the gold standard. Shortly afterward, as a member of the party's resolutions

God's will and cursing wealth for its iniquity." Republicans countered Bryan's moral evangelism and attacks on privilege (Bryan repeatedly preached that "every great economic question is in reality a great moral question") by predicting chaos if he should win. While Bryan raced around the country giving twenty speeches a day, Mark Hanna invited hundreds of thousands of people to McKinley's home in Canton, Ohio, where the candidate plied them with speeches on moderation and prosperity. Leaving moralizing to the Democrats, Republican candidates adopted the pragmatic, pluralistic approach of promising something for everyone. They particularly stressed the new jobs that a protective tariff would create and a policy of welcoming immigrants, both of which appealed to urban working-class voters.

Election results revealed that the political standoff had finally ended. McKinley, symbol of Republican pragmatism and new economic order, beat

> **Election Results** Bryan by over 600,000 popular votes and by 271 to 176 in the electoral college (see map, page 602). It was the most lopsided presidential election since 1872.

Democrats and Populists had done all they could to rally the nation. Bryan had tried to offset the huge Republican campaign chest, estimated at between $3.5 million and $7 million, by traveling 18,000 miles and giving over six hundred speeches. But lean campaign finances and obsession with silver undermined his effort. Silver especially prevented Populists from building the urban-rural coalition that would have given them political breadth. Reformer Henry Demarest Lloyd summarized the matter succinctly: "Free silver," he wrote, "is the cow bird of the reform movement. It waited till the nest had been built by the sacrifices and labor of others, and then it laid its eggs in it, pushing out the others which it smashed to the ground." Farmers' demands for an expanded currency found little support. Urban workers shied away from the silver issue because they feared that high prices would result. Labor leaders like Samuel Gompers of the AFL, though partly sympathetic, would not join with Populists because they viewed farmers as businessmen, not as workers. And socialists such as Daniel DeLeon denounced Populists as "retrograde" because, unlike socialists, they still believed in free enterprise. Thus the Populist crusade collapsed in 1896. Although Populists and

William McKinley (1843–1901) ran for president in 1896 on a platform that linked business prosperity with national prestige and economic well-being. *Library of Congress.*

fusion candidates made a few gains in state and congressional elections, the Bryan-Watson ticket polled only 222,600 votes nationwide.

As president, McKinley signed the Gold Standard Act (1900), which required that all paper money be backed by gold. A seasoned politician, personable and attractive, McKinley was best

> **The McKinley Presidency** known for his expertise in crafting high protective tariffs; as a congressman from Ohio, he had guided passage of record high rates in 1890. He accordingly supported the Dingley Tariff of 1897, which raised duties even higher—though it did expand reciprocity provisions. During McKinley's presidency domestic tensions subsided; an upward swing of the business

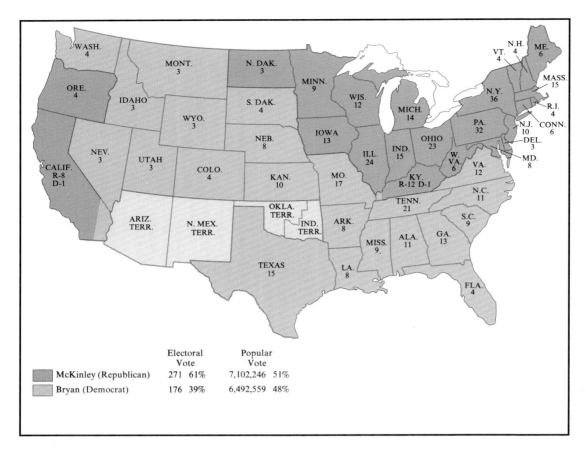

	Electoral Vote	Popular Vote
McKinley (Republican)	271 61%	7,102,246 51%
Bryan (Democrat)	176 39%	6,492,559 48%

Presidential Election, 1896

cycle and increased money supply from new gold discoveries in Alaska, Australia, and South Africa helped restore prosperity. Freed from care of the economy, McKinley spent time on foreign affairs. A strong believer in the need to open new markets abroad, he encouraged imperialistic ventures in Latin America and the Pacific (see Chapter 22). Good times and victory in war enabled McKinley to beat Bryan again in 1900, using the slogan "The Full Dinner Pail."

The 1896 election ended the old equilibrium and realigned national politics. The Republican party, which had begun in the 1850s as a party of moral evangelism against slavery, had

> **Political Realignment**

become the party of the majority of voters by emphasizing economic progress and broadening its social base to include urban workers. The Democratic party had miscalculated on the silver issue and had held its support only in the South; it would take the next three decades to refashion a broader

appeal. After 1896, however, party loyalties were not as potent as they once had been. Suspicions of party politics increased, even to the point at which some people chose not to vote at all, and voter participation rates declined. A new kind of politics was brewing, one in which technical experts and scientific organization would attempt to supplant the back-room deals and favoritism that had characterized the previous age.

The Populists had made the most concerted effort to combat special privilege and corruption but had foundered because too many people were benefiting from a generally expanding economy. Ironically, by 1920 many Populist reform goals would be achieved, including regulation of railroads, banks, and utilities; shorter working hours; a variant of the subtreasury system; a graduated income tax; direct election of senators; and the secret ballot. Those reforms succeeded because a variety of groups united behind them. Immigration, urbanization, and industrialization had transformed the United States into a pluralistic society where compromise among interest groups had become a political fact of life. The election of 1896 and the end of the Gilded Age equilibrium confirmed that transformation.

Suggestions for Further Reading

General

Sean Denis Cashman, *America in the Gilded Age* (1984); Harold U. Faulkner, *Politics, Reform, and Expansion, 1890–1900* (1959); Ray Ginger, *The Age of Excess,* 2nd ed. (1975); H. Wayne Morgan, *From Hayes to McKinley* (1969); H. Wayne Morgan, ed., *The Gilded Age* (1970); Nell Irvin Painter, *Standing at Armageddon: The United States, 1877–1919* (1987); Alan Trachtenberg, *The Incorporation of America: Culture and Society in the Gilded Age* (1982); R. Hal Williams, *Years of Decision: American Politics in the 1890s* (1978).

Parties and Political Issues

Beverly Beeton, *Women Vote in the West: The Suffrage Movement, 1869–1896* (1986); Christine Bolt, *American Indian Policy and American Reform* (1987); John H. Dobson, *Politics in the Gilded Age* (1972); Eleanor Flexner, *Century of Struggle: The Women's Rights Movement in the United States* (1959); Elisabeth Griffith, *In Her Own Right: The Life of Elizabeth Cady Stanton* (1984); J. Rogers Hollingsworth, *The Whirligig of Politics: The Democracy of Cleveland and Bryan* (1963); Ari A. Hoogenboom, *Outlawing the Spoils: The Civil Service Movement* (1961); Richard J. Jensen, *The Winning of the Midwest* (1971); David M. Jordan, *Roscoe Conkling of New York* (1971); Matthew Josephson, *The Politicos* (1938); Morton Keller, *Affairs of State* (1977); Paul Kleppner, *The Third Electoral System, 1853–1892* (1979); Paul Kleppner, *The Cross of Culture* (1970); Michael E. McGerr, *The Decline of Popular Politics* (1986); Robert D. Marcus, *Grand Old Party* (1971); Walter T. K. Nugent, *Money and American Society* (1968); A. M. Paul, *Conservative Crisis and the Rule of Law: Attitudes of Bar and Bench, 1887–1895* (1969); David J. Rothman, *Politics and Power: The United States Senate, 1869–1901* (1966); John G. Sproat, *The Best Men: Liberal Reformers in the Gilded Age* (1968).

The Presidency

Kenneth E. Davison, *The Presidency of Rutherford B. Hayes* (1972); Lewis L. Gould, *The Presidency of William McKinley* (1981); Margaret Leech and Harry J. Brown, *The Garfield Orbit* (1978); Horace Samuel Merrill, *Bourbon Leader: Grover Cleveland and the Democratic Party* (1957); H. Wayne Morgan, *William McKinley and His America* (1963); Allan Peskin, *Garfield* (1978); Thomas C. Reeves, *Gentleman Boss: The Life of Chester Alan Arthur* (1975); H. J. Sievers, *Benjamin Harrison,* 3 vols. (1952–1968).

Currents of Protest

William M. Dick, *Labor and Socialism in America* (1972); John P. Diggins, *The American Left in the Twentieth Century* (1973); Ray Ginger, *Bending Cross: A Biography of Eugene Victor Debs* (1969); John Laslett, *Labor and the Left* (1970); Nick Salvatore, *Eugene V. Debs: Citizen and Socialist* (1982); Carlos A. Schwantes, *Coxey's Army* (1985); David Shannon, *The Socialist Party of America* (1955).

Populism and the Election of 1896

Peter H. Argersinger, *Populism and Politics: William Alfred Peffer and the People's Party* (1974); Paolo Coletta, *William Jennings Bryan: Political Evangelist* (1964); Paul W. Glad, *McKinley, Bryan, and the People* (1964); Paul W. Glad, *The Trumpet Soundeth: William Jennings Bryan and His Democracy* (1964); Lawrence Goodwyn, *Democratic Promise: The Populist Moment in America* (1976); Sheldon Hackney, *Populism to Progressivism in Alabama* (1969); Steven Hahn, *The Roots of Southern Populism* (1983); John D. Hicks, *The Populist Revolt* (1931); Richard Hofstadter, *The Age of Reform: From Bryan to FDR* (1955); Stanley L. Jones, *The Election of 1896* (1964); J. Morgan Kousser, *The Shaping of Southern Politics* (1974); Walter T. K. Nugent, *The Tolerant Populists* (1963); Norman Pollack, *The Populist Response to Industrial America* (1962); Allan Weinstein, *Prelude to Populism: Origins of the Silver Issue* (1970); C. Vann Woodward, *Tom Watson* (1938).

Thomas Edison, of all people, would have known if something was not working properly. He perfected and promoted so many items of modern mass technology—the light bulb, phonograph, and motion-picture projector, among others—that he had good reason to view his world optimistically. But he did not. With the perceptiveness of a good inventor, Edison found American society flawed and perplexing. Writing to his friend Henry Ford in 1912, Edison observed that

> in a lot of respects we Americans are the rawest and crudest of all. Our production, our factory laws, our charities, our relations between capital and labor, our distribution—all wrong, out of gear. We've stumbled along for a while, trying to run a new civilization in old ways, but we've got to start to make this world over.

21

THE PROGRESSIVE ERA, 1895–1920

Americans had always been preoccupied with reforming their society, with "making it over," and between the 1890s and the end of the First World War, the reform spirit intensified. More and more people tried to address the problems of their time directly, to impose order on a confusing world, and, especially, to create a conflict-free society. Their efforts, inspired by a complicated mixture of calculated self-interest and unselfish benevolence, shaped what can be called the Progressive era.

During the 1890s, a severe depression, frightening labor violence, political upheaval (see Chapter 20), and foreign entanglements (see Chapter 22) shook the nation. Although many promises of technology had been fulfilled, great numbers of Americans continued to suffer from poverty and disease. In the minds of many, industrialists had become monsters, controlling markets, wages, and prices in order to maximize profits. Government seemed corroded by bosses and their henchmen, who used politics to enrich themselves rather than address critical problems. Society seemed to be fragmenting into little bits as conflicts created by urbanization and industrialization multiplied.

At the same time, however, there was cause for optimism. The fervor caused by Populism had died down; the economic depression seemed to be over; the nation had just completed a victorious war (see Chapter 23); and a new political age symbolized by

Teddy Roosevelt campaigning for president, summer of 1912. Oil over photograph. *The Granger Collection.*

dynamic leaders such as Theodore Roosevelt and Woodrow Wilson was dawning. This environment served both to heighten concern over continuing social and political problems and to raise hopes that the problems could be fixed.

From this environment emerged a broad, complex reform campaign, so many-sided that to identify its unifying characteristics is hard. By the 1910s many reformers were calling themselves progressives, and a new political party by that name had formed to embody their principles. Since that time historians have used the term *progressivism* to refer to the reform spirit in general, while disagreeing over the movement's meaning and membership. The era between 1895 and 1920 can nonetheless be characterized by a series of movements, each aimed in one way or another at renovating or restoring American society, its values, and its institutions.

The urge for reform had many sources. Industrialization had brought unprecedented productivity, awesome technology, and a cornucopia of consumer goods. But it had also included labor strife, waste of natural resources, and abuse of corporate power. Rapidly growing cities facilitated the amassing and distribution of goods, services, and cultural amenities but also magnified problems of poverty, disease, crime, and political corruption. Massive influxes of immigrants and the rise of a new class of managers and professionals shook the foundations of old social classes. And the depression that crippled the nation in the 1890s made many leading citizens realize what working people had known for some time: the central promise of American life was not being kept; equality of opportunity—whether economic, political, or social—was a myth.

Progressives tried to surmount these problems by organizing ideas and actions around three basic themes. First, they sought to end abuses of power. Attacks on unfair privilege, monopoly, and corruption were not new in 1900; Jacksonian reformers of the 1830s and 1840s (see Chapter 12) and Populists of the 1890s (see Chapter 20) are only two of many examples of such a tradition. In the Progressive era, however, the attacks became more strenuous. Trustbusting, consumers' rights, and good government became vital political issues.

Second, progressives aimed to supplant corrupt power with the power of reformed institutions such as schools, charities, medical clinics, and the family. Although they wanted to protect individual rights, they abandoned old individualistic assumptions such as the notion that hard work and good character automatically assured success and that the poor had only themselves to blame for their plight. Instead, progressives acknowledged that society and its institutions had power to help or harm the individual, and they believed they must provide opportunity for everyone. Their revolt against unchanging categories of thought challenged, but often failed to change, entrenched attitudes toward women's role, race relations, public education, legal and scientific thought, and morality.

Third, progressives wanted to apply principles of science and efficiency on a nationwide scale to all economic, social, and political institutions. Their aim was to minimize social and economic disorder and to establish cooperation, especially between business and government, that would end wasteful competition and labor conflict.

Befitting their name, progressives had strong faith in the ability of humankind to create a better world. They often used such phrases as "humanity's universal growth" and "the upward spiral of human development." Judge Ben Lindsey of Denver, who spearheaded reform in the treatment of juvenile delinquents, expressed the progressive creed when he wrote, "In the end the people are bound to do the right thing, no matter how much they fail at times." More than ever before, Americans looked to government as an agent of the people that could and should intervene in social and economic relations to protect the common good and substitute public interest for self-interest.

The Progressives

The Progressive era emerged out of the new political atmosphere that formed after the tumultuous election of 1896 (see pages 599–601) and the issues raised by urban reformers in the previous half-century (see pages 546–549). As the twentieth century dawned, the loyalty that political parties had once commanded eroded, and voter turnouts declined. In presidential elections, voter participation dropped from Gilded Age levels of over 80 percent of the eligible electorate to almost 60 percent in northern states and under 30 percent in southern

IMPORTANT EVENTS

1893	Anti-Saloon League founded
1895	Booker T. Washington's Atlanta Compromise speech
1898	*Holden* v. *Hardy*
1900	McKinley re-elected
1901	McKinley assassinated; Roosevelt assumes the presidency
1903	Elkins Act
1904	*Northern Securities* case Roosevelt elected president
1905	Niagara Falls Convention *Lochner* v. *New York*
1906	Hepburn Act Pure Food and Drug Act
1907	Economic panic
1908	Taft elected president *Muller* v. *Oregon*
1909	NAACP founded Payne-Aldrich Tariff
1910	White Slave Traffic Act Ballinger-Pinchot controversy
1912	Roosevelt runs for president on the Progressive (Bull Moose) ticket Wilson elected president
1913	Sixteenth and Seventeenth Amendments ratified Underwood Tariff Federal Reserve Act
1914	Federal Trade Commission Act Clayton Anti-Trust Act Sanger indicted
1916	Wilson re-elected Federal Farm Loan Act
1919	Eighteenth Amendment ratified
1920	Nineteenth Amendment ratified

states, where blacks had been excluded from the polls. Parties and elections, it seemed, were losing their function of providing Americans with a means of influencing government policies.

The political system was opening up to various and shifting interest groups, each of which championed its own brand of reform. Voluntary associations had been common to local

> **Issues of Reform**

life since the 1790s, but after the 1890s many organizations became nationwide in scope and tried to shape government policy. These organizations included professional associations, such as the American Bar Association; women's organizations, such as the National American Woman Suffrage Association; issue-oriented lobbies, such as the National Consumers League; civic clubs, such as the National Municipal League; and associations oriented toward minority groups, such as the National Negro Business League, the Society of American Indians, and the Association for the Study of Negro Life and History. Members of these organizations hoped to advance their own interests and to educate others about their goals. They made politics much more fragmented and issue-focused than in earlier eras.

Although ideas of moral regeneration, political democracy, and antimonopolism lingered from the rural-based Populist movement, prevailing issues of the Progressive era were mostly urban. The progressive quest for social justice, educational and legal reform, and streamlining of government actually extended urban-reform goals of the previous half-century. Between 1890 and 1920 the proportion of the nation's population living in cities rose from 35 percent to over 51 percent; the number of places with fifty thousand or more people rose

The Progressives ▶ 607

Judge Ben Lindsey (1869–1943) of Denver was a progressive reformer who worked for better legal protection for children. Typical of many reformers of his era, Lindsey had an earnest faith in the ability of humankind to build a better world. *Library of Congress.*

from 58 to 144. Recognition of the consequences of such changes, plus easier communications by mail, telephone, and telegraph, stimulated urban reformers to exchange information and consolidate their efforts. Formation of the National Municipal League in 1895 and the National Civic Federation in 1900 signaled the beginning of the new reform era. The National Municipal League served as a forum for debates on civic reform issues such as patronage versus civil service, nonpartisan elections, and municipal ownership of public utilities. The National Civic Federation broadened discussion of social reforms, such as workers' compensation and arbitration of labor disputes.

Organizations and individuals who accepted the three progressive themes—opposition to abuse of power, reform of social institutions, quest for cooperation and scientific efficiency—existed in almost all levels of society. The new middle class, men and women in the professions of law, medicine, social work, religion, teaching, and business, formed the vanguard of reform. Offended by inefficiency and immorality in business, government, and human

relations, these people set out to apply scientific techniques they had learned in their professions to problems of the larger society.

Many middle-class progressive reformers were motivated by personal indignation at corruption and injustice and felt frustrated by abusers of power. This feeling was voiced by journalists whom Theodore Roosevelt dubbed *muckrakers* (alluding to a character in John Bunyan's *Pilgrim's Progress* who rejected a crown for a muckrake). These writers, unlike journalists who merely reported events, fed the public's taste for scandal and sensation by investigating and attacking social, economic, and political wrongs. Their fact-filled articles in *McClure's, Cosmopolitan,* and other popular magazines, as well as books, exposed such offenses as the sale of tainted meat, fraudulent insurance, and prostitution. Lincoln Steffens's articles in *McClure's,* later published as *The Shame of the Cities* (1904), ranked among the highlights of muckraker journalism. Steffens hoped his surveys of bosses' misrule would inspire mass outrage and, ultimately, reform. Other well-known muckraking efforts included Upton Sinclair's *The Jungle* (1906), a novel that attacked the meat-packing industry, Ida M. Tarbell's scathing history of Standard Oil (1904), Burton J. Hendrick's *Story of Life Insurance* (1907), and David Graham Phillips's *Treason of the Senate* (1906).

Middle-class indignation also revealed itself in opposition to party politics, a reflection of the interest-group political system that arose in the 1890s. Male political reformers (women could not vote and therefore were seldom involved in these discussions) had distaste for the bargaining and self-serving that they believed infected boss-ridden parties. They felt, as journalist William Allen White did, that machines and bosses should "be reduced to mere political scrap iron by the rise of the people." When reformers referred to "the people," however, they all too often meant middle-class people like themselves, excluding the white native-born working class, blacks, and immigrants. To improve the political process, these progressives advocated such reforms as nominating candidates through direct primaries instead of party caucuses and nonpartisan elections to prevent the fraud and bribery bred by party loyalties.

> **Political Reformers**

To involve more people and make legislators more responsible, they advocated three reform devices: the initiative, which would enable voters to propose new laws on their own; the referendum, which would enable voters to accept or reject a law; and the recall, which would allow voters to remove officials and judges from office before their terms were up. Their goal, like that of the business consolidation movement, was efficiency. Government would be reclaimed by replacing the favoritism of the boss system with rational, accountable management chosen by a responsible electorate.

Middle-class progressive reformers recoiled from party politics, not from government. They turned to government for aid in achieving most of their goals, for they were convinced that only government offered them the leverage they needed. Members of professions in which systematic investigation and efficient management were paramount also agreed with muckrakers that knowledge was the key to progress. Science and scientific method—planning, control, predictability—were central to their values. Just as corporations were applying scientific management to achieve economic efficiency (see page 502), progressives used expertise and planning to achieve social and political efficiency.

Progressive spirit also stirred some elite business leaders. Successful executives like Alexander Cassatt of the Pennsylvania Railroad supported some government regulation and political reforms to protect their interests from more radical political elements. Others, like E. A. Filene, founder of a Boston department store, and Thomas L. Johnson, wealthy streetcar magnate, were humanitarians who worked unselfishly for social justice. Business leaders guided organizations like the Municipal Voters League and U.S. Chamber of Commerce, which supported limited political and economic reform. They aimed to stabilize society by organizing schools, hospitals, and local government like efficient businesses. Women of elite classes often led reform organizations like the YWCA, which sponsored aid and education for growing numbers of unmarried working women who had moved away from their families, and the Women's Christian Temperance Union, the largest women's organization of its time, which participated in numerous causes besides those linked with drinking.

> **Upper-Class Reformers**

Not all progressive reformers had middle- or upper-class standing. During this era vital elements of what would become modern American liberalism grew out of the working-class urban experience. By 1900, many urban workers were pressing for government intervention to ensure safety and promote welfare. They wanted improvements in housing and health, safe factories, shorter working hours, workers' compensation, and other "bread and butter" reforms. Often these were the very people who were or who supported political bosses, supposedly the enemies of reform. Workers knew that bosses needed to cultivate support among their constituents and would cater to everyday needs. In fact bossism was not necessarily at odds with humanitarianism. Thus when "Big Tim" Sullivan, a boss in New York City's Tammany Hall political machine, was asked why he supported a law requiring shorter working hours for women, he explained, "I had seen me sister go out to work when she was only fourteen and I know we ought to help these gals by giving 'em a law which will prevent 'em from being broken down while they're still young."

> **Working-Class Reformers**

After 1900, voters from inner-city districts populated by working-class families elected a number of progressive legislators who had trained in the arena of machine politics. People like New York's Alfred E. Smith and Robert F. Wagner, Massachusetts's David I. Walsh, and Illinois's Edward F. Dunne—all of whom came from immigrant backgrounds—became important reform spokesmen at state and national levels. They were most successful when they allied with other reformers to pass laws aiding labor and social welfare. The chief goal of these legislators was to establish government responsibility for alleviating hardship that resulted from urban-industrial growth. They opposed such reforms as prohibition, Sunday closing laws, civil service, and nonpartisan elections, all of which conflicted with their constituents' interests.

Some deeply frustrated workers wanted more than progressive reform. They wanted a different society. These people turned to the socialist movement, a blend of immigrant intellectuals, industrial workers, disaffected Populists, and western miners and lumbermen. Some factions had more impact than others. The radical union known as the Industrial Workers of the World—the IWW, or "Wobblies" (see page 518)—organized strife-torn strikes in western lumber and mining camps, in the steel town of McKees Rocks, Pennsylvania (1907), and in the textile mills of Lawrence, Massachusetts (1912). Led by former miner "Big Bill" Haywood, along with charismatic seventy-five-year-old "Mother" Jones and the young radical Elizabeth Gurley Flynn, the IWW reached out to unskilled laborers, promising to unite all workers by enabling them to control their own factories. IWW membership probably never exceeded 150,000, however, and the organization faded during the First World War when federal prosecution—and persecution—sent many of its leaders to jail.

Socialists

The majority of socialists united behind Eugene V. Debs (see page 595), the tall, dynamic railroad organizer who drew nearly 100,000 votes in the 1900 presidential election. Although Debs was never able to develop a consistent program beyond opposition to war and bourgeois materialism, he was a spellbinding speaker for the radical cause. His speaking tours touched increasing numbers of disenchanted workers and intellectuals. As a candidate for the Socialist party, Debs won 400,000 votes for the presidency in 1904, and in 1912, at the pinnacle of his and his party's career, he polled over 900,000.

With stinging rebukes of exploitation and unfair privilege, Debs and other socialists like Milwaukee's Victor Berger and New York's Morris Hillquit made attractive overtures to reform-minded people. Some, such as settlement-house worker and child-labor reformer Florence Kelley, joined the socialist cause. But most progressives avoided radical attacks on free enterprise. Municipal ownership of public utilities was as far as they would go toward changing the system. Indeed, progressives had too much at stake in the capitalist system to overthrow it. Thus even in Wisconsin, where progressivism was most highly developed, progressives would not join with Berger's more radical group. California progressives even formed a temporary alliance with reactionaries to prevent socialists from gaining power in Los Angeles. And few humanitarian reformers objected when in 1918 Debs was jailed for giving an antiwar speech.

It would be a mistake to assume that a progressive spirit touched all of American society between 1895 and 1920. Large numbers of people, heavily represented in Congress, disliked government interference in economic affairs—except when it strengthened the tariff—and saw nothing wrong with existing power structures. In Washington, "old-guard" Republicans like Senator Nelson W. Aldrich of Rhode Island and House Speaker Joseph Cannon of Illinois championed this ideology. Outside government, this outlook was represented by big business leaders like J. P. Morgan, John D. Rockefeller, and E. H. Harriman, and by countless other capitalists who insisted that real progress would result from maintaining the profit incentive.

Progressive reformers operated from the center of the ideological spectrum. Moderate, concerned, sometimes contradictory, they believed on the one hand that the laissez-faire system was obsolete and on the other that a radical shift away from the fundamentals of capitalism was dangerous. Like Jeffersonians, they believed in the conscience and will of the people; like Hamiltonians, they opted for a strong central government to act in the interest of conscience. The goals of progressive reformers were both idealistic and realistic. As minister-reformer Walter Rauschenbusch wrote, "We shall demand perfection and never expect to get it."

Though their objectives sometimes differed from those of middle-class progressive reformers, socialists also became a more active group in the early nineteenth century. Socialist parades on May Day, such as this one in 1910, were meant to express the solidarity of all working people. *Library of Congress.*

Governmental and Legislative Reform

What were the responsibilities of government? Answers to this question in the early twentieth century were much different from those of the previous century. Because the United States had been born from mistrust of government authority, theorists traditionally had held that democratic government should be small and unobtrusive, interfering in private affairs only in unique circumstances and withdrawing once balance had been restored. In the late 1800s this conception weakened. Corporations pursued government aid and protection for their enterprises. Discontented farmers organized to seek government regulation of railroads and other monopolistic businesses. City dwellers, accustomed to favors furnished by political machines,

came to expect government to act positively on their behalf.

By the turn of the century, professionals and intellectuals were accepting the notion that government could and should exert more power to ensure justice and well-being. They were becoming convinced that a simple, inflexible government was ineffective in a complex industrial age and that public power was needed to counteract inefficiency, corruption, and exploitation. But before reformers could effectively use such power, they would have to capture government from politicians whose greed had soiled the democratic system. Thus an important thrust of progressive activity was the effort to remove corruption from government.

Reformers first attacked this problem in cities (see pages 546–549). Between 1870 and 1900, opponents of the boss system tried to recast government through structural reforms such as civil service, nonpartisan elections, and tighter scrutiny of public expenditures. A few reform leaders ac-

Robert M. La Follette (1855–1925) was one of the most dynamic of progressive politicians. As governor of Wisconsin, he sponsored a program of political reform and business regulation known as the Wisconsin Plan. In 1906 he entered the U.S. Senate and continued to champion progressive reform. The National Progressive Republican League, which La Follette founded in 1911, became the core of the Progressive Party. *Library of Congress.*

tively supported poverty relief, housing improvement, and prolabor laws. But most worked chiefly for efficient—meaning economical—government. After 1900 reform momentum brought into being city manager and city commission forms of government (in which urban officials were chosen for their professional expertise, not their political connections) and public ownership of utilities (to prevent gas, electric, telephone, and streetcar companies from profiting at the public's expense and to contain these companies' monopoly power).

Reformers discovered, however, that the city was too small an arena for the changes they sought. State and federal governments offered more promising opportunities for effecting reform through legislation. Because of their faith in a strong, fair-minded executive, progressives looked to governors and other elected officials to extend and protect reforms that had been achieved at the local level. Reformers' goals varied from one region or state to another. In the Plains and Far West, they rallied behind railroad regulation and such governmental reforms as the initiative and referendum. In the South they continued the Populist crusade against big business and autocratic politicians. In the urban-industrial Northeast and Midwest, reformers directed attention to corrupt political machines and unsafe labor conditions.

The reform movement produced a number of skillful, influential, and in some instances charismatic governors who used executive power to achieve change. Their ranks included Braxton Bragg Comer of Alabama and Hoke Smith of Georgia, who introduced business regulations and other reforms in the South; Albert Cummins of Iowa and Hiram Johnson of California, who battled railroads that dominated their states; and Woodrow Wilson of New Jersey, whose administrative reforms were copied by other governors. Such men were not saints, however. Smith supported disfranchisement of blacks, and Johnson worsened discrimination against Japanese-Americans.

▶ **Progressive Governors**

The most notable progressive governor was Wisconsin's Robert M. La Follette. A self-made, small-town lawyer whose short, compact build and thick, bristling hair suited his combative personality, La Follette rose through the ranks of the state Republican party to the governorship in 1900. As governor he initiated a multipronged reform program that included direct primaries, more equitable taxes, and regulation of railroad rates. He also established commissions staffed with experts, whose investigations supplied La Follette with facts and figures that he used in fiery speeches to muster public support for his policies. After three terms as governor, La Follette was elected senator and carried his progressive ideals into national politics. "Fighting Bob" had a rare ability to take a tempered, scientific approach to reform while still appealing to the people with moving rhetoric. His goal, he once asserted, "was not to 'smash' corporations, but to drive them out of politics, and then to treat them exactly the same as other people are treated."

Not all state leaders were as successful as La Follette. To be sure, the crusade against party politics and corruption did accomplish some permanent changes. By 1916 all but three states had direct primaries, and many states had adopted the initiative, referendum, and recall. Political reformers achieved a major goal in 1912 when the states ratified the Seventeenth Amendment, which provided for the direct election of United States senators (formerly elected by state legislatures, which often were corrupted by private interests). But political reforms did not always bring about desired results. Party bosses, better organized and more experienced than reformers, were still able to control elections. The initiative, referendum, and recall often failed because special-interest groups could influence outcomes by using large funds to lobby the public and organize the voting. Moreover, political reformers found that the courts aided entrenched power in stifling change.

New state laws aimed at bettering social welfare had greater impact than political reforms, especially in factories. Broadly interpreting their powers

> **Progressive Legislation**

to protect the health and safety of their citizens, many states enacted factory inspection laws, and by 1916 nearly two-thirds of the states required compensation for most victims of industrial accidents. A coalition of labor and humanitarian groups supported these laws and even induced some legislatures to grant aid to mothers with dependent children. Under pressure from the National Child Labor Committee, nearly every state set a minimum age for employment (varying from twelve to sixteen) and prohibited employers from working children more than eight or ten hours a day. Such laws, however, were hard to enforce because they seldom provided for the close inspection of factories that full enforcement required. Also, families that needed extra income encouraged their children to work and to lie about their ages. Several groups also joined forces to limit working hours for women. After the Supreme Court upheld Oregon's ten-hour limit in 1908, many more states passed laws protecting female workers. And efforts of the American Association for Old Age Security began to succeed in 1914, when Arizona established old-age pensions. The courts struck down the law, but interest in pensions remained, and in the 1920s many states enacted laws to provide for needy elderly people.

Defenders of laissez faire and free enterprise opposed most of the new regulatory measures. They were motivated by self-interest or a belief that such government programs undermined individual initiative and responsibility, which they believed to be the basis of the free market system. Government interference, they contended, also contradicted natural law—survival of the fittest. The National Association of Manufacturers coordinated the battle

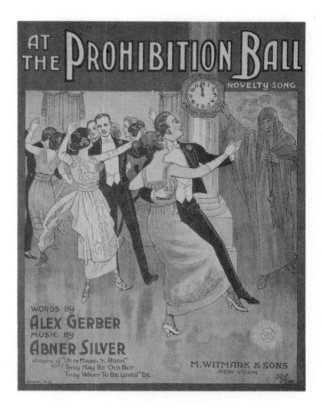

Though not supported by all progressive reformers, the constitutional amendment prohibiting the manufacture, sale, and transportation of alcoholic beverages (Eighteenth Amendment) was passed during the progressive era. The measure was intended to uplift morality and protect health. Social satirists exaggerated the belief that no fun could be had after prohibition went into effect. This sheet music cover from 1919 shows party-goers trying to squeeze in one last minute before the new law would take effect at midnight. *Sheet Music Collection, The John Hay Library, Brown University. Photo by Brooke Hammerle.*

against regulation of business and working conditions. Legislators friendly to special interests connived to weaken new laws by failing to fund their enforcement.

Reformers themselves were not always certain about what was progressive, especially in human behavior. The main problem seemed to be whether

> **Moral Reform**

it was possible to create a desirable moral climate through legislation. Some reformers, such as members of the Social Gospel movement (see page 547), believed that only church-based inspiration and humanitarian work, rather than legislation, could transform society.

In addition to their crusade against drunkenness, moral reformers stirred up emotions over accusations that evil men were seducing innocent young women into prostitution—or white slavery, as it was called. In this posed photograph printed in a 1910 antivice publication, *The White Slave Hell: or, With Christ at Midnight in the Slums of Chicago*, the man has supposedly gotten the woman drunk and is about to lure her into a life of sin. *Collection of Perry R. Duis. From* The Saloon.

Other people believed that state intervention was necessary to achieve purity, especially in drinking habits and sexual behavior.

Formation of the Anti-Saloon League in 1893 marked a new turn in the long campaign against drunkenness and its effects on society. This organization joined with the Women's Christian Temperance Union (founded in 1873) to publicize the fact that alcoholism caused liver disease and other health problems. The League was especially successful in shifting the focus away from individual responsibility for temperance to the saloon and the alleged link between the drinking that saloons encouraged and the accidents, poverty, and threat to industrial productivity that were consequences of drinking.

The war against saloons prompted a large number of states, counties, towns, and city wards to restrict the sale and consumption of liquor. By 1900 almost one-fourth of the nation's population lived in communities with such restrictions. But as consumption of alcohol, especially beer, increased after 1900, reformers became convinced that a national law was the only solution. By 1917 they had converted to their cause such notables as Supreme Court Justice Louis D. Brandeis and former president William Howard Taft. In 1918 they induced Congress to pass the Eighteenth Amendment (ratified in 1919 and implemented in 1920), prohibiting the manufacture, sale, and transportation of intoxicating liquors. Not all prohibitionists were progressive reformers, and not all progressives were prohibitionists. Yet the Eighteenth Amendment can be seen as an outcome of the progressive urge to change society and elevate morality through reform legislation.

Public outrage seethed after 1900 when muckraking journalists exposed interstate and international rings that kidnaped young women and forced them to become prostitutes, a practice called white slavery. Middle-class moralists, already alarmed by a perceived link between immigration and prostitution, prodded governments to investigate the problem and recommend corrective legislation. The Chicago Vice Commission, for example, undertook a "scientific" survey and published its findings, called *The Social Evil in Chicago,* in 1911. The report underscored the poverty, ignorance, and desperation that drove women, especially immigrants and blacks, to prostitution. Above all, however, it asserted that

> it is a man and not a woman problem which we face today—commercialized by men—supported by men—the supply of fresh victims furnished by men. . . . So long as there is lust in the hearts of men [the Social Evil] will seek out some method of expression. Until the hearts of men are changed we can hope for no absolute annihilation of the Social Evil.

Investigations such as the Chicago study showed that there seemed to be rising numbers of prostitutes, but they failed to prove that organized rings of men deliberately entrapped young women into prostitution. It appears, rather, that women were making their own choices to enter "the life," choices that not only reflected their own economic needs but also made moralists concerned about the alleged dangers of young women's sexuality, especially when it was channeled in the wrong way. Reformers nonetheless believed they could attack prostitution by punishing those who promoted it. In 1910 Congress passed the Mann, or White Slave Traffic, Act, prohibiting interstate and international transportation of women for immoral purposes. By 1915 nearly every state had outlawed brothels and the soliciting of sex.

Like prohibition, the Mann Act reflected growing sentiment that state and national governments could improve human behavior by restricting it. Reformers believed that the source of evil was not original sin but the social environment. If evil were human-made, then it could be human-destroyed. Thus human intervention, in the form of laws, could help create a heaven on earth.

New Ideas in Education, Law, and the Social Sciences

While legislation anchored the reform impulse, equally important changes were occurring in schools, courts, and settlement houses. Preoccupation with efficiency and scientific management challenged educators, judges, and social scientists to solve problems of modern mass society. Darwin's theory of evolution had upset traditional beliefs in a God-created world; immigration had replaced social uniformity with diverse nationalities; and technology had shaken old habits of production and consumption. Ways of thinking and acting had to be found that would be meaningful for the new era yet preserve what was best from the past.

Changing patterns of school attendance encouraged new ways of thinking. As late as the 1870s, when rural families needed children to do farm work and schools were located far apart, Americans attended school for an average of only four years. By 1900, however, swelling cities contained multitudes of children who were removed from farm work and had more time for school. Also, urban taxpayers were providing revenues to make extended mass education possible. Boosted by compulsory-attendance laws, enrollments in public schools rose from 6.9 million in 1870 to 17.8 million in 1910. During the same period the number of public high schools grew from five hundred to over ten thousand.

Reformers had long envisioned education as a means of bettering society. In 1883, psychologist G. Stanley Hall, whose ideas strongly influenced John Dewey, noted that the experi-

Progressive Education ences of modern urban schoolchildren differed greatly from those of their farm-bred parents and grandparents. In the early nineteenth century, school curricula chiefly taught moralistic pieties. *McGuffey's Reader,* used throughout the nation, contained homilies such as "By virtue we secure happiness" and "One deed of shame is succeeded by years of penitence." Hall and Dewey, however, asserted that modern education had to prepare children for productive citizenship and self-fulfilling lives. The child, not subject matter, should be the focus of school policy, and schools should serve as community centers and instruments of social progress. Above all, said Dewey, education must relate directly to experience. Children should be encouraged to discover for themselves. Knowledge relevant to students' lives should replace rote memorization and outdated subjects.

Progressive education, based on Dewey's theories in *The School and Society* (1899) and *Democracy and Education* (1916), was a uniquely American phenomenon. Like American economic theory, it emphasized growth. To Dewey, personal growth, not mastery of a given body of knowledge, was the goal of human existence. Because people grew fastest mentally in their youth, and because the family could no longer perform educational functions it had fulfilled in agrarian society, schools had to assume responsibility for cultivating intelligence and ingenuity. From kindergarten (pioneered by German educator Friedrich Froebel) through high school, children were supposed to learn through experience. In the Laboratory School that Dewey and his wife Alice directed at the University of Chicago, children examined, built, and discussed objects just as they would outside school.

Personal growth also became the driving principle behind college education. The purpose of American colleges and universities had traditionally been that of their Euro-

Growth of Colleges and Universities pean counterparts: to train a select few for the professions of law, medicine, teaching, and religion. But in the late 1800s, institutions of higher education multiplied, spurred by public aid and an increase in the number of people who

The objective of progressive education was to free children from the rigid classroom of the past, where pupils had to sit quietly at attention, and enable them to learn by doing and making things. Rather than make the subject matter the major focus of the learning process, progressives made children the center of attention. *Library of Congress.*

could afford tuition. Between 1870 and 1910 the number of colleges and universities grew from 563 to nearly 1,000. Curricula expanded as educators sought to make learning attractive to more students and to keep up with technological and social changes. Harvard University, under President Charles W. Eliot, pioneered in substituting electives for required courses and experimenting with new teaching methods. Public universities, such as the University of Wisconsin, achieved distinction in new areas of study.

Much of the expansion in college enrollments, especially in the Midwest and West, was prompted by the Morrill Land Grant Act of 1862 (see pages 412 and 485). Land-grant colleges offered a wide variety of courses, ranging from classics and natural science to carpentry and farming. Many of these schools considered athletics vital to a student's growth, and intercollegiate sports became a central feature of student life as well as a source of school pride and alumni contributions. Southern states, in keeping with separate-but-equal policies, set up segregated land-grant colleges for blacks. *Separate*

was more descriptive of these institutions than *equal,* however. Blacks continued to suffer inferior educational opportunities in the few state institutions and in many of the private, all-black colleges that existed throughout the South.

As colleges and universities expanded, so did the enrollment of women. Between 1890 and 1910 the number of females enrolled in institutions of higher learning swelled from 56,000 to 140,000. By the latter date, 106,000 women attended coeducational institutions (many of which were state universities aided by the Morrill Act); the rest attended women's colleges. By 1920, 283,000 women attended college, accounting for 47.3 percent of total enrollment. Their numbers disproved earlier objections that women were unfit for higher learning because they were mentally and physically inferior to men, but discrimination lingered in admissions and curriculum policies. Most women were encouraged (indeed, they usually sought) to take home economics courses rather than science and mathematics, and most medical schools, including Harvard and Yale, refused to admit women.

Chapter 21: The Progressive Era, 1895–1920

While they were developing new approaches to knowledge, American educators adopted the prevailing attitude of business: more is better. They justifiably congratulated themselves for drawing more people into schools and for making instruction more meaningful. By 1920, 78 percent of all children between ages five and seventeen were enrolled in public elementary and high schools; another 8 percent were in private and parochial schools. These figures represented a huge increase over the attendance rate of 1870. And there were 600,000 college and graduate students in 1920, compared with 52,000 in 1870. Yet few people looked beyond the numbers to assess how well schools were doing their job. The faith that schools could promote equality and justice as well as personal growth and responsible citizenship underwent little critical analysis.

Law, like education, exhibited new emphases on experience and scientific principles. An influential proponent of the new point of view was Harvard

Progressive Legal Thought

scholar Roscoe Pound, whose writings urged that social experience should influence legal thinking. In practice, Oliver Wendell Holmes, Jr., associate justice of the Supreme Court between 1902 and 1932, led the attack on the view of law as universal and unchanging, like the Ten Commandments. "The life of the law," said Holmes, sounding like Dewey, "has not been logic; it has been experience." The view that law should reflect society's needs challenged the practice of invoking precedents in an inflexible way that often obstructed social legislation. Louis D. Brandeis, a brilliant lawyer who later joined Holmes on the Supreme Court, carried legal reform one step further by insisting that judges' opinions be based on factual, scientifically gathered information about social realities. In the landmark case *Muller* v. *Oregon* (1908), Brandeis mustered extensive scientific data showing the harmful effects of long hours to convince the Supreme Court to uphold Oregon's law limiting women's working hours.

New legal thought, however, met some resistance. Judges raised on laissez-faire economic theory continued to overturn the kind of law progressives thought necessary for effective reform. Thus in 1905 the Supreme Court revoked a New York law limiting bakers' working hours (*Lochner* v. *New York*) in spite of Holmes's forceful

dissent. As in other cases in which it struck down reform, the Court's majority argued that the Fourteenth Amendment protected an individual's right to make contracts without government interference and that this protection superseded reform sentiments. Also, judges weakened federal regulations by invoking the Tenth Amendment, which prohibited the federal government from interfering in matters reserved for state supervision. Thus the judiciary's use of constitutional principles governing freedom of contract and the division of government powers impeded reform.

The judiciary during the Progressive era was not entirely negative. Courts upheld some regulatory measures, particularly those affecting the safety of the general public. A string of decisions, beginning with *Holden* v. *Hardy* (1898) in which the Supreme Court upheld Utah's mining regulations, supported the use of state police powers to protect health, safety, and morals. Judges also recognized federal police powers and Congress's authority over interstate commerce in sustaining such federal legislation as the Pure Food and Drug Act, the Meat Inspection Law (see page 626), and the Mann Act (see page 615). In these instances citizen welfare took precedence over the Tenth Amendment.

Still, the concept of general welfare posed thorny legal problems. Even if one agreed that law should reflect society's needs, which part of society should be represented? The United States was a mixed nation, and religion and ethnicity deeply influenced law. In many places a native white Protestant majority required Bible reading in public schools (thereby offending Catholics and Jews), stipulated that business establishments close on Sundays, restricted the religious practices of Mormons and other groups, prohibited interracial marriage, and enforced racial segregation. Although Holmes asserted that laws should be made for "people of fundamentally differing views," were, or are, such laws possible in a nation of so many ethnic, racial, and religious interest groups?

At about the same time, social science—the study of society and its institutions—experienced changes like those overtaking law and education. In

Social Science

economics, for example, a group of young scholars used statistics to argue that laws governing economic relationships were not carved in stone. Instead, they claimed, economic theory should reflect prevailing social conditions.

Some of the most lasting progressive reforms were in the areas of health and welfare. Women often were in the vanguard of these movements. In this photograph, a member of the Visiting Nurses Association provides medical aid to the mother of an immigrant family. *Western Heritage Museum, Omaha, with permission of Visiting Nurses Association.*

Richard T. Ely of Johns Hopkins University and the University of Wisconsin, an early spokesman for this point of view, argued that opposition to government interference in social and economic affairs had been outmoded by industrialization. He believed that practical solutions to current problems should be derived through "the united efforts of Church, state, and science." A new breed of sociologists led by Lester Ward, Albion Small, and Edward A. Ross agreed, adding that citizens should engage in planning to cure social ills rather than passively waiting for problems to solve themselves. In the field of psychology, female researchers were challenging age-old beliefs that women's minds were different from, and inferior to, men's.

Meanwhile, progressive historians Frederick Jackson Turner, Charles A. Beard, and Vernon L. Parrington were examining the past as a means of explaining current issues in American society and motivating social change. Beard, for example, believed with other progressives that the American Constitution was a flexible document subject to growth and change, not the inviolable product of wise forefathers. His famous book, *Economic Interpretation of the Constitution* (1913), argued that a group of merchants and business-oriented lawyers had created the Constitution to defend private property; thus if it had served special interests in one age, it could be changed to serve broader interests in another age. Political scientists like Woodrow Wilson emphasized the practical over the theoretical, advocating expansion of government power as a means to ensure justice and progress. To some degree these new ideas inspired reformers to use government to confront the effects of industrialization and urbanization.

Social scientists joined with physicians and organizations such as the National Consumers League

National Consumers League and Public Health Reform

(NCL) to bring about some of the most far-reaching of progressive reforms: those in public health. Founded by Josephine Shaw, a socially prominent Massachusetts widow, the NCL initially worked to improve the wages and conditions of young women employed in department stores. After settlement worker Florence Kelley became NCL's general secretary, the organization expanded its activities to include women's suffrage, protection of child laborers, and removal of potential health hazards. Local branches supported such consumer protection measures as the licensing of food vendors and inspection of dairies. They also urged city governments to fund neighborhood clinics that provided health education and medical care to the poor. Their efforts spurred a movement for consumer and health awareness that has continued to the present.

Between the end of the nineteenth century and the First World War, a new breed of men and women pressed for institutional change as well as political reform. Largely middle-class in background, trained by new professional standards, confident that new ways of thinking would bring progress, these people helped to broaden government's role in meeting the needs of a mature industrial society. Their questioning extended beyond their immediate goals and jostled conventional attitudes toward race and gender.

Challenges to Racial and Sexual Discrimination

W. E. B. Du Bois, the forceful black scholar and teacher, ended an essay in his book *The Souls of Black Folk* (1903) with a call that heralded the twentieth-century civil rights movement: "By every civilized and peaceful method," he wrote, "we must striving for "the right which the world accords to men"—freedom and equality. The progressive

By "men" Du Bois meant all human beings, not just one sex. But his statement and its context suggest the dilemma that vexed the two largest groups of underprivileged Americans in the early 1900s: women and nonwhites. Both lived in a society dominated by white native-born males. Both suffered from disfranchisement, discrimination, and humiliation. And for centuries both groups had been striving for "the right which the world accords to men"—freedom and equality. The progressive challenge to old ideas and customs gave impetus to

blacks' and women's struggles for their rights, but it posed a dilemma as well. Should women and blacks strive to become just like white men, with white men's values and power as well as their rights? Or was there something unique about racial and sexual identity that should be retained at the risk of sacrificing some gains? Both groups wavered between accepting and rejecting the culture from which they had been excluded.

The problems of blacks in white American society remained regional in scope until well into the twentieth century, though important shifts were beginning to occur. In 1900 only one in ten blacks lived in the North. The rest lived in southern states, where repressive Jim Crow laws had multiplied in the 1880s and 1890s. Southern blacks were not only denied legal and voting rights but were officially segregated in almost all walks of life. They faced constant exclusion and violence. In 1910 only 8,000 out of 970,000 high-school-age blacks in the entire South were enrolled in high schools. Between 1900 and 1914 white mobs lynched over a thousand blacks.

Blacks began to migrate northward in the 1880s, accelerating their rate of departure after 1900. But job and housing discrimination, inferior schools, and segregated neighborhoods characterized northern as well as southern cities. White humanitarians contributed to discrimination by maintaining separate and inferior institutions for blacks, rather than integrating them with whites. A half-century after the abolition of slavery, most whites still agreed with historian James Ford Rhodes who said that blacks were "innately inferior and incapable of citizenship."

Black leaders differed over how—and whether —to achieve assimilation. In the wake of emancipation, ex-slave Frederick Douglass had urged "ultimate assimilation through self-assertion, and on no other terms." Other blacks, who favored isolation from cruel white society, supported migration back to Africa or establishment of all-black communities in Oklahoma Territory and Kansas. Still others advocated militancy. According to one black writer, "Our people must die to be saved and in dying must take as many along with them as it is possible to do with the aid of firearms and all other weapons."

Most blacks, however, could neither escape nor conquer white society. They had to find other routes to improvement. Self-help, a strategy ar-

This photograph shows black college students learning to operate cheese presses at Hampton Institute, in Virginia, a school like Tuskegee Institute which followed Booker T. Washington's philosophy that by acquiring skills and working hard, blacks could convince whites they were worthy of equal rights. Founded in 1870, Hampton was one of the first black colleges and also pioneered in education for Indians. *Collection, The Museum of Modern Art, New York. Gift of Lincoln Kirstein.*

Booker T. Washington

ticulated by educator Booker T. Washington, was one of the most popular alternatives. Born in 1856 to slave parents, Washington worked his way through school and in 1881 founded Tuskegee Institute in Alabama, a vocational school for blacks. There he developed the philosophy that blacks' hopes for assimilation lay in at least temporarily accommodating themselves to whites. Rather than fighting for political rights, he said, blacks should work hard, acquire property, and prove they were worthy of their rights. Washington voiced his views in a widely acclaimed speech at the Atlanta Exposition in 1895. "Dignify and glorify common labor," he urged in what became known as the Atlanta Compromise. "Agitation of questions of racial equality is the extremest folly." Envisioning a society where blacks and whites would remain apart but share the same goals, Washington observed that "in all things that are purely social we can be as separate as the fingers, yet one as the hand in all matters essential to mutual progress."

Whites, including progressives, welcomed Washington's policy of accommodation because it urged patience and reminded black people to stay in their place. White businesspeople, reformers, and politicians chose to regard Washington as representative of all blacks, because he said what they wanted to hear. Yet though Washington endorsed separate-but-equal policy, he projected a subtle racial pride that would find more direct expression in black nationalism later in the twentieth century, when some blacks would urge control of their own businesses and schools. Washington never argued that blacks were inferior to whites; he instead asserted that they could enhance their dignity through self-improvement.

But to some blacks Booker T. Washington seemed to favor second-class citizenship, which they considered degrading. It was a southern-based philosophy that did not attract northern, well-educated blacks, such as William Monroe Trotter, fiery editor of the *Boston Guardian,* and social scientist T. Thomas Fortune. In 1905 a group of "anti-Bookerites" convened near Niagara Falls and pledged a more militant pursuit of such rights as unrestricted voting, equal access to economic opportunity, integration, and equality before the law. Spokesperson for the Niagara movement was W. E. B. Du Bois, a vociferous critic of the Atlanta Compromise. A New Englander with a Ph.D. from Harvard, Du Bois blended the backgrounds of a progressive and a black elite. He had an undergraduate degree from all-black Fisk University and had studied in Germany, where he learned about scientific investigation. He returned to assume a faculty position at all-black Atlanta University. Du Bois used scientific methods to compile fact-filled sociological studies of black ghetto dwellers, and he wrote poetically for the cause of civil rights. Du Bois initially supported the Atlanta Compromise and treated Washington politely, but he could not accept submission to white domination. "The way for a people to gain their reasonable rights," Du Bois asserted, "is not by voluntarily throwing them away." Blacks needed, instead, to agitate for what was rightfully theirs.

W. E. B. Du Bois

Du Bois showed that accommodation was an unrealistic strategy, but his own solution may have been just as fanciful. A blunt elitist, Du Bois believed that an intellectual vanguard of cultivated, highly trained blacks, which he called the Talented Tenth, would save the race by setting an example to whites and uplifting other blacks. Such sentiment had more attraction for middle-class white liberals than for black sharecroppers. Thus when Du Bois and his allies formed the National Association for the Advancement of Colored People (1909), which aimed to use legal redress in the courts to end racial discrimination, the leadership consisted chiefly of white progressives. By 1914 the NAACP had fifty branch offices and over six thousand members, but rarely did its activities touch sharecropping and laboring families except in its fight against lynching in the South.

Whatever strategy they pursued—accommodation or agitation—black Americans faced continued oppression. In fact, those who managed to acquire property and education encountered increased resentment, especially when they fought openly for civil rights. Black editor and reformer Ida B. Wells, who wrote a book in support of anti-lynching legislation, suffered destruction of her property and threats against her life. The federal government only aggravated conditions. Under the administration of Woodrow Wilson, discrimination within the federal government expanded; southern cabinet members supported racial separation in rest rooms, restaurants, and offices of government buildings and balked at hiring black workers. Commenting on Wilson's racism in 1913, Booker T. Washington wrote, "I have never seen the colored people so discouraged and so bitter as they are at the present time." And disfranchisement, instituted by southern states in the late nineteenth century (see pages 597–598), still precluded blacks from becoming full American citizens. Booker T. Washington seemed to accept disfranchisement, hoping blacks would eventually regain the vote through education and hard work. Du Bois believed that suffrage was essential to protect blacks' social and economic rights.

Blacks still sought to fulfill the American dream of success, but many wondered whether membership in a corrupt white society should be part of their quest. Du Bois voiced these doubts poignantly, writing that "one ever feels his twoness—an American, a Negro, two souls, two thoughts, two unreconciled strivings, two warring ideals in one dark body." Somehow blacks would have to reconcile that "twoness" by combining racial pride with national identity. As Du Bois wrote in 1903, a black

> would not Africanize America, for America has too much to teach the world and Africa. He would not bleach his Negro soul in a flood of white Americanism, for he knows that Negro blood has a message for the world. He simply wishes to make it possible for a man to be both a Negro and an American.

That simple wish would haunt the nation for decades to come.

The dilemma of identity haunted Native Americans as well, but it had an added dimension of tribal loyalty. Since the 1880s, Native Americans had belonged to white-led Indian reform organizations, but in 1911 they formed their own association, the Society of American Indians (SAI), to advance their interests. The SAI consisted of educated, middle-class Indian men and women, though men held most leadership positions. The SAI worked for better education, civil rights, and healthcare. It also sponsored American Indian Days to cultivate native pride and offset Anglo images of Native Americans represented in Wild West shows.

The SAI's emphasis on racial pride, however, was squeezed between pressures for assimilation of Indians on the one side and tribal allegiance on the other. Its small membership had trouble representing the diverse and unconnected Indian peoples of America, and its attempt to establish a governing body in which all tribes were represented faltered. Some tribal governments no longer existed to select representatives, and most members of the SAI simply represented their own points of view. At the same time, the goal of achieving acceptance into white society proved elusive. Individual hard work always encountered white prejudice and patronizing, and attempts to redress grievances through legal action bogged down for lack of funds. Ultimately, the SAI had to rely on rhetoric and moral exhortation, which had little effect on poor and powerless Indians, who seldom knew the SAI even existed. Torn by doubts and internal disputes, the association folded in the early 1920s.

During this time, the progressive challenge to social relations also stirred women to seek liberation from the confines of hearth and home. Their struggle raised questions of identity that resembled those faced by blacks. What tactics should women use to achieve equality, and what should be their role in society? Writer Henry James summed up the dilemma inherent in such questions when he complained that women who wanted to become just like men were disregarding their own uniqueness. Could women achieve equality with men and at the same time change male-dominated society?

Answers involved a subtle but important shift in women's politics. Before about 1910, those engaged in the quest for women's rights referred to themselves as "the woman move-

"The Woman Movement" ment." This label characterized women striving to move beyond the home into social and welfare activities, higher education, and paid labor. Like some black and Indian leaders, they argued that legal and voting rights were needed to accompany such moves. These women's rights advocates based their claims on the theory that women's special, even superior, traits as guardians of morals and the family would humanize all of society. Settlement-house founder Jane Addams,

for example, supported women's suffrage by asking, "If women have in any sense been responsible for the gentler side of life which softens and blurs some of its harsher conditions, may not they have a duty to perform in our American cities?"

The women's club movement defined a particularly female dimension of progressive era reform. Originated as literary and educational organizations, women's clubs consisted of

Women's Clubs middle-class women who began entering public affairs in the late nineteenth century. Because they were excluded from office holding, these reformers were drawn less to efforts to revise government than to drives for social betterment, a concept called "social housekeeping." As governments began assuming functions formerly filled by women in households, families, and voluntary associations, they drew women into the political arena more than ever before. But rather than press for reforms such as trustbusting, nonpartisan elections, and direct primaries, women tended to work for goals such as factory inspection, regulation of children's and women's labor, housing reform, education improvement, and pure food and drug laws. Such efforts were not confined to white women. The National Association of Colored Women, founded in 1895, fourteen years ahead of the National Association of Colored People, was the nation's first black social service organization, establishing a variety of activities ranging from nurseries and kindergartens to retirement homes.

Around 1910, however, some of those concerned with women's place in society began using a new term to refer to their efforts: *feminism*.

Feminism Whereas members of the woman movement spoke of duties and moral purity, feminists spoke of rights and self-development because they were more explicitly conscious of their identity as women. Feminism, however, contained an inherent contradiction. On the one hand, feminists argued that all women should unite together in the struggle for rights because they had commonality: society and nature had made them different from men. On the other hand, feminists also insisted that sex-typing in society—treatment of women differently from men—must wither because it resulted in discrimination against women. Thus, feminists were saying that women should unite as a gender group in pursuit of ending all gender-based distinctions.

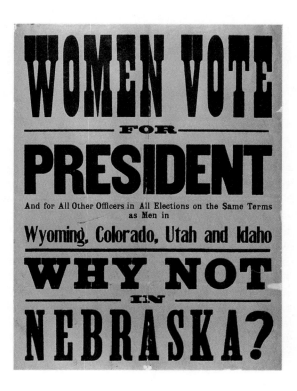

This women's suffrage flag shows stars for only those states in which women were allowed to vote. The poster from Nebraska was part of the propaganda used by one women's group in the campaign for the vote. *Flag: Museum of History and Technology, Smithsonian Institution; poster: Nebraska State Historical Society.*

Feminism focused especially on economic independence and sexual independence. In 1898, Charlotte Perkins Gilman previewed feminist goals in her book *Women and Economics*, declaring that domesticity and female innocence were obsolete and attacking male monopoly on economic opportunity. She argued that women must enter the modern age by taking paid jobs in industry and the professions and that domestic chores such as cooking, cleaning, and childcare should be handled by paid employees.

Feminists also supported what they called "sex rights," meaning a single sexual standard for men and women but also recognition of women's sexual drives. A number of them joined the birth-control movement led by Margaret Sanger. As a visiting nurse in New York's East Side immigrant neighborhoods, Sanger distributed information about contraception in hopes of preventing unwanted

pregnancies and their tragic consequences among poor women. Her crusade captured the attention of middle-class women who wanted to limit their own families and to control the growth of immigrant masses. It also roused opposition from men and women who saw birth-control as a threat to the family and morality. In 1914, foes caused Sanger to be indicted for sending obscene literature (articles on contraception) through the mails, forcing her to flee the country for a year. Sanger persevered and in 1921 formed the American Birth Control League, which enlisted physicians and social workers to convince judges to allow distribution of birth-control information. Most states still prohibited sale of contraceptives, but the issue had entered the realm of public discussion.

Feminist debates over work and class pervaded the suffrage movement, which achieved victory in 1920 when enough states ratified the Nineteenth

Amendment, giving women the vote in federal elections. Until the 1890s, the suffrage crusade was led by elite women who believed that the political system needed more representation from refined and educated persons, such as themselves, and that working-class women would defer to the betters of their sex on political matters. Elizabeth Cady Stanton, stalwart of the woman movement who long had fought for equality, voiced this viewpoint when she said that enfranchisement for "educated women" would best promote "woman's influence in public life."

But feminists, represented by Stanton's own daughter, Harriott Stanton Blatch, ardently opposed this logic. Blatch focused on work, saying that all women worked, whether it was paid labor or unpaid housework (though like Gilman she urged that women be paid for whatever work they did), and that all women's efforts contributed to society's betterment. To her, achievement rather than wealth and refinement was the major criterion for public influence. Thus women should have the vote not necessarily to increase the role of elites in public life but to promote and protect women's economic roles. This rationale, however, contained ambiguities. It implicitly (sometimes explicitly) advocated that all women work for pay, especially outside the home. But in doing so, it overlooked the exploitation of working-class women who already were in the labor force. The tension between the needs of middle- and upper-class women on the one hand and poor, laboring women on the other haunted the suffrage movement.

Regardless of theoretical arguments, suffragists achieved some successes. By 1912 nine states, all in the West, allowed women to vote in state and local elections, and women pressed increasingly for national suffrage. Tactics ranged from the moderate but persistent propaganda campaigns of the National American Woman Suffrage Association, led by Carrie Chapman Catt, to active picketing and marching by the National Woman's party, led by feminist Alice Paul. All these activities heightened public awareness. More decisive, however, was women's participation during the First World War as factory laborers, medical volunteers, and municipal workers (see pages 681–682). Their efforts convinced legislators that women could shoulder public responsibilities and gave final impetus to passage of the suffrage amendment.

All the activities by women's clubs, suffragists, and feminists failed to create an interest group united or powerful enough to dent political, economic, and social systems run by men. Like blacks, women knew that voting rights meant little until people's attitudes changed. The progressive era helped women to clarify issues that concerned them, but major reforms would await the future. As the feminist Crystal Eastman, echoing Du Bois, observed in the aftermath of the suffrage crusade,

> Men are saying perhaps, "Thank God, this everlasting women's fight is over!" But women, if I know them, are saying, "Now at last we can begin." . . . Now they can say what they are really after, in common with all the rest of the struggling world, is *freedom*.

Theodore Roosevelt and the Revival of the Presidency

The Progressive era's theme of reform—in politics, institutions, and social relations—drew attention to government, especially the federal government, as the foremost agent of change. At first, however, the federal government seemed incapable of assuming such responsibility. Dominated by two political parties that resembled private clubs more than bodies of impartial statesmen, the federal government acted mainly for special interests when it acted at all. Then suddenly, in September 1901, the climate changed. The assassination of President William McKinley by anarchist Leon Czolgosz vaulted Theodore Roosevelt, the young, vigorous vice president, into the White House.

Political manager Mark Hanna had warned fellow Republicans against nominating Roosevelt for the vice presidency in 1900. "Don't any of you realize," Hanna asked after the nominating convention, "that there's only one life between that madman and the Presidency?" As governor of New York, Roosevelt angered party bosses by showing sympathy for regulatory legislation, so Republican leaders rid themselves of their pariah by pushing him into national politics. Little did they realize that they were about to present the nation with its most forceful president since Lincoln, a man who would infuse the office with much of its twentieth-century character.

In marked contrast to his predecessors, Theodore Roosevelt lacked the dignified appearance of a president. He stood five-foot-nine but looked

> **Theodore Roosevelt**

shorter. Very nearsightedly, he was helpless without his metal-rimmed glasses. He had big, prominent teeth and talked in a high-pitched voice. As a youth he had suffered from asthma, yet throughout his life he was driven by an obsession to overcome his physical limitations and exert, in his public life as well as his private life, what he and his contemporaries called manliness. In his teens he practiced diligently to become an expert marksman and horseman. As a Harvard student he competed on boxing and wrestling teams. In the 1880s he went to live on a Dakota ranch, where he roped cattle and brawled with other cowboys.

Descendant of a Dutch aristocratic family, Roosevelt had wealth to indulge in such pursuits. But he also inherited a sense of civic responsibility that he translated into a career in public office. He served three terms in the New York State Assembly, ran for mayor of New York City in 1886 (finishing third), and served on the federal Civil Service Commission, as New York City's police commissioner, and as assistant secretary of the navy. In this series of offices Roosevelt earned a reputation as a combative, politically crafty leader. He also distinguished himself as a historian with his *The Naval War of 1812* (1882) and *The Winning of the West* (1889).

In 1898 Roosevelt thrust himself into the Spanish-American War by organizing a volunteer cavalry brigade, called the Rough Riders, to fight in Cuba (see page 648). His dramatic act excited the public, though it had little impact on the war's outcome. Nevertheless, Roosevelt returned a folk hero (people called him Teddy, a name he disliked) and was elected governor of New York, then vice president.

As president, Roosevelt became a progressive hero. At heart, though, he had unique qualities. His brash patriotism, admiration for big business, and dislike of anything he considered effeminate recalled the previous era of unbridled expansion when raw power prevailed in social and economic affairs. Yet Roosevelt came to conclusions similar to those reached by progressives. His sense of history convinced him that the kind of small government Jefferson had hoped for would not suffice in the

Theodore Roosevelt (1858–1919) liked to think of himself as a great outdoorsman, one who loved the most rugged countryside and one who believed that he and his country should serve as examples of "manliness." *California Museum of Photography, University of California.*

industrial era. Instead, economic development necessitated a Hamiltonian system of government powerful enough to guide national affairs. Like his supporters, Roosevelt believed in the wisdom and talents of a select few, whose superior backgrounds and education qualified them to coordinate public and private enterprise. "A simple and poor society," he observed, "can exist as a democracy on the basis of sheer individualism. But a rich and complex society cannot so exist."

Roosevelt's presidency inaugurated the federal regulation of economic affairs that has characterized twentieth-century American history. Roosevelt

> **Regulation of Trusts**

first turned his attention to big business, where the combination movement had produced giant trusts that controlled almost every sector of the economy. Although Roosevelt has a reputation as a trustbuster, he actually believed in consolidation as the most efficient means to achieve material progress. Rather than return to uncontrolled competition, he preferred to distinguish between good and bad trusts and to prevent bad ones from manipulating markets. Thus he instructed the Justice Department to use antitrust laws to prosecute railroad, meat-packing, and oil trusts, which he believed had unscrupulously exploited the public. Roosevelt's policy triumphed in 1904 when the Supreme Court, convinced by the government's arguments, ordered dissolution of the Northern Securities Company, the huge railroad combination created by J. P. Morgan and his powerful business allies. (Roosevelt chose, however, not to attack other gigantic trusts, such as U.S. Steel, another of Morgan's creations.)

When prosecution of Northern Securities began, Morgan reportedly collared Roosevelt and offered, "If we have done anything wrong, send your man to my man and they can fix it up." The president refused, but he was more sympathetic to such arrangements than his rebuff might suggest. He favored cooperation between business and government. Rather than prosecute, he urged the Bureau of Corporations (of the newly created Department of Labor and Commerce) to work with companies on mergers and other forms of expansion. Through investigation and cooperation the administration exerted pressure on business to regulate itself.

Roosevelt also pushed for regulatory legislation, especially after 1904, when he won a resounding electoral victory by garnering the votes of progressives and businesspeople alike. After a year of wrangling with business lobbyists in Congress, he succeeded in 1906 in getting passage of the Hepburn Act, which imposed stricter control over railroads and expanded the powers of the Interstate Commerce Commission. The act gave the ICC more authority to set railroad rates, though it did allow the courts to overturn rate decisions. Progressives like Robert La Follette deplored the fact that Roosevelt had compromised with business representatives like Senator Nelson W. Aldrich of Rhode Island to assure the bill's passage. But Roosevelt's aim was to reaffirm the principle of government regulation rather than risk defeat over more idealistic objectives.

Roosevelt showed similar willingness to compromise on legislation to ensure pure food and drugs.

> **Pure Food and Drug Laws**

For decades reformers had been urging government regulation of patent medicines and processed meat. The outcry against fraud and adulteration heightened in 1906 with publication of Upton Sinclair's *The Jungle,* a fictionalized exposé of Chicago meat-packing plants. Sinclair, a young socialist more interested in freeing workers from oppression than in muckraking, shocked public sensibilities by describing scandalous conditions like the following:

> There was never the least attention paid to what was cut up for sausage; there would come all the way back from Europe old sausage that had been rejected, and that was mouldy and white—it would be dosed with borax and glycerine, and dumped into the hoppers, and made over again for home consumption. . . . There would be meat stored in great piles in rooms; and the water from the leaky roofs would drip over it, and thousands of rats would race about on it. It was too dark in these storage places to see well, but a man could run his hand over these piles of meat and sweep off handfulls of dried dung of rats. These rats were a nuisance, and the packers would put poisoned bread out for them; they would die, and then rats, bread, and meat would go into the hoppers together.

On reading the novel, Roosevelt ordered an investigation. Finding Sinclair's descriptions accurate, he supported the Pure Food and Drug Act and the Meat Inspection Act, both passed in 1906. Like the Hepburn Act, these laws reinforced government regulation. But as part of the compromise to obtain their passage, the government had to pay for inspections and meatpackers could appeal adverse decisions in court. In addition, companies were not required to provide date-of-processing information on their canned goods. Most large companies welcomed the legislation anyway, because it helped them regularize their business, force out smaller competitors, and restore falling confidence in American beef and other kinds of meat in foreign markets.

Roosevelt's policy on labor issues resembled his stance toward business. When, for example, the United Mine Workers struck coal-mine owners in 1902, the president intervened by using the progressive tactics of investigation and arbitration. Mine workers, led by feisty John Mitchell, wanted higher pay and an eight-hour day, but owners stubbornly refused to recognize the union or arbitrate grievances. As winter approached and fuel shortages threatened, Roosevelt mustered public opinion. He warned that he would use federal troops to reopen the mines, thereby forcing management to accept arbitration of the dispute by a special commission. The commission decided in favor of higher wages and reduced hours but also declared that owners did not have to recognize the union, though management did have to deal with grievance committees elected by the miners. The decision, according to Roosevelt, created a "square deal" for all. The strike settlement illustrated Roosevelt's belief that the president or his agents should have a say in which labor demands were legitimate and which were not—just as he could help to guide business regulation. In Roosevelt's mind there were good and bad labor organizations (socialists, for example, were bad), just as there were good and bad business combinations.

On the issue of conservation, Roosevelt displayed the same mix of flamboyant executive action and quiet compromise that he applied to other domestic matters. He built a reputation as a determined conservationist, warning Congress in 1907, "We are prone to think of the resources of this country as inexhaustible; this is not so." A lover of the outdoors, Roosevelt used presidential authority to add almost 150 million acres to the national forests and to preserve vast areas of water and coal from private plunder. In 1902 he used his influence to secure passage of the National Reclamation Act, sponsored by Senator Francis G. Newlands of Nevada, which set aside proceeds of western public land sales for the purpose of financing irrigation projects. He sympathized with conservationist Gifford Pinchot, who was the government's chief forester, and in 1908 called forty-four governors and five hundred natural-resource experts to a national Conservation Congress. True to the progressive spirit, Roosevelt wanted a "well-conceived plan" for resource management, a plan for ordered growth rather than mere preservation of nature as it was. But compromises and factors beyond his control weakened his scheme. Timber and mining companies shunned supervision of their wasteful practices, and Congress never authorized enough funds to enforce federal regulations.

Roosevelt also had to compromise his principles in the face of economic crisis. In 1907 a financial panic caused by overspeculation forced some New York banks to close to prevent frightened depositors from withdrawing money. J. P. Morgan helped to stem the panic by persuading other financiers to

> **Conservation**

stop dumping their securities. In return for Morgan's aid, Roosevelt approved a deal allowing U.S. Steel to absorb its competitor, the Tennessee Iron and Coal Company—an act that flouted Roosevelt's trustbusting aims.

During his last year in office, Roosevelt moved further away from the Republican party's traditional alliance with big business. He lashed out at the irresponsible actions of "malefactors of great wealth" and supported stronger regulation of business and heavier taxation of the rich. Having promised in 1904 that he would not seek re-election, Roosevelt backed his friend Secretary of War William Howard Taft for the nomination in 1908, hoping that Taft would continue to pursue Roosevelt initiatives. Democrats nominated William Jennings Bryan for the third time, but the "Great Commoner" lost again. Aided by Roosevelt, who still had strong popular influence, Taft won by 1.25 million popular votes and a 2-to-1 margin in the electoral college.

Early in 1909 Roosevelt went to Africa to shoot game (he saw no contradiction between hunting and conservation), leaving Taft to face political problems that his predecessor had managed to postpone. Foremost among them were tariff rates, which had risen to excessive levels. Honoring Taft's pledge to cut rates, the House passed a bill sponsored by Representative Sereno E. Payne that provided for numerous downward revisions. As in the past, protectionists in the Senate prepared to amend the House bill and revise rates upward. But Senate progressives, led by La Follette, organized a stinging attack on the ways the tariff benefited vested interests. Taft was caught between reformers, who claimed they were carrying on in Roosevelt's antitrust spirit, and protectionists, who still controlled the Republican party. In the end, Senator Nelson W. Aldrich of Rhode Island and other protectionists restored many of the cuts, and Taft, more reluctant than Roosevelt to interfere in the legislative process, signed what became known as the Payne-Aldrich Tariff. To many progressives, Taft had failed the test of filling Roosevelt's shoes.

Progressive and conservative wings of the Republican party were rapidly drifting apart. Soon after the tariff controversy a group of insurgents in the House, led by George Norris of Nebraska, chal-

> **Taft Administration**

lenged Speaker "Uncle Joe" Cannon of Illinois, whose power over committee assignments and the scheduling of debate could make or break a piece of legislation. Taft first supported then abandoned the insurgents, who nevertheless managed to liberalize procedures by enlarging the important Rules Committee and removing its appointments from Cannon's control. Meanwhile, Taft also angered conservationists by allowing Secretary of the Interior Richard A. Ballinger to remove 1 million acres of forest and mineral land from the reserved list and to fire Gifford Pinchot when he protested a questionable sale of coal lands in Alaska.

In reality Taft was as sympathetic to reform as Roosevelt was. He prosecuted more trusts than Roosevelt; expanded the national forest reserves; signed the Elkins Act of 1903, which bolstered the regulatory powers of the ICC; and supported such labor reforms as the eight-hour day and mine safety legislation. The Sixteenth Amendment, which legalized federal income tax, and the Seventeenth Amendment, which provided for the direct election of United States senators, were initiated during Taft's presidency (and ratified in 1913). Like Roosevelt, Taft was forced to compromise with big business, but he lacked Roosevelt's ability to maneuver and publicize issues he supported. Roosevelt, who had worked to expand presidential power, had also infused the office with vitality. "I believe in a strong executive," he once asserted. "I believe in power." Taft, however, believed in the strict restraint of law. He had been a successful lawyer and judge (he returned to the bench as chief justice of the United States between 1921 and 1930). His caution and unwillingness to offend disappointed those who were used to Roosevelt's impetuosity.

Thus in 1910, when Roosevelt returned from Africa boasting over three thousand animal trophies, he found his party worn and tormented. Reformers, angered by Taft's apparent insensitivity to their cause, formed the National Progressive Republican League and rallied behind Robert La Follette for president in 1912, though many hoped Roosevelt would run. Another wing of the party stood loyal to Taft. Roosevelt, disappointed by Taft's performance (particularly his refusal to back Pinchot), began to speak out and to rekindle public attention. He filled speeches with references to "the welfare of the people" and to stronger regulation of business. When La Follette became ill early in 1912, Roosevelt, proclaiming himself fit as a "bull moose," threw his hat in the ring for the Republican presidential nomination.

Taft's supporters controlled the convention and nominated him for a second term, but Roosevelt forces formed a third party—the Progressive or Bull Moose party—and nominated the fifty-three-year-old former president. Meanwhile, Democrats endured forty-six ballots before selecting as their candidate New Jersey's progressive governor Woodrow Wilson. The Socialists, by now an organized and growing party, again nominated Eugene V. Debs. The ensuing campaign exposed voters to the most thorough evaluation of the American system in nearly a generation.

Woodrow Wilson and the Extension of Reform

In his acceptance speech before the Progressive party, Theodore Roosevelt had proclaimed, "We stand at Armageddon and we battle for the Lord." But on inauguration day 1913, it was Woodrow Wilson who assumed command of the forces of good. "The Nation," he exhorted,

> has been deeply stirred by a solemn passion. Stirred by the knowledge of wrong, of ideals lost, of government too often debauched and made an instrument of evil. The feelings with which we face this new age of right and opportunity sweep across our heartstrings like some air out of God's own presence, where justice and mercy are reconciled and the judge and the brother are one.

The election's outcome illustrated the extent to which the electorate had been swept up by the moral fervor of such pronouncements. Wilson won with 42 percent of the popular vote—he was a minority president, though he did capture 435 out of 531 electoral votes (see map). Roosevelt received about 27 percent of the popular vote. Taft finished a poor third, polling 23 percent of the popular vote and only 8 electoral votes. Debs won 902,000 votes, 6 percent of the total, but no elec-

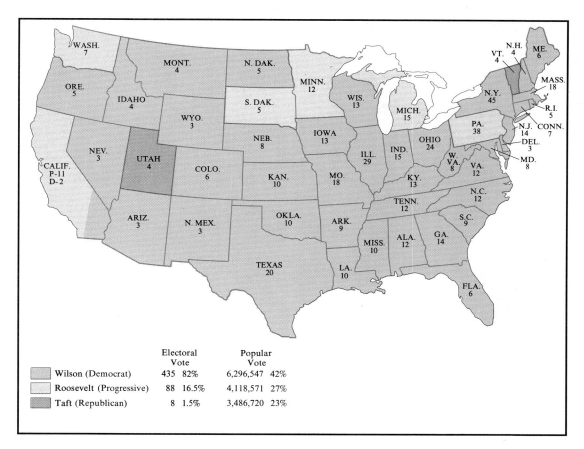

Presidential Election, 1912

	Electoral Vote		Popular Vote	
Wilson (Democrat)	435	82%	6,296,547	42%
Roosevelt (Progressive)	88	16.5%	4,118,571	27%
Taft (Republican)	8	1.5%	3,486,720	23%

toral votes. Thus fully three-quarters of the electorate supported some alternative to the restrained approach to government that Taft represented.

The campaign had featured sharp debate over the fundamentals of progressive government. On one side stood Roosevelt with a system called the

The New Nationalism and the New Freedom

New Nationalism, a term coined by reform editor Herbert Croly. Roosevelt foresaw a new era of national unity in which governmental authority would balance and coordinate economic activity. He would not destroy big business, which he saw as an efficient way to organize production. Rather, he would establish regulatory commissions, groups of experts who would protect citizens' interests and ensure wise use of concentrated economic power. "The effort at prohibiting all combinations has substantially failed," he claimed. "The way out lies . . . in completely controlling them."

Wilson offered a more idealistic scheme in his New Freedom, based on ideas of progressive lawyer Louis D. Brandeis. Wilson believed that concentration of economic power threatened individual liberty, that monopolies had to be broken so that the marketplace could again become open. But he did not want to restore laissez faire. Like Roosevelt, Wilson would enhance governmental authority to protect and regulate. "Freedom today," he declared, "is something more than being let alone. Without the watchful . . . resolute interference of the government, there can be no fair play between individuals and such powerful institutions as the trust." But Wilson stopped short of the cooperation between big business and big government inherent in Roosevelt's New Nationalism. In the campaign at least, he spoke in evangelical tones of economic emancipation, the need to "come out of a stifling cellar into the open . . . breathe again and see the free spaces of the heavens."

Looking sober and stubborn, Woodrow Wilson (1856–1924) used a preacher's moralism and an academic's reasoning to raise citizens' expectations for the fulfillment of his idealistic promises. *National Portrait Gallery, Smithsonian Institution, Transfer from the National Museum of American Art; Gift of the City of New York through the National Art Committee, 1923.*

Roosevelt and Wilson stood closer together than their rhetoric implied. In spite of his faith in experts as regulators, Roosevelt harbored sentiments for individual freedom as strong as Wilson's. And Wilson was not really hostile to concentrated power. Both men strongly supported equality of opportunity (though chiefly for whites), conservation of natural resources, fair wages, and social betterment for all classes. Perhaps more important, both would expand government activity through strong personal leadership and bureaucratic reform. Thus, even though he received a minority of the total vote in 1912, Wilson could interpret the election results as a popular mandate to subdue trusts and broaden the federal government's concern for social reform.

The public had often fondly referred to Roosevelt as Teddy or TR, but no one ever called Thomas Woodrow Wilson Tommy or WW. The son of a

Woodrow Wilson

Presbyterian minister, Wilson was born in 1856 and raised in the South. Both his mother, Janet Woodrow, and his first wife, Ellen Axson, were daughters of Presbyterian ministers. Wilson chose to become an academic rather than a cleric. He earned a B.A. at Princeton, studied law at Virginia, received a Ph.D. from Johns Hopkins, and became professor of history, jurisprudence, and political economy. Between 1885 and 1908 he published several books on American history and government that established him as a respected scholar. Wilson's manner and bearing reflected his background. Tall, lean, and stiff, he seemed to stare coldly through his pince-nez glasses. He exuded none of Roosevelt's flamboyance; in contrast to Roosevelt's lecturing, Wilson sermonized.

Yet Wilson was an effective and charismatic leader. A superb orator, he could inspire intense loyalty with religious images and an eloquent expression of American ideals. Wilson's convictions had led him early into reform. In 1902 he became president of Princeton, where he upset tradition with curricular reforms and battles against aristocratic elements in the university. In 1910 New Jersey Democrats, eager for respectability, nominated Wilson for governor. After winning the election, Wilson repudiated the party bosses and directed passage of progressive legislation. He was not good at administration, often losing his temper and stubbornly refusing to compromise. But his accomplishments attracted national attention and won him the Democratic nomination for president in 1912.

As president, Wilson had to blend New Freedom ideals with New Nationalism precepts, and in so doing he set the direction of federal economic policy for much of the twentieth century. The corporate merger movement had proceeded so far that restoration of free competition was impossible. Thus Wilson could only acknowledge economic concentration and try to prevent its abuse by expanding government's regulatory powers. His administration moved toward that end with passage in 1914 of the Clayton Anti-Trust Act and a bill creating the Federal Trade Commission (FTC). The Clayton Act extended the Sherman Anti-Trust Act of 1890 by outlawing quasi-monopolistic practices

Wilson's Policy on Business Regulation

such as price discrimination (whereby a company tried to destroy competition by lowering prices in some regions but not others) and interlocking directorates (management of two or more competing companies by the same executives). The FTC, which replaced the Bureau of Corporations, was to investigate corporations and issue cease-and-desist orders against unfair trade practices. As in ICC rulings, accused companies could appeal FTC orders in the courts. Nevertheless, the FTC represented a further step in the protection of consumers.

Wilson increased federal regulation of finance with the Federal Reserve Act of 1913. The law established the nation's first central banking system since Andrew Jackson had destroyed the Second Bank of the United States (see pages 359–360). Twelve newly created district banks would hold the reserves of member banks throughout the nation. (The act created many banks rather than one, to allay the agrarian fear of a monolithic eastern banking power, which had doomed the central bank in Jackson's time.) District banks would loan money to member banks at a low interest rate, called the *discount rate*. By adjusting this rate (and thus the amount of money a bank could afford to borrow), district banks could increase or decrease the amount of money in circulation. In other words, depending on the nation's needs, the reserve bank could loosen or tighten credit. Monetary affairs would no longer depend on the supply of gold, and interest rates would be fairer, especially for small borrowers.

Perhaps the only act of Wilson's first administration that promoted free competition was the Underwood Tariff, passed in 1913. For years rising

> **Tariff and Tax Reform**

prices had thwarted consumers' desires for the material benefits of the industrial age. Some prices were unnaturally high because government tariffs had discouraged the importation of cheaper foreign materials and manufactured products. The Underwood Tariff encouraged imports by drastically reducing or eliminating tariff rates. To recover revenues lost due to reductions, the act levied a graduated income tax on United States residents—an option made possible earlier that year when the Sixteenth Amendment was ratified. The income tax was tame by today's standards. Incomes under $4,000 were exempt; thus almost all factory workers and farmers escaped the tax. People and corporations earning $4,000 to $20,000 had to pay a 1 percent tax, and rates for higher incomes rose gradually to a maximum of 6 percent on earnings over $500,000. Such rates made no holes in pockets of the rich. The income tax, however, did become an institutional feature of American life.

In 1916 the First World War (see Chapter 23) and the approaching presidential campaign prompted Wilson to support stronger reforms. Concerned that food shortages might result if farmers could not borrow money to sustain production, the president backed the Federal Farm Loan Act of 1916. The measure created twelve federally supported banks (not to be confused with the Federal Reserve banks) that would lend money at moderate interest rates to farmers who belonged to credit institutions—a watered-down version of what Populists had agitated for a generation earlier. To stave off railroad strikes that might disrupt transportation at a time of national emergency, Wilson pushed passage of the Adamson Act of 1916, which mandated an eight-hour day and time-and-a-half for overtime for railroad laborers. Early that year, he pleased progressives by appointing Louis D. Brandeis, the "people's advocate," to the Supreme Court, though an antisemitic backlash almost blocked Senate approval of the first Jewish justice on the Court. Finally, Wilson courted the support of social reformers by backing laws that outlawed child labor and provided workers' compensation for federal employees who suffered from injury or illness.

In selecting a candidate to oppose Wilson in 1916, Republicans snubbed Theodore Roosevelt, who wanted the nomination, in favor of Charles

> **Election of 1916**

Evans Hughes, former reform governor of New York and Supreme Court justice. Wilson ran on a platform of peace, progressivism, and preparedness. Many voters were attracted by the Democratic party's campaign slogan: "He Kept Us Out of War." Hughes led a fractured party, and he could not muzzle Roosevelt, whose bellicose speeches suggested that Republicans would drag Americans into the world war. Wilson received 9.1 million votes to Hughes's 8.5 million, and the president barely won the electoral college by a 277-to-254 count. The Socialist party, which had earned 902,000 votes four years earlier, dropped to 600,000, largely because Wilson's reforms had attracted some socialists and the ailing Eugene Debs was not the party's standard-bearer.

Wilson's second term and subsequent United States involvement in the First World War saw a shift away from competition toward interest-group politics and government regulation. During his first term Wilson had become convinced that laws, not regulatory commissions that could easily fall under the influence of the very interests they were meant to regulate, should govern social and economic behavior. But wartime crisis and the desire for re-election had persuaded him to adopt a different attitude. The war effort required government coordination of production and cooperation between public and private sectors. The War Industries Board (see page 679) exemplified this cooperation. The private businesses regulated by the board submitted to its direction on condition that their own profit motives would continue to be satisfied.

After the war the Wilson administration dropped most cooperative and regulatory measures, including farm price supports, guarantees of collective bargaining, and high taxes. This move away from regulation would stimulate a new era of business ascendancy in the 1920s (see Chapter 24).

The Progressive Era in Perspective

In 1912 Thomas Edison had cautioned uneasily, "We've got to start to make this world over." By 1920 not many Americans agreed. A quarter-century of reform, climaxing in participation in the First World War, had wrought momentous changes. Government, economy, and society as they had existed in the nineteenth century were gone forever. Public concern over poverty and injustice had risen to new heights. But for every American who suffered some form of deprivation, three or four enjoyed unprecedented material comforts; and this majority could not sustain reform indefinitely. Although the effects of the progressive era lingered and in some cases expanded after the First World War, a mass consumer society had begun to refocus people's attention from reform to materialism.

The Progressive era was characterized by a welter of confusing and sometimes contradictory goals. Certainly there was no single progressive move-

ment. On the national level, reform programs ranged from Roosevelt's New Nationalism, with its faith in big government as a coordinator of big business, to Wilson's New Freedom, with its promise to dissolve economic concentrations and legislate open competition. At state and local levels, reformers pursued causes as varied as neighborhood improvement, government reorganization, public ownership of utilities, betterment of working conditions, and moral revival. Although local organizations and national associations coordinated their efforts on particular issues, reformers with different goals often worked at cross-purposes.

The failure of many progressive initiatives testifies to the strength of opposition to reform as well as ambiguities within the reform movements themselves. By asserting constitutional and liberty-of-contract maxims, courts struck down some key progressive legislation, most notably the federal law prohibiting child labor. In states and cities, adoption of the initiative, referendum, and recall did not encourage greater participation in government; either those mechanisms were seldom used or they became tools of special interests. On the federal level, new regulatory agencies rarely had resources for thorough investigations; they had to obtain information from the companies they were meant to police. Thus in many respects, progressives failed to redistribute power; in 1920, as in 1900, government remained under the influence of business and industry, a condition that many people considered quite satisfactory.

Yet in spite of all their weaknesses, the numerous reform movements that characterized the Progressive era did refashion the nation's future. Trustbusting, however faulty, forced industrialists to become more sensitive to public opinion, and reforms initiated by insurgents in Congress partially diluted the power of dictatorial politicians. Progressive legislation gave government important tools to protect consumers against price fixing and dangerous products. The income tax was a first step toward building government revenues and redistributing wealth. Social reformers soothed some of the festering sores of urban life. But perhaps most important, progressives challenged old ways of thinking. They raised questions about the quality of American life that, though they remained unresolved, made the nation more aware of its principles and promises.

Suggestions for Further Reading

General

Richard Abrams, *The Burden of Progress* (1978); John W. Chambers, *The Tyranny of Change: America in the Progressive Era* (1980); Arthur Ekirch, *Progressivism in America* (1974); Louis Filler, *The Muckrakers*, rev. ed. (1980); Samuel P. Hays, *The Response to Industrialism* (1957); Richard Hofstadter, *The Age of Reform: From Bryan to FDR* (1955); William R. Hutchinson, *The Modernist Impulse in American Protestantism* (1976); Gabriel Kolko, *The Triumph of Conservatism* (1963); David W. Noble, *The Progressive Mind*, rev. ed. (1981); Nell Irvin Painter, *Standing at Armageddon: The United States, 1877–1919* (1987); James Weinstein, *The Corporate Ideal in the Liberal State, 1900–1918* (1968); Robert Wiebe, *The Search for Order* (1968).

Regional Studies

Dewey Grantham, *Southern Progressivism: The Reconciliation of Progress and Tradition* (1983); Sheldon Hackney, *Populism to Progressivism in Alabama* (1969); Richard L. McCormick, *From Realignment to Reform: Political Change in New York State, 1893–1910* (1981); George E. Mowry, *The California Progressives* (1951); David P. Thelen, *Robert La Follette and the Insurgent Spirit* (1976); David P. Thelen, *The New Citizenship: Origins of Progressivism in Wisconsin* (1972); C. Vann Woodward, *Origins of the New South* (1951).

Legislative Issues and Reform Groups

Norman H. Clark, *Deliver Us from Evil: An Interpretation of American Prohibition* (1976); Allen F. Davis, *Spearheads for Reform: The Social Settlements and the Progressive Movement, 1890–1914* (1967); Ruth Rosen, *The Lost Sisterhood: Prostitution in America, 1900–1918* (1982); James H. Timberlake, *Prohibition and the Progressive Crusade* (1963); Walter I. Trattner, *Crusade for the Children* (1970); Irwin Yellowitz, *Labor and the Progressive Movement in New York State* (1965). (For works on socialism, see the listings under "Currents of Protest" at the end of Chapter 20.)

Education, Law, and the Social Sciences

Jerold S. Auerback, *Unequal Justice: Lawyers and Social Change in Modern America* (1976); Loren P. Beth, *The Development of the American Constitution, 1877–1917* (1971); Lawrence Cremin, *The Transformation of the School: Progressivism in American Education* (1961); Martin S. Dworkin, ed., *Dewey on Education* (1959); Thomas L. Haskell, *The Emergence of Professional Social Science* (1977); David W. Marcell, *Progress and Pragmatism: James, Dewey, Beard, and the American Idea of Progress* (1974); Philippa

Strum, *Louis D. Brandeis, Justice for the People* (1984); David Tyack and Elizabeth Hansot, *Managers of Virtue: Public School Leadership in America, 1820–1980* (1982); Lawrence Veysey, *The Emergence of the American University* (1970).

Women

Lois Banner, *Women in Modern America: A Brief History*, 2nd ed. (1984); Ruth Borden, *Women and Temperance* (1980); Nancy F. Cott, *The Grounding of American Feminism* (1987); Carl N. Degler, *At Odds: Women and the Family in America* (1980); Eleanor Flexner, *Century of Struggle: The Women's Rights Movement in the United States* (1959); Linda Gordon, *Woman's Body, Woman's Right: A Social History of Birth Control in America* (1976); David Kennedy, *Birth Control in America: The Career of Margaret Sanger* (1970); Alice Kessler-Harris, *Out to Work: A History of Wage-Earning Women in the United States* (1982); Aileen Kraditor, *The Ideas of the Women's Suffrage Movement* (1965); Ellen Condliffe Lagemann, *A Generation of Women: Education in the Lives of Progressive Reformers* (1970); William L. O'Neill, *Everyone Was Brave: The Rise and Fall of Feminism in America* (1969); William L. O'Neill, *Divorce in the Progressive Era* (1967); Rosalind Rosenberg, *Beyond Separate Spheres: Intellectual Roots of Modern Feminism* (1982); Elyce J. Rotella, *From Home to Office: U.S. Women and Work, 1870–1930* (1981); Sheila M. Rothman, *Woman's Proper Place* (1978).

Blacks

John Dittmer, *Black Georgia in the Progressive Era, 1900–1920* (1977); George Frederickson, *The Black Image in the White Mind* (1971); Louis R. Harlan, *Booker T. Washington: The Wizard of Tuskegee, 1901–1915* (1983); Louis R. Harlan, *Booker T. Washington: The Making of a Black Leader, 1856–1901* (1972); Jacqueline Jones, *Labor of Love, Labor of Sorrow: Black Women, Work and the Family from Slavery to the Present* (1985); Charles F. Kellogg, *NAACP* (1970); August Meier, *Negro Thought in America, 1880–1915* (1963); Elliot M. Rudwick, *W. E. B. Du Bois* (1969); Donald Spivey, *Schooling for the New Slavery: Black Industrial Education* (1978).

Roosevelt, Taft, and Wilson

John M. Blum, *Woodrow Wilson and the Politics of Morality* (1956); John M. Blum, *The Republican Roosevelt*, 2nd ed. (1954); Paolo E. Coletta, *The Presidency of William Howard Taft* (1973); John Milton Cooper, Jr., *The Warrior and the Priest: Woodrow Wilson and Theodore Roosevelt* (1983); William Harbaugh, *The Life and Times of Theodore Roosevelt* (1961); Arthur S. Link, *Wilson*, 5 vols. (1947–1965); Arthur S. Link, *Woodrow Wilson and the Progressive Era* (1954); Edmund Morris, *The Rise of Theodore Roosevelt* (1979); George E. Mowry, *The Era of Theodore Roosevelt* (1958); James Pednick, Jr., *Progressive Politics and Conservation: The Ballinger-Pinchot Affair* (1968).

Nicaragua? Panama? Mexico? Where should a canal linking the Gulf of Mexico and the Pacific Ocean be dug? American shipping and business interests thought a new interoceanic route essential to continued United States commercial expansion and to the health of the American economy. They joined politicians, diplomats, and navy officers to insist that the United States control any canal. In 1869 all marveled at the completion of the Suez Canal, a waterway that greatly facilitated travel between the Indian Ocean and Mediterranean Sea and enhanced British power. Surely that tremendous feat could be duplicated in the Western Hemisphere and swell United States power. But where?

22

THE QUEST FOR EMPIRE, 1865–1914

Navy Captain Robert W. Shufeldt knew exactly where—the Isthmus of Tehuantepec in southern Mexico (see map, page 657). Such an interoceanic canal, he argued, would become an extension of the Mississippi River. The canal would permit a boat "to load in Saint Louis and discharge her freight in California with but little more than the risk of inland navigation." And, the isthmian canal "converts the Gulf of Mexico into an American lake." Shufeldt dreamed too that the new waterway would help extend "our Empire" to Asia. The Pacific, "the ocean bride of America," would marry West to East. "Let us see to it that no rival flag floats upon [America's] Pacific bosom."

A tall, imposing man known for his independence and impatience, Shufeldt lobbied for the Tehuantepec route. In mid-1870 Congress voted $30,000 for a study. Shufeldt then met with President Ulysses S. Grant, who favored an American-dominated isthmian canal and believed that it would help make Mexico "an integral part of our own dominions." Named to head the Tehuantepec survey expedition, Shufeldt took engineers to the region in November 1870. He completed his report the following summer, and it rang with optimistic, machine-age rhetoric: "There is no obstacle to the construction of a canal which engineering, science, and liberal capital cannot overcome." He recommended a canal of 140 locks, deep and wide enough to accommodate nine-tenths of the world's commerce. But the United States Inter-Oceanic Canal Commission rejected Tehuantepec in favor of Nicaragua,

United States Fleet in the Straits of Magellan the Morning of February 8, 1908 (detail) by Henry Reuterdahl. Oil on canvas. *Courtesy United States Naval Academy Museum.*

Captain Robert Wilson Shufeldt (1822–1895) became one of the United States's noted naval expansionists. Besides lobbying for a canal to link the Gulf of Mexico with the Pacific Ocean, the tall, imposing Shufeldt dreamed of an American empire stretching far into Asia. *Library of Congress.*

whose Lake Nicaragua provided a much larger water supply. In the end, Panama, not Nicaragua, became the canal site—but not until the early twentieth century and under less-than-peaceful circumstances (see page 658).

Shufeldt contented himself with the thought that the United States's "controlling influence upon this hemisphere" ensured Washington's control of a canal, wherever located. He soon turned his expansionist zeal toward Asia, the Middle East, and Africa. In the 1870s and 1880s he sailed his United States Navy vessels to Liberia, Zanzibar, Aden, Japan, Korea, China, and other far-distant lands in search of markets for the increased production of American factories and farms. Most Americans heard little about Shufeldt's global exploits and

knew even less about the unusual places he visited on behalf of the United States government. But the American people did not make foreign policy—the men who governed in Washington, D.C., did, and they were expansionists and imperialists whose "destiny is always to expand," as the Russian diplomat who negotiated the sale of Alaska to the United States remarked. In the early nineteenth century, Americans had already purchased Louisiana, annexed Florida, Oregon, and Texas, pushed Indians out of the path of white migration westward, seized California and other western areas from Mexico, and acquired the Gadsden Purchase. Through the sale of their products abroad since the beginning of the republic they had developed a lucrative foreign trade that involved them deeply in world affairs. Not much, the Russian regretted, "escaped the lust of Americans."

This chapter explores the sources of American expansionism and the building, managing, and protecting of an overseas empire through a variety of methods in the late nineteenth and early twentieth centuries. The United States's empire ultimately stretched from Latin America to Asia, and it faced threats from restless nationalists, commercial competitors, and other imperial nations. The global American empire also aroused critics at home. As anti-imperialists, these dissenters engaged imperialists in a momentous debate, especially at the turn of the century, over the fundamental course of American foreign policy.

Most Americans applauded *expansionism*—the outward movement of goods, dollars, ships, people, and ideas—as a traditional feature of their nation's history. But many became uneasy with *imperialism*—the imposition of control over other peoples, denying them the freedom to make their own decisions and undermining their sovereignty. Imperial control could be imposed in several ways, both formally (by annexation, colonialism, or military occupation) and informally (by economic domination, political manipulation, or the threat of intervention). As the informal methods indicate, *imperialism* did not refer only to the taking of territory, although that is how most Americans then and now have interpreted the term.

Expansionism and Imperialism Defined

Many Americans in the late nineteenth century disparaged territorial imperialism as unbefitting

1861–69	Seward is secretary of state	**1900**	Second Open Door note
1866	Transatlantic cable completed		U.S. exports total $1.5 billion
	France withdraws from Mexico		McKinley re-elected
1867	Alaska and Midway acquired	**1901**	Theodore Roosevelt becomes

1861–69   Seward is secretary of state

1866   Transatlantic cable completed
France withdraws from Mexico

1867   Alaska and Midway acquired

1868   Burlingame Treaty with China

1870   Senate rejects annexation of
Dominican Republic

1871   *Alabama* claims settled

1878   U.S. products monopolize awards
at Paris World's Fair

1883   Advent of New Navy

1887   U.S. gains naval rights to Pearl
Harbor

1889   First Pan-American Conference

1890   Mahan, *The Influence of Sea
Power upon History*

1893   Severe depression begins
Turner's frontier thesis
Hawaiian revolution begins

1895   Crisis over Venezuela
Cuban revolution begins
Japan defeats China

1896   McKinley elected president

1898   Sinking of the *Maine*
Spanish-American-Cuban-Filipino
War
Hawaii and Wake Island annexed

1899   Senate passes Treaty of Paris
United Fruit Company founded
First Open Door note
Outbreak of Philippine
Insurrection

1900   Second Open Door note
U.S. exports total $1.5 billion
McKinley re-elected

1901   Theodore Roosevelt becomes
president
Aguinaldo captured
Hay-Pauncefote Treaty

1903   Panama breaks from Colombia
U.S. granted canal rights in
Panama
Platt Amendment

1904   Roosevelt Corollary

1905   Taft-Katsura Agreement
Portsmouth Conference
U.S. imposes financial supervision
on the Dominican Republic

1906   San Francisco segregates Asian
schoolchildren
U.S. invades Cuba

1907   Great White Fleet
Gentleman's agreement with
Japan

1908   Root-Takahira Agreement

1910   Mexican Revolution begins

1912   U.S. troops enter Cuba again
U.S. troops occupy Nicaragua

1914   U.S. troops invade Mexico
First World War begins
Panama Canal opens

the United States, and they opposed joining other great powers in the scramble for colonies in Asia and Africa. Would not an overseas territorial empire, with lands and peoples noncontiguous to the United States, undermine institutions at home, invite perpetual war, and violate honored principles? The United States became interested more in the "annexation of trade" than in the annexation of territory, as Secretary of State James G. Blaine declared in 1890. The key questions became: When did expansionism become nonterritorial imperialism, and when did expansionism, to remain successful, require colonies? By the early twentieth century, the United States possessed a fair number of colonies and Americans had become imperialists—albeit more informal than formal imperialists.

In this expansionist era, the federal government did not always adequately fund the vehicles of expansion, and most Americans were too caught up in the daily bustle of machine-age life to give much attention to foreign matters. Washington, for example, neglected the navy until the 1880s and maintained a foreign service weakened by the political spoils system. Most businessmen ignored foreign commerce in favor of the dynamic domestic marketplace. Still, the direction of American foreign policy after the Civil War became unmistakable: Americans intended to exert their influence beyond the continental United States, to reach for more space, more land, more markets, and more international power. A pattern of accelerating activity abroad culminated in the tumultuous decade of the 1890s, when doubters' voices were drowned out by shouts for war and foreign territory, and when American power was sufficient to deliver both.

The Domestic Roots of Expansionism and Empire

The Civil War had temporarily interrupted expansionism, but after that searing conflict leaders worked to heal sectional wounds and put the United States back on its traditional expansionist course. The 1876 centennial celebration emphasized national unity. Confederate and Union soldiers met to exchange captured flags. Pride

> **Nationalism**

welled up when American machines earned top marks at world fairs. At the 1878 Paris World's Fair, American exhibitors won more awards than any other nation's representatives. Patriotic societies like the Daughters of the American Revolution (founded in 1890) championed nationalism.

The inflated rhetoric of American exceptionalism and manifest destiny revived. To Reverend Josiah Strong, author of the influential book *Our Country* (1885), Americans were a special, God-favored Anglo-Saxon race destined to lead others. "As America goes, so goes the world," he claimed. To Social Darwinists, Americans stood as a superior people who would surely overcome all competition and thrive. "The rule of the survival of the fittest applies to nations as well as to the animal kingdom," claimed American diplomat John Barrett. The humorist Finley Peter Dunne captured the American mood by putting words in the mouths of his fictional Irish-American characters: "'We're a gr-reat people,' said Mr. Hennessy, earnestly. 'We ar-re,' said Mr. Dooley. 'We ar-re that. An' th best iv it is, we know we are.'"

With such chauvinistic attitudes, Americans scouted new frontiers to conquer. Secretary of State William H. Seward wanted Cuba; President Grant coveted Santo Domingo; and others envisioned new outposts in the Pacific Ocean. Religious leaders contemplated the conversion of "natives" and "savages" to Christianity. "Don't stay in this country theorizing," implored an officer of the Student Volunteer Movement, founded by college students in the 1880s. "A hundred thousand heathen a day are dying without hope because we are not there teaching the Gospel to them." Businesspeople and farmers talked of untapped overseas markets. Nationalists spoke of exporting America's superior political principles and practices to other peoples and of building an enlarged modern navy of the first order.

The arguments for expansion and empire seemed all the more urgent when Americans anticipated the closing of the frontier at home. In 1893 Frederick Jackson Turner of the University of Wisconsin postulated his frontier thesis. Turner claimed that an ever-expanding continental frontier had shaped the American character. That "frontier has gone, and with its going has closed the first period of American history." Professor Turner did not explicitly say that a

> **Turner's Frontier Thesis**

new frontier had to be found overseas. But some thought that was what he meant when he wrote in his famous article "The Significance of the Frontier in American History" that he doubted that "the expansive character of American life has now entirely ceased. Movement has been its dominant fact, and, unless this training has no effect upon a people, the American energy will continually demand a wider field for its exercise."

Foreign policy has always sprung from the domestic setting of a nation—its needs, wants, moods, and ideals. The leaders who guided America's expansionist foreign relations were the same people who kindled the spirit of national growth at home, celebrated the wonders of the machine age, championed the transcontinental railroad, forcefully removed Native Americans from the paths of white settlement, and built America's bustling cities and giant corporations. They understood the close relationship between domestic developments and foreign relations—that, for example, railroads made it possible for Iowa farmers to transport their crops to seaboard cities and then on to foreign markets. The farmers' livelihood thus became tied to world market conditions, the outcomes of foreign wars, and the viability of the principle of freedom of the seas, which stood as a reminder to other nations that American goods on American ships should be free to cross the oceans, even during foreign war.

The threads of domestic and foreign events and policies became densely interwoven in other ways. Periodic depressions fostered the belief that the country's surplus production must be sold in foreign markets to restore and sustain economic well-being at home. By promoting economic health, these markets would also contribute to domestic social and political stability. Blaine put it this way: "With these markets secured new life would be given to our manufactories, the product of the Western farmer would be in demand, the reasons for and inducements to strikers with all their attendant evils would cease." The tariff question also linked domestic and world affairs. Tariff increases (see pages 584, 601, 627, 631) designed to protect American industry and agriculture from foreign competition adversely affected those who sold to America, prompting them to enact retaliatory tariffs on American products. In Cuba and Hawaii, American tariff revisions actually induced economic crises, which fed revolutions that ultimately served American interests.

The massive influx of immigrants also stirred diplomatic as well as domestic questions. Ideas of racial superiority and Jim Crow practices at home, moreover, influenced American policies toward Asian and Latin American peoples of color, who were considered inferior. And some ambitious politicians tried to enhance their political reputations at home by flexing the national muscle in the world arena. In general, then, the major domestic questions that preoccupied Americans from the Civil War to the First World War were closely intertwined with the nation's diplomacy.

The spokesmen for expansion and empire belonged to what scholars have labeled the foreign policy elite, or opinion leaders in politics, business, labor, agriculture, religion, journalism, education, and the military. Better read and better traveled than most Americans, more cosmopolitan than provincial in outlook, and politically active, they believed that United States prosperity and security depended upon the exertion of American influence abroad. These opinion leaders dominated the making of foreign policy. Unlike domestic policy, foreign policy is seldom shaped by the people. Most Americans simply do not follow international relations or express themselves on foreign issues. Indeed, studies have suggested that no more than 10 to 20 percent of the voting public was alert to world affairs in the late nineteenth century. This small group, whom Secretary of State Walter Q. Gresham called "the thoughtful men of the country," expressed the opinion that counted. Increasingly in the late nineteenth century, and especially in the 1890s, they urged not only expansionism, but both formal and informal imperialism. Those members of the political elite who, like President Grover Cleveland, favored economic expansion and United States hegemony (that is, dominance) in South America, but not the annexation of overseas territory, gradually lost ground.

Ambitious and clannish, the imperialists often met informally in Washington, D.C., to talk about building a bigger navy and an isthmian canal, establishing colonies, and selling surpluses abroad. They gathered at Henry Adams's house on H Street or at the nearby home of John Hay, who became secretary of state in 1898; and they dined together at the Metropolitan Club. Theodore Roosevelt, appointed assistant secretary of the navy in 1897, was among

Foreign Policy Elite

them; so were Senator Henry Cabot Lodge, who became a member of the Foreign Relations Committee in 1895, and corporate lawyer Elihu Root, who would later serve as both secretary of war and secretary of state. These luminaries kept up the drumbeat for empire.

With a mixture of self-interest and idealism typical of American thinking on foreign policy, advocates of empire believed that imperialism benefited both Americans and those who came under their control. When they intervened in other lands or lectured weaker states, Americans defended their behavior on the grounds that they were extending the blessings of liberty and prosperity to less-fortunate people. For those imperialists who were also progressive reformers, interventions allowed Americans to remake foreign societies in the American model. To critics at home and abroad, however, American paternalism appeared hypocritical. They charged that to coerce foreigners to behave like Americans violated cherished American ideals. For example, to impose on resentful Filipinos an American-style political system, United States officials censored the press, jailed critics, and picked candidates for public office. From this experience, Filipinos probably learned more about how to fix elections than about how to make democracy work. The persistent American belief that other people cannot solve their own problems and that only the American model of development is appropriate produced what historian William Appleman Williams has called "the tragedy of American diplomacy."

Factory, Farm, and Foreign Affairs

Many businesspeople and farmers savored expansion and ultimately endorsed empire. They looked to profits from foreign sales. "It is my dream," cried the governor of Georgia in 1878, to see "in every valley . . . a cotton factory to convert the raw material of the neighborhood into fabrics which shall warm the limbs of Japanese and Chinese." Fear generated foreign trade as well, for the nation's farms and factories produced more than Americans could consume. Foreign commerce, it was as-

sumed, served as a safety valve to avert or relieve economic depression. Surpluses had to be exported, economist David A. Wells warned, or "we are certain to be smothered in our own grease."

The tremendous economic growth of the United States after the Civil War stimulated foreign trade, a larger navy to protect this lucrative commerce, a more efficient foreign service, a

Growth of Foreign Trade

call for more colonies, and a more activist foreign policy. In 1865 United States exports totaled $234 million; in 1900, $1.5 billion (see figure). By 1914, at the outbreak of the First World War, American exports had reached $2.5 billion, prompting some Europeans to protest an "American export invasion." In the 1870s the United States began to enjoy a long-term favorable balance of trade (exporting more than it imported). Most of America's products went to Britain, Europe, and Canada, but increasing amounts flowed to new markets in Latin America and Asia. Agricultural goods accounted for about three-fourths of the total exports in 1870 and about two-thirds in 1900. Manufactured goods led foreign sales for the first time in 1913, when the United States ranked third behind only Britain and Germany in such exports.

Grains, cotton, meat, and dairy products topped the export list in 1900, providing farmers with needed foreign outlets. Over half the annual cotton crop was exported each year. Wisconsin cheesemakers shipped to Britain; the Swift and Armour meat companies exported refrigerated beef to Europe; and American farmers became Europe's largest supplier of wheat. To sell American grain abroad, James J. Hill of the Great Northern Railroad distributed wheat cookbooks translated into several Asian languages.

America's ambitious entrepreneurs and large businesses looked to foreign markets, especially in the 1890s, when it became clear that industrial production was outdistancing consumption. Rockefeller's Standard Oil sold abroad, notably in Germany, England, and Cuba. In the 1870s and 1880s about two-thirds of all American petroleum was exported, and in succeeding decades the figure was about one-half. Fifteen percent of America's iron and steel and 50 percent of its copper were sold abroad by the turn of the century, making many workers in those industries dependent on exports. George Westinghouse marketed his air brakes in Europe; almost as many Singer sewing machines

Chapter 22: The Quest for Empire, 1865–1914

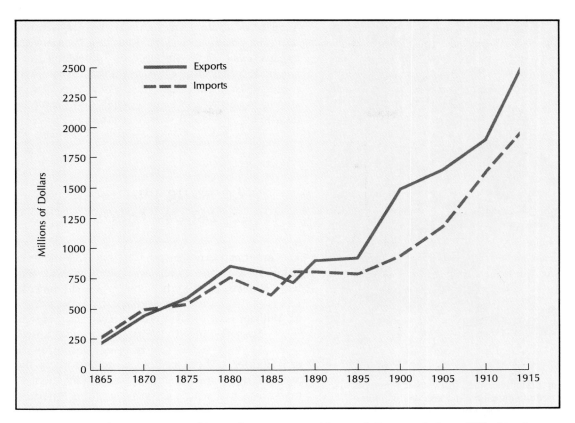

United States Trade Expansion, 1865–1914 *Source: From Thomas G. Paterson, J. Garry Clifford, and Kenneth J. Hagan,* American Foreign Policy: A History. *3rd edition. Copyright 1988. Used by permission of D.C. Heath and Company.*

were exported as were sold at home; and Cyrus McCormick's "reaper kings" harvested the wheat of Russian fields. Photography baron George Eastman, whose business operated around the globe, remarked that greater foreign sales allowed Americans to "distribute our eggs and pad the basket at the same time." As well, direct American investments abroad reached $3.5 billion by 1914, placing the United States among the top four investor countries.

Especially in Latin America, United States economic expansion grew impressively and aroused Washington's diplomatic interest in its neighbors to the South. United States exports to Latin America, which exceeded $50 million in the 1870s, climbed to over $120 million in 1900 and topped $300 million in 1914. Investments by United States citizens in Latin America amounted to a towering $1.26 billion in 1914. In 1899 two of the largest

▶ **Economic Expansion in Latin America**

banana importers merged to form the United Fruit Company. Owning much of the land (over 1 million acres in 1913) and the railroad and steamship lines of Central America, United Fruit became a major economic and political force in the region. It developed transportation, cultivated land, and fought to eradicate yellow fever and malaria. As for Mexico, American capitalists came to own its railroads and mines. By 1910, Americans controlled 43 percent of Mexican property and produced more than half that nation's oil.

Economic expansion abroad became both a reason and a mechanism for exerting political influence. Dunne's Mr. Dooley put it simply: "I tell ye, th' hand that rocks th' scales in th' grocery store is th' hand that rules th' wurruld." Indeed, by the early twentieth century American economic interests were influencing policies on taxes and natural resources in countries like Cuba and Mexico. American interests were responsible for drawing Hawaii into the American imperial net and for

Factory, Farm, and Foreign Affairs

Singer sewing machines joined many other American products in penetrating global markets. In 1890 three-quarters of the sewing machines sold in the world were Singers. The caption for this company-sponsored photograph of the king of Ou (Caroline Islands, in the Pacific) read: "The Herald of Civilization—Missionary Work of the Singer Manufacturing Company." *Courtesy, Robert B. Davies,* Peacefully Working to Conquer the World.

spreading American cultural values abroad. Religious missionaries and Singer executives, for example, joined hands in promoting the "civilizing medium" of the sewing machine. "The world is to be Christianized and civilized," declared Josiah Strong. "And what is the process of civilizing but the creating of more and higher wants. Commerce follows the missionary."

American leaders believed selling, buying, and investing in foreign marketplaces were important to the United States. Why? First, because of profits. But also because the problems of overproduction and unemployment, and hence social tensions, would be relieved at home, because a vigorous foreign trade symbolized national power, because economic ties permitted political influence to be exerted abroad, and because economic expansion helped spread the American way of life, creating a world more hospitable to Americans. Most

Americans championed economic expansion. Anti-imperialists, however, drew the line between expansionism and imperialism: profitable and fair trade relationships, yes; exploitation, no. And, some advised, American business activity abroad should not draw the United States into unwanted diplomatic crises and wars. But it did.

Looking Outward, 1860s–1880s

The American empire grew gradually, sometimes haltingly, in the years following the Civil War. William H. Seward became one of its chief architects. As senator from New York

> **William H. Seward**

(1849–1861) and secretary of state (1861–1869), he argued articulately for extension of the American frontier. "There is not in the history of the Roman Empire an ambition for aggrandizement so marked as that which characterized the American people," he once said. Seward envisioned a large, coordinated American empire encompassing Canada, the Caribbean, Cuba, Central America, Mexico, Hawaii, Iceland, Greenland, and Pacific islands. This empire would be built not by war but by a natural process of gravitation toward the attractive, republican United States. Commerce would hurry the process, he thought, noting that the merchants of Venice and Britain had become "masters of the world." To ensure the unity of this American empire, Seward appealed for a canal across Central America, a transcontinental American railroad to link up with Asian markets, and a telegraph system to speed communications.

Most of Seward's grandiose plans did not reach fruition in his own day. In 1867, for example, he signed a treaty with Denmark to buy the Danish West Indies (the Virgin Islands). Shortly afterward a hurricane and tidal wave wrecked St. Thomas, diminishing its value in the eyes of many senators. (The senators were also reluctant to hand Republican Seward a diplomatic triumph while he was supporting Democrat Andrew Johnson during the president's impeachment proceedings.) The treaty was shelved, and the Virgin Islanders, who had voted for annexation, had to wait until 1917.

Most of Seward's plans for acquiring territory were blocked by a combination of anti-imperialists and political foes. Anti-imperialists like Senator Carl Schurz and E. L. Godkin, editor of the magazine *The Nation*, believed that the country already had enough unsettled land and that the creation of a showcase of democracy and prosperity at home would best persuade other peoples to adopt American institutions and principles. Some anti-imperialists, sharing the racism of the times, opposed the annexation of territory populated by "inferior" dark-skinned people, such as Santo Domingo or slavery-plagued Cuba.

Although political foes sought to punish Seward by denying him his imperial dreams, he did enjoy some successes. When an American naval officer seized the Midway Islands in 1867, Seward laid claim to them for the United States. That same year he paid Russia $7.2 million for the 591,000 square miles of Alaska—a real bargain for land twice the size of Texas. Seward extolled the Russian territory's rich natural resources, and the Senate voted overwhelmingly for the treaty. He also shepherded the Burlingame Treaty (1868) through the Senate. This treaty with China provided for free immigration between the two countries and pledged Sino-American friendship. (A new treaty in 1880 permitted Congress to suspend Chinese immigration to the United States, which it did two years later to satisfy anti-Asian bias in the Far West.) The secretary's forceful handling of French interference in Mexico also furthered his reputation. In 1861, Napoleon III had placed Archduke Ferdinand Maximilian of Austria on the throne in Mexico. Preoccupied with the Civil War, Seward could do little to help the Mexicans dislodge the intruding Europeans. But in 1866, as American troops headed for the Mexican border, Seward cited the Monroe Doctrine and told the French to get out. Napoleon, troubled at home and now opposed by both Mexicans and Americans, abandoned his venture.

Seward's dream of a world knit together into a giant communications system was satisfied. In 1866, through the persevering efforts of Cyrus Field, an underwater transatlantic cable linked European and American telegraph networks. Backed by J. P. Morgan's capital, James A. Scrymser strung telegraph lines to Latin America, reaching Chile in 1890. Information about markets, diplomatic crises, and war flowed

> **International Communications**

William H. Seward (1801–1872) boldly envisioned a great American empire—both territorial and commercial. This ambitious, talkative secretary of state added Alaska and the Midway Islands to the United States domain, but anti-imperialists and political foes thwarted his plans for other territories. *Culver Pictures.*

steadily and quickly. Whereas delivery of surface mail from Washington, D.C., to European capitals often took from ten to twenty-one days, the transatlantic cable enabled the State Department to make same-day contact.

Officials made good use of the telegraph system in 1873, when Spain was attempting to quell a rebellion in its colony of Cuba. In November the Spanish seized the gun-running Cuban ship *Virginius* and executed some Americans on board. Washington quickly used the telegraph to manage the crisis before American war fever carried the United States into a serious conflict. (Spain later paid an indemnity of $80,000, and the crisis passed.) In general, drawn closer to one another by improvements in communications and transportation, nations found that faraway events became more important to their prosperity and security. Technology shrank the globe.

Seward's successor, Hamilton Fish (1869–1877), inherited the knotty and emotional problem of the *Alabama* claims. The *Alabama* and other vessels built by Great Britain for the Confederacy during the Civil War had preyed on Union shipping. Senator Charles Sumner demanded that Britain pay $2 billion in damages or cede Canada to the United States, but Fish patiently took the question to the bargaining table. In 1871 Britain and America signed the Washington Treaty, whereby the British apologized and agreed to the creation of a tribunal, which later awarded the United States $15.5 million. Disputes over fishing rights along the North Atlantic coast and the hunting of seals in the Bering Sea near Alaska also dogged Anglo-American relations and would continue to do so for decades. Yet the two powers, however competitive, were coming to the conclusion that rapprochement rather than confrontation best served their interests. American politicians still tried to "twist the lion's tail" to score political points at home, but the trend toward Anglo-American accommodation was not reversed.

Secretary Fish also had to deal with President Grant's ambitious designs on the Dominican Republic. The president was impressed by the island's raw materials and its potential as a market for American textiles, and the navy liked the harbor at Samaná Bay. Grant's personal secretary, Orville Babcock, negotiated a treaty of annexation. But Senator Sumner smelled a rat in Babcock, who through private intrigue stood to gain financially from the venture. Civil war, moreover, engulfed the Dominican Republic. Political rivalry also complicated the question. "No wild bull ever dashed more violently at a red rag than he does at anything that he thinks the President is interested in," Fish said of Sumner's political motives. In 1870 the Senate rejected the treaty.

Another venture in the Pacific succeeded. In 1878 the United States gained rights to a naval station at the strategic port of Pago Pago in Samoa,

Samoa several islands four thousand miles from San Francisco on the trade route between Australia and America. The Germans and British also coveted the islands. Year by year tensions grew. To avoid war, Germany, Britain, and the United States met in Berlin in 1889 and, without consulting the Samoans, carved Samoa into three parts. A decade later the United States annexed part of the islands, including Pago Pago.

In Latin America United States interests became extensive. Trade with the region flourished; investments grew; and the navy's presence expanded.

Pan-American Conference The convening in 1889 of the first Pan-American Conference in Washington, D.C., bore witness to growing ties. Secretary Blaine sponsored the meeting to improve commercial relations. The Latin American conferees toured United States factories and then negotiated several general agreements. To perpetuate inter-American cooperation, they founded the Pan American Union, which in 1907 moved into elegant new quarters in Washington, D.C., financed by Andrew Carnegie.

As the United States acquired new territories and markets and extended its influence abroad, the call went out for an improved and enlarged navy. Captain Alfred T. Mahan became a

New Navy major popularizer for the "New Navy." Because foreign trade was vital to United States well-being, he argued, the nation required an efficient navy to protect its shipping; in turn, a navy required colonies for bases. "Whether they will or no," Mahan wrote, "Americans must now begin to look outward. The growing production of the country demands it." Mahan became president of the Naval War College in Newport, Rhode Island, founded in 1884, and there gave lectures that were published as *The Influence of Sea Power upon History* (1890). This widely read book sat on every serious expansionist's shelf. German, Japanese, and British leaders turned its pages. Theodore Roosevelt and Henry Cabot Lodge eagerly consulted Mahan, sharing his belief in the linkage between trade, navy, and colonies.

Until its modernization, the American navy was in a sorry state. Many of its wooden ships were rotting. Its shipyards had become infamous for political patronage and waste. But in 1883 Congress authorized construction of the first steel-hulled warships. American factories went to work to produce steam engines, high-velocity shells, powerful guns, and precision instruments. Andrew Carnegie, displaying none of the pacifism that would later distinguish him, exclaimed, "There may be millions for us in armor," and signed a highly profitable naval contract. Businesspeople seeking men-of-war escorts for their commercial vessels and scouts for new trade opportunities cheered the birth of the New Navy.

Gradually, but especially in the 1880s, the United States Navy shifted from sail to steam and from wood to steel. New Navy ships like the *Maine,* the *Oregon,* the *Boston,* and the *Columbia* thrust the United States into naval prominence. The *Columbia* held the naval record for average sea speed, and the other three figured in the imperialist ventures of the 1890s. Many of the steel vessels were named for states and cities to kindle patriotism and local support for naval expansion. The enlarged navy gave the United States the tools to expand and build a greater empire.

Crises in the 1890s: Hawaii, Venezuela, and Cuba

"The Real British Lion," according to this 1895 American cartoon, was an ugly hog threatening to engulf the globe. The Venezuelan crisis stimulated this Anglophobic view. *New York Evening World.*

When the United States became engaged in a number of crises in the 1890s, the New Navy warships were put to the test. For decades the Hawaiian Islands had commanded American attention. This major Pacific way station became important for trade with Asia and had long been a site of missionary work. Its undeveloped but strategic port of Pearl Harbor tempted naval expansionists, and the vast sugar plantations of the islands attracted American entrepreneurs. In 1875 the United States signed a treaty granting Hawaiian sugar duty-free entry into the American market; the Hawaiian sugar industry boomed and became dependent on mainland business. Six years later Secretary Blaine warned other nations away from the islands, declaring them "essentially a part of the American system." In 1887 the United States gained naval rights to Pearl Harbor. When the Congress revised the tariff laws in the early 1890s, however, it eliminated the special provision for Hawaiian sugar. American planters in Hawaii suffered losses as sugar exports to the United States declined precipitously. To gain exemption from American tariffs, a group of planters called the Annexation Club plotted a revolution.

In January 1893 the white minority overthrew the native monarch, Queen Liliuokalani. Their success stemmed in part from the support of the chief American diplomat in Honolulu, John L. Stevens, who saw to it that sailors from the warship *Boston* encircled the royal palace. Stevens informed Washington that the "Hawaiian pear is now fully ripe, and this is the golden hour for the United States to pluck it." Against the protests of Japan, whose nationals accounted for about 40 percent of Hawaii's population (Americans equaled only 5 percent), President Benjamin Harrison sent a treaty of annexation to the Senate. But incoming President Grover Cleveland, who disapproved of forced annexation, withdrew it. Five years later, on July 7, 1898, during the Spanish-American-Cuban-Filipino War, President William McKinley successfully maneuvered annexation through Congress.

The Venezuelan crisis of 1895 also gave the United States an opportunity to express its expansive mood. For decades Venezuela and Great Britain had squabbled over the border between Venezuela and British Guiana. The disputed territory contained rich gold deposits and the mouth of the Orinoco River, the commercial gateway to northern South America. Venezuela asked for American help. President Cleveland de-

> **Revolution in Hawaii**

> **Venezuelan Crisis**

cided that the "mean and hoggish" British had to be warned away. In July 1895, Secretary of State Richard Olney sent the British a brash message that Cleveland compared to a twenty-inch gun—in the naval parlance of the time, a huge weapon. Olney lectured the British that the Monroe Doctrine prohibited European intervention in the Western Hemisphere, whose states "are friends and allies, commercially and politically, of the United States." The spread-eagle words that followed were clearly directed at an international audience: "To-day the United States is practically sovereign on this continent, and its fiat is law upon the subjects to which it confines its interposition."

This statement of United States hegemony did not impress the British, who rejected American interference in what they considered a local issue. American jingoistic nationalists clamored for action. "Let the fight come if it must; I don't care whether our sea coast cities are bombarded or not; we would take Canada," snorted Theodore Roosevelt. But neither London nor Washington wanted war. The British, seeking international friends to counter intensifying competition from Germany, quietly retreated from the crisis. In 1896 an Anglo-American arbitration board divided the disputed territory. Throughout the deliberations Venezuela was barely consulted. Thus the United States displayed a trait common to imperialists: a disregard for the rights and sensibilities of small nations.

In 1895 another crisis rocked Latin America: the Cuban revolution against Spain. From 1868 to 1878 the Cubans had battled their mother country. Slavery was abolished but independence denied, and Spanish rule continued to be repressive. The Cuban insurgents waited for another chance. José Martí, one of the heroes of Cuban history, collected money, arms, and men in the United States. As in the case of Hawaii, a change in American tariff policy hastened the revolution. The Wilson-Gorman Tariff (1894) imposed a duty on Cuban sugar, which had been entering the United States duty-free under the McKinley Tariff (1890) and a reciprocity agreement with Spain. The Cuban economy, highly dependent on exports, was thrown into turmoil.

> **Cuban Revolution**

From American soil, Martí launched a revolution that became gruesome in its human and material costs. Outnumbered rebels burned sugar-cane fields and razed mills, conducting an economic war and using guerrilla tactics to avoid head-on clashes with Spanish soldiers. "It is necessary to burn the hive to disperse the swarm," explained Cuban leader Máximo Gomez. The Spanish retaliated under the command of Valeriano Weyler, soon dubbed "Butcher." He instituted a policy of "reconcentration": an estimated 300,000 Cubans of all ages were herded into fortified towns and camps to separate the insurgents from their many supporters among the Cuban people and to break the rebels' morale. Hunger, starvation, and disease in the resettlement camps led to mass deaths; tens of thousands perished. Weyler's forces also ransacked the countryside. The island's economy deteriorated badly, and American investments of $50 million became jeopardized. American imports from Cuba (mostly tobacco and sugar), which had amounted to $76 million in 1894, slumped to $15 million in 1898; American exports to the island dropped by half in the same period.

As tragic stories of atrocity and destruction reached the United States—and were played up by the American yellow press (see page 572)—people grew angry with the Spanish and sympathetic toward the insurrectionists, whose ranks were swelling with each Weyler barbarity. In late 1897 a new government came to power in Madrid. The Spanish modified reconcentration and promised that Cuba would be given some autonomy. Americans waited to see if the new reforms would subdue the rebellious island and restore peace.

President William McKinley came to office an imperialist. He wanted foreign bases for a larger navy; he recognized that surplus production had to be exported; and he echoed the belief that American supremacy was essential in the Western Hemisphere. The 1896 Republican platform on which McKinley ran demanded both an enlarged American empire (Hawaii, the Virgin Islands, and a Nicaraguan canal) and Cuban independence. In his annual message in December 1897, McKinley surveyed the Cuban crisis, ruling out American intervention while Spain was walking the path of reform. McKinley wanted to avoid war if at all possible.

Events in the first few months of 1898 sabotaged the Spanish reforms and exhausted American patience. Early in January, antireform pro-Spanish loyalists and army personnel rioted in Havana. Many Americans lost faith in Madrid's ability to make its

Sinking of the Maine reforms work. After the riots, Washington officials ordered the battleship *Maine* to Havana harbor to demonstrate United States concern and protect American citizens. On February 15 explosions ripped the *Maine,* killing 260 American officers and crew. Americans were quick to blame Spain for the disaster.

Spain's image in the United States had been further undermined a week earlier when William Randolph Hearst's inflammatory *New York Journal* published a stolen private letter from Enrique Dupuy de Lôme, the Spanish minister in Washington. In the letter de Lôme scorned McKinley as "weak and a bidder for the admiration of the crowd" and revealed Spanish determination to fight on in Cuba. In March an irritated McKinley asked for $50 million in defense funds, and Congress complied unanimously. The naval board created to investigate the sinking of the *Maine* then reported that a mine had caused the explosion. (A study by Admiral Hyman G. Rickover in 1976 refuted that conclusion, blaming the explosion on an internal accident.) The panel did not assign responsibility, but restless Americans blamed Spain—if not for the catastrophe, then at least for creating an atmosphere that permitted it to happen.

The impact of these events greatly reduced McKinley's diplomatic options. He decided to send Spain an ultimatum. In late March the United States insisted that Spain accept an armistice, end reconcentration altogether, and designate McKinley as arbiter. Implicit was the demand that Spain grant Cuba its independence. Yet no Spanish government could have given up Cuba and remained in office. Madrid nonetheless made concessions. It abolished reconcentration and accepted an armistice on the condition that the insurgents agree first.

Wanting more, McKinley began to write a war message to Congress. After completing it, however, he received the news that Spain had gone one step further and declared a unilateral armistice. The weary McKinley—who was taking medication in order to sleep—hesitated, but he could no longer tolerate the chronic disorder just ninety miles off the American coast. As Senator Lodge explained, "We cannot go on indefinitely with this strain, this suspense, and this uncertainty, this tottering upon the verge of war."

In his message of April 11, the president asked Congress for authorization to use force, as "an impartial neutral," to effect "a rational compromise between the contestants." McKinley listed American grievances and the reasons the United States had to end the turmoil: first, the "cause of humanity"; second, the protection of American life and property; third, the "very serious injury to the commerce, trade, and business of our people"; fourth, referring to the destruction of the *Maine,* the "constant menace to our peace." At the very end of his statement McKinley mentioned Spain's recent concession but made little of it.

McKinley's War Message

The Spanish-American-Cuban-Filipino War

Congress debated for over a week and then on April 19 declared Cuba free and independent, directing the president to use force to remove Spanish authority from the island. The legislators also passed the Teller Amendment, which disclaimed any American intention to annex Cuba. McKinley beat back a congressional amendment to recognize the rebel government, for he believed the Cubans unready for self-government; they would first need a period of American tutoring.

Diplomacy had failed. By the time the Spanish concessions came forth, events had already pushed the antagonists to the brink. Washington might have been more patient, and Madrid might have faced the fact that its once-grand empire had disintegrated. But the Cuban insurgents would settle for nothing less than independence, which Spain could not easily grant and which the United States could achieve only through war. Striking in the Cuban crisis, as in the Venezuelan crisis, was the American insistence that the United States would set the rules for nations in the Western Hemisphere. Great Britain had backed down in 1895, but Spain stood firm in 1898.

The motives of the Americans who favored war were mixed and complex. McKinley's April message expressed a humanitarian impulse to stop the bloodletting, concern for commerce and property, and the psychological need to end the

Motives for War

nightmarish anxiety once and for all. Republican politicians advised McKinley that they would lose the upcoming congressional elections unless the Cuban question was solved. Many businesspeople, who had been hesitant before the crisis of early 1898, joined many farmers in the belief that removing Spain from Cuba would open new markets for surplus production—to which the depression of the 1890s had given urgency.

Inveterate imperialists saw the war as an opportunity to fulfill what Senator Lodge called the "large policy." Naval enthusiasts could prove the worth of the New Navy. Some religious leaders also saw merit in war. Social Gospel advocate Washington Gladden remarked that "in saving others we may save ourselves." Conservatives, alarmed by violent labor strikes and Populism, welcomed war as a national unifier. One senator commented that "internal discord" was disappearing in the "fervent heat of patriotism. . . . You will not see another [Eugene] Debs riot for many years." Sensationalism also figured in the march to war. Assistant Secretary of the Navy Theodore Roosevelt and others too young to remember the Civil War looked on war as adventure. The yellow press exaggerated stories of atrocities. Anglo-Saxon supremacists like politician Albert Beveridge shouted, "God's hour has struck." Underlying all explanations for this war was the spirit and reality of expansionism, which had been moving the nation ever outward in the last half of the nineteenth century.

More than 263,000 regulars and volunteers served in the army and another 25,000 in the navy during the war. Most of this total never left the United States. The typical volunteer was a white, young (early twenties), unmarried, native-born, working-class American. For some, glory flowed from what John Hay called a "splendid little war." Roosevelt could hardly contain himself. As he said of his motley unit of Ivy Leaguers and cowboys, the Rough Riders, they were "children of the dragon's blood, and if they had no outland foe to fight and no outlet for their vigorous and daring energy, there was always the chance of their fighting one another." The Rough Riders were actually undisciplined and not always effective warriors, but largely because of Roosevelt's self-serving publicity efforts they got a good press.

The war was hardly splendid. Over 5,400 Americans died, but only 379 of them in combat. The rest fell to malaria and yellow fever spread by mosqui-

toes. Food was bad and medical care was unsophisticated. Soldiers were issued heavy woolen uniforms in a tropical climate, and the stench of body odor sickened many. Black troops, about 10,000 in number, saw no relief from racism and Jim Crow. Their regiments were segregated, and they were constantly insulted as "coons" and "niggers." Cafes, saloons, and other public places refused to serve them. Race riots broke out; one in Tampa in early June sent twenty-seven blacks and several whites to the hospital. In Macon, Georgia, black soldiers tore down a park sign reading "No Dogs and Niggers Allowed" and chopped down a persimmon tree famous in the region as a lynching site. Whites in the South, where most troops were stationed, resented the appearance of status that the military uniform gave to blacks and used threats and violence to intimidate those who suggested that a war to free the Cubans might help to break down the color line at home. One angry black Iowan announced: "I will not go to war. I have no country to fight for. I have not been given my rights." But most volunteers, black and white, shared the attitude of a soldier who wrote to his parents back in Pennsylvania: "The boys are all in good health and spirits, and think they can whip the world."

Before Americans began to fight and die in Cuba, the first news of war actually came from faraway Asia. It surprised many Americans, ignorant about the steady United States push into the Pacific, about the dreams of farmers and businesspeople for a huge market in China, and about the foreign policy elite's knowledge of the Spanish colony of the Philippines. On May 1, 1898, Commodore George Dewey's New Navy ship the *Olympia*, leading an American squadron, steamed into Manila Bay, the Philippines, and wrecked the outweighed and outgunned Spanish fleet. Dewey became an instant hero. So pleased was McKinley that he hurried to promote Dewey to the rank of admiral. Dewey's sailors had to be handed volumes of the *Encyclopaedia Britannica* to acquaint them with this strange land, but officials in Washington knew that Manila ranked with Pearl Harbor and Pago Pago as a choice harbor. Histories used to credit (or blame) Theodore Roosevelt for having ordered Dewey to Manila. The story goes that one day in February when the navy secretary

Conditions in the Army

Dewey in the Philippines

On July 1, 1898, American troops stormed Spanish positions on San Juan Hill near Santiago, Cuba. Casualties from heavy fire were high for both sides—hundreds dead and thousands wounded. A *Harper's* magazine correspondent reported a "ghastly" scene after the battle, and the American painter William Glackens (1870–1938) put to canvas what he saw. Santiago surrendered on July 17, propelling the United States to victory in the Spanish-American-Cuban-Filipino War. *Wadsworth Atheneum, Hartford, Gift of Henry Schnakenberg.*

was away, Assistant Secretary Roosevelt usurped authority and cabled Dewey to take on coal, rest at Hong Kong, and head for Manila the moment war with Spain broke out. Actually Roosevelt was following established policy; McKinley himself approved Roosevelt's instructions to Dewey. In fact, during the short war, McKinley became deeply involved in both tactical and strategic decisions from his White House war room, where busy telegraphic equipment kept him abreast of daily events.

Author Sherwood Anderson observed that fighting Spain was "like robbing an old gypsy woman in a vacant lot at night after a fair." Facing rebels and Americans in both Cuba and the Philippines, Spanish resistance collapsed rapidly. American ships had early blockaded Cuban ports to prevent Spain from reinforcing and resupplying its army on the island. On July 3, the Spanish Caribbean squadron,

trapped in Santiago harbor, made a desperate attempt to escape but was destroyed by American warships. American troops did not get into a ground war until after June 22, the day several thousand of them landed near Santiago de Cuba and laid siege to the western city. On July 17 the Spanish garrison at Santiago capitulated. Several days later, American forces assaulted the Spanish island-colony of Puerto Rico, 3,435 square miles in size with nearly 1 million people. And Manila could not withstand the pressure from Americans and Filipino insurgents led by Emilio Aguinaldo. Losing on all fronts, Madrid sued for peace. Spain and the United States signed an armistice on August 12, thus ending a war that should be called—to reflect where it was fought and whose interests were at stake—the Spanish-American-Cuban-Filipino War. "Let's see what we get by this," said Secretary of

State William R. Day as he twirled the large globe in his office.

In Paris in December, American and Spanish negotiators agreed on the peace terms: independence for Cuba; cession of the Philippines, Puerto Rico, and Guam (an island in the Pacific) to the United States; and American payment of $20 million to Spain for the new American territories. Filipino nationalists tried to persuade American officials to set their nation free but were rebuffed. The American empire now stretched deep into Asia; and the annexation of Wake Island (1898), Hawaii (1898), and Samoa (1899) gave American traders, missionaries, and naval promoters other steppingstones to China. Puerto Rico provided a long-desired base in the Caribbean that could help protect an American-built isthmian canal.

> **Treaty of Paris**

Taste of Empire: Imperialists and Anti-Imperialists Debate

During the war the *Washington Post* detected "a new appetite, a yearning to show our strength. . . . The taste of empire is in the mouth of the people." But as the debate over the Treaty of Paris intensified in the United States, it became evident that many Americans found the taste sour. Anti-imperialists like Mark Twain, William Jennings Bryan, William Graham Sumner, Andrew Carnegie, Charles Francis Adams, Jr., and Senator George Hoar argued vigorously against annexation of the Philippines. They were disturbed that a war to free Cuba had led to an empire that reached into Asia. Their arguments varied. Some appealed to principle, citing the Declaration of Independence and the Constitution: the conquest of people against their will violated the concept of self-determination. Philosopher William James charged that the United States was losing its special place among nations; it was, he warned, about to "puke up its heritage." To those who believed the Filipinos were not yet fit for self-

> **Anti-Imperialist Arguments**

government, former Senator Carl Schurz mockingly replied that Manila's city council was probably less corrupt than Chicago's. Others protested that the dispatch of troops overseas by the president, as commander-in-chief, greatly increased the power of the presidency and subverted the constitutional checks-and-balances system. Other anti-imperialists argued that the United States could acquire markets without having to subjugate foreign peoples.

Reform-minded critics of the treaty emphasized domestic priorities, including the improvement of race relations. "Until our nation has settled the Negro and Indian problems," said Booker T. Washington, "I do not believe that we have a right to assume more social problems." A black politician from Massachusetts—who had just protested a lynching in Georgia that included mutilation of the black man's body by souvenir hunters—cried that the United States was exhibiting quite a spectacle to the world: "offering liberty to the Cubans with one hand, cramming liberty down the throats of the Filipinos with the other, but with both feet planted upon the neck of the negro." Other anti-imperialists warned that the absorption of dark-skinned peoples would undermine white Anglo-Saxon purity.

Samuel Gompers and other labor leaders worried about the possible undercutting of American labor—and the union movement—by what Gompers called the "half-breeds and semi-barbaric people" of the new colonies. Might not they be imported as cheap contract labor to drive down the wages of American workers? Might not this new empire require a large standing army that would take workers away from their jobs? Would not exploitation of the weak abroad become contagious and lead to further exploitation of the weak at home? Would not an overseas empire drain interest and resources from pressing domestic problems, delaying reform? Gompers charged, in fact, that imperialism was an attempt "to divert the attention of our people from the ills from which we suffer at home."

The imperialists answered their critics with references to patriotism, destiny, and commerce. They sketched a scenario of American greatness: merchant ships plying the waters to boundless Asian markets; naval vessels cruising the Pacific to protect American interests; missionaries uplifting inferior peoples. It was America's

> **Arguments for Empire**

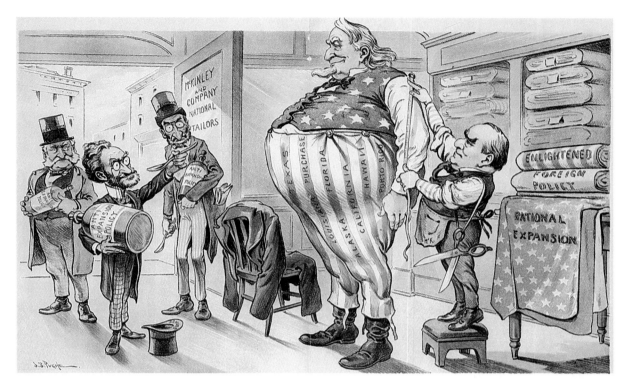

"Declined with thanks" reads this 1900 *Puck* magazine cartoon. President William McKinley measures Uncle Sam, fattened by several imperialist meals, as a group of anti-imperialists led by Carl Schurz futilely attempts to administer an antidote. The message was clear: the United States would continue to expand. *Library of Congress.*

duty, they insisted, quoting a then-popular Rudyard Kipling poem, to "Take Up the White Man's Burden." Furthermore, insurgents were beginning to resist American rule, and it was cowardly to pull out under fire. Germany and Japan, two major international competitors, were snooping around the Philippine Islands, seemingly ready to seize them if the United States did not. National honor dictated that Americans keep what they had shed blood to take earlier. Senator Beveridge asked: "Shall [history] say that, called by events to captain and command the proudest, ablest, purest race of history in history's noblest work, we declined that great commission?"

The anti-imperialists entered the debate with many handicaps. Possession of the Philippines was an accomplished fact; the anti-imperialists' role was thus a negative one. Then, too, they were internally divided, never able to launch an effective campaign. Although many of them belonged to the Anti-Imperialist League, they differed on so many domestic issues that it was difficult for them to speak with one voice on a foreign question. They were

also inconsistent: Gompers favored the war but not the postwar annexations; Carnegie would accept colonies if they were not acquired by force; Hoar voted for the annexation of Hawaii but against that of the Philippines. The imperialists sneered that some of their critics were hypocrites, showing more concern for Filipinos than for American Indians, blacks, unskilled workers, or destitute immigrants. Hay commented privately that Carnegie "does not seem to reflect that the government is in a somewhat robust condition after shooting down several [striking] American citizens in his interest at Homestead."

On February 6, 1899, the Senate passed the Treaty of Paris by a 57-to-27 vote. Republicans, except for Hoar and Senator Eugene Hale of Maine, voted with their president; 22 Democrats voted no, but 10 voted for the treaty. The latter group was probably influenced by Bryan, who had served as a colonel during the war; he urged a favorable vote in order to end the war and then push for Philippine independence. An amendment promising independence as soon as the Filipinos formed a

The missionary Grace Roberts teaches the Bible to Chinese women in Manchuria in 1903. The prominent American flag reveals that Americanism went hand in hand with overseas religious work. The mission force was feminized—a majority of missionaries were women. *ABCFM pictures, courtesy of Houghton Library, Harvard University.*

stable government was defeated only by the tie-breaking ballot of the vice president.

The anti-imperialists lost, but Bryan carried the debate into the election of 1900 as the Democratic standard-bearer against McKinley. In that unsuccessful campaign Bryan charged that imperialism benefited only American economic interests. To repudiate the principle of self-government in the Philippines would weaken it at home. "It is not necessary to own people to trade with them," Bryan protested. But McKinley would not apologize for American imperialism. "It is no longer a question of expansion with us," he told a midwestern audience. "If there is any question at all it is a question of contraction; and who is going to contract?"

Asian Troubles: Open Door in China, Filipino Insurrection, and Japan

In 1895, the same year as the advent of the Cuban revolution and the Venezuelan crisis, Japan claimed victory over China in a war of only eight months. Outsiders had been pecking away at China—known as the Sick Man of Asia—since the 1840s, but the Japanese onslaught intensified the international scramble. The Germans carved out a sphere of interest in Shandong; the Russians moved into Manchuria and the Liaodong peninsula; the French grabbed some provinces; and the British drove in stakes too. Japan controlled Formosa and Korea as well as parts of China proper (see map, page 654). Within their spheres, the imperial powers built fortified bases, leased territory, and claimed exclusive economic privileges. American religious leaders, whose missions in China had doubled to one thousand in the 1890s, and business interests, who saw trade opportunities threatened, petitioned Washington to halt the dismemberment before they were closed out. What good were the Philippines as steppingstones to China if there was nothing left to step into?

Secretary Hay recognized that the United States could not force the imperial powers out of China, but he was determined to protect American commerce. In September 1899 Hay sent the imperial nations a note asking them to respect the principle of equal trade opportunity—an Open Door—for all nations in their spheres. Germany, France, and the others sent evasive replies, privately complaining that the United States was seeking for free the trade rights the others had gained and maintained at considerable military and administrative cost. Then in 1900, a secret Chinese society called the Boxers revolted against the foreigners in their midst and laid siege to the foreign legations in Beijing (Peking). The United States joined the imperialists in sending troops to Beijing to lift the siege. Hay, in a second Open Door note dated July 3, 1900, instructed the other nations to preserve China's territorial integrity. He also called again for "equal and impartial trade." Hay's protests notwithstanding, China continued for years as fertile soil for foreign exploitation, especially for the Japanese.

> **Open Door Policy**

Hay's foray into Asian politics settled little, but the Open Door policy thereafter became a central element in United States diplomacy. Actually, the Open Door had long been an American principle, for as a trading nation the United States opposed barriers to international commerce and demanded equal access to markets. After 1900, when the United States began to emerge as the premier world trader, the Open Door policy became an instrument first to pry open markets and then to dominate them, not just in China but in the rest of the world as well. But the Open Door was not just a policy; it was also an ideology. The tenets of this ideology were that America's domestic well-being required exports, that foreign trade would suffer interruption unless the United States intervened abroad to implant American principles and keep foreign markets open, and that the closing of any area to American products, citizens, or ideas threatened the survival of the United States itself.

In the Philippines, meanwhile, the United States antagonized its new colonials, or "wards," as McKinley labeled them. Emilio Aguinaldo, the Philippine nationalist leader, believed that Dewey had promised independence for his country. But after the victory, Aguinaldo was ordered out of Manila and isolated from decisions affecting his nation. American racial slurs and paternalistic attitudes infuriated nationalistic Filipinos, and they felt betrayed by the Treaty of Paris. Once again Mr. Dooley caught the mood: "In ivry city in this unfair land we will erect schoolhouses an' packin' houses an' houses of correction; and we'll larn ye our language, because 'tis aisier to larn ye ours than to larn oursilves yours. An' we'll give ye clothes, if ye pay f'r them; an' if ye don't, ye can go without."

> **Philippine Insurrection**

In January 1899, an uncowed Aguinaldo proclaimed an independent Philippine Republic. Soon the Filipinos took up arms. Before the Philippine Insurrection was suppressed in 1901, more than 5,000 Americans and more than 200,000 Filipinos lay dead. Americans burned villages, tortured people, and introduced a variant of the reconcentration policy. It was the American practice not to take prisoners. Anti-imperialists cried foul, but President Roosevelt remarked that "we haven't a single incident in the Philippines as bad as the massacre at Wounded Knee." This reference to the massacre of Native Americans in South Dakota (see page 473) seemed appropriate, because Americans stationed at the Philippine front often spoke of the "savage" Filipino insurgents who might "injun up" on them. One soldier from Kansas declared that the Philippines "won't be pacified until the niggers are killed off like the Indians." Twenty-six of thirty United States Army generals ordered to the Philippines from 1898 through 1902 had had prior experience battling Indians in the American West.

After Aguinaldo's capture in 1901, the United

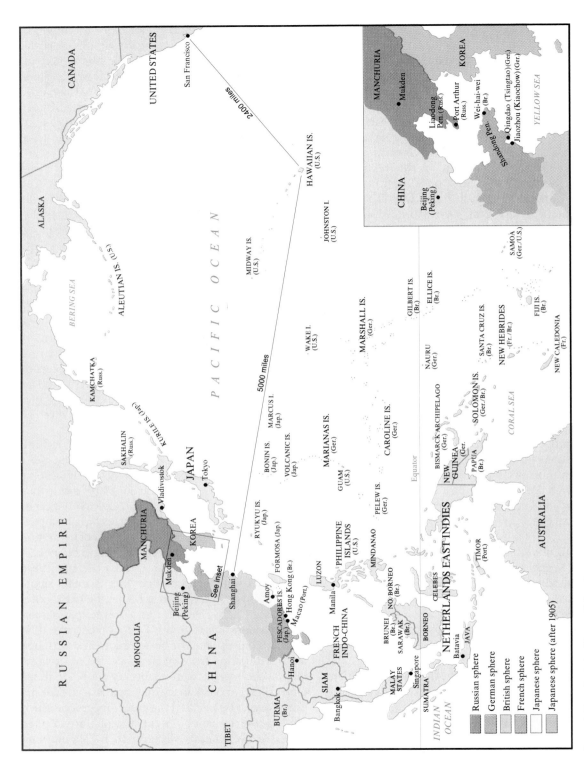

Imperialism in Asia: Turn of the Century

This 1900 photograph was titled "Our young Filipinos in holiday attire at the Fourth of July celebration, Manila, P.I." The quizzical looks on the faces of these children suggest that they may not have fully understood life as colonials in the American empire, but their parents certainly did. After taking the Philippines from Spain in the 1899 Treaty of Paris, the United States blocked Philippine independence, went to war against Filipino nationalists, and imposed stern American rule on the islands. *Library of Congress.*

States imposed its regime on the Philippines. Through a policy of "bread and guns," public works programs were introduced. The architect Daniel Burnham, who led the City Beautiful movement in the United States, planned modern Manila. English was declared the official language; American teachers were imported to staff schools; and the University of the Philippines was founded (1908) to train a native American-oriented elite. The Americanization of the Philippines even included the introduction of basketball. Political imprisonment under a sedition act silenced critics. The Philippine economy grew as a satellite of the United States economy. In 1916 the Jones Act promised Filipino independence, but not until thirty years later was Aguinaldo's dream realized.

Possession of the Philippines meant American participation in the turbulent politics of Asia. The major contender for influence in the area was Japan, and the Open Door policy did not stop its advances. When competition for Manchuria and Korea led to the Russo-Japanese War (1904–1905), Japan scored quick victories over the stunned Russians. Roosevelt mediated the crisis at the Portsmouth Conference in New Hampshire. The peace settlement, he hoped, would preserve a balance of power in Asia. It did not. In 1905, in the Taft-Katsura Agreement, the United States conceded Japanese hegemony over Korea in return for Japan's pledge not to undermine the American posi-

Japanese-American Rivalry

This cloth bandana celebrated President Theodore Roosevelt's receipt of the Nobel Peace Prize in 1906 for helping to end the Russo-Japanese War. First awarded in 1901, the prize was established by the bequest of the Swedish inventor-industrialist Alfred Bernhard Nobel. The irony of giving a peace prize to a man who often seemed eager to go to war was well illustrated at the top of the bandana, where Roosevelt the Rough Rider charges on horseback into battle in the Spanish-American-Cuban-Filipino War. *Museum of American Political Life, University of Hartford. Photo by Sally Anderson-Bruce.*

tion in the Philippines. (Roosevelt soon came to think of the vulnerable Philippines as America's Achilles' heel.) To alert Japan to American naval power and to persuade Congress to increase the navy's budget, Roosevelt in 1907 sent the "Great White Fleet" on a world tour. Duly impressed, the Japanese began to build a bigger navy of their own.

Troubles with Japan boiled to the surface in 1906 when the San Francisco School Board, reflecting the anti-Asian bias of West Coast Americans, ordered the segregation of all Chinese, Koreans, and Japanese in a special school. Tokyo protested this discrimination against its citizens. The following year, President Roosevelt quieted the crisis by striking a gentleman's agreement with Tokyo restricting Japanese immigration to the United States; San Francisco then rescinded its offending segregation order. Relations with Tokyo were jolted again in 1913 when the California legislature denied Japanese residents the right to own property in the state.

Despite the Root-Takahira Agreement (1908), in which the United States recognized Japan's interests in Manchuria and Japan again pledged the security of American possessions in the Pacific, Japanese-American relations deteriorated. Japan became alarmed by President William Howard Taft's ineffective attempt at dollar diplomacy, inducing American bankers to join an international consortium to build a Chinese railway. *Dollar diplomacy* was an effort to use private funds to serve American diplomatic goals and at the same time to garner profits for American financiers. Realizing neither purpose, Taft's venture seemed

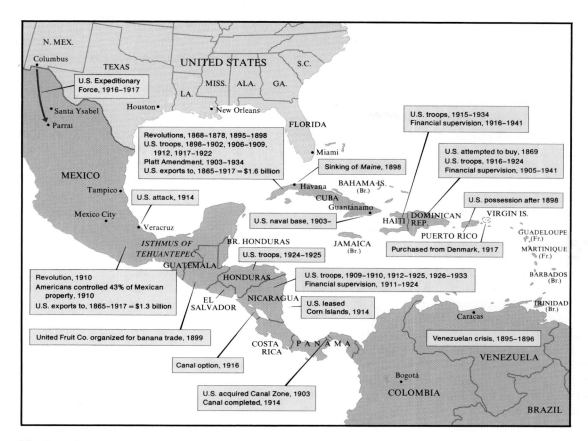

The United States and Latin America

only to embolden the Japanese to solidify and extend their holdings in China, whose nationalistic revolution of 1911 proved incapable of stopping relentless Japanese aggression. When the First World War broke out in Europe, Japan seized Shandong and some Pacific islands from the Germans. In 1915 Japan issued its Twenty-One Demands, virtually insisting on hegemony over all of China. As parts of China passed into Japan's hands, Americans, angry but lacking adequate countervailing power in Asia, could only protest.

The Fruits and Tasks of Empire in Latin America

If the United States demonstrated feebleness in Asia, it revealed strength in Latin America (see map). Although the Teller Amendment outlawed annexation, it did not rule out American control of postwar Cuba. American troops remained there until 1902. American officials also wrote the Platt Amendment and then forced the Cubans to append it to their constitution. A frank avowal of United States hegemony, the Platt Amendment provided

> **Platt Amendment for Cuba**

that Cuba could not make a treaty with another nation that might impair its independence. In short, all treaties had to be approved by the United States. Most important, Cuba granted the United States "the right to intervene" to preserve the island's independence and to maintain domestic order. Cuba was also required to undertake a sanitation program and to lease to the United States a naval base (Guantánamo). These violations of Cuban sovereignty, formalized in a 1903 treaty, governed Cuban-American relations until 1934. The Cubans, like the Filipinos, resisted their new masters: they marched in the streets against the Platt Amendment. A revolution in 1906 prompted Roosevelt, who disparaged Caribbean peoples as "dagoes" and "darkeys," to invade Cuba once again with troops. The marines stayed until 1909, were ordered back for a short time in 1912, and occupied Cuba again from 1917 to 1922. José Martí had warned Cubans from the beginning that the United States posed a threat: "I know the Monster, because I have lived in its lair."

The United States presence left an imprint on Cuban life. The North Americans helped to improve transportation, expand the public school system, found a national army, and improve sugar production. Walter Reed's experiments, based on the theory of Cuban physician Carlos Finlay, proved that the mosquito transmitted yellow fever; sanitary engineers soon controlled the insect and eradicated the disease from the island. United States individuals and corporations soon acquired title to more than 60 percent of Cuba's rural lands and came to dominate the island's sugar, mining, and tobacco industries and utilities. North American investments in Cuba grew from $50 million before the revolution to $220 million by 1913, and American exports to the island rose from $26 million in 1900 to $196 million in 1917. As historian Louis A. Pérez, Jr., has so aptly written, "the beneficiaries of North American rule were North Americans." No wonder that Cuban nationalists nurtured strong anti-Yankee views.

Panama became the site of one of Theodore Roosevelt's boldest expansionist ventures. American fascination with an isthmian canal was long-standing. But three obstacles had to be overcome. First, the Clayton-Bulwer Treaty with Britain (1850) provided for joint control of a Central American canal. President Theodore Roosevelt persuaded the British, who were cultivating United States friendship and who knew that their influence in the region was diminishing, to step aside (Hay-Pauncefote Treaty of 1901). Second, Colombia was driving a hard bargain in talks over a canal to be cut through its province of Panama. Roosevelt urged Panamanian rebels to declare independence from Colombia, and he sent American warships to the isthmus to ensure the success of the rebellion. In 1903 the United States signed a treaty with the new nation of Panama: the United States was awarded a canal zone and long-term rights to its control; Panama was guaranteed its indepen-

> **Panama Canal**

dence. Colombians would not easily forget this despoiling of their sovereignty. Third, the cost of constructing a canal was enormous. Roosevelt, having overcome the British and Colombian problems, pressed an obliging Congress for substantial funds.

The completion of the Panama Canal in 1914 marked a major technological achievement. The special bearings and gears used to operate the locks were manufactured by a Wheeling, West Virginia, firm; some fifty Pittsburgh factories and shops made the various bolts and steel girders; and the General Electric Company produced the electrical apparatus. People greeted the canal's opening the way people in the 1960s hailed the landing on the moon. During the canal's first year of operation, over one thousand merchant ships squeezed through its locks. (Ten years later the annual rate was five thousand, equal to the traffic through the Suez Canal.) The United States fortified the zone with conspicuous sixteen-inch guns, the nation's largest.

The rest of the Caribbean, as Captain Shufeldt had predicted, became an American lake. "Speak softly and carry a big stick," Roosevelt intoned. He did wield a big stick, but he seldom curbed his bombastic rhetoric or his drive to expand the American empire. Worried that Latin American nations that had defaulted on huge debts owed to Europeans were sparking European intervention (as when England, Germany, and Italy sent warships to Venezuela in 1902), the president in 1904 decided to issue the Roosevelt Corollary to the Monroe Doctrine. He warned Latin Americans to stabilize their politics and finances. "Chronic wrongdoing," he lectured, might require "intervention by some civilized nation" (the United States). "In flagrant cases of such wrongdoing or impotence," the United States would have to assume the role of "an international police power." Roosevelt and his successors were not bluffing. From 1900 to 1917, when the United States entered the First World War, American troops intervened in Cuba, Panama, Nicaragua, the Dominican Republic, Mexico, and Haiti. American officials took over customs houses (as in the Dominican Republic, from 1905 to 1941) to control tariff revenues and thus government budgets; they renegotiated foreign debts with American banks; they trained national guards and ran elections.

The United States set out to police its neighbors

> **Roosevelt Corollary**

Thomas May's 1907 cartoon displayed many features of imperialism: naval might, racism (Cubans as little black children being instructed by a paternalistic Uncle Sam), and United States possession of the power to grant or to deny "freedom." Through the Platt Amendment, economic domination, and military occupations (troops were landed again in 1906), the United States kept Cuba subservient. *From* Detroit Journal. *Permission from* The Detroit News.

to the south in the name of order. Whether achieved by the landing of marines, the development of a national guard, a managed electoral process, bold declarations, a manipulated economy, or dollar diplomacy, Americans deemed order necessary to guarantee United States security and prosperity. After Roosevelt helped to slice off Panama from Colombia and initiated construction of the Panama Canal, Washington would not tolerate disturbances that might threaten the vital waterway. Order was believed essential to American commerce and investment too. Between 1900 and 1917 American exports to Latin America swelled from $132 million to $309 million, and imports from Latin America increased even more. Investments in sugar, tobacco, transportation, and banking also rose impressively. Finally, order seemed imperative to Americans eager to remake Latin American societies in the image of the United States. "When properly directed there is no people not fitted for self-government," President Woodrow Wilson remarked. "Every nation needs to be drawn into the

tutelage of America" and taught "the habit of law and obedience." The United States possessed few colonies but had developed an empire nonetheless—an informal one largely marked by economic and political control rather than formal annexation.

One of the assumptions that governed United States policy toward Europe was that European nations should not intervene in Western Hemispheric affairs; the Monroe Doctrine, European officials now knew, had power behind it. Another assumption of American policy toward Europe was that the United States should stand outside continental embroilments. A third was that America's best interests lay in cooperation with Great Britain. The balance of power in Europe was precarious, and seldom did an American president involve the United States directly. At Germany's request, Roosevelt helped to settle a Franco-German clash over Morocco by mediating a settlement at Algeciras, Spain (1906). But the president drew American criticism for entangling the United States in a European problem. Americans endorsed the ultimately futile Hague peace conferences (1899 and 1907) and negotiated various arbitration treaties, but on the whole they stayed outside Europe's embittered arena.

A major offshoot of the German-British rivalry was London's quest for American friendship. The makings of the "great rapprochement" had been

	developing since the late nine-
Anglo-	teenth century. When the British
American	supported Americans in the war
Rapproche-	of 1898, stepped aside in the Hay-
ment	Pauncefote Treaty (1901) to per-
	mit the building of an American

canal, virtually endorsed the Roosevelt Corollary, and withdrew their warships from the Caribbean, Americans warmed toward them. The British overtures paid off in 1917 when the United States threw its arms and men into the First World War on the British side.

From the Civil War to the First World War, expansionism and imperialism rested at the core of American foreign policy. By 1914 Americans held extensive interests in a world made smaller by modern technology. Ideas of racial supremacy, the belief that the nation needed foreign markets to absorb surplus production so that the domestic economy could thrive, a mission to uplift the less fortunate, and emotional appeals to national greatness—all fed the appetite for foreign adventure and commitments. The instruments of expansion and empire were the machines produced by American entrepreneurs and inventors. The underwater cable, steel warships, the Panama Canal, the exportation of American products across the globe, and the rifles toted by American soldiers into Philippine jungles and into the streets of Latin American capitals—all facilitated the imperial odyssey.

The outward reach of American policy from Secretary of State Seward to President Wilson met opposition from domestic critics, congressional doubters, other imperial nations, and proud and resentful nationalists; but the trend was never seriously diverted. In the future, Americans who sincerely believed that they had been helping others to enjoy a better life would come to feel betrayed when their foreign clients questioned American tutelage or openly rebelled. But August 1914 presented an immediate and different problem: the outbreak of war in Europe.

Suggestions for Further Reading

General

"American Empire, 1898–1903," *Pacific Historical Review,* 48 (1979), entire issue; Robert L. Beisner, *From the Old Diplomacy to the New, 1865–1900,* 2nd ed. (1986); Charles S. Campbell, *The Transformation of American Foreign Relations, 1865–1900* (1976); Richard D. Challener, *Admirals, Generals, and American Foreign Policy, 1889–1914* (1973); James A. Field, Jr., "American Imperialism," *American Historical Review,* 83 (1978), 644–668; Willard B. Gatewood, Jr., *Black Americans and the White Man's Burden* (1975); John A. S. Grenville and George B. Young, *Politics, Strategy, and American Diplomacy* (1967); David Healy, *United States Expansionism* (1970); Patricia Hill, *The World Their Household* (1985) (on women missionaries); Ronald J. Jensen, *The Alaska Purchase and Russian-American Relations* (1975); George F. Kennan, *American Diplomacy, 1900–1950* (1951); Walter LaFeber, *The New Empire* (1963); Ernest R. May, *American Imperialism* (1968); Milton Plesur, *America's Outward Thrust* (1971); David M. Pletcher, *The Awkward Years* (1962); Emily Rosenberg, *Spreading the American Dream* (1982); Rubin F. Weston, *Racism in United States Imperialism* (1972); William Appleman Williams, *The Tragedy of American Diplomacy,* new ed. (1988).

Theodore Roosevelt and Other Expansionists

Howard K. Beale, *Theodore Roosevelt and the Rise of America to World Power* (1956); John M. Blum, *The Republican Roosevelt* (1954); John M. Cooper, Jr., *The Warrior and the Priest: Woodrow Wilson and Theodore Roosevelt* (1983); Lewis L. Gould, *The Presidency of William McKinley* (1981); William H. Harbaugh, *The Life and Times of Theodore Roosevelt* (1975); Frederick Marks III, *Velvet on Iron* (1979) (on Roosevelt); Frank Merli and Theodore A. Wilson, eds., *Makers of American Diplomacy* (1974); Edmund Morris, *The Rise of Theodore Roosevelt* (1979); Ernest N. Paolino, *The Foundations of the American Empire* (1973) (on Seward); William C. Widenor, *Henry Cabot Lodge and the Search for an American Foreign Policy* (1980). For works on Woodrow Wilson, see the listings at the end of Chapter 23.

Economic Expansion

See the works by Beisner, Campbell, and LaFeber cited above; William H. Becker, *The Dynamics of Business-Government Relations* (1982); Robert B. Davies, *Peacefully Working to Conquer the World: Singer Sewing Machines in Foreign Markets, 1854–1920* (1976); David M. Pletcher,

"Rhetoric and Results: A Pragmatic View of American Economic Expansionism, 1865–98," *Diplomatic History,* 5 (1981), 93–105; Tom Terrill, *The Tariff, Politics, and American Foreign Policy, 1874–1901* (1973); Mira Wilkins, *The Emergence of the Multinational Enterprise* (1970); William Appleman Williams, *The Roots of the Modern American Empire* (1969).

The American Navy

Benjamin F. Cooling, *Gray Steel and Blue Water Navy* (1979); Frederick C. Drake, *The Empire of the Seas* (1984) (on Shufeldt); Kenneth J. Hagan, *American Gunboat Diplomacy and the Old Navy, 1877–1889* (1973); Kenneth J. Hagan, ed., *In Peace and War,* 2nd ed. (1984); Walter R. Herrick, *The American Naval Revolution* (1966); Peter Karsten, *The Naval Aristocracy* (1972); Robert Seager II, *Alfred Thayer Mahan* (1977); Ronald Spector, *Admiral of the New Empire* (1974) (on Dewey).

The Spanish-American-Cuban-Filipino War

Graham A. Cosmas, *An Army for Empire* (1971); Richard Hofstadter, "Cuba, the Philippines, and Manifest Destiny," in *The Paranoid Style in American Politics,* ed. Richard Hofstadter (1967); Walter LaFeber, "That 'Splendid Little War' in Historical Perspective," *Texas Quarterly,* 11 (1968), 89–98; Gerald F. Linderman, *The Mirror of War: American Society and the Spanish-American War* (1974); Ernest R. May, *Imperial Democracy* (1961); Joyce Milton, *The Yellow Journalists* (1989); Julius Pratt, *Expansionists of 1898* (1936); David F. Trask, *The War with Spain in 1898* (1981).

Anti-Imperialism and the Peace Movement

Robert L. Beisner, *Twelve Against Empire* (1968); Kendrick A. Clements, *William Jennings Bryan* (1983); Merle E. Curti, *Peace or War* (1936); Charles DeBenedetti, *Peace Reform in American History* (1980); C. Roland Marchand, *The American Peace Movement and Social Reform, 1898–1918* (1973); Thomas J. Osborne, *"Empire Can Wait": American Opposition to Hawaiian Annexation, 1893–1898* (1981); David S. Patterson, *Toward a Warless World* (1976); E. Berkeley Tompkins, *Anti-Imperialism in the United States* (1970). See also works listed at the end of Chapter 23.

Relations with Cuba and Latin America

Samuel F. Bemis, *The Latin American Policy of the United States* (1943); Arturo M. Carrión, *Puerto Rico* (1983); David Healy, *Drive to Hegemony: The United States in the Caribbean, 1898–1917* (1989); Walter LaFeber, *Inevitable Revolutions* (1983) (on Central America); Walter LaFeber, *The Panama Canal* (1979); Lester D. Langley, *The United States and the Caribbean, 1900–1970* (1980); Lester D. Langley, *Struggle for the American Mediterranean* (1980); David McCullough, *The Path Between the Seas* (1977) (on the Panama Canal); Allan R. Millett, *The Politics of Intervention* (1968) (on Cuba); Dana G. Munro, *Intervention and Dollar Diplomacy in the Caribbean, 1900–1921* (1964); Louis A. Pérez, Jr., *Cuba* (1988); Dexter Perkins, *The Monroe Doctrine, 1867–1907* (1937); Ramon Ruiz, *Cuba* (1968); Karl M. Schmitt, *Mexico and the United States, 1821–1973* (1974); Josefina Vázquez and Lorenzo Meyer, *The United States and Mexico* (1985).

Asia and the Pacific

Charles S. Campbell, *Special Business Interests and the Open Door Policy* (1951); Warren I. Cohen, *America's Response to China,* 2nd ed. (1980); John K. Fairbank, *The United States and China,* 4th ed. (1983); Michael Hunt, *The Making of a Special Relationship* (1983) (on China); Jane Hunter, *The Gospel of Gentility: American Women Missionaries in Turn-of-the-Century China* (1984); Akira Iriye, *Across the Pacific* (1967); Jerry Israel, *Progressivism and the Open Door* (1971); Paul M. Kennedy, *The Samoan Tangle* (1974); Robert McClellan, *The Heathen Chinee: A Study of American Attitudes Toward China, 1890–1905* (1971); Thomas J. McCormick, *China Market* (1967); Charles E. Neu, *The Troubled Encounter* (1975) (on Japan); Merze Tate, *The United States and the Hawaiian Kingdom* (1965); Paul A. Varg, *The Making of a Myth: The United States and China, 1897–1912* (1968); Marilyn Blatt Young, *The Rhetoric of Empire* (1968).

The Philippines: Insurrection and Colony

John M. Gates, *Schoolbooks and Krags: The United States Army in the Philippines, 1898–1902* (1973); Brian M. Linn, *The U.S. Army and Counterinsurgency in the Philippine War, 1898–1902* (1989); Glenn A. May, *Social Engineering in the Philippines* (1980); Stuart C. Miller, *"Benevolent Assimilation"* (1982); Julius Pratt, *America's Colonial Experiment* (1950); Daniel B. Schirmer, *Republic or Empire?* (1972); Peter Stanley, *A Nation in the Making* (1974); Richard E. Welch, *Response to Imperialism: American Resistance to the Philippine War* (1972); Walter L. Williams, "United States Indian Policy and the Debate over Philippine Annexation," *Journal of American History,* 66 (1980), 810–831.

Britain and Canada

Kenneth Bourne, *Britain and the Balance of Power in North America, 1815–1908* (1967); Robert C. Brown, *Canada's National Policy, 1883–1900* (1964); Alexander E. Campbell, *Great Britain and the United States, 1895–1903* (1960); Charles S. Campbell, *From Revolution to Rapprochement: The United States and Great Britain, 1783–1900* (1974); Adrian Cook, *The Alabama Claims* (1975); Bradford Perkins, *The Great Rapprochement* (1968).

"Oh my God, what am I to do?" murmured Woodrow Wilson. Just moments before he had been holding Ellen Axson Wilson's hand when she died after years of suffering kidney disease. Two days earlier, on August 4, 1914, as he kept vigil at her bedside, the president had drafted a message offering American mediation to end the menacing war the European nations had just begun. Seldom have such painful personal and official burdens fallen on a president at the same time.

In twenty-nine years of marriage Ellen Axson Wilson had been central to his well-being and success. Woodrow Wilson cherished her loyalty, intelligence, and strength in the family. She was a southern woman, born into a Presbyterian minister's family, educated at a small Georgia women's college, and dedicated to making a pleasant home for her husband and daughters. Ellen Axson Wilson was also a painter, avid reader of Shakespeare and Wordsworth, and mother who made her children's clothing, nursed them through scarlet fever, and planned the family budget. A well-managed and serene household mattered to her. "A woman's place is to keep one little spot in the world quiet," she said. She was not, in today's sense, an emancipated woman, although she once complained about having to stay home "like the fixtures." Yet she did not confine herself to the home, often entering her husband's political world to discuss issues with decision makers.

Now, at a time of wrenching bereavement, when the partner who had always helped him in times of crisis was gone, Woodrow Wilson faced momentous decisions about America's place in the First World War. In his private grief he found it difficult to concentrate on affairs of state. Wilson had always striven to practice self-control; nations, too, he had long believed, should demonstrate the "dignity of self-control." Yet, as the president entered the era of the First World War, both personal and national self-control, however imperative, seemed elusive. He sought to achieve both, but soon personal and national tragedy, not achievement, marked his record.

The Great War in Europe shocked Woodrow Wilson and the American people. For years Americans had witnessed and partici-

23

AMERICA AT WAR, 1914–1920

Americans Arriving in Paris, July 14, 1918 (detail) by eyewitness artist J. F. Bouchor. Oil on canvas. *U.S. Military Academy, West Point Museum. Photo by Henry Groskinsky.*

The Wilson family: from left to right, Margaret, Ellen Axson Wilson (1860–1914), Eleanor, Jessie, and President Woodrow Wilson (1856–1924). Ellen Axson Wilson died just as the First World War was breaking out. The president married again in 1915, just as a major national debate over American preparedness for war was heating up. *Library of Congress.*

pated in the international competition for colonies, markets, and weapons supremacy. But full-scale war seemed unthinkable in the modern age of progress. "Civilization is all gone, and barbarism come," moaned one social reformer after hearing the gruesome news from the European battlefields. The French and Germans, observed *Harper's Weekly,* were using "huge death engines to mow down men and cities," and "we go about in a daze, hoping to awake from the most horrid of nightmares."

For almost three years President Wilson kept America out of the world war. He sought to protect American interests as a neutral trader and to improve the nation's military posture, all the while lecturing the belligerents to rediscover their humanity and to respect international law. But American neutrality, lives, and property fell victim to British and German naval warfare. In early 1917 the president asked Congress for a declaration of war

with his characteristic crusading zeal. America joined the battle not just to win the war but to reform the postwar world.

The American people, even after more than a decade of progressive reform, remained heterogeneous and fractious during the war. In 1914 labor-capital confrontations—like the Ludlow Massacre in Colorado, in which two women and eleven children were killed when state militia attempted to break a miners' strike—still claimed headlines. Racial antagonisms were evident in Wilson's decision to segregate federal buildings in Washington, D.C., and by continued lynchings of blacks (fifty-one in 1914). Nativists protested the fast pace of immigration; 1.2 million immigrants entered the United States in 1914 alone. Ethnic groups eyed one another suspiciously. Many women articulated the case for equality among the sexes and for female suffrage, while many men restated the case for traditional subordination.

IMPORTANT EVENTS

1914	American troops invade Mexico	**1918**	Wilson announces Fourteen Points
	First World War begins		Sedition Act
1915	Germany declares war zone around British Isles		Eugene Debs imprisoned
			U.S. troops at Château-Thierry
	German U-boat sinks *Lusitania*		U.S. troops intervene in Russia
	Bryan resigns in protest		Flu epidemic
1916	Gore-McLemore resolution loses		Republicans win congressional elections
	U.S. troops invade Mexico again		Armistice
	Sussex torpedoed	**1919**	Paris Peace Conference at Versailles
	National Defense Act		May Day bombs
	Wilson re-elected		American Legion founded
1917	Germany declares unrestricted submarine warfare		Red Summer; Chicago race riot
	Zimmermann telegram		Steel strike
	Russian Revolution		Communist Party of the U.S. founded
	U.S. entry into First World War		Wilson suffers stroke
	Selective Service Act		Senate rejects Treaty of Paris
	Espionage Act		*Schenck* v. *U.S.*
	Race riot in East St. Louis, Illinois	**1920**	Palmer Raids (Red Scare)
	War Industries Board created		Nineteenth Amendment ratified
	War Revenue Act		
	Fuel crisis due to severe winter		

The war experience accentuated and intensified the nation's social divisiveness. Whites who did not like the migration of southern blacks to work in northern defense plants resisted their new neighbors, and race riots revealed once again the depth of racial prejudice. German-Americans were denounced as traitors, and war hawks harassed pacifists. The federal government itself, eager to arouse patriotism, trampled on civil liberties to silence critics. And, as communism implanted itself in Soviet Russia, America suffered a postwar Red Scare that did further damage to its reputation as a free and democratic society. In the aftermath of war, groups that sought to consolidate gains made during the war vied with those who sought to restore the prewar status quo.

America's participation in the war also wrought massive changes and accelerated trends already in motion. Wars are emergencies, and during such times the normal way of doing things surrenders to the extraordinary and exaggerated. This period witnessed greater powers for the presidency, the military draft, unprecedented centralization and integration of the economy, increased standardization of products, and unusual cooperation between government and business. The war experience also helped cause the splintering and fading of the progressive movement, although reformers did put wartime effort into such issues as prohibition and women's suffrage. But, Jane Addams remarked sadly, "the spirit of fighting burns away all those impulses . . . which foster the will to justice."

The United States came out of the war a major power in a disrupted and economically hobbled world. Yet Americans who had marched to battle as if on a crusade grew disillusioned. They recoiled from the spectacle of the victors squabbling over the spoils, and they chided Wilson for failing to deliver his promised "peace without victory." As in the 1790s, 1840s, and 1890s, Americans engaged in a fundamental national debate about foreign policy. The president appealed for American membership in a new international organization, the League of Nations, which he touted as a vehicle for reforming world politics. But the Senate killed his diplomatic offspring, fearful that it might entangle Americans once again in Europe's problems, impede the growth of the American empire, and compromise the country's traditional unilateralism in international affairs. On many fronts, then, Americans during the era of the First World War were at war with themselves.

Neutrality and Unneutrality

The war that erupted in August 1914 grew from years of European competition over trade, colonies, allies, and armaments. Two powerful alliance systems had formed: in the Triple Alliance were Germany, Austria-Hungary, and Italy; the Triple Entente combined Britain, France, and Russia. All had imperial ambitions, but Germany seemed particularly bold as it rivaled Britain for world leadership. Strategists said that Europe enjoyed a balance of power, but a series of crises in the Balkans (southeastern Europe) started a chain of events that shattered the "balance" and propelled the European nations into battle.

Slavic nationalists in the Balkans sought to attach to Serbia, an independent Slavic nation, regions like Bosnia, a province of the Austro-Hungarian Empire (see map). In June 1914 at Sarajevo (a city in Bosnia), the heir to the Austro-Hungarian throne was assassinated by a member of the Black Hand, a Slavic terrorist group using Serbia as a base. Austria-Hungary, long worried that a large Slavic state—an enlarged Serbia—would grow on its southern border, consulted its Triple Alliance partner Germany, which urged toughness. Serbia called upon its Slavic friend Russia for help. Russia looked to its ally France. When Austria-Hungary declared war against Serbia in late July, on the

> **Outbreak of the First World War**

grounds that the Serbian government tolerated anti-Austrian terrorists, Russia began to mobilize its armies. Having goaded Austria-Hungary toward war and now certain that war was coming its way, Germany struck first, declaring war against Russia on August 1 and against France two days later. What would the British do? They hesitated, but when Germany slashed into Belgium to get at France, Britain declared war against Germany on August 4. Eventually Turkey joined the Central Powers of Germany and Austria-Hungary, and Japan and Italy teamed up with the Allies of Britain, France, and Russia. Japan took advantage of the European war to seize Germany's Chinese sphere of influence, Shandong, and to expand Tokyo's power in China. The world was aflame.

President Wilson at first sought to distance America from the conflagration by issuing a proclamation of neutrality. He also asked Americans to refrain from taking sides, to exhibit "fine poise" and "the dignity of self-control." Privately, the president said that "we definitely have to be neutral, since otherwise our mixed populations would wage war on each other." The United States, he fervently hoped, would stand as the pre-eminently sane, civilized nation in a deranged international environment.

Wilson's lofty appeal for American neutrality and unity at home collided with three realities. First, ethnic groups in the United States naturally took sides. Many German-Americans and anti-British Irish-Americans (Ireland was then trying to break free from British rule) cheered for the Central Powers. Americans of British and French ancestry applauded the Allies. Anglo-American traditions and slogans like "Remember Lafayette," as well as the sheer number of Americans with roots in the Allied nations, drew a majority to the Allied cause. To them the war was a matter of democracy against autocracy. Germany's attack on neutral Belgium at the start of the war confirmed in many minds that Germany had become the archetype of unbridled militarism, the defiler of innocent women and children.

> **Ethnic Ties to Europe**

Second, America's economic links with the Allies also rendered neutrality difficult, if not impossible. England had long been one of the nation's best customers. Now the British flooded the United States with new orders for products, includ-

> **Trade and Loans**

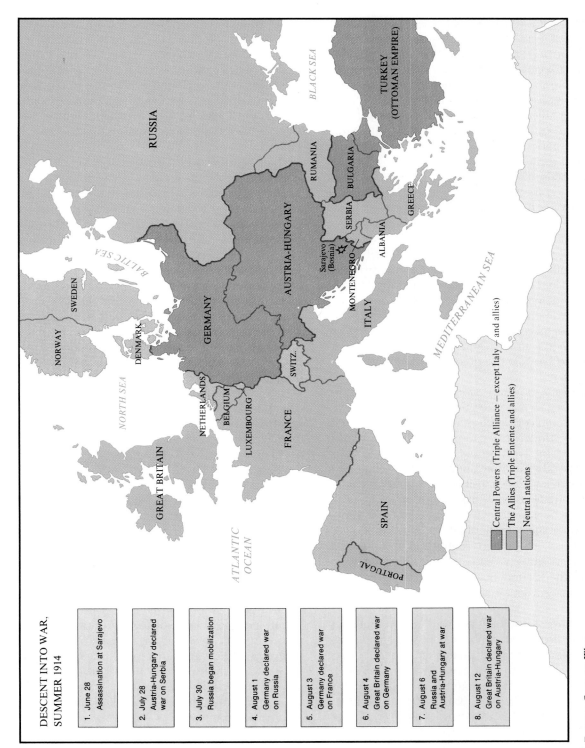

DESCENT INTO WAR, SUMMER 1914

1. **June 28**
   Assassination at Sarajevo

2. **July 28**
   Austria-Hungary declared war on Serbia

3. **July 30**
   Russia began mobilization

4. **August 1**
   Germany declared war on Russia

5. **August 3**
   Germany declared war on France

6. **August 4**
   Great Britain declared war on Germany

7. **August 6**
   Russia and Austria-Hungary at war

8. **August 12**
   Great Britain declared war on Austria-Hungary

Central Powers (Triple Alliance — except Italy — and allies)

The Allies (Triple Entente and allies)

Neutral nations

RUSSIA

TURKEY (OTTOMAN EMPIRE)

BLACK SEA

RUMANIA

BULGARIA

SERBIA

GREECE

ALBANIA

AUSTRIA-HUNGARY

Sarajevo (Bosnia)

MONTENEGRO

ITALY

SWEDEN

NORWAY

BALTIC SEA

DENMARK

GERMANY

SWITZ.

MEDITERRANEAN SEA

NETHERLANDS

BELGIUM

LUXEMBOURG

FRANCE

NORTH SEA

GREAT BRITAIN

ATLANTIC OCEAN

SPAIN

PORTUGAL

Europe Goes to War

▶ 667

ing arms. Sales to the Allies helped pull the economy out of its recession. In 1914 American exports to England and France totaled $753 million; in 1916 the figure spurted to $2.75 billion. In the same period, however, exports to Germany dropped from $345 million to only $29 million. Much of the American-Allied trade was financed through private American loans, amounting to $2.3 billion during the period of neutrality; in stark contrast, Germany received only $27 million.

The Wilson administration, which at first frowned on the transactions, came to see them as necessary to the economic health of the United States. Without loans to help the Allies pay for American products, one of Wilson's key advisers gloomily told the president, the United States would suffer "restriction of output, industrial depression, idle capital, idle labor, numerous failures, financial demoralization, and general unrest and suffering among the laboring classes." From Germany's perspective, the linkage between the American economy and the Allies meant that the United States had become the quite-unneutral Allied arsenal and bank.

Americans, however, were caught in a dilemma: for the United States to cut its economic ties with Britain would constitute an unneutral act in favor of Germany. Under international law, Britain (which controlled the seas) could buy contraband (war-related goods) and noncontraband from neutrals. It was Germany's responsibility, not America's, to stop the trade in ways that international law prescribed—by an effective blockade of the enemy's territory or the seizure of all goods from belligerent (British) ships and contraband from neutral (American) ships. From Germany's perspective, of course, the United States's huge trade with the Allies was an act of unneutrality that had to be stopped.

The third reason neutrality did not work derived from the pro-Allied sympathies of Wilson administration officials. Shortly after Ellen Wilson's death, the president received a note

Pro-Allied Sympathies from another man who had lost his wife, British Foreign Secretary Edward Grey. Wilson, moved by the thoughtful message, replied "that we are bound together by common principle and purpose." He was talking not about their shared personal tragedies but about their agreement that a German victory would destroy "free industry and enter-

prise" and government by law. If Germany won the war, Wilson prophesied, "it would change the course of our civilization and make the United States a military nation." Wilson's chief advisers and diplomats—Edward House (Wilson's assistant), Secretary of State Robert Lansing, and Ambassador to London Walter Hines Page—held similar anti-German views that often translated into pro-Allied policies.

The president and his aides also believed that Wilsonian principles stood a better chance of international acceptance if Britain, rather than the Central Powers, sat astride the postwar

Wilso-nianism world. "Wilsonianism"—the cluster of ideas espoused by Wilson—consisted of traditional American principles. Wilson's ideal world was to be open in every sense: no barriers to commerce, no impediments to democratic politics, no secret diplomatic deals. Empires were to be opened up in keeping with the principle of self-determination, and armaments were to be reduced. Wilson envisioned free market, nonexploitative capitalism and political constitutionalism for all nations to ensure the good society and world peace. His critics complained that Wilson often violated his own tenets in his eagerness to force them upon others. All agreed, though, that such ideals served the American national interest; in this way idealism and realism were married.

Wilson also articulated the traditional belief in American exceptionalism. America, he believed, had a mission to reform international relations and other societies. American progressivism was to be projected onto the world. "We created this Nation," he intoned, "not to serve ourselves, but to serve mankind." Wilson's missionary zeal blended with a pragmatism that bespoke his understanding of the balance of world power and America's major position in the world economy. His inheritance was the expansionism and imperialism that characterized American foreign policy before the First World War. Like his predecessors he believed that even unsavory methods—such as military intervention—sometimes became necessary to protect American interests.

To say that American neutrality was never a real possibility, given ethnic loyalties, economic ties, and Wilsonian preferences, is not to say that Wilson sought to enter the war. He emphatically wanted to keep the United States out and in fact did so for two-and-a-half years. Time and again, Wilson tried to mediate the crisis so that one power would not crush another. The president remarked in early 1917 that "we are the only one of the great white nations that is free from war today, and it would be a crime against civilization for us to go in." But go in the United States finally did. Why?

Americans got caught in the Allied–Central Power crossfire. British naval policy was designed to sever neutral trade with Germany in order to cripple the German economy. The British, "ruling the waves and waiving the rules," declared a blockade of water entrances to Germany; defined a broad list of contraband (including foodstuffs), which was not supposed to be shipped to Germany by neutrals; mined the North Sea; and harassed neutral shipping by seizing cargoes. American vessels bearing goods for Germany seldom reached their destination. To counter German submarines, the British flouted international law by arming their merchant ships and flying neutral (sometimes American) flags. Wilson frequently protested British violations of neutral rights, pointing out that neutrals had the right to sell and ship noncontraband goods to belligerents without interference. But London often deftly defused American criticism by paying for confiscated cargoes, and provocative German actions made British behavior seem less serious by comparison.

> **British Naval Policy**

Germany struggled to lift the blockade and to end American-Allied commerce. Unable to win the war on land, German leaders looked for victory at sea by using submarines. In February 1915 Berlin announced that it was creating a war zone around the British Isles; all enemy ships in the area would be sunk. Neutral vessels were warned to stay out so as not to be attacked by mistake, and passengers from neutral nations were warned to stay off enemy ships. Writing diplomatic messages on his own typewriter, President Wilson stiffly informed Germany that the United States was holding it to "strict accountability" for any losses of American life and property.

Wilson was interpreting existing international law in the strictest sense. Such law held that an attacker had to warn a passenger or merchant ship before attacking, so that passengers and crew could disembark safely into lifeboats. That rule predated the emergence of the submarine as a major weapon,

> **The Submarine and International Law**

yet Wilson refused to make adjustments. The Germans thought him unfair. As they saw it, the slender, frail, and sluggish *unterseebooten* could not surface to warn ships of their imminent destruction. Surfacing would deny the U-boats the advantage of surprise. A surfaced submarine became a sitting target for a British deck gun or hand grenade, and British vessels had standing orders to ram U-boats and sink them. Finally, the time required to evacuate passengers usually gave the distressed ship adequate opportunity to radio for help to a British destroyer in nearby waters. Berlin frequently complained to Wilson that he was denying the Germans the one weapon they could use to break the British economic stranglehold, disrupt the Allies' substantial connection with American producers and bankers, and win the war. To all concerned—British, Germans, and Americans—this naval warfare seemed a matter of life and death, a vital question of national survival.

Wilson, the Submarine, and War

Over the next few months the U-boats sank ship after ship. In May the sinking of the *Lusitania* stunned Wilson. When the swift, luxurious British passenger liner left New York City with more than twelve hundred passengers aboard, it also carried a cargo of food and contraband, including 4.2 million rounds of ammunition for Remington rifles. Before "Lucy's" departure, the newspapers carried an unusual announcement from the German embassy: travelers on British vessels were warned that Allied ships in war-zone waters "are liable to destruction." Few passengers paid attention to the notice; few shifted to an American vessel for the transatlantic trip. On May 7, off the Irish coast, submarine U-20 unleashed torpedoes at the four-stacked vessel. The *Lusitania* sank quickly, taking to their deaths 1,198 people, 128 of them Americans.

Even if the ship was carrying armaments, argued Wilson, the sinking was a brutal assault on innocent people. But he ruled out a military response. Secretary of State William Jennings Bryan advised

"Here's money for your Americans. I may drown some more," says the imperious German kaiser to the incredulous President Wilson. This anti-German cartoon appeared in April 1916 after Germany expressed "profound regret" for causing American deaths almost a year earlier when a U-boat sunk the British liner *Lusitania.* The Germans offered an indemnity, but they also defended their use of submarines as necessary to break the British blockade. Not until 1925 did a claims commission determine that Germany should pay $2.5 million in damages to American claimants who had suffered losses because of the *Lusitania* disaster. Life *Magazine, April 13, 1916. The Boston Athenaeum.*

Reaction to the Sinking of the *Lusitania*

that Americans be prohibited from travel on belligerent ships and that passenger vessels be prohibited from carrying war goods. "Germany has a right to prevent contraband going to the Allies," wrote Bryan, "and a ship carrying contraband should not rely on passengers to protect her from attack—it would be like putting women and children in front of an army." Bryan also urged Wilson to forward protest notes to both London and Berlin.

The president moved deliberately. He rejected Bryan's counsel and sent a note to Berlin insisting on the right of Americans to sail on belligerent ships and demanding that Germany cease its inhumane submarine warfare. "Weasel words" from "the word-lover in the White House," shouted Theodore Roosevelt, one of many jingoists who clamored for war. When the Germans replied to Wilson that he should rethink the relationship between international law and the submarine, the president fumed. After a stormy White House meeting marked by Bryan's charge that the cabinet was pro-Allied, Wilson dispatched a second letter to Germany reiterating the demand that submarines be kept in port. When the president refused to ban American travelers from belligerent ships, Bryan resigned in protest—an uncommon act for unhappy secretaries of state, who usually leave quietly. The pro-Allied Robert Lansing was elevated to the top diplomatic post. To criticism that he was pursuing a double standard favoring the Allies, Wilson responded that the British were taking cargoes and violating property rights, but the Germans were taking lives and violating human rights. Wilson's attitude toward Germany had noticeably hardened.

Germany, seeking to avoid war with America, ordered its U-boat commanders to halt attacks on passenger liners. But in mid-August another British vessel, the *Arabic,* was sunk and two American lives were lost. The Germans hastened to pledge that never again would an unarmed passenger ship be attacked without warning. But the sinking of the *Arabic* fueled the debate over American passengers on belligerent vessels. Why not require Americans to sail on American craft? asked critics. From August 1914 to March 1917 only three Americans died on an American ship (the tanker *Gulflight* in May 1915), while about 190 were killed on belligerent ships.

In early 1916 Congress began to debate the Gore-McLemore resolution, which would prohibit Americans from traveling on armed merchant vessels or on ships carrying contraband. The resolution, it was hoped, would prevent incidents like the sinking of the *Lusitania* from hurtling the United States into war. But Wilson would tolerate no interference in the presidential making of foreign policy (he had just sent House to European capitals to mediate an end to the war) and no restrictions on American travel. The resolution, he argued, would destroy the "whole fine fabric of international law." After

Gore-McLemore Resolution

heavy politicking, the House defeated the resolution 276 to 142 and the Senate followed suit 68 to 14. If America's goal was to avoid entry into the First World War, Wilson's critics have pointed out, passage of the Gore-McLemore resolution would have avoided or at least delayed a German-American confrontation over the submarine without undercutting American interests or besmirching national honor.

In March 1916 an attack on the *Sussex,* a French vessel crossing the English Channel, took the United States a step closer to war. Four Americans on that ship, which the U-boat commander mistook for a minelayer, were injured. Stop the marauding submarines, Wilson lectured Berlin, or he would sever diplomatic relations. Again the Germans backed off, pledging not to attack merchant vessels without warning. At about the same time, relations with Britain soured. The British crushing of the Irish Easter Rebellion and further restriction of American trade with the Central Powers aroused American anger.

Sentiment for peace remained strong, as evidenced by Wilson's victory on a peace platform in the 1916 election. After his triumph, Wilson futilely labored once again to bring the belligerents to the conference table. In early 1917 he advised them to temper their acquisitive war aims, appealing for a "peace without victory."

In early February 1917, Germany startled the Wilson administration by launching unrestricted submarine warfare. All vessels, belligerent or neutral, warship or merchant, would be attacked if sighted in the declared war zone. This bold decision represented a calculated risk that submarines could impede munitions shipments from America to England and thus defeat the Allies before Americans could be mobilized and ferried across the Atlantic to enter the fight. Wilson quickly broke diplomatic relations with Berlin. Everybody waited for the inevitable collision.

> **Unrestricted Submarine Warfare**

With this German challenge to American neutral rights and economic interests came a German threat to American security. In late February, the British intercepted, decoded, and handed to the American government a telegram addressed to the German minister in Mexico from German

> **Mexican Revolution and Zimmermann Telegram**

Foreign Secretary Arthur Zimmermann. The minister was instructed to tell the Mexican government that if it joined a military alliance against the United States, Germany would help Mexico to recover the territories it had been forced to give up to its northern neighbor in 1848. Zimmermann hoped, as he expressed it to other German officials, to "*set new enemies on America's neck*—enemies which give them plenty to take care of over there."

American officials took the message seriously, because at the time Mexican-American relations were extremely tense. The Mexican Revolution, a bloody civil war with strong anti-American overtones, had spilled across the Rio Grande, and the Mexican government was threatening to nationalize American properties. Wilson had twice ordered American troops onto Mexican soil: in 1914 at Veracruz, to avenge a slight to the American uniform and flag; and again in 1916 in northern Mexico, where General John J. "Black Jack" Pershing spent months trying to capture the elusive Pancho Villa after his raid on an American border town. Lansing and Wilson agreed that Zimmermann's telegram constituted "a conspiracy against this country."

Soon after learning of Zimmermann's ploy, Wilson asked Congress for "armed neutrality" to defend American lives and commerce. He requested the specific authority to arm American merchant ships and the more general power to "employ any other instrumentalities or methods that may be necessary." In the midst of the debate, Wilson released Zimmermann's telegram to the press; Americans expressed outrage. Still, antiwar Senators Robert M. La Follette and George Norris, among others, saw the armed-ship bill as a blank check for the president to move the country to war, and they filibustered it to death. Wilson, denouncing them as a "little group of willful men," proceeded to arm America's commercial vessels anyway. The action came too late to prevent the sinking of several American ships. War cries echoed across the nation. In late March, after agonizing in private for some time, Wilson called Congress into special session.

On April 2, 1917, the president stepped before a hushed Congress. Solemnly he chided the Germans for "warfare against mankind." Passionately and eloquently Wilson explained American grievances: Germany's violation of the principle of freedom of the seas, disruption of

> **Wilson's War Message**

Jeanette Rankin (1880–1973) was the first woman to sit in the House of Representatives (elected in 1916) and the only member of Congress to vote against American entry into both world wars (in 1917 and 1941). A native of Montana, Rankin became a social worker and woman's suffrage activist. A lifelong pacifist, she led a march in Washington—at age eighty-seven—to protest the Vietnam War. *Brown Brothers.*

American commerce, the attempt to stir up trouble in Mexico, and violation of human rights by killing innocent Americans. The "Prussian autocracy" had to be punished by the "democracies." Russia was now among the latter, he was pleased to report, because the Russian Revolution had ousted the czar just weeks before. Wilson's most famous words rang out: "The world must be made safe for democracy." Congress quickly declared war against Germany by a vote of 373 to 50 in the House and 82 to 6 in the Senate. The first woman ever to sit in Congress, Montana's Jeannette Rankin, elected in 1916, cast a ringing "no" vote that won her high ranking in the pantheon of American pacifism. "Peace is a woman's job," she believed, "because men have a natural fear of being classed as cowards if they oppose war" and because mothers should protect their children from death-dealing weapons.

For principle, for morality, for honor, for commerce, for security—for all these reasons the United States took up arms against Germany. The submarine was certainly the culprit that drew a reluctant president and nation into the maelstrom. Yet critics like Bryan, Gore, McLemore, La Follette, and Rankin did not think that the U-boat alone was responsible for the American descent into war. They emphasized Wilson's rigid definition of international law, which did not take account of the submarine's tactics. They faulted his contention that Americans could travel anywhere, even on a belligerent ship loaded with contraband, in time of war. They criticized his policies as unneutral. But they lost the debate. Although Americans might agree that Wilson's decisions were anti-German, they seemed to accept his view that the Germans had to be checked to ensure an open and orderly world in which American principles and interests would be safe.

In the most general sense, America went to war to reform world politics, not to destroy Germany. By early 1917 Wilson seemed to believe that after the war America would not be able to claim a seat at the peace conference unless it had been a combatant. At the peace conference, Wilson intended to put into constitutional form the principles he thought essential to a stable world order, to promote democracy and the Open Door, and to outlaw revolution and aggression. If he remained the representative of a neutral nation, he could only "call through a crack in the door" at the postwar conference. In the end, Woodrow Wilson decided for war to gain an American-fashioned peace.

Taking Up Arms and Winning the War

Even before the war decision, the United States had been preparing for combat. Encouraged by such groups as the National Security League and the Navy League and by mounting public outrage against Germany's submarine warfare, the president in 1915 began to plan a substantial military build-up. As the debate over preparedness swirled about the nation's capital, Wilson took a new bride, the widowed Edith Bolling Galt, and went on a two-week honeymoon. When the Wilsons returned in early 1916, Senator La Follette and House Majority Leader Claude Kitchin, among others, vowed to block preparedness. Some pacifist progressives, like Oswald Garrison Villard, Paul Kellogg, and Lillian Wald, had organized in late 1915 an antiwar coalition, the American Union Against Militarism. As well, Jane Addams and suffragist Carrie Chap-

Peace Movement

man Catt had founded the Women's Peace party. The businessman Andrew Carnegie, who in 1910 had established the Carnegie Endowment for International Peace with $10 million in U.S. Steel bonds, helped to finance the peace groups. So did Henry Ford, who spent half a million dollars in late 1915 to send a "peace ship" to Europe to propagandize for a negotiated settlement. "If I had my way," said Ford, "I'd throw every ounce of gunpowder into the sea and strip soldiers of their insignias." Socialists like Eugene Debs added their voices to the peace movement.

The various messages of these antiwar advocates were that war drained a nation of its youth, resources, and impulse for reform; that it fostered a repressive spirit at home; that it violated Christian morality; and that wartime business barons reaped huge profits at the expense of the people. Furthermore, Europe's Great War was self-serving. The very outbreak of the war, they argued, proved that an increase in armaments, such as had occurred in Europe before the war, only precipitated hostilities. Militarism and conscription, Addams pointed out, were what millions of immigrants had left behind in Europe. Were they now—in the United States—to be forced into the decadent system they had escaped?

But the peace movement was splintered, some of its followers endorsing peace but not pacifism, and it could not prevent passage of the National Defense Act of 1916. This legislation provided for increases in the army and National Guard and for summer training camps modeled on the one in Plattsburg, New York, where a slice of America's social and economic elite had trained in 1915 as "citizen soldiers." The Navy Act, providing for a three-year naval expansion program, soon followed. To pay part of the huge cost of these undertakings, Congress passed the Revenue Act in 1916. Backers of the bill believed that businesspeople should pour back into the national treasury a portion of the profits they were sure to derive from the

Government posters attempted to rally Americans to the armed forces. The artist Howard Chandler Christy often used the traditional theme of war as masculine enterprise in his government-sponsored recruiting posters. *Private collection.*

new defense contracts. The act, which antipreparedness people applauded, raised the surtax on high incomes and corporate profits, imposed a federal tax on large estates, and significantly increased the tax on the gross receipts of munitions manufacturers.

To raise an army after the declaration of war, Congress in May 1917 passed the Selective Service Act, requiring the registration of all males between the ages of twenty and thirty (later

The Draft

changed to eighteen and forty-five). National service, proponents believed, would not only prepare the nation for battle but also promote efficiency, order, democracy, personal sacrifice, and nationalism, and, as one general put it, "heat up the melting pot." Where else but in an army tent could a Boston Brahmin, a butcher, a college student, a dairy farmer, and the son of a washerwoman be brought

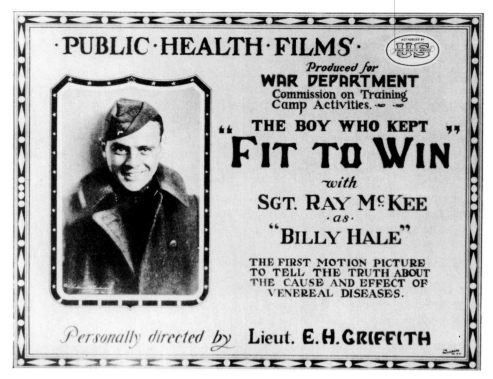

This Commission on Training Camp Activities poster promoted a film about venereal disease intended to combat the serious, sexually transmitted threat to the American military. The film was first titled *Fight to Fight*; after the war, the name was changed to *Fight to Win*. In 1919 the New York State Board of Censors declared the film obscene. *Social Welfare History Archives Center, University of Minnesota.*

together? Critics, on the other hand, feared that "Prussianism," not democratization, would be the likely outcome.

On June 5, 1917, over 9.5 million men signed up for the "great national lottery." By war's end, 24 million men had been registered by local draft boards. Over 4.8 million served in the armed forces, 2 million of whom fought in France. About 16 percent of the male labor force was drawn into military service; millions of laborers received deferments from military duty because they worked in war industries or had personal dependents. Over 300,000 men evaded the draft by failing to show up when called, and 4,000 were classified as conscientious objectors (many more applied for that classification but failed to receive it or changed their minds after induction).

Hundreds of thousands of citizens volunteered to the sound of the popular song "Johnny Get Your Gun." Asked why he joined the army, one soldier replied that he was eager "to see a little of the

biggest scrap the world has ever known." Other volunteers gave different answers: "Girls like soldiers"; they wanted to become men; they were homeless; they wanted to "kick the Kaiser." The typical soldier was a draftee between twenty-one and twenty-three years old, white, single, and poorly educated (most had not attended high school). Perhaps as many as 18 percent were foreign-born, and 400,000 were black. Some women became navy clerks; others served in the U.S. Army Signal Corps and Nurse Corps. On college campuses, 150,000 students entered the Student Army Training Corps or similar navy and marine units.

Camp life sapped the fresh recruits of some of their enthusiasm for war. They put in seventeen-hour days. Calisthenics, kitchen duty, target practice, grounds maintenance ("policing the area"), and bayonet drills consumed their regimented time. They ate well but slept on straw mattresses and marched around uncomfortably in olive-drab

Chapter 23: America at War, 1914–1920

Like most African-American troops in the First World War, these soldiers were assigned to noncombat tasks— here the assembling of coffins in France. The irony did not go unnoticed that the United States sent abroad a segregated army to make the world "safe for democracy." *National Archives.*

uniforms and leggings. There were never enough weapons to go around, so some trained without. At officer training camps, the army turned out "ninety-day wonders." Although some soldiers imbibed Wilson's idealism, others were ignorant of the reasons they were going to war. This ignorance of purpose so alarmed Wilson administration officials that they put a copy of the president's war message in every knapsack.

American leaders worried that the young soldiers, once away from their homes, would be tempted by vice—especially by the houses of prostitution and saloons that quickly surrounded training centers. To protect the supposed novices with "invisible armor," the government created the Commission on Training Camp Activities to coordinate the work of the YMCA and other groups that dispensed food, showed movies, held athletic contests, and distributed books. Men in uniform were not permitted to drink. Alarmed by the spread of venereal disease, commission officials declared

▶ **Commission on Training Camp Activities**

"sin-free" zones around military bases and lectured the soldiers that they could still preserve their manhood if they practiced "sexual continence" (abstention). Besides facing the danger of a disabling disease, "a man who is thinking below the belt is not efficient," the recruits were told. American Federation of Labor President Samuel Gompers thought the moralizing ridiculous and the prohibitions unenforceable, because "real men will be men." But Navy Secretary Josephus Daniels answered that "men must live straight if they would shoot straight."

Jim Crow was in the army too. Fearing "arrogant, strutting representatives of black soldiery in every community," as Senator James K. Vardaman of Mississippi snarled, many politicians opposed the drafting of blacks. But the army needed men, white and black. The NAACP and W. E. B. Du Bois urged blacks to join the fight for "world liberty," for they thought that a war to make the world safe for democracy might blur the color line at home. Military leaders actually segregated facilities, discouraged blacks from becoming officers, and assigned black recruits to menial labor. Racist slang echoed through the camps. In Houston, Texas, angry black soldiers took up arms against whites who had been goading them, killing thirteen. After brief "trials," thirteen blacks were executed; another six were hanged after an unsuccessful appeal of their death sentences; others were court-martialed and given long prison terms.

In Europe, the head of the American Expeditionary Forces (AEF), General John J. Pershing, insisted that his troops remain an independent American army. He was not about to put his AEF "doughboys"—called such by the French because the Americans looked so clean compared to French soldiers mired in trench warfare—under the leadership of Allied commanders who had become wedded to unimaginative and deadly trench warfare, producing military stalemate and ghastly casualties on the Western front. Zigzag trenches fronted by barbed wire and mines stretched across France. Beyond the muddy and stinking trenches lay "no man's land," denuded by artillery fire. When ordered out, soldiers would charge the German lines, also a maze of trenches. Machine guns mowed them down; chlorine gas, first used by Germany in 1915, poisoned them. Little was gained. At the Battle of the Somme in 1916 the British and French suffered 600,000 dead or wounded to earn only 125 square miles (the Germans lost 500,000 men).

The influx of American men and materiel decided the outcome of the First World War. With both sides virtually exhausted, the Americans tipped the balance toward the Allies. Actually, the American forces, successfully convoyed across the Atlantic by the United States Navy, did not engage in much combat until after the lull of the severe winter of 1917–1918. In March 1918, after knocking Russia out of the war, closing the eastern front, and shifting troops to France, the Germans launched a major offensive. By May, Kaiser Wilhelm's forces had stormed to within fifty miles of Paris, the French capital. In late May, troops of the U.S. First Division helped blunt the German advance at Cantigny (see map). In June the U.S. Second Division fought the Germans at Château-Thierry in the Belleau Wood; before American soldiers won, 5,183 of 8,000 marines died or were wounded after they made almost sacrificial frontal attacks against German ma-

> **Americans in Combat in France**

chine guns. American troops marched on, fighting Germans in the Second Battle of the Marne, an Allied victory that seemed to turn the tide against the Germans. In September French and American forces took St. Mihiel. That month, too, the Allies began their massive Meuse-Argonne offensive. More than a million Americans joined British and French troops in weeks of fierce combat during cold, rainy weather. More than 26,000 Americans died in that campaign before the Allies claimed the Argonne Forest on October 10.

Firsthand war, American soldiers in France soon learned, certainly differed from popular, abstract slogans that glorified American participation. They came to know the muck and putrid smell of trench warfare and the horrors of poison gas. Some suffered battle shock: violent tremors, dazed eyes, listless arms and legs. By today's standards army medicine and psychiatry were primitive. Away from the front lines, Red Cross canteens staffed by women volunteers served the soldiers as way stations in a strange land, offering haircuts, food, and recreation. American troops might even have met some American literary figures. Early in the war e e cummings, John Dos Passos, Ernest Hemingway, and others had volunteered for ambulance service in Allied countries because they thought it a humane thing to do. But another motive drove them, too, as Dos Passos explained candidly: "What was war like? We wanted to see with our own eyes. . . . I wanted to see the show."

For some young warriors, "the show" played in cafés and brothels—just as officials had feared. In Paris, where no less than forty major houses of prostitution thrived, it became a common if cruel saying that the British were drunkards, the French were whoremongers, and the Americans were both. Despite Pershing's lecture that "sexual intercourse is not necessary for good health," soldiers indulged. Venereal disease became a serious problem. At one point, French Prime Minister Georges Clemenceau offered licensed, supposedly health-inspected prostitutes in "special houses" to the American army. When the generous Gallic offer was received in Washington, Secretary of War Newton Baker gasped, "For god's sake . . . don't show this to the President or he'll stop the war." By war's end, data revealed that about 15 percent of America's soldiers had become afflicted with venereal disease,

> **Problem of Venereal Disease**

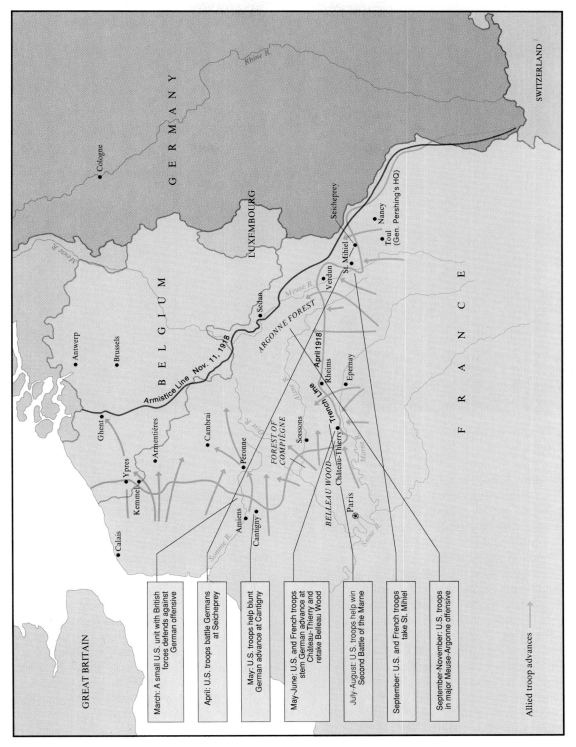

American Troops at the Western Front, 1918

March: A small U.S. unit with British forces defends against German offensive

April: U.S. troops battle Germans at Seicheprey

May: U.S. troops help blunt German advance at Cantigny

May–June: U.S. and French troops stem German advance at Château-Thierry and retake Belleau Wood

July–August: U.S. troops help win Second Battle of the Marne

September: U.S. and French troops take St. Mihiel

September–November: U.S. troops in major Meuse-Argonne offensive

Allied troop advances

GREAT BRITAIN

GERMANY

BELGIUM

LUXEMBOURG

FRANCE

SWITZERLAND

Cologne

Rhine R.

Meuse R.

Antwerp

Brussels

Ghent

Ypres

Kemmel

Calais

Armentières

Cambrai

Péronne

Amiens

Cantigny

Somme R.

FOREST OF COMPIÈGNE

Soissons

BELLEAU WOOD

Château-Thierry

Paris

Seine R.

Marne R.

Rheims

Epernay

Trench Line April 1918

Sedan

Armistice Line   Nov. 11, 1918

ARGONNE FOREST

Verdun

St. Mihiel

Seicheprey

Nancy

Toul
(Gen. Pershing's HQ)

An American soldier of Company K, 110th Infantry Regiment, receives aid during fighting at Verennes, France. *National Archives.*

costing the army 7 million days of active duty and $50 million. Periodic inspections, chemical prophylactic treatments, and the threat of court-martial for infected soldiers kept the problem from being even more disastrous—and kept the AEF in the field to help win the First World War.

American victories in the fall of 1918 spelled doom for Germany. Its ground war a shambles, its submarine warfare a dismal failure, its troops and cities mutinous, and abandoned

> **Casualties**

by Turkey and Austria, Berlin sued for peace. The armistice was signed on November 11, 1918. The belligerents then counted their awesome casualties: 8 million soldiers and 6.6 million civilians dead and 21.3 million people wounded. Of these numbers, the United States suffered more than 200,000 soldiers wounded, and more than 50,000 American soldiers died in battle (another 62,000 American soldiers died from disease—many from the worldwide flu epidemic of 1918).

President Wilson welcomed the armistice not only because it ended the bloodletting, but also because it was signed on *his* terms. The combatants

> **The Fourteen Points**

agreed that the president's Fourteen Points, which he had enunciated in January, would guide the peace negotiations. The Allies initially balked, but Wilson scared them into acceptance by threatening a separate peace with Germany. The Fourteen Points summarized "Wilsonianism." The first five called for diplomacy in the "public view," freedom of the seas, lower tariffs, reductions in armaments, and the decolonization of empires. Points 6 through 13 appealed for self-determination for national groups in Europe. For Wilson the fourteenth point was the most important, the mechanism for achieving all the others: "a general association of nations" or League of Nations. Having won the war, the resolute Wilson set out to win the peace and build a stable world order following American principles.

The Home Front

"It is not an army that we must shape and train for war," declared the president, "it is a nation." The United States was a belligerent for only nineteen months, but the war had a tremendous impact on domestic America. The federal government quickly geared the economy to war needs and marshaled public opinion for the sacrifices and adjustments imposed by belligerency. As never before, the state intervened in American life. An unprecedented concentration of bureaucratic power developed in Washington, D.C. To progressives of the New Nationalist persuasion, the expansion and centralization of government power were welcome. To others they seemed an excessive and dangerous development. "War is the health of the state," said radical intellectual Randolph Bourne.

The federal government and private business became partners during the war. Dollar-a-year executives flocked to the nation's capital from major

Business-Government Cooperation

companies; they retained their corporate salaries while serving in official administrative and consulting capacities. Early in the war, the government relied on several industrial committees for advice on purchases and prices. But evidence of self-interested businesspeople cashing in on the national interest aroused public protest. The chief of the aluminum advisory committee, for example, was also president of the largest aluminum company in America. The committees were disbanded in July 1917 in favor of the War Industries Board (WIB). The government, however, continued to work closely with business through trade associations, which grew significantly in number. Business-government cooperation was also stimulated by the suspension of antitrust laws; by cost-plus contracts, which guaranteed companies a healthy profit and a means to pay higher wages to head off labor strikes; by the Webb-Pomerene Act (1918), which granted immunity from antitrust legislation to companies that combined to operate in the export trade; by the virtual abandonment of competitive bidding; and by a floor placed under prices to ensure profits.

Hundreds of new government agencies, staffed largely by businesspeople, came into being to wage the war. Some of the superagencies placed un-

The National Association of Manufacturers, a business organization, published this poster to support economic mobilization at home, to dissuade workers from striking by appealing to their patriotism, and to make the point that wars are won not only on battlefields but also in factories. *The State Historical Society of Wisconsin.*

precedented controls on the economy. The Food Administration, led by Herbert Hoover, undertook programs to improve production and conserve food through voluntary action; it also set prices and regulated distribution. Americans were urged to grow "victory gardens" in their backyards and to eat meatless and wheatless meals. The Railroad Administration took over the snarled and financially troubled railway industry. When strikes threatened the telephone and telegraph companies, the federal government seized and ran them.

The largest and potentially most powerful of the wartime agencies was the War Industries Board. Designed as a clearinghouse to coordinate the national economy and headed after early 1918 by

War Industries Board

financier Bernard Baruch, the WIB faced the enormous task of satisfying both Allied and domestic needs. It made purchases, allocated supplies, and fixed prices. This often meant satisfying business requests for price increases. The WIB ordered the standardization of goods to save materials and streamline production. The number of colors of typewriter ribbon, for example, was reduced from 150 to 5. Although the WIB seemed all-powerful, in reality it had to conciliate competing interest groups and compromise with the businesspeople whose advice it so valued.

The performance of the mobilized economy was mixed, but it delivered enough men and materiel to France to ensure the defeat of the Central Powers. About a quarter of all American production was diverted to war needs. Farmers enjoyed boom years as they put more acreage into production and watched prices go up. Induced to produce more at a faster pace, farmers mechanized as never before. From 1915 to 1920 the number of tractors in American fields jumped tenfold. Gross farm income for the period from 1914 to 1919 increased from $7.6 billion to $17.7 billion. Although manufacturing output leveled off in 1918, some industries enjoyed substantial increases because of wartime demand. Steel reached a peak production of 45 million tons in 1917, twice the prewar figure. The cigarette industry profited from the marked wartime increase in the consumption of tobacco, from 26 billion cigarettes in 1916 to 48 billion in 1918. The gross national product in 1920 was 237 percent higher than in 1914.

Massive assignments had to be completed in a hurry, and mistakes were made. Weapons deliveries fell short of demand; the bloated bureaucracy of the War Shipping Board failed to build enough ships. As the mercury dipped in the severe winter of 1917–1918, millions of Americans found that they could not get coal, because the coal companies had held back on production to raise prices and railroads did not have enough coal cars. Harbors froze, closing out coal barges, and the federal government seemed immobilized. People died of pneumonia or freezing: a Brooklyn man went out in the morning to forage for coal and returned to find his two-month-old daughter frozen to death in her crib. In January, blizzards shut down midwestern railroads and factories, impeding the war effort.

If the fuel crisis could be blamed on the weather, inflation was directly attributable to government policy. Although inflation was **Inflation** partly caused by demand exceeding supply because of increases in

Allied buying, the government's liberal credit policies and fixing of prices at high levels also encouraged it. As a result, the wholesale price index was 98 percent higher in 1918 than it had been in 1913. By fixing prices on raw materials rather than on finished products, the government lost control of inflation. By bowing to the political pressure of southerners who wanted cotton left unregulated, the government permitted runaway cotton prices. Clothing tripled in cost and food prices more than doubled. A quart of milk that cost 9 cents in 1914 climbed to 17 cents in 1920.

Tax policies during the war months were designed to pull some of the profits reaped from high prices into the treasury. The Wilson administration believed that wealth as well as labor should be conscripted. Still, the government financed only one-third of the war through taxes. The other two-thirds came from loans, including Liberty Bonds sold to the American people through aggressive campaigns. The War Revenue Act of October 1917 provided for a more steeply graduated personal income tax, a corporate income tax, an excess profits tax, and increased excise taxes on alcoholic beverages, tobacco, and luxury items. Although these taxes did curb excessive corporate profiteering, they had several loopholes. Sometimes companies inflated costs to conceal profits or paid high salaries and bonuses to their executives. Four officers of Bethlehem Steel, for example, divided bonuses of $2.3 million in 1917 and $2.1 million the next year. Corporate net earnings for 1913 totaled $4 billion; in 1917 they had risen to $7 billion; and in 1918, after the tax bite and the war's end, they still stood at $4.5 billion. Patriotism and profits had to be partners, the federal government believed, in order for the United States to win the war.

Organized labor sought a partnership with government too, but its gains were far less spectacular. For unions the war seemed to offer opportunities for recognition and better pay. **Wartime** Gompers threw the AFL's loyalty **Labor** to the Wilson administration, promising to deter strikes. He and other moderate labor leaders were rewarded with appointments to high-level wartime government agencies. The National War Labor Board, created to mediate labor disputes, ruled out strikes and lockouts but required management to deal with already organized unions. From roughly 2.7 million in 1916, union membership climbed to over 4 million in 1919. The AFL could not curb strikes by the radical Industrial Workers of the World (IWW) or rebellious AFL locals, especially those with a high proportion of antiwar socialists as members. In the nineteen war months, over six thousand strikes expressed workers' discontent with their wages, working conditions, and inflation. Laborers benefited from the full-employment wartime economy, which increased their total earnings and gave many of them time-and-a-half pay for overtime work. Given the high cost of living, however, workers saw little improvement in their economic standing.

When 16 percent of the male work force trooped off to battle, and when immigration dropped off and some aliens departed to fight for their homelands, depriving business of **Women in the Work Force** much-needed labor, the call went out to women, blacks, and Mexican-Americans (see pages 705–706) to fill vacancies. Munitions makers in Bridgeport, Connecticut, for example, dropped leaflets from airplanes urging women to work in their factories. Although the number of women in the work force increased slightly, the real story was that many shifted from one job to another, sometimes into formerly male domains. Some white women left domestic service for factories, moved from clerking in department stores to stenography and typing, and departed textile mills for employment in firearms plants. Twenty percent or more of all workers in the wartime manufacture of electrical machinery, airplanes, and food were women. As white women took advantage of the new opportunities, black women took some of their places in domestic service and in textile factories. For the first time department stores employed black women as elevator operators and cafeteria waitresses, though they favored light-skinned blacks for these highly visible positions. Overall, most working women remained concentrated in sex-segregated occupations ("women's jobs") as typists, nurses, teachers, and domestic servants.

The movement of women into jobs that had been the preserve of males generated controversy. Some male workers complained that women were destabilizing the work environment with their higher productivity; women answered that they were used to seasonal employment and piecework and hence worked at a faster pace. Some men protested that women were undermining the wage system by

When men trooped off to war, women took industrial jobs as never before. These women are trimming shell fuses in a munitions plant. *UPI/Bettmann Archive.*

working for lower pay; women pointed out that male-dominated companies discriminated against them and unions denied them membership. Finally, male employees resented the spirit of independence evident among women whose labor was now greatly valued. The female workers in a Vermont machine-tool company addressed a crude poem to their harping male cohorts:

> We're independent now you see,
> Your bald head don't appeal to me,
> I love my overalls;
> And I would rather polish steel
> Than get you up a tasty meal.
> Or go with you to balls.
> Now, only premiums good and big,
> Will tempt us maids to change our rig.
> And put our aprons on;
> And cook up all the dainty things,
> That so delighted men and kings
> In days now past and gone.[1]

When the war was over, women lost many of the gains they had made. The attitude that women's

---

[1] Originally appeared in the *Springfield Reporter,* December 5, 1917. Reprinted by permission of *The Eagle Times.*

proper sphere was the home changed very little. Married working women found their family relationships growing tense; husbands and children resented the disruption of home life. Moreover, reformers complained that working mothers were neglecting their children, failing to prepare good meals, and coming home so tired that their housework suffered. Day nurseries were scarce and beyond the means of most working-class families, and few employers provided childcare facilities. Whether married or single—and the great majority of working women were unmarried—women lost their jobs to the returning veterans. "During the war they called us heroines," cried Mary McDowell of the University of Chicago Settlement, "but they throw us on the scrapheap now."

Women participated in the war effort in other ways. As volunteers, they made clothing for refugees and soldiers, rolled bandages, served at Red Cross facilities, and taught French to nurses assigned to the war zone. Many joined the activities of the Women's Committee of the Council of National Defense, whose leaders included Ida Tarbell and Carrie Chapman Catt. A vast network of state, county, and town volunteer organizations, the council publicized government mobilization programs, encouraged home gardens, sponsored drives to sell Liberty Bonds, and continued the push for social welfare reforms. This patriotic work, praised by men who would decide whether women should be granted the vote, improved the prospects for passage of the Nineteenth Amendment (see pp. 623–624).

Wartime mobilization wrought significant changes for the black community. Wartime jobs in the North provided an escape from southern lynchings, political disenfranchisement,

Black Migration to the North

low wages, sharecropping, tenancy, crop liens, debt peonage, floods, and boll-weevil-stricken cotton crops. During the war years, southern blacks undertook a great migration to northern cities to work in railroad yards, packing houses, steel mills, shipyards, and coal mines. In the decade from 1910 to 1920, Cleveland's black population swelled by over 300 percent, Detroit's by over 600 percent, and Chicago's by 150 percent, much of the increase occurring between 1916 and 1919. All told, about a half-million black Americans uprooted themselves to move north. Most were young (in their early twenties), skilled or semi-skilled, unmarried males seeking economic opportunity. One black man explained in a letter to a friend in Mississippi why he found the North attractive: "I just begin to feel like a man. . . . I don't have to humble to no one. I have registered. Will vote the next election."

New jobs and improved opportunities could not erase the fact that blacks, both North and South, continued to be a minority in a white society. When the United States entered the First World War, there was not one black judge in the entire country and segregation was social custom. The Ku Klux Klan began to revive, and racist films like D. W. Griffith's *The Birth of a Nation* (1915) fed prejudice. Lynching statistics exposed the wide gap between American declarations of humanity in the war and the American practice of inhumanity at home: between 1914 and 1920, 382 blacks were lynched, some of them in military uniform.

Northern whites who resented the "Negro invasion" vented their anger in riots. In East St. Louis, Illinois, in July 1917, whites opposed to black employment in a defense plant rampaged through the streets; nine whites and about forty blacks lost their lives. In the bloody "Red Summer" of 1919, race riots rocked two dozen cities and towns. The worst race war occurred in Chicago, a favorite destination for migrating blacks. In the very hot days of July 1919, a black youth swimming at a segregated white beach was hit by a thrown rock and drowned. Rumors spread, tempers flared, and soon blacks and whites were battling one another. Stabbings, burnings, and shootings went on for days until state police restored some calm. Thirty-eight people died—fifteen whites and twenty-three blacks; more than five hundred others were injured.

For some white Americans, this sad record meant that the nation should direct its missionary zeal at the reform not of foreign societies but of its own. Some black leaders spoke out similarly, displaying more militancy than Booker T. Washington, who died in 1915, would have countenanced. Insisting on equality and an end to segregation, W. E. B. Du Bois vowed a struggle: "We return. We return from fighting. We return fighting." The black poet Claude McKay of New York expressed in 1919 a self-assertion and self-defense that prefigured later black protest:

If we must die—let it not be like hogs
Hunted and penned in an inglorious spot,

While round us bark the mad and hungry gods,
Making their mock at our accursed lot.

Like men we'll face the murderous, cowardly pack,
Pressed to the wall, dying but fighting back![2]

The Attack on Civil Liberties

"Woe be to the man that seeks to stand in our way in this day of high resolution," warned President Wilson. Dissenters who questioned his war decision and the draft soon faced an official and unofficial campaign to silence them. Jingoists warped truth and incited violence; civil liberties were trampled; and an "Americanization" crusade cut a gaping wound in American democracy. The targets of abuse were the hundreds of thousands of Americans and aliens who refused to support the war: pacifists from all walks of life, conscientious objectors, socialists, the Industrial Workers of the World, the debt-ridden tenant farmers of Oklahoma who staged the Green Corn Rebellion against the draft, the Non-Partisan League, reformers like Robert La Follette and Jane Addams, and countless others.

Shortly after the declaration of war in 1917, the president appointed George Creel, a progressive journalist, to head the Committee on Public Information. The CPI was a propaganda

Committee on Public Information
agency pure and simple. Employing some of the nation's most talented writers and scholars, the CPI set out to shape and mobilize public opinion by means of anti-German tracts; speeches by "four-minute men," who visited thousands of schools and churches; films like *America's Answer* (1918); and "self-censorship" of the press. The CPI encouraged people to spy on their neighbors and report any suspicious behavior. "Not a pin dropped in the home of any one with a foreign name," Creel claimed, "but that it rang like thunder on the inner ear of some listening sleuth." Exaggeration, fear-mongering, distortion, half-truths—such were the stuff of the CPI's "mind mobilization."

---

[2] From "If We Must Die," by Claude McKay. Reprinted by permission of Twayne Publishers.

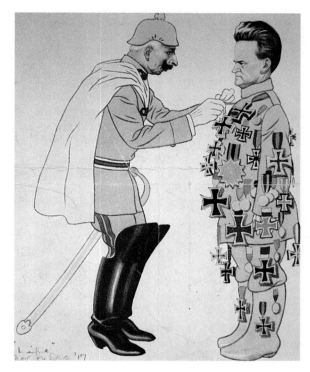

Some critics thought Senator Robert La Follette (1885–1925) a traitor for his opposition to American participation in the First World War. This harsh cartoon from *Life* magazine shows the Wisconsin reformer receiving awards from the German kaiser. La Follette believed that a majority of Americans, if asked in a referendum, would vote his way. "The poor . . . who are the ones called upon to rot in the trenches, have no organized power," he lamented. *The State Historical Society of Wisconsin.*

The Wilson administration also guided through an obliging Congress the Espionage Act (1917) and the Sedition Act (1918). The first statute forbade

Silencing Dissenters
"false statements" designed to impede the draft or promote military insubordination and banned from the mails materials considered treasonous. The Sedition Act made it unlawful to obstruct the sale of war bonds and to use "disloyal, profane, scurrilous, or abusive" language against the government, the Constitution, the flag, and the military uniform. These loosely worded laws gave the government wide latitude to crack down on those with whom it differed. Fair-minded people could disagree over what constituted false or abusive language, but in the feverish home-front atmosphere of the First World War and under the threat of federal prosecution, the Justice Depart-

ment's definition prevailed. Over two thousand people were prosecuted under the acts and many others were intimidated into silence.

Stories of arrests and an intellectual reign of terror began to make the news. Three Columbia University students were picked up in mid-1917 for circulating an antiwar petition. The liberal-left journal *The Masses* and Tom Watson's *The Jeffersonian* were denied use of the mails and forced to shut down. Jane Addams was put under Justice Department surveillance, causing her, by her own admission, to moderate her appeals for peace. The producer of *The Spirit of '76,* a film about the American Revolution complete with redcoats shooting minutemen, was given a ten-year prison sentence for, according to the judge, questioning the "good faith of our ally, Great Britain."

In the summer of 1918, with a government stenographer present, Socialist party leader Eugene Debs delivered a spirited oration extolling socialism and freedom of speech—including the freedom to criticize the Wilson administration for taking America into the war. Federal agents arrested him. Debs told the court what many dissenters—and later many jurists and scholars—thought of the Espionage Act: it was "a despotic enactment in flagrant conflict with democratic principles and with the spirit of free institutions." Handed a ten-year sentence, Debs remained in prison until late 1921, when he received a pardon (see page 761).

State and local governments joined the campaign. Because towns had Liberty Bond quotas to fill, they sometimes bullied "slackers" through public humiliation into making purchases. Officials banned what they considered "pro-German" books from public schools; the governor of Iowa prohibited the use of any language but English in schools; and Pittsburgh banned Beethoven's music. Everywhere teachers who questioned the war faced dismissal by hostile school boards.

Across the nation, supporters of "Americanization" or "100% Americanism" exploited the emotional atmosphere to press immigrants to throw off their Old World cultures. To fuse a superpatriotic national unity, the CPI set up Loyalty Leagues in ethnic communities. Companies offered English-language and naturalization classes in their factories and refused jobs and promotions to those who did not make adequate strides toward learning English. What began as education gave way to repression.

Encouraged by official behavior, groups like the American Protective League, the Sedition Slammers, and the American Defense Society took it upon themselves to cleanse the nation through vigilantism. German books were burned in Nebraska and a German-American miner in Illinois was wrapped in a flag and lynched. In Tulsa, a mob whipped IWW members and then poured tar into their bleeding sores. Nor were universities shelters for unorthodox ideas. In a celebrated case, antiwar Professor J. M. Cattell, a distinguished psychologist at Columbia University, was fired. His colleague Charles Beard, a historian with prowar views, resigned in protest: "If we have to suppress everything we don't like to hear, this country is resting on a pretty wobbly basis."

The point was just that: Wilson and his officers tried to crush what they did not like to hear. In particular, the administration concentrated on the IWW and the Socialist party. The war emergency and the frank opposition of those two radical organizations gave progressives and conservatives alike an opportunity to throttle their political rivals. Standing for revolution against capitalism and often violent in its tactics, the IWW aroused bitter opposition (see pages 518, 610). Soon after the declaration of war, government agents raided union meetings and arrested IWW leaders. The army was sent into western mining and lumber regions to put down IWW strikes on the pretense that they were pro-German. Under the immigration acts, alien members of the IWW were deported. Town after town evicted the "Wobblies," and by the end of the war most of the union's leaders were in jail. The Socialist party fared little better: others besides Debs were imprisoned. The new Civil Liberties Bureau (forerunner of the American Civil Liberties Union) defended many dissenters, but even its head, Roger Baldwin, was jailed as a conscientious objector.

The Supreme Court, itself attuned to the pulse of the times, upheld the Espionage Act. Justice Oliver Wendell Holmes, in *Schenck* v. *U.S.* (1919), expressed the Court's unanimous opinion that in time of war the First Amendment could be restricted: "Free speech would not protect a man falsely shouting fire in a theater and causing panic." If words "are of such a nature as to create a clear and present danger that they will bring about the substantial evils that Congress has a right to prevent," Holmes went on, free speech could be limited. In another case, *Abrams* v. *U.S.* (1919), the Court voted 7 to 2 (with Holmes and Brandeis in the minority) that the Sedition Act was constitutional. This time Holmes, writing the minority opinion, expressed concern that the "free trade in ideas" was being jeopardized.

The Red Scare

The line between wartime suppression of dissent and the postwar Red Scare is not easily drawn. Both were directed against suspected internal enemies; both put on the mask of patriotism to harass radicals and deprive them of their constitutional rights; and both had government sanction. In the last few months of the war, guardians of Americanism began to label dissenters not only pro-German but pro-Bolshevik. After the Bolshevik Revolution in the fall of 1917, American hatred for the Kaiser's Germany was readily transferred to Communist Russia. When the new Russian government under V. I. Lenin made peace with Germany in early 1918, Americans grew angry that the closing of the eastern front would give the Germans the chance to move troops west. Many lashed out at American radicals, casually applying the term "Red" to people of varying beliefs, such as anarchists, Wobblies, Socialists, pacifists, Communists, union leaders, and reformers.

The ordeal of Victor Berger illustrates the blending of the wartime and postwar suppression of civil liberties. A Socialist of German descent and former congressman from Wisconsin, Berger was indicted under the Espionage Act for denouncing American entry into the European war. Nonetheless, in 1918 the voters of Milwaukee elected him once again to Congress. In early 1919 he was convicted and sentenced to twenty years in federal prison. The House of Representatives thereupon refused to admit him, its members absurdly charging that he was both pro-German and pro-Bolshevik. While out on bail pending an appeal of his conviction, Berger won the special election held to replace him. The House again blocked his admission. Berger's ordeal did not end until 1921, when the Supreme Court reversed his conviction. He was elected to Congress again in 1924; this time he took his seat.

> **Case of Victor Berger**

An early sign of the Wilson administration's anti-Bolshevism was the president's ordering of five thousand American troops to northern Russia in June 1918. Then, a month later, he sent another ten thousand soldiers to Siberia, where they joined other Allied contingents. Wilson did not consult Congress; he announced that the military expeditions were intended to guard Allied supplies and Russian railroads from German seizure and to rescue a group of Czechs who wished to return to their homeland to fight the Germans. Wilson also worried that the Japanese were building influence in Siberia and closing the Open Door. But he also hoped to smash the infant Bolshevik government. The Allied governments were blunter about this goal than Wilson, for they feared that Bolshevism might spread across Europe. (Indeed, there were short-lived uprisings in Germany and Hungary in early 1919.) Not only did Wilson attempt to subvert Lenin's regime by military means; he participated in an economic blockade of Russia, sent arms to anti-Bolshevik forces, refused to recognize the Bolshevik government, and later blocked Russian participation in the Paris Peace Conference. American troops did not leave Siberia until spring 1920. These interventions in civil war–torn Russia immediately embittered Washington-Moscow relations—a legacy that would persist deep into the twentieth century.

> **Intervention in Russia**

At home, too, the Wilson administration moved against radicals and others imprecisely defined as Bolsheviks or Communists. After the war Americans were edgy: the war had disrupted race relations, the workplace, and the family; it had increased the cost of living; postwar unemployment loomed; and in 1919 the Russian Communists established the Comintern to promote world revolution. Already hardened by wartime violations of civil liberties, Americans found it easy to blame their postwar troubles on new scapegoats.

Dramatic events sparked the Red Scare. First came a rash of labor strikes in 1919. All told, over 3,300 strikes involving 4 million laborers occurred that year, including a Seattle general strike in January that sent ripples of fear across the nation. America, said Wilson's press secretary with exaggeration, was poised between "organization and anarchy." On May 1 (May Day), bombs were sent through the

> **Labor Strikes, 1919**

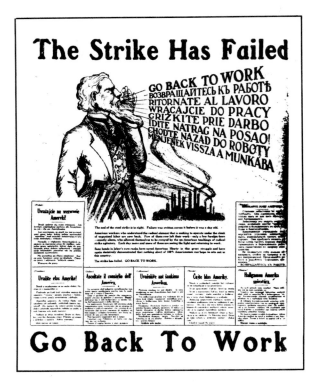

This United States Steel Corporation advertisement appeared in a Pittsburgh newspaper as part of the steel industry's campaign to break the strike called by unions grouped under the National Committee for Organizing Iron and Steel Workers. The strike by at least a quarter million workers of many nationalities began in September 1919, but ended without success in early 1920, although the eight-hour day finally came to the steel industry in the 1920s. *The Historical Society of Western Pennsylvania.*

mails to prominent Americans; most of the devices were intercepted and dismantled. Police never captured the conspirators. The common and not-unreasonable assumption was that anarchists and others bent on the destruction of the American way of life were responsible. Next came the Boston police strike in September; some thought it part of a Bolshevik conspiracy. The governor of Massachusetts, Calvin Coolidge, gained fame by proclaiming that nobody had the right to strike against the public safety. State guardsmen were brought in to replace the striking police force.

Events in the steel industry in September seemed more ominous. Conservative steel executives grew alarmed with the successful efforts of the National Committee for Organizing Iron and Steel Workers, whose honorary chairman was Samuel Gompers of the American Federation of Labor. Many workers still put in twelve-hour days seven days a week and went home to squalid living quarters. They looked to local steel unions, organized by the committee, to improve their conditions. After postwar unemployment in the industry climbed and the United States Steel Corporation refused to meet with committee representatives, some 250,000 workers walked out for the right to collective bargaining, shorter hours, and a living wage. The steel barons sent agents to club strikers, hired strikebreakers, and depicted strike leaders as Bolsheviks bent on revolution. The steel companies won; the strike collapsed in early 1920.

One of the leaders of the steel strike was William Z. Foster, a radical who later joined the Communist party. His presence in a labor movement seeking legitimate bread-and-butter goals permitted political and business leaders to dismiss the steel strike as a foreign threat orchestrated by American radicals. There was actually no conspiracy, and the American left was badly splintered. After breaking away from the Socialist party, John Reed and Benjamin Gitlow founded the Communist Labor party in the summer of 1919. That September the Communist Party of the United States, largely composed of aliens, was launched. Neither Communist party commanded much of a following—perhaps about 70,000 members total—and in 1919 the harassed Socialist party could muster no more than 30,000 members.

Although divisiveness among radicals was actually symptomatic of weakness, both progressives and conservatives interpreted the advent of the new parties as a strengthening of the radical menace. That is certainly how the American Legion saw the matter. Organized in May 1919, the veterans' organization soon became a standard-bearer for the Red Scare. The editor of the *London Daily News* visited the United States in 1919 and recalled what he witnessed: the nation was "hag-ridden by the spectre of Bolshevism. . . . 'Radical' covered the most innocent departure from conventional thought with a suspicion of desperate purpose. 'America,' as a wit of the time said, 'is the land of liberty—the liberty to keep in step.'"

Attorney General A. Mitchell Palmer insisted on conformity. A progressive, a Quaker, and an aspirant to the 1920 Democratic presidential nomination, Palmer claimed that the "blaze of rev-

A. Mitchell Palmer

olution" was "eating its way into the homes of the American workmen, its sharp tongues of revolutionary heat . . . licking the altars of the churches, leaping into the belfry of the school bell, crawling into the sacred corners of American homes, burning up the foundations of society." To stamp out the radical fire, Palmer created a new Bureau of Investigation and appointed J. Edgar Hoover to run it. Hoover organized a file of thousands of index cards bearing the names of alleged radical individuals and organizations. During 1919 agents jailed IWW members; and in December, Palmer saw to it that 249 alien radicals, including the anarchist Emma Goldman, were deported to Soviet Russia.

Again, state and local governments took their cue from Washington. The New York State legislature expelled five duly elected Socialist members. States passed peacetime sedition acts under which hundreds of people were arrested. Vigilante groups and mobs flourished once again, their numbers swelled by returning veterans. In November 1919, in Centralia, Washington, a town beset by emotional antiradicalism, four American Legionnaires were shot when they broke from an Armistice Day parade in an apparent attempt to storm the IWW hall. Several Wobblies were arrested and later convicted of murder; one, an ex-soldier, was taken from jail by a mob, beaten, castrated, and then shot.

The Red Scare reached a climax in January 1920 when the attorney general staged his Palmer Raids. Using information gathered by Hoover, government agents in thirty-three cities

Palmer Raids

broke into meeting halls, poolrooms, and homes without search warrants. More than four thousand people were thrown into overcrowded jails and denied counsel. In Boston, some four hundred people were kept in detainment on bitterly cold Deer Island; two died of pneumonia, one leaped to his death, and another went insane. Because of court rulings and the courageous efforts of Assistant Secretary of Labor Louis Post, most of the victims of government arrests were released and not deported, although in 1920–1921 nearly six hundred were sent abroad.

Palmer's disregard for elementary civil liberties soon drew criticism. Civil libertarians and lawyers pointed out that Palmer's blatant tactics ignored the Constitution, that many of the arrested "Communists" had committed no crimes, and that some were not even radicals. Palmer's call for a peacetime sedition act alarmed leaders of many political persuasions. His dire prediction that major violence would mar May Day 1920 proved mistaken. Palmer's exaggerations, his scenarios of Bolshevik conspiracy, simply exceeded the truth so far that he lost credibility. With the steel strike over, the threat of Bolshevism in Europe receding, and the nation settling down into a postwar routine of business as usual, Palmer could no longer count on stampeding the public. Finally, even officials in the Wilson administration refused to cooperate with him. Assistant Secretary of Labor Louis Post and immigration commissioner Frederick Howe blocked Palmer's attempts at wholesale deportations, charging him with gross violations of human rights.

The campaign against free speech in the period from 1917 through 1920 left casualties. Critics, radical or otherwise, became afraid to speak their minds. Debate, so essential to democracy, was curbed. Reform suffered as reformers either joined in the antiradicalism or became victims of it. The radical movement was badly weakened, the IWW becoming virtually extinct and the Socialist party paralyzed. The government's war on its critics and disrespect for the Bill of Rights left an indelible blot on Wilson's political record. The president made it appear that his critics were attacking the nation itself, when in fact they were questioning the policies of his administration. Wilson's intolerance of those who disagreed with him seemed to bespeak a distrust of democracy. At the least it illustrated that some progressives would use coercion and authoritarian methods to achieve their goal of a reformed society. Senator La Follette thought the sorry experience demonstrated what was for him the supreme issue: "the encroachment of the powerful few upon the rights of the many."

The Peace Conference and League Fight

As the Red Scare was threatening American democracy, Woodrow Wilson was struggling to make his Fourteen Points a reality. When the president departed for the Paris Peace Conference in December 1918, he faced obstacles erected by his political enemies, by the Allies, and by himself. Some observers suggested that the ambitious and overly confident Wilson underestimated his task. During the 1918 congressional elections, Wilson had urged a vote for the Democrats as a sign of support for his peace goals. But the American people, probably voting less in response to foreign policy issues than to domestic questions like inflation, did just the opposite. The Republicans gained control of both houses, signaling trouble for Wilson in two ways. First, any peace treaty would have to be submitted for approval to a potentially hostile Senate; second, Wilson's stature had been diminished in the eyes of foreign leaders. Wilson aggravated his political problems by not naming a senator to his advisory American Peace Commission, refusing to take any prominent Republican with him to Paris, and failing to consult with the Senate Foreign Relations Committee before he sailed for Paris. Analysts thought he had lost his political senses.

Another obstacle in Wilson's way was the Allies' determination to impose a harsh, vengeful peace on the Germans. Georges Clemenceau of France, David Lloyd George of Britain, and Vittorio Orlando of Italy—with Wilson, the Big Four—were formidable adversaries. They had signed secret treaties during the war and expected to enlarge their empires at Germany's expense. They scoffed at the headstrong, self-impressed president who wanted to deny them the spoils of war. Sizing up Wilson as a theologian self-consciously wielding United States power, they challenged his blueprint for peace. "God gave us the Ten Commandments, and we broke them," remarked Clemenceau. "Wilson gives us the Fourteen Points. We shall see."

The Paris Peace Conference at the palace of Versailles was a meeting of the titans—"the clearing house of the Fates," as a contemporary put it. Much of the business of the conference

Paris Peace Conference was conducted by the Big Four behind closed doors, and critics quickly pointed out that Wilson had thus abandoned the first of his Fourteen Points, which urged diplomacy in the "public view." The victors demanded that Germany pay a huge reparations bill. Wilson called for a small indemnity, fearing that a resentful and economically hobbled Germany might turn to Bolshevism or disrupt the postwar community in some other way. Unable to moderate the Allied position, the president reluc-

tantly gave way, agreeing to a clause blaming the war on the Germans and to the creation of a reparations commission to determine a figure (later set at $33 billion).

As for decolonization (the breaking up of empires) and the principle of self-determination, Wilson only partially overcame the land-grabbing mood of the conference. The conferees placed former German and Turkish colonies under the control of other imperial nations in a League-administered "mandate" system. France and Britain, for example, obtained parts of the Middle East, and Japan gained authority over Germany's colonies in the Pacific. The mandate system was a half-way station between outright imperial domination and independence. In other compromises, Japan was granted influence over China's Shandong peninsula, and France was permitted occupation rights in Germany's Rhineland. Elsewhere in Europe, however, Wilson's prescriptions fared better. Out of Austria-Hungary and Russia came the new independent states of Austria, Hungary, Yugoslavia, Czechoslovakia, and Poland. Wilson and his colleagues also built a *cordon sanitaire* of new westward-looking nations (Finland, Estonia, Latvia, and Lithuania) around Russia to quarantine the Bolshevik contagion.

Wilson worked harder on the charter for the League of Nations than on anything else. In the long run, he believed, the League would moderate

League of Nations the harshness of the Allied peace terms and temper imperial ambitions. He devised a League that reflected the power of large nations like the United States: an influential council of five permanent members (great powers) and elected delegates from smaller states; an assembly for discussion; and a World Court. The "backbone" of the League covenant, said Wilson, was Article 10:

> The Members of the League undertake to respect and preserve as against external aggression the territorial integrity and existing political independence of all Members of the League. In case of any such aggression or in case of any threat or danger of such aggression the Council shall advise upon the means by which this obligation shall be fulfilled.

This collective-security provision, with the entire League charter, became part of the peace treaty.

German representatives at first refused to accept the punitive Treaty of Paris but then signed it in June 1919. In so doing they gave up 13 percent of

Germany's territory, 10 percent of its population, all of its colonies, and a huge portion of its national wealth. Secretary Lansing and others prophesied that the League could not function in the poisoned atmosphere of revenge and humiliation. But Wilson, filled with America's traditional missionary zeal, was euphoric: "The stage is set, the destiny disclosed. It has come about by no plan of our conceiving, but by the hand of God, who led us into this way."

Americans vigorously debated the treaty. In March 1919, as the conferees in Paris were hammering out the accord, thirty-nine senators (enough to deny the treaty the necessary two-thirds vote) signed a petition stating that the League's structure did not adequately protect American interests. Wilson lamented the "pygmy" minds of his antagonists but persuaded the peace conference to exempt the Monroe Doctrine and domestic matters from League jurisdiction. Having made these concessions to senatorial advice, Wilson would budge no more.

The Treaty Debated

Journalist Walter Lippmann asked: "How in our consciences are we to square the results with the promises?" Criticism mounted: Wilson had bastardized his own principles; he had conceded Shandong to Japan; he had personally killed a provision affirming the racial equality of all peoples. The treaty did not mention freedom of the seas, and tariffs were not reduced. Negotiations had been conducted in private, and reparations promised to be punishing. Senator La Follette joined others in complaining that the League was an imperialist assemblage that would perpetuate empire. Conservative critics like Senator Henry Cabot Lodge of Massachusetts feared that the League would limit American freedom of action in world affairs, stymie American expansion, and intrude on domestic questions. Racist nationalists wanted no part of an organization that bestowed the vote on nonwhite peoples. And Article 10 raised serious questions: Would the United States be obligated to use armed force to ensure collective security? And what about colonial rebellions, such as in Ireland or India? Would they be disturbances of the peace that the League would feel compelled to crush?

Wilson pleaded for understanding and lectured his opponents. Did they not realize that compromises were necessary given the awesome, stubborn resistance of the Allies, who had threatened to jetti-

THEY WON'T DOVETAIL
—Bronstrup in San Francisco *Chron*

This cartoonist took the anti-League of Nations view that the proposed charter for the international organization was incompatible with American constitutional procedures—in short, that American laws could be restricted by the League or that, as in the case of Article 10 of the charter, decisions for war could circumvent Congress's power to declare war. *Library of Congress.*

son the conference unless Wilson made concessions? Did they not recognize that the League would rectify wrongs? Could they not see that membership in the League would give the United States "leadership in the world"? Senator Lodge remained unimpressed. A Harvard-educated Ph.D. and partisan Republican, he ridiculed Wilson's charter as poor scholarship. Lodge packed the Foreign Relations Committee with League critics and prolonged public hearings. He introduced reservations to the treaty: one stated that the nation's immigration acts could not be subject to League decision; another held that Congress had to approve any obligation under Article 10.

In September 1919, Wilson embarked on a speaking tour of the United States. Growing more exhausted every day, he dismissed his critics as "absolute, contemptible quitters." When he met Irish-American and German-American hecklers, he lashed out in Red Scare language: "I cannot say too often—any man who carries a hyphen about him carries a dagger which he is ready to plunge into the vitals of the Republic." In Colorado, while delivering another passionate speech, the president collapsed. A few days later, in Washington, D.C., he suffered a stroke that paralyzed his left side. Although his mind remained alert, he became grumpy and peevish, fearful of displaying weakness and unable to conduct the heavy business of the presidency. Told by advisers to placate senatorial critics so the treaty would have a chance of passing, Wilson stubbornly refused to "dip [his] colors to dishonorable compromise." From Democrats in the Senate he demanded loyalty—a vote against all reservations.

The Senate first tested the treaty's strength in November. In two votes, one on the treaty with reservations (39 to 55) and one without (38 to 53),

> **Senate Rejection of the Treaty**

the Senate rejected it. A group of sixteen "Irreconcilables" (most of whom were Republicans), determined to defeat any treaty and voted "nay" each time. Republicans either opposed the treaty altogether or favored reservations; Democrats, on the whole, voted for the treaty without reservations. Again in March 1920, the treaty fell short of the necessary two-thirds vote (49 to 35). Had Wilson permitted Democrats to compromise, he could have achieved his fervent goal of American membership in the League of Nations.

Who or what was responsible for the defeat of the treaty? Wilson's stroke incapacitated the president, sapping his energy and his ability to lead effectively; yet even a healthy Wilson would likely have set his jaw against compromise. Certainly his concessions to a harsh peace at Paris undercut his case in the United States, but it seems that two-thirds of the Senate were willing to forgive his errors in Versailles if he would accept some reservations. The bitter personal feud between Wilson and Lodge does not account for enough—it does not, for example, explain the determination of the Irreconcilables.

Wilson's refusal to compromise with his senatorial foes certainly doomed the treaty. Why were

> **Collective Security vs. Unilateralism**

Wilson's critics so committed to crippling Article 10, and why was the president so adamant against its revision? At the core of the debate lay a basic issue of American foreign policy: whether the United States would endorse collective security or continue to travel the path of unilateralism articulated in George Washington's Farewell Address and the Monroe Doctrine. In a world dominated by imperialist states unwilling to subordinate their selfish, acquisitive ambitions to an international organization, Americans preferred their traditional nonalignment and freedom of choice over binding commitments to collective action. Woodrow Wilson failed to create a new world order through reform; he promised more than he could deliver.

The Experience of War

As the war ground to a close in Europe, historian Albert Bushnell Hart observed that "it is easy to see that the United States is a new country." What had changed? America emerged from the war years an unsettled mix of the old and the new. The war exposed the heterogeneity of the American people and the deep divisions among them: white versus black, nativist versus immigrant, capital versus labor, "dry" versus "wet," men versus women, radical versus progressive or conservative, pacifist versus interventionist, nationalist versus internationalist. Race riots, labor strikes, the Americanization movement, the suppression of civil liberties, the Red Scare, the League fight, and male resentment of female workers—all underscored the distempers of the times. It is no wonder that after 1920 Americans would seek relief in "normalcy" and want to escape from what John Dewey called the "cult of irrationality."

During the war the federal government intervened in the economy and influenced people's everyday lives as never before. In the period 1916

> **Enlarged Federal Role**

to 1919 annual federal expenditures increased 2,500 percent, and war expenses ballooned to $33.5 billion. The total cost of the war was probably triple that figure, since future generations would have to pay veterans' benefits and interest on loans. Centralization of control in Washington, D.C., and mobilization of the home front served as a model for the future. The partnership of government and business in managing the wartime economy contributed to the further development of a mass society through the standardization of products and the promotion of efficiency.

Wartime business-government cooperation also encouraged the growth of trade associations, which numbered about two thousand by 1920. After the war these industry-wide groups would continue to lobby to protect their interests and to minimize competition. Wilsonian wartime policies also nourished the continued growth of oligopoly through the suspension of antitrust laws. A 1920 Supreme Court decision not to dissolve the giant U.S. Steel Corporation symbolized the persistent trend toward bigness. After a short postwar recession, business power revived to dominate the next decade. American labor, by contrast, entered what one historian has called its lean years.

America's changed place in world affairs also held significance for later generations. By 1920 the United States had become the world's leading economic power, producing 40 percent of its coal, 70 percent of its petroleum, and half its pig iron. It rose to first rank in world trade. During the war years, American companies expanded overseas. Goodyear went into the Dutch East Indies for rubber; copper interests dug new mines in Chile; and Swift and Armour reached into South America. American economic expansionists took advantage of the war to nudge the Germans and British out of markets, especially in Latin America. The United States also shifted from a debtor to a creditor nation, becoming the world's leading banker.

The disillusionment common to so many Americans after the disappointment of Versailles did not cause the United States to adopt a policy of isolationist withdrawal (see Chapter 26). Although the League of Nations began to operate without United States membership, Americans became curious onlookers who even occasionally participated in League activities. But in general Americans stood against intervening in European affairs until the Europeans first set their own house in order.

The carnage of the war stimulated new appeals for arms control and revitalized the peace movement. At the same time, the military became more professional. The Reserve Officer Training Corps (ROTC) became permanent; military "colleges" provided upper-echelon training; and the Army Industrial College, founded in 1924, pursued business-military cooperation in the area of logistics and planning. The National Research Council, created in 1916 with government and Carnegie and Rockefeller funds, continued after the war as an alliance of scientists and businesspeople engaged in research relating to national defense. As before the war, the tendencies toward disarmament on the one hand and preparedness on the other continued to compete.

The international system born in these years was unstable and fragmented. Espousing decolonization, nationalist leaders like Ho Chi Minh

Unstable International System

of Indochina and Mohandas K. Gandhi of India, taking to heart the Wilsonian principle of self-determination, vowed to achieve independence for their peoples. Communism became a new and disruptive force in world politics, and the Russians bore a grudge against those invaders who had futilely tried to thwart their revolution. The new states in Central and Eastern Europe proved weak, dependent on outsiders for security. Germans bitterly resented the harsh peace settlement. And the war debts and reparations problems would dog international order for years.

The war experience also changed Americans' mood. The war was grimy and ugly, far less glorious than Wilson's lofty rhetoric had it. People recoiled from the photographs of bodies dangling from barbed wire, poison-gas victims, and battle-shocked faces. American soldiers were eager to return home. Apparently tired of idealism and cynical about their ability to right wrongs, they craved the latest baseball scores. Still, for the doughboys the army years were memorable, a turning point in their lives. They shed some of their parochialism, as the title of a popular song hinted: "How 'Ya Gonna Keep 'Em Down on the Farm, After They've Seen Paree?" And they made lasting friendships that would be cemented by membership in the American Legion. A young soldier from Missouri, Harry S Truman of Battery D, would never lose touch with his wartime buddies, and when he became president in 1945 he would bring some of them into the White House as advisers.

Those progressives who had believed entry into the war would deliver the millennium now marveled at their naiveté. Many lost their enthusiasm for crusades, and many others turned away in disgust from the bickering of the victors. Randolph Bourne commented that progressives felt "like brave passengers who have set out for the Isles of

Stirred by Woodrow Wilson's passionate appeals for victory in 1917, thirty-three-year-old Missourian Harry Truman enlisted in the National Guard. "I wouldn't be left out of the greatest history-making epoch the world has even seen," he said. He became a First Lieutenant for Battery D of the 129th Field Artillery of the 35th Division and saw action in the Saint Mihiel and Meuse-Argonne campaigns. A Truman biographer, William E. Pemberton, has written that the war experience "taught him the value of organization and basic management principles. . . . He also developed a great admiration for military men, leading him as president to appoint more military leaders to high positions than any other president in the twentieth century." *Harry S Truman Library.*

the Blest only to find that the first mate has gone insane and jumped overboard." Some felt betrayed, distraught that the Great War had not proven exceptional. William Allen White angrily wrote to a friend that the Allies "have—those damned vultures—taken the heart out of the peace, taken the joy out of the great enterprise of the war, and have made it a sordid malicious miserable thing like all the other wars in the world."

Woodrow Wilson himself had remarked soon after taking office in 1913, before the Great War, that "there's no chance of progress and reform in an administration in which war plays the principal part." From the perspective of 1920, looking back on distempers at home and abroad, Wilson would have to agree with other Americans that progress and reform had been dealt blows.

Suggestions for Further Reading

General

John W. Chambers, *The Tyranny of Change* (1980); Allen F. Davis, *American Heroine* (1974) (on Jane Addams); Otis L. Graham, Jr., *The Great Campaigns* (1971); Ellis W. Hawley, *The Great War and the Search for a Modern Order* (1979); Henry F. May, *The End of American Innocence* (1964); Emily S. Rosenberg, *Spreading the American Dream* (1982); Bernadotte Schmitt and Harold E. Vedeler, *The World in the Crucible: 1914–1919* (1984); Ronald Steel, *Walter Lippmann and the American Century* (1980); David P. Thelan, *Robert M. La Follette and the Insurgent Spirit* (1976); John A. Thompson, *Reformers and War* (1987).

Woodrow Wilson, His Diplomacy, and the First World War

Thomas A. Bailey and Paul B. Ryan, *The Lusitania Disaster* (1975); Edward H. Buehrig, ed., *Wilson's Foreign Policy in Perspective* (1957); Frederick S. Calhoun, *Power and Principle* (1986); Kendrick A. Clements, *Woodrow Wilson, World Statesman* (1987); John W. Coogan, *The End of Neutrality* (1981); John M. Cooper, Jr., *The Warrior and the Priest* (1983); Patrick Devlin, *Too Proud to Fight* (1975); Robert H. Ferrell, *Woodrow Wilson and World War I* (1985); Lloyd C. Gardner, *Safe for Democracy: The Anglo-American Response to Revolution, 1913–1923* (1984); Ross Gregory, *The Origins of American Intervention in the First World War* (1971); Manfred Jonas, *The United States and Germany* (1984); N. Gordon Levin, Jr., *Woodrow Wilson and World Politics* (1968); Arthur S. Link, ed., *Woodrow Wilson and a Revolutionary World, 1913–1921* (1982); Arthur S. Link, *Woodrow Wilson: Revolution, War and Peace* (1979); Arthur S. Link, *Wilson,* 5 vols. (1947–1965); Ernest R. May, *The World War and American Isolation, 1914–1917* (1959); Robert E. Osgood, *Ideals and Self-Interest in American Foreign Relations* (1953); Frances W. Saunders, *Ellen Axson Wilson* (1985); Daniel M. Smith, *The Great Departure* (1965); Barbara Tuchman, *The Zimmermann Telegram* (1958); Edwin A. Weinstein, *Woodrow Wilson: A Medical and Psychological Biography* (1981).

The American Military and the First World War

Arthur E. Barbeau and Florette Henri, *The Unknown Soldiers: Black American Troops in World War I* (1974); John W. Chambers, *To Raise an Army* (1987); J. Garry Clifford, *The Citizen Soldiers* (1972); Edward M. Coffman, *The War to End All Wars* (1968); Harvey A. DeWeerd, *President Wilson Fights His War* (1968); Marvin E. Fletcher, *The Black Soldier and Officer in the United States Army, 1891–1917* (1974); Thomas C. Leonard, *Above the Battle* (1978); Donald Smythe, *Pershing* (1986); David Trask, *The United States in the Supreme War Council* (1961); Russell F. Weigley, *The American Way of War* (1973).

The Home Front

Allan M. Brandt, *No Magic Bullet* (1985) (on venereal disease); William J. Breen, *Uncle Sam at Home* (1984) (on the Council of National Defense); Valerie Jean Conner, *The National War Labor Board* (1983); Alfred W. Crosby, Jr., *Epidemic and Peace, 1918* (1976); Robert D. Cuff, *The War Industries Board* (1973); Allen F. Davis, "Welfare, Reform, and World War I," *American Quarterly,* 19 (1967), 516–533; Edward R. Ellis, *Echos of Distant Thunder* (1975); Charles Gilbert, *American Financing of World War I* (1970); Maurine W. Greenwald, *Women, War, and Work* (1980); Frank L. Grubbs, Jr., *The Struggle for Labor Loyalty* (1968); David M. Kennedy, *Over Here* (1980); Seward W. Livermore, *Politics Is Adjourned* (1966); Frederick C. Luebke, *Bonds of Loyalty: German-Americans and World War I* (1974); John F. McClymer, *War and Welfare: Social Engineering in America, 1890–1925* (1980); Barbara J. Steinson, *American Women's Activism in World War I* (1982); Stephen L. Vaughn, *Holding Fast the Inner Lines* (1979) (on CPI); Neil A. Wynn, *From Progressivism to Prosperity: World War I and American Society* (1986).

Black Americans on the Home Front

Robert V. Haynes, *A Night of Violence: The Houston Riot of 1917* (1976); Florette Henri, *Black Migration* (1975); Thomas C. Holt, "Afro-Americans," in *Harvard Encyclopedia of American Ethnic Groups,* ed. Stephan Thernstrom (1980); Elliot M. Rudwick, *Race Riot at East St. Louis, July 2, 1917* (1964); William M. Tuttle, *Race Riot: Chicago in the Red Summer of 1919* (1970).

Wartime Dissent, Civil Liberties, and the Red Scare

David Brody, *Labor in Crisis: The Steel Strike of 1919* (1965); Charles Chatfield, *For Peace and Justice: Pacifism in America, 1914–1941* (1971); Stanley Coben, *A. Mitchell Palmer* (1963); Charles DeBenedetti, *Origins of the Modern Peace Movement* (1978); Robert L. Friedheim, *The Seattle General Strike* (1965); Sondra Herman, *Eleven Against War* (1969); Donald Johnson, *The Challenge to American Freedoms* (1963); C. Roland Marchand, *The American Peace Movement and Social Reform, 1898–1918* (1973); Paul L. Murphy, *World War I and the Origin of Civil Liberties* (1979); Robert K. Murray, *Red Scare* (1955); H. C. Peterson and Gilbert C. Fite, *Opponents of War, 1917–1918* (1968); Richard Polenberg, *Fighting Faiths* (1987) (on the *Abrams* case); William Preston, *Aliens and Dissenters: Federal Suppression of Radicals, 1903–1933* (1966); Francis Russell, *A City in Terror: 1919—The Boston Police Strike* (1975); James Weinstein, *The Decline of Socialism in America, 1912–1923* (1967).

The Bolshevik Revolution and United States Intervention

Peter G. Filene, *Americans and the Soviet Experiment, 1917–1933* (1967); John L. Gaddis, *Russia, the Soviet Union, and the United States* (1978); George F. Kennan, *The Decision to Intervene* (1958); George F. Kennan, *Russia Leaves the War* (1956); Christopher Lasch, *The American Liberals and the Russian Revolution* (1962); John Thompson, *Russia, Bolshevism, and the Versailles Peace* (1966); Betty M. Unterberger, *America's Siberian Expedition, 1918–1920* (1956); William Appleman Williams, *American-Russian Relations, 1781–1947* (1952).

Paris Peace Conference and League Fight

Lloyd Ambrosius, *Woodrow Wilson and the American Diplomatic Tradition* (1987); Thomas A. Bailey, *Woodrow Wilson and the Great Betrayal* (1945); Thomas A. Bailey, *Woodrow Wilson and the Lost Peace* (1944); Inga Floto, *Colonel House in Paris* (1973); Herbert Hoover, *The Ordeal of Woodrow Wilson* (1958); Warren F. Kuehl, *Seeking World Order* (1969); Arno Mayer, *Politics and Diplomacy of Peacemaking* (1967); Keith Nelson, *Victors Divided* (1973); Ralph A. Stone, *The Irreconcilables* (1970); Arthur Walworth, *Wilson and the Peacemakers* (1986); William C. Widenor, *Henry Cabot Lodge and the Search for an American Foreign Policy* (1980).

The Aftermath of War

Stanley Cooperman, *World War I and the American Mind* (1970); Malcolm Cowley, *Exile's Return* (1951); Paul Fussell, *The Great War and Modern Memory* (1975); Stuart I. Rochester, *American Liberal Disillisionment in the Wake of World War I* (1977); Stephen R. Ward, ed., *The War Generation: Veterans of the First World War* (1975).

Edward Albert Filene's most famous innovation was the "Automatic Bargain Basement," a section of his Boston department store in which prices automatically declined when merchandise failed to sell after a given period. Copied and elaborated by merchants across the country, the "bargain basement" became synonymous with the concept of offering goods in large variety at low prices. An immigrant's son, Filene believed his merchandising idea would give consumerism a good name and cause his store to be overrun with "hard-boiled" customers looking for values rather than bargains. "It is economic treason," he preached, "to shop carelessly."

But E. A. Filene was more than just a conscientious retailer; he was, one associate observed, "as near to being the philosopher of our machine economy as we have yet produced." If "machine economy" is defined as a consumer economy based upon mass production and mass communications, the characterization is apt. In his numerous writings, as well as in his marketing innovations, Filene set the tone for much of the American outlook of the 1920s.

Filene concluded that mass production was about to create a world of abundance in which trouble-free prosperity would ensure freedom and peace. The basis of prosperity, he wrote in 1929, was "the buying power of the masses, which has been created by scientific mass methods in production and distribution." As prosperity spread throughout the world, it would "become a bulwark against war." Filene was also a reformer; he established unemployment and medical insurance for his employees, sponsored a program for city betterment in Boston, endowed a foundation to collect data for the purpose of informing economic policymaking, and supported high wages for all workers. But most of all, Filene had deep faith in the benefits of consumerism. If producers would increase wages and reduce prices through mass production, he wrote, "those products which almost all people want will all but sell themselves." And once such abundance was achieved, "men's minds will inevitably turn to other and higher issues."

24

THE NEW ERA OF THE 1920s

Sixth Avenue Elevated at Third Street, 1928 (detail) by John Sloan. Oil on canvas. *Whitney Museum of American Art. Purchase 36.1.54.* This painting is reproduced in its entirety on page 725.

Filene only had to look around him to justify his faith, for during the 1920s the flower of consumerism reached full bloom. Although poverty dogged small farmers, workers in declining industries, and nonwhites living in urban slums, the majority of the population enjoyed a high standard of living. Spurred by advertising and new forms of credit, Americans eagerly bought automobiles, radios, real estate, and stocks. As in the Gilded Age, government policies supported the interests of business, as Congress, the Supreme Court, and three Republican presidents directed their efforts toward maintaining a favorable climate for profits. Yet important reforms were accomplished at state and local levels of government, solidifying and extending reforms of the Progressive era.

In many ways the decade was a time of complexities. Its frivolous stunts, contests, and fads were balanced by an outburst of creativity in literature, music, and art, and by significant advances in science and technology. Changes in work habits, family responsibilities, and healthcare fostered new uses of time and new attitudes about proper behavior. Material bounty and increased leisure time enticed Americans into a variety of new amusements, including games, sports, and movies. Winds of change also stirred up waves of reaction. New, more liberal values repelled various groups, such as the Ku Klux Klan, immigration restrictionists, and religious fundamentalists. Such groups reacted by trying to restore a society in which everyone had the same beliefs, people knew their place, and deviants were not tolerated.

However, troubling clouds were gathering. The consumer culture that dominated everyday life caused Americans to ignore rising debts and other increasingly negative economic signs. And just before the decade closed, the whole system came crashing down, not only shattering E. A. Filene's vision but also bringing the new era to a brutal close.

Big Business Triumphant

The decade of business ascendancy did not begin very brightly. Besides political wrangling over ratification of the Treaty of Paris and the Red Scare (see Chapter 23), the nation suffered a frightening economic decline. For two years after the First World War, heavy consumer spending drove prices up. Then in 1920 people stopped buying. Export trade and industrial output dropped as wartime orders ended. Farm income plunged as the result of falling exports, and farmers' share of the national wealth continued to decline throughout the decade. Unemployment, around 2 percent in 1919, passed 12 percent in 1921. Railroad and mining industries suffered declining profits, and layoffs spread through New England as textile companies abandoned outdated factories for the raw materials and cheap labor of the South.

Recovery began in 1922 and continued unevenly until 1929. Electric motors were responsible for much of the expansion. By 1929 electricity powered 70 percent of American industry, and thousands of steam engines had been relegated to the scrap heap. Assembly-line production also contributed to economic health, adding countless new consumer products to the market. New metal alloys, chemicals, synthetic materials, and preserved foods became commonplace. As Americans acquired more spending money and as leisure time expanded, service industries boomed. More people could afford the goods and services of department and specialty stores, restaurants, beauty and barber shops, and movie theaters. This new consumerism was fueled by refined methods of credit, especially the installment or time-payment plan ("a dollar down and a dollar forever," one critic quipped). Of 3.5 million automobiles sold in 1923, some 80 percent were bought on credit.

Postwar Economic Recovery

Behind the prosperity, an economic revolution was peaking. First, the consolidation movement that had bred trusts and holding companies in the late nineteenth century reached a new stage. Although Progressive-era trustbusting had harnessed big business to some extent, it had not halted oligopoly—control of a whole industry by a few large firms. By the 1920s oligopolies dominated not only production but marketing, distribution, and even financing. In such businesses as automobile manufacturing, steel production, meat processing, and railroads, a few sprawling companies predominated. Oligopolistic firms, like General Electric, General Motors, and U.S. Steel, developed management techniques to maximize profits and minimize market uncertainties.

1919	Eighteenth Amendment ratified		**1923–24**	Exposure of government scandals
1920	Nineteenth Amendment ratified Harding elected president First commercial radio broadcast		**1924**	National Origins Act Coolidge elected president
1920–21	Postwar deflation and depression		**1925**	Scopes trial
1921	Federal Highway Act Immigration quotas established Sacco and Vanzetti convicted Sheppard-Towner Act		**1927**	Sacco and Vanzetti executed Lindbergh's transatlantic flight Babe Ruth hits 60 home runs *The Jazz Singer,* the first movie with sound
1922	Economic recovery		**1928**	Stock market soars Hoover elected president

1923	Harding dies; Coolidge assumes
	  the presidency
	Peak of Ku Klux Klan activity
	Equal rights amendment
	  introduced
			1929	Stock market crashes; depression
				  begins

The organizational movement that had begun around 1900 also matured in the 1920s. Myriad business and professional associations sprang up to protect members' interests. Retailers and small manufacturers formed trade associations to pool information and coordinate planning. Farm bureaus and cooperative associations promoted scientific agriculture, lobbied for government protection, and tried to stabilize markets. Lawyers, engineers, and social scientists cooperated with business to promote economic growth. Big business had begun to dominate American economic life in the late nineteenth century, but these consolidated, corporate forms of activity now pervaded so many segments of the economy that in many ways they marked the real separation of the twentieth century from the nineteenth. In this outburst of expansion, many Americans shed their fear of big business, swayed in part by testimonials of probusiness propagandists. "Among the nations of the earth today," one writer proclaimed in 1921, "America stands for one idea: *Business*. . . . Thru business, properly conceived, managed and conducted, the human race is finally to be redeemed."

Government reflected this outlook. As corporations became more national in scope, they looked increasingly to the federal government for assistance in promoting economic growth. In 1921 Congress reduced taxes on corporations and wealthy individuals, and in 1922 it raised tariff rates in the Fordney-McCumber Tariff Act. Presidents Warren G. Harding, Calvin Coolidge, and Herbert Hoover appointed strong cabinet officers who pursued policies favorable to business. Regulatory agencies such as the Federal Trade Commission and Interstate Commerce Commission cooperated with corporations more than they regulated them.

Government Support of Business

The Supreme Court, led by Chief Justice and former president William Howard Taft, became a powerful policymaking body, exerting authority as aggressively as in the Gilded Age to protect business and private property. Its key decisions sheltered business from government regulation and undermined attempts by organized labor to achieve its ends through strikes and legislation. In 1922 Taft ruled in *Coronado Coal Company* v.

The River Rouge plant of the Ford Motor Company, with its bewildering patchwork of smokestacks, towers, passageways, scaffolding, and buildings, signifies the complexity and power of the twentieth-century corporation. *George Eastman House, International Museum of Photography.*

United Mine Workers that a striking union, like a trust, could be prosecuted for illegal restraint of trade. Yet in *Maple Floor Association* v. *U.S.* (1929), the Court gave support to trade associations that had formed to gather and disseminate antiunion information, by effectively exempting them from antitrust laws. The Court also struck down labor reform in cases such as *Bailey* v. *Drexel Furniture Company* (1922), which voided restrictions on child labor, and *Adkins* v. *Children's Hospital* (1923), which overturned a minimum-wage law for women because it infringed on liberty of contract.

Organized labor, which had gained ground during the Progressive era, suffered other setbacks during the 1920s. Public opinion, influenced by prosperity and probusiness rhetoric, turned against workers who disrupted everyday life with strikes. The federal government frequently stifled union attempts to exercise power. Early

> **Suppression of Labor Unions**

in the decade, for instance, the Justice Department used troops and court injunctions to end strikes by steel, mine, and railroad workers. Meanwhile, large corporations counteracted the appeal of unions by offering pensions, profit sharing (which actually amounted to the withholding of wages for later distribution), and company-sponsored social and sporting events—a policy known as welfare capitalism. Employers also received aid from legislators in establishing measures that ensured open shop conditions (prohibiting mandatory employment of union members) over closed (union) shop employment. And workers, concerned over meeting family needs with secure employment, shied away from unions and the uncertain class solidarity they promoted. In such a climate, union membership fell from 5.1 million in 1920 to 3.6 million in 1929.

A Business-Minded Presidency

During the 1920s a series of Republican presidents extended Theodore Roosevelt's notion of government-business cooperation—though they often made government a compliant coordinator rather than the active director Roosevelt had advocated. A symbol of the decade's goodwill toward business was President Warren G. Harding, a Republican elected in 1920 at a time when the populace wanted to avoid national and international crusades. Democrats had nominated Governor James M. Cox of Ohio, who supported Woodrow Wilson's fading hopes for United States membership in the League of Nations (see pages 688–690). But the efforts of Cox and his running mate, Franklin D. Roosevelt of New York, failed to attract voters. Harding, who kept his opinion on the League vague, captured 16.1 million popular votes to only 9.1 million for Cox. The total votes cast in the 1920 presidental election increased by 36 percent over 1916, reflecting the participation of women voters for the first time.

A small-town newspaper publisher and senator from Ohio, Harding selected some capable assistants, notably Secretary of States Charles Evans Hughes, Secretary of Commerce Herbert Hoover,

Harding Adminis- tration Secretary of the Treasury Andrew Mellon, and Secretary of Agriculture Henry C. Wallace. Harding also backed some important reforms. He helped streamline the budget, supported antilynching legislation, approved bills assisting farm cooperatives and liberalizing farm credit, and, unlike his predecessor Wilson, was generally tolerant on civil liberties issues.

Harding's problem was that he had too many predatory friends. His father once reputedly remarked, "Warren, it's a good thing you wasn't born a gal. You'd be in the family way all the time—you can't say no." Harding said yes too often, appointing friends who infested government with corruption. Charles Forbes of the Veterans Bureau served time in Leavenworth prison after being convicted of fraud and bribery in connection with government contracts. Thomas W. Miller, custodian of alien property, was jailed for accepting bribes. Attorney General Harry Daugherty was implicated in a scheme of accepting bribes and in other fraudulent acts; he escaped prosecution only by refusing to testify against himself. In the most notorious case, a congressional inquiry in 1923 and 1924 revealed that Secretary of the Interior Albert Fall had accepted bribes to lease government property to private oil companies. For his role in the affair, called the Teapot Dome scandal after a Wyoming oil reserve that had been turned over to Mammoth Oil Company, Fall was fined $100,000 and spent a year in jail. He was the first cabinet officer ever to be so disgraced.

In June 1923, few Americans knew how corrupt Harding's administration had become. The president, however, was disillusioned. Amid rumors of mismanagement and crime, he told journalist William Allen White, "My God, this is a hell of a job. I have no trouble with my enemies. . . . But my friends, my God-damned friends . . . they're the ones that keep me walking the floor nights." On a speaking tour that summer, Harding became ill and died in San Francisco on August 2. His death preceded revelation of the Teapot Dome scandal, but some people later believed that Harding had committed suicide rather than face the brewing storm. Most evidence, however, points to death from natural causes, probably a heart attack. At any rate, Harding was truly mourned. A warm, dignified-looking man who relished a good joke or an evening of poker and drinking, he seemed right for a

nation that had just experienced racking upheaval at home and abroad.

Harding's successor, Vice President Calvin Coolidge, was far more solemn. A dour New Englander (Alice Roosevelt Longworth, Theodore's daughter, once quipped that Coolidge looked as if he had been weaned on a pickle), Coolidge had an undistinguished record as Republican governor of Massachusetts. He first attracted national attention by his firm stand against striking Boston policemen in 1919, a policy that won him the vice-presidential nomination in 1920. Usually, however, he was content to let events take their course, prompting columnist Walter Lippmann to grumble, "It is a grim, determined, alert inactivity, which keeps Mr. Coolidge occupied constantly."

Coolidge had great respect for private enterprise; he once remarked, "The man who builds a factory builds a temple. The man who works there, worships there." Fortunately for him,

Coolidge Prosperity his presidency coincided with extraordinary business prosperity. Aided by Andrew Mellon, whom he retained as secretary of the treasury, and other cabinet officers, his administration balanced the budget, reduced government debt, lowered income-tax rates (especially for the rich), and began construction of a national highway system. With his generally tightfisted fiscal policies he won business support. Congress took little initiative during these years and assented to most measures recommended by the cabinet and by business associations such as the U.S. Chamber of Commerce. The only disruptions arose over farm policy. Responding to farmers' complaints of falling prices, Congress twice passed bills to establish government-backed price supports for staple crops (the McNary-Haugen bills of 1927 and 1928). But Coolidge vetoed the measure both times.

"Coolidge prosperity" was the determining issue in the presidential election of 1924. That year both major parties ran candidates who accepted business supremacy. Republicans nominated Coolidge with little dissent. At their national convention Democrats first debated heatedly whether to condemn the Ku Klux Klan, voting 542 to 541 against condemnation. Then they endured 103 ballots before breaking a deadlock between southern prohibitionists who favored former Secretary of the Treasury William G. McAdoo and antiprohibition easterners who backed New York's Governor Al-

Basically a shy and introverted person, Calvin Coolidge was content to let business have free rein in the pursuit of profits. This cartoon shows Coolidge accompanying the lively performance of big business with an instrument and song of praise. *Culver Pictures.*

Extensions of Reform

The triumph of business influence prompted some political analysts to claim that progressivism had died. They were partly right; concern for social

> **Extension of Progressive Reforms**

and economic justice that had moved the previous generation faded in the 1920s. Yet many of the Progressive era's achievements were sustained and expanded in these years. Federal trustbusting declined, but regulatory commissions and other government agencies still monitored business activities and worked to reduce wasteful practices. In Congress a corps of reformers, led by George Norris of Nebraska and Robert La Follette of Wisconsin, kept progressive causes alive by supporting labor legislation, federal aid to farmers, and a government-owned hydroelectric dam at Muscle Shoals, Alabama. (Business-oriented politicians wanted to sell or lease the dam and its nitrate plant to private interests.)

Most reform, however, occurred at state and local levels. Following initiatives begun before the First World War, thirty-four states instituted or expanded workers' compensation laws in the 1920s. At the same time many states established old-age pensions and other welfare programs. In cities, social scientists gathered data and drew maps in a systematic effort to identify and solve urban problems. Planning became a common feature of urban government; by 1926 every major city and many smaller ones had planning and zoning commissions that aimed to harness physical growth to the common good. Social workers continued to strive for better housing and poverty relief. During the 1920s the nation's state houses, city halls, and universities trained a new generation of reformers who would eventually influence national affairs during the New Deal government of the 1930s.

Indian affairs stirred some reform interest, though the generally apathetic stance of the federal government forced reformers to take adversary positions toward federal officials. No

> **Indian Affairs**

longer a threat to whites' ambitions, largely because of reduced numbers, Native Americans had become like other minorities: objects of discrimi-

fred E. Smith. They finally settled on John W. Davis, a corporation lawyer from New York. Remnants of the progressive movement, along with various farm, labor, and Socialist groups, formed a new Progressive party and nominated Robert M. La Follette, the aging reformer from Wisconsin. The party revived issues unresolved in previous generations: public ownership of utilities, aid to farmers, decreased restraint on organized labor, increased regulation of business.

Election results resembled those of 1912 in reverse: the two probusiness candidates captured most of the votes. Coolidge beat Davis by 15.7 million to 8.4 million popular votes, 382 to 136 electoral votes. Like Taft in 1912, La Follette finished a poor third, receiving a respectable but ineffective 4.8 million popular votes and only 13 electoral votes. The electorate thus endorsed the status quo and voiced their expectation for a period of extended prosperity.

Though armed with the vote for the first time in the 1920s, women generally failed to participate in elections in proportions higher than those of men. Nevertheless, some women took their new responsibilities seriously. Here the members of a women's political organization prepare to attend a convention. *UPI/Bettmann Archive.*

nation and of pressures to assimilate. Severalty, the policy of allotting land to individual Indians rather than to tribes (see page 472), had failed to make Native Americans self-supporting. Indian farmers suffered from poor soil, lack of irrigation, poor medical care, overcut forests, and white cattle thieves. Attached to their land, natives showed little desire to move to cities. Whites still hoped to convert natives into productive citizens but in a way that remained insensitive to Indian culture. Reformers especially criticized Indian women, who refused to adopt middle-class homemaking methods and balked at sending their children away to boarding school.

Some reformers realized that citizenship would have to come at the Indians' pace and with their consent. Organizations such as the Indian Rights Association, the American Indian Defence Association, and the General Federation of Women's Clubs worked to obtain racial justice and social services for Indians. Under President Hoover, the Bureau of Indian Affairs was reorganized and expenditures were increased for health, education, and welfare. Yet much of the money went to enlarge the bureaucracy rather than into Indian hands, and paternalism continued to characterize policy toward Native Americans.

Certain continuities characterized women's politics even after the achievement of suffrage in 1920 (see page 623). Rather than become enmeshed in party politics, women tended to remain tied to voluntary organizations whose specialized memberships helped develop modern pressure-group politics. Whether their issue was birth control, peace, education, Indian affairs, or opposition to lynching, women in these associations tried to publicize their cause and lobby legislators rather than elect their own candidates. Although they often allied with men's organiza-

> **Women and Politics**

tions working for similar ends—and therefore were not exclusively feminist—they did achieve legislative victories especially helpful to women. Lobbying by several women's groups succeeded in 1921 when Congress passed the Sheppard-Towner (Maternity and Infancy) Act, which allotted funds to states to help set up maternity and pediatric clinics. (The measure was rescinded in 1929 when Congress, under pressure from private physicians, cut off funding.) In 1922 the Cable Act reversed an old law under which an American woman who married a foreigner would take on her husband's citizenship; under the new law such a woman was allowed to retain United States citizenship.

Women now were voters, however, and as such faced a dilemma in electoral politics. Given that male party leaders were not likely to yield their power and would welcome only those women who accepted a party's platform and candidates, should women form their own party? The National Woman's Party, which before suffrage had been the champion of feminism, still stressed female solidarity in the quest for equal rights. But in doing so, it sustained the old paradox of mobilizing women as a class to erase discrimination against the class of women (see pages 623–624). Other groups, such as the League of Women Voters, which evolved out of the National American Woman Suffrage Association, tried to avoid creating a female voting bloc, preferring instead to lobby for issues of interest to women while at the same time integrating women into politics with, rather than constantly struggling against, men. To the dismay of women's political groups, however, newly enfranchised female voters participated in elections in the same small proportions as did men. They, like men, seemed caught up in the diversions of the new era's materialism.

Materialism Unbound

Poor Richard's Almanac would have sold poorly in the 1920s. Few Americans of that era had much interest in the virtues of thrift and sobriety that Benjamin Franklin had preached. They grew more attracted to acquisition, amusement, and salesmanship. Instead of traditional homilies like

"Waste not, want not," they succumbed to the advice of an advertising executive: "Make the public want what you have to sell. Make 'em pant for it." With such an attitude Americans attained the highest standard of living they had yet experienced. Poverty and social injustice still blighted the country, but many people shared the belief, as journalist Joseph Wood Krutch put it, that "the future was bright and the present was good fun at least."

Between 1919 and 1929 the gross national product—the total value of all goods and services produced in the United States—swelled by 40 percent.

Expansion of the Consumer Society

Wages and salaries also increased (though not as much), while cost of living remained relatively stable. People had more purchasing power, and they spent as Americans had never spent. In an article in *Survey* magazine, Eunice Fuller Barnard contrasted one family's expenditures in 1900 with those of 1928:

1900

2 bicycles	$ 70
wringer and washboard	$ 5
brushes and brooms	$ 5
sewing machine (mechanical)	$ 25
Total	$ 105

1928

automobile	$ 700
radio	$ 75
phonograph	$ 50
washing machine	$ 150
vacuum cleaner	$ 50
sewing machine (electric)	$ 60
other electrical equipment	$ 25
telephone (year)	$ 35
Total	$1,145[1]

Barnard added that certain items, such as education and medical care, had become costlier. Yet she re-

[1] From Paul Carter, *Another Part of the Twenties,* © 1977, Columbia University Press. By permission.

garded the change as worthwhile. She would rather pay more for a quart of milk knowing that it was safer and purer than the product of a generation earlier. "When some of us bewail the higher cost of living we may be talking about the higher cost of *better* living," Barnard concluded.

The benefits of modern technology were reaching more people than ever before. By 1929 two-thirds of all Americans lived in dwellings that had electricity, compared with one-sixth in 1912. In 1929 one-fourth of all families owned electric vacuum cleaners and one-fifth had electric toasters. Many could afford these and other items such as radios, washing machines, and movie tickets only because more than one family member worked or because the breadwinner took a second job. Nevertheless, new products and services were available to more than just the rich.

Of all the era's technological and economic wonders, the automobile was the vanguard. During the 1920s automobile registrations soared from 8 million to 23 million. Mass produc-

Effects of the Automobile tion and competition brought down prices, making cars affordable even to some working-class families. By 1926 a Ford Model T cost under $300 and a Chevrolet sold for $700—at a time when workers in manufacturing earned about $1,300 a year and clerical workers about $2,300. At these prices, people could consider the car a necessity rather than a luxury. "There is no such thing as a 'pleasure automobile,' " proclaimed an ad in a Nashville, Tennessee, newspaper in 1925. "You might as well talk of 'pleasure fresh air,' or of 'pleasure beef steak.' . . . The automobile increases length of life, increases happiness, represents above all other achievements the progress and the civilization of our age."

The motor car altered society as much as the railroad had seventy-five years earlier. Public officials were forced to pay more attention to safety regulations and traffic control. (In 1924 General Electric Company produced the first timed stop-and-go traffic light.) Changes in design provided new opportunities for youths to escape watchful parents. By 1927, five-sixths of all autos were enclosed (in 1919 most had had open tops), making for a privacy that bred fears of "houses of prostitution on wheels." The growing choice of models (there were 108 different automobile manufactur-

The huge expansion of electrical appliances in the 1920s created a demand for a new kind of service, electrical repair shops. Here, a flourishing repair establishment offers a full range of services "day and night." *University of Louisville Photographic Archives, Caufield and Shook Collection.*

ers in 1923) and colors allowed owners to suit their personal tastes in a growing mass society. Most important, the car was the ultimate symbol of social equality. As one writer observed in 1924, "It is hard to convince Steve Popovich, or Antonio Branca, or plain John Smith that he is being ground into the dust by Capital when at will he may drive the same highways, view the same scenery, and get as much enjoyment from his trip as the modern Midas."

Americans' newly acquired taste for driving necessitated extensive construction of roads and abundant supplies of fuel. Since the late 1800s farmers and bicyclists had been pressing for improved roads; after the First World War motorists joined the campaign, prompting cities and states to improve local arteries. Important advances came in 1921 when Congress passed the Federal Highway

"Everyone owns a car but us"~

You, too, can own an automobile without missing the money, and *now*, is the time to buy it—through the easiest and simplest method ever devised:

Ford Weekly Purchase Plan

Thousands of families, who thought a car was out of the question because of limited incomes, found that they could easily, quickly and surely buy a car of their own under this remarkable plan

Ford Motor Company
Detroit

IT IS EASY TO OWN A CAR BY USING THIS PLAN

By the 1920s, not only was an automobile affordable, especially through installment payments such as the "Ford Weekly Purchase Plan," but also there was strong social pressure on families to own one. As this advertisement so vividly illustrates, Americans were made to feel that they needed an automobile for the pleasure and status it would bring them. *Library of Congress.*

Act, which provided federal aid for state roads; and in 1923 when the Bureau of Public Roads planned a national highway system.

The oil industry, already vast and powerful, shifted emphasis from products providing illumination and lubrication to products providing propulsion. In 1920 the United States produced about 65 percent of the world's oil, much of it controlled by the Standard Oil trust. But already Americans were tasting a bitter future (see page 971) as corporate and government officials warned of fuel shortages and shrinking reserves. Early in 1920 a U.S. Geological Survey report stated that "unless our consumption is checked, we shall by 1925 be dependent on foreign oilfields." In some parts of the country companies limited the amount of gasoline

people could buy and doubled the price. But the crisis had a dubious flavor. Just after price hikes occurred, the State Department persuaded the British to grant Standard Oil a share in British-controlled Iraqi oilfields. Immediately thereafter, the crisis abated.

More than ever, the taste for automobiles and other goods and services was whetted by advertising. By 1929 total advertising earnings reached $3.4 billion, more than was spent on all types of formal education. For many, advertising became the language of a new gospel. In his best-selling *The Man Nobody Knows* (1925), advertising executive Bruce Barton called Jesus "the founder of modern business" because he "picked up twelve men from the bottom ranks of business and forged them into an organization that conquered the world." About the same time, a pamphlet entitled *Moses, Persuader of Men* declared, "Moses was one of the greatest salesmen and real-estate promoters that ever lived," demonstrating that advertising could be ecumenical. Advertising theorists also adopted psychological principles and practical cynicism in asserting that, with proper influences, any person's tastes could be manipulated.

> **Advertising**

Although daily newspaper circulation declined during the 1920s, other media assumed vital advertising functions. By 1929 over 10 million families owned radios, which bombarded them almost continuously with advertisements. Station KDKA in Pittsburgh pioneered in commercial radio broadcasting beginning in 1920; by 1922 there were 508 such stations. By 1929 Americans were spending $850 million a year on radio equipment, and the National Broadcasting Company, which had begun to assemble a network of radio stations three years earlier, was charging advertisers $10,000 to sponsor an hour-long show. Commercial intermissions at movie houses and highway billboards also reminded viewers to buy. Packaging and product display became sciences, with the objective of creating demand.

Although poor people could not afford many of the products and services, some new trends touched the working classes, especially those living in cities. Indoor plumbing and electricity became more common in private residences, and canned foods, varied diets, ready-made clothes, and mass-produced shoes became more affordable. A little cash and a lot of credit enabled many to purchase an automobile. And even if a family could not afford a radio, vacuum cleaner, or vacation right away, there was always hope. Spending became a national pastime. No wonder many people wanted Henry Ford to run for president in 1924.

Cities, Migrants, and Suburbs

The expansion of consumerism bespoke not only an economically mature nation but an urbanized one. In 1920 for the first time the federal census revealed that a majority of Americans, 51.4 percent, lived in urban areas (places with 2,500 or more people), a sign that the city had become the locus of national experience. Indeed, the growth of both services and industry derived from and responded to urbanization. Industries such as steel, oil, and auto production boosted cities like Detroit, Birmingham, and Houston; service and retail trades accounted for expansion in Atlanta, Minneapolis, and Seattle. The most explosive growth occurred in areas of warm climate—Miami and San Diego—where promises of comfort and profit attracted thousands of speculators.

> **Continuing Urbanization**

The trend toward urbanization continued during the 1920s, as an estimated 6 million Americans left their farms for nearby or distant cities. Midwestern migrants, particularly young single people, moved to regional centers or to California. A steady stream of southerners moved into burgeoning industrial cities of the South or followed railroad lines north.

Blacks accounted for a sizable portion of the migrants. Crushed by tenant farming and lured by industrial jobs, 1.5 million blacks moved cityward during the 1920s, accelerating a trend that began a decade earlier (see page 664). Black populations of New York, Chicago, Detroit, and Houston doubled during these years. Forced by necessity and discrimination to seek the cheapest housing, newcomers squeezed into ghettos—low-rent districts from which escape was difficult at best. Unlike white migrants, who were free to move away from inner-city districts if and when they could afford to do so, blacks found better housing closed to them.

The only way they could expand housing opportunities was to spill into nearby neighborhoods, a process that sparked resistance and violence. Fears of such expansion prompted white neighborhood associations to adopt restrictive covenants, whereby homeowners pledged not to sell their property to blacks.

In response partly to their new urban experiences and partly to race riots and threats, thousands of blacks in northern cities joined movements that glorified black independence. The most influential of these black nationalist groups was the Universal Negro Improvement Association (UNIA), headed by Marcus Garvey, a Jamaican immigrant who believed blacks should separate themselves from corrupt white society. Proclaiming "I am the equal of any white man," Garvey cultivated race pride through militant mass meetings and parades. He also promoted black capitalism to demonstrate blacks' management skills. His newspaper, the *Negro World,* refused to publish ads for hair straighteners and skin-lightening cosmetics, and his Black Star shipping line was intended to help blacks emigrate to Africa.

> **Marcus Garvey**

The UNIA declined in the mid–1920s when the Black Star line went bankrupt (unscrupulous dealers had sold the line dilapidated ships) and when antiradical fears prompted government prosecution (ten of the organization's leaders were arrested on charges of anarchism and Garvey was deported for mail fraud). Black middle-class leaders like W. E. B. Du Bois opposed the UNIA. Nevertheless, the organization attracted a huge following (contemporaries estimated it at 500,000; Garvey claimed 6 million) in New York, Chicago, Detroit, and other cities. Garvey's speeches had served notice that blacks had their own aspirations, which they could and would translate into action.

The newest immigrants to American cities came from Mexico and Puerto Rico. As in the nineteenth century, Mexicans moved north to work as agricultural laborers in the Southwest, but in the 1920s a large number also flowed into growing cities like Denver, San Antonio, Los Angeles, and Tucson. Like other immigrant groups, Mexicans generally lacked resources and skills, and men greatly outnumbered women. Victims of white prejudice, Mexicans crowded into low-rent, inner-city districts

> **Mexican and Puerto Rican Immigrants**

During and after the First World War, thousands of southern blacks migrated northward, taking railroad routes into cities like Chicago, New York, and St. Louis. In these cities blacks found new job opportunities and better housing but also racial tension and violence. *The Phillips Collection, Washington.*

where they often were deprived of decent city services, such as sanitation, schools, and police protection. Yet their communities, called *barrios,* provided an environment in which immigrants could sustain customs and values of the homeland and develop institutions to help them adapt to American society.

The 1920s also saw a great influx of Puerto Ricans to the mainland (Puerto Rico had been a United States possession since 1898; see page 649). A shift in the island's economy from sugar to coffee production had created a surplus population willing to move and attracted by contracts from American employers seeking cheap labor. Most Puerto Rican migrants moved to New York City where they formed *barrios* in parts of Brooklyn and Manhattan. Besides manufacturing, Puerto Ricans found jobs in hotels, restaurants, and domestic service. Puerto Rican and Mexican communities contained some educated elites—doctors, lawyers, business own-

ers—who served as ethnic leaders. Puerto Rican *barrios,* which contained nearly equal numbers of women and men, also developed their own consumer institutions, such as *bodegas* (grocery stores), restaurants, and boarding houses.

As urban growth peaked, suburban growth accelerated. Although towns had existed around the edges of urban centers since the nation's earliest years, prosperity and easier trans-

Growth of the Suburbs portation—mainly the automobile —made the urban fringe more accessible in the 1920s. Between 1920 and 1930, suburbs of Chicago (such as Oak Park and Evanston), Cleveland (such as Shaker Heights), and Los Angeles (such as Burbank and Inglewood) grew five to ten times as fast as the central cities. Most suburbs were middle- and upper-class bedroom communities; some, like Highland Park (near Detroit) and East Chicago, were industrial suburbs.

Westwood Hills Westwood Hills

The possibility of luxurious life in a planned suburban community, such as this one in southern California, beckoned to middle- and upper-class families during the 1920s. While New England colonial style bungalows were popular in the suburban East and Midwest, the Spanish colonial revival style was favored by western architects and developers. *Los Angeles County Museum of Natural History.*

With their own police, fire protection, and water and gas services, many suburbs resisted annexation to core cities. Suburbanites wanted to escape big-city crime, dirt, and taxes, and they fought to preserve local control. "Under local government," one suburban editor reasoned, "we can absolutely control every objectionable thing that may try to enter our limits—but once annexed we are at the mercy of city hall." Particularly in the Northeast and Midwest, the fierce independence of growing suburbs choked off expansion by the central city and divided metropolitan areas in ways that would cause problems for future generations.

Bulging cities and suburbs fostered the new mass culture that gave the decade its character. Most of the consumers who jammed shops, movie houses, and sporting arenas and who embraced fads like crossword puzzles, miniature golf, and marathon dancing were city and suburb dwellers. Cities and suburbs were the places where people defied law and morality by patronizing speakeasies (illegal saloons), wearing outlandish clothes, and listening to jazz. They were also the places where women, ethnic and racial minorities, and religious denominations strained hardest to adjust to the new era. Yet the ideal of small-town society survived. While millions thronged cityward and intellectuals carped that small towns stifled personal growth, Americans reminisced about the innocence and simplicity of a world gone by. This was the dilemma of a modern nation: how could one anchor oneself in a world of rampant material and social change?

Cities, Migrants, and Suburbs

Life

Commuters' Number

Suburbanization and the demands of white collar work created new schedules and roles in the middle-class family. Here the housewife, now the chief consumer and household manager, sews a button on the sleeve of the breadwinner husband while he gulps coffee and reads his paper before rushing to catch his commuter train. *Library of Congress.*

New Rhythms of Everyday Life

Amid all the change, Americans developed new social values and new ways of using time. Increasingly, people were splitting their daily lives into three distinct compartments: work, family, and leisure. Each type of time was altered in the 1920s. For many people, time on the job shrank. Among industrial workers the five-and-a-half-day workweek (half a day on Saturday) was becoming common. Many white-collar employees enjoyed two days off and worked a forty-hour week. Annual vacations were becoming a standard job benefit for white-collar workers, whose numbers grew by 40 percent.

Family time is harder to measure, but certain figures suggest important changes. As birth control became more widely practiced, birthrates dropped noticeably between 1920 and 1930. As a result, family size decreased. Among American women who married in the 1870s and 1880s, well over half who survived to age fifty had five or more children; of those who married in the 1920s, however, just 20 percent had five or more children. Over the same period the divorce rate rose. In 1920 there was 1 divorce in every 7.5 marriages; in 1929 the national ratio was 1 in 6, and in many cities it was 2 in 7. Lower birthrates, more divorce, plus longer life expectancy meant that adults were devoting a smaller portion of their lives to parental and other family tasks.

The availability of ready-to-wear clothes, preserved foods, and mass-produced furniture meant that family members spent less time producing household necessities. Wives still

Household Management

spent most of their day cleaning, cooking, mending, and raising children, but new machines lightened some of their tasks. Especially in middle-class households, electric irons and washing machines made tedious chores less burdensome. Gas- and oil-powered central heating and hot-water heaters eliminated the hauling of wood, coal, and water, the upkeep of a kitchen fire, and the removal of ashes.

As a result, housewives filled their time differently from their forebears—though they spent as much, if not more, time on domestic responsibilities. Although the new technology was supposed to make life easier for women, it also created new demands on their time. By eliminating servants, who had helped with cleaning, cooking, and childcare, machines shifted the entire job of household management onto the wife herself. Instead of being a producer of food and clothing as women had been, the wife became chief consumer, shopping and making sure the family spent its money wisely.

Prudent expenditure of family money was related to a major revolution in American food habits. Before 1920, nutritionists believed that poor health resulted from eating harmful foods; their remedy was to cut down on or abstain from certain foods like spices, garlic, and onions. The discovery of vitamins between 1915 and 1930 prompted nutritionists to advocate the consumption of certain foods to prevent illness. Giant food companies scrambled to advertise their products as filled with vitamins and minerals beneficial to growth and health. Not only did the producers of milk and canned fruits and vegetables exploit the vitamin craze, but other companies made lofty claims that were hard to dispute because little was known about these invisible, tasteless ingredients. For example, Fleischmann's advertised its yeast cakes as the ultimate health food, "the richest known source of water soluble vitamins." C. W. Post claimed that his Grape-Nuts contained *"iron, calcium, phosphorus,* and *other mineral elements* that are taken right up as vital food by the millions of cells in the body."

In addition, the ready availability of washing machines, hot water, and commercial soap put great pressure on wives to keep everything clean. Advertisers tried to coax women into buying products by making them feel guilty for not giving enough attention to cleaning the home, caring for children, and tending to personal hygiene. "Are you unpopular with your own children?" asked makers of Listerine mouthwash. If so, the ad advised, "More often than you would imagine . . . halitosis is at fault. Children are quick to resent it. . . . Realizing this, [caring mothers] eliminate any risk of offending by the systematic use of Listerine in the mouth. Every morning. Every night." Thus, while the industrial and service sectors became more specialized as a result of technological advances, housewives retained a wide variety of tasks and added new ones as well.

While family time shifted and work time decreased, nonwork, nonfamily activities expanded. More people spent more years in school. High school enrollment quadrupled between 1910 and 1929; by 1929 over one-third of all high school graduates went on to college. As the use of electricity spread, people stayed up later at night to read or listen to the radio. They filled expanding leisure time with automobile rides, sports events, motion pictures, shopping, and other forms of amusement.

In general, more rest and better diets made Americans healthier. Between 1920 and 1930 life expectancy at birth increased from fifty-four to sixty years, and infant mortality decreased by two-thirds. Sanitation and research in bacteriology and immunology combined with better nutrition to reduce the risks of life-threatening diseases such as tuberculosis and diphtheria. Medical progress did not benefit all groups equally, however. Rates of stillbirth and infant mortality were 50 to 100 percent higher among blacks than among whites, and incidences of tuberculosis in urban slums remained alarmingly high. Moreover, the death rate from automobile accidents rose 150 percent, and deaths from heart disease and cancer—diseases of old age—increased about 15 percent. Nevertheless, Americans in general were living longer: the total number of people age sixty-five and over grew 35 percent between 1920 and 1930, while the rest of the population increased only 15 percent.

Rising numbers and worsening economic conditions of the elderly stirred interest in old-age pensions and other forms of assistance. The industrial system put a premium on youth and agility, pushing older people into poverty from forced retirement and reduced income. Recognizing the needs of aging citizens, most European countries had established state-supported pension systems in the early 1900s. But many Americans believed that people should prepare for old age by saving in their youth; pensions, they felt, smacked of socialism. As late as 1923 the Pennsylvania Chamber of Commerce labeled old-age assistance "un-American and socialistic . . . an entering wedge of communistic propaganda."

Old Age and Retirement

Yet something had to be done. A large majority of all inmates in state pauper institutions were older people, and almost one-third of Americans age sixty-five and older were financially dependent on someone else. Only a few companies had retirement plans; most, including the federal government, did not provide for retired employees. Noting that the government fed retired horses until they died, one postal worker complained, "For the purpose of drawing a pension, it would have been better had I been a horse than a human being." Resistance to pensions finally broke at the state level in the 1920s. Led by Isaac Max Rubinow and Abraham Epstein, reformers persuaded voluntary associations, labor unions, and legislators to accept the principle of old-age support through pensions, insurance, and retirement homes. By 1933 almost every state provided at least minimal assistance to needy elderly, and the way had been opened for a national program of old-age insurance.

New fashions in clothing and beach wear that freed the body from old restraints did not always meet with the approval of moralists. In this scene a guardian of virtue measures the length of a bathing suit to be sure it did not overstep limits of decency. *Library of Congress.*

With more people spending time away from work and family, new values were inevitable. Especially among the middle class but among the working class too, clothes became a means to personal expression and freedom. Both men and women wore more casual and gaily colored styles than their parents would have considered. The line between inappropriate and acceptable behavior blurred as smoking, swearing, and frankness about sex became more common. Thousands who had never read psychoanalyst Sigmund Freud's theories were certain that he prescribed an uninhibited sex life as the key to mental health. Birth-control advocate Margaret Sanger, who a decade earlier had been accused of promoting race suicide and had fled the country, gained a large following in respectable circles. Newspapers,

> **Social Values**

magazines, motion pictures, and popular songs (such as "Hot Lips" and "Burning Kisses") made certain that Americans did not suffer from "sex starvation." A typical movie ad announced "brilliant men, beautiful jazz babies, champagne baths, midnight revels, petting parties in the purple dawn, all ending in one terrific smashing climax that makes you gasp."

Other trends contributed to the breakdown of old values. Because child-labor laws and compulsory-school-attendance laws kept children in school longer than was common in earlier generations, schools and peer groups played a greater role in socializing children. In earlier times, different age groups had common activities: children worked with older people in the fields, and young apprentices worked with older journeymen and craftsmen. Now, however, graded school classes, sports, clubs, and other activities constantly brought together children who were the same age, separating them from the company and influence of adults. In addition, parents tended to rely less on family tradition and more on childcare manuals in raising children. Old-age homes, public health clinics, and workers' compensation reduced family responsibilities even further.

In spite of shrinkage in the employment opportunities that had been created by the First World War, women continued to stream into the labor force. By 1930, 10.8 million women held paying jobs, an increase of over 2 million since the war's end. The sex segregation that had long characterized occupations continued; most female workers held jobs at which few men worked. Over a million women were teachers and nurses. Some 2.2 million were typists, bookkeepers, and office clerks, a tenfold increase since 1920; another 736,000 were store clerks. Increasing numbers took jobs as waitresses and hairdressers. Almost 2 million women worked in factories, though their numbers grew very little over the decade. Whatever the employment, wages paid to women seldom equaled more than half of the wages paid to men.

> **Jobs for Women**

Entry into work outside the home extended women's family roles. Although women worked for a combination of reasons, the economic needs of their families shaped most women's job experiences. The consumerism of the 1920s prompted working-class and middle-class families to satisfy their wants by living beyond their means or by sending women and children into the labor force. In previous eras, most of these extra wage earners were young and single. In the 1920s, the proportion of the work force that contained married women rose by 30 percent, and numbers of employed married women swelled from 1.9 million to 3.1 million. Figures conceal countless widows, divorcées, and abandoned women who held jobs and who, like married women, likely had children to support. The vast majority of married women remained out of the work force (only 12 percent were employed in 1930), but they did so because social pressures and the demands of housework and childcare prevented them from joining. Black women were the exception; their proportions in the work force were twice those of white women.

Extended kin, such as grandmothers and aunts, helped with childcare while black mothers took outside employment, but such family arrangements did not lessen the economic burdens of black households beset by poverty and discrimination.

Feminists in the 1920s focused on the issue of women in the labor force, but they did not fully understand the motivations of many female workers. Women's earlier functions as producers of food and clothes, said feminists, had lapsed into passive roles as child nurturers and homemakers; the result was economic dependency. The way to restore married women's sense of worth in a money-oriented society was through gainful employment. A job, asserted *Harper's* editor Dorothy Bromley, would make a married women "a full-fledged individual who is capable of molding her own life."

> **Economic Feminism**

Because feminists stressed economic independence, they tended to oppose protective legislation that limited hours and improved conditions in industries that monopolized female workers and thereby prevented women from entering male-dominated jobs in which skill levels and pay were higher. Feminists believed married and single women should challenge the sexual division of labor. They heeded the call for equal pay and equal opportunity voiced by Alice Paul, leader of the National Women's party, who in 1923 supported an equal rights amendment to the Constitution. But other women, especially in the working class, had doubts. They did not trust the competitive, individualistic environment of job markets, and they had been raised in cultures that assigned women the responsibility of maintaining cooperation within their families and neighborhoods. Once again the question of whether women should be like or different from men posed thorny questions.

Employed or not, women were exposed to alternative images of femininity. Short skirts and bobbed hair, regarded as signs of sexual freedom, became common among office workers and store clerks as well as among college coeds. Several studies claimed that sexual experimentation, including premarital sex, increased among young women during the decade. The most popular models of female behavior were not chaste, modest heroines but movie

> **Alternative Images of Femininity**

vamps like Clara Bow, known as the "It Girl," and Gloria Swanson, known for torrid love affairs on and off the screen. Not every woman was a flapper, as the young independent-minded woman was called, but many women were asserting social equality with men. As one observer described the "new woman":

> She takes a man's point of view as her mother never could. . . . She will never make you a hatband or knit you a necktie, but she'll drive you from the station . . . in her own little sports car. She'll don knickers and go skiing with you, . . . she'll dive as well as you, perhaps better, she'll dance as long as you care to, and she'll take everything you say the way you mean it.

These new trends represented a sharp break with the more restrained culture of the nineteenth century. But social change, as always, did not proceed smoothly. As the decade wore on, various groups prepared to defend against threats to older, more familiar values.

Lines of Defense

In the spring of 1920 the leader of a newly formed organization decided to hire two public relations experts to recruit members. Using modern advertising techniques, the promoters, Edward Clarke and Elizabeth Tyler, canvassed communities in the South, Southwest, and Midwest, where they found thousands of men eager to pay $10 to join and another $6 for a uniform made of white cloth. For their efforts, Clarke and Tyler pocketed $2.50 out of each membership fee. No one could argue with their success. By 1923 the organization claimed 5 million members.

This was no ordinary civic club like the Lions or Kiwanis; it cultivated a special kind of social consciousness. It was the Ku Klux Klan, a revived version of the hooded order that had terrorized southern communities after the Civil War, and its appeal was based on fear. As one pamphlet distributed by Clarke and Tyler put it, "Every criminal, every gambler, every thug, every libertine, every girl ruiner, every home wrecker, every wife beater, every dope peddler, every moonshiner, every white slaver, every Rome-controlled newspaper, every black spider—is fighting the Klan. Think it over, which side are you on?"

The Klan was the most sinister reactionary movement of the 1920s. Reconstituted in 1915 by William J. Simmons, an Atlanta evangelist and insurance salesman who wanted to purify southern culture, the new Invisible Empire revived the hoods, intimidating tactics, and mystical terms of its forerunner. (Local societies were klaverns, its leader the Imperial Wizard, its books of rituals the kloran.) The new Klan was broader in membership and objectives than the old. Its chapters fanned outward from the deep South and for a time wielded frightening power in all other regions of the country. Unlike the first Klan, which terrorized mostly emancipated blacks, the new Klan directed its venom toward a variety of racial and religious groups.

▶ **Ku Klux Klan**

One brief phrase expressed Klan goals: "Native, white, Protestant supremacy." *Native* meant no immigration, no "mongrelization" of white Protestant culture. According to Imperial Wizard Hiram Wesley Evans, *white* supremacy was a matter of survival. "The world," he warned, "has been so made so that each race must fight for its life, must conquer, accept slavery, or die. The Klansman believes the whites will not become slaves, and he does not intend to die before his time." Evans praised *Protestantism* for permitting "unhampered individual development." The Catholic Church, on the other hand, prevented immigrants from assimilating and suppressed free conscience by enslaving people to priests and a foreign pope.

Using threatening assemblies, violence, and political pressure, Klan members menaced many communities in the early 1920s. Assuming the role of moral protector, they meted out vigilante justice to assumed bootleggers, wife beaters, and adulterers; they forced schools to adopt Bible readings and stop teaching the theory of evolution; and they campaigned against Catholic and Jewish political candidates. By the mid-1920s, however, the Invisible Empire was on the wane, outnumbered by immigrants and their offspring and rocked by scandal. (In 1925 Indiana Grand Dragon David Stephenson allegedly kidnaped and raped a women who later died either from taking poison or from an infection caused by bites on her body; Stephenson was convicted of second-degree murder on grounds that he was responsible for her suicide.) The Klan's negative, exclusive brand of patriotism and purity could not compete in a pluralistic society.

◀

The Ku Klux Klan had no monopoly on bigotry; intolerance still pervaded American society. Since the 1880s a number of groups had been urging an end to free immigration. Huge influxes of Catholic and Jewish immigrants, nativists charged, clogged inner-city slums, upset traditional norms with their drinking habits, and stubbornly held to alien religious and political beliefs. As self-styled expert Madison Grant wrote in *The Passing of the Great Race* (1916): "These immigrants adopt the language of the native American, they wear his clothes, they steal his name and they are beginning to take his women, but they seldom adopt his religion or understand his ideals."

Fear of radicalism, left over from the Red Scare of 1919, fueled antiforeign sentiments. The most notorious outburst of hysteria occurred in 1921,

> **Sacco and Vanzetti**

when a court convicted Nicola Sacco and Bartolomeo Vanzetti, two immigrant anarchists, of murdering a guard and paymaster during a robbery in South Braintree, Massachusetts. Sacco and Vanzetti's main offenses seem to have been their political beliefs and Italian origins, since evidence failed to prove their involvement in the robbery. Judge Webster Thayer nevertheless openly sided with the prosecution, privately calling the defendants "those anarchist bastards." Appeals by protesters failed to win a new trial, and the two Italians, who remained calm and dignified throughout their ordeal, were executed in August 1927. Their deaths chilled those who had looked to the United States as the land that nurtured freedom of belief.

Meanwhile, the move to restrict immigration was gathering support. Labor leaders warned that a flood of aliens would depress wages and raise unemployment. Business executives who formerly had opposed restrictions because immigrant laborers were easy to exploit changed their minds when they realized that mechanization and the hiring of black workers could enable them to keep labor costs low. Drawing support from these and other nativists, Congress set yearly immigration quotas for each nationality.

The quotas favored northern and western Europeans, reflecting the prejudices of the nativists against new immigrants from southern and eastern Europe. The Emergency Quota

> **Immigration Quotas**

(Johnson) Act of 1921 stipulated that annual immigration of a given

Advocates of immigrant restriction intensified their campaigns in the 1920s with propaganda such as this cartoon, which argues that the only way to prevent hoards of Europeans from invading the country was to funnel them in such a way so that only a small fraction of them could reach American shores. *Library of Congress.*

nationality could not exceed 3 percent of the number of immigrants from that nation residing in the United States in 1910. This law, meant to be temporary, did not satisfy restrictionists' aims, so Congress replaced it with the National Origins Act of 1924. The new law set the quota at 2 percent of each nationality residing in the United States in *1890,* further limiting southern and eastern Europeans, since far fewer members of those groups lived in the United States in 1890 than in 1910. Congress amended the National Origins Act in 1927, moving the base year to 1920 and fixing a limit of 150,000 immigrants a year—including 65,721 from Great Britain and 25,957 from Germany but only 5,802 from Italy and 2,712 from Russia. The laws excluded Asians but set no quotas for peoples from the Western Hemisphere. Soon Canadians, Mexicans, and Puerto Ricans became the largest groups of newcomers (see figure, page 714).

The impulse to ensure moral purity also stirred religious fundamentalists. Millions of Americans sought certainty in a rapidly changing world by fol-

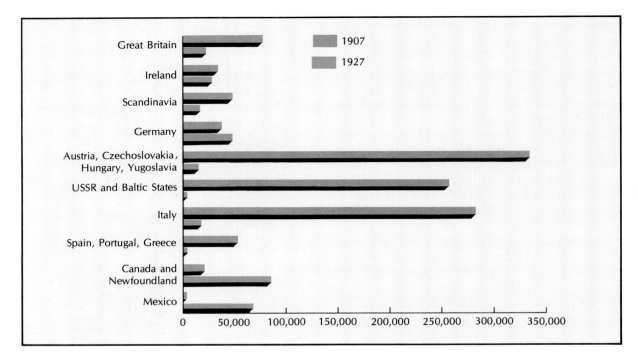

Immigration, 1907 and 1927

lowing evangelical branches of Protestantism that accepted a literal interpretation of the Bible. For them, unquestioning faith was not only a means to salvation but a traditional and comforting defense against the skepticism and irreverence of a materialistic, hedonistic society.

In 1925 Christian fundamentalism clashed with new scientific theory in a celebrated case in Dayton, Tennessee. Early that year the Tennessee legislature passed a law forbidding public school instructors to teach the theory that humans had evolved from lower forms of life rather than from Adam and Eve. Shortly thereafter, high school teacher John Thomas Scopes was arrested for violating the law (he had volunteered to serve in a test case). Scopes's trial that summer became a headline event, with William Jennings Bryan, former secretary of state and three-time presidential candidate, arguing for the prosecution, and a team of civil liberties lawyers headed by Clarence Darrow arguing for the defense. Hordes of news correspondents crowded into town, and radio stations broadcast the trial.

Although Scopes was convicted—clearly he had broken the law—modernists claimed victory. The testimony, they believed, showed fundamentalism

> **Scopes Trial**

to be at odds with secular social trends. The trial's climax occurred when Bryan took the witness stand as an expert on religion and science. Responding to Darrow's probing, Bryan asserted that Eve had truly been created from Adam's rib, that a big fish had swallowed Jonah, and that God had created the world in six days—though a "day" might have lasted a million years. The liberal press mocked Bryan's uncritical faith; humorist Will Rogers quipped, "I see you can't say that man descended from the ape. At least that's the law in Tennessee. But do they have a law to keep a man from making a jackass of himself?" Nevertheless, fundamentalists nursed their wounds and steadfastly pursued their cause of faith and salvation.

Ku Klux Klan rallies, immigration restriction, and fundamentalist protests might be seen as last gasps of a rural society yielding to modern urban-industrial values. Yet city dwellers swelled the ranks of these defensive movements. Nearly half the Klan's members lived in cities, especially in working-class neighborhoods, where fear of invasion by blacks and foreigners was strong. Even urban reformers backed laws limiting immigration, seeing them as a means of controlling poverty and quickening the assimilation of foreigners. Cities also housed hundreds of pentecostal churches, which attracted whites struggling between the middle and lower classes. Such people were swayed by the pageantry and closeness to God offered by these churches. Using elaborately staged services, radio broadcasts, and modern advertising techniques, cult leaders such as Aimee Semple McPherson of Los Angeles stirred revivalist fervor. Finally, many urban dwellers supported prohibition. Middle-class Protestants and even some Catholics and Jews believed that by eliminating the temptation of drink they could win the battle against poverty, vice, and corruption.

Americans' emotional responses to events during the 1920s were part of an attempt to sustain old, local ways in a fast-moving, materialistic world. Occasionally Americans lashed out at minority cultures and seemingly hedonistic trends in behavior. Millions of otherwise decent Americans firmly believed that nonwhites and immigrants were inferior people who imperiled existing values. Evangelists who preached against evolution were rare compared to the clergy and teachers of all faiths who condemned drinking, dancing, new styles of dress, and new sexual habits.

Even as they worried about losing old values, most Americans tried to adjust to the new order in one way or another. Few refrained from listening to the radio or attending movies, activities that proved less corrupting than critics feared. Radio featured harmless music, news, and homey drama. Movie producers bowed to pressure from legislators in 1927 and instituted self-censorship, forbidding nudity, rough language, and plots that did not end with justice triumphant. More than ever, Americans sought fellowship in civic organizations. Membership swelled in Rotary, Kiwanis, Lions, Elks, and women's clubs, and the number of community chests—associations that coordinated civic and welfare projects—grew from 12 in 1919 to 361 in 1930. Perhaps most important, more and more people were finding release in a world of leisure.

The Age of Play

During the 1920s Americans developed an almost insatiable thirst for recreation. In 1919 they spent $2.5 billion on leisure activities; by 1929 such expenditures topped $4.3 billion, a figure not again equaled until after the Second World War. Spectator amusements—movies, theater, sports—accounted for about 21 percent of the figure for 1929. Individual recreation, from participation sports to reading, hobbies, music, and travel, took up the remainder.

Entrepreneurs responded quickly. The decade marked the flowering of fads, frivolities, and what contemporaries called ballyhoo, a blitz of publicity that lent exaggerated importance to some person or event. New games and fancies were particularly attractive to middle-class families with large spendable incomes. In the early 1920s the Chinese tile game of mahjong was the rage. Merchants could not import enough of the games, so dozens of American manufacturers began to produce them. By the mid-1920s people were turning to crossword puzzles, which mass-circulation newspapers and magazines had begun printing a decade earlier. In 1924 the new publishing firm of Simon and Schuster brought out a book of crossword puzzles with a pencil attached—anyone who did a crossword puzzle with a pen was labeled a foolish optimist—and the volume became an instant best seller. A few years later fun seekers adopted miniature golf as their new craze. By 1930 some thirty thousand miniature golf courses featuring tiny castles, windmills, and waterfalls dotted cities and towns across the country. Throughout the decade dance crazes like the Charleston riveted public attention, aided by radio music and the growing popularity of jazz.

In addition to being active participants in leisure activities, Americans were avid spectators, particularly of movies and sports. In total capital investment, motion pictures became **Movies** one of the nation's leading industries. Nearly every community had at least one theater, whether it was a hundred-seat Bijou on Main Street or a big-city picture palace with ornate walls, fountains in the lobby, and thousands of cushioned seats. In 1922 movies attracted 40 million viewers a week; by 1930 the number had reached 100 million—at a time when total population was just over 120 million and total weekly church attendance was under 60 million. The introduction of sound in *The Jazz Singer* in 1927 and of color a few years later made movies even more attractive and realistic. Movie producers presented fantasy and vicarious escape rather than a serious new art form. The most popular films were mass spectacles such as Cecil B. DeMille's *The Ten Commandments* (1923) and *The King of Kings* (1927); lurid dramas such as *Souls for Sale* (1923) and *A Woman Who Sinned* (1924); and slapstick comedies starring Fatty Arbuckle, Harold Lloyd, Buster Keaton, and Charlie Chaplin. Ironically, the comedies, with their poignant satire of the human condition, carried the most thought-provoking messages.

Spectator sports also boomed. Each year millions packed stadiums and parks to watch athletic events. By late 1920s gate receipts from college football alone surpassed $21 million. In an age when technology and mass production had robbed experiences and objects of their uniqueness, sports provided unpredictability and drama that people craved. Newspapers and radio captured and exaggerated this drama, feeding news to an eager public and often overpromoting events with unrestrained narrative. Thus in 1920 the otherwise staid *New York Times* resorted to wild hyperbole to summarize a tennis match between William Tilden, the national champion, and challenger William Johnston:

> The Tilden-Johnston struggle will go down on the records as the most astounding exhibition of tennis, the most nervewracking battle that the courts have ever seen. . . . Tilden and Johnston played five acts of incredible melodrama, with a thrill in every scene, with horrible errors leading suddenly to glorious achievements, with skill and courage and good and evil fortune. . . . Tilden's victory was a triumph for supertennis.

With reporting like this, sports promoters did not need to buy advertisements.

Baseball, with its drawn-out suspense, infinite variety of plays, and potential for statistics keeping, attracted a huge following. After a scandal in 1919, in which eight members of the Chicago White Sox were accused of taking bribes to lose World Series games (they were acquitted in 1921 though some appear to have been guilty), the two major professional leagues appointed Kenesaw Mountain Landis, a federal district judge, as baseball commissioner. Landis gave the game renewed respectability by rooting out allegedly dishonest players. At the same time, the nature of the game changed. Discovering that home runs aroused excitement, the leagues redesigned the ball to make it livelier. Thereafter, attendance at major-league games skyrocketed. In 1921 a record 300,000 people attended the six-game World Series between the New York Giants and New York Yankees. That same year millions more gathered regularly to watch local teams take on nearby rivals.

Sports, movies, and the news gave Americans a galaxy of heroes. As society became more anonymous and the individual less significant, people clung to heroic personalities as a

Sports Heroes means of identifying with the unique. Names such as Tilden in tennis, Gertrude Ederle in swimming (in 1926 she became the first woman to swim across the English Channel), and Bobby Jones in golf became household words, but boxing, football, and baseball produced the biggest sports heroes. Heavyweight champion Jack Dempsey, a powerful brawler from Manassa, Colorado, attracted the first of many million-dollar gates in his fight with Georges Carpentier in 1921. Harold "Red" Grange, running back for the University of Illinois football team, thrilled thousands and became the idol of sportswriters. During his senior year in 1925, Grange was offered huge contracts by real-estate and motion-picture companies and collected $42,000 for his first two games as a professional with the Chicago Bears.

Baseball's major hero was George Herman "Babe" Ruth, who began his career as a pitcher but found he could use his prodigious strength to better advantage hitting home runs. Ruth hit 29 of them in 1919, 54 in 1920 (the year he moved from the Boston Red Sox to the New York Yankees), 59 in 1924, and 60 in 1927—each year a record. His exaggerated gestures on the field, defiant lifestyle, and boyish grin endeared him to millions. He became a national legend. Known for overindulgence in food, drink, and women, Ruth missed almost two months of the 1925 season when he was hospitalized with "the stomach ache that was heard round the world." But he usually made fans forget his excesses by appearing at public events and making special efforts to visit children in hospitals.

If Americans identified with the physical exploits of sports stars, they fulfilled a yearning for romance and adventure through adulation

Movie Stars and Public Heroes of movie stars. Films and the personal lives of Douglas Fairbanks, Gloria Swanson, Charlie Chaplin, and others were discussed in par-

Babe Ruth was not only one of the era's most successful sports heroes but also a celebrated media personality. Wherever he went, he was besieged by reporters and photographers from the popular press, and his words and off-field antics made the news almost daily.

lors and pool halls across the country. Perhaps the decade's most ballyhooed personality was Rudolph Valentino, whose Latin machismo made women swoon and prompted men to copy his pomaded hairdo and slick sideburns. Valentino's films exploited the era's new-found sexual liberalism and flirtation with evil. Playing a sheik who passionately snatched women into his arms and carried them into his tent, he combined the roles of seducer and abductor. When Valentino died of complications from ulcers and appendicitis at the age of thirty-one, the press turned his funeral into a public extravaganza. Crowds lined up for over a mile to file past his coffin.

News promoters created their own heroes beyond athletics and entertainment. For two weeks in 1925, newspapers kept readers on edge with reports on the plight of Floyd Collins, trapped in a Kentucky cave. Rescuers eventually found Collins dead, but not before the entire country had idolized him as a hero battling nature. Flagpole sitters, marathon dancers, and other record seekers regularly occupied front pages. The most notable news hero was Charles A. Lindbergh, the pilot whose daring nonstop solo flight across the Atlantic in 1927 was cheered by millions. A modest, independent midwesterner whom writers dubbed the Lone Eagle, Lindbergh accepted fame but did not try to profit from it. Because his quiet personality contrasted so starkly with the ballyhoo that surrounded him, Americans honored him even more fervently.

In part adulation of Lindbergh may have reflected guilt over betrayal of traditional virtues of restraint and moderation, for in their quest for fun and individual expression—liberties that prohibition seemed to deny—Americans became law-

Prohibition

Rudolph Valentino became the idol of men and women alike in *The Sheik,* his most famous movie. With flashing eyes and wanton smile, Valentino carries a swooning woman to his tent. This immensely popular movie earned a million dollars for Paramount Pictures. *Museum of Modern Art Film Still Archive.*

breakers and supporters of crime. The Eighteenth Amendment (1919) and federal law that prohibited the manufacture, sale, and transportation of alcoholic beverages (see page 614) worked well at first. Per capita consumption of liquor dropped, arrests for drunkenness diminished, and the price of illegal booze rose higher than the average worker could afford. But beyond passing supportive laws, legislators saw little need to enforce Prohibition. In 1922 Congress gave the Prohibition Bureau only three thousand employees and less than $7 million for nationwide enforcement.

Prohibition was especially effective in regions where temperance movements had historically been successful. In fact, some people believe that it might have succeeded more widely if it applied only to hard liquor and not to beer or wine. After about 1925 the noble experiment broke down in cities, where desire for personal freedom over-

whelmed weak enforcement. The law allowed manufacture of beer for dilution into near-beer and sale of alcohol for medicinal and sacramental purposes, but bootleggers cleverly obtained and sold such spirits for other purposes. Smuggling and home manufacture of liquor were rampant. Hundreds of thousands of people made their own wine and bathtub gin, and bootleg importers along the country's long borders and shorelines easily evaded the few patrols that attempted to curb them.

Local officials realized it was impractical to devote their scarce resources to strict enforcement of Prohibition. Drinking, like gambling and prostitution, was a business that had willing customers. Criminal organizations were quick to capitalize on this fact. The most notorious of such mobs belonged to Al Capone, a burly tough who seized control of illegal liquor and vice organizations in

Al Capone

Chicago and exercised his influence through bribery, intimidation, and violence. With his armed force of gangsters, Capone was able to influence local politics as well as vice operations until 1931, when a federal court convicted and imprisoned him for income-tax evasion.

It is important to recognize that Prohibition and its weak enforcement did not create organized crime. Gangs like Capone's had provided illegal goods and services long before the 1920s. As Capone explained it, "Prohibition is a business. All I do is supply a public demand. I do it in the least harmful way I can." Americans wanted their liquor and their freedom; Capone took advantage of these desires.

Thus during the 1920s Americans were caught between two value systems. On the one hand, the Puritan tradition of hard work, sobriety, and restraint—"Waste not, want not"—still prevailed, especially in rural areas where new diversions were unavailable. On the other hand, a liberating age of play beckoned. At no previous time in American history had so many opportunities for recreation existed. Not just mass entertainment such as nightclubs, movies, sports, and radio, but individual amusements such as stamp collecting, puzzle working, and playing and listening to music became commonplace. Most of these activities were not illegal or immoral, but many people were increasingly willing to break the law or shun moral tradition if such restrictions interfered with their personal quest for pleasure. As Walter Lippmann wrote in 1931, "The high level of lawlessness is maintained by the fact that Americans desire to do so many things which they also desire to prohibit."

Cultural Currents

Tension between value systems pulled artists and intellectuals in new directions. Rejection of old beliefs prompted experimentation in literature, art, and music. Fear that materialism and conformity were being fostered by mass society gave this movement a bitterly critical tinge. Yet critics seldom voiced a radical message; they had no urge to destroy modern society, only to protect the individual from vulgar forces.

Many of the era's leading literary figures, finding vulgar materialism hostile to their art, became disillusioned and were known as the Lost Generation. A number of them, including novelist Ernest Hemingway and poets Ezra Pound and T. S. Eliot, moved to Europe. Others, such as novelists William Faulkner and Sinclair Lewis, remained in America but assailed what they saw happening around them. Along with innovative forms of expression and realistic portrayals of emotions, these writers also produced biting social commentary.

Literature of Alienation

Dominant themes of social criticism were middle- and upper-class materialism and the impersonality of modern society. F. Scott Fitzgerald's *This Side of Paradise* (1920) and *The Great Gatsby* (1925); Lewis's *Babbitt* (1922), *Arrowsmith* (1925), and *Elmer Gantry* (1927); and Eugene O'Neill's plays exposed Americans' overemphasis on money. Edith Wharton explored the clash of old and new moralities in novels such as *The Age of Innocence* (1921). Ellen Glasgow, the South's literary historian, lamented the trend toward modern impersonality in *Barren Ground* (1925). Willa Cather looked to previous eras for moral strength in her novel *My Antonia* (1918). The powerful antiwar sentiments of John Dos Passos's *Three Soldiers* (1921) and Hemingway's *Farewell to Arms* (1929) were skillfully interwoven with passionate critiques of the impersonality of modern relationships.

A spiritual discontent quite different from that of white writers inspired a new generation of young black artists. Middle class and well educated, these writers often rejected the amalgamation of black and white cultures, exalting the militantly assertive "New Negro," proud of his or her African heritage. Most of them lived in Harlem, the black section of upper Manhattan. In this "Negro Mecca" black intellectuals and artists, aided by a few white patrons, celebrated modern black culture in what became known as the Harlem Renaissance.

Harlem Renaissance

The popular black musical comedy "Shuffle Along," which opened in May 1921, is often credited with beginning the Harlem Renaissance. The show, written by lyricist Noble Sissle and composer Eubie Blake, included catchy songs such as "Love

Florence Mills was a talented black artist whose singing career received a major boost from her performance in the musical comedy "Shuffle Along," a show that heralded the beginning of the Harlem Renaissance. *Photo by James VanDerZee.*

Will Find a Way" and "I'm Just Wild About Harry." More importantly, it boosted the careers of black performing artists such as singers Florence Mills, Josephine Baker, and Mabel Mercer. Harlem in the 1920s also fostered a number of gifted writers, among them Langston Hughes, whose poems captured the mood and rhythm of blues and jazz; Countee Cullen, a poet with moving lyrical skills; and Claude McKay, whose militant verses invoked rebellion against bigotry. Jean Toomer's poems and his novel *Cane* (1923) portrayed black life with passionate realism, and Alain Locke's essays gave direction to the artistic renaissance. The movement also included visual artists such as Aaron Douglas, a painter who illustrated many of the books published by Harlem Renaissance authors; James A. Porter, whose paintings became part of every im-

portant exhibition of black artists; and Augusta Savage, who sculpted busts of many famous black personalities and who became the object of controversy in 1923 when the French government rejected her application to attend a summer art school because of her race.

Issues of identity vexed many participants in the Harlem Renaissance. Although black intellectuals and artists took pride in their African heritage and culture, they also realized that black Americans had to assert themselves and come to terms with themselves as Americans. Thus Locke urged that the New Negro should "lay aside the status of beneficiary and ward for that of a collaborator and participant in American civilization." As well, Hughes wrote, "We younger Negro artists who create now intend to express our individual dark-skinned selves without fear or shame. If white people are pleased we are glad. If they are not, it doesn't matter. We know we are beautiful."

The Jazz Age, as the decade of the 1920s is sometimes called, owed its name to music that grew out of black urban culture. Evolving from African and black American folk music, early **Jazz** jazz communicated unrestrained freedom that black people seldom knew in their public, working, or political lives. With its emotional rhythms and emphasis on improvisation, jazz blurred the distinction between composer and performer and created new intimacy between performer and audience.

As blacks moved north from the Mississippi Delta, they brought jazz with them. By the 1920s dance halls and bars featured jazz, sometimes popularized by white musicians such as Paul Whiteman and Bix Biederbecke. Gifted black performers like trumpeter Louis Armstrong, trombonist Kid Ory, and singer Bessie Smith enjoyed wide fame. Phonograph records and radio, better suited than sheet music to the spontaneity of jazz, helped to popularize it. In fact, jazz boosted the recording industry immensely, and music recorded by black artists and bought by millions of black purchasers (sometimes called race records) gave black Americans a distinctive place in the new consumer culture. More important, jazz endowed America with its most distinctive art form.

In many ways the 1920s were the most creative years the nation had yet experienced. Influenced by jazz and experimental writing, painters such as

Georgia O'Keeffe and John Marin tried to forge a unique American style of painting. European composers and performers still dominated classical music, but Americans such as Henry Cowell, who pioneered electronic music, and Aaron Copland, who built orchestral and vocal works around native folk motifs, began careers that later won wide acclaim. George Gershwin blended jazz, classical, and folk musical forms in his serious compositions (*Rhapsody in Blue,* 1924, and *Concerto in F,* 1925), musical dramas (*Funny Face,* 1927), and numerous hit tunes. In architecture the skyscraper boom drew worldwide attention, and Frank Lloyd Wright's "prairie-style" houses, churches, and schools reflected the magnificence of the American landscape. At the beginning of the decade, essayist Harold Stearns had complained that "the most . . . pathetic fact in the social life of America today is emotional and aesthetic starvation." By 1929 such a contention was hard to support.

The Election of 1928 and the End of the New Era

Whatever doubts intellectuals may have had about materialism in the 1920s faded before the confident rhetoric of politics. Herbert Hoover epitomized that confidence in his speech accepting the Republican nomination for president in 1928. "We in America today," Hoover boasted, "are nearer to the final triumph over poverty than ever before in the history of any land. . . .We have not yet reached the goal, but, given a chance to go forward with the policies of the last eight years, we shall soon, with the help of God, be in sight of the day when poverty will be banished from this nation."

Hoover was an apt candidate for Republicans in 1928 (Coolidge chose not to run for re-election), because he fused old values of success through individual hard work with new

Herbert Hoover emphasis on collective action. A Quaker from West Branch, Iowa, orphaned at age ten, Hoover worked his way through Stanford University and became a wealthy mining engineer. During and after the First World War, he distinguished himself as

United States food administrator and head of food relief for Europe. As secretary of commerce under Harding and Coolidge, Hoover expanded Theodore Roosevelt's New Nationalism. Recognizing the extent to which large nationwide associations had come to dominate commerce and industry, Hoover mounted a campaign to stimulate cooperation between business and government. He took every opportunity to make the Department of Commerce a center for the promotion of business, encouraging the formation of trade associations, holding conferences, sponsoring studies, and issuing reports, all aimed at improving production, marketing, and profitability. His active leadership prompted one observer to quip that Hoover was "Secretary of Commerce and assistant secretary of everything else."

As Hoover's opponent, Democrats chose Governor Alfred E. Smith of New York, whose career contrasted markedly with that of Hoover. Whereas Hoover had rural, native, Protestant, business roots and had never run for public office, Smith was an urbane, gregarious politician of immigrant stock whose career was rooted in New York City's Tammany Hall. His relish for the give-and-take of the city streets is illustrated by an incident from the campaign. When a heckler taunted Smith by shouting, "Tell them all you know, Al. It won't take long!" Smith unflinchingly retorted, "I'll tell them all we both know, and it won't take any longer!" Smith was the first Roman Catholic to run for president on a major party ticket. As such, he had considerable appeal among urban ethnic groups, who were voting in increasing numbers, but he lost southern and rural votes for the same reason. During his governorship, Smith had compiled a strong record as a promoter of progressive reforms and civil rights, but his campaign failed to build a reform coalition of farmers and city dwellers because he stressed issues that were not likely to unite these groups. He openly opposed Prohibition, and he struck back at charges that his Catholicism made him a servant of the pope.

Although Smith waged a spirited campaign, Hoover, who stressed the nation's prosperity, won the popular vote by 21 million to 15 million, the electoral vote by 444 to 87. But Smith's candidacy had important effects on the Democratic party. Smith carried the nation's twelve largest cities,

This lithograph by artist James Rosenberg represents the day of wrath, *dies irae,* from a Latin hymn that alludes to the Day of Judgment. To Rosenberg, the day of judgment was marked by the stock market crash of 1929, when all of Wall Street seemed to come tumbling down. *Philadelphia Museum of Art.*

national problems. In time, Hoover and his experts believed, they could establish a stable social order based on cooperation between government and various civic groups.

If the Hoover administration was optimistic, so were most Americans. Reverence for what Hoover called "the American system," which now included such exciting products as radios and refrigerators, ran high. The belief that individuals were responsible for their own condition, that unemployment or poverty suggested personal failing, was widespread. Prevailing thought also held that changes in the business cycle were natural and therefore not to be tampered with.

This confidence was jolted in the fall of 1929 when stock prices suddenly plunged. Analysts explained the drop as a temporary condition caused by a "lunatic fringe." But on October 24, Black Thursday, panic selling set in. The price of many stocks hit record lows; some sellers could find no buyers. Stunned crowds gathered outside the frantic New York Stock Exchange, buzzing about the apparent seriousness of the decline. At noon, banking leaders met at the headquarters of J. P. Morgan and Company to halt the skid. To restore faith, they put up $20 million and ceremoniously began buying stocks like U.S. Steel. The mood changed and some stocks rallied. The bankers, it seemed, had saved the day.

Stock Market Crash

But as news of Black Thursday spread across the country, fearful investors decided to sell their stocks rather than risk further drops. On Black Tuesday, October 29, stock prices plummeted again. The market settled into a grim pattern of declines and weak rallies. Hoover, who had never approved of what he called the "fever of speculation," assured Americans that the economy was sound. He shared the popular assumption that the stock market's ills could be quarantined and that the economy was strong enough to endure until the stock market righted itself.

Instead of reversing, the crash ultimately helped to unleash a devastating depression. The economic downturn did not come suddenly (see Chapter 25); it was more like a leak in a punctured tire than a blowout. The hidden weakness of the economy in the 1920s underlay the depression. Had conditions been as strong as businesspeople maintained,

which formerly had given majorities to Republican candidates, and lured millions of foreign-stock voters to the polls for the first time. From 1928 onward, the Democratic party would solidify this urban base, which when combined with its traditional strength in the South made the party a formidable force in national elections.

Democrats and Republicans both had reasons to be encouraged in 1928. In his inaugural address, Hoover proclaimed a New Day, "bright with hope."

Hoover's Administration

His cabinet, composed mostly of businessmen, included six millionaires devoted to the existing order. To the lower ranks of government Hoover appointed mostly young professionals who agreed with him that scientific methods could be applied to solve

the nation would have stood a better chance of weathering the Wall Street crash. In fact, however, some historians suggest that the stock market collapse merely moved an ongoing recession into depression.

There were several interrelated causes of the weak economy and ultimately the Great Depression. The first was overproduction. Throughout the 1920s farmers produced more and more to compensate for declining crop prices and mounting debts. Industries like coal, railroads, and textiles were in distress long before 1929; the automobile and construction industries also faced troubles early. These weaknesses meant that by 1929 major sectors of the economy were not expanding; owners were not investing funds to build new plants and hire more workers. Instead, unsold inventories were stacking up in warehouses, and laborers were being laid off.

> **Over-production**

The onset and severity of the depression can also be attributed to underconsumption. Production (supply) had outstripped consumption (demand). Wages and mass purchasing power had lagged behind the industrial surge of the 1920s; workers who produced the new consumer products ultimately could not afford to buy them. Farmers suffered economic distress and had to trim their purchases. As industries declined, they held wages down and sent home laborers, who lacked the money to buy goods. Thus a sizable nonconsuming group had grown before 1929.

> **Under-consumption**

Underconsumption also resulted from the unequal distribution of income. As the rich got much richer in the 1920s, others made only modest gains. Average per capita disposable income (income after taxes) rose about 9 percent between 1920 and 1929, but the income of the wealthiest 1 percent rose 75 percent, accounting for most of the increase. Much of this increase was put into luxuries, savings, and stock market investments instead of being spent on consumer goods.

American business was unbalanced because oligopolies (see page 696) dominated each industry. In 1929 the top two hundred nonfinancial corporations controlled 49 percent of corporate wealth. Many corporations built pyramid-like empires supported by shady, though legal, manipulation of

> **Oligopolies**

assets. When one part of the edifice collapsed, the entire structure crumbled.

The depression also derived from pell-mell, largely unregulated, speculation on the stock market. Corporations and banks invested huge sums in stocks, and some even speculated in their own issues. Brokers sold stocks to buyers who put up little cash, borrowed in order to purchase, and then used as collateral for loans the stocks they had bought but not fully paid for. When stock prices collapsed, so did brokerage firms, banks, and investment companies. Needing cash, brokers demanded that buyers repay their loans. Buyers tried to do so by withdrawing their savings from banks or selling their stocks at a loss for whatever they could get. Bankers, meanwhile, also needed cash, and they put pressure on brokers, tightening the vise further. The more obligations that went unmet, the more the system crumbled.

> **Speculation on the Stock Market**

International economic troubles constitute a fifth explanation for the crash and depression. As the world's leading creditor and trader, the United States was deeply involved with the world economy. Billions of dollars in loans had flowed to Europe during the First World War and during postwar reconstruction. Yet in the late 1920s American investors were beginning to keep their money at home, to invest it in the more exciting and lucrative stock market. Europeans, unable to borrow more funds and unable to sell their goods easily in the American market because of high tariffs, began to buy less from the United States and to default on their crippling debts left over from the First World War. Pinched at home, they raised their own tariffs, further disabling international commerce, and withdrew their investments from America. Reacting to the collapse of European economies, Hoover complained that "the European disease had contaminated the United States." He would have been more accurate had he said that the European and American illnesses were mutually infectious.

> **Inter-national Economic Troubles**

Finally, government policies and practices contributed to the crash and depression. The federal government failed to regulate wild speculation, contenting itself with occasional scoldings of bank-

Failure of Federal Policies ers and businesspeople. It neither checked corporate power nor raised income taxes to encourage a more equitable distribution of income. The Federal Reserve Board pursued easy credit policies before the crash, charging low discount rates, or interest rates, on its loans to member banks, even though it knew that easy money was financing the speculative mania.

In 1929 neither the experts nor the people on the street realized what factors had brought on the depression, partly because of their optimism and partly because the state of economic analysis and statistics gathering was primitive compared to what it is today. Conventional wisdom, based on the experience of previous depressions, held that little could be done to correct economic problems; they simply had to run their course, like a common cold. So in 1929 people waited for the deflation to bottom out, never realizing that the era of expansion and frivolity had come to an end and that the nation's culture and politics, as well as its economy, would have to be rebuilt.

Suggestions for Further Reading

Overviews of the 1920s

Frederick Lewis Allen, *Only Yesterday* (1931); John Braeman et al., eds., *Change and Continuity in Twentieth Century America: The 1920s* (1968); Paul A. Carter, *Another Part of the Twenties* (1977); Ellis Hawley, *The Great War and the Search for a Modern Order* (1979); John D. Hicks, *Republican Ascendancy* (1960); William E. Leuchtenburg, *The Perils of Prosperity* (1958); Robert Lynd and Helen Lynd, *Middletown* (1929); Donald R. McCoy, *Coming of Age* (1973); George Soule, *Prosperity Decade* (1947).

Business and the Economy

Irving L. Bernstein, *The Lean Years: A History of the American Worker, 1920–1933* (1960); Alfred D. Chandler, *Strategy and Structure* (1962); James J. Flink, *The Car Culture* (1975); Stephen Fox, *The Mirror Makers: A History of American Advertising and Its Creators* (1984); Allan Nevins, *Ford*, 2 vols. (1954–1957); J. W. Prothro, *The Dollar Decade* (1954); John Rae, *The Road and the Car in American Life* (1971); Robert Zieger, *Republicans and Labor, 1919–1929* (1969).

Politics and Law

Christine Bolt, *American Indian Policy and American Reform* (1987); David Burner, *Herbert Hoover* (1979); David Burner, *The Politics of Provincialism* (1968); Nancy F. Cott, *The Grounding of American Feminism* (1988); Paula Elder, *Governor Alfred E. Smith: The Politician as Reformer* (1983); J. Joseph Huthmacher, *Massachusetts People and Politics* (1959); Matthew Josephson and Hannah Josephson, *Al Smith* (1970); Allan J. Lichtman, *Prejudice and the Old Politics: The Presidential Election of 1928* (1979); Richard Lowitt, *George W. Norris* (1971); Donald R. McCoy, *Calvin Coolidge* (1967); Alpheus Mason, *The Supreme Court from Taft to Warren* (1958); Robert K. Murray, *The Harding Era* (1969); Andrew Sinclair, *The Available Man* (1965); George Tindall, *The Emergence of the New South* (1967); James Weinstein, *The Decline of Socialism in America, 1912–1925* (1967); Joan Hoff Wilson, *Herbert Hoover: The Forgotten Progressive* (1975).

Blacks and Latinos

Rodolfo Acuna, *Occupied America: A History of Chicanos* (1980); E. D. Cronon, *Black Moses: The Story of Marcus Garvey* (1955); Kenneth Kusmer, *A Ghetto Takes Shape* (1976); Matt S. Meier and Feliciano Rivera, *The Chicanos* (1972); Gilbert Osofsky, *Harlem: The Making of a Ghetto* (1965); Mark Reisler, *By the Sweat of Their Brows* (1976) (on Mexican-Americans); Ricardo Romo, *East Los Angeles: History of a Barrio* (1983); Virginia E. Sanchez, *From Colonia to Community: The History of Puerto Ricans in New York, 1917–1948* (1983); Alan Spear, *Black Chicago* (1967); Judith Stein, *The World of Marcus Garvey* (1986); Theodore Vincent, *Black Power and the Garvey Movement* (1971).

Women and the Family

W. Andrew Achenbaum, *Shades of Gray: Old Age, American Values, and Federal Policies Since 1920* (1983); William H. Chafe, *The American Woman: Her Changing Social, Economic, and Political Role* (1972); Howard P. Chudacoff, *How Old Are You? Age in American Culture* (1989); Ruth Schwartz Cowan, *More Work for Mother* (1983); David H. Fischer, *Growing Old in America* (1977); Linda Gordon, *Woman's Body, Woman's Right: A Social History of Birth Control in America* (1976); J. Stanley Lemons, *The Woman Citizen: Social Feminism in the 1920s* (1973); Sheila Rothman, *Woman's Proper Place* (1978); Lois Scharf, *To Work and to Wed* (1980); Susan Strasser, *Never Done: A History of American Housework* (1982); Winifred D. Wandersee, *Women's Work and Family Values, 1920–1940* (1981).

Lines of Defense

David M. Chalmers, *Hooded Americanism: The History of the Ku Klux Klan* (1965); Norman F. Furnis, *The Fundamentalist Controversy* (1954); Joseph R. Gusfeld, *Symbolic Crusade* (1963); John Higham, *Strangers in the Land: Patterns of American Nativism* (1955); Kenneth T. Jackson, *The Ku Klux Klan and the City* (1967); G. L. Joughin and E. M. Morgan, *The Legacy of Sacco and Vanzetti* (1948); William G. McLoughlin, *Modern Revivalism* (1959); Andrew Sinclair, *Prohibition: The Age of Excess* (1962).

Mass Culture

Erik Barbouw, *A Tower of Babel: A History of Broadcasting in the United States to 1933* (1966); Robert Creamer, *Babe* (1974); Kenneth S. Davis, *The Hero, Charles A. Lindbergh* (1959); Susan J. Douglas, *Inventing American Broadcasting* (1987); Paula Fass, *The Damned and the Beautiful: American Youth in the 1920s* (1977); Harvey J. Levenstein, *Revolution at the Table: The Transformation of the American Diet* (1988); Randy Roberts, *Jack Dempsey, The Manassa Mauler* (1979); Philip T. Rosen, *The Modern Stentors: Radio Broadcasting and the Federal Government, 1920–1933* (1980); Robert Sklar, *Movie-made America* (1976).

Literature and Thought

Mary Campbell, *Harlem Renaissance: Art of Black America* (1987); Robert Crunden, *From Self to Society: Transition in American Thought, 1919–1941* (1972); George H. Douglas, *H. L. Mencken* (1978); Gloria T. Hull, *Color, Sex and Poetry: Three Woman Writers of the Harlem Renaissance* (1987); Nathan I. Huggins, *Harlem Renaissance* (1971); David L. Lewis, *When Harlem Was in Vogue* (1981); Roderick Nash, *The Nervous Generation: American Thought, 1917–1930* (1969); Marvin K. Singleton, *H. L. Mencken and the American Mercury Adventure* (1962); Kenneth M. Wheller and Virginia L. Lussier, eds., *Women and the Arts and the 1920s in Paris and New York* (1982).

Sixth Avenue Elevated at Third Street painted by John Sloan in 1928. A detail of this painting appears at the beginning of Chapter 24, on page 694. Oil on canvas, 30 × 40 inches. *Collection of Whitney Museum of American Art. Purchase 36.1.54.*

Butch Beuscher was fifty-six years old when he was laid off from the job he had held for twenty-nine years—boilermaker in the Dubuque, Iowa, railroad shops. The year was 1931, and businesses and farms across the country were collapsing. Butch's wife, Tessie, was a part-time seamstress, but since her customers were also unemployed or irregularly employed, her earnings declined until they rarely exceeded three or four dollars a week. The Beuschers had a partially paid-up insurance policy, but they also had a mortgaged home and ten children, four of whom still lived at home. As their income plummeted, the family lived off money borrowed on the insurance policy, Tessie's earnings, and credit from the grocery store. Their unpaid bills mounted as did the overdue notices for mortgage and property-tax payments. Then, in the fall of 1933, Butch announced that the family would have to face facts. "We ought to try to get relief," he said. Tessie recalled gasping at the suggestion that they apply to the government for welfare, but there was no alternative.

25

THE GREAT DEPRESSION AND THE NEW DEAL, 1929–1941

Statistics—the Beuschers' among them—begin to tell the story of the Great Depression's human tragedy. The stock market crash in October 1929 had shocked investors and caused a financial panic (see page 722). Between 1929 and 1933 a hundred thousand businesses failed; corporate profits fell from $10 billion to $1 billion; and the gross national product was cut in half. Banks failed by the thousands. Americans who believed that saving was a virtue, a path to material fulfillment, discovered that their deposits had disappeared with the banks.

Americans lost jobs as well as savings. Although most people remained employed, day after day thousands of men and women received severance slips. At the beginning of 1930 the number of jobless reached at least 4 million; by November it jumped to 6 million. When President Herbert Hoover left office in 1933, about one-fourth of the labor force was idle—13 million workers—and millions more were underemployed, working only part-time. Unemployment placed strains on relations within the family. Blacks and other minorities sank deeper into destitution. Working women heard renewed calls for their return to the home in order to open places for males in the labor market. Overall, the eco-

Transients Cooking Their Dinner in the Snow Near a Coal Chute, DeKalb, Illinois (detail). Oil on canvas painting by J. Porter, 1975, after a photograph taken of the scene in 1938 with a Univex camera (purchased for 50 cents) by Ivan E. Prall. *Collection of Ivan E. Prall.*

nomic catastrophe aggravated old tensions: labor versus capital, white versus black, male versus female.

Elected amid prosperity and optimism, Herbert Hoover spent the years from late 1929 to his departure from office in early 1933 presiding over a gloomy and sometimes angry nation. Iowa farmers in 1932 emptied milk cans into drainage ditches as a way of protesting low prices, and in the same year thousands of unemployed veterans of the First World War encamped in Washington, D.C., to demand their military bonuses. Hoover, however, was somber and appeared cold and indifferent to the people's suffering. Although he activated the federal government more than any of his predecessors had done in an economic crisis, he opposed direct relief payments for the unemployed. When Hoover refused to take measures strong enough to relieve people's hardships, voters turned him out of office in the election of 1932. His successor in the White House was Franklin D. Roosevelt, the governor of New York, who promised vigorous action and projected hope in a time of despair.

From the first days of his presidency Roosevelt displayed a buoyancy and a willingness to experiment that helped to restore public confidence in the government and the economy. He acted not only to reform the banks and securities exchanges, but also to provide central planning for industry and agriculture and direct government relief for the jobless. After shoring up the banks, Roosevelt proposed a succession of laws to aid landowning farmers, blue-collar workers, business and local governments facing bankruptcy, the unemployed, the elderly, and even impoverished writers and artists. This sweeping legislation was based on the concept of "pump priming," or deficit financing, to stimulate consumer buying power, business and industrial activity, and ultimately employment by pouring billions of federal dollars into the economy.

Roosevelt's New Deal inspired opposition from both the left and the right. Businesspeople and economic conservatives found it fiscally irresponsible; demagogues and left-wing politicians thought it too conservative. Ultimately Roosevelt prevailed, however, revitalizing the progressive movement, vastly expanding both the scope of the federal government and the popularity of the Democratic party, and in the process establishing America's welfare system.

During these years several million workers seized the chance to organize for better wages and working conditions. The new Congress of Industrial Organizations (CIO) established unions in major industries like automobiles, steel, and meat packing. Blacks registered political and economic gains too, though in general they benefited less from the New Deal than did whites. Some federal agencies actually worked against blacks; on the other hand, black advisers took posts in the White House, and Native Americans discovered that New Dealers respected their culture and tribal rights.

Two-and-a-half million additional women workers joined the labor force during the 1930s. But female workers were segregated in low-income jobs, and New Deal legislation excluded many women from Social Security coverage and minimum-wage protection. Still, there was progress on the political front, as a "women's network" of government and Democratic party officials worked effectively in Washington for social welfare and social justice.

Roosevelt was re-elected in 1936, but soon thereafter his fortunes began to wane. The spate of relief and reform legislation came to an end in 1938, but by that time the New Deal had transformed the United States. Although the New Deal was not a revolution, its legacy is evident today. Farmers still plant according to federal crop allotments. The elderly and disabled still collect Social Security payments. The Federal Deposit Insurance Corporation still insures bank deposits. The Securities and Exchange Commission still monitors the stock exchanges. One goal the New Deal did not accomplish—putting back to work all the people who wanted jobs. That would await the nation's entry into the Second World War in 1941.

Hard Times: America's Worsening Depression, 1929–1933

As the Great Depression deepened in the early 1930s, its underlying causes—problems such as overproduction and underconsumption—grew in severity (see pages 723–724). So too did another

▼

1931	Scottsboro affair
	Moratorium on First World War debts and reparations
1932	Reconstruction Finance Corporation established
	Bonus March
	Franklin D. Roosevelt elected president
1933	13 million Americans unemployed
	National bank holiday
	Agricultural Adjustment Act
	Tennessee Valley Authority
	National Industrial Recovery Act
	Twentieth (Lame Duck) Amendment ratified
	Twenty-first Amendment repeals Eighteenth (Prohibition) Amendment
1934	Townsend's Old Age Revolving Pensions plan
	Huey Long's Share Our Wealth Society
	Indian Reorganization (Wheeler-Howard) Act
	Democratic victories in congressional elections
	Coughlin's National Union for Social Justice
1935	Emergency Relief Appropriation Act
	Works Progress Administration
	Schechter v. *U.S.* invalidates NIRA
	National Labor Relations (Wagner) Act
	Social Security Act
	Huey Long assassinated
	Committee for Industrial Organization (CIO) established
1936	*U.S.* v. *Butler* invalidates AAA
	Roosevelt defeats Landon
1937	United Auto Workers' sit-down strikes
	Court-packing plan
	N.L.R.B. v. *Jones & Laughlin* upholds Wagner Act
	Memorial Day Massacre
	Farm Security Administration
1937–39	Business recession
1938	AFL expels CIO unions
	Fair Labor Standards Act
	10.4 million Americans unemployed
1939	Marian Anderson's concert at the Lincoln Memorial
1940	Roosevelt defeats Willkie
1941	March on Washington Movement
	Fair Employment Practices Committee (FEPC) established

Causes of the Deepening Depression

cause: instability in the banking industry. What happened to America's banks illustrates the cascading nature of the depression. Banks tied into the stock market or foreign investments were badly weakened; some failed. When nervous Americans made runs on banks to salvage their threatened savings, a powerful momentum—panic—took command. In 1929, 659 banks folded; in 1930 the number of failures more than doubled to 1,350. The Federal Reserve Board blundered after the crash, as it had before it (see page 724). In 1931 the board drastically raised the discount rate, tightening the money market at a time when just the opposite was needed: loosening to spur borrowing and spending. That year, 2,293 banks shut their doors, and another 1,453 ceased to do business in 1932.

As unemployment soared in the early 1930s, people's fortunes hit bottom. In Detroit, auto workers roamed from plant to plant, only to discover padlocked gates. Western apple growers sent their surplus to the cities, where a new class of street-corner entrepreneurs peddled apples at five cents apiece. A Minneapolis woman described her futile daily vigil at the city unemployment office: "So we sit in this room like cattle waiting for a nonexistent job, willing to work to the farthest atom of energy, unable to work, unable to get food and lodging, unable to bear children. Here we must sit in this shame looking at the floor, worse than beasts at a slaughter."

During these years people's diets deteriorated, malnutrition became common, and the undernourished fell victim more easily to disease. Some people quietly lined up at Red Cross **Deterio-** and Salvation Army soup kitchens **ration of** or queued in breadlines. Others **Health** ate only potatoes, crackers, or dandelions, or scratched through garbage cans for bits of food. Milk consumption decreased to such an extent that Kentucky miners called it "medicine." Pregnant women went without essential foods like eggs and vegetables, and doctors reported increases in tuberculosis, typhoid, dysentery, and heart and stomach disorders. Millions of Americans were not only hungry and ill; they were cold. Unable to afford fuel, they huddled in unheated tenements and shacks. Families doubled up in crowded apartments, but some who were unable to pay the rent were evicted, furniture and all. Urban jungles, bitterly called "Hoovervilles," sprouted up, constructed from packing boxes and other debris usually carted away as junk. Several hundred women took to sleeping in Chicago's Lincoln and Grant parks; in Oakland, California, hundreds of people lived in leftover concrete waste ducts of Sewer-Pipe City.

In the countryside, hobbled long before the depression struck, economic hardship deepened. Between 1929 and 1933 farm income was cut in half. Although farm prices dropped 60 **Plight of the** percent, production decreased **Farmers** only 6 percent as individual farmers struggled to make up for lower prices by producing more, thereby creating an excess. The surplus that so depressed agricultural prices could not be exported because foreign demand had shrunk. Drought, foreclosure, clouds of hungry grasshoppers, and bank failures further plagued American farmers. Some became transients in search of jobs or food. Dispossessed tenant farmers—husbands, wives, and children—walked the roads of the South. Hundreds of thousands of other people jumped aboard freight trains or hitchhiked. The California Unemployment Commission reported in 1932 that an "army of homeless" had trooped into the state and moved constantly from place to place, forced by one town after another to move on.

Across America economic woe also burdened marriage patterns and family life. People postponed marriage, and married couples postponed having children. Divorces also declined, but desertions rose as husbands unable to provide for their families simply took off. Families were beset in other ways as well. With less opportunity for outside recreation, family members were forced to spend more time together, which increased the tension in families suffering unemployment and crowded living quarters. Out-of-work fathers felt ashamed, resenting their diminished role. "A child who was playing irritated him," recalled the son of an unemployed Waterloo, Iowa, tool-and-die maker. "It wasn't just my own father. They all got shook up."

Most Americans met the crisis not with protest or violence but with bewilderment and an inability to fix the blame. They scorned businesspeople and bankers, of course, but often they **Farmers'** blamed themselves as well, as the **Holiday** traditional ideology of the self-**Association** made man had taught them to do. Some people were angry, and scattered protests raised the specter of popular revolt. Farmers in the Midwest prevented evictions and slowed foreclosures on farm properties by harassing sheriffs, judges, and lawyers. They also conspired at auctions to bid very low on foreclosed land and then turned over the property to its relieved former owners. In Nebraska, Iowa, and Minnesota, farmers protesting low prices put up barricades, stopped trucks, and dumped milk and vegetables on the road. Some of these demonstrations were organized by the Farmers' Holiday Association, whose leader, Milo Reno, encouraged farmers to take a holiday—to keep their products off the market until they commanded a better price.

Isolated protests also sounded in cities and in mining regions. In Chicago, Los Angeles, and Phil-

Plagued by dust storms and evictions, thousands of tenant farmers and sharecroppers were forced to leave their land during the Great Depression. Known as "Okies" and "Arkies," they took off for California with their few belongings. These refugees from drought-stricken Oklahoma experienced car trouble and were stalled on a New Mexico highway. *Library of Congress.*

adelphia, the unemployed marched on city halls. In Harlan County, Kentucky, miners struck against wage reductions. Mine owners responded with strikebreakers, bombs, the National Guard, the closing of relief kitchens, and evictions from company-owned housing.

The most spectacular confrontation shook Washington, D.C., in the summer of 1932. Congress was considering a bill authorizing immediate issuance of bonuses totaling $2.4 billion already allotted to First World War veterans because of their service, but not due for payment until 1945. To lobby for the bill, fifteen thousand unemployed veterans and their families converged on the tense nation's capital, calling themselves the Bonus Expeditionary Force (BEF). They camped in crude shacks on vacant lots and in empty government buildings. President Hoover threw his weight against the bonus bill, but the House passed it. The showdown came in the Senate, which voted "no" after much debate. One BEF

> **Bonus Expedition- ary Force**

member shouted: "We were heroes in 1917, but we're bums today." Many of the bonus marchers then left Washington, but several thousand stayed on during the summer. Hoover grew impatient, carelessly labeled them "insurrectionists" and Communists, and refused to meet with them.

In July, General Douglas MacArthur, assisted by Major Dwight D. Eisenhower and Major George S. Patton, met the veterans and their families with cavalry, tanks, and bayonet-bearing soldiers. The BEF hurled back stones and bricks. What followed shocked the nation. Men and women were chased down by horsemen; children were tear-gassed; shacks were set afire. Hoover's image as a humanitarian was further tarnished. When presidential hopeful Franklin D. Roosevelt heard about the attack on the Bonus Army, he turned to his friend Felix Frankfurter and said: "Well, Felix, this will elect me."

With capitalism on its knees, American Communists in various parts of the nation organized "unemployment councils" to arouse class con-

Massed on the steps of the Capitol in July 1932, veterans of the First World War demanded the immediate payment of their bonuses. Not only did President Hoover refuse, but just a few days later, he ordered the army to drive the Bonus Marchers from Washington. The army tossed tear gas bombs into groups of defiant veterans and set fire to their makeshift housing. *UPI Newsphotos.*

sciousness and to agitate for jobs and food. In March 1930 they conducted urban demonstrations, some of which ended in violent clashes with local police. With the slogan "Fight—Don't Starve," they led a hunger march on Washington, D.C., in 1931. Their tangles with authority publicized the real human tragedy of the depression. Still, total party membership in 1932 remained small at twelve thousand. The Socialist party, which argued with both capitalists and Communists, fared better. More reformist than radical, the Socialists ran well in municipal elections after the stock market crash but scored few victories. Indeed, few despairing Americans looked to left-wing parties and doctrines, protest marches, or violence for relief from their misery. They turned instead to institutions of considerable longevity and stability: their local, state, and federal governments.

> **Communist Party**

Hoover Holds the Line

When urgent daily appeals for government relief for the jobless reached the White House, Hoover at first became defensive, if not hostile. "We cannot legislate ourselves out of a world depression; we can and will work ourselves out," he replied. Hoover rejected direct relief because he believed it would undermine character and individualism. To a growing number of Americans, Hoover seemed heartless and inflexible at a time when humanitarianism and action were called for. But true to his beliefs, the president urged people to help themselves and their neighbors. He applauded private voluntary relief through the Red Cross and other charitable agencies. Yet when the need was greatest, donations declined. State and urban officials found their treasuries drying up too. Phila-

Chapter 25: The Great Depression and the New Deal, 1929–1941

delphia, after hiring the unemployed to paint city buildings, exhausted its relief funds by 1931, leaving 57,000 families without assistance. These Philadelphians got no sympathy from Secretary of the Treasury Andrew Mellon, who advised Hoover to "let the slump liquidate itself. Liquidate labor, liquidate stocks, liquidate the farmers, liquidate real estate. . . . It will purge the rottenness out of the system."

Hoover's Anti-depression Remedies As the depression intensified, Hoover's opposition to federal action diminished. He rejected Mellon's insensitive counsel, hesitantly and gradually energizing the White House and federal agencies to take action—more action than the government had taken before. He met with business and labor leaders, winning pledges from them to maintain wages and production and to avoid strikes. He urged state governors to increase their expenditures on public works. And he created the President's Organization on Unemployment Relief (POUR) to generate private contributions for relief of the destitute. Unfortunately, POUR chairman, president of the American Telephone and Telegraph Company Walter Gifford, seemed a man of limited concern and vision. Asked by a senator to specify the nation's relief requirements, Gifford said he had no precise information. The incredulous senator leaned forward: "Do you know what the relief needs are in the rural districts of the United States?" Gifford answered simply, "No."

If POUR proved ineffective, Hoover's spurring of federal public works projects (including the Hoover and Grand Coulee dams) did provide some jobs. Help also came from the Federal Farm Board, created before the depression under the Agricultural Marketing Act of 1929. An outcome of Hoover's emphasis on cooperation among individuals, groups, and government, the Farm Board supported agriculture prices by lending money to cooperatives to buy products and keep them off the market. But the board soon found itself short of money, and unsold surplus commodities jammed warehouses. The federally sponsored and privately funded National Credit Corporation assisted faltering banks, but it barely slowed the number of bank failures. To retard the collapse of the international monetary system, Hoover announced a moratorium on the payment of First World War debts and reparations (1931).

Herbert Hoover (1874–1964), the wealthy mining engineer and businessman, headed a relief program during the First World War and served as secretary of commerce in the 1920s. His reputation for compassion was tarnished when as president he faced the Great Depression and seemed heartless in his response to massive human suffering. *Library of Congress.*

Reconstruction Finance Corporation The president reluctantly asked Congress to charter the Reconstruction Finance Corporation (RFC). Created in 1932 and eventually empowered with $2 billion, the RFC was designed to make loans to banks, insurance companies, and railroads and later to state and local governments. The theory behind the RFC was that it would lend money to large entities at the top of the economic system, and benefits would filter down to people at the bottom. Liberal Republican Representative Fiorello La Guardia of New York labeled the plan a "millionaires' dole." It did not work; banks continued to collapse and small companies to go into bankruptcy. Few Americans took comfort in Hoover's prediction that prosperity was "just around the corner."

Despite warnings from prominent economists, Hoover also signed the Hawley-Smoot Tariff (1930). A congressional compromise serving special interests, the tariff raised duties by about one-third. Besides fulfilling a Republican party pledge, Hoover argued that the tariff would help farmers and manufacturers by keeping foreign goods off the market. Actually, the tariff further weakened the economy by making it even more difficult for foreign nations to sell their products and thus earn money to buy American products and pay off their First World War debts.

> **Hawley-Smoot Tariff**

Like most of his contemporaries, Hoover believed that a balanced budget was sacred and deficit spending sinful. In 1931 he appealed for a decrease in federal expenditures and an increase in taxes. The following year he supported a sales tax on manufactured goods, which liberal Democrats charged was an attempt to avoid higher income and corporate taxes. The sales tax was defeated, but the Revenue Act of 1932 raised corporate, excise, and personal income taxes. Hoover seemed caught in a contradiction: he urged people to spend to spur recovery, but his tax policies deprived them of spending money. He never did balance the budget. Nor did he seek repeal of the legal loopholes that permitted the partners of J. P. Morgan and other wealthy Americans to escape paying any income taxes in 1931 and 1932.

Although Hoover expanded public works projects and approved loans to some institutions, he vetoed a variety of relief bills presented to him by the Democratic Congress. In rejecting a public power project for the Tennessee River, he argued that its cheap electricity would compete with power from private companies. Hoover's traditionalism also was well demonstrated by his handling of Prohibition. Despite the Eighteenth Amendment, Americans were producing and drinking liquor with grand illegality and hypocrisy. Although the law was not and could not be enforced, Hoover resisted the mounting public pressure for repeal. Opponents argued not only that Prohibition encouraged crime, but that its repeal would stimulate economic recovery in Milwaukee and St. Louis, increase demand for grain, and revive the nation's old beer, liquor, and pretzel factories. But the president would not, he said, tamper with the Constitution, and the liquor industry,

> **Hoover's Traditionalism**

having no socially redemptive value, was best left depressed. Instead, Hoover pushed for better enforcement of the Eighteenth Amendment, and during the presidential election campaign of 1932 he stood firm against repeal.

During his presidency, Hoover held the line. Clinging to his old viewpoints, he stretched government activities as far as he thought he could without violating his cherished principles. Still, because Hoover mobilized the resources of the federal government as never before, some historians have depicted him as a bridge to the New Deal of the 1930s. If nothing else, he prepared the way for massive federal activity by giving private enterprise the opportunity to solve the depression—and to fail in the attempt.

Franklin D. Roosevelt and the Election of 1932

Herbert Hoover and the Republican party faced dreary prospects in 1932. The president kept pointing to international causes for the economic crisis, when Americans were less concerned with abstract explanations than with tomorrow's meal. He grumbled and grew impatient with critics. But what soured public opinion most was that Hoover seemed not to lead at a time when innovative generalship was required. So unpopular had he become by 1932 that Republicans who did not want to be associated with a loser ran independent campaigns. The president made few major speeches, rarely left Washington, and when he did venture out was frequently jeered and booed. On the final day of the campaign, when Hoover returned to California to vote, his motorcade was interrupted by stink bombs.

Franklin D. Roosevelt enjoyed a different reputation. Born into the upper class of tradition and privilege, the smiling, ingratiating governor of New York appealed to people of all classes, races, and regions, and he spoke to the American penchant for optimism. He had served for eight years as the assistant secretary of the navy under Woodrow Wilson, and in 1920 he had been the robust vice-presidential candidate of the Demo-

> **Franklin D. Roosevelt**

cratic party. The Democratic ticket went down to defeat, but Roosevelt suffered a more devastating loss the next year when he was struck by polio and totally paralyzed in both legs.

What should Roosevelt do next? Should he retire from pubic life, a rich invalid? His answer and his wife Eleanor's was no. Throughout the 1920s Franklin and Eleanor contended with his new handicap. Rejecting self-pity, Roosevelt worked to rebuild his body. People who had known him before commented that polio had made him a "twice-born man" and that his fight against the dread disease had given him "new moral and physical strength." As Roosevelt explained it: "If you had spent two years in bed trying to wiggle your big toe, after that anything would seem easy."

For her part, Mrs. Roosevelt learned to do things for herself, such as driving a car; and she began to shape her own career in public life, giving

> **Eleanor Roosevelt**

speeches and participating in the activities of the League of Women Voters, the Women's Trade Union League, and the Democratic party. Two of her strongest commitments came to be equal opportunity for women and for African-Americans, and she wanted to alleviate the suffering of the poor. On these issues, she served as her husband's conscience.

Elected governor of New York in 1928, after the stock market crash Roosevelt launched relief programs and an unemployment commission. Roose-

> **Roosevelt as Governor of New York**

velt's governorship coincided with Hoover's presidency, and both coincided with the onset of the Great Depression. But whereas Hoover appeared hardhearted and unwilling to help the jobless, Roosevelt seemed just the opposite. He urged unemployment insurance and direct relief payments for the jobless. Under his leadership New York's Temporary Emergency Relief Administration (1931) became the first state agency to mobilize on behalf of the poor. Aid to the unemployed, Roosevelt declared, "must be extended by Government, not as a matter of charity, but as a matter of social duty."

Roosevelt was more willing than Hoover to experiment. As governor of New York, he advocated creating jobs in publicly funded reforestation, land reclamation, and hydroelectric power projects. He endorsed and worked for old-age pensions and

In November 1930 Franklin D. Roosevelt (1882–1945) read the good news. Re-elected governor of New York by 735,000 votes, he immediately became a leading contender for the Democratic presidential nomination. Note Roosevelt's leg braces, rarely shown in photographs because of an unwritten agreement by photographers to shoot him from the waist up. *UPI/Bettmann Archive.*

Franklin D. Roosevelt and the Election of 1932

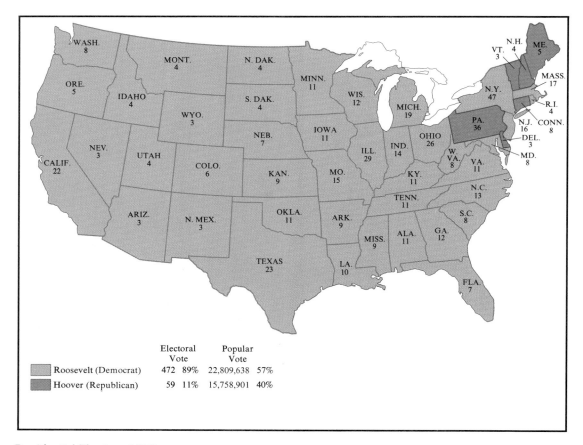

Presidential Election, 1932

	Electoral Vote		Popular Vote	
Roosevelt (Democrat)	472	89%	22,809,638	57%
Hoover (Republican)	59	11%	15,758,901	40%

protective legislation for labor unions. Roosevelt warned people not to dismiss such experimentation "with the word radical. Remember the radical of yesterday is almost [always] the reactionary of today." After he was re-elected in 1930 by a record-setting plurality of 735,000 votes, politicians had to take a serious look at his vote-getting ability.

To prepare a national political platform, Roosevelt surrounded himself with a brain trust (originally called the "Brains Trust") of lawyers and university professors. Bigness was unavoidable in the modern American economy, these experts reasoned; thus the cure for the nation's ills was not to go on a rampage of trustbusting but to place large corporations, monopolies, and oligopolies under effective government regulation. "We are no longer afraid of bigness," declared Columbia University professor Rexford G. Tugwell, speaking in the tradition of

> **Roosevelt's "Brains Trust"**

Theodore Roosevelt's New Nationalism. "We are resolved to recognize openly that competition in most of its forms is wasteful and costly; that larger combinations in any modern society must prevail."

Roosevelt and his brain trust agreed that it was essential for the government to restore purchasing power to farmers, blue-collar workers, and the middle classes, and that the way to do so was to cut production. If the demand for a product remained constant and the supply were cut, they reasoned, the price would rise. Producers would make higher profits, and workers would earn more money. This method of combating a depression has been called the economics of scarcity. Roosevelt and Hoover both campaigned as fiscal conservatives committed to the balanced budget. But unlike Hoover, Roosevelt also advocated immediate and direct relief to the unemployed. Finally, Roosevelt and his advisers rejected Hoover's explanation that the depression was international, not domestic, in origin.

Chapter 25: The Great Depression and the New Deal, 1929–1941

They demanded that the federal government engage in centralized economic planning and experimentation to bring about recovery.

Upon accepting the Democratic nomination, Roosevelt called for a "new deal for the American people." The two party platforms differed little, but the Democrats were willing to abandon Prohibition and to launch federal relief. More people went to the polls in 1932 than in any election since the First World War. In a crisis-ridden moment Americans calmly, even routinely, followed tradition and exchanged one government for another. Roosevelt's 22.8 million popular votes far outdistanced Hoover's 15.8 million; 57 percent of the popular vote went to the Democrat, 40 percent to the Republican, and 3 percent to minor party candidates. Hoover won only 59 electoral votes compared to Roosevelt's 472 (see map). Cities continued the trend, begun in 1928, of voting Democratic. Democrats also won overwhelming control of the Senate and the House.

1932 Election Results

The presidential election of 1932 had never been much of a contest, but once elected, Roosevelt had to wait until his inauguration on March 4 to act. (As a result of that crucial loss of time, the Twentieth Amendment to the Constitution—the Lame Duck Amendment—was ratified in 1933; it moved all future inaugurations to January 20.) It was a troubled four months. Millions of jobless Americans walked the streets; prices for agricultural and manufactured goods continued to plummet; industrial production sank to new depths. While farmers in the Farmers' Holiday movement poured milk into ditches, another kind of holiday was observed in some states: the bank holiday. Throughout the United States, depositors demanding their savings lined up in front of banks. Banks with insufficient funds on hand to pay depositors had to close their doors and declare themselves insolvent. In February, Michigan and Maryland suspended banking operations, and by March 4 thirty-six other states, including New York, had followed suit.

On the afternoon of March 2, 1933, President-elect Roosevelt and his family and friends boarded a train for Washington, D.C., and the inauguration ceremony. Roosevelt was carrying with him rough drafts of two presidential proclamations, one summoning a special session of Congress, the other declaring a national bank holiday, suspending banking transactions throughout the nation.

A gloomy Hoover and a buoyant Roosevelt ride to the inauguration in 1933. This magazine cover was never published, apparently because the editors of the *New Yorker* thought it inappropriate after an attempted assassination on the president-elect. *Franklin D. Roosevelt Library.*

Launching the New Deal and Restoring Confidence

"First of all," declared the newly inaugurated president, "let me assert my firm belief that the only thing we have to fear is fear itself—nameless, unreasoning, unjustified terror." In his inaugural address Roosevelt scored his first triumph as president, instilling hope and courage in the rank and file. He attacked the nation's bankers, accusing them of having "fled from their high seats in the temple of our civilization." He invoked "the analogue of war," proclaiming that, as in the First World War, the American people must march forward "as a trained and loyal army willing to sacrifice for the good of a common discipline." If need be, he asserted, "I shall ask the Congress for the one remaining instrument to meet the crisis—broad Executive power to wage a war against the emergency, as great as the power that would be given to me if we were in fact invaded by a foreign foe."

On March 5, Roosevelt declared a four-day national bank holiday and summoned Congress to an emergency session. Congress convened on March 9 to launch what observers would call the First Hundred Days. This was also the beginning of what historians would call the First New Deal (1933–1934). Roosevelt's initial legislative requests were cautious; portions had even been drafted by Hoover's advisers before leaving office. The first measure, the Emergency Banking Relief Bill, was introduced on March 9, passed sight unseen by unanimous House vote, approved 73 to 7 in the Senate, and signed by the president that evening. The act confirmed Roosevelt's emergency actions and provided for the reopening, under Treasury Department license, of banks that were solvent and the reorganization and management of those that were not. It also prohibited the hoarding and export of gold. It was, however, a conservative law that upheld the status quo and left the same bankers as before in charge. This was a special disappointment to those who had taken seriously the antibanker rhetoric of Roosevelt's inaugural address. Complained one representative, "The President drove the money-changers out of the Capitol on March 4th—and they were all back on the 9th."

On the next day, March 10, another conservative New Deal bill was introduced in Congress; ten days later it became law. Called the Economy Act, its purpose was to balance the federal budget by chopping veterans' benefits and allowances by $400 million and reducing by $100 million the pay of federal employees. Under Roosevelt, the budget balancers won a battle that could not have been won under Hoover. Although this legislation was deflationary and would decrease rather than increase the amount of money in circulation, the important point was that Roosevelt had acted and had done so boldly.

On Sunday evening, March 12, the president broadcast the first of his fireside chats, and 60 million people heard his comforting voice on their

First Fireside Chat

radios. His message: banks were once again safe places for depositors' savings. On Monday morning the banks opened their doors, but instead of queuing up to withdraw their savings, people were waiting outside to deposit their money. The bank runs were over; people had regained confidence in their political leadership, their banks, even their economic system.

Roosevelt next pursued a measure, the Beer-Wine Revenue Bill, that was not only deflationary but would actually take money out of people's pockets. It would generate revenues by legalizing the sale of low-alcohol wines and beers and levying a tax on them. (Congress proposed the repeal of Prohibition in February 1933 in the Twenty-first Amendment, and the states ratified it in December 1933.) To many, levying new taxes seemed a strange way to restore purchasing power to people who could not afford to buy what they needed. Roosevelt knew that. "I realize well," he wrote a friend, "that thus far we have actually given more of deflation than of inflation. . . . It is simply inevitable that we must inflate." He added that his "banker friends may be horrified" by the large-scale federal spending that was to come.

Beginning in mid-March, Roosevelt did seek congressional authorization to spend. On March 16, he sent to Congress the Agricultural Adjustment Bill to restore farmers' purchasing power. If overproduction was the cause of farmers' problems—falling prices and mounting surpluses—then the government had to encourage farmers to grow less food. Under the domestic allotment plan, the government would pay farmers to reduce their acreage or plow under crops already in the fields. Farmers would receive payments based on parity, a system of regulated prices for corn, cotton, wheat, rice, hogs, and dairy products that would allow them the same purchasing power they had had during the prosperous period of 1909 to 1914. In effect, the government was making up the difference between the actual market value of farm products and the income farmers needed to make a profit. The funds for the subsidies would come from taxes levied on the processors of agricultural commodities.

Roosevelt's farm plan immediately encountered vehement opposition. How could there be crop

Launching the First New Deal

Agricultural Adjustment Act

surpluses when some Americans were hungry and even starving? Underconsumption, people argued, was the result of a maldistribution of wealth and power as well as of goods and services. Some politicians wanted to put more money into circulation by coining silver, printing greenbacks, altering the gold content of the dollar, or going off the gold standard altogether. Cheap money, they contended, would make it easier for farmers to repay their debts. On May 12, Congress finally overcame opposition to the domestic allotment plan and passed the Agricultural Adjustment Act (AAA). A month later the Farm Credit Act also became law, providing short- and medium-term loans that enabled many farmers to refinance their mortgages and hang on to their homes and land.

Meanwhile, other relief measures became law. On March 21 the president requested three kinds of massive relief: a job corps called the Civilian

> **Civilian Conserva-tion Corps**

Conservation Corps (CCC), direct cash grants to the states for relief payments to needy citizens, and public works projects. Ten days later Congress approved the CCC. Within four months, 1,300 camps were in operation and 300,000 young men between the ages of eighteen and twenty-five were planting trees, clearing camping areas and beaches, and building bridges, dams, reservoirs, fish ponds, and fire towers. More than 2.5 million young men eventually lived and worked in CCC camps. Then on May 12, Congress passed the Federal Emergency Relief Act, which authorized $500 million in aid to state and local governments.

Roosevelt's proposed plan for public works became Title II of the National Industrial Recovery Act (NIRA). Passed on June 16, NIRA established in the Public Works Administration (PWA) a fund of $3.3 billion to hire the unemployed to build roads, sewage and water systems, public buildings, ships, naval aircraft, and a host of other projects. The purpose of the PWA was to prime the economic pump to spur economic recovery. Roosevelt resorted to pump priming only as a last-ditch measure. He remained orthodox in his views, anxious to return to a balanced budget at the earliest opportunity.

If the AAA was the agricultural cornerstone of the New Deal, the National Industrial Recovery Act was the industrial cornerstone. The NIRA was a testimony to the New Deal belief in national planning as opposed to an individualistic, intensely

RESETTLEMENT ADMINISTRATION
Rescues Victims
Restores Land to Proper Use

Under the Agricultural Adjustment Act, farmers received government payments for not planting crops or for destroying crops that had already been planted. Some farmers, however, needed help of a different kind. The Resettlement Administration, established by executive order in 1935, was authorized to resettle destitute farm families from areas of soil erosion, flooding, and stream pollution to homestead communities. This poster was done by Ben Shahn. *Library of Congress.*

> **Economic Planning under the NIRA**

competitive, laissez-faire economy. It was essential, the planners argued, for businesses to end cutthroat competition and raise prices by limiting production. Like the War Industries Board (WIB) during the First World War, the NIRA exempted businesses from antitrust laws by establishing the National Recovery Administration (NRA). Under the auspices of the NRA, competing businesses met with representatives of workers and consumers to draft codes of fair competition, which limited production and established prices. With businesses en-

Under construction near Knoxville, Tennessee, the Norris Dam became an essential component of the massive Tennessee Valley Authority. Senator George Norris of Nebraska, for whom the dam was named, had long urged the federal government to produce and distribute electric power to the impoverished residents of the valley. *New Britain Museum of American Art, John Butler Talcott Fund, photo by Irving Blomstrann.*

joying new concessions, workers wanted a share of the pie too. Congress responded with Section 7(a) of the NIRA, which guaranteed their right to unionize and to bargain collectively.

One of the boldest programs enacted by Congress during this period concerned the badly depressed Tennessee River valley, which ran through Tennessee, North Carolina, Kentucky, Virginia, Mississippi, Georgia, and Alabama. For years progressives had advocated government operation of the Muscle Shoals electric power and nitrogen facilities on the Tennessee River. Roosevelt's Tennessee Valley Authority (TVA), established in May 1933, was a much broader program. Its dams would not only control floods but also generate hydroelectric power, reclaim and reforest land, and prevent soil erosion. The TVA would produce and sell nitrogen fertilizers to private citizens and nitrate explosives to the government, dig a 650-mile navigation channel from Knoxville to Paducah, and construct public power facilities as a yardstick for determin-

ing fair rates for privately produced electric power. The goal of the TVA was nothing less than enhancement of the economic well-being of the entire Tennessee River valley (see map).

Congress finally adjourned on June 16. During the First Hundred Days, Roosevelt had delivered fifteen messages to Congress, and fifteen significant laws had been enacted (see table, page 742), including the Federal Securities Act, to compel brokers to tell the truth about new securities issues, and the Banking Act of 1933, to set up the Federal Deposit Insurance Corporation for insuring bank deposits. On April 19 the United States had abandoned the gold standard, no longer guaranteeing the gold value of the dollar abroad. Freed from the gold standard, the Federal Reserve System could expand the supply of currency in circulation, thus enabling monetary policy to become another weapon for economic recovery.

End of the First Hundred Days

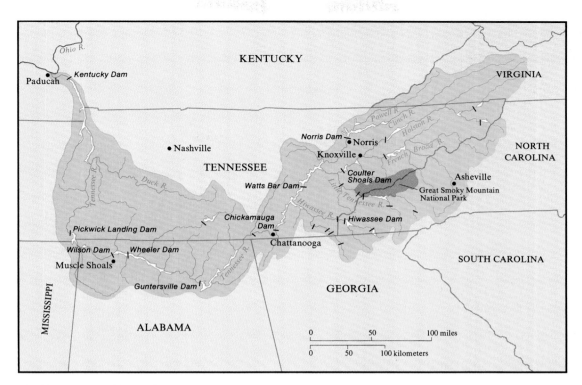

The Tennessee Valley Authority

Within a few months of Roosevelt's taking office, the United States had rebounded from shock, hysteria, and near-collapse. Columnist Walter Lippmann wrote that at the time of the inauguration, the country was a collection of "disorderly panic-stricken mobs and factions. In the hundred days from March to June we became again an organized nation confident of our power to provide for our own security and to control our own destiny."

Throughout the remainder of 1933 and the spring and summer of 1934, more New Deal bills became law, benefiting farmers, the unemployed, investors, homeowners, and workers. The Commodity Credit Corporation, organized in 1933, bolstered crop prices by lending money to farmers against their underpriced crops and allowing farmers to withhold their crops from the market until prices rose. Additional hundreds of millions of federal dollars were appropriated for unemployment relief and public works. Finally, in 1934 legislation established the Securities and Exchange Commission, the National Labor Relations Board, and the Federal Housing Administration.

Representing interest-group democracy at work, the New Deal seemed to promise something for every group. In the midst of this coalition of interests was President Roosevelt, the artful broker, and this broker state was working. Following New Deal legislation, the unemployment figure fell steadily to 13 million in 1933 and then to 9 million in 1936. Net farm income rose from just over $3 billion in 1933 to $5.85 billion in 1935. Manufacturing salaries and wages also increased, jumping from $6.25 billion in 1933 to almost $13 billion in 1937.

> **Interest-Group Democracy**

There was no doubt about the popularity of either the New Deal or Roosevelt during those early years of his presidency and programs. In the 1934 congressional elections, the Democrats gained ten seats in the House and ten in the Senate. The New Deal, according to Arthur Krock of the *New York Times,* had won "the most overwhelming victory in the history of American politics." As for Roosevelt, "he has been all but crowned by the people," wrote William Allen White.

Launching the New Deal and Restoring Confidence

NEW DEAL ACHIEVEMENTS

	Labor	Agriculture	Business and Industrial Recovery	Relief	Reform
1933	Section 7(a) of NIRA	Agricultural Adjustment Act Farm Credit Act	Emergency Banking Act Economy Act Beer and Wine Revenue Act Banking Act of 1933 (guaranteed deposits) National Industrial Recovery Act	Civilian Conservation Corps Federal Emergency Relief Act Home Owners Refinancing Act Public Works Administration Civil Works Administration	TVA Federal Securities Act
1934	National Labor Relations Board				Securities Exchange Act
1935	National Labor Relations (Wagner) Act	Resettlement Administration Rural Electrification Administration		Works Progress Administration and National Youth Administration	Banking Act of 1935 Social Security Act Public Utilities Holding Company Act Revenue Act (wealth tax)
1937		Farm Security Administration			
1938	Fair Labor Standards Act	Agricultural Adjustment Act of 1938			

Source: Adapted from Charles Sellers, Henry May, and Neil R. McMillen, A Synopsis of American History, 6th ed. Copyright © 1985 by Houghton Mifflin Company. Reprinted by permission.

Reactions Against the First New Deal

There was more than one way to read employment and income statistics and election returns. For example, although unemployment had dropped from a high of 13 million (25 percent) in 1933 to 9 million (16.9 percent) in 1936, it had been only 1.5 million (3.2 percent) in 1929. And although manufacturing wages and salaries had reached almost $13 billion in 1937, that figure was almost $1.5 billion less than the total for 1929. In other words, regardless of the New Deal's successes, it had a long way to go before reaching predepression standards.

With the arrival of partial economic recovery, many businesspeople and conservatives became vocal critics of the New Deal. Some charged that there was too much taxation and government regulation. Others criticized the deficit financing of relief and public works. According to still others, the New Deal was subverting individual initiative and self-reliance by providing welfare payments.

Conservative Critics of the New Deal

If businesspeople felt the government was their enemy, others thought the government favored business too much. Critics argued that business leaders had dominated the drafting of NRA codes, which, they claimed, favored industry's needs over those of workers and consumers. In time criticism grew. Farmers, labor unions, individual entrepreneurs, and antitrust critics complained that the NRA set prices too high and favored large producers over small businesses. The federal courts also began to scrutinize the constitutionality of the legislation in cases brought by critics.

The AAA also came under attack, because of its encouragement of cutbacks in production. In 1933, farmers had plowed under 10.4 million acres of cotton and slaughtered 6 million pigs—at a time when people were ill clothed and ill fed. Although for landowning farmers the program was successful, to the average person such waste was shocking. Tenant farmers and sharecroppers were also supposed to receive government payments for taking crops out of cultivation, but very few of them, especially if they were black, received what they were entitled to.

Furthermore, the AAA's hopes that landlords would keep their tenants on the land even while cutting production were not fulfilled. In the South the number of sharecropper farms dropped from 776,278 in 1930 to 541,291 in 1940. The result was a homeless population. Joining the migration were the "Okies" and "Arkies," who took to the road in the mid-1930s to escape the "Dust Bowl" areas of Oklahoma, Arkansas, and the rest of the Great Plains. Plaguing these farmers were drought, searing winds, eroded soil, and grasshoppers. "Everywhere you looked," recalled a North Dakota farmer, "you could see the grasshoppers coming in swarms." But worse than the grasshoppers was the dust. "We had days," the farmer said, "when you didn't see the sun."

As dissatisfaction mounted, so too did the appeal of various demagogues, who presented an analysis of American society that people understood: big wealth and power were ruling people's lives from distant cities, eroding community morale, and ruining family farms and small businesses. Father Charles Coughlin, a Roman Catholic priest whose weekly radio sermons offered a curious combination of anticommunism, anticapitalism, and anti-Semitism, was one of the best-known demagogues. For a while Coughlin supported the New Deal, but he opposed the AAA's plowing under of crops and slaughtering of livestock. In late 1934, Coughlin organized the National Union for Social Justice and began to criticize the New Deal for having "out-Hoovered Hoover."

Demagogic Attacks on the New Deal

Another challenge to the New Deal came from Dr. Francis E. Townsend. Under Townsend's Old Age Revolving Pensions plan, the government would pay monthly pensions of $200 to all citizens over age sixty on condition that they spent the money in the same month they received it. Townsend claimed his plan would not only aid the aged but cure the depression by pumping enormous purchasing power into the economy. The plan was fiscally impossible, but it addressed a real need.

Then there was Huey Long, "the Kingfish," perhaps the most successful demagogue in American history. In 1928, Long was elected governor of Louisiana with the slogan "Every Man a King, But No One Wears a Crown." As a United States senator (elected in 1930), Long at first supported the New Deal, but he found the Economy Act and the NRA too conservative and began to believe that Roosevelt had fallen captive to big business. Long countered in 1934 with the Share Our Wealth Society, which advocated the seizure by taxation of all incomes over $1 million and all inheritances over $5 million. With those funds, the government would furnish each family a homestead allowance of $5,000 and an annual income of $2,000. By mid-1935, Long's movement claimed 7 million members, and few doubted that Long aspired to the presidency. An assassin's bullet extinguished his ambition in September 1935, but the Share Our Wealth movement persisted under a new leader, the vitriolic anti-Semite Gerald L. K. Smith.

Some politicians of the 1930s, like Floyd Olson, governor of Minnesota, declared themselves Socialists. Olson sought a third party that would "preach the gospel of government and collective ownership

Senator Huey Long (center) had a mass following in the 1930s, and he had presidential ambitions. But he was assassinated in 1935, the same evening this photograph was taken. Long fell into the arms of James O'Connor (left), a political crony, while Louisiana's Governor O. K. Allen (right) seized a pistol and dashed into the corridor after the murderer shouting, "If there's shooting, I want to be in on it." *National Archives.*

> **Left-Wing Critics of the New Deal**

of the means of production and distribution." In neighboring Wisconsin the left-wing Progressive party re-elected Robert La Follette, Jr., to the Senate in 1934, sent seven of the state's ten representatives to Washington, and placed La Follette's brother Philip in the governorship. And the old muckraker Upton Sinclair won the Democratic gubernatorial nomination in California in 1934 on the platform End Poverty in California (EPIC).

Perhaps the most controversial alternative to the New Deal was the Communist Party of the United States of America (CPUSA). Membership in the CPUSA remained small until 1935, when the party leadership changed its strategy. Proclaiming "Communism is Twentieth Century Americanism," the CPUSA disclaimed any intention of overthrowing the United States government and began to cooperate with left-wing labor unions, student groups, and writers' organizations. At its high point for the decade in 1938, the CPUSA had 55,000 members.

In addition to challenges from the right and the left, the New Deal was threatened by the Supreme Court. Many New Deal laws had been hastily drafted and enacted, and the ma-

> **Supreme Court Decisions Against the New Deal**

jority of the justices feared that this legislation had vested too much power in the presidency. In January 1935, in *Panama Refining Co.* v. *Ryan,* the Court struck down part of the NIRA. By granting the president power to prohibit interstate and foreign shipment of oil, the Court ruled, Congress had unconstitutionally delegated legislative power to the executive branch. On May 27 the Court unanimously struck down the whole NIRA (*Schechter* v. *U.S.*) on the grounds that it gave excessive legislative power to the White House and that the commerce clause of the Constitution did not give the federal government authority to regulate intrastate businesses. Roosevelt's industrial recovery program was dead. In January 1936 his farm program met a similar fate when the Court invalidated the AAA (*U.S.* v. *Butler*), deciding that agriculture was a local problem and thus, under the Tenth Amendment, subject to state, not federal, action.

As Roosevelt looked ahead to the presidential election of 1936, he saw that he was in danger of losing his capacity to lead and to govern. His coalition of all interests was breaking up; radicals and demagogues were offering Americans alternative programs; and the Supreme Court was dismantling the New Deal. In the spring and summer of 1935, Roosevelt took the initiative once more, and the New Deal scored some of its biggest victories. So impressive was the new legislation that some historians have called it the Second New Deal.

The Second New Deal and the Election of 1936

There was an important difference between the First and Second New Deals. In 1933 and 1934 the chief legislative goal had been the recovery of the economy, so Roosevelt had cooperated with business. Beginning in 1935, however, he denounced business leaders for placing their selfish interests above the national welfare. The Second New Deal aimed at reforming the economy. Roosevelt also was being pushed left by the liberal Congress that had been elected in 1934, by the demagogues, and by the unions' growing ranks.

The first triumph of the Second New Deal was an innocuous-sounding but momentous law called the Emergency Relief Appropriation Act, which Congress passed and Roosevelt signed in April 1935. The act authorized the president to issue executive orders establishing massive public works programs for the jobless, including the Works Progress Administration (WPA). Later renamed the Work Projects Administration, the WPA ultimately employed more than 8.5 million people on a total of 1.4 million projects. By the time it was terminated in 1943, the WPA had built over 650,000 miles of highways,

▶ **Works Progress Administration**

streets, and roads, 125,000 public buildings, and 8,000 parks, as well as numerous bridges, airports, and other structures. But the WPA did more than lay bricks. Its Federal Theatre Project brought plays, vaudeville shows, and circuses to cities and towns across the country, and its Federal Writers' Project hired writers like John Cheever, Claude McKay, John Steinbeck, and Richard Wright to write local guidebooks and regional and folk histories.

Besides the WPA, the Emergency Relief Appropriation Act funded other relief and public works measures. The Resettlement Administration (RA) resettled destitute families and organized rural homestead communities and suburban greenbelt towns for low-income workers. The Rural Electrification Administration (REA) distributed electricity to isolated rural areas. And the National Youth Administration (NYA) sponsored work relief programs for young adults and part-time jobs for students.

As significant as these achievements were, Roosevelt wanted new legislation, some of it aimed at controlling the activities of big business. The Supreme Court had condemned the government-business cooperation that had been the foundation of the First Hundred Days. Businesspeople had become increasingly critical of Roosevelt and the New Deal. Now Roosevelt determined that if big business would not cooperate with government, government should "cut the giants down to size" through antitrust suits and heavy corporate taxes. In June 1935 he asked Congress to enact five major bills: a labor bill sponsored by Senator Robert Wagner, a Social Security bill, a banking bill, a measure to regulate public-utilities holding companies, and a "soak-the-rich" tax bill.

The summer of 1935 constituted the Second Hundred Days; when they were over, the president had everything he had requested. On July 5 the National Labor Relations (Wagner) Act granted workers the right to unionize and bargain collectively with management. When the Supreme Court had struck down the NIRA, labor unions had lost their federal protection. The new Wagner Act, however, was stronger than Section 7(a) of the NIRA. It empowered the National Labor Relations Board to ensure democratic union elections and to eradicate unfair labor practices by employers, such as the firing of workers for union membership.

▶ **Roosevelt's Second Hundred Days**

In *Gulliver's Travels,* Jonathan Swift's famous satire, Captain Lemuel Gulliver was staked to the ground by the tiny people called Lilliputians. In this 1935 cover illustration of *Vanity Fair,* the same fate befalls Uncle Sam. In this attack on the Roosevelt administration, each rope helping to immobilize Uncle Sam bears the initials of a New Deal agency. *Copyright © 1935, 1963 by the Condé Nast Publications, Inc.*

On August 15 Roosevelt signed the Social Security Act, which established old-age insurance. According to the law, workers who paid Social Security taxes out of their wages would receive retirement benefits at age sixty-five. Social Security was a conservative measure: the government did not pay for old-age benefits; workers and their bosses did. The tax was regressive because the more workers earned, the less they were taxed proportionally; and it was deflationary because it took out of people's pockets money that it did not repay for years. Finally, the law excluded many people from coverage—farm workers, domestic servants, and many hospital and restaurant workers. These occupations included many women and people of color.

> **Social Security Act**

Nevertheless, the Social Security Act was a milestone. The federal government acknowledged its responsibility to establish a system of insurance not only for the aged but also for the temporarily jobless. To assist the unemployed, the act established a cooperative federal-state system of unemployment compensation funded by a payroll tax paid by the employer and by matching state funds. It also authorized grants to the states for the relief of dependent children and disabled people, and it funded public health programs.

In the next two weeks Roosevelt gained the remainder of what he had asked for, including the Revenue (Wealth Tax) Act of 1935. The Wealth Tax Act, which some critics saw as the president's attempt to "steal Huey's thunder," did not result in a redistribution of income, though it did increase the income taxes paid by the wealthy. It also imposed a new tax on excess business profits, and it increased taxes on inheritances, large gifts, and profits from the sale of property.

The Second Hundred Days indicated not only that the president was once again in charge but that he was set to run for re-election. The campaign

> **Election of 1936**

was less heated than might have been expected, however. The Republican nominee, Governor Alf Landon of Kansas, criticized Roosevelt, but he did not advocate wholesale repeal of the New Deal. The followers of Father Coughlin, Dr. Townsend, and the late Senator Long banded together in the Union party and nominated Representative William Lemke of North Dakota. The Socialists nominated Norman Thomas; the Communists, Earl Browder.

The president and the Democratic party swept to a landslide victory. Roosevelt polled 27.8 million votes to Landon's 16.7 million; Lemke, Thomas, and Browder together received slightly over 1 million. The Democrats carried every state but Maine and Vermont and won huge majorities in the House and Senate. Some observers worried that the two-party system was about to collapse.

By 1936 Roosevelt and the Democrats had forged what observers have called the "New Deal coalition." In the 1920s and 1930s the sons and daughters of 13 million southern and

> **New Deal Coalition**

eastern European immigrants were reaching voting age and swelling the ranks of their parents' traditional party. In addition, the 6 million Americans who had migrated from farms to cities in the 1920s were looking to the government for help, and before long they too were gravitating to the Democratic party. The growing strength of the party in the cities converged with the New Deal's response to social distress to make Roosevelt the champion of the urban masses, many farmers, and members of labor unions. The new unions of the Congress of Industrial Organizations (CIO) fused the interests of millions of workers, native-born and foreign-born, black and white, male and female, skilled and unskilled (see pages 748–750). The New Deal coalition also included black voters in northern cities, most of whom had been Republicans prior to the 1930s; now they cast their lot with the Democratic party. Many lifelong Socialists began to vote Democratic. Finally, the party included the "Solid South," the eleven states of the Confederacy that had voted Democratic since the end of Reconstruction. The Democratic party had become the dominant half of the two-party system.

Roosevelt's Second Term: Court Packing and Other Failures

Despite the bold and unprecedented steps of his first term, Roosevelt faced a darkening horizon during his second term. The economy faltered again between 1937 and 1939, bringing renewed unemployment and suffering. And Europe drew closer to war, threatening to drag the United States into the conflict (see Chapter 26). To gain support for his foreign and military policies, Roosevelt began to court conservative politicians who were long-time opponents of his domestic reforms. The eventual result was the demise of the New Deal.

In several instances Roosevelt caused his own defeat. The Supreme Court had invalidated much of the work of the First Hundred Days; now Roosevelt feared it would do the same with the fruits of the Second Hundred Days. Four of the justices steadfastly opposed the New Deal; three generally approved of it; and two were swing votes. What the federal judiciary needed, the president claimed, was a more enlightened and progressive world view. So in February 1937 he sent to Congress his Judiciary Reorganization Bill.

What Roosevelt requested was the authority to add a federal judge whenever an incumbent who had already served at least ten years failed to retire

> **Roosevelt's Court-packing Plan**

within six months of reaching age seventy. He wanted the power to name up to fifty additional federal judges, including six to the Supreme Court. Roosevelt envisioned using the bill to create a Supreme Court sympathetic to the New Deal. Opposition to Roosevelt's attempt to pack the Court was widespread and vocal. Opponents thundered that the president's true aim was to become a dictator. Liberals joined Republicans and some conservative Democrats in resisting the bill. In the end Roosevelt had to concede defeat. The bill he signed into law in August made pensions available to retiring judges but denied him the power to increase the number of judges.

This episode had an ironic final twist. During the public debate over court packing, the two swing-vote justices began to vote in favor of liberal, pro–

ALL I SAID
WAS "GIMME
SIX MORE
JUSTICES!"

President Roosevelt's plan to expand the membership of the Supreme Court was met by angry opposition, not only from his political opponents but from others in the nation. *Library of Congress.*

New Deal rulings. In the spring of 1937, the Court upheld a Washington state minimum-wage statute; the Wagner Act (*N.L.R.B.* v. *Jones & Laughlin Steel Corp.*, ruling that Congress's power to regulate interstate commerce involved also the power to regulate the production of goods for interstate commerce); and the Social Security Act, all by 5-to-4 votes. Moreover, the new pensions encouraged judges past age seventy to retire, and the president appointed seven new associate justices in the next four years, including such notables as Hugo Black, Felix Frankfurter, and William O. Douglas.

Another New Deal setback was the renewed economic recession of 1937–1939. Roosevelt had never abandoned his commitment to the balanced budget. In 1937, confident that

> **Recession of 1937–1939**

most of the problems of the depression had been solved, he began to order drastic cutbacks in government spending. At the same time, the Federal Reserve Board, concerned about a 3.6 percent inflation rate, tightened credit. The two actions sent the economy into a tailspin: unemployment climbed from 7.7 million in 1937 to 10.4 million in 1938. Soon Roosevelt was forced to resume deficit financing. But even with sudden in-

fusions of relief, unemployment still stood at 9.5 million in 1939.

In the spring of 1938, with conflict over events in Europe commanding more and more of the nation's attention, the New Deal came to an end. Roosevelt sacrificed further domestic reforms in return for conservative support for his programs of military rearmament and preparedness. The last significant New Deal laws enacted were the National Housing Act of 1937, which established the U.S. Housing Authority, and in 1938 a new Agricultural Adjustment Act and the Fair Labor Standards Act, which not only forbade labor by children under age sixteen but also established the minimum wage and the forty-hour workweek for many, but by no means all, workers.

Industrial Workers and the Rise of the CIO

From the New Deal, working people gained the right to organize labor unions and bargain collectively with their bosses. On enactment, Section 7(a) of the NIRA inspired the vigorous recruitment of union members. Organizers for the United Mine Workers (UMW) told coal miners, "President Roosevelt wants you to join the union," and many thousands did so. By October 1933 an additional 1.5 million workers had enlisted in unions, bringing total membership to 4 million. With passage of the Wagner Act in mid-1935, labor union recruiting received another big boost; within three years total membership surpassed 7 million.

These gains did not always come easily. Management put up determined resistance in the 1930s, relying upon the police or hiring armed thugs to intimidate workers and break up strikes. Violence surfaced in the steel, automobile, and textile industries and among the lumber workers of the Pacific Northwest and the teamsters in the Midwest. In 1934 there was a general strike of workers in San Francisco.

Labor confronted yet another obstacle in the AFL craft unions' traditional skepticism and hostility toward industrial unions. Craft unions typically consisted of skilled workers in a particular trade, such as carpentry or plumbing. Industrial unions,

Rivalry Between Craft and Industrial Unions

on the other hand, represented all the workers, skilled and unskilled, in a given industry. The UMW and the International Ladies' Garment Workers Union were industrial rather than craft unions. Ever since its establishment in 1886, the American Federation of Labor had been dominated by craft unions. But gains in the 1930s were far more impressive in industrial unions than in craft unions, with hundreds of thousands of workers organizing in such industries as autos, garments, rubber, and steel.

The leaders of craft and industrial unions struggled for control of the growing labor movement. Personifying this power struggle were William Green of the AFL and John L. Lewis of the UMW. Lewis was probably the most colorful and tenacious labor leader in the nation's history, a fighter with a flair for the dramatic. But he presided over only one of the many unions within the AFL, whereas Green held power as president of the entire federation. Attempts to reconcile the craft and industrial union movements failed, and in late 1935 Lewis resigned as vice president of the AFL. He and other industrial unionists within the AFL formed the Committee for Industrial Organization (CIO). When the AFL's Executive Council demanded that the CIO disband, Lewis replied: "The American Federation of Labor is standing still, with its face toward the dead past." In 1938 the AFL expelled the CIO unions, and the CIO reorganized itself as the Congress of Industrial Organizations. By that time CIO membership stood at 3.7 million, more than the AFL's 3.4 million.

The CIO, which in the 1930s evolved into a pragmatic, "bread and butter" labor organization, organized millions of workers who had never before had an opportunity to join a

Sit-down Strikes

union. One of these unions, the United Auto Workers (UAW), scored a major victory in late 1936. The union, thirty thousand strong, demanded recognition from General Motors, Chrysler, and Ford. When GM refused, the workers launched a sit-down strike. Beginning in the Fisher Body plant in Flint, Michigan, they refused to leave the building. To discourage the strikers, GM managers turned off the heat. When that tactic failed, they called the police, who were met by a barrage of iron bolts, coffee mugs, and pop bottles. When the police resorted to tear gas, the strikers turned the plant's water hoses on them.

The strike lasted for weeks. GM obtained a court order to evacuate the plant, but the strikers continued, risking imprisonment and fines. With the support of their families and neighborhoods, the workers maintained rigid discipline. Community women organized an "emergency brigade" to picket and deliver food and supplies to the strikers. In 1937 the UAW prevailed: GM agreed to recognize the union. Chrysler signed a similar agreement, but Ford held out for four more years, a time of bloody encounters between the UAW and union-busting hoodlums hired by the Ford Service Department.

What made the sit-down strike significant was that it spread to all kinds of workers: textile, glass, and rubber workers, dime-store clerks, janitors, dressmakers, and pie bakers began using the technique. Some people condemned the sit-down as a trespass on private property; others endorsed it, including muckraker Upton Sinclair, who wrote that "for 75 years big business has been sitting down on the American people, and now I am delighted to see the process reversed." Most important, participation in the sit-downs bestowed self-respect upon the strikers. One man proudly compared his actions to those of Davy Crockett. "Yes sir, Chevy [Plant] No. 4 was my Alamo."

In 1937, the Steel Workers Organizing Committee (SWOC) signed a contract with the nation's largest steelmaker, U.S. Steel, that guaranteed an

Memorial Day Massacre

eight-hour day and a forty-hour week. Other steel companies refused to go along, however. Confrontations between these so-called little steel companies and the SWOC led to violence. On Memorial Day in Chicago, strikers and their families had joined with sympathizers in a peaceful picket line in front of the Republic Steel plant. Suddenly and without provocation the police opened fire. They continued to shoot into the crowd even as people turned away and began to run. Ten were killed. All had been shot in the back.

As senseless as the Memorial Day Massacre was, its occurrence was not surprising. During the 1930s industries had hired private police agents and accumulated large stores of arms and ammunition for use in deterring workers from organizing and joining unions. Through it all, the CIO continued to

On Memorial Day 1937, Chicago police used guns, clubs, and tear gas to break up a peaceful picket line at a Republic Steel plant. Ten people were killed and forty wounded in the Memorial Day Massacre. *Wide World Photos.*

enroll new members. By 1938 industrial unions had enlisted 600,000 miners, 375,000 steelworkers, 400,000 auto workers, 300,000 textile workers, 250,000 ladies' garment workers, and 100,000 agricultural and packing-house workers. By the end of the decade the CIO had succeeded in organizing most of the nation's mass-production industries.

Mixed Progress for People of Color

The depression sank the vast majority of blacks deeper into the mire of fear, political disfranchise-

Blacks in the Depression
ment, Jim Crow segregation, and privation. In 1930 about three-fourths of all blacks lived in the South. Almost all were prohibited

from voting or serving on juries; they were denied access to hospitals, universities, public parks, and swimming pools; and they were not hired except for the least desirable, most menial jobs. Blacks living in rural areas (56.9 percent in 1930) were propertyless sharecroppers, tenants, or wage hands caught in a cycle of poverty, disease, and illiteracy. Black life expectancy was more than ten years lower than white life expectancy (46.7 years versus 57.1). And the specter of the lynch mob's noose was a growing threat to black people. In 1929, seven black men were lynched; in 1930, twenty; and in 1933, when the depression was at its worst, twenty-four.

Racism also plagued blacks living in the North. Southern blacks who migrated to the northern cities discovered that employers discriminated against them. Black unemployment rates ran high; in Pittsburgh 48 percent of black workers were jobless in 1933, compared with 31 percent of white laborers.

Blacks were aware that Herbert Hoover shared prevailing white racial attitudes. Hoover sought a lily-white GOP and was attempting to push blacks out of the Republican party in order to attract white southern Democrats. He appointed few blacks to federal office, disbanded the Negro division of the Republican National Committee, rejected appeals for an antilynching law, and continued the segregation of the army and federal buildings in the nation's capital. Hoover's philosophy of individualism, opportunity, and fair play was, like signs posted across the country, "For Whites Only."

In 1930, the president showed his racial insensitivity by nominating Judge John J. Parker of North Carolina to the Supreme Court. Ten years earlier Parker had endorsed the disfranchisement of blacks; the NAACP remembered Parker's speech and protested the nomination. The American Federation of Labor joined the protest, and this combined pressure plus liberal votes in the Senate defeated Parker's nomination, 41 to 39. Unmoved, Hoover stood by his nominee throughout.

Then came Scottsboro, a civil rights case that symbolized the ugliness of race relations in the depression era. One afternoon in March 1931, when a

Scottsboro Trials

freight train pulled in at Paint Rock, near Scottsboro, Alabama, armed sheriff's deputies arrested nine blacks, charging them with roughing up some white hoboes and throwing them off the train earlier in the day. Two white women who were removed from the same train claimed that the blacks had raped them. Medical evidence later showed that the women were lying, perhaps to save themselves from arrest as prostitutes. But within two weeks eight of the so-called Scottsboro boys were convicted of rape by all-white juries and sentenced to death.

After several trials, Haywood Patterson, the first defendant, was ordered to die. But a Supreme Court ruling intervened, this time because it was evident that in Alabama blacks were systematically excluded from juries. Patterson faced a new trial in 1936. Found guilty again, he was given a seventy-five-year jail sentence. Four of the other youths were sentenced to life imprisonment. Not until 1950 were all five out of jail—four by parole and Patterson by escaping from his work gang.

Blacks coped with their white-circumscribed environment and fought back against racism in a variety of ways. The NAACP, though internally divided, lobbied quietly against a long list of injustices, and A. Philip Randolph's Brotherhood of Sleeping Car Porters defended the rights of black workers. In Harlem the militant Harlem Tenants League fought rent increases and evictions, and in some cities black consumers began to boycott white merchants. But America's white leaders made few concessions. Only the Supreme Court, which declared the Texas "white primary" law unconstitutional and attempted to check the abuse in the Scottsboro trials, provided a measure of protection for black Americans in the early 1930s.

With the election of Franklin D. Roosevelt, blacks' attitudes toward government changed, as did their political affiliation. For black Americans—an important segment of the New Deal coalition—Franklin D. Roosevelt would become the most appealing president since Abraham Lincoln. Part of the reason was the courageous way he bore his physical disability. Blacks, who suffered from a handicap of their own—racism—knew what courage was. Moreover, Roosevelt seemed a decided improvement over Hoover, and in his fireside chats and through his personal magnetism and buoyancy the new president spoke directly to them. When they saw pictures of black visitors at the White House and read about Roosevelt's Black Cabinet, they were heartened. Most important, through the WPA and other relief programs, the New Deal aided black people in their struggle for economic survival.

The Black Cabinet, or black brain trust, was unique in United States history. Never before had there been so many black advisers at the White

Black Cabinet

House, and never had they been highly trained professionals. There were black lawyers, journalists, and Ph.D.s; black experts on housing, labor, and social welfare. William H. Hastie and Robert C. Weaver, holders of advanced degrees from Harvard, served in the Department of Interior. Mary McLeod Bethune, a college president, was director of the Division of Negro Affairs of the National Youth Administration. There were also among the New Dealers some whites who had committed themselves to first-class citizenship for African-Americans. Foremost among these people was Eleanor Roosevelt. In 1939, when the acclaimed black contralto Marian Anderson was barred from performing in Washington's Constitution Hall by its owners, the Daughters of the

American Revolution, Mrs. Roosevelt arranged for Anderson to sing on Easter Sunday at the Lincoln Memorial.

The president himself, however, remained uncommitted to black civil rights. Fearful of alienating southern whites, he never endorsed two key goals of the civil rights struggle: a fed-

> **Antiblack Effects of the New Deal**

eral law against lynching and abolition of the poll tax. Furthermore, some New Deal programs functioned in ways that were definitely hostile to black Americans. The AAA, rather than benefiting black tenant farmers and sharecroppers, actually forced many of them off the land. The Federal Housing Administration (FHA) refused to guarantee mortgages on houses purchased by blacks in white neighborhoods. The CCC was racially segregated, as was much of the TVA, which constructed all-white towns and handed out skilled jobs to whites first. Finally, waiters, cooks, hospital orderlies, janitors, farm workers, and domestics, many of whom were black, were excluded from Social Security coverage and from the minimum-wage provisions of the Fair Labor Standards Act of 1938.

In short, though blacks benefited, they did not get their fair share. Despite these shortcomings, blacks overwhelmingly supported Roosevelt's New Deal for the benefits they did receive. And at election time, black voters showed their gratitude by giving Roosevelt large majorities.

Confronted with the mixed message of the New Deal, many blacks turned only reluctantly to the Democratic party while others, concluding that ultimately they could depend only on themselves, organized self-help and direct-action movements. In 1934, black tenant farmers and sharecroppers joined with poor whites to form the Southern Tenant Farmers' Union. In the North, blacks boycotted stores in Don't Buy Where You Can't Work campaigns, launched Jobs for Negroes movements, and started tenants' unions to fight high rents. In 1935 a race riot erupted when rumors swept Harlem that police had beaten to death a black youth. Mobs of poor and angry people smashed store windows and raided shelves. Working-class blacks criticized the NAACP for ignoring the economics of second-class citizenship and for being too middle class and legalistic in its war on racism. Although the NAACP was scoring notable victories in opening up graduate and professional schools to black students, crit-

ics charged that these gains benefited only the middle class, not the masses who above all needed jobs.

Nowhere was the trend toward direct action more evident than in the March on Washington Movement in 1941. In that year billions of federal

> **March on Washington Movement**

dollars flowed into American industry as the nation prepared for the possibility of another world war. The government funds generated thousands of new jobs, but discrimination deprived blacks of their fair share. One executive notified black job applicants that "the Negro will be considered only as janitors and in other similar capacities." So in early 1941, A. Philip Randolph, president of the Brotherhood of Sleeping Car Porters, proposed that blacks march on the nation's capital to demand equal access to jobs in defense industries.

By midsummer thousands of blacks were ready to march. Fearing that the march might provoke riots and Communists might infiltrate the movement, Roosevelt announced that if the march were canceled, he would issue an executive order prohibiting discrimination in war industries and in the government. The result was Executive Order No. 8802, issued on June 25, 1941, which established the Fair Employment Practices Committee (FEPC). The March on Washington Movement anticipated future trends in the civil rights movement. It was all-black; its tactic was direct action—a threat by the masses to take to the streets; and the beneficiaries of the movement were the urban working class, not the black middle class.

During the early 1930s, another group, American Indians, sank further into malnutrition and disease. In Oklahoma, where the Choctaws, Cherokees, and Seminoles lived with over twenty other tribes on infertile soil, three-fourths of all Indian children were undernourished. Tuberculosis swept through the reservations. At the heart of the problem was a 1929 ruling by the U.S. comptroller general that landless tribes were ineligible for federal aid. Not until 1931 did the Indian Bureau take steps to relieve the suffering. A federal relief program was launched to provide flour from the Red Cross, surplus clothing from the War Department, and seed from the Department of Agriculture. Yet, when Congress substantially increased the bureau's budget that year, much of the money went to hire more bureaucrats.

Mary McLeod Bethune, pictured here with her friend and supporter Eleanor Roosevelt, became the first African-American woman to head a federal agency as director of the Division of Negro Affairs of the National Youth Administration. *Franklin D. Roosevelt Library.*

The New Deal took a very different approach from earlier administrations to fulfilling its duty to Native Americans. As a result, Indians benefited more directly than blacks from the New Deal. Roosevelt appointed John Collier commissioner of Indian affairs. In the 1920s, as founder of the American Indian Defense Association, Collier had crusaded for tribal landownership and an end to the allotment policy established by the Dawes Severalty Act of 1887 (see pages 472–473). "The allotment act," Collier had written, "contemplates total landlessness for the Indians of the third generation of each allotted tribe." First, the Dawes Act sought to dissolve Indian tribes by dividing tribal lands among tribal members—160 acres to each head of

A New Deal for American Indians

family and 80 acres to each single adult. Many Indians in turn sold their allotments to white ranchers, miners, and farmers. Second, reservation land remaining after the distribution of allotments was opened for settlement to non-Indian homesteaders. The result was that after 1887, Indian landholdings dropped from 138 million acres to 48 million acres, 20 million of which were arid or semiarid.

Passed by Congress in 1934, the Indian Reorganization (Wheeler-Howard) Act aimed to reverse this process by restoring lands to tribal ownership and forbidding future division of Indian lands into individual parcels. Other provisions of the act enabled tribes to obtain loans for economic development and to establish self-government. Under Collier, the Bureau of Indian Affairs also encouraged the per-

Violence erupted in October 1933 in California's San Joaquin Valley. When Mexican farm workers struck, the growers evicted them and their families. The growers also fired upon workers holding strike meetings at Pixley and Arvin, killing three. This group of Mexican women was bound for the picket line to protest for food relief for the hungry families. *Library of Congress.*

petuation of Indian religions and cultures. One order stated: "No interference with Indian religious life or expression will hereafter be tolerated. The cultural history of Indians is in all respects to be considered equal to that of any nonIndian group." Collier's reforms would stand until 1953 (see pages 857–858).

Mexican-Americans also suffered extreme hardship during the depression, but no government programs benefited them. During these years many

> **Depression Hardships for Mexican-Americans**

Mexicans and Mexican-Americans packed up their belongings and moved south of the border, sometimes willingly, sometimes deported by immigration officials or forced out by California officials eager to purge them from the relief rolls. As an inducement, the government offered free one-way train tickets to Mexico. From 1929 through 1934, about 425,000, mostly from Texas, California, Indiana, and Illinois, returned to Mexico.

According to the federal census, the Mexican-born population dropped from 617,000 in 1930 to 377,000 in 1940. One reason was that many employers had changed their minds about the desirability of hiring Mexican-American farm workers. Before

the 1930s farmers had boasted that Mexican-Americans were a cheap, docile labor supply and would not join unions. But in the 1930s Mexican-Americans belied their image by engaging in prolonged and sometimes bloody strikes. During one protest in the strawberry fields of El Monte, California, workers established their own union, which waged two dozen strikes from 1933 to 1936. In united action in the San Joaquin valley in October 1933, eighteen thousand cotton pickers walked off their jobs and set up a "strike city" after being evicted from the growers' camps. Shortly after, their union hall was riddled with bullets and two strikers died.

The New Deal offered little help to these Mexican-Americans. The AAA was created to assist property-owning farmers, not migratory farm workers. The Wagner Act did not cover farm workers' unions, nor did the Social Security Act or the Fair Labor Standards Act cover farm laborers. One New Deal agency, the Farm Security Administration (FSA), was established in 1937 to help farm workers, in part by setting up migratory labor camps. But the FSA came too late to help Mexican-Americans, most of whom had by that time been replaced by dispossessed white farmers. Between 1935 and

1940 more than 350,000 Okies and Arkies fled to California from Oklahoma, Arkansas, Texas, and other drought-stricken "Dust Bowl" states. As early as 1936 they made up 85 to 90 percent of the state's migratory work force, compared to less than 20 percent before the depression. In just a few years, however, Mexican-Americans would be back. With the onset of the Second World War, the United States would again need Mexican-Americans to work in the fields and on the railroads.

Women, Work, and the Depression

During the depression women had to work overtime to maintain themselves and their families. In *It's Up to the Women* (1933), Eleanor Roosevelt wrote that during such periods, wives and mothers often had to bear a heavier responsibility than husbands and fathers. "The women know," she asserted, "that life must go on and that the needs of life must be met. . . ." With families experiencing severe income reductions, wives and mothers followed the maxim "Use it up, wear it out, make it do, or do without." Making do, Eleanor Roosevelt wrote, meant "endless little economies and constant anxiety for fear of some catastrophe such as accident or illness which may completely swamp the family budget." Women bought day-old bread and cheap cuts of meat; they relined old coats with blankets and saved string, rags, and broken crockery for possible future use. In short, many families with reduced incomes were able to maintain their standard of living only because of astute women shoppers or because women substituted their own labor in the home for goods and services they used to purchase. Husbands and fathers shared these financial concerns, but it was usually women's responsibility to do the family budgeting; it was estimated that wives and mothers in the 1930s allocated over 80 percent of all family income.

> **Wives and Mothers Face the Depression**

While they were cutting corners to make ends meet, women were also seeking paid work outside the home. In 1930 over 10.5 million women were paid workers; ten years later, the female labor force topped 13 million. Despite these statistics, most Americans believed that women should not work outside the home, that they should strive instead to be good wives and mothers, and that women who worked were doing so for "pin money" to buy frivolous things. The experience of teachers provides an example. Of the 1,500 urban school systems surveyed by the National Education Association in 1930–1931, 77 percent refused to hire married women as teachers and 63 percent fired female teachers who married while employed.

Another popular argument of the 1930s held that male unemployment stemmed directly from women working. When a Gallup poll in 1936 asked whether wives should work if their husbands had jobs, 82 percent of the respondents (including 75 percent of the women) answered no. Severe job discrimination resulted from these attitudes. Most insurance companies, banks, and public utilities had policies against married women working, and from 1932 to 1937 federal law prohibited more than one family member from working for the civil service. Because wives usually earned less than their husbands, they were the ones who quit their government jobs.

Such thinking missed the point, for two reasons. First, women were heavily concentrated in certain occupations or "women's jobs," including clerical positions (49 percent of all employees were women), teachers (81 percent), telephone operators (95 percent), and nurses (98 percent). Men rarely sought these "feminized" jobs and probably would not have been hired had they applied for such work. Second, most women workers (72 percent in 1930) were single, not married; they were thus self-supporting. But since the economy had become so segregated into "men's jobs" and "women's jobs," the problem for these women was that, on balance, their wages lagged far behind those for men.

Other women workers were married; they worked to keep their families from slipping into poverty. Married women constituted 35 percent of the female work force in 1940, an increase from 29 percent in 1930 and 15 percent in 1900. But the assistance of working wives with family expenses did not improve their status. As the sociologists Robert and Helen Lynd observed at the time: "The men, cut adrift from their usual routine, lost most of their sense of time and dawdled helplessly and dully about the streets; while in the homes the women's world remained largely intact and the round of cooking, housecleaning, and mending became if anything more absorbing." Even while women were making increased contributions to the family, their husbands, including those without jobs, still exercised authority as family decision makers.

The New Deal did take into account women's needs, but only if reminded forcefully to do so by the women activists who advised the government.

Women in the New Deal

The historian Susan Ware has written that there was in Washington a women's network of government and Democratic party officials who were united by their attitudes toward social reform and the role of women in politics and government. Many were long-time personal friends and professional allies who had worked together in the National Consumers' League, Women's Trade Union League, and other organizations. Most were social feminists who believed that working women needed protective laws for their health and safety on the job. The network's most prominent member was Eleanor Roosevelt, who was her husband's valued adviser. Frances Perkins, the secretary of labor, was the nation's first woman cabinet officer. Other historic New Deal appointments included the first woman federal appeals judge and the first women ambassadors. Molly Dewson, head of the Democratic party's Women's Division, noted with pride: "The change from women's status in government before Roosevelt is unbelievable."

Even with increased participation by women, however, New Deal provisions for women were mixed. The maximum-hour and minimum-wage provisions mandated by the NRA won women's applause. Women workers in the lowest-paying jobs, many of them laboring under sweatshop conditions, had the most to gain from these standards. At the same time, some NRA codes mandated pay differentials based on gender, so that women's minimum wages were lower than men's. Federal relief agencies, such as the Civil Works Administration and the Federal Emergency Relief Administration, put only one woman to work for every eight to ten men placed in relief jobs. A popular New Deal program, the Civilian Conservation Corps, was limited to young men. And women who were low-income workers, especially in agriculture and domestic service, were not protected by the 1935 Social Security Act or the 1938 Fair Labor Standards Act.

The Election of 1940 and the Legacy of the New Deal

As the presidential election of 1940 approached, many people wondered whether Roosevelt would run for a third term (no president had ever served more than two terms). Roosevelt himself seemed undecided until May 1940, when Adolf Hitler's military advances in Europe apparently convinced him to stay on. He confided his decision to no one, however, and even sent a message to the Democratic convention that he did not want to be renominated. But at a timely moment, loudspeakers broadcast the chant "We want Roosevelt!" throughout the convention hall, and delegates began to snake-dance up and down the aisles. Roosevelt wanted the nomination, but he also wanted the appearance of a draft. He was nominated on the first ballot and selected Secretary of Agriculture Henry A. Wallace as his running mate.

The Republican candidate was Wendell Willkie, a utilities executive who had been an anti–New Deal Democrat throughout most of the 1930s. As a politician Willkie was an unknown, and as late as April 1940 he did not have a single delegate to the Republican convention, scheduled to open in two months. In May, however, with the Nazi invasion of the Low Countries and France, Willkie's support mounted in public opinion polls. Other anti–New Deal Democrats joined with eastern Republicans to boost his candidacy, painting him as an internationalist who would halt the Nazi advance before it reached England. On the sixth ballot Willkie defeated New York's Thomas E. Dewey.

Willkie campaigned against the New Deal, contending that its meddling in the affairs of business had failed to return the nation to prosperity. He also criticized the government's lack of military preparedness. But Roosevelt pre-empted the defense issue by beefing up military and naval contracts. As workers streamed into the factories to fill the new orders, unemployment figures dropped as well. In his speeches Roosevelt reminded workers that it was his administration that had provided the defense jobs. When Willkie reversed his approach and accused Roosevelt of being a warmonger, the president promised, "Your boys are not going to be sent into any foreign wars."

Willkie never did come up with an effective campaign issue, and on election day Roosevelt received 27 million votes to Willkie's 22 million. In the electoral college Roosevelt buried Willkie 449 to 82. Willkie did manage to win the farm and small-town vote in the Midwest, but as in 1936 Roosevelt triumphed in the cities, primarily among working-class, lower-income, and black voters. Although the New Deal was over at home, Roosevelt was still riding a wave of public approval.

Any analysis of the New Deal must begin with Franklin Delano Roosevelt. Assessments of his career varied widely during his presidency. Most

Franklin D. Roosevelt Assessed

historians have considered him a truly great president, citing his courage, his buoyant self-confidence, his willingness to experiment, and his capacity to inspire the nation during the most somber days of the depression. Those who have criticized him have charged that he was too pragmatic, that he failed to formulate a bold and coherent strategy of economic recovery and political and economic reform.

Although scholars have debated Roosevelt's performance, they all agree that he transformed the presidency. "Only Washington, who made the office, and Jackson, who remade it," Clinton Rossiter, the political scientist, observed, "did more than Roosevelt to raise it to its present condition of strength, dignity, and independence." Scholars in a later era would charge that Roosevelt had initiated "the imperial presidency" (see page 970). But whether for good or ill, Roosevelt strengthened not only the presidency but the whole federal government. "For the first time for many Americans," the historian William Leuchtenburg has written, "the federal government became an institution that was directly experienced. More than state and local governments, it came to be *the* government." In the past, the federal government had served as a regulator of railroads, corporations, and other businesses; during the New Deal it became a guarantor and stimulator as well.

The New Deal laid the foundation of America's welfare system on which subsequent presidential administrations would build. For the first time

Origins of America's Welfare System

the federal government acknowledged a responsibility to bring relief to the jobless and the needy, and for the first time it resorted to deficit spending in order to stimulate the economy. Millions of Americans benefited from government programs that are still operating today.

Yet the economy itself remained basically capitalistic under the New Deal. The profit motive and private property remained fundamental to the system. Some redistribution of wealth did result from the New Deal, but the wealthy survived as a class. In 1929, for example, the most well-to-do 5 percent of the population received 30 percent of the total family income. By 1941, their share had shrunk but was still a healthy 24 percent. Most of the income lost by the wealthy ended up in the pockets of the middle and upper-middle classes, not of the poor (see table, page 758).

The New Deal brought about limited change in the nation's power structure. Beginning in the 1930s, business interests had to share their political clout with others. Labor gained influence in Washington, and farmers got more of what they wanted from Congress and the White House. But there was no real increase in the power of African-Americans and other minorities. If people wanted their voices to be heard, they had to organize in labor unions, trade associations, or other special-interest lobbies.

The New Deal was a liberal, evolutionary reform program that did not represent a revolutionary break with the past. New Deal ideas such as the TVA and Social Security had been around for decades, and prominent New Dealers had been involved in reform movements since the Progressive era. Historians generally view the New Deal as a reform movement that benefited middle-class Americans. William Leuchtenburg has concluded that the New Deal "swelled the ranks of the bourgeoisie but left many Americans—sharecroppers, slum dwellers, most Negroes—outside of the new equilibrium."

The New Deal failed in its fundamental purpose: to put people back to work. As late as 1939, over 10 million men and women were still jobless. That

New Deal Failure to Solve Unemployment

year unemployment was 19.1 percent; over the next two years it fell no lower than 14.6 percent. What plagued the nation throughout the 1930s was underconsumption: people and businesses did not purchase enough goods to sustain high levels of employment. In the end it was not the New Deal but massive government spending during the Second World War that put people back to

DISTRIBUTION OF TOTAL FAMILY INCOME[a] AMONG VARIOUS SEGMENTS OF THE POPULATION, 1929–1944 (IN PERCENTAGES)

Year	Poorest Fifth	Second Poorest Fifth	Middle Fifth	Second Wealthiest Fifth	Wealthiest Fifth	Wealthiest 5 Percent
1929	12.5		13.8	19.3	54.4	30.0
1935–1936	4.1	9.2	14.1	20.9	51.7	26.5
1941	4.1	9.5	15.3	22.3	48.8	24.0
1944	4.9	10.9	16.2	22.2	45.8	20.7

[a]Monetary and nonmonetary income.

Source: Adapted from U.S. Bureau of the Census, Historical Statistics of the United States, Colonial Times to 1970, *Bicentennial Edition (Washington, D.C.: U.S. Government Printing Office, 1975), p. 301.*

work. In 1941, as a result of mobilization for war, unemployment would drop to 9.9 percent, and in 1944, at the height of the war, only 1.2 percent of the labor force would be jobless.

In some ways, the New Deal's most lasting accomplishments were its programs to ameliorate the suffering of unemployment. The United States has suffered several economic recessions since 1945, but American presidents, including Republicans, have "primed the pump" during these periods of slump. Prior to the New Deal, the United States had experienced a major depression every fifteen or twenty years—1819, 1837, 1857, 1873, 1893, 1907, 1921, 1929. But since the New Deal, thanks to unemployment compensation, Social Security, and other measures, the United States has experienced no return to the national nightmare of the Great Depression.

Suggestions for Further Reading

Hoover and the Worsening Depression

William W. Barber, *Herbert Hoover, the Economists, and American Economic Policy, 1921–1933* (1986); Michael A. Bernstein, *The Great Depression: Delayed Recovery and Economic Change in America, 1929–1939* (1988); David Burner, *Herbert Hoover* (1979); Carl N. Degler, "The Ordeal of Herbert Hoover," *Yale Review,* 52 (1963), 563–583; Martin L. Fausold, *The Presidency of Herbert C. Hoover* (1985); Milton Friedman and Anna Schwartz, *The Great Contraction, 1929–1933* (1965); Susan Kennedy, *The Banking Crisis of 1933* (1973); Charles Kindleberger, *The World in Depression, 1929–1939* (1973); Donald J. Lisio, *The President and Protest: Hoover, Conspiracy, and the Bonus Riot* (1974); James S. Olson, *Herbert Hoover and the Reconstruction Finance Corporation, 1931–1933* (1977); Albert B. Romasco, *The Poverty of Abundance: Hoover, the Nation, the Depression* (1965); Jordan A. Schwarz, *Interregnum of Despair* (1970); Richard N. Smith, *An Uncommon Man* (1984).

The New Deal

Barton J. Bernstein, "The New Deal: The Conservative Achievements of Liberal Reform," in Barton J. Bernstein, ed., *Towards a New Past* (1968), 263–288; Paul K. Conkin, *The New Deal,* 2nd ed. (1975); Peter Fearon, *War, Prosperity, and Depression* (1987); Otis L. Graham, Jr., *Encore for Reform: The Old Progressives and the New Deal* (1967); Ellis W. Hawley, *The New Deal and the Problem of Monopoly* (1966); William E. Leuchtenburg, *Franklin D. Roosevelt and the New Deal* (1963); Robert S. McElvaine, *The Great Depression* (1984); James S. Olson, *Saving Capitalism: The Reconstruction Finance Corporation and the New Deal, 1933–1940* (1988); Albert U. Romasco, *The Politics of Recovery: Roosevelt's New Deal* (1983); Harvard Stikoff, ed., *Fifty Years Later: The New Deal Evaluated* (1985).

Franklin D. Roosevelt

James MacGregor Burns, *Roosevelt: The Lion and the Fox* (1956); Kenneth S. Davis, *FDR: The New Deal Years, 1933–1937* (1986); Frank Freidel, *Franklin D. Roosevelt,* 4 vols.

(1952–1973); Joseph P. Lash, *Eleanor and Franklin* (1971); William E. Leuchtenburg, *In the Shadow of FDR* (1983); Arthur M. Schlesinger, Jr., *The Age of Roosevelt,* 3 vols. (1957–1960).

Voices from the Depression

James Agee, *Let Us Now Praise Famous Men* (1941); Ann Banks, ed., *First-Person America* (1980); Federal Writers' Project, *These Are Our Lives* (1939); Robert S. McElvaine, ed., *Down and Out in the Great Depression: Letters from the Forgotten Man* (1983); Studs Terkel, *Hard Times: An Oral History of the Great Depression* (1970); Tom E. Terrill and Jerrold Hirsch, eds., *Such as Us: Southern Voices of the Thirties* (1978).

Alternatives to the New Deal

Alan Brinkley, *Voices of Protest: Huey Long, Father Coughlin, and the Great Depression* (1982); Harvey Klehr, *The Heyday of American Communism* (1984); R. Alan Lawson, *The Failure of Independent Liberalism, 1930–1941* (1971); Mark Naison, *Communists in Harlem During the Depression* (1983); James T. Patterson, *Congressional Conservatism and the New Deal* (1967); Leo Ribuffo, *The Old Christian Right: The Protestant Far Right from the Great Depression to the Cold War* (1983); Frank A. Warren, *An Alternative Vision: The Socialist Party in the 1930s* (1976); T. Harry Williams, *Huey Long* (1969).

Labor

John Barnard, *Walter Reuther and the Rise of the Auto Workers* (1983); Irving Bernstein, *A Caring Society: The New Deal, the Worker, and the Great Depression* (1985); Irving Bernstein, *Turbulent Years: A History of the American Worker, 1933–1941* (1969); Irving Bernstein, *The Lean Years: A History of the American Worker, 1920–1933* (1960); Melvin Dubofsky and Warren Van Tine, *John L. Lewis: A Biography* (1977); Sidney Fine, *Sit-Down: The General Motors Strike of 1936–1937* (1969); John W. Hevener, *Which Side Are You On? The Harlan County Coal Miners, 1931–1939* (1978); August Meier and Elliott Rudwick, *Black Detroit and the Rise of the UAW* (1979); David Milton, *The Politics of U.S. Labor: From the Great Depression to the New Deal* (1980).

Agriculture

David E. Conrad, *The Forgotten Farmers: The Story of Sharecroppers in the New Deal* (1965); Lowell K. Dyson, *Red Harvest: The Communist Party and American Farmers* (1982); Theodore M. Saloutos, *The American Farmer and the New Deal* (1982); John L. Shover, *Cornbelt Rebellion: The Farmers' Holiday Association* (1965); Walter J. Stein, *California and the Dust Bowl Migration* (1973); Donald Worster, *Dust Bowl: The Southern Plains in the 1930s* (1979).

People of Color

Francisco E. Balerman, *In Defense of LaRaza: The Los Angeles Mexican Consulate and the Mexican Community, 1929–1936* (1982); Dan T. Carter, *Scottsboro,* rev. ed. (1979); Laurence M. Hauptman, *The Iroquois and the New Deal* (1981); Abraham Hoffman, *Unwanted Mexican Americans in the Great Depression: Repatriation Pressures, 1929–1939* (1974); Laurence C. Kelly, *The Assault on Assimilation: John Collier and the Origins of Indian Policy Reform* (1983); John B. Kirby, *Black Americans in the Roosevelt Era: Liberalism and Race* (1980); Donald J. Lisio, *Hoover, Blacks, and Lily-Whites* (1985); Donald L. Parman, *The Navajos and the New Deal* (1975); Kenneth Philp, *John Collier's Crusade for Indian Reform, 1920–1954* (1977); Mark Reisler, *By the Sweat of Their Brow: Mexican Immigrant Labor in the United States, 1900–1940* (1976); Harvard Sitkoff, *A New Deal for Blacks* (1978); Nancy J. Weiss, *Farewell to the Party of Lincoln: Black Politics in the Age of FDR* (1983); Raymond Wolters, *Negroes and the Great Depression: The Problem of Economic Recovery* (1970); Robert L. Zangrando, *The NAACP Crusade Against Lynching, 1909–1950* (1980).

Women

Julia Kirk Blackwelder, *Women of the Depression: Caste and Culture in San Antonio, 1929–1939* (1984); Glen H. Elder, Jr., *Children of the Great Depression: Social Change in Life Experience* (1974); Lois Scharf, *To Work and to Wed: Female Employment, Feminism, and the Great Depression* (1980); Winifred Wandersee, *Women's Work and Family Values, 1920–1940* (1981); Susan Ware, *Holding Their Own: American Women in the 1930s* (1982); Susan Ware, *Beyond Suffrage: Women in the New Deal* (1981); Jeane Westin, *Making Do: How Women Survived the '30s* (1976).

Cultural and Intellectual History

Daniel Aaron, *Writers on the Left: Episodes in American Literary Communism* (1961); Andrew Bergman, *We're in the Money: Depression America and Its Films* (1971); Jerre Mangione, *The Dream and the Deal: The Federal Writers' Project, 1935–1943* (1972); Alice Goldfarb Marquis, *Hopes and Ashes: The Birth of Modern Times, 1929–1939* (1986); David P. Peeler, *Hope Among Us Yet: Social Criticism and Social Solace in Depression America* (1987); Richard H. Pells, *Radical Visions and American Dreams: Culture and Social Thought in the Depression Years* (1973); Warren I. Susman, "The Culture of the Thirties," in Warren I. Susman, *Culture as History* (1984), 150–183; Edmund Wilson, *The American Earthquake* (1958).

On December 24, 1921, prisoner #9653 strode out of Atlanta's federal penitentiary. After a train ride to Washington, D.C., he entered the White House to meet the man who had just pardoned him. "Well," said the congenial President Warren G. Harding, "I have heard so damned much about you, Mr. Debs, that I am now very glad to meet you personally." They had a good talk, and Eugene V. Debs told reporters that Harding was a "gentleman" who "possesses human impulses." The First World War now over for him, Debs went home to Terre Haute, Indiana.

It seemed unusual for a conservative, probusiness Republican who had supported the American effort in the First World War to pardon Eugene V. Debs, the anticapitalist Socialist party leader who from his jail cell, had run against Harding for the presidency in 1920 and had won nearly one million votes. Because of his antiwar views, Debs had been handed a ten-year sentence for violating the wartime Sedition Act. President Woodrow Wilson had snarled a firm "no" to pardoning this "traitor." Harding was more compassionate. But, most important, he believed that Debs's continued imprisonment simply reminded Americans of a troubled past they should try to forget.

26

DIPLOMACY IN A BROKEN WORLD, 1920–1941

Debs's release was one of Harding's ways of saying that the United States was liquidating the war and returning to what he called "normalcy." "I thought the spirit of clemency was quite in harmony with the things we were trying to do here in Washington." What "things"? A return to peacetime, free from missionary zeal, overseas crusades, huge military expenditures, and domestic divisiveness. Interpreting his 1920 victory as a repudiation of Wilson's League of Nations, Harding also wished to shelve that issue. The United States would not again become "entangled" in "Old World affairs," he insisted.

The president took several other steps in November 1921 to demonstrate his resolve to put the war behind the nation. He buried the Unknown Soldier in Arlington Cemetery to initiate, he said, "a new and lasting era of peace." He signed peace treaties with the defeated Central Powers, until then technically still at war with the United States because the Senate had rejected the Treaty

Secretary of the Navy Claude Swanson, President Roosevelt, and former Secretary of the Navy Josephus Daniels reviewing the fleet, May 31, 1934. Oil over photograph. *UPI/Bettmann Newsphotos.*

travel?
adventure?
answer—Join the Marines!
ENLIST TODAY FOR 2-3 or 4 YEARS

This recruiting poster in the era of independent internationalism promised exciting military duty. The United States government fulfilled the promise by sending the marines to intervene abroad, especially in the Caribbean and Central America. The violent interventions and occupations, however, were hardly as fun-filled as artist James Montgomery Flagg here suggested. And, anti-imperialist critics asked, once you are on the jaguar's back, how do you get off? *Library of Congress.*

of Paris. Harding wanted these peace treaties "so that we may put aside the last remnant" of the war. That month too he opened an international conference in Washington, where the United States insisted on a major reduction in naval armaments to ensure a stable world order. Harding's pardon of Debs was thus but one part of a concerted attempt to heal the wounds of the First World War and to chart a new foreign policy for a warless future.

Harding's desire to shove the war into the past and his emphasis on avoiding entanglements with Europe should not be interpreted to mean that Americans cut themselves off from international affairs after the First World War. To be sure, many Americans had become disillusioned with their war experience. But they remained quite active in the world in the 1920s—from gunboats on Chinese rivers to negotiations in European financial centers to interventions in Latin America. The most useful description of interwar foreign policy is *independent internationalism*. That is, the United States was active on a global scale but retained its independence of action, its traditional unilateralism. Even if they had wanted to, Americans could not have escaped the tumult of international relations; their interests were too far-flung and too vast— colonies, client states, overseas naval bases, investments, trade, missionaries.

At the same time, many Americans called themselves *isolationists*. By that label they meant that they wanted to isolate themselves from Europe's political squabbles, from military alliances and interventions, and from commitments like the League of Nations that might restrict their freedom of choice. Americans, then, were isolationists in their desire to avoid war but independent internationalists in their behavior.

The desire to avoid war led American leaders to search for nonmilitary means to exercise power. In the aftermath of the First World War, Americans had grown disenchanted with military methods of achieving order and protecting American prosperity and security. "We can never herd the world into the paths of righteousness with the dogs of war," Herbert Hoover said. American diplomats thus increasingly emphasized conferences, moral lectures and calls for peace, nonrecognition of disapproved regimes, arms control, and economic and financial ties in accord with the principle of the Open Door. They pulled the marines out of and fashioned a Good Neighbor policy for Latin America.

The United States, however, failed to create a stable world order, largely because severe economic problems undercut stability. The debts and reparations bills left over from the First World War bedeviled leaders in the 1920s, and the Great Depression of the 1930s further disrupted world trade and finance. The depression threatened America's prominence in the international marketplace, but it also spawned revolutions in Latin America and political extremism, militarism, and war in Europe and Asia. As Nazi Germany and Japan traveled the road to world war, the United States sought neutrality.

Yet in the late 1930s, especially after the outbreak of European war in September 1939, Americans,

IMPORTANT EVENTS

1921	Washington Conference opens
1922	Mussolini comes to power in Italy
	Fordney-McCumber Tariff
1924	Dawes Plan for German reparations
	U.S. departs Dominican Republic
1926	American troops occupy Nicaragua
1927	Jiang Jieshi attacks Communists in China
1928	Kellogg-Briand Pact
1929	Onset of the Great Depression
	Young Plan for German reparations
1930	Hawley-Smoot Tariff
1931	Japan seizes Manchuria
1932	Stimson Doctrine
1933	Hitler comes to power in Germany
	U.S. recognition of Soviet Russia
	Good Neighbor policy announced
1934	Batista comes to power in Cuba
	Reciprocal Trade Agreements Act
	Export-Import Bank founded
1935	Italy invades Ethiopia
	Neutrality Act
1936	U.S. votes for nonintervention at Pan American Conference
	Outbreak of Spanish Civil War
	Neutrality Act
1937	Neutrality Act
	"China incident"
	Roosevelt's quarantine speech
1938	Mexico nationalizes American-owned oil companies
	Munich Conference
1939	Nazi-Soviet pact
	Germany invades Poland
	Second World War begins
	U.S. repeals arms embargo
1940	Soviets invade Finland
	Committee to Defend America by Aiding the Allies formed
	Tripartite Pact
	Destroyer-bases deal
	America First Committee formed
	Selective Training and Service Act
1941	Lend-Lease Act
	Germany attacks the Soviet Union
	U.S. freezes Japanese assets
	Atlantic Charter
	Greer incident
	Japan attacks Pearl Harbor
	U.S. enters Second World War

along with President Franklin D. Roosevelt, changed their minds. They believed that Germany and Japan had become unacceptable menaces to the national interest because they intended to build exclusive, self-sufficient spheres of influence based upon military power and economic domination. Roosevelt first appealed for American military preparedness and then worked to abandon neutrality in favor of aiding Britain and France. German victory in Europe, he reasoned, would imperil Western political principles, destroy traditional American economic ties, threaten America's influence in the Western Hemisphere, and place at the pinnacle of European power a fanatical man—Adolf Hitler—whose ambitions and barbarities seemed to know no limits.

At the same time, Japan seemed determined to dismember America's friend China, to emasculate the Open Door principle by creating a closed economic sphere in Asia, and to endanger the American colony of the Philippines. To deter Japanese expansion in the Pacific, the United States ultimately cut off supplies of vital American products like oil. Yet economic warfare had the effect not of containing Japan but rather of intensifying antagonisms. Japan's surprise attack on Pearl Harbor in December 1941 finally brought the United States into the Second World War.

A fundamental clash of orders or systems explains why diplomacy failed and war came. On the one hand, Germany and Japan preferred a world divided into closed spheres of influence. On the other, the United States sought conditions that would ensure it continued international stature and domestic well-being: a liberal, capitalist world order in which all nations enjoyed the freedom to trade with and invest in all other nations. The United States prided itself on its democratic system; Germany and Japan embraced authoritarian regimes with strong military influence. When the United States protested, Berlin and Tokyo reminded Washington of the United States's exclusive sphere in Latin America under the Monroe Doctrine. Axis (German and Italian) and Japanese leaders also charged that Americans were applying a double standard. Had not the United States itself built an empire through conquest, military occupation, and economic privilege, at times violating avowed American principles? Americans rejected such comparisons and claimed that their expansionism had benefited not just themselves but the rest of the world. Because of such different objectives and outlooks, conflict was certainly inevitable. But a difficult question remains: was it inevitable that this clash of systems would lead to war?

The Search for Peace and Order in the 1920s

In the early 1920s Secretary of State Charles Evans Hughes predicted that "there will be no permanent peace unless economic satisfactions are enjoyed." Like the nation's business leaders, Hughes expected continued United States economic expansion to bring about international stability: out of economic prosperity, it was predicted, would spring a world free from political extremes, revolution, arms races, aggression, and war. Such a world never developed.

Europe lay in shambles at the end of the First World War. In the years 1914 to 1921 Europe suffered 60 million casualties from world war, civil war, massacre, epidemic, and famine. Both Germany and France lost 10 percent of their workers. Crops, livestock, factories, trains, forests, bridges—little was spared. The plight of Europeans drew American sympathy and aid. The American Relief Administration delivered food to needy Europeans, including Soviet citizens wracked by famine in 1921 and 1922. All told, private charities and official relief programs delivered foodstuffs worth more than half a billion dollars.

American peace efforts joined American humanitarianism to try to create international stability. During the 1920s and 1930s peace societies advocated numerous strategies to ensure world order: cooperation with the League of Nations, membership in the World Court, disarmament and arms reduction, curbs on exploitative business ventures, arbitration of international disputes, the outlawing of war, and strict neutrality in times of belligerency. Organizations like the Fellowship of Reconciliation, the Women's International League for Peace and Freedom, and the National Council for Prevention of War struggled to remind Americans of the carnage of the First World War and the futility of war as a solution to international problems. Antiwar films like *What Price Glory?* (1926) and *Submarine* (1928) emphasized the cruelties of military combat.

Peace Movement

At the time, the Washington Conference (November 1921–February 1922) seemed a substantial step toward arms control. The United States discussed with eight other nations (Britain, Japan, France, Italy, China, Portugal, Belgium, and the Netherlands) limits on naval armaments. Britain, the United States, and Japan—the three major naval powers—were facing a costly naval arms race, and they welcomed the opportunity to deflect it. As Secretary Hughes argued, arms competition had to stop because huge military expenditures endangered economic rehabilitation.

Washington Conference

In the Five-Power Treaty the delegates set a ten-year moratorium on the construction of capital ships (battleships and aircraft carriers) and established a total tonnage ratio of 5:5:3:1.75:1.75 among the five top nations (Britain, the United States, Japan, France, and Italy). The first three nations actually agreed to dismantle some existing vessels to meet the ratio. They also pledged not to build new fortifications in their Pacific possessions (such as the Philippines for the United States). In the Nine-Power Treaty, the conferees reaffirmed the Open Door in China, recognizing Chinese sovereignty. In the Four-Power Treaty, the United States, Britain, Japan, and France agreed to respect each other's Pacific possessions. The treaties represented a rare example of mutual disarmament. But they did not limit submarines, destroyers, or cruisers; nor did they provide enforcement powers for the Open Door declaration. Subsequent conferences in the 1930s produced meager results, and rearmament rather than disarmament became the thrust of the times.

Peace advocates also placed their hopes on the Kellogg-Briand Pact of 1928, a treaty eventually signed by sixty-two nations. The signatories agreed

> **Kellogg-Briand Pact**

to "condemn recourse to war for the solution of international controversies, and renounce it as an instrument of national policy." The treaty's backers billed it as a first step in a long journey toward international cooperation and the outlawry of war. The document passed the Senate 85 to 1, but many senators thought it no more than a moral statement because it lacked provisions for enforcement. Although weak, the pact reflected popular sentiment that war was barbaric and wasteful, and it prompted people to think about the important issues of peace and war.

The League of Nations, also looked to as a peacemaker, exhibited conspicuous feebleness, not because the United States refused to join, but because members themselves usually chose not to use it to settle disputes. Starting in the mid-1920s, American officials participated discreetly in League meetings on public health, prostitution, drug trafficking, and other questions. By 1930, American "observers" had sat in on over forty League conferences. Individual American jurists like Charles Evans Hughes served on the World Court in Geneva, although the United States also refused to join that institution. Neither the World Court, the League of Nations, nor the Kellogg-Briand Pact proved capable of keeping the peace because economic troubles upended world order.

"Come on in. I'll treat you right. I used to know your daddy." Clarence D. Batchelor's haunting cartoon recalled the human tragedy of the First World War. The artist won a Pulitzer Prize for this antiwar statement. *Library of Congress.*

Instability: The World Economy and the Great Depression

While Europe struggled to recover from the ravages of the First World War and United States economic influence became conspicuous around the world, the international economy wobbled. Then the world economy collapsed in the 1930s after the Great Depression hit. Cordell Hull, secretary of state from 1933 to 1944, often said that economic conditions defined the character of international relations. Hull pointed to political extremism, border squabbles, resurgent militarism, and increased

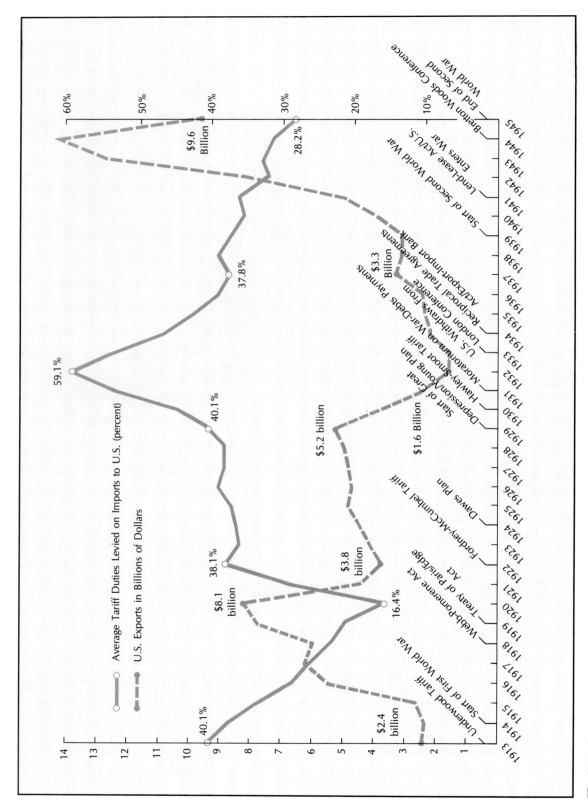

The United States in the World Economy *Source: U.S. Department of Commerce, Historical Statistics of the United States: Colonial Times to 1970* (Washington, D.C., 1975).

military expenditures as products of maimed economies. "We cannot have a peaceful world, we cannot have a prosperous world," he advised, "until we rebuild the international economic structure." Hull proved right; the depression so disoriented world politics that it ranks as one of the main causes of the Second World War.

For those leaders who, like Hughes and Hull, believed that American economic expansion would stabilize world politics, the prominent United States position in the international economy seemed opportune. By the late 1920s the United States produced about half the world's industrial goods, ranked first among exporters ($5.4 billion worth of shipments in 1929), and acted as the financial capital of the world (see figure). During the period from 1914 to 1930 private investments abroad grew fivefold, to over $17 billion. To cite some examples, General Electric joined international cartels and invested heavily in Germany; American companies began to exploit Venezuela's rich petroleum resources; in the Middle East, American companies began to challenge the British for control of oil resources. Britain and Germany lost ground to American businesses in Latin America, where Standard Oil was active in eight nations, the United Fruit Company was a huge landowner, and International Telephone and Telegraph dominated Cuba's communications network.

> **U.S. Economic Expansion**

The United States government facilitated business activities abroad through the 1918 Webb-Pomerene Act (which excluded from antitrust prosecution those combinations set up for export trade); the 1919 Edge Act (which permitted foreign branch banks); and the overseas offices of the Department of Commerce (which gathered important market information). The federal government also stimulated and monitored foreign loans made by American investors, discouraging those that might be used for military purposes. "Any student of modern diplomacy knows," claimed one American diplomat, "that in these days of competition, capital, trade, agriculture, labor and statecraft all go hand in hand if a country is to profit."

Europeans warily watched American economic expansion while they branded Americans stingy for their handling of war debts and reparations. Twenty-eight nations became entangled in the web of inter-Allied debts, which totaled $26.5 billion, about half of it owed to the United States. Europeans urged Americans to erase the debts as a magnanimous contribution to the war effort. During the war, they charged, Europe had bled while America profited. But American leaders insisted on repayment. "They hired the money, didn't they?" President Coolidge reportedly said. Other Americans argued that the victorious European nations had gained vast lands and resources through the war; to cancel their debts would be to increase their spoils even more. Senator George Norris of Nebraska, emphasizing domestic priorities, declared that the United States could build highways in "every county seat" if only the Europeans would pay their debts.

> **War Debts**

The debts question was linked to Germany's $33 billion reparations bill. Hobbled by inflation and economic disorder, Germany began to default on its payments. Americans grew worried that German economic troubles would spawn radicalism.

> **German Reparations**

To keep Germany afloat, American bankers loaned millions of dollars to the floundering nation. A triangular relationship developed: American investors' money flowed to Germany; German reparations payments went to the Allies; the Allies then paid some of their debts to the United States. The American-crafted Dawes Plan of 1924 greased the financial tracks by reducing Germany's annual payments, extending the repayment period, and providing still more loans. The United States also gradually scaled down Allied obligations, cutting the debt by half during the 1920s.

The triangular arrangement, however, was dependent on continued German borrowing in the United States, and in 1928 and 1929 American lending abroad declined sharply in the face of more lucrative opportunities in the stock market. The American-negotiated Young Plan of 1929, which reduced Germany's reparations, salvaged little as the international economy sputtered and collapsed. That year the British rejected an ingenious offer from President Hoover to trade their debt altogether for British Honduras (Belize), Bermuda, and Trinidad. By 1931, when Hoover declared a moratorium on payments, the Allies had paid back only $2.6 billion. Wracked by the Great Depression, which began in 1929 (see Chapter 25), they defaulted on the rest. World trade, heavily dependent on an easy and safe exchange of currencies, also faltered: from 1929 to mid-1933, it declined in value by 40 percent. American exports slumped from $5.4 billion to $2.2 billion at the same time.

By the early 1930s, United States economic power had failed to sustain a healthy world economy. Americans might have worked for a comprehensive, multinational settlement. **Economic Nationalism** Instead of raising their tariff rates, as they did in the acts of 1922 (Fordney-McCumber) and 1930 (Hawley-Smoot), they might have lowered them so that Europeans could sell their goods in the United States and thus earn dollars to pay off their debts. By 1932 about twenty-five nations had retaliated against the American tariff by imposing similar restrictions on American imports. In short, economic nationalism gained momentum. The selfish and vengeful Europeans might have trimmed Germany's huge indemnity. The Germans might have borrowed less from abroad and taxed themselves more. The Soviets might have agreed to pay rather than repudiate Russia's $4 billion indebtedness. Many nations, in short, shared responsibility for the economic cataclysm.

Referring to the world economic emergency in his first inaugural address in 1933, President Franklin D. Roosevelt said that he favored a "practical policy of putting first things first." In other words, he would work to restore world trade, but he would attend first to the emergency at home. Roosevelt thereupon barred American cooperation in international monetary stabilization at the London Conference (1933). Hull disagreed with the president, bemoaning Roosevelt's decision as yet another example of the world's conspicuous nose-dive into economic nationalism and political disequilibrium.

A start-up of world trade, the secretary of state insisted, would not only help the United States pull itself out of the economic doldrums but would also **Reciprocal Trade Agreements Act** boost the chances for global peace. Calling the protective tariff the "king of evils," Hull successfully pressed Congress to pass the Reciprocal Trade Agreements Act in 1934. This important piece of legislation, which would guide American economic foreign policy thereafter, empowered the president to reduce American tariffs by as much as 50 percent through special agreements with foreign countries. The central feature of the act was

the *most-favored-nation principle,* whereby the United States was entitled to the lowest tariff rate set by a nation with which it had an agreement. For example, if Belgium and the United States granted each other most-favored-nation status, and if Belgium negotiated an agreement with Germany that reduced the Belgian tariff on German typewriters, American typewriters would receive the same low rate.

In 1934 Hull also sponsored the creation of the Export-Import Bank, a government agency that provided loans to foreigners for the purchase of American goods. The bank not only stimulated trade but became a formidable diplomatic weapon, allowing the United States to exact concessions through the approval or denial of loans. But Hull's ambitious programs—examples of America's independent internationalism—brought only mixed results in the short term.

Sphere of Influence in Latin America

In United States policy toward Latin America the interwar themes of independent internationalism, isolationism, nonmilitary means, economic expansion, and the destabilizing impact of the Great Depression became prominent. Before the First World War the United States had thrown an imperial net over much of the region by means of the Platt Amendment, the Roosevelt Corollary, construction of the Panama Canal, military intervention, and economic domination. A patronizing attitude permeated United States activities in the region. A leading State Department officer told the Foreign Service School that Latins were incapable of political progress because of their temperament, the tropical climate, and their "low racial quality." They were, however, "very easy people to deal with if properly managed." And managed they were. By the 1920s American-built schools, roads, telephones, and irrigation systems were evident in Latin America. United States financial advisers supervised government budgets in the Caribbean, and in 1920 American soldiers were occupying Cuba, the Dominican Republic, Haiti, Panama, and Nicaragua.

William E. Borah (1865–1940), chairman of the Senate Foreign Relations Committee (left), and Henry L. Stimson (1867–1950), secretary of state (right), were often at odds. The Idaho senator became a passionate anti-imperialist and isolationist who protested United States interventions in Latin America. Because of critics like Borah, Secretary Stimson sought nonmilitary means to maintain United States hegemony in the Western Hemisphere. *Library of Congress.*

A famous Argentine writer, Manuel Ugarte, asserted that the United States had become a new Rome: it annexed wealth rather than territory, enjoying the "essentials of domination" without the "dead-weight of areas to administrate and multitudes to govern." To such criticisms the American ambassador to Chile replied that "American capital will be the controlling factor in public and private finance in these countries. . . . American civilization, material and cultural, is bound to impress itself upon, and I believe, benefit these peoples. If anti-American critics wish to describe this as our 'imperialism' let them make the most of it."

Criticism of American Imperialism

"Imperialism" was exactly what some United States critics saw and protested—especially the military interventions. Senator William Borah of Idaho insisted that Latin Americans be granted the right of self-determination. Others protested that the president was usurping constitutional power by ordering troops abroad without a congressional declaration of war. Businesspeople feared that nationalists would direct their anti-Yanqui feelings against American *gringos* and their property. A double standard also troubled the United States. Secretary of State Henry L. Stimson outlined the problem in 1932 when he was protesting Japanese incursions in China: "If we landed a single soldier among those South Americans now . . . it would put me absolutely in the wrong in China, where Japan has done all this monstrous work under the guise of protecting her nationals with a landing force."

Turning away pragmatically from unpopular military intervention, the United States tried other methods of maintaining its influence in Latin America: Pan-Americanism, support for strong native leaders, the training of national guards, economic penetration, Export-Import Bank loans, and political subversion. Although the process began before his presidency, Franklin D. Roosevelt gave it a name in 1933: the Good Neighbor policy. It meant that the United

Good Neighbor Policy

States would be less blatant in its domination—less willing to defend exploitative business practices, less eager to send in military expeditions, and less wary of consultation with Latin Americans. "Give them a share," FDR recommended. In 1936, for example, the United States restored some sovereignty to Panama and increased that nation's income from the canal. Roosevelt's popularity in Latin America grew enormously for this and other such acts.

United States interests in the hemisphere also grew. From 1914 to 1929, direct American investments in Latin America (excluding bonds and securities) jumped from almost $1.3 billion to $3.5 billion. In the same period American exports to the area tripled in value. In country after country Latin Americans understood the repercussions of American economic and political decisions. The price Americans set for Chilean copper determined the health of the Chilean economy. American oil executives bribed Venezuelan politicians for tax breaks. In Honduras, where United Fruit and Standard Fruit accounted for most of the nation's revenue, American interests so manipulated and disrupted politics that American troops were sent there in 1924 to restore calm and protect property. What was more, American businesses drew substantially greater sums out of Latin America in profits than they put in as investments. Latin American nationalists complained that their resources were being drained away and that many of their own businesspeople put their profits not into investments at home but into New Orleans and New York banks.

The training of national guards went hand in hand with support of dictators. Some Latin American dictators rose to power through the ranks of a national guard trained by the United States. For example, before the United States withdrew its troops from the Dominican Republic in 1924, American personnel created a guard. One of its first officers was Rafael Leonidas Trujillo, who became head of the national army in 1928. Trujillo became president in 1930 through fraud and intimidation and ruled the Dominican Republic with an iron fist until his assassination in 1961. "He may be an S.O.B.," Roosevelt supposedly remarked, "but he is our S.O.B."

> **National Guard in the Dominican Republic**

In Nicaragua the experience was similar. United States troops occupied Nicaragua from 1912 to 1925 and returned in late 1926 during a civil war.

> **Somoza and Sandino in Nicaragua**

Washington claimed that it was only trying to stabilize Nicaragua's politics, but critics at home and abroad saw a case of United States imperialism. Nationalistic Nicaraguan opposition, led by César Augusto Sandino, who denounced the Monroe Doctrine as meaning "America for the Yankees," helped prompt Washington to end the occupation. In 1933 the United States Marines departed; but they left behind a powerful national guard headed by General Anastasio Somoza, who "always played the game fairly with us," according to the top-ranked American military officer there. With American backing, the Somoza family ruled Nicaragua from 1936 to 1979 through corruption, political suppression, and torture. The revolutionaries who overthrew the Somoza dictatorship in 1979 called themselves Sandinistas in honor of the man who, more than three decades earlier, had battled the American marines and had been assassinated by Somoza henchmen.

The marine occupation of black, French-speaking Haiti from 1915 to 1934 also produced a very negative legacy. American officials censored the Haitian press, manipulated elections, wrote the constitution, jailed or killed thousands of protesters, managed government finances, and created a national guard. The National City Bank of New York became the owner of the Haitian Banque Nationale, and the United States became Haiti's largest trading partner. The American high commissioner, General John H. Russell of Georgia, boasted that the Haitian president "has never taken a step without first consulting me." Black leaders in the United States decried this blatant manipulation of foreigners. James Weldon Johnson of the National Association for the Advancement of Colored People reported after a fact-finding trip that Haitians forced to work without pay (the *corvée* system) to build roads "were in the same category with the convicts in the negro chain gangs" of the American South. Indeed, Jim Crow had cut deeply into Haiti.

> **Occupation of Haiti**

When in 1929 Haitians protested violently against American rule, and after an official investigative commission told President Hoover that the occupation had failed to bring benefits to the Haitian people, Washington decided to withdraw its soldiers. Haiti continued to suffer Latin America's highest

In this 1927 photograph American marines are reading comic strips to Nicaraguan children. United States troops actually spent most of their time chasing César Augusto Sandino and his revolutionary forces. Sandino's resistance to United States occupation made him a national hero in Nicaragua. *National Archives.*

illiteracy rate, lowest per capita income, and poorest health, as well as dictatorship and police-state repression. Speaking for many of his compatriots, one Haitian called Americans "exploiters" and asked, "How can they teach us when they have so much to learn themselves?"

The Cubans too grew restless under American domination. By 1929 American investments in the Caribbean nation totaled $1.5 billion, up from $220 million in 1913. Most of this money was bound up in the Cuban sugar industry, about two-thirds of which was in American hands. The American military uniform was conspicuous at the naval base at Guantánamo Bay. Still, during the Cuban revolution of 1933, in open defiance of United States warships cruising offshore, Professor Ramon Grau San Martín became president. Grau declared the Platt Amendment, which accorded the United States the right to

> **Cuban Revolution of 1933**

intervene in Cuban affairs, null and void. His government also seized some American-owned mills, did not repay American bank loans, and talked of land reform. Unsettled by this display of nationalism, United States officials refused to recognize the Grau government and successfully plotted in 1933–1934 with army sergeant Fulgencio Batista to overthrow it. During the dictatorial Batista era, which lasted until 1959, Cuba protected American investments and granted the United States military sites. In return Havana received military aid, Export-Import Bank loans, abrogation of the Platt Amendment, and a favorable sugar tariff.

Mexico, torn by revolution and civil war, presented the United States with a unique case. Woodrow Wilson had sent troops to neighboring Mexico in 1914 and 1916 in an attempt to install a pro–United States government, but the military expeditions only united the Mexican people against the United States. In 1917 the Mexicans adopted a new

At the 1928 Pan American Conference in Havana, Cuba, Latin American representatives applauded the courageous delegate from El Salvador when he introduced a resolution declaring that "no state has the right to intervene in the internal affairs of another." United States delegate Charles Evans Hughes would not tolerate such anti-American, noninterventionist sentiment. He blocked passage, as this cartoon by J. N. "Ding" Darling shows. *Des Moines Register and Tribune Company.*

Confrontation with Mexico constitution specifying that all "land and waters" and all subsoil raw materials (like oil) belonged to the Mexican nation. This nationalistic document represented a threat to American landholdings and petroleum interests. A weak, undeveloped Latin American nation on the United States border had issued a direct challenge to the hemisphere's hegemonic power. If Washington's attention and resources had not been diverted to the First World War, some observers noted, the United States might have taken drastic action against Mexico.

Washington and Mexico City wrangled for years over the rights of American economic interests. Then, in 1938, Mexico boldly expropriated the property of all foreign-owned petroleum companies. The United States countered by reducing purchases of Mexican silver and encouraging a business boycott of the upstart nation. But President Roosevelt decided to compromise because he feared the Mexicans would sell their oil to Germany and Japan. In 1941 the United States conceded that Mexico owned its raw materials and could treat them as it saw fit, and Mexico compensated American companies for their lost property. Although American investments and trade continued to claim an important share of Mexican business, United States power had been diminished. Mexico's defiance of its giant neighbor became an inspiring symbol for other Latin American nationalists.

Roosevelt's movement toward nonmilitary methods—the Good Neighbor policy—can be seen also in Pan-Americanism. Throughout the 1920s the United States had refused to abandon its right of intervention in Latin America. But in 1936, at the Pan American Conference in Buenos Aires, United States officials endorsed nonintervention. Although United States interventionism of a nonmilitary sort remained conspicuous in Latin America, the new policy marked a distinct change from the days of the Roosevelt Corollary and expeditions of marines. One payoff was the Declaration of Panama (1939), wherein Latin American governments drew a security line around the hemisphere and warned aggressors away. In exchange for more trade and foreign aid, Latin Americans also reduced their sales of raw materials to Germany, Japan, and Italy and increased shipments to the United States. On the eve of the Second World War, then, the United States's sphere of influence was virtually intact, and most Latin American regimes backed United States diplomatic objectives.

Upheaval in Europe

In depression-wracked Germany, where 6 million workers were unemployed in the early 1930s, Adolf Hitler came to power in 1933. Like Benito Mussolini, who had gained control of Italy in 1922, Hitler was a fascist. Fascism (called Nazism, or National Socialism, in Germany) was a collection

Hitler's Germany

Chapter 26: Diplomacy in a Broken World, 1920–1941

The bold, militaristic Adolf Hitler (1889–1945), with the ever-present Nazi swastika on his sleeve, ruled Germany from 1933 to 1945. Here he salutes marchers in Nuremberg, 1937. The anti-Semitic Hitler denounced the United States as a "Jewish rubbish heap" of "inferiority and decadence" that was "incapable of conducting war." *Hugo Jaeger,* Life *Magazine,* © *Time, Inc.*

of ideas and prejudices that included supremacy of the state over the individual; of dictatorship over democracy; of authoritarianism over freedom of speech; of a regulated, state-oriented economy over a free market economy; and of militarism and war over peace. The Nazis vowed not only to revive German economic and military strength but to cripple communism and to "purify" the German "race" by subjugating and ultimately destroying Jews.

In 1933, resentful of the punitive terms of the 1919 Treaty of Paris, Hitler pulled Germany out of the League of Nations, ended reparations payments, and began to rearm. Secretly laying plans for the conquest of neighboring states, he watched admiringly as Mussolini's troops invaded the African nation of Ethiopia in 1935. The next year Hitler ordered his goose-stepping troops into the Rhineland, an area the Treaty of Paris had declared demilitarized. Germany's timid neighbor France did not resist this aggressive action. "The world belongs to the man with guts!" crowed Hitler.

Soon the aggressors began to join hands. In the fall of 1936 Italy and Germany formed an alliance called the Rome-Berlin Axis. Shortly thereafter Germany and Japan united against the Soviet Union in the Anti-Comintern Pact. To these events Britain and France responded with a policy of appeasement, hoping to curb Hitler's expansionist appetite by permitting him a few nibbles. But the policy eventually proved disastrous; taking advantage of European caution, the German leader continually raised his demands.

In those hair-trigger times, a civil war in Spain turned into an international struggle. From 1936 to 1939 the Loyalist Republicans battled the fascist-backed insurgents under Francisco Franco. Hitler and Mussolini sent military aid to Franco; the Soviet Union assisted the Loyalists. France and Britain held to the fiction of a nonintervention pledge that even Italy and Germany had signed. About three thousand American volunteers known as the Lincoln Battalion joined the fight on

Spanish Civil War

the side of the Republicans. When Franco won in 1939, his victory tightened the grip of fascism on the European continent.

Early in 1938 Hitler once again tested the limits of European patience when he sent his soldiers into Austria to annex that nation. In September of the same year he seized the Sude-

> **Munich and Poland**

ten region of Czechoslovakia. Appeasement reached its peak that month at the Munich Conference when France and Britain, without consulting the helpless Czechs, agreed to allow Hitler this one last territorial bite. British Prime Minister Neville Chamberlain returned home to proclaim "peace in our time," confident he had satiated the dictator. But in March 1939 Hitler swallowed the rest of Czechoslovakia. Poland was next on his list. Scuttling appeasement, London and Paris announced they would stand by their ally Poland. Undaunted, Berlin signed the Nazi-Soviet Pact with Moscow and launched attacks against Poland on September 1. Britain and France declared war on Germany two days later. The Second World War had begun.

As the world spiraled toward war, the Soviet Union played a key role and stood as a special problem in American foreign relations. Following Wilsonian precedent, the Republi-

> **Relations with the Soviet Union**

can administrations of the 1920s had not recognized the Soviet government, arguing that the Bolsheviks had refused to pay more than $600 million for confiscated American-owned property and had repudiated Russian debts. To Americans the Communists were also godless, radical malcontents bent on destroying the American way of life through world revolution. Yet American businesses like General Electric and International Harvester began to enter the Soviet marketplace, offering technology and machinery. Henry Ford himself signed a contract in 1929 to build a huge automobile plant using mass-production methods called *Fordizatsia*. By 1930 the Soviet Union had become the largest buyer of American farm and industrial equipment.

In the early 1930s, however, trade began to slump. To stimulate business and help the United States pull out of the depression, some businesspeople began to lobby for diplomatic recognition of the Soviet Union. "We would recognize the Devil with a false face if he would contract for some pitchforks," quipped Will Rogers. President Roosevelt agreed that a change in policy was necessary, not only because it would improve trade, but because nonrecognition had failed to alter the Soviet system and closer Soviet-American relations might deter the Japanese.

Practicing personal, one-on-one diplomacy, Roosevelt negotiated in 1933 with Soviet Commissar for Foreign Affairs Maxim Litvinov. They hammered out agreements, some of them vague in language: United States recognition, future discussion of the debts question, a Soviet promise to forgo propagandistic or subversive activities in the United States, and religious freedom and legal rights for Americans in the Soviet Union. The first American embassy in Moscow opened in 1934, but within a few years Soviet-American relations had once again become embittered. Especially upsetting to Americans was the Soviet Union's 1939 pact with Nazi Germany and its grabbing half of Poland after Soviet troops invaded that abused nation. For his part, Soviet leader Josef Stalin believed that the West's appeasement of Hitler had left no choice but to cut a deal with the Nazi ruler.

Isolationism, Roosevelt, and the Neutrality Acts

As depression-induced authoritarianism, racial hatred, and military expansion descended upon Europe and Asia in the 1930s, Americans reasserted their isolationist beliefs (see page 762). The First World War left them with powerful negative lessons: that war disrupts reform movements, undermines civil liberties, dangerously expands federal and presidential power, deranges the economy through inflation and windfall profits for business, and accentuates racial and class tensions (see Chapter 23). A 1937 Gallup poll found that nearly two-thirds of the people asked about the First World War thought American participation had been a mistake. Conservative isolationists feared higher taxes and increased federal power if the nation went to war again. Liberal isolationists spoke of the need to give domestic problems priority and to spend less on the military. Senator Gerald P. Nye of

North Dakota, for example, complained that the federal government appropriated more for the care of National Guard horses than for the Children's Bureau. Critics of many persuasions predicted that in attempting to spread democracy abroad, Americans would lose it at home. The vast majority of isolationists opposed fascism and disapproved aggression, but many resented the fact that some Europeans looked to the United States to do what they themselves refused to do: block Hitler.

Although isolationist thought was strongest in the Midwest and among anti-British ethnic groups, especially German- and Irish-Americans, it was a

▶ **Isolationist Thought**

truly national phenomenon that cut across socioeconomic, ethnic, party, and sectional lines and attracted a majority of the American people. Isolationist leadership in the 1930s included Republicans like Congressman Hamilton Fish of New York, Senator William Borah of Idaho, and former president Herbert Hoover; Democrats like Congressman Maury Maverick of Texas; Socialists like Norman Thomas; Communists and Nazi sympathizers; and pacifists like Congresswoman Jeannette Rankin of Montana. It also included publisher Robert R. McCormick of the *Chicago Tribune,* historian Charles Beard, scientist Albert Einstein, and the popular, anti-Semitic radio priest Charles E. Coughlin. What united these people was the opinion that there were alternatives to American involvement in yet another Old World war that would surely damage the national interest.

Some liberal isolationists, critical of business practices at home, charged that corporate "merchants of death" were undermining the national interest by assisting the aggressors. From 1934 to 1936 a congressional committee chaired by Senator Nye held hearings on the role of business interests in the American decision to enter the First World War. The hearings did not prove that businesspeople and financiers had dragged reluctant Americans into that war, but they did uncover evidence that corporations had bribed foreign politicians to improve arms sales in the 1920s and 1930s and had lobbied against arms control. Records show that isolationists were correct to suspect American business ties with Nazi Germany and fascist Italy. Twenty-six of the top one hundred American corporations in 1937 had contractual agreements with Germany. And after Italy attacked Ethiopia in 1935, American petroleum, copper, and iron and steel scrap exports to Italy increased substantially, despite Roosevelt's call for a moral embargo on such commerce. Du Pont, Standard Oil, General Motors, and Union Carbide executives apparently agreed with a Dow Chemical Company officer who stated, "We do not inquire into the uses of the products. We are interested in selling them." (One exception was the Wall Street firm of Sullivan and Cromwell, which severed lucrative ties with Germany to protest the persecution of Jews.)

President Franklin D. Roosevelt shared isolationist views in the early 1930s. Like his famous older cousin Theodore, Franklin as a young man had believed that the United States should exert leadership in the world community and flex its military muscle to ensure American security and prosperity. FDR was an expansionist and interventionist who had imbibed the belief that Americans knew what was best for other societies (as assistant secretary of the navy under Wilson, he had helped write and impose on Haiti a new constitution). But during the interwar period, like most Americans, Roosevelt talked less about preparedness and more about disarmament and the horrors of war.

Roosevelt revealed his and the nation's preference to avoid European squabbles when he signed a series of neutrality acts. Congress sought to

▶ **Neutrality Acts**

protect the nation by stopping contacts that had compromised American neutrality two decades earlier. The Neutrality Act of 1935 prohibited arms shipments to either side in a war once the president had declared the existence of belligerency. Roosevelt had wanted the authority to name the aggressor and apply an arms embargo against it alone, but Congress was reluctant to leave such matters to the president's discretion. The Neutrality Act of 1936 forbade loans to belligerents. After a joint resolution in 1937 declared the United States neutral in the Spanish Civil War, Roosevelt embargoed arms shipments to both sides. The Neutrality Act of 1937 introduced the cash-and-carry principle: warring nations wishing to trade with the United States would have to pay cash for their purchases and carry the goods away in their own ships. The act also forbade Americans from traveling on the ships of belligerent nations.

Expressing prevailing isolationist opinion and making a pitch for the pacifist vote in the upcoming

In April 1937, when isolationism was strong and neutrality acts were law, these University of Chicago students left their classes to join a national antiwar demonstration. *Wide World Photos.*

election, Roosevelt gave a stirring speech in August 1936 at Chautauqua, New York: "I have seen war. . . . I have seen blood running from the wounded. I have seen men coughing out their gassed lungs. . . . I have seen the agony of mothers and wives. I hate war." He promised that the United States would remain distant from European conflict. During the Czech crisis of 1938 Roosevelt actually endorsed appeasement. The United States, he wrote to Hitler, had "no political involvements in Europe." The results of the Munich Conference, he commented on another occasion, elicited a "universal sense of relief."

Roosevelt's Antiwar Views

But Roosevelt became deeply troubled by the arrogant behavior of the "three bandit nations"— Germany, Italy, and Japan. He expressed disgust with Nazi persecution of the Jews and with Japanese slaughter of Chinese civilians (see pages 778–779). Privately he snarled against the refusal of the British and French to collar Hitler in their own backyards, and he worried that the United States was militarily ill prepared to confront the aggressors.

The United States did not neglect its military. Roosevelt's New Deal public works programs included millions for the construction of new ships. In 1935 the president requested the largest peacetime defense budget in American history; three years later, in the wake of Munich, he asked Congress for funds to build up the air force. "Had we had this summer 5,000 planes and the capacity immediately to produce 10,000 per year," he told advisers, "Hitler would not have dared to take the stand he did." (Whether Hitler would have been deterred by a militarily superior United States is debatable, given the Führer's view of Americans as a mongrel race incapable of playing an important role in foreign affairs.) The president also began to cast about for ways to encourage the British and French to show more backbone. One result was his agreement in January 1939 to sell bombers to France.

In his annual message early in 1939, the president lashed out at the international lawbreakers. Soon afterward he urged Congress to repeal the arms embargo and permit the sale of munitions to

Chapter 26: Diplomacy in a Broken World, 1920–1941

belligerents on a cash-and-carry basis. Roosevelt knew that repeal would aid Britain, which dominated the seas. When the Senate Foreign Relations Committee voted down repeal, Roosevelt raged: "I think we ought to introduce a bill for statues of [Senators] Austin, Vandenberg, Lodge and Taft . . . to be erected in Berlin and put the swastika on them."

When Europe fell into the abyss of war in September 1939, Roosevelt declared neutrality. But unlike Woodrow Wilson, he did not ask Americans to be neutral in thought, and he

> **Repeal of the Arms Embargo**

pressed again for repeal of the arms embargo. Senator Arthur Vandenberg, an isolationist from Michigan, roared back that the United States could not be "an arsenal for one belligerent without becoming a target for the other." After much debate, however, Congress in November lifted the embargo on contraband and approved cash-and-carry exports of arms. Roosevelt was ready to aid the Allies—but short of war.

Japan, China, and a New Order in Asia

If United States power was massive in Latin America and limited in Europe, it was minuscule in Asia. Still, the United States had interests in Asia that needed defense: the Philippines and Pacific islands, religious missions, trade and investments, and the Open Door in China. Americans came to believe that Japan threatened these interests, because the Japanese seemed bent on subjugating China and unhinging the Open Door doctrine of equal trade and investment opportunity. Pearl Buck's best-selling novel *The Good Earth* (1931), made into a widely distributed film six years later, confirmed their opinion with its image of the noble, persevering Chinese peasant. In traditional missionary fashion, Americans believed they were China's special friend, its protector and uplifter. "With God's help," Senator Kenneth Wherry of Nebraska proclaimed, "we will lift Shanghai up and up, ever up, until it is just like Kansas City."

But the Chinese themselves were uneasy about the American presence in Asia and, like the Japa-

Jiang Jieshi (1887–1976) and his wife Soong Meiling were *Time* magazine's 1937 Man and Wife of the Year. Their anticommunism and resistance to Japanese aggression earned Jiang's regime favor in the United States. *Reprinted by permission from* Time, *the Weekly Newsmagazine; Copyright Time Inc. 1938.*

nese, wished to exclude white foreigners from Asia. The highly nationalistic Chinese Revolution of 1911 still rumbled in the 1920s; antiforeign riots damaged American property and imperiled American missionaries, business representatives, and sailors. Chinese nationalists complained that Americans joined with other imperialists in the practice of extraterritoriality (the exemption of foreigners accused of crimes from Chinese legal jurisdiction) and demanded an end to this affront to Chinese sovereignty.

In the late 1920s Jiang Jieshi (Chiang Kai-shek) emerged as the leader of this convulsed nation.

> **Rise of Jiang Jieshi in China**

Jiang ousted Communists from the Guomindang party, forcing Mao Zedong and his followers to flee to the hills. Americans ap-

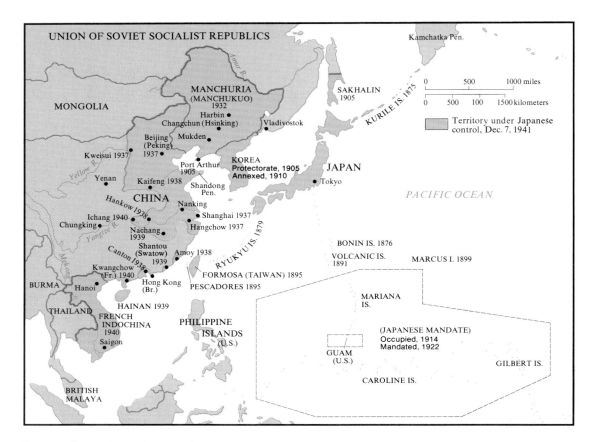

Japanese Expansion Before Pearl Harbor

plauded this display of anti-Bolshevism and Jiang's conversion in 1930 to Christianity. Jiang's new wife, Soong Meiling, also won their hearts. The American-educated daughter of a Chinese businessman, Madame Jiang spoke flawless English, dressed in Western fashion, and cultivated close social and political ties with prominent Americans. Warming to Jiang, United States officials signed a treaty in 1928 restoring control of tariffs to the Chinese. American gunboats and marines remained in China, however.

The Japanese grew increasingly suspicious of United States–Chinese ties. In the early twentieth century Japanese-American relations were seldom cordial. Japan intruded more and more into China, driving economic and political stakes into Manchuria, Shandong, and neighboring Korea. The Japanese were determined not only to oust Western imperialists from Asia but also to dominate Asian territories that produced the raw materials their island nation depended on. Proud Japanese also resented the discriminatory immigration law of 1924 (see page 713), which excluded them from entry into the United States. Despite the Washington Conference treaties of 1922, naval competition continued; in fact, American naval officers, betting on a future war with Japan, used that country as the imaginary enemy on the war-game board at the Naval War College. Finally, although the volume of Japanese-American trade was twice that of Chinese-American trade, commercial rivalry strained relations between Japan and the United States. American producers and workers whose profits and jobs were threatened by the importation of inexpensive Japanese goods, especially textiles, organized "Buy America" campaigns and boycotts.

Relations deteriorated further after the Japanese military seized Manchuria in September 1931 (see

Japanese Seizure of Manchuria

map). Only nominally a Chinese region, Manchuria was important to the Japanese both as a buffer against the Russians and as a vital source of coal, iron, timber, and food. More than half of Japan's foreign investments rested in Manchuria; the South Manchurian Railway, which the Chinese wanted to take over, linked the extensive Japanese holdings. "We are seeking room that will let us breathe," said a Japanese politician, arguing that his tiny, heavily populated nation (65 million people in an area slightly smaller than California) needed to expand in order to survive. Although the seizure of Manchuria violated the Nine-Power Treaty and the Kellogg-Briand Pact, the United States did not have the power to compel Japanese withdrawal. The American response therefore went no further than a moral lecture called the Stimson Doctrine (1932): the United States would not recognize any impairment of China's sovereignty or of the Open Door policy, Secretary of State Henry L. Stimson declared.

Hardly cowed by protests from Western capitals, Japan continued to harry China. In mid-1937 full-scale Sino-Japanese war erupted, although Tokyo preferred to call it the "China incident" to maintain the fiction that it had not violated the Kellogg-Briand Pact. The Japanese seized cities and bombed innocent civilians. Senator Norris, an isolationist who moved further away from his isolationism with each new Japanese thrust, condemned the Japanese as "disgraceful, ignoble, barbarous, and cruel, even beyond the power of language to describe." In an effort to help China, Roosevelt refused to declare the existence of war, thus not invoking the Neutrality Acts and thereby allowing the Chinese to buy weapons in the United States. In a stirring speech denouncing the aggressors in October 1937, he called for a "quarantine" to curb the "epidemic of world lawlessness." People who thought Washington had been too gentle with Japan cheered. Confirmed isolationists warned that the president was edging toward war. Actually, Roosevelt had formulated no program to halt the Japanese. When in late 1937 Japanese aircraft sank the American gunboat *Panay,* an escort for Standard Oil Company tankers on the Yangtze River, Roosevelt demanded an apology but stopped short of retaliation. He was much relieved when Tokyo apologized and offered to pay for damages.

Japan's declaration of a "New Order" in Asia "banged, barred, and bolted" the Open Door, as one American official observed. Alarmed, the Roosevelt administration found small ways to assist China and thwart Japan in 1938 and 1939. Military

Japanese soldiers in the streets of Shanghai, China, September 1937, after fierce fighting with Chinese troops. Shanghai was battered by Japanese bombing raids and shelling from offshore warships. After suffering huge casualties, Jiang Jieshi's forces retreated in defeat. "The defense of Shanghai," historian Barbara Tuchman has written, "made the world China-conscious." *Wide World Photos.*

equipment flowed to the Chinese, as did a $25 million loan. Secretary of State Hull declared a moral embargo against the shipment of airplanes to Japan. The United States Navy continued to grow, helped by a billion-dollar congressional appropriation in 1938. In mid-1939 the United States abrogated the 1911 Japanese-American trade treaty; yet America continued to ship oil, cotton, and machinery to Japan. The administration hesitated to initiate economic sanctions because such economic pressure might spark a Japanese-American war at a time when Germany posed the more serious threat. When war broke out in Europe in 1939, Japanese-American relations were stalemated.

Collision Course, 1939–1941

"What worries me, especially," President Roosevelt told interventionist William Allen White in late 1939, "is that public opinion over here is patting itself on the back every morning and thanking God for the Atlantic Ocean [and the Pacific]." The European war, he went on, seriously jeopardized American security, and the American people had better recognize their precarious place in world affairs. Polls showed that Americans strongly favored the Allies and that most supported aid to Britain and France—but the great majority emphatically wanted the United States to remain at peace. Troubled by this conflicting advice—defeat Hitler, aid the Allies, but stay out of war—the president between 1939 and 1941 gradually moved the nation from neutrality to undeclared war and then to war itself.

During those tense months of inching toward belligerency, isolationist sentiment declined. Alarmed by the swift defeat of one European nation after another, some liberals left the isolationist fold, which became more and more the province of conservatives. Die-hard isolationists organized the America First Committee in the fall of 1940; interventionists, meanwhile, joined the Committee to Defend America by Aiding the Allies (formed in mid-1940). Roosevelt called the isolationists "ostriches" and charged that some were pro-Nazi subversives—"conscious disorganizers or unwitting dupes." The White House began to turn over to the Federal Bureau of Investigation letters that criticized Roosevelt's foreign policy.

In September 1939 Poland succumbed to German stormtroopers in two weeks (see map). In November Soviet forces marched into Finland,

> **Fall of France**

prompting Roosevelt to denounce "this dreadful rape"; by March 1940 Finland had been defeated. The following month Germany invaded Denmark and Norway, a month later the Netherlands and Belgium. "The small countries are smashed up, one by one, like matchwood," sighed the new British Prime Minister Winston Churchill. In May 1940 several German divisions attacked France. By early June they had pushed French and British forces to the English Channel. At Dunkirk, more than 300,000 Allied soldiers, leaving their equipment on the beaches, frantically escaped to Britain on a flotilla of small boats. France's collapse stunned Americans, who wondered if the Nazis would next quickly conquer Britain.

After a worried Roosevelt tried futilely to draw the belligerents to the peace table, he told his advisers that though he was "not willing to fire the first shot," he was waiting for some incident to bring the United States into the war. In the meantime, assuring people that New Deal reforms would not have to be sacrificed to achieve military preparedness, Roosevelt began to aid the beleaguered Allies to prevent the fall of Britain. In May 1940 he had ordered the sale of surplus First World War equipment to Britain and France. In July he cultivated bipartisan support by naming Republicans Henry L. Stimson and Frank Knox, ardent backers of aid to the Allies, secretaries of war and the navy respectively. In September, by executive agreement, he traded fifty old American destroyers for leases to eight British bases, including Newfoundland, Bermuda, and Jamaica.

Two weeks later Roosevelt signed into law the hotly debated and narrowly passed Selective Training and Service Act, the first peacetime military

> **Selective Service Act**

draft in American history. The act called for the registration of all men between the ages of twenty-one and thirty-five. Soon more than 16 million men had been signed up, and draft notices began to be delivered. Ironically, Roosevelt won re-election that fall with promises of peace: "Your boys are not going to be sent into any foreign wars." Republican candidate Wendell Willkie, who in the emerging spirit of bipartisanship had not made an issue of foreign policy, snapped, "That hypocritical son of a bitch! This is going to beat me!" It did.

Roosevelt claimed that the United States could keep out of the war if America enabled the British to win. The United States must become the "great arsenal of democracy." In January

> **Lend-Lease Act**

1941 the administration sent the controversial Lend-Lease bill to Congress. Because Britain was broke, the president said, the United States should lend rather than sell weapons, much as a neighbor lends a garden hose to fight a fire. Roosevelt's analogy did not persuade strict isolationist Senator

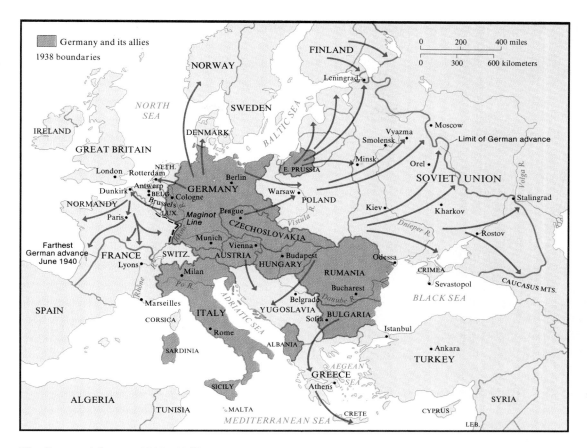

The German Advance, 1939–1942

Burton K. Wheeler of Montana, who shouted out another comparison: Lend-Lease was "the New Deal's triple A foreign policy; it will plow under every fourth American boy." But in March 1941, with pro-British sentiment running high, the House passed the Lend-Lease Act 317 to 71; the Senate followed suit 60 to 31. The initial appropriation was $7 billion, but by the end of the war the amount had reached $50 billion, over $31 billion of it for England.

To ensure the safe delivery of Lend-Lease goods, Roosevelt ordered the navy to patrol halfway across the Atlantic and sent American troops to Greenland. In June 1941 Hitler struck the Soviet Union (two months earlier, in anticipation of just such an attack, the Soviets had signed a neutrality treaty with Japan, thereby reducing the chances that they would have to fight a two-front war). In July, arguing that Iceland was essential to the defense of the Western Hemisphere, Roosevelt dispatched four

thousand marines there. He also sent Lend-Lease aid to the Soviet Union. If the Soviets could hold off the more than two hundred German divisions engaged in the east, Britain would gain some breathing time. Churchill, who had thundered loudly against the Communists for years, now applauded aid to the Soviets: "If Hitler invaded Hell I would make at least a favorable reference to the Devil in the House of Commons."

In August 1941 Churchill and Roosevelt met for four days off Newfoundland. They got along well, trading naval stories, paying deference to one another, and taking pleasure in the fact that Churchill was half American. "It is fun to be in the same decade with you," Roosevelt later wrote to his new friend.

"Atlantic Charter" Conference

At this conference the two leaders issued the Atlantic Charter, a set of war aims reminiscent of Wilsonianism (see pages 668, 678): collective se-

President Franklin D. Roosevelt (1882–1945) (left) and Prime Minister Winston S. Churchill (1874–1965) (right) confer on board a ship in the quiet waters of Placentia Bay, near Newfoundland. At this August 1941 summit meeting, they signed the Atlantic Charter. When Churchill returned to England, he told his war cabinet that Roosevelt had promised to "wage war" against Germany and do "everything" to "force an incident." Although these words forecast FDR's policies for the remainder of 1941, they stopped short of a firm American commitment to war. *Franklin D. Roosevelt Library, Hyde Park, New York.*

curity, disarmament, self-determination, economic cooperation, and freedom of the seas. Later, on January 1, 1942, twenty-six nations signed the Declaration of the United Nations, pledging allegiance to the charter. According to Churchill, the president told him in Newfoundland that although he could not ask Congress for a declaration of war against Germany, "he would wage war" and "become more and more provocative."

In September 1941, there occurred the incident Roosevelt had been waiting for: the American destroyer *Greer* was fired on (but not hit) by a German submarine. In a special national radio broadcast the president protested German "piracy" and announced a policy he had privately promised to Churchill: American naval vessels would now convoy British merchant ships all the way to Iceland and shoot German submarines, the "rattle-

snakes of the Atlantic," on sight. Roosevelt practiced deliberate deception in the *Greer* case, for he did not mention that the *Greer* had been tailing a German U-boat for hours and radioing the submarine's location to British airplanes hunting the ship with depth charges. He and his advisers thought it necessary to manipulate public opinion in order to scare Americans into defending Britain.

The United States had in essence entered into an undeclared war with Germany. When in early October a German submarine torpedoed the American destroyer *Kearny* off the coast of Iceland, the president announced that "the shooting has started. And history has recorded who fired the first shot." When later that month the destroyer *Reuben James* went down with the loss of over one hundred American lives, Congress scrapped the cash-and-carry policy and further revised the Neutrality Acts to permit the transport of munitions to England on armed American merchant ships. When would war be declared? tense observers asked themselves.

In retrospect it seems ironic that the Second World War came to the United States by way of Asia, where Roosevelt so wanted to avoid it in order to concentrate American resources on the defeat of Germany.

> **Cutoff of Trade with Japan**

In September 1940, after Germany, Italy, and Japan had signed the Tripartite Pact, Roosevelt slapped an embargo on shipments of aviation fuel and scrap metal to Japan. Because the president believed the petroleum-thirsty Japanese would consider a cutoff of oil a life-or-death matter, he did not stop that vital commodity. But after Japanese troops occupied French Indochina in July 1941, Washington froze Japanese assets in the United States, virtually ending trade (including oil) with Japan.

Tokyo recommended a high-level meeting between President Roosevelt and Prime Minister Prince Konoye, but the United States rejected the idea. American officials insisted that the Japanese first agree to respect China's sovereignty and territorial integrity and to honor the Open Door policy—in short, to get out of China. Although the American public, according to polls in the fall of 1941, seemed willing to risk war with Japan to thwart further aggression, Roosevelt was not ready for an Asian war; Europe still claimed first priority. Still, he would not back down in Asia, and he supported Secretary of State Hull's hard-line policy against Japan's pursuit of the Greater East Asia Co-Prosperity Sphere—the name Tokyo gave to the vast Asian region it intended to dominate.

Roosevelt told his advisers to string out Japanese-American talks to gain time—time to fortify the Philippines and time to check the fascists in Europe. "Let us do nothing to precipitate a crisis," he told the cabinet in November 1941. By breaking the Japanese code through Operation Magic, Americans learned that Tokyo had committed itself to war with the United States if shipments of oil did not resume. In late November the Japanese rejected American proposals that they withdraw from Indochina. On December 1 decoding experts informed the president that Japanese task forces were being ordered into battle. Why not attack first? asked aide Harry Hopkins. No, said Roosevelt, "we would have to wait until it came." Secretary Stimson explained later that the United States let Japan fire the first shot so as "to have the full support of the American people" and "so that there should remain no doubt in anyone's mind as to who were the aggressors."

The Japanese plotted a daring raid on Pearl Harbor in Hawaii. A flotilla of Japanese aircraft carriers crossed 3,000 miles of ocean undetected. On the morning of December 7, 350 planes stamped with a red sun—representing the Japanese flag—swept down on the unsuspecting

> **Pearl Harbor**

American naval base and nearby airfields, killing more than 2,400 people, sinking or damaging eight battleships, and smashing aircraft (three American Pacific aircraft carriers, at sea, escaped the disaster). Roosevelt was distressed that his proud navy had been caught by surprise, but like many Americans he felt relief after the weeks of tension.

How could the stunning attack on Pearl Harbor have happened? Americans asked. Roosevelt did not, as some critics charged, conspire to leave the fleet vulnerable to attack so that the United States could enter the Second World War through the "back door" of Asia. The base was not ready—not on red alert—because a message of warning from Washington, mistakenly transmitted by a slow method, arrived too late. Base commanders were relaxed, thinking Hawaii too far from Japan to be a target for all-out attack. They expected the assault to come at British Malaya, Thailand, or the Philippines. The terrible tragedy at Pearl Harbor stemmed from mistakes, not conspiracy.

On December 8, referring to the previous day as a "date which will live in infamy," Roosevelt asked Congress for a declaration of war against Japan. A unanimous vote in the Senate and a 388 to 1 vote in the House thrust America into war. (Representative Jeannette Rankin of Montana alone voted "no," matching her vote against entry into the First World War.) Three days later Germany and Italy declared war against the United States. Winston Churchill was pleased that America was now fully at war. "Hitler's fate was sealed," he wrote in his memoirs. "Mussolini's fate was sealed. As for the Japanese, they would be ground to powder. . . . I went to bed and slept the sleep of the saved and thankful."

The war was now a global conflict. The old emphasis on independent internationalism, on economic and nonmilitary means to peace, seemed archaic at that moment. The Great Depression, which had brought on so much of the international

December 7, 1941. The daring Japanese attack on Pearl Harbor, Hawaii, caught the United States by surprise. Rescuers struggle to save survivors of one of the crippled American warships, the USS *West Virginia*. *U.S. Army.*

havoc, also faded in memory as the economy geared up for war. The Neutrality Acts, which had been designed to insulate the United States from European troubles, had been gradually revised and retired. President Roosevelt had wanted to avoid American entry into a second world war, yet he sought also to aid the Allies and thwart Japanese aggression. What he had tried to avoid he could not. He ultimately believed that the United States, deeply involved in international affairs and with economic and strategic interests to protect, had to prevent the world from being divided into exclusive spheres of influence, some of which would be ruled by fascists and militarists. The perennial American desire to set things right also compelled action. As publisher Henry Luce put it in his best-selling book *American Century* (1941), the United States must "exert upon the world the full impact of our influence, for such purposes as we see fit and by such means as we see fit."

As they had so many times before, Americans flocked to the colors. Isolationists now joined the president in spirited calls for victory. "We are going to win the war, and we are going to win the peace that follows," Roosevelt predicted.

Suggestions for Further Reading

General and 1920s Foreign Policy

Thomas H. Buckley, *The United States and the Washington Conference, 1921–1922* (1970); Warren I. Cohen, *Empire Without Tears* (1987); Frank Costigliola, *Awkward Domin-ion* (1984) (on Europe); Robert H. Ferrell, *American Diplo-macy in the Great Depression* (1957); Peter G. Filene, *Americans and the Soviet Experiment, 1917–1933* (1967); Melvyn P. Leffler, *The Elusive Quest* (1979); Elting E. Morison,

Turmoil and Tradition (1964) (on Stimson); Arnold A. Offner, *The Origins of the Second World War* (1975); Emily S. Rosenberg, *Spreading the American Dream* (1982); Michael S. Sherry, *The Rise of American Airpower* (1987); Raymond Sontag, *A Broken World, 1919–1939* (1971); Joan Hoff Wilson, *Herbert Hoover* (1975).

The Peace Movement and Kellogg-Briand Pact

Charles Chatfield, *For Peace and Justice: Pacifism in America, 1914–1941* (1971); Charles DeBenedetti, *The Peace Reform in American History* (1980); Charles DeBenedetti, *Origins of the Modern American Peace Movement, 1915–1929* (1978); Robert H. Ferrell, *Peace in Their Time* (1952); Lawrence Wittner, *Rebels Against War* (1984).

The United States in the World Economy

Frederick Adams, *Economic Diplomacy* (1976); Derek H. Aldcroft, *From Versailles to Wall Street, 1919–1929* (1977); Herbert Feis, *The Diplomacy of the Dollar, 1919–1932* (1950); Lloyd C. Gardner, *Economic Aspects of New Deal Diplomacy* (1964); Michael J. Hogan, *Informal Entente* (1977) (on Anglo-American relations); Charles Kindleberger, *The World in Depression* (1973); Stephen J. Randall, *United States Foreign Oil Policy, 1919–1948* (1986); Mira Wilkins, *The Maturing of Multinational Enterprise* (1974); Joan Hoff Wilson, *American Business and Foreign Policy, 1920–1933* (1971).

Latin America

Cole Blasier, *The Hovering Giant* (1976); Bruce J. Calder, *The Impact of Intervention* (1984) (on the Dominican Republic); Alton Frye, *Nazi Germany and the American Hemisphere, 1933–1941* (1967); Irwin F. Gellman, *Good Neighbor Diplomacy* (1979); David Green, *The Containment of Latin America* (1971); Walter LaFeber, *Inevitable Revolutions* (1983) (on Central America); Lester D. Langley, *The United States and the Caribbean, 1900–1970* (1980); Neil Macaulay, *The Sandino Affair* (1967); Lorenzo Meyer, *Mexico and the United States in the Oil Controversy, 1917–1942* (1977); Richard Millett, *Guardians of the Dynasty* (1977) (on Nicaragua); Louis A. Pérez, *Cuba* (1988); Louis A. Pérez, *Cuba Under the Platt Amendment* (1986); Stephen G. Rabe, *The Road to OPEC* (1982) (on Venezuela); Robert I. Rotberg, *Haiti* (1971); Karl M. Schmitt, *Mexico and the United States, 1821–1973* (1974); Robert F. Smith, *The United States and Revolutionary Nationalism in Mexico, 1916–1932* (1972); Bryce Wood, *The Making of the Good Neighbor Policy* (1961).

Isolationism and Isolationists

Warren I. Cohen, *The American Revisionists* (1967); Wayne S. Cole, *Roosevelt and the Isolationists, 1932–1945* (1983); Wayne S. Cole, *America First* (1953); Manfred Jonas, *Isolationism in America, 1935–1941* (1966); Thomas C. Kennedy, *Charles A. Beard and American Foreign Policy* (1975); Richard Lowitt, *George W. Norris,* 3 vols. (1963–1978); John Wiltz, *In Search of Peace: The Senate Munitions Inquiry, 1934–1936* (1963).

Europe, the Coming of World War II, and Roosevelt

Edward Bennett, *Recognition of Russia* (1970); James MacGregor Burns, *Roosevelt: The Lion and the Fox* (1956); J. Garry Clifford and Samuel R. Spencer, Jr., *The First Peacetime Draft* (1986); James V. Compton, *The Swastika and the Eagle* (1967); David H. Culbert, *News for Everyman: Radio and Foreign Affairs in Thirties America* (1976); Robert Dallek, *Franklin D. Roosevelt and American Foreign Policy, 1932–1945* (1979); Robert A. Divine, *The Reluctant Belligerent,* 2nd ed. (1979); Robert A. Divine, *Roosevelt and World War II* (1969); Waldo H. Heinrichs, Jr., *Threshold of War* (1988); Manfred Jonas, *The United States and Germany* (1984); Warren F. Kimball, *The Most Unsordid Act: Lend-Lease, 1939–1941* (1969); Thomas R. Maddux, *Years of Estrangement* (1980) (on relations with the Soviet Union); Arnold A. Offner, *American Appeasement* (1969); Julius W. Pratt, *Cordell Hull,* 2 vols. (1964); David Reynolds, *The Creation of the Anglo-American Alliance, 1937–1941* (1982); Bruce Russett, *No Clear and Present Danger* (1972); David F. Schmitz, *The United States and Fascist Italy, 1922–1944* (1988); Richard Steele, *Propaganda in an Open Society: The Roosevelt Administration and the Media, 1933–1941* (1985).

China, Japan, and the Coming of War in Asia

Charles A. Beard, *President Roosevelt and the Coming of the War, 1941* (1948); Dorothy Borg and Shumpei Okomoto, eds., *Pearl Harbor as History* (1973); R. J. C. Butow, *Tojo and the Coming of War* (1961); Warren I. Cohen, *America's Response to China,* 2nd ed. (1980); Roger Dingman, *Power in the Pacific* (1976); Herbert Feis, *The Road to Pearl Harbor* (1950); Waldo H. Heinrichs, Jr., *American Ambassador* (1966) (on Grew); Akira Iriye, *The Origins of the Second World War in Asia and the Pacific* (1987); Akira Iriye, *Across the Pacific* (1967); Akira Iriye, *After Imperialism: The Search for a New Order in the Far East, 1921–1931* (1965); Charles Neu, *The Troubled Encounter* (1975); Paul W. Schroeder, *The Axis Alliance and Japanese-American Relations, 1941* (1958); Jonathan Utley, *Going to War with Japan* (1985).

Pearl Harbor

Martin V. Melosi, *The Shadow of Pearl Harbor* (1977); Gordon W. Prange, *Pearl Harbor* (1986); Gordon W. Prange, *At Dawn We Slept* (1981); John Toland, *Infamy* (1982); Roberta Wohlstetter, *Pearl Harbor* (1962).

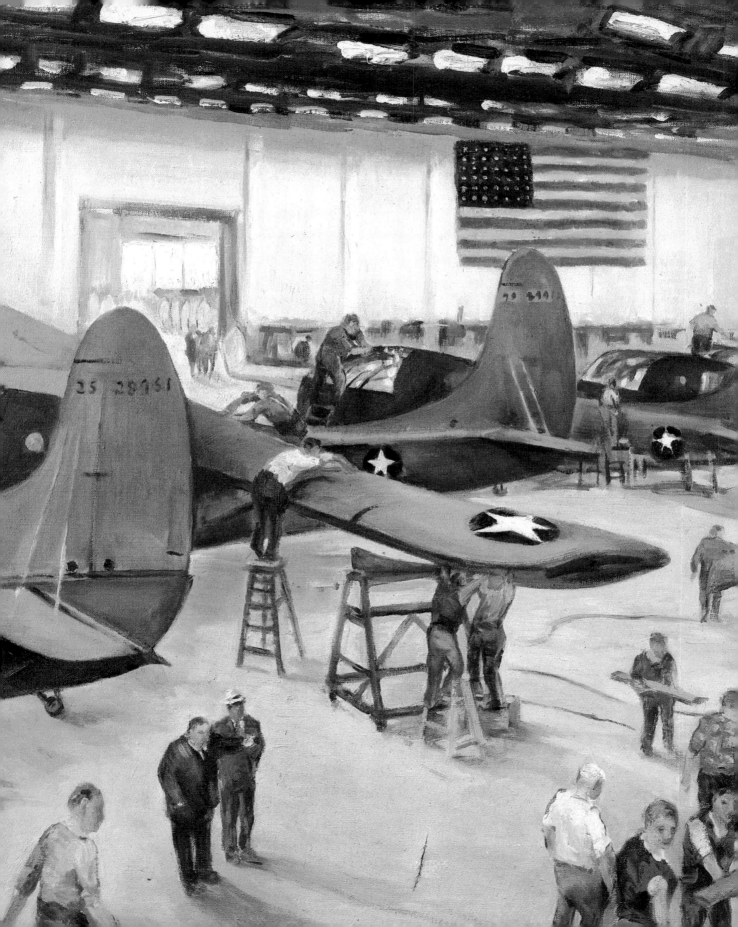

Elliott Johnson was dining with three friends in a Chinese restaurant in Portland, Oregon, when he learned of the attack. It was December 7, 1941. Bursting through the double doors of the kitchen came the restaurant owner; the portable radio he was carrying told the news of the Japanese bombing of Pearl Harbor. "We were furious," Johnson recalled. "No one's gonna come in our country. We immediately went to the marine recruiting headquarters," where they joined a line two blocks long. But before Johnson could enlist, the recruiter barked at him: "Step out of line, you're getting a Dear John letter from the President." The next day, Johnson received the letter; and on January 12, he was inducted into the army.

Two-and-a-half years later, as a lieutenant in charge of an artillery company, Johnson participated in the D-Day invasion of Europe. On the morning of June 6, 1944, he remembered, "we took off." Johnson and his men were aboard a 300-foot long "landing ship tank" (LST), which had "a great mouth in front of which was the ramp" for unloading the soldiers and supplies. While the craft was approaching Normandy beach, Johnson saw another LST take "a direct hit and go up in a huge ball of flames" and "there were bodies floating, face down, face up." The young naval officer at the helm of Johnson's LST announced that he "wasn't gonna take us up that beach. . . . We could swim ashore, but we'd never make it, we were loaded with so much paraphernalia. So I ended up taking my gun out on him. Shoved it in his mouth. . . . He finally got us to where we were in about three feet of water and he said, 'I just can't go any more.' Fine, let down the ramp."

Like many soldiers, sailors, and marines, Elliott Johnson found that during the Second World War his life changed in profound ways. For one thing, it took the war "to hammer it home to me: I am totally averse to killing and warfare. I saw it with my own eyes and it didn't do a dadratted thing. And the wonderful boys we lost over there. It took four years out of my life." Contrary to Johnson, most home-front Americans believed that their nation had fought for noble purposes and that war was a proper instrument of national policy. But whether overseas or at home, few disagreed

27

THE SECOND WORLD WAR AT HOME AND ABROAD, 1941–1945

The O-2 by Guy Wiggins, 1943 (detail). Oil on canvas. Painted for the Pratt-Read Corporation (manufacturers of ivory piano keyboards), showing the company's wartime production of cargo and training gliders. *Courtesy Grogan & Company.*

that the Second World War was a watershed in the country's development.

For forty-five months Americans fought abroad to subdue the Nazi and Japanese aggressors. After military engagements against fascists in North Africa and Italy, American troops joined the dramatic crossing of the English Channel on D-Day in June 1944. The massive invasion forced the Germans to retreat through France to Germany. Battered by merciless bombing raids, leaderless after Adolf Hitler's suicide, and pressed by a Russian advance from the east, the Nazis capitulated in May 1945. In the Pacific, Americans drove the Japanese from one island after another before turning to the just-tested atomic bombs that demolished Hiroshima and Nagasaki and helped spur a Japanese surrender in August.

Throughout the war the Allies—Britain, Russia, and the United States—were held together by their common goal of defeating Germany. But they squabbled over many issues: when the second, or western, front would be opened; how a new international organization would be structured; how Eastern Europe, liberated from the Germans, would be reconstructed; how Germany itself would be governed after defeat. At the end of the war Allied leaders seemed more intent on keeping and expanding their own nations' spheres of influence than on building a community of mutual interest. The United States and the Soviet Union emerged from the war as major competitors in a world facing the task of reconstruction. The prospects for postwar international cooperation seemed bleak, and the advent of an atomic age with nuclear weapons frightened people everywhere.

The atomic bomb was a milestone in world affairs, but events on the home front transformed American life in different ways. The nation united behind the war effort, collecting scrap iron, rubber, and old newspapers and planting victory gardens. But more than national unity and enthusiasm were required to win the war. Essential to victory was the successful mobilization of all sectors of the economy—industry, finance, agriculture, and labor. The federal government had the monumental task of coordinating these several elements, as well as a couple of new ones: higher education and science. For this was a scientific and technological war, supported by the development of new weapons like radar and the atomic bomb.

For millions of Americans the war was a time to relocate in other parts of the country. Between 1941 and 1945, over 16 million men and women served in the armed forces. They traveled to new duty stations in the United States and abroad, acquired new skills, and broadened their horizons. But at war's end they were older, both physically and emotionally, and many felt they had sacrificed the best years of their lives. Also on the move during the Second World War were blacks, Mexican-Americans, and whites who migrated to war-production centers in the North and the West. For numerous African-Americans, the war offered new economic and political opportunities, encouraging them to demand their full rights as citizens. But it also provided the ingredients of racial violence; in 1943, race riots erupted across the country.

Employers' negative attitudes toward women workers eased during the Second World War, and millions of married middle-class women, many of them over age thirty-five, took jobs in war industries. For some, work was an economic necessity; for others, it was a patriotic obligation. Whatever the motivation, paying jobs brought women benefits—financial independence and enhanced self-esteem—that many were reluctant to give up at war's end.

The United States underwent profound change during the course of the war. Its big businesses got even bigger, as did its labor unions. The federal government also experienced tremendous growth in its budget and bureaucracy. Furthermore, the experiences of the First World War and the New Deal proved an inadequate guide in this longer, more demanding conflict. For all of these reasons the Second World War was a turning point in American history.

Winning the Second World War

"We are now in the midst of a war, not for conquest, not for vengeance, but for a world in which this Nation, and all that this Nation represents, will be safe for our children." President Franklin D. Roosevelt was speaking just two days after the surprise attack on Pearl Harbor. Few Americans knew much about the principles of the Atlantic Charter

1941	Japan attacks Pearl Harbor; U.S. enters Second World War
1942	National War Labor Board established
	War Production Board established
	Internment of more than 110,000 Japanese-Americans in "relocation centers"
	War Manpower Commission established
	Bataan Death March
	Battles of Coral Sea and Midway
	Office of War Information established
	Manhattan Project established
	Allied invasion of North Africa
	Republican gains in Congress
	Synthetic-rubber program begins
1943	Russian victory at Stalingrad
	Strikes by soft-coal and anthracite miners
	Office of War Mobilization established
	War Labor Disputes (Smith-Connally) Act
	Race riots in Detroit, Harlem, and 45 other cities
	Allied invasion of Italy
	Teheran Conference
1944	Roosevelt requests Economic Bill of Rights
	War Refugee Board established
	Supreme Court upholds Japanese-American internment
	GI Bill of Rights
	Normandy landings (D-Day)
	Dumbarton Oaks Conference
	Roosevelt re-elected
	U.S. retakes the Philippines
1945	Yalta Conference
	Battles of Iwo Jima and Okinawa
	Roosevelt dies; Truman assumes the presidency
	United Nations founded
	Germany surrenders
	Potsdam Conference
	First atomic bomb exploded in test at Alamogordo, New Mexico
	Atomic bombs devastate Hiroshima and Nagasaki
	Japan surrenders

(see page 781) or about United States war aims. But practically without exception they believed with Roosevelt that they were defending their homes and families against aggressive and satanic Japanese and Nazis. After all, had not Japan started the war with its bombs on Hawaii?

America's men and women responded to Roosevelt's call to the colors. In 1941, even though Selective Service had been functioning for a full year, the grand total of people serving on active duty was only 1,801,000. In 1942 the number more than doubled to 3,859,000, and that was merely the beginning. In 1943 it more than doubled again to 9,045,000, and in 1945 the number of women and men serving in the army, navy, and marines peaked at 12,124,000. Such a massive force was necessary to fight a world war on two fronts.

Despite the near unity of Americans' support for the war effort, various government leaders worried that women and men would become wary of lofty rhetoric about the future, remembering how Woodrow Wilson had promised so much and delivered too little during the era of the First World War. Concerned that public morale would lag as the war dragged on, the army hired prominent Hollywood director Frank Capra to produce a series of prop-

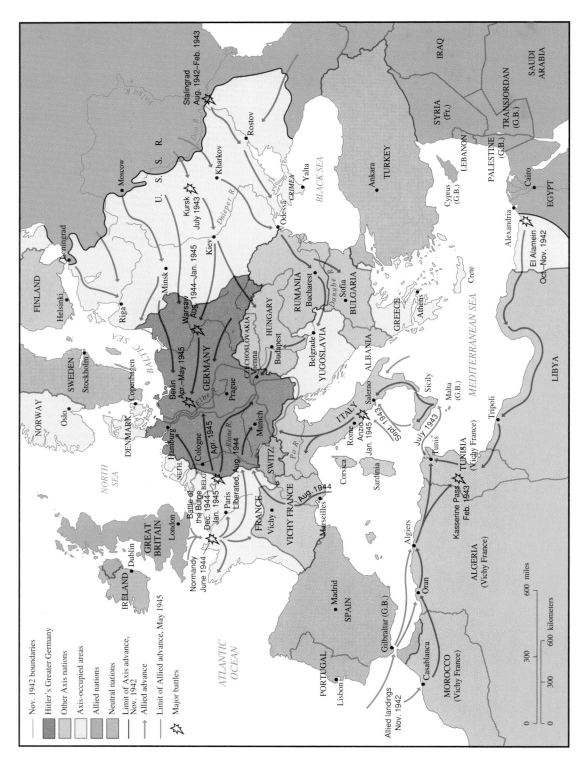

The Allies on the Offensive in Europe, 1942–1945

Legend:
- Nov. 1942 boundaries
- Hitler's Greater Germany
- Other Axis nations
- Axis-occupied areas
- Allied nations
- Neutral nations
- Limit of Axis advance, Nov. 1942
- Allied advance
- Limit of Allied advance, May 1945
- ✪ Major battles

Map labels include:
IRAQ, SAUDI ARABIA, TRANSJORDAN (G.B.), SYRIA (Fr.), LEBANON, PALESTINE (G.B.), Cairo, EGYPT, Alexandria, El Alamein Oct.–Nov. 1942, Cyprus (G.B.), TURKEY, Ankara, BLACK SEA, CRIMEA, Yalta, Odessa, Stalingrad Aug. 1942–Feb. 1943, Rostov, Don R., Dnieper R., Kharkov, Kursk July 1943, Moscow, Kiev, U. S. S. R., Minsk, Aug. 1944–Jan. 1945, Warsaw Aug. 1944–Jan. 1945, Leningrad, Riga, Helsinki, FINLAND, Stockholm, SWEDEN, NORWAY, Oslo, BALTIC SEA, Copenhagen, DENMARK, Hamburg, NETH., BELG., GERMANY, Berlin Apr.–May 1945, Elbe R., Prague, CZECHOSLOVAKIA, Vienna, Munich, Rhine R., Cologne Apr. 1945, SWITZ., Po R., ITALY, Rome, Anzio Jan. 1945, Salerno Sept. 1943, Sardinia, Corsica, Sicily, July 1943, Malta (G.B.), MEDITERRANEAN SEA, Crete, Athens, GREECE, ALBANIA, YUGOSLAVIA, Belgrade, Budapest, HUNGARY, RUMANIA, Bucharest, Danube R., Sofia, BULGARIA, Tripoli, LIBYA, TUNISIA (Vichy France), Tunis, Kasserine Pass Feb. 1943, Algiers, ALGERIA (Vichy France), Oran, Casablanca, MOROCCO (Vichy France), Allied landings Nov. 1942, PORTUGAL, Lisbon, SPAIN, Madrid, Gibraltar (G.B.), ATLANTIC OCEAN, NORTH SEA, GREAT BRITAIN, London, IRELAND, Dublin, FRANCE, VICHY FRANCE, Vichy, Paris Liberated, Aug. 1945, Aug. 1944, Marseilles, Battle of the Bulge Dec. 1944–Jan. 1945, Normandy June 1944

Scale: 0, 300, 600 miles; 0, 300, 600 kilometers

aganda films called *Why We Fight.* In these widely distributed films and in the popular mind, the Allies were heroic partners in a common effort against evil.

Actually, wartime relations among the United States, Great Britain, and the Soviet Union ran hot and cold. Although winning the war claimed top priority, Allied leaders knew that military decisions had political consequences. If one ally became desperate, for instance, it might sue for a separate peace. Moreover, the position of troops at the end of the war might determine the politics of the region they occupied. Thus an undercurrent of suspicion ran beneath the surface of Allied cooperation.

Roosevelt, British Prime Minister Winston Churchill, and Soviet Premier Josef Stalin differed vigorously over the opening of a second, or western,

> **Second-Front Controversy**

front. After Germany conquered France in 1940 and invaded Russia in 1941, the Russians bore the brunt of the war until mid-1944, suffering heavy casualties. By late 1941, before the fierce Russian winter stalled their onslaught, German troops had reached the edge of Moscow and Leningrad and had slashed deeply into the Ukraine, taking Kiev. Stalin pressed for a British-American landing on the northern coast of Europe to draw German troops away from the eastern front, but Churchill would not agree. The Russians therefore did most of the fighting and dying on land, while the British and Americans concentrated on getting Lend-Lease supplies across the Atlantic and harassing the Germans from the air with attacks on factories and civilians alike. When Secretary of State Cordell Hull bemoaned the 200,000 American casualties suffered from 1941 to 1943, a Russian official replied, "We lose that many each day before lunch. You haven't got your teeth in the war yet."

Roosevelt was particularly sensitive to the suggestion that Americans were shirking their responsibility by avoiding an invasion of Europe. He feared that Russia might be knocked out of the war, leaving Hitler free to send his goose-stepping soldiers into England. In 1942 Roosevelt told the Russians they could expect the Allies to open a second front later that year. The move across the English Channel, later tagged Operation OVERLORD, was exactly what Stalin sought to take pressure off his wracked country. But Churchill balked. "To postpone that evil day, all his arts, all his eloquence, all

his great experience was spent," the prime minister's chief military adviser later wrote. Churchill feared heavy losses in a premature cross-channel invasion. Although American Generals George C. Marshall and Dwight D. Eisenhower argued for a direct attack on the heart of German power, Churchill held out for a series of small jabs at the enemy's Mediterranean forces. American officials suspected that Churchill's strategy derived from his desire to recover British imperial power in the Mediterranean.

Churchill won the debate. Instead of attacking France, the western Allies invaded North Africa in November 1942 in Operation Torch (see map). To reduce fascist French resistance to the invasion, the Americans agreed to recognize the pro-Nazi Vichy French regime in North Africa—a "deal" many critics denounced as unsavory. Roosevelt deemed the bargain justified in order to get Americans into combat. "We are striking back," the cheered president declared. News from Russia also buoyed Roosevelt. In the battle for Stalingrad (September 1942 to January 1943), probably the turning point of the European war, the Red Army defeated the Germans in bloody block-by-block fighting, forcing Hitler's divisions to retreat. But shortly after Stalingrad, the president once again angered the Russians by declaring another delay in launching the second front. Marshal Stalin was not mollified in the summer of 1943 by the Allied invasion of Italy. When Italy surrendered in September, it capitulated to American and British officers; Russian officials were not invited to participate. Stalin grumbled that the arrangement smacked of a separate peace and wondered if Roosevelt and Churchill's policy of unconditional surrender for the Axis, announced that January at the Anglo-American conference at Casablanca, had been violated.

With the Grand Alliance badly strained, Roosevelt sought reconciliation through personal diplomacy. The three Allied leaders met in Teheran, Iran, in December 1943. Stalin dismissed Churchill's repetitious justifications for further delaying the second front. Roosevelt had had enough too; with Stalin he rejected Churchill's proposal for another peripheral attack, this time through the Balkans to Vienna. The three finally agreed to launch OVERLORD in early 1944. An appreciative Russia promised to aid the Allies against Japan once Germany was defeated.

More than 4,000 ships and 3 million American, British, Canadian, and French troops participated in the D-Day invasion of Europe, making this the largest invasion fleet ever assembled. After landing at Normandy, France, the troops pushed gradually inland and entered Germany in September 1944. *Combat Art Division, U.S. Navy.*

Like a coiled spring bursting free, the second front opened in the dark morning hours of June 6, 1944: D-Day. Two hundred thousand Allied troops under the command of General **D-Day** Eisenhower scrambled ashore in Normandy, France, in the largest amphibious landing in history. Thousands of ships ferried the men within a hundred yards of the sandy beaches. Landing craft and soldiers became entangled in sharp obstacles; they triggered mines and were pinned down by fire from cliffside pillboxes. Meanwhile, airborne troops dropped behind German lines. Although heavy aerial and naval bombardment and the clandestine work of underground saboteurs had softened up German defenses, the fighting was ferocious. One soldier felt like a "pigeon at a trap shoot."

After digging in at now-famous places like Utah and Omaha beaches and gaining reinforcements, Allied forces broke through disorderly German lines and gradually pushed inland, reaching Paris in August. That same month another force invaded southern France and threw the stunned Germans back. Allied troops soon spread across the countryside, liberating France and Belgium and entering Germany itself in September. In December, Ger-

man panzer divisions counterattacked in Belgium's Ardennes Forest, hoping to push on to Antwerp to halt the flow of Allied supplies through that major Belgian port. After weeks of heavy fighting in what has come to be called the Battle of the Bulge —because of the noticeable dent in the Allied line—the Allies pushed the enemy back once again. Meanwhile, battle-hardened Russian troops marched through Poland and cut a path to the German capital, Berlin. American forces crossed the Rhine in March 1945 and captured the heavily industrial Ruhr valley. Some units peeled off to enter Austria and Czechoslovakia, where they met up with Russian soldiers. As the Americans marched east, a new president took office in Washington. Franklin D. Roosevelt died on April 12, and Harry Truman became the commander-in-chief. Eighteen days later, in bomb-ravaged Berlin, defended largely by teenage boys and old men, Adolf Hitler killed himself. On May 8 Germany surrendered.

Allied strategists had devised a "Europe first" formula: knock out Germany first and then concentrate on an isolated Japan. Nevertheless, the Pacific theater claimed headlines throughout the war, for the American people regarded Japan as the United States's chief enemy. The treacherous Japanese—

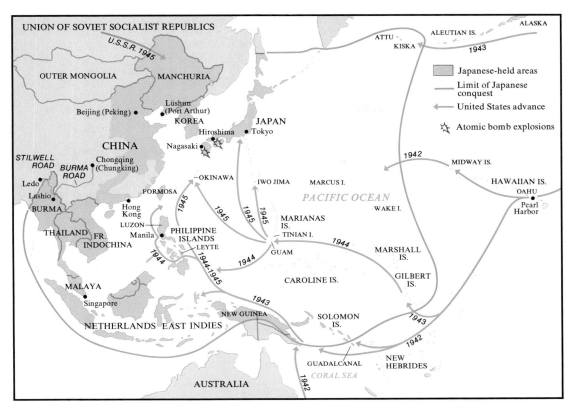

The Pacific War *Source: From Paterson et al.,* American Foreign Policy: A History, *copyright 1988, p. 398. Reprinted by permission of D.C. Heath and Company.*

"monkeys" and "bastards," boomed Admiral William Halsey—had to be repaid for Pearl Harbor. But other American losses followed Pearl Harbor. By mid-1942 Japan had seized the Philippines, Guam, Wake, Hong Kong, Singapore, Malaya, and the Netherlands East Indies. In the Philippines in 1942, Japanese soldiers forced American and Filipino prisoners, weak from insufficient rations, to walk sixty-five miles, clubbing, shooting, or starving to death about ten thousand of them. The Bataan Death March intensified American hatred of the Japanese.

In April 1942, Americans began to hit back. They bombed Tokyo, and in May, in the momentous Battle of the Coral Sea, carrier-based United States planes halted a Japanese advance toward Australia (see map). The next month American forces defeated the Japanese at Midway, sinking four of the enemy's valuable aircraft carriers. Thanks to the success of Operation Magic—the work of American experts who deciphered the secret code used by the Japanese to transmit messages—American

naval officers knew ahead of time the approximate date and direction of the Japanese assault. The Battle of Midway was a turning point in the Pacific war, breaking the Japanese momentum and relieving the threat to Hawaii. Thereafter, Japan was never able to match American manpower, sea power, air power, or economic power. Still, the war in Asia was contested until the very end. "There are no breathers in this schedule," exclaimed General H. H. Arnold in the football jargon of the time. "You take on Notre Dame every time you play!"

Even after victory in Europe, the war in Asia raged on. American strategy was to "island-hop" toward Japan itself, skipping the most strongly fortified points whenever possible and taking weaker ones. Americans also set out to sink the Japanese merchant marine, in an effort to strand the Japanese armies in their island outposts and to cut off raw materials from the factories of the home islands. The first American offensive—at Guadalcanal in the Sol-

> **American Offensive in the Pacific**

This scorched watch, found in the rubble at Hiroshima, stopped at the time of the blast at 8:16. The shock waves and fires caused by the atomic bomb leveled great expanses of the city. Radiation released by the bomb caused lingering deaths for thousands who survived the explosion. *Watch: John Launois/Black Star; Hiroshima: National Archives.*

omon Islands in summer and fall 1942—gave troops their first taste of jungle warfare: thick vegetation, mosquitoes, scorpions, tropical heat, and rotting gear. From the Solomons the United States military pushed relentlessly on, colliding with the entrenched enemy in the Gilberts, Marshalls, and Marianas in 1943 and 1944. In June 1944 the navy smashed Japanese forces in the Battle of the Philippine Sea. In October, General Douglas MacArthur landed at Leyte to reclaim the Philippines for the United States. Then in early 1945 both sides took heavy losses at Iwo Jima and Okinawa. In desperation, Japanese pilots began suicide (*kamikaze*) attacks, flying their planes directly into American ships.

Hoping to avoid a humiliating unconditional surrender (and to preserve the emperor's sovereignty), Japanese leaders refused to admit defeat. They hung on while American bombers leveled their cities. In one staggering attack on Tokyo on May 23, 1945, American planes dropped napalm-filled bombs that engulfed the city in a firestorm. Eighty-three thousand people died; observers described the ghastly scene as a mass burning.

Chapter 27: The Second World War at Home and Abroad, 1941–1945

Impatient for victory, American leaders began to plan a fall invasion of the Japanese islands, an expedition that was sure to bring high casualties. But the successful development of an atomic bomb by American scientists provided another route to victory. The secret atomic program, known as the Manhattan Project, began in August 1942 and cost $2 billion. The first atomic bomb was exploded in the desert near Alamogordo, New Mexico, on July 16, 1945. On August 6 the Japanese city of Hiroshima was destroyed by an atomic blast. At 8:16 that morning, the bomb exploded, having been dropped a minute earlier from an American B-29 named *Enola Gay*. A flash of dazzling light shot across the sky; then a huge purplish mushroom cloud boiled forty thousand feet into the atmosphere. Dense smoke, swirling fires, and suffocating dust soon engulfed the ground for miles. Much of the city was leveled almost instantly. Approximately 130,000 people were killed; tens of thousands more suffered painful burns and nuclear poisoning. As Hiroshima suffered its unique nightmare, Washington, D.C., celebrated its military and scientific triumph. "This is the greatest thing in history," exclaimed President Truman on hearing of the successful mission.

American planes continued their devastating conventional bombing and scattered leaflets over other Japanese cities warning that they too would face atomic terror unless the Japanese empire surrendered. On August 9 another atomic attack flattened Nagasaki, killing at least sixty thousand people. The next day a sobered President Truman suspended the further atomic bombing of Japan. He had belated qualms about killing "all those kids." Four days later the Japanese, who had been sending out peace feelers since June, surrendered. The victors promised that the Japanese emperor could remain as the nation's titular head. Formal surrender ceremonies were held September 2 aboard the battleship *Missouri*. The Second World War was over.

Most Americans agreed with President Truman that the atomic bombing of two Japanese cities had been necessary to end the war as quickly as possible and to save American lives.

Why the Atomic Bomb Was Used Use of the bomb to achieve victory had, in fact, been the primary assumption of the Manhattan Project. At the highest government levels and among atomic scientists, alternatives had been discussed: detonate the bomb on an unpopulated Pacific island, with international observers as witnesses; blockade and bomb Japan conventionally; follow up Tokyo's peace feelers; encourage a Russian declaration of war. But Truman's aides had rejected these options on the grounds that they would take too long and would not convince the tenacious Japanese that they had been beaten. Then, too, memories of Pearl Harbor played a part. "When you have to deal with a beast you have to treat him as a beast," Truman said.

Diplomatic considerations also sped the decision to use the bomb. Leaders envisioned the real and psychological power the bomb would bestow on the United States. It might serve as a deterrent against aggression; it might intimidate Russia into making concessions in Eastern Europe; it might end the war in the Pacific before Russia could claim a role in the management of Asia. "If it explodes, as I think it will," Truman remarked, "I'll certainly have a hammer on those boys" (the Russians).

Economic Effects of the War at Home

The Second World War was won at great cost not only abroad but also on the American home front. While the guns boomed in Europe and Asia, the war changed American lives and institutions. One month after Pearl Harbor, President Roosevelt established the War Production Board (WPB). First on the WPB's list of tasks was the conversion from civilian to military production. Factories that had manufactured silk ribbons began to turn out silk parachutes; automobile companies switched to the production of tanks and airplanes; adding-machine companies converted to make automatic pistols. Factories had to be expanded and new ones built. The WPB was so successful that the production of durable goods more than tripled. For example, manufacture of military aircraft, which had totaled 6,000 in 1940, jumped to over 47,000 in 1942 and 85,000 in 1943.

The wartime emergency spurred the establishment of totally new industries, the best known of

The federal government used a variety of methods to exhort home-front Americans to obey wartime regulations. This Office of War Information poster suggested that the gas cheat was betraying his patriotic duty to support American troops. *National Archives.*

which was synthetic rubber. The Japanese, in their conquest of the South Pacific in the weeks following Pearl Harbor, had captured 90 percent of the world's supply of crude rubber. Although the American government resorted to conservation measures, including a national speed limit and gasoline rationing to save wear and tear on tires, neither conservation nor recycling could meet wartime needs. So with an investment of $700 million, the government underwrote the creation of a synthetic-rubber industry based on petroleum. By war's end the nation that had been the world's largest importer of rubber had become the world's largest exporter of rubber—all of it synthetic. New industries introduced new pollutants: smog (first detected in Los Angeles in 1943); artificially made radioactive elements; and petrochemical wastes from such new products as plastics, detergents, and DDT.

To gain the cooperation of business, the WPB and other government agencies met business more than halfway. The government guaranteed profits

▶ **Government Incentives to Business**

in the form of cost-plus-fixed-fee contracts, generous tax write-offs, and exemption from anti-trust prosecution. And it allowed prime contractors to distribute subcontracts as they saw fit, including those involving scarce war-related materials. These rewards made sense for a government—and a nation—that wanted vast quantities of war goods manufactured in the shortest possible time.

From mid-1940 through September 1944 the government awarded contracts totaling $175 billion, no less than two-thirds of which went to the top one hundred corporations. General Motors received 8 percent of the total; big awards also went to other automobile companies, as well as to aircraft, steel, electrical, and chemical companies. Almost all these industries had been dominated by big corporations at the beginning of the war; the billions of dollars they received in government contracts only accentuated their dominance. Although no one had yet coined the expression "military-industrial complex"—President Dwight Eisenhower would do so in 1961 (see page 875)—the web of military-business interdependence had begun to be woven.

In science and higher education the big also got bigger. To develop radar and do other research, Massachusetts Institute of Technology received contracts valued at $117 million. California Institute of Technology was in second place with contracts totaling $83 million, followed by Harvard, Columbia, the University of California, Johns Hopkins, and the University of Chicago. The most spectacular result of a government contract with a university was the atomic bomb; its testing was run by the University of California at Berkeley.

Big labor also grew bigger during the war. Union membership ballooned from 8.5 million in 1940 to 14.75 million in 1945. Less than a week after Pearl Harbor, a White House labor-management conference produced a no strike–no lockout pledge to guarantee uninterrupted war production. "When the nation is attacked," declared John L. Lewis, the gruff president of the United Mine Workers union, "every American must rally to its defense. All other considerations become insignificant." In 1942, to minimize labor-management conflict, President

◀ Chapter 27: The Second World War at Home and Abroad, 1941–1945

Roosevelt created the National War Labor Board (NWLB), sometimes referred to as the Supreme Court for labor disputes. Unions were permitted to enroll as many new members as possible, but workers were not required to join a union. Thus the NWLB forged a compromise between the unions' demand for a closed shop, in which only union members could be hired, and management's interest in open shops.

When the NWLB attempted to limit wage increases to increases in the cost of living, there were wildcat strikes and other work stoppages that tripled the production time lost in

> **Wartime Labor Strikes**

1943. "Strikes are spreading at an alarming rate," bemoaned a member of the NWLB, "and unless they are checked immediately, the 'no strike–no lockout' agreement will become meaningless." The worst labor disruptions of 1943 came in the coal fields, where 450,000 soft-coal miners and 80,000 anthracite miners struck. "When the mine workers' children cry for bread, they cannot be satisfied [with words]," declared John L. Lewis, who seemed to forget his earlier patriotic commitment to sacrifice.

Public hostility grew toward organized labor in general and toward John L. Lewis in particular. To discourage further work stoppages, Congress passed the War Labor Disputes (Smith-Connally) Act of June 1943. The act conferred on the president the authority to seize and operate any strike-bound plant deemed necessary to the national security, and it established a mandatory thirty-day cooling-off period before any new strike could be called. The Smith-Connally Act also gave the NWLB the legal authority to settle labor disputes for the duration of the war. Over the course of the war the NWLB handled close to eighteen thousand disputes, reducing time lost due to strikes to one-third the peacetime level.

Although the war demanded sacrifices from Americans, it also brought new highs in personal income. Savings deposits jumped from $32.4 billion in 1942 to $51.4 billion in 1945. It was an even more bountiful time both for corporations, which doubled their net profits between 1939 and 1943, and for employees, whose wages and salaries rose more than 135 percent from 1940 to 1945. The government did not tax this extra income as heavily as it might have. Instead it resorted to deficit financing and borrowed approximately 60 percent of the cost of the war, about half of it in the form of war bonds sold to patriotic citizens. The national debt skyrocketed from $49 billion in 1941 to $259 billion in 1945.

Agriculture also made an impressive contribution to the war effort, not only through hard work but through the introduction of labor-saving machinery to replace the men and women who had gone to the front or migrated to war-production centers. Farming was in the midst of a transition from the family-owned and -operated farm to the large-scale, mechanized agribusiness dominated by banks, insurance companies, and farm co-ops. The Second World War accelerated the trend, for wealthy financial institutions were better able than family farmers to pay for expensive new machinery. From 1940 to 1945 the value of American agricultural machinery rose from $3.1 billion to $6.5 billion, and the average acreage per farm jumped from 175 to 195. The use of the new machines and fertilizers boosted farm output per labor-hour by 25 percent. At the same time the farm population fell from 30.5 million to 24.4 million. Like business and labor, agriculture was becoming more consolidated as it contributed to the war effort.

At the head of the burgeoning national economy stood the federal government, whose size and importance, like that of business and labor, was mushrooming: from 1940 to 1945 the

> **Growth in the Federal Government**

federal bureaucracy expanded from 1.1 million workers to 3.4 million. The executive branch, which included the Office of the Commander-in-Chief and bore the responsibility for directing the war effort, grew the most. Besides raising the armed forces, mobilizing industrial production, pacifying labor and management, and controlling inflation, the executive also had to manage the labor supply. Through the War Manpower Commission (WMC), established in 1942 and composed of representatives of various agencies, the government determined where labor was most needed, allocated labor between industry and the armed forces, and recruited new workers.

Although the WMC was far from successful in accomplishing its goals, another government agency, the Office of Price Administration (OPA), did succeed in combating inflation by fixing price ceilings on commodities and introducing rationing programs. Consumers became skilled in handling ration stamps, each worth ten points—red for

B-17 pilots return from a training flight in their Flying Fortress Pistol Packin' Mama. WAF pilots ferried the planes for the Air Corps. *U.S. Air Force Photo.*

meats and cheese, blue for canned goods—and car windows displayed "A" stamp decals for gasoline. In addition, the OPA issued a series of proclamations and rules that governed the behavior of landlords, employers, rationing boards, wholesalers, retailers, and consumers. In May 1943, as economic mobilization became increasingly bogged down in red tape, President Roosevelt created the Office of War Mobilization, which became, in effect, a court of appeal in disputes between conflicting civilian and military claims.

Although government-business-labor relations were sometimes bitter and slowed production, Americans were generally ready to make personal sacrifices. They knew the war would be costly and long. In previous conflicts Americans had flocked to the colors with flags, wild rallies, and militaristic songs, but in the Second World War they fought with a grim, realistic determination. To elicit the people's enthusiasm, the Office of War Information took charge of domestic propaganda and hired Hollywood filmmakers and New York advertising copywriters to sell the war. But as historian Allan Nevins observed, "In this war there was . . . no such straw fire of frothy enthusiasm." Most Americans

wanted to leave behind their concerns about the war, so the motion pictures produced and books published during this war were typically light, fluffy, sentimental escapes from the harsh realities of life. In 1861, 1898, and 1917, Nevins wrote, Americans had thought that "the war would be easy. They knew full well in 1941 that it wouldn't."

The Military Life

To American service people in Asia and in Europe, the Second World War was a grimy job. Like cartoonist Bill Mauldin's popular GI characters Willy and Joe, who were more interested in tasty food and dry socks than in abstractions, they were eager to get it over with. So too were the 16.4 million other GIs who served during wartime. The largest of the services was the army, which, at the war's conclusion in 1945, had 8.3 million soldiers, including 100,000 WACS (Women's Army Corps). Although women were prohibited from engaging in combat duty, they worked at a variety of noncombat

Chapter 27: The Second World War at Home and Abroad, 1941–1945

jobs, not only in the WACS but as WAVES (Women Accepted for Volunteer Emergency Service) in the navy, as pilots in the WASPS (Women Air Service Pilots), and as members of the Coast Guard and the Marine Corps Women's Reserve. The WASPS taught basic flying, towed aerial targets for gunnery practice, and flight-tested military aircraft.

American troops served overseas for an average of about sixteen months. Some never returned: total deaths exceeded 405,000; total wounded, 670,000. In terms of human life, the cost of the war was second only to that of the Civil War. Still, compared with losses suffered by other nations, United States figures were low. Less than 1 percent of the population was killed or wounded in the war; the Soviet Union lost 8 percent of its population—about 20 million people.

Many soldiers and sailors who had never been more than a few miles from home became homesick. GIs joked, somewhat bitterly, about having found a home in the army. But this loneliness was minor compared with the intense fear that soldiers admitted to feeling in battle. Combat veterans told a group of psychologists that a man who burst out weeping was "not regarded as a coward unless he made no apparent effort to stick to his job." Some Americans became looters. One veteran explained that when soldiers took a town, they "wanted something to drink. Then they wanted a woman. And then they wanted to go out and see what they could loot."

But if combat's cruelties robbed many GIs of their innocence, military service itself broadened the horizons of millions of men and women. "Take these kids from the hills," noted one GI, "the service opened their eyes some. . . . And some of these guys from Chicago, why they'd never been outside of Chicago." They talked about fellows 'from the sticks' and they'd never been out in the 'sticks'—they'd never even known what the 'sticks' were."

Broadening of GIs' Horizons

Among the millions of people who had left their homes and neighborhoods were men and women who had experienced same-sex attraction in peacetime. Freed in wartime of their familial environments and serving in sex-segregated units, they acted upon their feelings. "When I first got into the navy—in the recreation hall, for instance," recalled a chief petty officer, "there'd be eye contact. . . . All of a sudden you had a vast network of friends. . . ."

"Just gimme a coupla aspirin. I already got a Purple Heart." The cartoonist Bill Mauldin became famous through his GI characters Willie and Joe, two battle-hardened veterans who hated officers almost as much as they hated the enemy. *By permission of Bill Mauldin and Wil-Jo Associates, Inc.*

The military court-martialed homosexuals, but gay relationships usually went unnoticed by the heterosexual world. Among the 150,000 women serving in the armed forces, the military environment created friendships and a positive identity among lesbians. "For many gay Americans," the historian John D'Emilio has written, "World War II created something of a nationwide coming out situation." Gay people went in different directions after the war; some went back in the closet, others moved to cities to lay the foundations for a gay subculture.

Wartime service not only broadened horizons but fostered soldiers' ambitions. A soldier from the Midwest, who reported that he found himself "living among fellows from all over the country," said, "I picked up a lot of ideas from them, not only [about] what the United States was really like—I mean the whole country—but about how to live my own life and to get more out of it. . . . I came out a lot more ambitious than I was before I went in." Finally, many GIs returned to civilian life with new skills they had learned in the military's technical schools. Some became fluent in foreign languages; others became medical technicians, electronics experts, and aircraft mechanics. Still others took advantage of the educational benefits offered in the GI Bill of Rights (1944) to study for a college degree (see pages 895–896).

Still, after two or three years abroad, men and women in the service returned to the United States not knowing what to expect from civilian life. Earlier in the war, troops had been given orientation lectures and booklets introducing them to the historical backgrounds and social customs of the foreign nations where they would serve. Now they were coming home, and yet, as one observer wrote, they were "to a surprising degree, foreigners in their own land." Returning soldiers also feared a postwar economic depression. A B-17 crew chief complained that people were "spending too much money and . . . not saving up for what's coming—you know, unemployment after the war."

What might have been most disturbing to GIs was the feeling that life at home had passed them by. For one thing, returning GIs were much older in experience and in exposure to brutality; they had lost their innocence. Many came back to the United States convinced that they had sacrificed their youth. Still worse, they found that home had changed as well. "Our friends are gone," one GI lamented. "The family and the town naturally had to go on even if we weren't there, and somehow it seems things have sort of closed in and filled that space we used to occupy."

Civil Liberties and the Internment of Japanese-Americans

Once the United States entered the war, American leaders had to consider whether enemy agents were operating within the nation's borders and threatening the war effort. It was clear that not all Americans were enthusiastic supporters of the nation's involvement in the war. After Pearl Harbor, several thousand "enemy aliens" were arrested and taken into custody, some of them Nazi agents who had accumulated firearms, shortwave radios, and

codes in the course of their work. Other people had conscientious objections to the war, particularly Quakers, Mennonites, and members of the Church of the Brethren. During the Second World War conscientious objectors (COs) had to have a religious (as opposed to moral or ethical) reason for refusing military service. About 25,000 qualified COs accepted noncombat service, most of them as medical corpsmen. An additional 12,000 were placed in civilian public service camps, where they worked at forestry or conservation or as orderlies in public health hospitals. Approximately 5,500, three-fourths of whom were Jehovah's Witnesses, refused to participate in any way; they were imprisoned.

The one enormous exception to the nation's generally creditable wartime civil liberties record was the internment in "relocation centers" of more than 110,000 Japanese-Americans. Of these people, 70,000 were Nisei, or native-born citizens of the United States. Their imprisonment was based not on suspicion or evidence of treason; their crime was their ethnic origin—the fact that they were of Japanese descent. As General John L. DeWitt, chief of the Western Defense Command, expressed it:

> Internment in "Relocation Centers"

> The Japanese race is an enemy race and while many second and third generation Japanese born on United States soil, possessed of United States citizenship, have become "Americanized," the racial strains are undiluted. . . . It, therefore, follows that along the vital Pacific Coast over 112,000 potential enemies, of Japanese extraction, are at large today.

With strained illogic he declared: "The very fact that no sabotage [by Japanese-Americans] has taken place to date is a disturbing and confirming indication that such action will be taken." DeWitt was not alone in his paranoia.

Charges of criminal behavior were never brought against Japanese-Americans; none was ever indicted or tried for espionage, treason, or sedition. Even their alleged crime, disloyalty to the United States, was not against the law. Nevertheless in 1942 more than 110,000 Japanese-Americans of all ages were rounded up and imprisoned. "It was really cruel and harsh," recalled Joseph Y. Kurihara, a citizen and a veteran of the First World War. "To pack and evacuate in forty-eight hours was an impossibility. Seeing mothers completely bewildered with children crying from want and peddlers taking advantage and offering prices next to robbery made me feel like murdering those responsible." After the war, Kurihara, along with 8,000 other Japanese-Americans, did the next best thing: he emigrated to Japan, a country he had never seen.

The internees were sent to flood-damaged lands at Relocation, Arkansas; to the intermountain terrain of Wyoming and the desert of western Arizona; and to other arid and desolate spots in the West. Although the names were evocative—Topaz, Utah; Rivers, Arizona; Heart Mountain, Wyoming; Tule Lake and Manzanar, California—the camps themselves were bleak and demoralizing. Behind barbed wire stood tar-papered wooden barracks where entire families lived in a single room furnished only with cots, blankets, and a bare light bulb. Toilets and dining and bathing facilities were communal; privacy was almost nonexistent. Besides their freedom, the Japanese-Americans lost property valued at $500 million, along with their positions in the truck-garden, floral, and fishing industries. Indeed, their economic competitors were among the most vocal proponents of their relocation.

The Supreme Court upheld the government's policy of internment. In wartime, the Court said in the *Hirabayashi* ruling (1943), "residents having ethnic affiliations with an invading enemy may be a greater source of danger than those of different ancestry." And in the *Korematsu* case (1944), the Court, with three justices dissenting, approved the removal of the Nisei from the West Coast. One dissenter, Justice Frank Murphy, denounced the decision as the "legalization of racism," and Justice Robert Jackson warned that the precedent established by the cases "lies about like a loaded weapon ready for the hand of any authority that can bring forward a plausible claim of an urgent need." The most damning appraisal of all came from Circuit Court Judge William Denman, who in an earlier ruling had written that "the identity of this doctrine with that of the Hitler generals . . . justifying the gas chambers of Dachau is unmistakable."

In 1983, forty-one years after he had been placed in a government camp, Fred Korematsu had the satisfaction of hearing a federal judge rule that he—and by implication all detainees—had been the victim of "unsubstantiated facts, distortions and misrepresentations of at least one military commander whose views were affected by racism." A

It was ironic that patriotism seemed to be alive even at this Japanese-American internment camp in Heart Mountain, Wyoming. On a subzero morning in 1943, Nisei internees, led by a Boy Scout drum-and-bugle corps, salute the American flag. *Hansel Mieth © 1943* Life *Magazine, Time Inc.*

year earlier, the government's special Commission on Wartime Relocation and Internment of Civilians had recommended compensating the victims of this policy. Because of "race prejudice, war hysteria and a failure of political leadership," the commission concluded, the government had committed "a grave injustice" to more than 110,000 people. Finally, in 1988, Congress voted to award $20,000 and a public apology to the surviving 60,000 Japanese-American internees.

Jobs and Racism on the Home Front

For other people of color in America, the Second World War would prove to be a mixed blessing, providing both the benefits of employment and the insults of racism. For many black Americans, the war was a turning point at which they determined

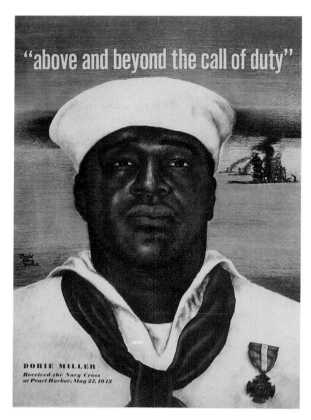

"above and beyond the call of duty"

DORIE MILLER
*Received the Navy Cross
at Pearl Harbor, May 27, 1942*

The first African-American hero of the Second World War was Dorie Miller, who won the Navy Cross. Miller's citation for bravery read: "Without previous experience [he] . . . manned a machine gun in the face of serious fire during the Japanese attack on Pearl Harbor, December 7, 1941, on the battleship *Arizona,* shooting down four enemy planes." *Library of Congress.*

to make a stand against racial discrimination. Several factors highlighted African-American involvement in the war: the presence of nearly 1 million black men and women in the armed services; the mass migration of blacks, particularly from the rural South to the urban North and West, to work in war industries; and the participation of black people in all kinds of wartime activities—buying war bonds, serving as air-raid wardens, and volunteering for the Red Cross.

At peak enrollment the army had over 700,000 black troops. An additional 187,000 enlisted in the navy, the Coast Guard, and the once all-white Marine Corps. In response to the March on Washington Movement of 1941 (see page 752), the Selective Service System and the War Department agreed to draft black Americans in proportion to their presence in the population: about 10 percent.

Although blacks served in segregated units, they made some real advances in the direction of racial equality during these years. For the first time the War Department sanctioned the

Black Troops training of blacks as pilots. After instruction at Tuskegee Institute in Alabama, pilots saw heroic service in such all-black units as the Ninety-ninth Pursuit Squadron, winner of eighty Distinguished Flying Crosses. Some blacks reached positions of leadership. In 1940 Colonel Benjamin O. Davis became the first black brigadier general. Wherever black people were offered opportunities to distinguish themselves, they proved that they could do the job. The performance of black marines in the Pacific theater was such that the corps commandant proclaimed: "Negro Marines are no longer on trial. They are Marines, period."

Set against these accomplishments, however, were serious failures in race relations. Race riots instigated by whites occurred on military bases, and white civilians assaulted black soldiers and sailors throughout the South. In North Carolina a white bus driver murdered a black soldier in full view of the passengers but was found not guilty. When the War Department issued an order in mid-1944 forbidding racial segregation in military recreation and transportation, the *Montgomery Advertiser* replied, "Army orders, even armies, even bayonets, cannot force impossible and unnatural social relations upon us."

Experiences such as these caused black soldiers and sailors to wonder what, in fact, they were fighting for. They recalled the remark of the governor of Tennessee, when blacks urged him to appoint African-Americans to local draft boards: "This is a white man's country. . . . The Negro had nothing to do with the settling of America." They noted that the Red Cross separated blood taken from whites and blacks, as if there were some difference. Many considered black participation in the First World War a mistake, for it had resulted not in social advances but in race riots and lynchings. Some even argued that the Second World War was a white man's war. But most telling was the charge that American racism was little different from German racism.

At the same time, there were positive reasons for blacks to participate in the war effort. Perhaps this was an opportunity, as the NAACP believed, "to persuade, embarrass, compel and shame our government and our nation . . . into a more enlightened attitude toward a tenth of its people." Proclaiming that in the Second World War they were waging a "Double V" campaign (for victory at home and abroad), blacks were more militant than before and readier than ever to protest. Membership in civil rights organizations soared. The NAACP, with 50,000 members in 1940, had 450,000 members by 1946. In 1942 civil rights activists founded the Congress of Racial Equality (CORE).

Because of the war, blacks found new opportunities in industry. Roosevelt's Executive Order 8802, issued in 1941 in response to the March on Washington Movement, required employers in defense industries to make jobs available "without discrimination because of race, creed, color or national origin." To secure defense jobs, 1.2 million blacks migrated from the South to the industrial cities of the North and West in the 1940s. Almost three-fourths settled in the urban-industrial states of California, Illinois, Michigan, New York, Ohio, and Pennsylvania. More than half a million became active members of CIO unions such as the United Auto Workers, the United Steel Workers, and the United Rubber Workers. Finally, black voters in northern cities were beginning to constitute a vital swing vote not only in presidential contests, but in local and state elections.

> **Black War Workers**

But along with the benefits of urban life came liabilities. The migrants had to make enormous emotional and cultural adjustments, and white hostility and ignorance made their task difficult. Southern whites who had migrated north brought with them the racial prejudices of the Deep South. Blacks competed with these whites for housing, jobs, and seats on buses; they rubbed elbows with them in city schools and parks and at the beaches. But just as significant was the ignorance of northern whites, more than half of whom believed in 1942 that blacks should be segregated in separate schools and neighborhoods; that black people were receiving all the opportunities they deserved; and that if blacks suffered economically, politically, or socially, it was their own fault. These attitudes encouraged racial violence.

Many people, black and white, feared that the summer of 1943 would be like 1919, another Red Summer. And indeed, almost 250 racial conflicts exploded in forty-seven cities that year. The worst of the 1943 race riots bloodied the streets of Detroit in June. At the end of thirty hours of rioting, twenty-five blacks and nine whites lay dead. White mobs, undeterred by police, had roamed the city attacking blacks. Blacks had hurled rocks at police and hauled white passengers off streetcars. This was outright racial warfare. In response to the riot a city councilman suggested that the city build a bigger ghetto and pen blacks up in it. Surveying the damage, an elderly black woman said, "There ain't no North any more. Everything now is South."

> **Race Riots of 1943**

The federal government did practically nothing to prevent further racial violence. From President Roosevelt on down, most federal officials put the war first, domestic reform second. Unquestionably many government leaders were racists themselves; Secretary of War Henry L. Stimson claimed that the riots were "the deliberate effort . . . on the part of certain radical leaders of the colored race to use the war for obtaining . . . racial equality and interracial marriages." But this time government neglect could not discourage African-Americans and their century-old civil rights movement. By war's end they were ready—politically, economically, and emotionally—to wage the struggle for voting rights and for equal access to public accommodations and institutions.

Not all racial violence was directed against blacks. To some whites, people of Mexican origin were as despicable as those whose roots were African. In 1942, American farms and war industries needed workers, and the United States and Mexico had agreed to the *bracero* program, whereby Mexicans were admitted to the United States on short-term work contracts. Although the newcomers suffered racial discrimination and segregation, they seized the economic opportunities that had become available. In Los Angeles, 17,000 people of Mexican descent found shipyard jobs where before the war none had been available to them. But ethic and racial animosities in the city rose during the war.

In 1943, whites, most of whom were sailors and soldiers, attacked Mexican-Americans in the Los

The bloodiest race riot of 1943 struck Detroit, where 34 people, 25 blacks and 9 whites, were killed. At the peak of the rioting a white mob overturned a black person's car, showering trolley passengers with burning gasoline. *UPI/Bettmann Archives.*

Angeles zoot-suit riot. Mexican-American teenagers had joined street gangs (*pachucos*), adopted ducktail haircuts, and donned "zoot suits": long coats (called "drapes") with wide, padded shoulders, pegged pants, wide-brimmed hats, and long watch chains. Whites' anger boiled over in June, and for four days mobs invaded Mexican-American neighborhoods. According to one report: "Procedure was standard: grab a zooter. Take off his pants and frock coat and tear them up or burn them. Trim the '. . . ducktail' haircut that goes with the screwy costume." Not only did white policemen look the other way during these assaults, but the city of Los Angeles even passed an ordinance that made it a crime to wear a zoot suit within city limits.

Such experiences made life difficult for people of Mexican descent within the United States. Although the war opened up brief economic opportunities for Mexican-Americans, these years were not the transformational experience that they were for African-Americans.

A Milestone for Women

If the Second World War was a turning point for African-Americans, it was equally or even more so for the women of America. During the Great Depression, when millions of men were unemployed, public opinion had been hostile to the hiring of women, but the war brought about a rapid increase in employment. Just when men were going off to war, industry had to recruit millions of new workers to supply the rapidly expanding need for military equipment. African-Americans, southern whites, teenage boys and girls, Mexicans and Mexican-Americans, and, above all, women filled these new jobs.

Well over 6 million women entered the labor force during the war years, increasing the number of working women 57 percent in less than five years. Two million took clerical jobs; another 2.5

Women workers mastered numerous manufacturing skills during the war. Working for the Consolidated Aircraft Corporation in Fort Worth, Texas, in 1942, this lathe operator was machining parts for transport planes. *The Saturday Evening Post © 1944 Curtis Publishing Company.*

million worked in manufacturing. The significance of the trend lay not in the numbers but in the kinds of women who were entering the work force. Seventy-five percent of the new women workers were married, and 3.7 million were not only married but mothers. Before the war the average woman wage earner had been young, single, and largely self-supporting; by 1945 more working women were married than single and more were over age thirty-five than under.

But statistics, no matter how impressive, tell only part of the story. There was a change in attitude toward heavy labor for women. Up to the early months of the war employers had insisted that women were not suited for industrial jobs. If women were allowed to work in factories, they would begin to wear overalls instead of dresses, their muscles would bulge, they might even drink whiskey and swear like men. As labor shortages began to threaten the war effort, employers did an about-

Women in War Production

face. "Almost overnight," said Mary Anderson, head of the Women's Bureau of the Department of Labor, "women were reclassified by industrialists from a marginal to a basic labor supply for munitions making." Women became riveters, lumberjacks ("lumberjills"), welders, crane operators, keel benders, tool makers, shell loaders, cowgirls, blast-furnace cleaners, locomotive greasers, police officers, taxi drivers, and football coaches.

The new employment opportunities increased women's geographic and occupational mobility. Especially noteworthy were the gains made by black women; over 400,000 quit work as domestic servants to enjoy the better working conditions, higher pay, and union benefits of industrial employment. Hundreds of thousands of others, black and white, abandoned menial jobs in dime stores, restaurants, laundries, and hospitals for higher-status, higher-paying jobs. To take these jobs, women uprooted themselves. Over 7 million women moved from their original counties of residence to new locations during the war. Many sought jobs in the rapidly expanding aircraft industry, which increased its employment of women from 4,000 in December 1941 to 310,000 two years later.

Public opinion quickly changed from hostility to support of women's war work. Posters and billboards urging women to "Do the Job HE Left Behind" soon began to appear. Newspapers and magazines, radio and movies proclaimed Rosie the Riveter a war hero. But very few people asserted that women's war work should bring about a permanent shift in sex roles. This was merely a response to a national emergency. Once the victory was won, women should go back to nurturing their husbands and children, leaving their jobs to returning GIs. From "a humanitarian point of view," stated the president of the National Association of Manufacturers, "too many women should not stay in the labor force. The home is the basic American institution." Wartime surveys showed, however, that many of the women wanted to remain in their jobs. Eighty percent of New York's women workers felt that way, as did 75 percent of Detroit's female laborers. "War jobs have uncovered unsuspected abilities in American women," explained one woman. "Why lose all these abilities because of a belief that 'a woman's place is in the home.' For some it is," she added, "for others not."

Although women increased their wages when they acquired better jobs, they still received lower pay than men, even for the same work. In 1945,

Discrimination Against Women and Children

women in manufacturing earned only 65 percent of what men were paid. An important reason for this inequality was the sex-segregated labor market. Although the wartime emergency caused some traditionally male jobs to be reclassified for women, most jobs were defined as either "women's work" or "men's work." Even in factories, most women worked in all-female shops.

Working women, particularly working mothers, suffered in other ways as well. Perhaps the most persistent problem was the near-absence of supportive services such as childcare centers and communal kitchens. Some of the most serious wartime social problems were a direct result of the lack of such services. During the war there were increases in juvenile delinquency, venereal disease, teenage pregnancy, and the incidence of "eight-hour orphans," or "latchkey children," left alone while their mothers worked eight-hour shifts in war

plants. In 1940 Congress passed the Lanham Act to provide federal aid to communities that had to absorb large war-related populations. Benefits included funds for daycare centers, hospitals, sewer systems, police and firefighting facilities, and recreation centers. But provision was made for the care of only 107,000 children. Many of the remaining children roamed the streets or were locked in cars or sent to all-day or even all-night movies. In an area of concentrated war industry in Los Angeles, one social worker counted forty-five infants locked in cars in a single lot.

Crime was another problem: juvenile arrests jumped 20 percent nationwide in 1943. The increase was greater for girls than for boys; in San Diego, arrests increased 55 percent for boys and 355 percent for girls. Some of these girls became prostitutes: in 1943, arrests for that crime climbed 68 percent. Among boys the most common crime was theft, but vandalism and violence were also problems.

Perhaps because of such statistics, the massive contributions children made to the war effort were often overlooked. Children contributed their own nickels and dimes to buy war stamps and bonds, and they pulled their wagons from house to house collecting old newspapers and tin cans. The Boy Scouts collected 109 million pounds of rubber and 370 million pounds of scrap metal. Even more significant was that thousands of young people went to work during the war. In 1940, for example, 900,000 boys and girls between the ages of fourteen and eighteen were employed. By the spring of 1944 their number had climbed to 3 million—one-third of their age group. Indeed, some observers felt that the most pressing social problem afflicting teenagers was not juvenile delinquency but failure to finish school. High school enrollments hit new lows during the war, prompting a back-to-school drive in 1944.

While millions of women and youths were entering the work force, hundreds of thousands of women were getting married. From 1939 to 1942

Increase in Marriage, Divorce, and Birth Rates

the marriage rate rose from 73 marriages per 1,000 unmarried women to 93 per 1,000. Some couples scrambled to get married so they could spend time together before the man was sent overseas. Some doubtless married and had children to qualify for military deferments. But the rush to get married was also fueled by prosperity. A justice of the peace in Yuma, Arizona, explained that the marriage rate "began going up as soon as those boys were given employment in those plants at San Diego and Los Angeles and were taken off WPA." He was not exaggerating; 90 percent of the marriage licenses in Yuma went to aircraft workers.

These hasty marriages often did not survive long military separations. As a result, divorces soared too, from 25,000 in 1939 to 359,000 in 1943 and 485,000 in 1945. As might be expected, the birthrate also climbed: total births rose from over 2.4 million in 1939 to 3.1 million in 1943. Many of these births were "good-bye babies," conceived as a hedge against the future before the father left for the war, a guarantee that the family would be perpetuated if he died in battle overseas.

Ironically, women's efforts to hold their families together during the war posed problems for returning fathers. Women war workers had brought home the wages; they had taken over the budgeting of expenses and the writing of checks. In countless ways they had proved they could hold the reins in their husbands' absence. When the husbands began returning home in the waning months of the war, many found that the pattern of life for their wives and children seemed to be complete without them. For some men, it was not just a case of appearances; they knew their families could survive and even prosper without them.

What of the women who wanted to remain in the labor market? Many were forced by employers, or by their husbands, to quit. Others chose to leave their jobs for a year or two but then returned to work. And throughout the rest of the 1940s and 1950s, millions more who had never worked took jobs.

Old institutions and children alike participated in the war effort. These boys from the Grand Street Settlement on New York City's Lower East Side collected metal for recycling. Beating pots, spoons, lids, and pans together, the boys attracted a gathering of onlookers as well as the attention of the tenant-dwellers to whom they directed their appeal. *Wide World Photos.*

The Decline of Liberalism and the Election of 1944

Another wartime trend was the decline of political liberalism. Even before Pearl Harbor, liberals had suffered major defeats. Some Democrats hoped to revive the reform movement during the war, but Republicans and conservative Democrats were on guard against such a move. New Dealers, warned Republican Senator Robert Taft of Ohio early in 1942, "are determined to make the country over under the cover of war if they can." Taft and his fellow conservatives successfully blocked reform.

Aided by a small turnout in November 1942, the Republicans scored impressive gains, winning forty-four new seats in the House and nine in the Senate and defeating Democratic governors in New York, California, and Michigan. Part of the Democrats' problem was that the war years, unlike the 1930s, were a time of full employment. Once people had acquired jobs and gained some economic security, they began to be more critical of New Deal policies. The New Deal coalition had always had the potential for fragmentation. Southern white farmers had little in common with northern blacks or white factory workers. And in northern cities, blacks and whites who had voted for Roosevelt in

Campaigning for re-election in 1944, President Roosevelt appeared emaciated and weary. Raindrops stood on the lenses of his glasses as he waved to crowds in New York City. Some people thought he had been foolhardy to campaign in the rain, but he needed to prove that he could still measure up to the demands of his office.
UPI/Bettmann Archives.

ness, and old age. If to accomplish those goals the government had to operate at a deficit, Roosevelt was willing to do so. But first he had to be re-elected.

In 1944 Franklin D. Roosevelt looked like an exhausted old man. His eyes were tired and puffy; he was almost bald; and the loose flesh that hung on his large frame made him appear emaciated. The president's personal physician pronounced "nothing organically wrong with him at all—he's perfectly O.K.," but rumors of his ill health persisted. Whether or not Roosevelt expected to survive his fourth term, he selected a running mate who was inexperienced in international affairs. His choice was Senator Harry S Truman of Missouri. During the war Truman had gained favorable publicity for chairing a senatorial watchdog committee on favoritism and waste in the awarding of defense contracts. A representative of both a border state and a big-city machine (the Pendergast machine in Kansas City), Truman was satisfactory both to southerners and to the bosses. An ardent and loyal New Dealer, the senator was also approved by liberals. There was little evidence, however, that he possessed the qualities of national and world leadership that he would need as president. Roosevelt did not take Truman into his confidence, failing even to inform his running mate about the atomic bomb project.

The Republicans were optimistic about their prospects for regaining the presidency. New York's Governor Thomas E. Dewey, who won the nomination on the first ballot, was a moderate who did not advocate repeal of the essentials of the New Deal— Social Security, unemployment relief, collective bargaining, and price supports for farmers—and he was cautious in his criticism of Roosevelt's foreign policy. But Dewey had one great liability, his public image. Short of stature and dull of personality, Dewey looked, as Alice Longworth, Theodore Roosevelt's daughter, described him, "like the bridegroom on a wedding cake."

Although Roosevelt won a fourth term, the margin of victory in the popular vote was his narrowest ever; it was the closest presidential election since 1916. Nevertheless, he won 53.4 percent of the popular vote and 432 electoral votes to Dewey's 99. It was the urban vote that returned Roosevelt to the White House. Wartime population shifts had much to do with the cities' new political clout. New work-

1940 were competing for jobs and housing and would soon collide in race riots.

With Republican victories in 1942, the alliance of conservative southern Democrats and Republicans became a formidable threat to New Deal programs. In 1942 and 1943 the conservative coalition actually abolished several New Deal relief and social welfare agencies, among them the Civilian Conservation Corps and the Work Projects Administration.

But though liberalism was enfeebled, it was far from dead. The liberal agenda began with a pledge to secure full employment. Roosevelt emphasized the concept in his Economic Bill of Rights, delivered as part of his 1944 State of the Union address. Every American had a right, the president declared, to a decent job; to sufficient food, shelter, and clothing; and to financial security in unemployment, ill-

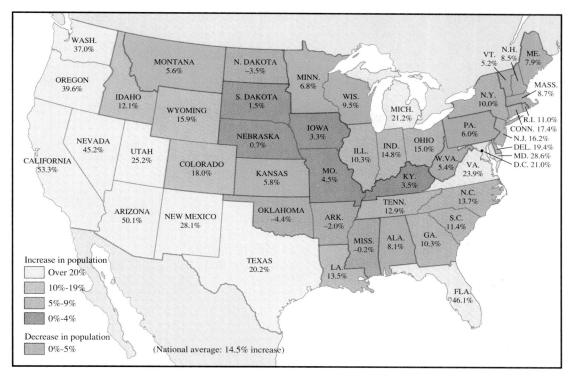

A Nation on the Move, 1940–1950 *Source: U.S. Bureau of the Census,* Portfolio of United States Census Maps, 1950 *(Washington: U.S. Government Printing Office, 1953), p. 4.*

ers—notably southern whites who had been lifelong Democrats and southern blacks who had never before voted—had migrated to the urban industrial centers (see map). Added to the urban vote was a less-obvious factor. Many voters seemed to be exhibiting what has been called "depression psychosis." Fearful that hard times would return once war contracts were terminated, they remembered New Deal relief programs and voted for Roosevelt. Finally, as Senator Taft conceded, the Republicans had "underestimated the difficulty of changing a President at the very height of a victorious war."

With victory within grasp, many Americans wanted Roosevelt's experienced hand to guide the nation, and the world, to a lasting international peace. But Roosevelt's death rendered that choice mute. The new president who would deal with the postwar world was Harry Truman.

A New President: Harry Truman

Wartime Diplomacy

The lessons of the post–First World War period weighed heavily on the minds of American diplomats throughout the war. Americans vowed to make a peace that would ensure a postwar world free from depression, totalitarianism, and war. The Atlantic Charter, so reminiscent of Woodrow Wilson's vision of an open world, was their general guide, tempered and compromised by the interests of the great powers. Thus American goals included the Open Door and lower tariffs; self-determination for liberated peoples; avoidance of the debts-reparations tangle that had plagued Europe after the First World War; expansion of the United States sphere of influence; and management of world affairs by what Roosevelt once called the Four Policemen: Russia, China, Great Britain, and the United States.

Although the major Allies concentrated on defeating the aggressors, their suspicions of one another undermined cooperation. More dogged

> **Allied Disagreement over Eastern Europe**

them than the timing of the second front and the Italian surrender. Eastern European questions proved the most difficult. The Russians sought to fix their boundaries where they had stood before Hitler attacked in 1941. In the case of Poland, this meant that the part of the country that the Soviets had invaded and captured in 1939 would become Russian territory. The British and Americans hesitated, preferring to deal with Eastern Europe at the end of the war. But the sustained drive of the Russian armies through the region on the heels of the retreating Germans persuaded Churchill to act. In an October 1944 agreement, he and Stalin struck a bargain: Russia would gain Rumania and Bulgaria as a sphere of influence; Britain would have the upper hand in Greece; and the two would share authority in Yugoslavia and Hungary. The two leaders, however, did not agree on Poland.

Poland was a special case. In 1943, Moscow had broken off diplomatic relations with the conservative Polish government-in-exile in London. The Poles had angered Moscow when they asked the International Red Cross to investigate German charges that the Russians had massacred thousands of Polish army officers in the Katyn Forest in 1940. Then an uprising in Warsaw in July 1944 complicated matters still further. Taking advantage of the nearness of Soviet troops, the Warsaw underground rose against the occupying Germans. To the dismay of the world community, Soviet armies stood aside as German troops slaughtered 166,000 people and devastated the city. Finally, in late 1944 and early 1945 the Soviets spawned a pro-Communist government in Lublin. Thus near the end of the war Poland had two competing governments, one in London, recognized by America and Britain, and another in Lublin.

Early in the war the Allies had begun talking about a new international organization. At Teheran in 1943 Roosevelt called for an institution controlled by the Four Policemen.

> **Creation of the United Nations Organization**

The next year, in a Washington, D.C., mansion called Dumbarton Oaks, American, British, Russian, and Chinese representatives conferred on the details. Since American participation had been endorsed in public opinion polls and congressional resolutions, United States diplomats proceeded with some assurance that their handiwork would not meet the legislative fate of Wilson's League of Nations. The conferees approved a preliminary charter for a United Nations Organization, providing for a supreme Security Council dominated by the great powers and a weak General Assembly (Roosevelt called it "an investigatory body only"). The Security Council would have five permanent members, each with veto power.

Disagreement surfaced when the United States pushed China forward as a great power entitled to permanent membership on the council. Churchill complained that China was a captive vote on the side of the United States. To mollify him, the United States reluctantly agreed to elevate France to a permanent seat. Russia accepted both France and China, believing that its veto power would protect its national interest against unfriendly decisions. But noting that the United States would have a group of sympathetic votes in the General Assembly among the Latin American states, and that Britain could muster support from members of its Commonwealth, the Soviets asked for a balancing of power. They wanted separate membership in the General Assembly for the sixteen Soviet republics. This issue was not resolved at Dumbarton Oaks, but the meeting proved a success nevertheless. The conferees had achieved 90 percent of their goals, Roosevelt pointed out. "Well, that is what we used to call in the old days a darn good batting average."

Diplomatic action on another problem, Nazi treatment of the Jews, proved to be a tragic failure. Even before the war, Nazi officials had targeted

> **Jewish Refugees from the Holocaust**

Jews throughout Europe for extermination. By war's end, about 6 million Jews had been forced into concentration camps and systematically killed by firing squads, unspeakable tortures, and gas chambers. The Nazis also exterminated as many as 250,000 gypsies. During the Nazi era, about 60,000 men were convicted of homosexuality; most ended up in concentration camps where they perished. Many others who survived the Holocaust could never forget the terror. During the depression the United States and other nations had refused to relax

◀   Chapter 27: The Second World War at Home and Abroad, 1941–1945

On April 11, 1945, prisoners in the Buchenwald concentration camp rose up against their SS jailers and liberated themselves. Parading arms stolen from the SS guards or smuggled into the camp, the inmates were in control when American troops arrived the next day. During the grisly years preceding the end of the war, however, the Nazis had murdered well over 6 million people in camps such as Buchenwald. *Margaret Bourke-White,* Life *Magazine © 1945 Time Inc.*

their immigration restrictions to save Jews fleeing persecution. The American Federation of Labor and Senator William Borah of Idaho, among others, argued that new immigrants would compete with American workers for scarce jobs, and public opinion polls supported their position. The fear of economic competition was fed by anti-Semitism. Bureaucrats applied the rules so strictly—requiring legal documents that fleeing Jews could not possibly provide—that otherwise qualified refugees were kept out of the country. From 1933 to 1945 less than 40 percent of the German-Austrian quota was filled.

Even the tragic voyage of the *St. Louis* did not change government policy. The vessel left Hamburg in mid-1939 with 930 desperate Jewish ref-

ugees who lacked proper immigration documents. Denied entry to Havana, the *St. Louis* headed for Miami, where Coast Guard cutters prevented it from docking. Aroused American citizens appealed to Washington, but the ship was forced to return to Europe. Some of those refugees took shelter in countries that were later overrun by Hitler's legions. "The cruise of the *St. Louis,*" wrote the *New York Times,* "cries to high heaven of man's inhumanity to man."

As news of the Nazi atrocities filled government files during the war years, American officials futilely attempted to persuade Latin American countries to accept refugees. They also approached the British, who proved unhelpful as well: they would not open Palestine. Some American leaders were themselves lax in their attention to the problem. The State Department officer in charge was Breckinridge Long, a Democratic politician who actually hindered private citizens' efforts to save victims.

When evidence mounted that Hitler intended to exterminate the Jews, British and American representatives met in Bermuda (1943) but came up with no plans. Secretary Hull made a discouraging report to the president, emphasizing "the unknown cost of moving an undetermined number of persons from an undisclosed place to an unknown destination." Appalled, Secretary of the Treasury Henry Morgenthau, Jr., charged that the State Department's foot-dragging made the United States an accessory to murder. "It takes months and months to grant the visa and then it usually applies to a corpse," he wrote bitterly. Early in 1944, stirred by Morgenthau's well-documented plea, Roosevelt created the War Refugee Board, which set up refugee camps in Europe and saved thousands from death.

But American officials waited too long to act, and they missed a chance to destroy the gas chambers and ovens at the extermination camp at Auschwitz in occupied Poland. They had aerial photographs and diagrams of the camp, but they argued that bombing it would detract from the war effort or prompt the Germans to step up the anti-Jewish terror. In 1944, American planes bombed synthetic oil and rubber plants in the industrial sector of Auschwitz, only five miles from the gas chambers and crematoria. "How could it be," historian David S. Wyman has asked, "that Government officials knew that a place existed where 2,000 helpless human beings could be killed in less than an hour, knew that this occurred over and over again, and yet did not feel driven to search for some way to wipe such a scourge from the earth?"

The Yalta Conference and a Flawed Peace

With the war in Europe nearing an end, and a host of political questions—including what to do with Germany—yet to be settled, President Roosevelt urged another summit meeting. The three Allied leaders met at Yalta, on the Russian Crimea, in early February 1945. Controversy has surrounded the conference ever since. Roosevelt was obviously ill. "His appearance could change in a couple of hours from looking like a ghost to looking okay," remarked the new Secretary of State Edward Stettinius, Jr. The sixty-two-year-old president suffered from hypertension, heart disease, and hardening of the arteries. His doctors prescribed rest, a reduction in cigarette smoking, and medication, but the president maintained a busy schedule. Critics of the Yalta agreements later charged that Roosevelt was too weak to resist the demands of a guileful Stalin and that he struck a poor bargain. The evidence suggests, however, that Roosevelt was mentally alert and that he managed to sustain his strength during negotiations.

The Yalta meeting has also been criticized because some of its agreements were secret (suggesting that the Allies had something to hide) and because it decided the fate of weakened nations like Poland and China without their consent. The truth is that some agreements were secret because they contained military information that had to be kept from the still undefeated Japanese and Germans. But the criticism that the Allies paid scant attention to small nations was well deserved. It exposed a pattern of wartime diplomacy, which assumed that the most powerful of the Allies would dominate international relations after the war.

Each of the Allies entered into the conference with definite goals. Britain sought a place for France in occupied Germany, a curb on Soviet influence in Poland, and protection for the vulnerable British Empire. Russia wanted reparations from Germany to assist in the massive task of rebuilding at home, possessions in Asia, continued influence in Poland, and a permanently weakened Germany so that Russia would never again suffer a German attack. The United States lobbied for the United Nations Organization, where it believed it could exercise influence; for a Soviet declaration of war against Japan; for recognition of China as a major power; and for compromise between rival factions in Poland.

Allied Goals at Yalta

Military positions at the time of the conference helped to shape the final agreements. Soviet troops had occupied much of Eastern Europe, including

Chapter 27: The Second World War at Home and Abroad, 1941–1945

The three Allied leaders—Winston Churchill, Franklin D. Roosevelt, and Josef Stalin—met at Yalta in February 1945. Having been president for twelve years, Roosevelt showed signs of age and fatigue. Two months later, he died of a massive cerebral hemorrhage. *Franklin D. Roosevelt Library.*

Poland, while the Western Allies were emerging from the Battle of the Bulge. In Asia the Japanese were still resisting the American advance. Millions of Japanese troops in China, Manchuria, Korea, and the home islands seemed ready to die to the last man for the empire. As near as victory was, Britain and the United States still needed the Soviets to win the war.

The unsettled issue of Poland preoccupied the conferees. Stalin repeatedly pointed out that twice in the century German armies had marched through Poland into Russian territory, killing millions. He insisted on a government friendly to Moscow—the Lublin regime—in order to prevent

another German onslaught. And he demanded boundaries that would give Poland part of Germany in the west and Russia part of Poland in the east. Churchill boiled over in protest; he wanted the London regime to return to Poland. A compromise was reached under Roosevelt's leadership: a boundary favorable to Russia in the east, postponement of the western boundary issue, and the creation of a "more broadly based" coalition government that would include members of the London government-in-exile. Free elections would be held sometime in the future. The agreement was vague, but given Soviet occupation of Poland, Roosevelt considered it "the best I can do."

The Yalta Conference and a Flawed Peace

As for Germany, the Big Three agreed that it would be divided into four zones, the fourth to go to France. On the question of reparations, Russia wanted a precise figure, but Churchill and Roosevelt said they would first have to determine Germany's ability to pay. Without the British, the Americans and Russians agreed that an Allied committee would consider the sum of $20 billion as a basis for discussion in the future, with half the amount to go to the Soviet Union.

Other issues found trade-offs. Stalin promised to declare war on Japan two or three months after Hitler's defeat. Since the atomic bomb was still on the drawing boards, American military leaders applauded the commitment. The Soviet premier also consented to sign a treaty of friendship and alliance with Jiang Jieshi (Chiang Kai-shek), America's ally in China, rather than with the Communist Mao Zedong. In return the United States agreed to Russia's taking the southern part of Sakhalin Island and Lushun (Port Arthur). To the Russians these concessions amounted to a recovery of holdings lost after the Russo-Japanese War in 1905. Regarding the new world organization, Roosevelt and Churchill granted the Soviets three votes in the General Assembly. (Fifty nations officially launched the United Nations Organization in May.) Finally, the conferees accepted the Declaration of Liberated Europe, pledging to establish order and to rebuild economies by democratic methods.

Yalta marked the high point of the Grand Alliance; each of the Allies came away with something, in the tradition of diplomatic give-and-take. But as the great powers jockeyed

Potsdam Conference
for influence at the close of the war, neither the spirit nor the letter of Yalta held firm. The crumbling of the alliance became evident at the Potsdam Conference, which took place between July 17 and August 2, 1945. Roosevelt had died in April, and Harry S Truman had replaced him. Truman was a novice at international diplomacy and less patient with the Russians. Stalin "seems to like it when I hit him with a hammer," he bragged in a letter to his wife Bess. "We had a tough meeting," he also wrote. "I reared up on my hind legs and told 'em where to get off and they got off." Truman seemed especially emboldened after he learned during the conference that the atomic test in New Mexico was successful. "Now I know what happened to Tru-

man," said Churchill. "When he got to the meeting after having read this report he was a changed man. He told the Russians just where they got off and generally bossed the whole meeting."

Despite the "brawl" at Potsdam, as Truman called it, the Big Three did agree on general policies toward Germany: complete disarmament, elimination of industry used for military production, and dissolution of Nazi institutions and laws. In a compromise over reparations, they decided that each occupying nation should take reparations from its own zone; but they could not agree on a total figure. To resolve other issues, such as peace treaties with Italy, Finland, and Hungary, the Big Three created the Council of Foreign Ministers.

Potsdam left much undone. As the war drew to a close, there was little that bound the Allies together. Roosevelt's cooperative style was gone; the spirit of Yalta was evaporating; the common enemy, Hitler, was defeated. And America, with the awesome atomic bomb in the offing to force defeat upon Japan, no longer needed, or even wanted, Russia in the Pacific war. Moreover, the victors were seeking to preserve and enlarge their spheres of influence. Britain claimed authority in Greece and parts of the Middle East; the Soviet Union already dominated much of Eastern Europe; and the United States continued its hegemony in Latin America. The United States also seized several Pacific islands as strategic outposts and laid plans to dominate a defeated Japan. Let the Americans have their Pacific bases, responded Churchill, "but 'Hands off the British Empire' is our maxim." Furthermore, American interests increased their stake in Middle Eastern oil during the war. By 1944, American petroleum companies controlled 42 percent of the proven oil reserves of the Middle East—a nineteen-fold increase since 1936. Both the British and the Russians complained about this new evidence of American expansionism.

Hitler once said, "We may be destroyed, but if we are, we shall drag a world with us—a world in flames." Indeed, *rubble* became the word most commonly invoked to describe the global landscape at the end of the war. Hamburg, Stuttgart, and Dresden had been laid waste; three-quarters of Berlin was in ruins. In England, Coventry and parts of London were bombed out. Across the continent transportation systems had been disrupted and water supplies contaminated. Everywhere ghostlike

Chapter 27: The Second World War at Home and Abroad, 1941–1945

people wandered about searching desperately for food and mourning those who would never come home. Russia had lost 20 million people; Poland 5.8 million; Germany 4.5 million. In all, about 35 million Europeans died as a result of the war. In Asia untold millions of Chinese and 2 million Japanese died.

Only one major combatant escaped these grisly statistics: the United States. Its cities were not burned and its fields were not trampled. American deaths from the war—405,399—were few compared with the losses of other nations. In fact, Americans came out of the Second World War more powerful than they had gone in. They alone had the atomic bomb. The American air force and navy were the largest anywhere. And though the United States demobilized the major part of its regular army after the war, it still had 2 million men in arms in 1946, 1.6 million in 1949. What is more, only the United States had the capital and economic resources to spur international recovery. America was, gloated Truman, a "giant." In the coming struggle to fashion a new world out of the ashes of the old, soon called the Cold War (see Chapter 28), the United States held a commanding position.

> **Postwar Strength of the United States**

Because of events at home and abroad, life for many Americans in 1945 was fundamentally different from what it had been before Pearl Harbor. The Academy Award–winning film for 1946 was *The Best Years of Our Lives,* the painful story of the postwar readjustments of three veterans and their families and friends. Not only veterans' lives had been changed by the experiences of war; with the advent of the Cold War, millions of younger men would also be inducted into the armed forces over the next thirty years. War and the expectation of war would become part of American life.

The Second World War was a powerful engine of social change in the United States. The gains made during the war by blacks and women were overdue, but other changes were less welcome. The war had stimulated the trend toward bigness not only in business and labor but also in government. In the next few years, government agencies that had been conceived as temporary would become permanent and would grow in size and influence. The results are well known—a Department of Defense (consolidating the War and Navy Departments), the Central Intelligence Agency (succeeding the Office of Strategic Services), the Atomic Energy Commission. The seeds of the military-industrial complex were sown in these years. At the same time, by blending New Deal ideology and wartime urgency, the government assumed the responsibility of assuring prosperity and stepping in when capitalism faltered. For better or worse—and clearly there were elements of both—the Second World War was a watershed in the nation's history.

Suggestions for Further Reading

Fighting the War

Stephen A. Ambrose, *Eisenhower: Soldier, General of the Army, President-Elect* (1983); Stephen A. Ambrose, *The Supreme Commander* (1970); Hanson Baldwin, *Battles Lost and Won* (1966); A. Russell Buchanan, *The United States in World War II,* 2 vols. (1964); Peter Calvocoressi and Guy Wint, *Total War* (1972); John W. Dower, *War Without Mercy: Race and Power in the Pacific War* (1986); R. Ernest Dupuy, *World War II* (1969); Kent R. Greenfield, *American Strategy in World War II* (1963); B. H. Liddell Hart, *History of the Second World War* (1970); Max Hastings, *OVERLORD: D-Day and the Battle of Normandy* (1984); D. Clayton James, *A Time for Giants: Politics of the American High Command in World War II* (1987); D. Clayton James, *The Years of MacArthur, 1941–1945* (1975); David Kahn, *The Codebreakers* (1967); Eric Larabee, *Commander in Chief* (1987); Richard M. Leighton and Robert W. Coakley, *Global Logistics and Strategy, 1940–1945,* 2 vols. (1955–1968); Samuel Eliot Morison, *The Two-Ocean War* (1963); Samuel Eliot Morison, *Strategy and Compromise* (1958); Forrest C. Pogue, *George C. Marshall,* 4 vols. (1963–1987); Ronald Schaffer, *Wings of Judgment: American Bombing in World War II* (1985); Bradley F. Smith, *The Shadow Warriors: O.S.S. and the Origins of the C.I.A.* (1983); Ronald H. Spector, *Eagle Against the Sun: The American War with Japan* (1984); Russell F. Weigley, *The American Way of War* (1973); Gordon Wright, *The Ordeal of Total War, 1939–1945* (1968).

Grand Alliance Diplomacy

Robert Beitzel, *The Uneasy Alliance* (1972); Russell Buhite, *Decisions at Yalta* (1986); James MacGregor Burns, *Roosevelt: The Soldier of Freedom* (1970); Thomas Campbell, *Masquerade Peace: America's UN Policy, 1944–1945* (1973); Winston S. Churchill, *The Second World War,* 6 vols. (1948–1953); Diane Clemens, *Yalta* (1970); Robert Dallek, *Franklin D. Roosevelt and American Foreign Policy, 1932–*

1945 (1979); Robert A. Divine, *Roosevelt and World War II* (1969); Robert A. Divine, *Second Chance: The Triumph of Internationalism in America During World War II* (1967); Henry L. Feingold, *Politics of Rescue* (1970); Herbert Feis, *Churchill, Roosevelt, and Stalin* (1957); George C. Herring, *Aid to Russia, 1941–1946* (1973); Akira Iriye, *Power and Culture: The Japanese-American War, 1941–1945* (1981); Gabriel Kolko, *The Politics of War* (1968); William R. Louis, *Imperialism at Bay: The United States and the Decolonization of the British Empire* (1978); William H. McNeill, *America, Britain, and Russia* (1953); Vojtech Mastny, *Russia's Road to the Cold War* (1979); Arthur D. Morse, *While Six Million Died* (1968); Keith Sainsbury, *The Turning Point* (1985); Gaddis Smith, *Diplomacy During the Second World War, 1941–1945,* 2nd ed. (1985); Michael Stoff, *Oil, War, and American Security* (1980); Mark Stoler, *The Politics of the Second Front* (1977); Christopher Thorne, *Allies of a Kind* (1977); David S. Wyman, *The Abandonment of the Jews: America and the Holocaust, 1941–1945* (1984).

The Home Front

John Morton Blum, *V Was for Victory: Politics and American Culture During World War II* (1976); Alan Clive, *State of War: Michigan in World War II* (1979); John Costello, *Virtue Under Fire: How World War II Changed Our Social and Sexual Attitudes* (1985); John D'Emilio, *Sexual Politics, Sexual Communities: The Making of a Homosexual Minority in the United States, 1940–1970* (1983); Mark Jonathan Harris et al., *The Homefront* (1984); Richard R. Lingeman, *Don't You Know There's a War On?* (1970); Gerald D. Nash, *The American West Transformed: The Impact of the Second World War* (1985); Geoffrey Perrett, *Days of Sadness, Years of Triumph: The American People, 1939–1945* (1973); Richard Polenberg, *War and Society* (1972); Studs Terkel, ed., *"The Good War": An Oral History of World War Two* (1984).

Mobilizing for War

David Brinkley, *Washington Goes to War* (1988); Bruce Catton, *The War Lords of Washington* (1948); George Q. Flynn, *The Mess in Washington: Manpower Mobilization in World War II* (1979); Eliot Janeway, *The Struggle for Survival* (1951); Daniel J. Kevles, *The Physicists* (1977); Paul A. C. Koistinen, *The Hammer and the Sword: Labor, the Military, and Industrial Mobilization, 1920–1945* (1979); William M. Tuttle, Jr., "The Birth of an Industry: The Synthetic Rubber 'Mess' in World War II," *Technology and Culture,* 22 (1981), 35–67; Harold G. Vatter, *The U.S. Economy in World War II* (1985); Gerald T. White, *Billions for Defense: Government Finance by the Defense Plant Corporation During World War II* (1980); Allen M. Winkler, *The Politics of Propaganda: The Office of War Information, 1942–1945* (1978).

Farmers and Workers, Soldiers and Sailors

John L. Blackman, Jr., *Presidential Seizure in Labor Disputes* (1967); Melvyn Dubofsky and Warren H. Van Tine, *John L. Lewis: A Biography* (1977); Lee Kennett, *G.I.: The American Soldier in World War II* (1987); Nelson Lichtenstein, *Labor's War at Home: The CIO in World War II* (1983); Bill Mauldin, *Up Front,* rev. ed. (1968); Davis R. B. Ross, *Preparing for Ulysses: Politics and Veterans During World War II* (1969); Joel Seidman, *American Labor from Defense to Reconversion* (1953); Samuel A. Stouffer et al., *The American Soldier,* 2 vols. (1949); Walter W. Wilcox, *The Farmer in the Second World War* (1947).

Japanese-American Internment

Commission on Wartime Relocation and Internment of Civilians, *Personal Justice Denied* (1982); Roger Daniels, *Concentration Camps U.S.A.* (1971); Morton Grodzins, *Americans Betrayed: Politics and the Japanese Evacuation* (1949); Bill Hosokawa, *Nisei: The Quiet Americans* (1969); Peter Irons, *Justice at War* (1983); Thomas James, *Exile Within: The Schooling of Japanese-Americans, 1942–1945* (1987); John Tateishi, ed., *And Justice for All: An Oral History of the Japanese-American Detention Camps* (1984); Jacobus tenBroek et al., *Prejudice, War and the Constitution* (1954); Michi Weglyn, *Years of Infamy* (1976).

Politics

Richard E. Darilek, *A Loyal Opposition in Time of War* (1976); James C. Foster, *The Union Politic: The CIO Political Action Committee* (1975); Maurice Isserman, *Which Side Were You On? The American Communist Party During the Second World War* (1982); Roland Young, *Congressional Politics in the Second World War* (1956).

African-Americans and Wartime Violence

A. Russell Buchanan, *Black Americans in World War II* (1977); Dominic J. Capeci, Jr., *Race Relations in Wartime Detroit* (1984); Dominic J. Capeci, Jr., *The Harlem Riot of 1943* (1977); Richard M. Dalfiume, *Desegregation of the U.S. Armed Forces* (1969); Lee Finkle, *Forum for Protest: The Black Press During World War II* (1975); Phillip McGuire, ed., *Taps for a Jim Crow Army: Letters from Black Soldiers in World War II* (1982); Mauricio Mazon, *The Zoot-Suit Riots* (1984); Harvard Sitkoff, "Racial Militancy and Interracial Violence in the Second World War," *Journal of American History,* 58 (1971), 661–681; Patrick S. Washburn, *A Question of Sedition: The Federal Government's Investigation of the Black Press During World War II* (1986); Neil A. Wynn, *The Afro-American and the Second World War* (1976).

Women at War

Karen T. Anderson, *Wartime Women: Sex Roles, Family Relations, and the Status of Women During World War II* (1981); D'Ann Campbell, *Women at War with America* (1984); William H. Chafe, *The American Woman: Her Changing Social, Economic, and Political Roles, 1920–1970* (1972); Sherna Berger Gluck, *Rosie the Riveter Revisited* (1987); Chester W. Gregory, *Women in Defense Work During World War II* (1974); Susan M. Hartmann, *The Home Front and Beyond* (1982); Margaret Randolph Higgonet et al., eds., *Behind the Lines: Gender and the Two World Wars* (1987); Sally Van Wagenen Keil, *Those Wonderful Women in Their Flying Machines* (1979); Alice Kessler-Harris, *Out to Work* (1982); Ruth Milkman, *Gender at Work: The Dynamics of Job Discrimination by Sex During World War II* (1987); Leila J. Rupp, *Mobilizing Women for War: German and American Propaganda, 1939–1945* (1978).

The Atomic Bomb and Japan's Surrender

Gar Alperovitz, *Atomic Diplomacy,* rev. ed. (1985); Barton J. Bernstein, ed., *The Atomic Bomb* (1976); Robert J. C. Butow, *Japan's Decision to Surrender* (1954); Committee for the Compilation of Materials on Damage Caused by the Atomic Bombs in Hiroshima and Nagasaki, *Hiroshima and Nagasaki* (1981); Herbert Feis, *The Atomic Bomb and the End of World War II* (1966); Gregg Herken, *The Winning Weapon* (1980); John Hersey, *Hiroshima,* rev. ed. (1985); Richard G. Hewlett and Oscar E. Anderson, *The New World* (1962); Richard Rhodes, *The Making of the Atomic Bomb* (1987); Martin J. Sherwin, *A World Destroyed* (1975); Leon V. Sigal, *Fighting to a Finish* (1988).

President Harry S Truman was exhausted on March 13, 1947, as his official plane flew him from Washington to his Florida vacation spot in Key West. "This terrible decision I had to make," he wrote his daughter Margaret that day, "had been over my head for about six weeks." He said he had learned at the Potsdam Conference of 1945 "that there is no difference in totalitarian or police states, call them what you will, Nazi, Fascist, Communist. . . . The attempt of Lenin, Trotsky, Stalin, et al., to fool the world . . . is just like Hitler's and Mussolini's so-called socialist states. Your Pop had to tell the world just that in polite language."

The day before, in a controversial speech to a joint session of Congress, the president had announced the Truman Doctrine. Without mentioning the Soviet Union by name, he equated its policies with the former "totalitarian regimes" of Germany and Japan. "I believe," he said, "that it must be the policy of the United States to support free peoples who are resisting attempted subjugation by armed minorities or by outside pressures." These words became the backbone of *containment,* a doctrine that in the coming years would lead the United States into armed conflict in Asia, the Middle East, and Latin America.

28

THE COLD WAR AND AMERICAN POLITICS, 1945–1953

The Cold War was a central theme of Truman's presidency at home as well as abroad. For one thing, Truman's rhetoric heightened fears that a Communist conspiracy was operating within the federal government. On March 21, just a week after his Truman Doctrine speech, the president announced another momentous decision. Through an executive order, he established the Employee Loyalty Program for the executive branch of the government. Henceforth, all agency heads had to ensure that each employee under their jurisdiction was a loyal American. In doubtful cases, the agency's director had to appoint a loyalty board to hear the evidence and make recommendations. For the first time, government officials had the authority to pass judgment on a job applicant's personal beliefs and past associations. People already on the job who were accused of disloyalty were presumed to be guilty, not innocent. Although some critics argued that Truman's anti-Communist actions were bellicose and a threat to civil liberties and that he shot from the hip, his decisiveness initially won him many followers nationally.

When Franklin D. Roosevelt died in office in April 1945, Truman had acceded to the presidency. Contrary to his later "Give 'em hell, Harry" image, Truman's immediate response to this challenge was a deep feeling of inadequacy. "I'm not big enough for this job," he confided to a friend. Even an experienced, well-respected president would have faced an enormous task in guiding the nation's transition from war to peace. But the new president was little more than an obscure politician. "Who is Harry Truman?" Americans asked themselves when they heard the news of Roosevelt's death. As a senator from Missouri, Truman had been a New Deal liberal. He was intelligent, warm, hardworking, and honest, a loving husband and father. But he was also short-tempered, impulsive, headstrong, and quick to call people names ("son of a bitch" was one of his favorites). Neither his virtues nor his defects, however, were well known at the time.

Although Roosevelt had chosen Truman as his running mate in 1944, he had left the vice president in the dark about crucial foreign and military policies, even including the development of the atomic bomb. "They didn't tell me anything about what was going on," Truman fretted after a month in the presidency. With the rapid deterioration of Soviet-American relations, however, the new president got a quick education.

In foreign affairs the theme of anticommunism revealed itself in Cold War policies that protected and expanded American overseas interests, challenged the Soviet Union, created alliance systems, rebuilt Western Europe and Japan, drew the United States into civil wars, and favored a military build-up over diplomacy. The United States emerged from the Second World War the most powerful nation on earth, but the world it faced seemed resistant to the exercise of that power. Much of Asia and Europe lay in ruins, requiring a huge reconstruction task, and civil wars and colonial rebellions rocked political stability. The United States and the Soviet Union scrambled to win friends and to drive in economic and strategic stakes. The two nations clashed constantly, "like two big dogs chewing on a bone," remarked Senator J. William Fulbright of Arkansas. Truman saw the Soviet threat as global and decided to project American power on a worldwide scale. This new globalism, with the containment doctrine as its guide, brought the United States into crisis after crisis. As Secretary of State Dean Acheson said, the United States was "playing for keeps" in a global contest with the Soviet Union and would go on creating "situations of strength."

Just five years after the Second World War, the Cold War turned hot on the peninsula of Korea. Although the threat of world war did not materialize, the Korean conflict significantly accelerated the process toward globalism. The United States began to enlarge its military power and to develop new nuclear weapons.

In domestic as well as in foreign policy, the new president got a crash course in the intricacies of governing the United States. In 1945, the nation's reconversion from war to peace was not smooth, and Truman managed to anger liberals, conservatives, farmers, consumers, and union members during his first year as president. In 1946, voters responded to inflation and a wave of strikes by electing a Republican Eightieth Congress. But just two years later, partly because of public approval of his decisive foreign policy, Truman confounded political experts by winning the presidency in his own right. Truman had continued to espouse the New Deal and to be loyal to the welfare system fashioned in the 1930s. He was also the first president ever to pledge federal support for racial equality. His upset victory in 1948 was proof that the New Deal coalition was alive and well.

As Truman's victory indicated, however, politics were volatile. The key domestic issues of the period—black civil rights and the anti-Communist witch hunt called McCarthyism—were the most highly charged of all. The outbreak of the Korean War in June 1950 intensified discontent at home. The military stalemate frustrated war-weary citizens; inflation began another upward climb; and evidence of corruption surfaced in the White House. Truman's popularity plummeted. In 1952, Americans cast their presidential votes for a war hero, General Dwight D. Eisenhower.

The Sources of the Cold War

After overseeing the final stages of Germany and Japan's defeat, President Truman participated in

1945	Yalta Conference	**1949**	North Atlantic Treaty
	Roosevelt dies; Truman assumes		Organization founded
	presidency		Russia explodes an atomic bomb
	Germany surrenders		Communist victory in China

1945
Yalta Conference
Roosevelt dies; Truman assumes
  presidency
Germany surrenders
Potsdam Conference
Japan surrenders
Truman's 21-point economic
  message to Congress

1946
Crisis over Iran
Employment Act of 1946
Churchill's Iron Curtain speech
Strikes by coal miners
Baruch Plan
Truman fires Secretary of
  Commerce Wallace
Inflation reaches 18.2 percent
Republicans win both houses of
  Congress

1947
Truman Doctrine
Truman's Employee Loyalty
  Program
Communist takeover in Hungary
Taft-Hartley Act
Kennan's "Mr. X" article
Marshall Plan announced
To Secure These Rights issued by
  the President's Committee on
  Civil Rights
National Security Act
Rio Pact

1948
Communist coup in
  Czechoslovakia
State of Israel founded
Berlin blockade and airlift
Truman elected president

1949
North Atlantic Treaty
  Organization founded
Russia explodes an atomic bomb
Communist victory in China

1950
Klaus Fuchs arrested as an atomic
  spy
Alger Hiss convicted of perjury
Hydrogen bomb project
  announced
McCarthy alleges Communists in
  government
Freedom to Serve issued by the
  President's Committee on
  Equality of Treatment and
  Opportunity in the Armed
  Services
NSC-68
Point Four Program launched
Korean War begins
Julius and Ethel Rosenberg
  arrested
Marine landing at Inchon
Internal Security (McCarran) Act
U.S. troops cross the 38th parallel
China enters the Korean War

1951
Armistice talks begin in Korea
Dennis et al. v. *U.S.*

1952
Hydrogen bomb exploded
Eisenhower elected president
Republicans win both houses of
  Congress

1953
Korean War ends

the rapid deterioration of Soviet-American relations—the Cold War. In this new conflict, competitive ideologies, propaganda, reconstruction programs, military alliances, atomic arms development, and spheres of influence condemned the world once again to instability and fear.

Some conflict was inevitable after the Second World War, because the international environment was so unsettled. First, the world was in serious economic trouble. Across Europe and Asia, factories, bridges, transportation and communications systems, and houses had been reduced to rubble.

People and governments in the postwar world faced the awesome task of rebuilding. In Berlin, which had been reduced to rubble, the future of the children and of subsequent generations depended upon their success. *John Philips* Life *Magazine © Time, Inc.*

> **Unsettled International Environment**

Agricultural production was low, and displaced persons wandered around in search of food and family members. How would this devastated world be pieced back together? America and Russia each offered a different model. Second, the collapse of Germany and Japan created power vacuums that drew the two major powers into collision as they sought to claim influence in countries where the Axis had once held sway. Third, political turmoil within nations spurred Soviet-American competition. In Greece and China, for example, where civil wars were waged between leftists and conservative regimes, the two powers favored different sides. Fourth, empires were disintegrating. In this process of decolonization, the European imperial nations were forced to withdraw by nationalist rebels and by their own financial constraints. New nations were born in the Middle East and Asia, and America and Russia competed to win them as friends who might provide military bases, resources, and markets.

Conflict also seemed inevitable because of the shrinkage of the globe. Because of the triumph of the airplane and the advent of the "air age," the world became more compact. Nations were brought closer together by faster travel; at the same time, they became more vulnerable to surprise attack from the air. The Americans and Soviets once again collided as they strove to establish defensive positions, sometimes far from home.

Conflict may have been inevitable because of those international conditions, but the Cold War may not have been. The national policies of the United States and the Soviet Union and their leaders' conduct of diplomacy worsened rather than resolved postwar issues. Both nations marched into the Cold War with a sense of righteousness that gave the contest an almost religious character. Each country saw the other as the world's bully. If Americans feared "communist aggression," Russians feared "capitalist encirclement." In mirror image, each side saw the other as the obstacle to international peace.

"We are in this thing all over the world to the

Chapter 28: The Cold War and American Politics, 1945–1953

extent few people realize," Secretary of State James F. Byrnes (1945–1947) told Truman's cabinet. Why were Americans "all over the world"? One reason was that they had determined never to repeat the experience of the 1930s: they vowed no more depressions that would spawn political extremism and in turn produce war, no more Munichs, no more appeasement. It seemed to Americans in the 1940s that Nazi Germany had been replaced by Soviet Russia, that communism was simply the flip side of the totalitarian coin. The popular term "Red fascism" captured this sentiment.

American officials also knew that the nation's economic well-being depended on an activist foreign policy. In the postwar years the United States was the largest supplier of goods to world markets: in 1947 its exports amounted to $14 billion. That trade was jeopardized by the postwar economic paralysis of Europe, traditionally America's major customer, and by discriminatory trade practices that violated the Open Door doctrine. "Any serious failure to maintain this flow," declared an assistant secretary of state, "would put millions of American businessmen, farmers, and workers out of business." Indeed, exports constituted about 10 percent of the gross national product; the automobile, steel, and machine-tool industries, among others, relied heavily on foreign trade. About half of America's wheat was shipped abroad, and surpluses of cotton and tobacco also required foreign outlets. Finally, the United States needed to export in order to pay for imports such as zinc, tin, and manganese. Economic expansionism, so much a part of pre–Cold War history, thus remained a central feature of postwar foreign relations.

New strategic theory also propelled the United States toward an activist, expansionist, globalist diplomacy. "As top dog, America becomes target No. 1," warned Air Force General Carl Spaatz. To be ready for a military challenge in the postwar air age, American strategists believed that the nation's defenses had to begin far beyond its own borders. Thus the United States felt compelled to acquire overseas bases to guard the approaches to the Western Hemisphere. Overseas bases would also permit the United States to launch offensive attacks with might and speed. When asked where the American navy would float, Navy Secretary James Forrestal declared: "Wherever there is a sea."

> **American Strategic Thinking**

President Truman, who shared these assumptions, had a personality that tended to increase international tensions. Whereas Franklin D. Roosevelt had been ingratiating, patient, and evasive, Truman was brash, impatient, and direct. He seldom displayed the appreciation of subtleties so essential to successful diplomacy; for him issues were sketched in black and white, not shades of gray. As a friendly Winston Churchill said of him, Truman "takes no notice of delicate ground, he just plants his foot firmly on it."

Shortly after Roosevelt's death, Truman met Soviet Commissar of Foreign Affairs V. M. Molotov at the White House. The president sharply berated Russia for violating the Yalta accords, a charge Molotov denied. When Truman shot back that the Soviets should honor their agreements, Molotov stormed out of the room. The president was pleased with his "tough method": "I gave it to him straight 'one-two to the jaw.'" But the Yalta agreements were vague; although Soviet actions in Poland had been heavy-handed, whether they were in violation of the agreements was a matter of interpretation. Nonetheless, Truman's simplistic display of toughness would become a trademark of American Cold War diplomacy.

As for the Soviets, they were not easy to get along with either. Dean Acheson, a high-ranking diplomat from 1945 to 1947 and secretary of state from 1949 to 1953, found them rude and abusive. This conservative graduate of Yale and Harvard Law School could, he said, talk with "everybody who was housebroken." The Russians, he asserted, were not: "I think it is a mistake to believe that you can, at any time, sit down with the Russians and solve problems." Indeed, Premier Josef Stalin's blunt *nyets* stung American ears. But more than Soviet style bothered Americans. Soviet territorial ambitions—and successes—included a portion of eastern Poland, the Baltic states of Lithuania, Latvia, and Estonia, and parts of Finland and Rumania. In Eastern Europe Soviet officials began to suppress non-Communists.

> **American Anti-Soviet Views**

For their part, the Soviets remembered how the hostile West had attempted to ostracize them before: "We were always outsiders," complained one Soviet diplomat. Driven by memories of the past, by fear of a revived Germany, by the huge task of reconstruction, and by Marxist-Leninist doctrine, the

Soviets suspected capitalist nations of plotting once again to extinguish the Communist flame. They protested that the Americans were surrounding them with hostile bases and practicing atomic and dollar diplomacy.

"After World War II," Senator J. William Fulbright remembered, "we were sold on the idea that Stalin was out to dominate the world." This view pitted a generous United States ready to rebuild a peaceful world against a selfish, uncooperative Soviet Union; Americans were forced to react defensively against expansionist Russians. But Fulbright came to believe that the Soviets probably never intended to dominate the world, and they certainly lacked the capability to do so. Russia emerged from the war with a weak military establishment, a hobbled economy, and obsolete technology. Knowing this, American leaders did not expect the Soviets to attack Western Europe or to start a war they obviously could not sustain. The Soviet Union was a regional power in Eastern Europe, not a global menace.

American officials nonetheless exaggerated the Soviet threat. There are several reasons, and they sum up the American global perspective in the early Cold War. First, President

> **Question of the Soviet Threat**

Truman liked things in black and white, as his aide Clark Clifford remarked. Nuances, ambiguities, and counterevidence were often glossed over to satisfy Truman's penchant for the simple answer. Second, military officers often overplayed the Soviet threat to persuade Congress to pass larger defense budgets. (Like the United States, the Soviet Union actually undertook a major demobilization of its armed forces.) Third, some Americans fixed their attention, as they had since the Bolshevik Revolution of 1917, on the utopian Communist goal of world revolution rather than on actual Soviet behavior, which was limited largely to regions along the Soviet border and to bombastic rhetoric. Fourth, American leaders feared that the terrible postwar conditions of poverty and social unrest abroad would leave United States strategic and economic interests vulnerable to political disorders that the Soviets might exploit. In other words, Americans feared less a direct Soviet attack and more the Soviets' potential seizing of opportunities to challenge American interests, perhaps through subversion.

Last and overall, the United States, flushed with its own strength, took advantage of the postwar power vacuum to expand its overseas interests and shape a peace on American terms. The American pursuit of nuclear superiority, outlying bases, raw materials and markets, supremacy in Latin America, control of the Atlantic and Pacific oceans, and air-transit rights across other nations aroused a growing number of opponents, in particular the Soviet Union. Americans overreacted to the criticism, unable to understand it except as further evidence of wicked Soviet obstructionism on a worldwide scale. George F. Kennan, one of the chief architects of Cold War policy, later regretted that Americans had created the image of the Soviet Union as "the totally inhuman and malevolent adversary," because this distorted view contributed to the American abandonment of diplomacy during the rash of crises that bedeviled the global community.

Cold War Crises and the Containment Doctrine

One of the first Soviet-American clashes came in Poland in 1945, when the Soviets refused to admit conservative Poles from London to the Communist government in Lublin, as agreed at

> **Soviet Domination of Eastern Europe**

Yalta. A visit to Stalin by former Roosevelt aide Harry Hopkins in May of that year brought about some broadening of the Lublin regime but did not change Poland's status as a subservient, Soviet-directed state where the Communists could not claim majority support. The Soviets also snuffed out civil liberties in the former Nazi satellite of Rumania. They allowed free elections to be held in Hungary and Czechoslovakia, but as the Cold War progressed and they came to fear American power more and more, they encouraged Communist coups. First Hungary (1947) and then Czechoslovakia (1948) succumbed to Soviet subversion. Yugoslavia was a unique case: its independent Communist government, led by Josip Broz Tito, successfully broke with Stalin in 1948.

To justify their actions the Soviets complained that the United States was reviving Russia's tradi-

A Soviet tank in Gdansk, Poland, April 1945. After driving the Germans from Poland, the Red Army stayed on to ensure the power of the Communist regime in that war-weary nation. *Sovfoto.*

tional enemy, Germany. Citing radio broadcasts that encouraged resistance, clandestine meetings with anti-Soviet groups, repeated calls for elections, and the extension or withholding of loans to gain political influence (dollar diplomacy), the Soviets protested that the United States was meddling in Eastern Europe. Russia also charged that the United States was pursuing a double standard—intervening in the affairs of Eastern Europe but expecting Russia to stay out of Latin America and Asia. The Soviets pointed to the lack of free elections in United States–backed Latin American dictatorships. Americans insisted that their spheres of influence were far more open, their methods far less repressive than the Soviets'. But protest as Washington did, it was unable to roll back Soviet influence in Eastern Europe.

Another issue that divided America and Russia was the atomic bomb. The Soviets believed that the Americans were practicing "atomic diplomacy"—

> **Atomic Diplomacy**

maintaining a frightening nuclear monopoly and bragging about it to scare the Soviets into diplo-matic concessions. At a stormy foreign ministers' conference in London in the fall of 1945, Soviet Commissar of Foreign Affairs V. M. Molotov asked Secretary of State James F. Byrnes if he had an atomic bomb in his side pocket. Byrnes replied that southerners "carry our artillery in our hip pocket. If you don't cut out all this stalling and let us get down to work, I am going to pull an atomic bomb out of my hip pocket and let you have it." Retiring Secretary of War Henry L. Stimson was one of the few who opposed the use of the bomb as a diplomatic lever. As he told the president in September 1945, if Americans continued to have "this weapon rather ostentatiously on our hip, their [the Soviets'] suspicions and their distrust of our purposes and motives will increase."

In this atmosphere of suspicion and distrust, the United States and the Soviet Union could not agree on the international control of atomic energy. The American proposal, called the Baruch Plan, provided for America's abandoning its monopoly after the world's fissionable materials had been brought under the authority of an international agency. The

Soviets retorted that this plan denied them the right to develop their own bomb while the United States continued its supremacy. Secretary of Commerce Henry A. Wallace understood why Moscow rejected the Baruch Plan: "We are telling the Russians that if they are 'good boys' we may eventually turn over our knowledge of atomic energy. . . ."

The two adversaries also collided over Iran. By wartime agreement, British, American, and Soviet troops occupied Iran. The Soviets had some influence in the north, near the Soviet-Iranian border, and the British dominated the country's rich oil industry. When American petroleum companies asked the Iranian government for an oil concession, Moscow sniffed a capitalist plot on its border. In March 1946, the date agreed on for troop withdrawal, the Soviets stayed on in violation of the wartime treaty. Americans angrily accused them of intending to take over Iran. The Soviets countered that American military advisers remained in Iran and that British oil interests ensured Anglo-American political influence in the Teheran government. When the American-dominated United Nations investigated only Soviet actions in Iran, Moscow ordered its delegation to boycott the international body.

Crisis in Iran

Still, Iranian and Soviet diplomats managed to negotiate a settlement in April: Soviet soldiers would leave Iran in exchange for an oil concession. Americans claimed a Cold War victory, believing their tough words had forced the Soviets to withdraw. (In 1947 they turned the tables by persuading the Iranians to go back on their promise of a Russian oil concession. Moscow cried that it had been double-crossed.)

Soviets and Americans clashed on every front in 1946. They could not agree on the unification of Germany, so they built up their zones independently. The new World Bank and International Monetary Fund, created at the 1944 Bretton Woods Conference to stabilize trade and finance, also became tangled in the Cold War struggle. The Soviets refused to join because the United States so dominated both institutions. In early 1946, Washington extended a $3.5 billion loan to Great Britain but turned down a similar Soviet request. Already smarting from an abrupt cutoff of Lend-Lease aid in mid-1945, the Soviets denounced the United States for using its reconstruction dollars in order to manipulate foreign governments.

When in early February 1946 Stalin gave a pre-election speech depicting a world threatened by capitalist acquisitiveness, the American chargé d'affaires in Moscow, George F. Kennan, concluded that Soviet fanaticism made even a temporary understanding impossible. Kennan's pessimistic "long telegram" to Washington fed the growing belief that only toughness would work with the Russians. On March 5, Winston Churchill made his stirring Iron Curtain speech, warning that Eastern European countries were being cut off from the West by Russia. With the approving Truman sitting on the stage, the former prime minister called for an Anglo-American partnership to resist the Russian menace. Stalin protested that "Russia was not attacking, she was being attacked."

Secretary of Commerce Henry A. Wallace, a critic of Truman's get-tough policy, feared the United States was substituting atomic and economic coercion for diplomacy. "'Getting tough,'" he told a Madison Square Garden audience in September 1946, "never brought anything real and lasting—whether for schoolyard bullies or businessmen or world powers. The tougher we get, the tougher the Russians will get." Truman fired Wallace from the cabinet, blasting him privately as "a real Commy and a dangerous man." The president crowed that he had now "run the crackpots out of the Democratic Party."

The Cold War escalated further on March 12, 1947, when in response to a request from the British, who could no longer afford to fund their Greek client government, the president asked Congress for $400 million in aid to Greece and Turkey, both of which were threatened by economic dislocation and Communist political pressure. To repeat Truman's famous words: "It must be the policy of the United States to support free peoples who are resisting attempted subjugation by armed minorities or by outside pressures." It was time to draw the line, to contain the Communist menace. The president's statement quickly became known as the Truman Doctrine. Critics correctly pointed out that there was no evidence that the Soviet Union was involved in the civil war in Greece; that the rebel National Liberation Front had good reason to resent the repressive and corrupt regime supported by the British; and that the resistance movement included non-Communists as well as Communists. Others suggested that aid should

Truman Doctrine

be channeled through the United Nations. But after much debate the Senate approved Truman's request 67 to 23. Using American dollars and military advisers, the Greek government defeated the insurgents in 1949.

In July 1947 George F. Kennan, now director of the State Department's policy-planning staff, offered another statement of what became known as the containment doctrine. Writing under the name "Mr. X" in the magazine *Foreign Affairs,* this expert on Soviet affairs advocated a "policy of firm containment, designed to confront the Russians with unalterable counterforce at every point where they show signs of encroaching upon the interests of a peaceful and stable world." Such a counterforce, Kennan argued, would check Soviet expansion and eventually foster a "mellowing" of Soviet behavior. Together with the Truman Doctrine, Kennan's article became a key manifesto of Cold War policy.

The highly regarded journalist Walter Lippmann was critical of the containment doctrine. In *The Cold War* (1947), Lippmann called containment

▶ **Debate over Containment** a "strategic monstrosity" that did not distinguish between those areas vital and those peripheral to American security. If American leaders thought every place on earth was of strategic importance, he reasoned, the nation's patience and resources would soon be drained. Nor did Lippmann share Truman's view that Russia was plotting to take over the world. Truman, he asserted, put too little emphasis on diplomacy.

Lippmann was happier with the Marshall Plan for the reconstruction of Western Europe. In 1946 and 1947 an unusually harsh winter swept over Europe. Coal supplies dwindled; meager food stores were exhausted. European nations, still reeling from the war, lacked the dollars to buy American goods. Especially in France and Italy, leftists and Communists gained in political influence. Americans, who had already spent billions of dollars on European relief and recovery by 1947, recalled the troubles of the 1930s: global depression, political extremism, war born of economic discontent. It could not be allowed to happen again. Western Europe, Dean Acheson emphasized, was the "keystone in the arch which supports the kind of a world which we have to have in order to conduct our lives."

On June 5, 1947, Secretary of State George C. Marshall (1947–1949) announced that the United States would finance a massive European recovery

In December 1949, with the arrival in Athens of a shipload of wheat and flour, American aid to Greece under the Marshall Plan exceeded 1 million tons. To celebrate, a parade through the main streets followed the unloading of the cargo at the harbor. *UPI/Bettmann Archives.*

▶ **Marshall Plan** program. Although Marshall did not exclude Eastern Europe or the Soviet Union, few American leaders believed that Russia and its allies would want to join an American-dominated project. And, indeed, they did not join. Launched in 1948, the Marshall Plan sent $12.4 billion to Western Europe before the program ended in late 1951 (see map, page 828). To stimulate business at home, the legislation provided that the foreign aid dollars must be spent in the United States.

The Marshall Plan was a mixed success. In Europe, it caused inflation, failed to solve a serious balance-of-payments problem, and took only tentative steps toward economic integration. But it also sparked impressive Western European industrial production and investment and started the region toward self-sustaining economic growth. By 1952 the focus of the program had shifted from recovery

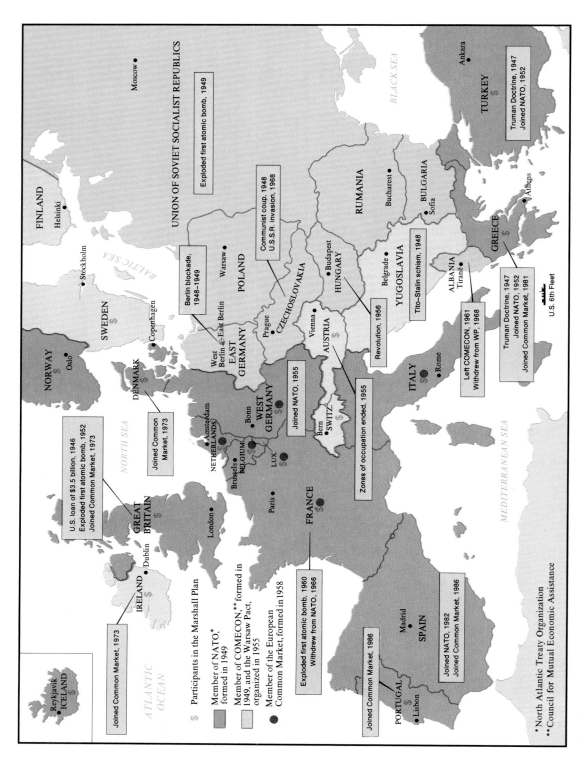

Divided Europe

Union of Soviet Socialist Republics

Exploded first atomic bomb, 1949

Moscow

FINLAND
Helsinki

SWEDEN
Stockholm

NORWAY
Oslo

DENMARK
Copenhagen

Berlin blockade, 1948–1949

West Berlin • East Berlin

POLAND
Warsaw

EAST GERMANY

Prague

CZECHOSLOVAKIA

Communist coup, 1948
U.S.S.R. invasion, 1968

Vienna

Budapest

HUNGARY

AUSTRIA

RUMANIA
Bucharest

Revolution, 1956

YUGOSLAVIA
Belgrade

Tito–Stalin schism, 1948

BULGARIA
Sofia

BLACK SEA

TURKEY
Ankara

Truman Doctrine, 1947
Joined NATO, 1952

GREECE
Athens

Truman Doctrine, 1947
Joined NATO, 1952
Joined Common Market, 1981

U.S. 6th Fleet

ALBANIA
Tiranë

Left COMECON, 1961
Withdrew from WP, 1968

Joined NATO, 1955

WEST GERMANY
Bonn

Zones of occupation ended, 1955

ITALY
Rome

Bern
SWITZ.

NETHERLANDS
Amsterdam

Brussels
BELGIUM
LUX.

FRANCE
Paris

Exploded first atomic bomb, 1960
Withdrew from NATO, 1966

U.S. loan of $3.5 billion, 1946
Exploded first atomic bomb, 1952
Joined Common Market, 1973

GREAT BRITAIN
London

Joined Common Market, 1973

IRELAND
Dublin

Joined Common Market, 1973

Joined Common Market, 1973

ICELAND
Reykjavik

ATLANTIC OCEAN

NORTH SEA

BALTIC SEA

MEDITERRANEAN SEA

SPAIN
Madrid

Joined NATO, 1982
Joined Common Market, 1986

PORTUGAL
Lisbon

Joined Common Market, 1986

$ Participants in the Marshall Plan

Member of NATO,* formed in 1949

Member of COMECON,** formed in 1949, and the Warsaw Pact, organized in 1955

Member of the European Common Market, formed in 1958

*North Atlantic Treaty Organization
**Council for Mutual Economic Assistance

to military assistance. From the beginning the Soviets blasted the Marshall Plan as the enslavement of Europe. They created a special propaganda agency—the Cominform—to harangue against it, but they also set up the Molotov Plan for Eastern Europe, which was a feeble imitation of the Marshall Plan.

To strengthen the nation's defenses, Truman worked with Congress to streamline the government's administrative structure under the National Security Act (July 1947). The act created the Department of Defense, the National Security Council (NSC) to advise the president, and the Central Intelligence Agency (CIA) to conduct spying and information gathering. By the early 1950s the CIA had expanded its functions to include covert (secret) operations aimed at overthrowing unfriendly foreign leaders and, as a high-ranking American official put it, stirring up economic trouble in "the camp of the enemy" through a "Department of Dirty Tricks." In 1953 the United States Information Agency was created to counter Soviet propaganda.

American officials also reached out to find new foreign friends and build new bases. In 1946, the United States granted the Philippines independence but maintained its old military, economic, and political ties. In 1947, American diplomats created the Rio Pact—a military alliance with Latin American countries. To enforce the Rio Pact, the United States helped found the Organization of American States (OAS) the following year. Under this and other agreements the Truman administration sent several military advisory missions to Latin America and to Greece, Turkey, Iran, China, and Saudi Arabia. In 1948, Americans activated an air base in Libya. In May of that year Truman—after vigorous debate with his Department of State—quickly recognized the new state of Israel, which had been carved out of the British-held territory of Palestine after years of Arab-Jewish dispute. America's perceived need for international allies joined the president's desire for Jewish-American votes in the upcoming election to hurry the decision.

One of the most electric moments in the Cold War came a month later. In June 1948 the Russians cut off Western access to the jointly occupied city of Berlin, located well inside the Soviet zone of Germany. Before the Soviets' bold

Berlin Blockade and Airlift move, the Americans, French, and British had agreed to fuse their zones into what became known as

West Germany. The three allies planned to integrate West Germany, including the three sectors of Berlin under their control, into the Western European economy, complete with a reformed German currency. The Soviets, fearing a resurgent Germany tied to the American Cold War camp, may have sparked the Berlin crisis to stimulate negotiations. But if they thought Truman would compromise, they guessed wrong. The president ordered a massive airlift of food, fuel, and other supplies to the isolated city. Finally, in May 1949, their image badly damaged, the Soviets lifted the blockade. They had spurred the very result they feared: the creation of the Federal Republic of Germany (West Germany) that month. In retaliation they founded the German Democratic Republic (East Germany).

On April 4, 1949, believing that a military shield should be added to the economic shield of the Marshall Plan, the United States, Canada, and much

Creation of NATO of Western Europe founded the North Atlantic Treaty Organization (NATO) (see map). The treaty aroused considerable debate at home, for not since 1778 had the United States entered a formal European military alliance. Senator Robert A. Taft of Ohio protested that NATO would provoke an arms race with Russia or cause American soldiers to be stationed in Europe. Others complained that the scheme gave the president power to send troops into combat without a congressional declaration of war and that it would cost too much, ultimately weakening the nation. Truman responded that NATO would give Europeans the will to resist, the confidence to thwart communism in their midst. And it would function as a "tripwire," bringing the full force of the United States to bear on the Soviet Union if it dared to cross the East-West line with troops—which it was not expected to do, with or without NATO. Quietly, administration spokesmen also indicated that NATO was designed to knit Western Europe together, to discourage some nations' tendency toward neutrality. The Senate ratified the treaty in July, 82 to 13. Truman then asked for a $1.5 billion Mutual Defense Assistance Act, to which Congress also consented, as it did to all of Truman's major foreign policy requests.

Just before passage of the military aid bill (September 1949), an American aircraft carrying sensitive equipment detected unusually high radioactivity in the atmosphere: the Soviets had exploded an atomic bomb. "This is now a different world," commented Senator Arthur Vandenberg of Michigan. The American nuclear monopoly was no more, and Western Europe seemed more vulnerable. The Communists were also winning the civil war in China (see pages 830–832), and Moscow was scoring propaganda points by advocating "peaceful coexistence" with the West. American leaders could have responded to this changed state of affairs with diplomatic negotiations. But Secretary of State Dean Acheson announced that there would be no "appeasement." The United States would instead build "situations of strength" around the world. In early 1950, Truman ordered production of the hydrogen bomb. In May, Congress finally endorsed funds for technical assistance to developing nations, to draw them into the American sphere of influence (a plan called the Point Four Program, after point 4 of Truman's 1949 inaugural address).

A month earlier, the National Security Council had delivered to the president a top-secret document numbered NSC-68. Predicting continued tension with the Communists and

NSC-68 describing a "shrinking world of polarized power," the report appealed for an enlarged military budget to counter the Soviet global design that American strategists perceived. The authors advised that public opinion would have to be mobilized behind huge defense expenditures. Administration officials worried about how to sell this strong prescription to the voters and budget-conscious congressional representatives. "We were sweating over it, and then—with regard to NSC-68—thank God Korea came along," recalled one of Dean Acheson's aides.

The Cold War in Asia

When the Korean War erupted in mid-1950, it came in the wake of vast changes in Asia. The Second World War had accelerated the process of decolonization begun during the First World War. Occupied with defending themselves and then with rebuilding after the war, imperial countries were no longer able to resist their colonies' demands for independence. Britain gave up India and what are

now Pakistan and Bangladesh in 1947, Burma and Ceylon in 1948. The Dutch reluctantly let go of Indonesia in 1949. Only the French fought on in Indochina, finally retiring from that outpost in 1954.

The defeat of Japan brought about the division of its empire among the victors. Korea was divided between the United States and the Soviet Union.

Reconstruction of Japan The Pacific islands (the Marshalls, Marianas, and Carolines) came under American control. Half of Sakhalin went to Russia as agreed at Yalta, and Formosa (Taiwan) was returned to the Chinese. As for Japan itself, the United States monopolized its reconstruction. Although the British and Russians asserted that they too had fought in the Asian theater and deserved a say in the occupation, Ambassador W. Averell Harriman answered that Washington was "very firm on the matter of keeping the power in American hands." Stalin wondered what the difference was between American domination of Japan and Russian domination of Rumania. But General Douglas MacArthur, who envisioned turning the Pacific Ocean into "an Anglo-Saxon lake," had the last word in Japan. As director of the American occupation, MacArthur wrote a democratic constitution for Japan, revitalized its economy, and destroyed the weapons of the Japanese military.

Although United States supremacy in Japan was an established fact, the Russians would not recognize it. Thus, after squabbling with Russia for years over a peace treaty with Japan, the United States finally signed a separate peace in 1951. The treaty restored Japan's sovereignty, ended the occupation, granted the United States a military base at Okinawa, and permitted American troops to be stationed in Japan. Tokyo and Washington also initialed a defense pact. The people who had been called beasts after their surprise attack on Pearl Harbor were now American allies in the Cold War. Along with Germany, Japan was, as Kennan noted, one of "our most important pawns on the chessboard of world politics."

Meanwhile, America's Chinese ally was faltering. The United States was feeding and fueling Jiang Jieshi's (Chiang Kai-shek's) Nationalist army in its

Chinese Civil War battle against Mao Zedong and Zhou Enlai's Communists. Immediately after the Second World War American troops had occupied northern China, flown Nationalist soldiers to

In this 1945 photograph taken at the Chinese Communists' headquarters at Yenan, Mao Zedong (1893–1976) stands with Lin Biao (at right), a war hero whom Mao had designated his "closest comrade in arms and successor." In 1971, however, Biao split from Mao and was reportedly shot down in a jet airplane while trying to escape from China. *Wide World Photos*.

Manchuria, and stayed on to advise Generalissimo Jiang. From 1945 to 1949 the United States sent China $3 billion in aid. But it soon became evident that Jiang was an unreliable friend. His government was corrupt and inefficient; he was out of touch with the rebellious peasants, whom the Communists enlisted with promises of land redistribution; and he tolerated a grossly unfair tax system. Journalist Theodore White thought the Nationalists combined "some of the worst features of Tammany Hall and the Spanish Inquisition," and Truman privately denounced them as "grafters and crooks." Jiang ignored American advice to root out corruption, halt inflation, and begin land reform. He also worked to disrupt the efforts of the Marshall mission (1945–1947) to negotiate a cease-fire and a coalition government. And he rejected American military advice. "We picked a bad horse," Truman admitted. Still, seeing Jiang as the only alternative to Mao, Truman backed him to the end.

American officials were divided on the question of whether Mao was a puppet of the Soviet Union. Some diplomats considered him an Asian Tito—Communist but independent—but most believed he was part of an international Communist movement and would thus give the Soviets a springboard into Asia. In the *White Paper* of 1949—a government report written to explain America's efforts to contain communism through aid to Jiang—Secretary Acheson overstated his case in saying that the "Communist leaders have foresworn their Chinese heritage and have publicly announced their subservience to a foreign power." Thus when the Chinese Communists made secret overtures to begin diplomatic talks in 1945 and again in 1949, American officials rebuffed them. Mao soon decided that he was "leaning to one side" in the Cold War—the Soviet side.

Actually, Americans had overestimated Mao's dependence on the Soviet Union. The Russians gave Mao little support, rejecting his interpretation of Marxism-Leninism and resenting his determination to resist their influence. For its own purposes Russia preferred a weak China under Jiang to a strong China under Mao, an attitude that derived from a long history of Sino-Russian rivalry.

In the fall of 1949, after numerous military setbacks, Jiang fled to the island of Formosa, and Mao proclaimed the People's Republic of China. Would the United States extend diplomatic recognition to Mao's new government? Truman hesitated; he tried unsuccessfully to persuade the British to wait. "Are we to refuse to recognize facts, however unpleasant they may be?" asked the British prime minister. "Are we to cut ourselves off from all contact with one-sixth of the inhabitants of the world?" But for several reasons Washington did just that. First, American officials were alarmed by a Sino-Soviet treaty of friendship signed in February 1950. Second, Mao's followers had harassed Americans and seized American-owned property in China. Third, Mao was now openly hostile to the United States, blaming it for prolonging the bloody civil war. Fourth, Secretary Dean Acheson simply wanted to "wait until the dust settles." He predicted that Mao would conquer Formosa, thus eliminating Jiang, and that frictions between Beijing and Moscow would ultimately convince Mao to sever his ties with the Soviets.

> **Nonrecognition of the People's Republic of China**

Still another reason lay behind the policy of nonrecognition. A noisy group of Republican critics called the China lobby, shattering the postwar spirit of bipartisanship, was seeking to blame Jiang's defeat on Truman. Publisher Henry Luce, Senator William Knowland of California, and Congressman Walter Judd of Minnesota won headlines by charging that the United States had "lost" China. Senator Joseph McCarthy of Wisconsin snorted that "egg-sucking liberals" and "queers" had sold China into "atheistic slavery."

Truman and Acheson answered that the United States had never had China to lose, that Jiang was not willing to help himself, and that large-scale military intervention in the Chinese civil war would have been costly and probably unending. Moreover, major involvement in China would have drained valuable resources from Europe, the primary front in the Cold War. "The United States cannot furnish determination, it cannot furnish the will, and it cannot furnish the loyalty of a people to its government," Acheson insisted—adding, "China lost itself." For reasons of both domestic politics and international relations, the United States did not open formal diplomatic relations with the People's Republic of China until 1979— thirty years after Mao's government came to power.

Reaching for some way to offset Jiang's collapse, the National Security Council urged the president to fortify "friendly and independent" states in Asia as a bulwark against Communist expansion. In February 1950 the United States recognized the French puppet regime of Bao Dai in Vietnam and a few months later decided to extend aid to the beleaguered French there. In April the National Security Council sent the president its alarming report NSC-68. In May more funds went to Jiang Jieshi in Formosa. It is in this context of globalist thought and action that America's response to war in Korea must be seen (see pages 844–845).

A Rough Transition at Home

Truman's crises abroad were matched by severe challenges at home. The atomic bombs that fell on Hiroshima and Nagasaki brought about victory much sooner than the economic planners had anticipated. Mid-1946 was the target date for victory, and administrators had planned a gradual conversion from a wartime to a peacetime economy. But in 1945 the war was over and important questions remained unanswered. What would be the effect of reconversion—the cancellation of war contracts, the termination of wage and price controls, and the end of wartime labor agreements? Would depression recur once the artificial stimulus of the war was withdrawn, throwing people out of work and sending prices downward? Or would Americans go on a buying spree, driving prices up to record highs? After all, during the Great Depression penny-pinched Americans could not afford to buy autos, houses, appliances, and other consumer durables. During the prosperity of the Second World War, civilian items such as these were not manufactured. Therefore, by 1945 Americans had bulging bank accounts, and they wanted to treat themselves.

Yet most Americans were pessimistic about the future. Even before the war's end, cutbacks in production had caused layoffs. Workers at Ford Motor Company's massive Willow Run plant outside

Postwar Job Layoffs Detroit, where nine thousand Liberator bombers had been produced, were let go in the spring of 1945. Ten days after the victory over Japan, 1.8 million people received pink slips and 640,000 filed for unemployment compensation. The peak of postwar unemployment came in March 1946, when 2.7 million people were seeking work.

Swelling the ranks of those seeking jobs were the millions of soldiers and sailors who received their discharges from the armed services in 1945 and 1946. Like the cancellation of government contracts, the demobilization of the armed forces was rapid. The army had expected to muster out 1.1 million people in the eighteen months between victory in Europe and in Japan, but the atomic bombings of Hiroshima and Nagasaki had cut that period to four months. The army's demobilization rate was increased fivefold, with a target of 5.5 million by July 1946. The navy hurriedly converted landing and cargo ships to troop carriers and returned 4 million GIs from abroad in the first year of peace. In mid-1945 the nation's armed forces stood at over 12 million. A year later, the figure had fallen to just over 3 million; in 1947 it hit 1.5 million. "The program we were following," Truman recalled, "was no longer demobilization—it was disintegration of our armed forces."

Truman declared his determination not only to combat unemployment but also to expand on New Deal programs begun in the 1930s. On September 6, 1945, he delivered to Congress

Truman's Reconversion Plan a twenty-one-point message urging extension of unemployment compensation, an increase in the minimum wage, adoption of permanent farm price supports, and new public works projects. Truman revived Roosevelt's Economic Bill of Rights: every able-bodied American had a right to a job. If the economy failed to provide one, the government should create it. Congress responded to Truman's message with the Employment Act of 1946, which announced that the government would use its resources, including deficit spending if necessary, to achieve "maximum employment, production, and purchasing power." The act established the Council of Economic Advisers to assist the president, but it fell short of Truman's hopes: Congress had deleted a commitment to absolute full employment.

Despite high unemployment in the immediate postwar period, the United States was not teetering on the brink of depression; in fact, after a brief period of readjustment, the economy would blast off into a quarter-century of unprecedented boom (see Chapter 30). People had plenty of savings to spend in 1945 and 1946, and suddenly there were new houses and cars for them to buy. Easy credit and the availability of new products from such war-inspired industries as synthetic rubber and electronics promoted the buying spree. As a result, though war production began to wind down in 1944, the gross national product (GNP) continued to rise in 1945. And though there was a slight dip in economic activity in 1946, the GNP jumped from $209 billion to $231 billion the next year. In 1948 it rose to $258 billion.

The nation's postwar economic problem was not depression; it was inflation, fueled by maddening shortages of consumer goods like meat and housing. Throughout 1945 and 1946 prices skyrocketed; the inflation rate for 1946 was 18.2 percent.

Meanwhile, though prices were spiraling upward, many people were earning less real income than they had earned during the war. Industrial workers complained that the National War Labor Board had limited them to cost-of-living pay increases. In fact, during the war manufacturing wages had risen 27 percent, largely due to the wartime increase in the average work week from 40.6 hours to 45.2 hours. But in 1945, the workers who had put in long hours of overtime were returning to the forty-hour paycheck. Although employers claimed they could not afford to guarantee workers the same take-home pay for fewer hours, most workers believed it was possible. The result was an impasse between management and labor and a spate of strikes. During the fall and early winter of 1945, daily absences due to strikes ballooned to 28.4 million, more than double the 1943 figure. But although such strikes were massive and frequent, they were peaceful compared with the fiery confrontations that had followed the First World War.

Throughout the period of reconversion the government hesitated to act in the face of competing special-interest groups. Big business and small business, management and labor, farmers and consumers, liberals and conservatives offered conflicting prescriptions, and to serve one interest was to risk offending others. For all these groups, Truman was the perfect scapegoat. "Sherman was *wrong,*"

In 1946, ex-servicemen picketed coal mines in Panther Valley, Pennsylvania, complaining that mine owners had hired outside help during the war and then had refused to lay these workers off in favor of the returning veterans, former coalminers themselves. *Wide World Photos.*

Truman told a Gridiron Dinner audience in December 1945. "I'm telling you I find peace is hell."

As severe as the discontent of farmers, factory workers, and consumers was in 1945, in 1946 it became worse. As volatile as labor-management relations were in 1945, the next year they exploded. Over 4.5 million men and women left their jobs to strike in 1946, more even than in 1919. Daily absences due to strikes totaled 113 million—four times as many as in 1945. One reason for workers' discontent was that while wages and salaries had declined slightly in 1946, net profits had reached all-time highs, jumping more than 50 percent from 1945 to 1946. Indignant that they were not sharing in the increased prosperity, workers forced nationwide shutdowns in the coal, automobile, steel, and electric industries and halted railroad and maritime transportation.

Upsurge in Labor Strikes

John L. Lewis's United Mine Workers was among the most powerful unions to walk off the job. Coal was the nation's primary source of energy in 1946. When soft-coal production stopped on April 1,

steel and automobile output plummeted, railroad service was canceled, thousands of people were laid off, and twenty-two states reinstituted wartime "dim-outs" to conserve coal. The miners' demands were legitimate—higher wages, a federal safety code, and a royalty of ten cents per ton to finance health services and welfare and pension funds. A two-week truce in May failed to produce a solution, so on May 21, with time running out and the country still desperate for coal, Truman ordered the seizure of the mines. Lewis and the government reached an accord a week later, and the miners returned to work. But within six months the agreement collapsed, and once again the government placed the operation of the mines under its direct control.

There was no doubt in 1946 about the growing unpopularity of labor unions and their leadership. Many Americans believed that the unions were responsible for strikes that not only restricted the output of consumer goods and inflated prices, but also threatened the national security. In May, when a nationwide railroad strike

Truman's Attack on the Unions

Chapter 28: The Cold War and American Politics, 1945–1953

was threatened, Truman hopped aboard the anti-union bandwagon. A special board appointed to mediate the dispute had managed to satisfy eighteen of the disgruntled unions, but two held out for a better settlement. In exasperation, Truman made a dramatic appearance before a joint session of Congress. If the government seized a strike-bound industry, he said, and the workers in that industry refused to honor a presidential order to return to work, "I [would] request the Congress immediately to authorize the President to draft into the Armed Forces of the United States all workers who are on strike against their government." He also requested authority to strip strikers of seniority benefits, to take legal action against union leaders, and to fine and even imprison them for contempt. Truman's speech alienated not only railroad workers but union members in general. Many dedicated themselves to defeating President Truman in the upcoming 1948 presidential election.

Truman fared little better in his direction of the Office of Price Administration. Now that the war was over, powerful interests wanted OPA controls lifted. Consumers were impatient with shortages and black-market prices, and manufacturers and farmers wanted to jack up prices legally. Yet when most controls expired in mid-1946 and inflation rose higher, people became angry. When the OPA price ceilings on beef expired in June, for example, the cost of beef soared, cattle ranchers beamed, and consumers grumbled. When the OPA reimposed ceilings in August, producers retaliated by withholding beef from the market. Soon consumers were standing in long lines at the butcher shop and buying beef through the black market. In an election year, they blamed the Democrats. "This is going to be a damn *beefsteak* election," groused Speaker of the House Sam Rayburn of Texas.

Truman's popularity rating plunged from 87 percent in late 1945 to 32 percent in 1946. Even liberals were unhappy with the president's performance. Truman had prompted the resignation of Harold Ickes, one of the two New Dealers left in the cabinet, by appointing a California oil and real-estate baron (who also happened to be a Democratic fund-raiser) as undersecretary of the navy. Fearing another Teapot Dome scandal, Ickes angrily denounced Truman's policy of "government by crony." Seven months later Truman fired Henry

Consumer Discontent

A. Wallace, the only remaining New Dealer, for making a speech critical of his containment policy (see page 826). By election time the president was out of favor with labor, consumers, farmers, liberals, and—because of his advocacy of welfare programs—conservative Democrats as well.

Republicans made the most of public discontent. "Got enough meat?" asked Republican Congressman John M. Vorys of Ohio. "Got enough houses? Got enough OPA? . . . Got enough inflation? . . . Got enough debt? . . . Got enough strikes?" When the votes were tabulated in the 1946 congressional election, the Republicans had won a majority in both houses of the Eightieth Congress and captured twenty-five of thirty-two nonsouthern governorships. The White House in 1948 seemed within their grasp.

The Eightieth Congress and the Election of 1948

The politicians who ruled the Eightieth Congress, both Republicans and southern Democrats, were committed conservatives. Although they supported Truman's foreign policy, they perceived the Republican landslide as a mandate to reverse the New Deal, to curb the power of government and of labor. Truman had had little success with the Seventy-ninth Congress; he would have even less success with this one. Ironically, however, it would be the Eightieth Congress that would help him to win the presidency in 1948. For if Truman had alienated labor, farmers, and liberals, the Eightieth Congress made them livid.

One extremely unpopular measure was the Taft-Hartley Act, which Congress adopted over Truman's veto in 1947. A revision of the Wagner Act of 1935, the bill prohibited the union, or closed, shop, in which only union members could be hired. It also permitted the states to ban the closed shop by passing "right-to-work" laws. Workers could still organize, elect a union to represent them, enroll new union members, bargain collectively, and strike. But the Taft-Hartley Act forbade union contributions to political funds in federal elections, required union leaders to sign

Taft-Hartley Act

non-Communist affidavits, and mandated an eighty-day cooling-off period in strikes that imperiled the national security. Although it was not the slave-labor act that union spokespersons said it was, responses to the act quickly distinguished supporters of labor from opponents. Truman's veto therefore vindicated him in the eyes of labor. Just a year earlier, labor leaders had pledged all-out war against the president; now they threw their resources behind him.

Throughout 1947 and into 1948 the Eightieth Congress offended numerous interest groups, which in turn swung back to Truman. For example, the president asked Congress for continued price supports for farmers; the Eightieth Congress responded with weakened price supports. The president requested nationwide health insurance; the Eightieth Congress refused. It was the same with federal funding of public housing and aid to public education; with broadened and increased unemployment compensation, old-age and survivors' benefits, and the minimum wage; with funds for land reclamation, irrigation, and public power; and with antilynching, anti–poll tax, and fair-employment legislation. Truman proposed; Congress rejected or ignored his requests.

Republicans seemed oblivious to public opinion. Not since 1928 had they been so confident of capturing the presidency, and most political experts agreed. "Only a political miracle,"

Campaign of 1948 stated *Time,* "or extraordinary stupidity on the part of the Republicans can save the Democratic party." At their national convention, Republicans strengthened their position by nominating for president and vice president the governors of two of the nation's most populous states: Thomas E. Dewey of New York and Earl Warren of California. Democrats revealed how fragmented they were when an alliance of big-city bosses and liberals tried to dump Truman in favor of General Dwight D. Eisenhower. But Eisenhower declined the overtures of both Democrats and Republicans, declaring that "lifelong professional soldiers should abstain from seeking high political office." In the end, Truman received the nomination.

Democrats were fighting against more than Republicans in 1948. After his dismissal from the cabinet, Henry Wallace decided to run for president on the Progressive party ticket, which advocated friendship and negotiation with the Soviet Union, condemned the Truman Doctrine as a "global Monroe Doctrine," supported desegregation, and advocated nationalization of oil companies, railroads, and other basic industries. Experts predicted that the Progressives would poll enough votes to dash the Democratic party's hopes for victory. A fourth party, the Dixiecrats (States Rights Democratic party), had bolted the Democratic party when the 1948 national convention adopted a pro–civil rights plank, and they nominated Governor Strom Thurmond of South Carolina. If Wallace's candidacy did not destroy Truman's chances, experts said, the Dixiecrats certainly would.

But Truman had ideas of his own. He called the Eightieth Congress into special session and demanded that it enact all the planks in the Republican platform. If Republicans really wanted to transform their ideals into law, said Truman, this was the time to do it. After Congress had met for two weeks and accomplished nothing of significance, Truman took to the road. Traveling more than 30,000 miles by train, he delivered scores of whistle-stop speeches denouncing the "do-nothing" Eightieth Congress. Still, no amount of furious campaigning by Truman seemed likely to change the predicted outcome. On election eve, the odds on a Truman victory were eighteen to one.

As the votes were counted early into the morning, it became clear that Truman had confounded the experts. The final tally was 24.1 million popular votes, 303 electoral votes, for Truman; 21.9 million popular votes, 189 electoral votes, for Dewey (see map, page 838). Not only had Truman won four more years in the White House, but the Democrats had also regained control of Congress—in the House by a majority of 93, in the Senate by 12.

How and why had the upset occurred? First, the United States was prosperous, at peace, and essentially united on foreign policy. Moreover, the Roosevelt legacy—the New Deal coalition—had endured; big cities, northern blacks, southern whites, ethnic Americans, and labor unions had rallied to Truman's support. Ironically, the extremist images of the Progressive and Dixiecrat parties helped Truman by making the Democratic party look moderate. The Democrats, for their part, did not hesitate to distort the facts by denouncing the Progressives as a pack of Communists. Rather than the predicted 5 million votes apiece, Wallace and Thurmond polled just a little over 1 million each.

So few pollsters predicted that President Harry S Truman (1884–1972) would win in 1948 that the *Chicago Tribune* announced his defeat before all the returns were in. Here a victorious Truman pokes fun at the newspaper for its premature headline. *UPI/Bettmann Archives.*

But in the end it was the farmers whose votes made the difference. Truman advocated continued high price supports for farmers; Republicans wanted to decrease supports. In the bumper-crop year of 1948, Republicans actually wanted to cut back on grain storage. As the harvest mounted, prices began to fall; corn dropped from $1.78 a bushel in September to $1.38 in mid-October. Ever ready, Truman told farmers that the Eightieth Congress had "stuck a pitchfork in the farmer's back." All of the border states and several important midwestern states went for Truman.

Truman entered his new term brimming with confidence. He believed that it was time for government to fulfill its responsibility to provide economic security for the poor and the elderly. As he worked on his 1949 State of the Union message, he penciled in an expression of his intentions: "I expect to give every segment of our population a fair deal." Little did Truman know that he had selected the label that historians would hereafter associate with his presidency: Fair Deal.

Truman on Civil Rights

The postwar years were a period of gathering strength for African-Americans. Truman and other politicians knew they would have to compete for the growing black vote in urban-industrial states like California, Illinois, Michigan, Ohio, Pennsylvania, and New York. Many Republicans cultivated the

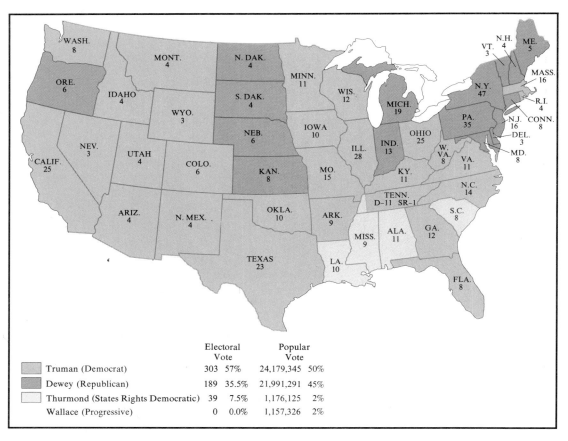

	Electoral Vote		Popular Vote	
Truman (Democrat)	303	57%	24,179,345	50%
Dewey (Republican)	189	35.5%	21,991,291	45%
Thurmond (States Rights Democratic)	39	7.5%	1,176,125	2%
Wallace (Progressive)	0	0.0%	1,157,326	2%

Presidential Election, 1948

black vote. Thomas Dewey, who as governor of New York had pushed successfully for the establishment of a fair employment practices commission, was particularly popular with blacks. In Harlem, which had gone Democratic by a 4-to-1 margin in 1938, Dewey won by large margins in 1942 and 1946.

Certainly, then, Truman had political reasons for supporting black civil rights. But he also felt a moral obligation to blacks. For one thing, he believed it was only fair that each American, regardless of race, should enjoy the full rights of citizenship. More than that, Truman was disturbed by the resurgence of racial terrorism. To combat aspirations for civil rights unleashed by the war, the Ku Klux Klan had taken to the road again, burning crosses and murdering blacks who had had the audacity to vote. Senator Theodore G. Bilbo of Mississippi had exhorted every "red-blooded Anglo-Saxon man in Mississippi to resort to any

means to keep . . . Negroes from the polls," and Eugene Talmadge had won the governorship of Georgia with the promise that "no Negro will vote in Georgia for the next four years." But what really horrified Truman was the report that police in Aiken, South Carolina, had gouged out the eyes of a black sergeant just three hours after he had been discharged from the army. Several weeks later, on December 5, 1946, Truman signed an executive order establishing the President's Committee on Civil Rights.

A year later the committee delivered its report, *To Secure These Rights*. Among the committee's recommendations, which would become the agenda for the civil rights movement for the

President's Committee on Civil Rights

next twenty years, were the enactment of federal antilynching, anti-segregation, and anti–poll tax laws. *To Secure These Rights* also called for laws guaranteeing vot-

Campaigning in Harlem on October 29, 1948, President Truman called for first-class citizenship for African-Americans. Truman recognized that black votes were crucial to his election effort in 1948. *Cornell Capa,* Life *Magazine* © *1948 Time, Inc.*

ing rights and equal employment opportunity, and for the establishment of a permanent commission on civil rights and a civil rights division within the Department of Justice. In February 1948, Truman sent a special message to Congress. The protection of citizens' rights, Truman said, was "the duty of every government which derives its powers from the consent of the governed." Congress made no formal response. Some southerners told Truman that with such a civil rights program, "You won't be elected dogcatcher in 1948." There is evidence that the president did not expect congressional action and that his real goal was the black vote in 1948. But whatever his motive, this was the first time since Reconstruction that a president had acknowledged the federal government's responsibility to protect African-Americans and strive for racial equality.

Truman also used the power of the executive to proclaim a policy of "fair employment throughout the federal establishment," and he created the Employment Board of the Civil Service Commission to

hear charges of discrimination. His Committee on Equality of Treatment and Opportunity in the Armed Services issued a report, *Freedom to Serve,* in 1950 stating that racial desegregation would "make for a better Army, Navy, and Air Force." Though strong, at times even fierce, opposition to desegregation existed within the military, by the outbreak of the Korean War segregated units were being phased out.

Blacks also benefited from a series of Supreme Court decisions. The trend toward judicial support of civil rights had begun in the late 1930s when the

Supreme Court Decisions on Civil Rights

NAACP established its Legal Defense Fund led by Thurgood Marshall. (In 1967 Marshall would become the first black Supreme Court justice.) Marshall and his colleagues were trying to destroy the separate-but-equal doctrine established in *Plessy* v. *Ferguson* (1896) by insisting on its literal interpretation. In higher education, the NAACP figured, the cost of racially separate

Jackie Robinson cracked the color line in major league baseball when he joined the Brooklyn Dodgers for the 1947 season. Robinson won rookie-of-the-year honors and was later elected to the Baseball Hall of Fame. In this game against the Philadelphia Phillies, Robinson stole home. *Wide World Photos.*

schools was prohibitive. "You can't build a cyclotron for one [black] student," the president of the University of Oklahoma acknowledged. As a result of NAACP lawsuits in the 1930s and 1940s, black students won admission to professional and graduate schools at a number of state universities. The NAACP also scored notable victories in several other cases. In 1944, in *Smith* v. *Allwright,* the Supreme Court outlawed the whites-only primaries held by the Democratic party in some southern states, branding them a violation of the Fifteenth Amendment. Two years later the Court declared segregation in interstate bus transportation unconstitutional (*Morgan* v. *Virginia*).

In 1947 the Department of Justice began to submit friend-of-the-court briefs on behalf of the civil rights movement, most notably in cases involving higher education and restrictive covenants (private agreements among white homeowners not to sell to blacks). In *Shelley* v. *Kraemer* (1948), the Court held that a racially restrictive covenant violated the equal protection clause of the Fourteenth Amendment. In the Thompson Restaurant case (*District of Columbia* v. *John R. Thompson Company*), a Justice Department brief helped to bring about the desegregation of restaurants and eventually hotels

in the District of Columbia. But most important was the attorney general's brief supporting the NAACP's effort to desegregate the nation's public schools. Although the Supreme Court did not decide the landmark *Brown* v. *Board of Education of Topeka* until 1954, the Truman administration's legal efforts helped overturn the separate-but-equal doctrine that had been the law of the land since *Plessy* v. *Ferguson* (see page 490).

A change in social attitudes accompanied these gains in black political and legal power. Books such as Gunnar Myrdal's *An American Dilemma* (1944) and Richard Wright's *Native Son* (1940) and *Black Boy* (1945) had increased white awareness of the social injustice that plagued blacks. A new black middle class had emerged, composed of college-educated activists, veterans, and union workers. Blacks and whites were working together in CIO unions and with service organizations such as the National Council of Churches, the Anti-Defamation League, the National Urban League, and the American Friends Service Committee. In 1947 a black baseball player, Jackie Robinson, cracked the major-league color barrier and electrified crowds with his spectacular hitting and base running.

Cold War pressures also benefited blacks. As the

Soviet Union was quick to point out, the United States could not pose as the leader of the free world, or condemn the denial of human rights behind the Iron Curtain, so long as it condoned racism at home. Nor could it convince new African and Asian nations of its dedication to human rights if African-Americans were subjected to segregation, disfranchisement, and racial violence. To win the support of nonaligned nations, the United States would have to live up to its own ideals. That the nation was not doing so was evident. Segregation was still an accepted practice in the 1950s, even if it was no longer the law of the land. Blacks continued to suffer job discrimination and disfranchisement. Nevertheless, in the ten years following the Second World War, African-Americans made considerable progress, more than in any period since Reconstruction.

McCarthyism

A common misconception about the postwar era is that anti-Communist hysteria began in 1950 with the furious speeches of Senator Joseph R. McCarthy. Actually, anticommunism had been part of the American political temper ever since the First World War and the Red Scare of 1919 and 1920. The Cold War heightened anti-Communist fears at home, and by 1950 they reached hysterical proportions. McCarthy did not create this hysteria; he manipulated it to his own advantage. He was the most successful and frightening redbaiter the country had ever seen.

What reason was there to fear Communist influence in the 1940s and 1950s? The party had never been strong, even during the hard times of the depression. When news of the

Communist Party Membership trial and execution of large numbers of anti-Stalinists in the Soviet Union reached America in 1937 and 1938, followed shortly by the

signing of the Nazi-Soviet Pact in August 1939, the party had quickly lost many of its members. With the German invasion of Russia in the summer of 1941, however, American attitudes toward the Soviet Union became more favorable. Suddenly the United States and Russia were allies in the war against Hitler.

At the same time anticommunism persisted in the United States. In 1940 Congress enacted the Alien Registration (Smith) Act, which made it unlawful to advocate the overthrow of the United States government by force or violence or to join any organization that did so. Politicians began playing on anti-Communist paranoia again. In the 1944 presidential campaign Dewey warned that the Democratic party was about to be captured by the Communists.

Then in March 1945 an incident occurred that tended to confirm anti-Communists' worst fears. In a raid on the offices of *Amerasia,* a little-known magazine whose editors sympathized with the Chinese Communists, the Office of Strategic Services confiscated classified government documents. People asked who had supplied the documents to the magazine, and why. Concern was also mounting in Canada, where in 1946 a royal commission issued a report claiming that Soviet spies were operating in the country. Among them, the report said, were a member of the Canadian Parliament and a scientist who had transmitted atomic secrets to a Soviet agent.

Spurred by these revelations, Truman in March 1947 ordered investigations into the loyalty of the more than 3 million employees of the United States

Truman's Loyalty Probe government. In 1950 the government began discharging people deemed "security risks," among them alcoholics, homosexuals, and debtors thought to be susceptible to blackmail. In most cases there was no question of these people's loyalty. Without the right to confront their accusers and demand evidence, however, many were ruined for life. Still others became victims of guilt by association—they knew people considered to be subversive, disloyal, or dangerous.

The wellspring of this fear of communism was the Cold War. Fear of internal subversion was intertwined with fear of external attack. It was no coincidence that Truman ordered the loyalty probe the same week he appeared before a joint session of Congress to announce his containment policy. His alarmist rhetoric heightened public anxiety.

Truman was not alone in peddling fear; conservatives and liberal Democrats joined him. Republicans used the same technique to attack the Democratic candidates for president in 1948 and 1952; liberal Democrats used it to discredit the far-left, pro-Wallace wing of their party. In many ways, the anti-Communist hysteria of the late 1940s was a phenomenon created by professional politicians and promoted by labor union officials, religious leaders, Hollywood moguls, and other influential figures.

People began to point accusing fingers at each other. "Reds, phonies, and 'parlor pinks,'" in Truman's words, seemed to lurk everywhere. Hollywood film personalities who had been ardent left-wingers were blacklisted; some writers and directors were sentenced to prison for contempt of Congress when they refused to provide names of alleged Communists. Schoolteachers and college professors were fired for expressing dissenting viewpoints, and in some communities "pro-Communist" books were removed from school libraries. In labor union elections and in struggles to dominate local parent-teacher associations, redbaiting became a convenient tactic for discrediting the opposition. The hysteria was particularly damaging to the labor movement, which forsook its class-conscious militancy in favor of patriotism and anti-communism. In the United Auto Workers, Walter Reuther used redbaiting to destroy his opposition and win the union's presidency. Union bulletin boards that had once bristled with strike notices and photographs of police clubbing strikers were now adorned with such slogans as "UAW Americanism for Us." At its 1949 convention, the CIO expelled eleven unions with a combined membership of over 900,000 for alleged Communist domination. All this occurred at a time when membership in the Communist party was rapidly declining, from a high of about 83,000 in 1947 to 55,000 in 1950 and 25,000 in 1954.

Despite the false accusations, there was cause for alarm—especially in 1949, which dramatist Arthur Miller called "the year it came apart." Throughout that year a former State Department official, Alger Hiss, was on trial for perjury for swearing to a grand jury that he had never passed classified documents to his accuser, former American Communist spy Whittaker Chambers, and in fact had not seen Chambers since 1936. When Truman and Secretary of State Dean Acheson came to his defense, charging that the Republicans were publicizing the case to divert attention from their own failures, some people began to suspect the worst. The Democrats, they decided, had something to hide. Republican

> **Hiss Trial**

Congressman Richard M. Nixon of California, a member of the House Committee on Un-American Activities, which had led the investigation of the Hiss case, harped constantly on that theme. Then two events shoved the Hiss trial off the front page. In September the Russians exploded their first atomic bomb, and on October 1 the Chinese Communists, finally victorious in the civil war, proclaimed the People's Republic of China. A howl of indignation arose from the China lobby; Truman and Acheson were now on the defensive.

The dawn of a new decade brought no end to the hysteria; indeed, 1950 saw more disquieting news. Hiss was convicted. Scotland Yard arrested Klaus Fuchs, a nuclear scientist, for turning over to Soviet agents secrets from the atomic-bomb project at Los Alamos, New Mexico. And President Truman announced that in response to the Russian atomic bomb, the United States would embark on a crash project to develop a hydrogen bomb. "How much more are we going to have to take?" wailed one right-wing Republican. "Fuchs and Acheson and Hiss and hydrogen bombs threatening outside and New Dealism eating away at the vitals of the nation. In the name of heaven, is this the best America can do?" Anti-Communists also exploited the hysteria to drive homosexuals from their jobs. "Sexual perverts," the Republican national chairman warned in 1950, "have infiltrated our government in recent years" and "were perhaps as dangerous as the actual Communists."

The ingredients of the situation were ripe for a demagogue: an irrational blurring of enemies, simplistic conspiracy theories, awareness that the Second World War had not ended the threat of war but had brought the new threat of nuclear holocaust. It was in this atmosphere that on February 9, 1950, Senator Joseph McCarthy mounted a rostrum in Wheeling, West Virginia, and gave a name to the hysteria: McCarthyism.

That day in Wheeling, McCarthy proclaimed, "The reason we find ourselves in a position of impotency is . . . because of the traitorous actions of those who have been treated so well by this nation." The State Department, he asserted, was "thoroughly infested with Communists," and the most dangerous person in the State Department was Dean Acheson. Reporters wrote that the senator claimed to have a list of 205 Communists

> **McCarthy's Attack on the State Department**

Congressman Richard M. Nixon appeared to take little satisfaction in the newspaper headline proclaiming Alger Hiss's perjury conviction in early 1950. As a member of the House Un-American Activities Committee, Nixon had led the investigation into charges that Hiss had been a Communist party member and a spy in the 1930s. *UPI/Bettmann Archives.*

working in the State Department; later McCarthy lowered the figure to "57 card-carrying members," then raised it to 81. No matter the number. What McCarthy needed was a winning campaign issue, and he had found it. Republicans, distraught over losing what had appeared to be a sure victory in 1948, were eager to support his attack. Here was a chance to discredit both Roosevelt's New Deal and Truman's Fair Deal. "A generation was on trial," wrote journalist Alistair Cooke.

McCarthy and McCarthyism gained momentum throughout 1950. Nothing seemed to slow the senator down, not even attacks by other Republicans. Seven Republican senators broke with their colleagues and publicly condemned McCarthy for his "selfish political exploitation of fear, bigotry, ignorance, and intolerance." A Senate committee reported that his charges against the State Depart-

ment were "a fraud and a hoax." But McCarthy had much to sustain him, including Julius and Ethel Rosenberg's 1950 arrest for conspiracy to commit espionage; during the war, at the Los Alamos atomic laboratory, they allegedly had recruited and supervised a spy.

Widespread support for anti-Communist measures was also apparent in the adoption, over Truman's veto, of the Internal Security (McCarran) Act of 1950. The act made it unlawful for anyone to "contribute to the establishment . . . of a totalitarian dictatorship," required members of "Communist-front" organizations to register with the government, and prohibited them from holding defense jobs or traveling abroad. In a telling decision in 1951 (*Dennis et al.* v. *U.S.*), the Supreme Court upheld the Smith Act, under which eleven Communist leaders had been convicted and imprisoned.

Meanwhile, McCarthy continued to display his unparalleled talent for demagoguery, making unsubstantiated charges, implying guilt by association, interpreting writings out of context, and telling outright lies. "It would seem easy to pin down the preposterous utterances," a reporter covering the Senate observed. "But no; McCarthy is as hard to catch as a mist—a mist that carries lethal contagion." There is no doubt that the outbreak of the Korean War in June 1950 made McCarthyism even more virulent than before.

The Korean War and Its Global Consequences

In the early morning hours of June 25, 1950, thousands of troops under the banner of the Democratic People's Republic of Korea (North Korea) moved across the 38th parallel into the Republic of Korea (South Korea). They "struck like a cobra," recalled General Douglas MacArthur. For years the two Koreas had skirmished along the border drawn for them by the great powers in 1945. Both regimes sought reunification of the divided country, but each on its own terms. Now it appeared that the North Koreans, heavily armed by the Russians, would realize their goal by force, for the South Koreans, armed by the Americans, soon disintegrated. When the news reached Washington, D.C., people recalled Pearl Harbor and braced themselves for a third world war.

For the thirty-third president, it was the 1930s all over again. "Communism was acting in Korea just as Hitler, Mussolini, and the Japanese had acted," Truman recalled. After huddling with his advisers, the president decided to intervene; he ordered MacArthur to send arms to South Korea and to attack North Korean forces from the air. Thinking beyond Korea, he directed the Seventh Fleet to patrol the waters between the Chinese mainland and Jiang's sanctuary, Formosa, thus inserting the United States once again into Chinese politics. Finally, on June 30, Truman ordered American troops into battle. "If Washington only will not hobble me," boasted MacArthur, "I can handle it with one arm tied behind my back." After the United Nation's Security Council, in the Soviet delegate's absence, voted to assist South Korea, MacArthur became United Nations commander.

Truman acted decisively for war because he believed, in the Cold War mentality of the time, that the Soviets had masterminded the North Korean attack. As an assistant secretary of state put it, the relationship between the Soviet Union and North Korea was "the same as that between Walt Disney and Donald Duck." There is little evidence that the Soviets began the Korean War, but at the time there was reason to believe that the Soviets were exploiting an opportunity to expand their influence. When most American troops had withdrawn from Korea in mid-1949, the Joint Chiefs of Staff had secretly declared South Korea nonvital to American security. In a public speech in January 1950, Secretary Acheson had drawn the American defense line in Asia through the Aleutians, Japan, and Okinawa to the Philippines. Although Formosa and Korea were clearly beyond that line, Acheson did say that those areas could expect United Nations (and hence American) assistance in the event of attack. Still, Stalin might have read Acheson's speech as an abandonment of South Korea. The Soviet Union may also have been willing to risk war to challenge China for leadership of the Communist world or to disrupt American peace negotiations with its longtime rival Japan.

Origins of the Korean War

But unanswered questions dog the thesis that Moscow started the Korean War. When the Security Council voted to aid South Korea, the Soviet delegate was absent because he was protesting the United Nations' refusal to seat the People's Republic of China. If the Soviets did foment the war in Korea, it is surprising that their delegate was not present to veto aid to South Korea. Were they caught off-guard? Other questions are also puzzling. Why did the Soviets give so little aid to the North Koreans once the war broke out? And why, when they were scoring important propaganda points by advocating peaceful coexistence, would they destroy their gains by igniting a war? Some scholars believe that the North Koreans began the war for their own nationalistic reasons. To suggest this is to emphasize the *Korean* rather than international origins of the conflict—to focus on the civil war between the North Korean Communists led by Kim Il-sung and the South Korean government ruled by Syngman Rhee.

In June 1950 such questions were not being asked. Truman and his aides never doubted that Russia or international communism was testing their policy of containment, that American prestige was at stake, and that failure to act in Korea would prompt Russian aggression in Iran or Berlin. Having bragged about toughness against communism, Truman could not refrain from acting against North Korea.

At first the war (Truman called it a "police action") went badly. The North Koreans, utilizing tanks and superior firepower, sent the South Korean army into chaotic retreat. The first American troops sent into battle tried to buy time for General MacArthur's effort to amass larger forces. Taking heavy casualties, American soldiers slowed but could not stop the North Korean advance. Within weeks the South Koreans and Americans found themselves pushed into the tiny Pusan perimeter at the base of South Korea. There they dug in.

MacArthur began to plan a daring operation: an amphibious landing at Inchon, several hundred miles behind North Korean lines (see map). Inchon seemed an inhospitable place for such an attack, with high tides, narrow approach channels, mud flats, and heavy enemy fortifications. The Joint Chiefs of Staff balked, but MacArthur insisted. After American naval guns and bombs pounded Inchon, United States Marines sprinted ashore on September 15, 1950. By nightfall, 18,000 American troops were inland, ready with tanks and vehicles to move against the South Korean capital of Seoul. They soon liberated Seoul and pushed the North Koreans back to the 38th parallel. Even before the landing at Inchon, Truman had decided to redefine the American war goal from the containment of North Korea to the reunification of Korea by force. Communism would not only be stopped; it would be rolled back. On September 27 Truman authorized United Nations forces (90 percent of them American) to cross the 38th parallel.

Within several weeks American troops had driven deeply into North Korea. In early November, American aircraft began strikes against bridges on the Yalu River, the border between North Korea and the People's Republic of China. The Chinese watched warily, wondering if the Americans who had supported Jiang Jieshi would soon stab at the People's

Inchon

Chinese Entry into the Korean War

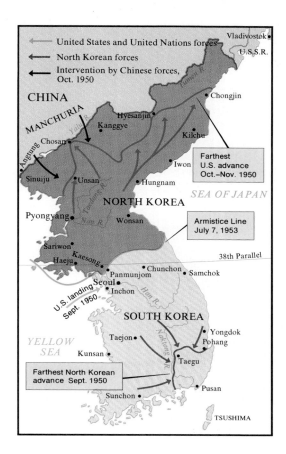

The Korean War, 1950–1953 *Source: From Paterson et al.,* American Foreign Policy: A History, *copyright 1988, p. 378. Reprinted by permission of D.C. Heath and Company.*

Republic. Mao issued public warnings that China could not permit the continued bombing of its transportation links with Korea or the annihilation of North Korea itself. MacArthur shrugged off the warnings, telling Truman that the Chinese would face the "greatest slaughter" if they entered the war. Officials in Washington agreed. But they were dead wrong.

In late October, Americans had tangled with some Chinese soldiers, who pulled back quickly after the encounter. This may have been one of many signals to the United States that American advances to the Chinese border should halt or else China would enter the war. A month later an unmoved MacArthur sent his Eighth Army northward in a new offensive. On November 26, tens of thousands of Chinese troops counterattacked, surprising the general's forces and driving them

This soldier was on patrol in Korea in September 1951. Although armistice talks had begun in July, the fighting continued for another two years. *Wide World Photos.*

pell-mell southward. Embarrassed, MacArthur demanded that Washington order a massive air attack on China. Truman hesitated, reflecting on the costs and consequences of a wider war. He hinted that he might use the atomic bomb, but he seemed chastened, uneager for a war that might drag on for years.

By March 1951 the military lines had stabilized around the 38th parallel. Truman contemplated negotiations, and the Soviets stated publicly that they favored a political settlement. MacArthur had other ideas. The theatrical general was making reckless public statements, calling for an attack on China or for Jiang's return to the mainland. Now was the time, he insisted, to smash communism by destroying its Asian flank. MacArthur also hinted that the president was practicing appeasement. Denouncing the concept of limited war (war without nuclear weapons, confined to one place), he told one member of Congress: "There is no substitute for vic-

Truman Fires MacArthur

tory." On April 10 Truman fired the general for insubordination. MacArthur, who had not set foot in the United States for over a decade, returned home to a ticker-tape parade and made a televised address to Congress that moved many in the audience to tears. One spellbound congressman murmured, "We saw a great hunk of God in the flesh."

Although Truman's popularity sagged, he withstood calls for his impeachment. The chairman of the Joint Chiefs of Staff, General Omar Bradley, spoke against MacArthur's provocative ideas. Escalation could bring Russia into battle, Bradley pointed out—American bombs had already fallen close to the Siberian port of Vladivostok. And it was unwise to exhaust America's resources in an Asian war that promised no victory when there were allies in Europe to be protected. Indeed, a showdown with Asian Communists, Bradley told a Senate committee, would be "the wrong war, at the wrong place, at the wrong time, and with the wrong enemy." MacArthur had overestimated his popularity and soon faded from the public eye.

Armistice talks began in July 1951, but the fighting and dying went on for two more years. Dwight D. Eisenhower, elected president in November 1952, went to Korea in December to fulfill a campaign pledge, but his postelection visit brought no settlement. After his inauguration, Eisenhower let it be known privately that he was considering using atomic weapons in Korea. He hoped the Chinese would be frightened into an agreement. The sticking point in the negotiations was the fate of the prisoners of war (POWs): thousands of North Korean and Chinese captives did not want to return home. In violation of international custom, American officials honored their wishes and refused to ship them back against their will. The price for this position proved high: an extended war and 32,000 more American casualties. On July 23, 1953, an armistice was finally signed. The combatants agreed to hand the POW question over to a special panel of neutral nations (which later gave prisoners their choice of staying or leaving). The North Korean–South Korean line was set close to the 38th parallel, the prewar boundary. Thus ended a frustrating war—a limited war that Americans, accustomed to victory, had not won. No celebrations greeted news of the end of the war. The experience was indeed sobering, as was the casualty list of 34,000 Americans dead in battle and 103,000 wounded. Total killed and wounded for all combatants in the Korean War was 1.9 million.

> **The POW Question**

The Korean War had major political consequences. The failure to achieve victory and the public's impatience with a limited war undoubtedly helped to elect Eisenhower (see pages 849–850). Bipartisanship in foreign policy eroded further, and the powers of the presidency grew as Congress deferred to Truman time and again. Truman had never gone to Congress for a declaration of war, for he believed that as commander-in-chief he had the authority to send troops to Korea. A few dissenters like Senator Robert Taft disagreed, but Truman saw no need to debate the matter. If he had asked for a declaration, he would have had majorities in both houses. But as Dean Acheson later explained, Truman did not wish to invite hearings and "ponderous questions" that might have "muddled up" presidential decisions.

The Korean War set off a great national debate. Conservative critics of globalism, like Taft, former

> **Debate over Globalist Policy**

ambassador to England Joseph P. Kennedy, and ex-president Herbert Hoover, suggested that America should reduce its overseas commitments and draw its defense line in the Western Hemisphere. If foreign nations were not willing to commit their own resources to defending themselves, the United States had no obligation to help them, they reasoned. But Republican John Foster Dulles countered that "a defense that accepts encirclement quickly decomposes." Truman himself joined the debate with bloated rhetoric exaggerating the Communist threat: "We are fighting in Korea so we won't have to fight in Wichita, or in Chicago, or in New Orleans, or on San Francisco Bay."

The advocates of global defense won the debate. Increased aid flowed to the French for their die-hard stand in Indochina; by 1954, when the French effort finally collapsed, the United States was paying three-fourths of the war's cost (see Chapter 31). South Korea and Formosa also became major recipients of American foreign aid. Australia and New Zealand joined the United States in a mutual defense agreement, the ANZUS Treaty (1951), which provided that an attack on any of the three countries would be considered an attack on all.

The Korean War, Acheson noted happily, removed "the recommendations of NSC-68 from the realm of theory and made them immediate budget issues." Indeed, the military budget shot up to $44 billion in 1953 (it had been $14 billion in 1949) and remained at $35 billion to $44 billion a year throughout the 1950s. The American military acquired new bases in Morocco (1951) and Spain (1953), among other places; developed the hydrogen bomb; and introduced a new long-range bomber, the B-52. The army sent six divisions to Europe, and the administration initiated plans to rearm West Germany. Proponents claimed that the logic of the containment doctrine required this global military watch, for if the threat was worldwide, the response had to be worldwide as well. "If you don't pay attention to the periphery," diplomat Dean Rusk warned, "the periphery changes. And the first thing you know the periphery is the center."

But the periphery did not in fact always become the center. Some areas were vital and others were not. Nor did a global watch ensure security. One member of Congress compared containment to "sending three policemen to surround a building that has 25 exits." And as Walter Lippmann had warned, blind allegiance to the containment doctrine did lead to repeated overseas ventures and alliances with questionable clients and dictators. Officials also assumed wrongly that threats to world peace always sprang from international Communist intrigue. They overlooked the local, non-Communist roots of many rebellions against the status quo, and they underestimated the independence of non-Soviet Communists. In the future, Americans would struggle in a revolutionary world where nationalism rather than communism was the driving force in international affairs—a force that would be subordinated neither to the United States nor to the Soviet Union.

Wartime Discontent and the Election of 1952

As Senator Joseph McCarthy raged on and Americans mobilized for the war in Korea, they remembered shortages in the last war and flocked to their

Korean War on the Home Front grocery stores for sugar, shortening, razor blades, and canned goods. Fearing that Detroit would have to convert to the manufacture of military vehicles, Americans bought cars in a hurry. Orders for military supplies flooded factories. Ford built engines for B-36 bombers; the American Locomotive Company contracted for medium-size tanks; other companies filled requests for boots, sandbags, bandages, and jackets. By the end of 1950 U.S. Steel was enjoying its greatest profits since 1917.

Fueled by panic buying and these huge federal expenditures, inflation, which had not been a problem since 1948, began to eat away at the economy again: prices rose 8 percent in the first eight months of the war. In January 1951, after six months of inflation, the government froze wages and prices. Although administering the controls proved to be a nightmare—especially after Truman's unconstitutional seizure of the steel industry in 1952, when it rejected a government-recommended wage increase—inflation had been brought un-

der control by mid-1951. Meanwhile, factories hummed, the gross national product grew, disposable personal income increased, and unemployment fell. Reform-minded Democrats were not altogether pleased, however, for defense mobilization was taking precedence over Fair Deal programs. "Every liberal movement has been stopped cold at the time of national emergency," groaned Senator Hubert Humphrey.

Draft boards registered men between the ages of eighteen and twenty-six and began to call them up. National guardsmen and reservists were elevated to active duty. There was no rush to join. "Everybody wants out; no one wants in," complained the director of the draft. Husbands and fathers thought single men should go first; parents wrote protest letters when in 1951 the military began to draft eighteen-and-a-half-year-olds. When the government announced that college students would be granted deferments, young people enrolled in universities. Other students hoped that the war would end before their graduation. But the war did not end quickly, and by mid-1952 American military personnel numbered 3.6 million, up from 1.5 million two years earlier.

As the 1952 presidential election approached, the Democrats foundered. Added to frustration with the war and hysteria over communism was the revelation of influence-peddling by some of Truman's cronies. Known as "five-percenters," these presidential appointees had offered government contracts in return for 5 percent kickbacks. In exchange for help in expediting the importation of perfume ingredients, Truman's military aide and friend Major General Harry Vaughn had accepted a freezer. An employee of the executive branch admitted under oath, "I have only one thing to sell and that is influence." In 1951 Truman's public approval rating slumped to an all-time low of 23 percent and hovered at that level for the next year. Joe Martin of Massachusetts, the House Republican minority leader, went so far as to call Truman "the worst President in history." Once again the Democratic party seemed doomed along with its leader—only this time the prediction was correct. Voters agreed with the 1952 Republican campaign slogan, "It's Time for a Change."

What sealed the fate of the Democratic party was the Republican candidate, General Dwight D. Eisenhower, who had changed his mind about the appropriateness of a military man running for

During the 1952 presidential campaign, Dwight D. Eisenhower received a delegation of Republican national committeewomen at his New York City headquarters. As the women chanted "I Like Ike," the Republican candidate opened his arms to welcome them. *UPI/Bettmann Archives.*

> **The Republican Ticket**

office. "Ike" was a bona fide war hero with a winning smile, a man who seemed to embody the virtues Americans most admired: integrity, decency, lack of pretense, and the ability to rise from humble beginnings. His running mate, Senator Richard M. Nixon of California, was less likable. Accused during the campaign of having been the beneficiary of a secret slush fund raised by wealthy Californians, Nixon went on television to deny the charge. The only gift his family had received, he explained, was a puppy named Checkers. His daughters loved the little dog, and "we're gonna keep it."

Eisenhower's unlucky Democratic opponent was Adlai Stevenson, the thoughtful, literate, and witty governor of Illinois. From the outset it was never much of a contest. Eisenhower promised to end the

Korean War. He remained cautiously silent on the subject of McCarthyism, but his running mate did not. Nixon scrambled for political points by referring to Stevenson as "Adlai the appeaser . . . who got a Ph.D. from Dean Acheson's College of Cowardly Communist Containment." The result was a landslide: Eisenhower won almost 34 million popular votes and 442 electoral votes, compared with the Democrats' 27 million popular and 89 electoral votes.

Dwight D. Eisenhower's 1952 presidential election victory was a great personal triumph. But several issues, including the Korean War, also stirred the voters. By election day, armistice negotiations in Korea had been dragging on for almost one-and-a-half years. There was still sporadic and heavy fighting, and Eisenhower had promised to visit Korea and end the war. Americans were also upset by White House corruption and allegations that Communists still worked in the State Department. All these factors coalesced to produce a record turnout of 61.5 million voters, 13 million more than in 1948. Many wanted to express their enthusiasm for Eisenhower, war hero and trusted statesman, who won the votes of Americans from a diversity of socioeconomic groups, educational levels, and religious faiths. He even captured four states in the once-solid Democratic South. Moreover, Eisenhower's coattails were long enough to carry other Republicans to victory; the party gained control of both houses of Congress, though with only a one-seat margin in the Senate (48 Republicans, 47 Democrats, 1 Independent).

Although Truman was highly unpopular when he left office in 1953, historians now rate him among the nation's ten best presidents. He came to

Truman's Presidential Legacy

office suddenly and with little experience, but in eight years he greatly strengthened the powers of the presidency. At the onset of the Cold War he announced policies to contain any presumed threat of Soviet expansion. During his presidency the Central Intelligence Agency, National Security Council, Council of Economic Advisers, and a unified Department of Defense were all created. Truman's main problems stemmed from his overreaction to the alleged threat of Communist subversion in government. His loyalty program ruined innocent people's lives and careers. In drumming up support for his foreign and military policies, Truman presented a frightening picture to the American people of the Communists' aims, and with his rhetoric he helped prepare the way for McCarthyism. Finally, he sent American troops to fight in Korea without a declaration of war from Congress.

At the same time, Truman was a New Dealer who fought for social welfare programs and legislation for farmers, workers, homeowners, retired persons, and people in need of healthcare. Above all, his Fair Deal, most of which was enacted during subsequent presidential administrations, included first-class citizenship for African-Americans. He showed his spunk and courage in 1948, when he pulled the biggest upset in American political history. When he left office in 1953, he had set the United States on a course from which it would not veer in the future, and he had cast a long shadow across the country's twentieth-century history.

Suggestions for Further Reading

Origins of the Cold War and Policy Toward Europe

Stephen Ambrose, *Rise to Globalism,* 5th ed. (1988); Richard J. Barnet, *The Alliance* (1983); Leonard Dinnerstein, *America and the Survivors of the Holocaust* (1982); John L. Gaddis, *The United States and the Origins of the Cold War, 1941–1947* (1972); James L. Gormly, *The Collapse of the Grand Alliance* (1987); Francis Harbutt, *The Iron Curtain* (1986); Gregg Herken, *The Winning Weapon* (1981); Michael Hogan, *The Marshall Plan* (1987); Laurence S. Kaplan, *The United States and NATO* (1984); Gabriel Kolko and Joyce Kolko, *The Limits of Power* (1972); Bruce Kuklick, *American Reparations Policy and the Division of Germany* (1972); Walter LaFeber, *America, Russia, and the Cold War, 1945–1984,* 5th ed. (1985); Melvyn Leffler, "The American Concept of National Security and the Beginnings of the Cold War, 1945–1948," *American Historical Review,* 89 (1984), 346–381; Alan Milward, *The Reconstruction of Western Europe* (1984); Thomas G. Paterson, *Meeting the Communist Threat* (1988); Thomas G. Paterson, *On Every Front: The Making of the Cold War* (1979); Thomas G. Paterson, *Soviet-American Confrontation* (1973); Thomas G. Paterson, ed., *Cold War Critics* (1971); Gaddis Smith, *Dean Acheson* (1972); William Taubman, *Stalin's American Policy* (1982); Adam Ulam, *The Rivals* (1971); Imanuel Wexler, *The Marshall Plan Revisited* (1983); Daniel Yergin, *Shattered Peace* (1977). Also see works cited in Chapter 27 on the diplomacy of the Second World War and the atomic bomb.

Truman Doctrine, Containment, and the Middle East

Richard M. Freeland, *The Truman Doctrine and the Origins of McCarthyism* (1972); John L. Gaddis, *Strategies of Containment* (1982); Charles Gati, ed., *Caging the Bear* (1974); John D. Iatrides, *Revolt in Athens* (1972); Howard Jones, *A New Kind of War* (1989); Bruce R. Kuniholm, *The Origins of the Cold War in the Near East* (1980); Deborah Larson, *Origins of Containment* (1985); William R. Louis, *The British Empire in the Middle East, 1945–1951* (1984); Aaron D. Miller, *Search for Security* (1980); Michael B. Stoff, *Oil, War, and American Security* (1980); Samuel F. Wells, Jr., "Sounding the Tocsin: NSC-68 and the Soviet Threat," *International Security,* 4 (1979), 116–158; Lawrence S. Wittner, *American Intervention in Greece, 1943–1949* (1982).

China, Japan, and Asia

Robert M. Blum, *Drawing the Line* (1982); Dorothy Borg and Waldo Heinrichs, eds., *Uncertain Years* (1980); Russell Buhite, *Soviet-American Relations in Asia, 1945–1954* (1982); Warren I. Cohen, *America's Response to China,* 2nd ed. (1980); Herbert Feis, *Contest over Japan* (1967); Herbert Feis, *The China Tangle* (1953); Akira Iriye, *The Cold War in Asia* (1974); E. J. Kahn, Jr., *The China Hands* (1975); William R. Louis, *Imperialism at Bay* (1978); Gary May, *China Scapegoat: The Diplomatic Ordeal of John Carter Vincent* (1979); Charles E. Neu, *The Troubled Encounter: The United States and Japan* (1975); Michael Schaller, *The American Occupation of Japan* (1985); Michael Schaller, *The U.S. Crusade in China, 1938–1945* (1978); William W. Stueck, Jr., *The Road to Confrontation: American Policy Toward China and Korea, 1947–1950* (1981); Christopher Thorne, *Allies of a Kind* (1978); Tang Tsou, *America's Failure in China, 1941–1950* (1963); Nancy B. Tucker, *Patterns in the Dust: Chinese-American Relations and the Recognition Controversy, 1949–1950* (1983).

Politics of the Truman Administration

Barton J. Bernstein, ed., *Politics and Policies of the Truman Administration* (1970); Bert Cochran, *Harry Truman and the Crisis Presidency* (1973); Robert J. Donovan, *Conflict and Crisis: The Presidency of Harry S Truman, 1945–1948* (1977); Robert J. Donovan, *Tumultuous Years: The Presidency of Harry S Truman, 1949–1953* (1982); Andrew J. Dunar, *The Truman Scandals and the Politics of Morality* (1984); Alonzo L. Hamby, *Beyond the New Deal: Harry S. Truman and American Liberalism* (1973); Susan Hartmann, *Truman and the 80th Congress* (1971); Donald R. McCoy, *The Presidency of Harry S Truman* (1984); William E. Pemberton, *Harry S. Truman* (1989); Gary Reichard, *Politics as Usual* (1988).

The Truman Administration and the Economy

Stephen K. Bailey, *Congress Makes a Law: The Story Behind the Employment Act of 1946* (1950); Jack Stokes Ballard, *The Shock of Peace: Military and Economic Demobilization After World War II* (1983); Richard O. Davies, *Housing Reform During the Truman Administration* (1966); R. Alton Lee, *Truman and Taft-Hartley* (1966); Arthur F. McClure, *The Truman Administration and the Problems of Postwar Labor* (1969); Maeva Marcus, *Truman and the Steel Seizure Case* (1977); Allen J. Matusow, *Farm Policies and Politics in the Truman Years* (1967).

The Election of 1948

Robert Divine, *Foreign Policy and U.S. Presidential Elections, 1940–1960* (1974); V. O. Key, *Southern Politics in State and Nation* (1949); Norman D. Markowitz, *The Rise and Fall of the People's Century: Henry A. Wallace and American Liberalism, 1941–1948* (1973); Richard Norton-Smith, *Thomas E. Dewey and His Times* (1982); Irwin Ross, *The Loneliest Campaign: The Truman Victory of 1948* (1968); Allen Yarnell, *Democrats and Progressives: The 1948 Presidential Election as a Test of Postwar Liberalism* (1974).

Civil Rights

William C. Berman, *The Politics of Civil Rights in the Truman Administration* (1970); Richard M. Dalfiume, *Desegregation of the U.S. Armed Forces* (1969); Richard Kluger, *Simple Justice: The History of* Brown *v.* Board of Education *and Black America's Struggle for Equality* (1975); Donald R. McCoy and Richard T. Ruetten, *Quest and Response: Minority Rights and the Truman Administration* (1973); Mark V. Tushnet, *The NAACP's Legal Strategy Against Segregated Education* (1987); Jules Tygiel, *Baseball's Great Experiment: Jackie Robinson and His Legacy* (1983).

McCarthyism

Michael R. Belknap, *Cold War Political Justice* (1977); David Caute, *The Great Fear* (1978); Larry Ceplair and Steven Englund, *The Inquisition in Hollywood* (1983); Richard M. Fried, *Men Against McCarthy* (1976); Robert Griffith, *The Politics of Fear: Joseph R. McCarthy and the Senate* (1970); Robert Griffith and Athan Theoharis, eds., *The Specter* (1974); Maurice Isserman, *If I Had a Hammer . . . : The Death of the Old Left and the Birth of the New Left* (1987); Stanley I. Kutler, *The American Inquisition* (1982); Victor Navasky, *Naming Names* (1980); William L. O'Neill, *A Better World: Stalinism and the American Intellectuals* (1983); David M. Oshinsky, *A Conspiracy So Immense: The World of Joe McCarthy* (1983); Richard Gid Powers, *Secrecy and Power: The Life of J. Edgar Hoover* (1987); Ronald Radosh and Joyce Milton, *The Rosenberg File* (1983); Thomas C. Reeves, *The Life and Times of Joe McCarthy* (1982); Walter and Miriam Schneir, *Invitation to an Inquest*, rev. ed. (1983); Ellen W. Schrecker, *No Ivory Tower: McCarthyism in the Universities* (1986); Athan Theoharis, *Seeds of Repression: Harry S Truman and the Origins of McCarthyism* (1971); Athan Theoharis and John Stuart Cox, *The Boss: J. Edgar Hoover and the Great American Inquisition* (1988); Allen Weinstein, *Perjury: The Hiss-Chambers Case* (1978).

The Korean War

Clay Blair, *The Forgotten War* (1988); Ronald J. Caridi, *The Korean War and American Politics* (1969); Bruce Cumings, *The Origins of the Korean War* (1980); Rosemary Foote, *The Wrong War* (1985); Joseph C. Goulden, *Korea* (1982); John Halliday and Bruce Cumings, *Korea: The Unknown War* (1989); Max Hastings, *The Korean War* (1987); Burton I. Kaufman, *The Korean War* (1986); Peter Lowe, *The Origins of the Korean War* (1986); Callum A. MacDonald, *Korea* (1987); Glenn D. Paige, *The Korean Decision* (1968); David Rees, *Korea: The Limited War* (1964); Michael Schaller, *Douglas MacArthur* (1989); Robert R. Simmons, *The Strained Alliance* (1975); John W. Spanier, *The Truman-MacArthur Controversy and the Korean War* (1959); I. F. Stone, *The Hidden History of the Korean War* (1952); Allen Whiting, *China Crosses the Yalu* (1960).

The signs of patriotism were everywhere. Whether scoring victories over Russian athletes at the Olympics, bragging about new records in automobile ownership, or marveling at the nation's powerful military machine, Americans celebrated their country as the best place on earth. Certainly it was better than the Soviet Union. And to trumpet that difference, sermonized the Presbyterian minister George M. Docherty on February 7, 1954, religion should be enlisted. Every morning American schoolchildren recited the famous words of the pledge of allegiance to the flag: "One nation, indivisible, with liberty and justice for all." With President Dwight D. Eisenhower sitting in his congregation that day, the Reverend Docherty implored political leaders to insert "under God" after "one nation" in the pledge. Nobody could utter *those* words in the Soviet Union, where atheistic Communists ruled. The president agreed, and Congress hastened to make the change.

29

AN AGE OF FRAGILE CONSENSUS, 1953–1961

This episode conjoining religion, patriotism, and politics befitted the 1950s, an age of consensus. In that decade Americans generally shared a belief in anticommunism and economic progress. Republican President Eisenhower, hardly the passive, ill-informed chief executive the Democrats tried to depict, was active in articulating the two beliefs and devising programs to satisfy them. But he moved cautiously and preferred a hidden-hand style to conspicuous displays of political arm-twisting.

Believing that Communists—even a few—posed a mortal danger to the American system, the Eisenhower administration expanded Truman's loyalty program, endorsed restrictive legislation, and purged the State Department. The president was reluctant to confront directly Senator Joseph McCarthy of Wisconsin, whose anti-Communist tactics proved reckless. McCarthy eventually destroyed himself with his excesses, but not before he had damaged many people and the nation itself. To maintain economic growth, Eisenhower pursued staunchly Republican goals: a balanced budget, reduced government spending, lower taxes, low inflation, private enterprise, a return of power to the states, and modest federal efforts to stimulate economic development. Eisenhower officials did not attempt to roll back the New Deal and Fair

Eisenhower visits the Far East, 1959. *Wayne Miller/Magnum Photos.*

Deal. In fact, however reluctantly, they expanded the welfare state.

Holding to their consensus thinking, white Americans celebrated their economic system for providing a high standard of living. But recurrent recessions and continued poverty in the midst of plenty raised doubts that economic progress had bestowed its benefits on all. An infant civil rights movement especially challenged the consensus view. Not only were most blacks at the bottom of the economic ladder; they were being denied their constitutional rights. How would blacks be brought into the consensus? The president, Congress, southern whites, black civil rights activists—all gave different answers as they debated the Supreme Court's 1954 *Brown* decision on desegregation.

In foreign affairs, too, Eisenhower's low-key style and the two features of the consensus—anticommunism and economic progress—were evident. Eisenhower essentially continued Truman's Cold War policies, applying the containment doctrine worldwide. To wage the Cold War, the administration relied on the threat of nuclear weapons and on interventions, some of them by a major new instrument of foreign policy, the Central Intelligence Agency (CIA). Many of the CIA's covert operations were directed against governments in the Third World, where new states were emerging from colonialism to nationhood. Americans feared that revolutionary nationalism and unrest in Third World countries would be exploited by Communists linked to a Soviet-led international conspiracy. But the United States faced serious obstacles and suffered numerous setbacks in its attempts to project and sustain American influence in the Third World. In Latin America, for example, nationalists who sought to end their nations' economic dependency upon North Americans hurled challenges at United States hegemony. The United States, then, intervened abroad not just to stop communism but also to protect American economic interests, which traditionally had contributed to economic growth at home.

President Eisenhower left office a disappointed man. The nuclear arms race had accelerated, race relations had deteriorated, and his vice president, Richard M. Nixon, had lost the 1960 presidential election to Senator John F. Kennedy of Massachusetts. The young Kennedy had criticized Eisenhower's domestic policies as inadequate to sustain economic progress for all Americans. And he had faulted Eisenhower's foreign policy for not winning the Cold War and for not aligning the Third World with the United States. Yet the consensus, however fragile, remained basically intact, for Kennedy too shared its premises. Scholars largely agree that for all the political rhetoric of the 1960 campaign the Eisenhower presidency was the kind most Americans desired in the 1950s age of consensus. Americans liked Eisenhower's traditionalism, caution, and moderation. "Ike" reassured them, and they trusted him.

Consensus and the Politics of the Eisenhower Presidency

Smiling Ike, with his folksy style, displays of confusion, garbled syntax, and frequent escapes from the Oval Office to the golf course, fueled Democratic charges that he failed to lead—"the bland leading the bland." But it was not that simple. Dwight D. Eisenhower was no stranger to hard work. His low-key, hidden-hand style was his way of playing down his political role and highlighting his role as chief of state. He was also timid about tangling directly with the vocal right wing of the Republican party. Eisenhower relied considerably upon staff work, delegated authority to departments, and shied away from close involvement in the legislative process. Sometimes this meant that he was not well informed on details, giving the impression that he was out of touch with his own government. He was not, and he remained a very popular president.

During Eisenhower's presidency most Americans clung to the status quo. It was a time of both national self-congratulation and national worry.

The Consensus Mood The British journalist Godfrey Hodgson, describing the "consensus mood," wrote that Americans were "confident to the verge of complacency about the perfectibility of American society, anxious to the point of paranoia about the threat of communism." Much as they might bicker about how the Cold War should be waged or about how the economy should be managed, they were one when it came to anticom-

1952	Eisenhower elected president First U.S. H-bomb exploded	**1957**	Eisenhower Doctrine Little Rock desegregation crisis Civil Rights Act *Sputnik* launched Recession
1953	Stalin dies Rosenbergs executed Oppenheimer case Termination policy for Native Americans Recession	**1958**	U.S. intervention in Lebanon NASA established Ouemoy-Matsu crisis again National Defense Education Act Adams resigns over scandal Berlin crisis

1954	St. Lawrence Seaway project
	   started
	Brown decision
	CIA intervention in Guatemala
	Quemoy-Matsu crisis
	Senate condemns Senator
	   McCarthy
		1959	Castro takes power in Cuba

		1960	Eighteen colonies become
			   independent nations
			Sit-in in Greensboro, North
			   Carolina
			SNCC formed
			U-2 incident
			Kennedy elected president
			Recession

1955	Bandung Conference Montgomery bus boycott begins		
1956	Highway Act Soviets invade Hungary Suez crisis Eisenhower re-elected	**1961**	Eisenhower warns against "military-industrial complex"

munism and a faith in economic progress. Most white Americans believed not only that the United States was the greatest nation in the world, but that its potential was boundless. For middle-class Americans who surrounded themselves with the symbols of economic success—automobiles, televisions, and houses in suburbia—the American dream seemed a reality (see Chapter 30). The liberal economist and Harvard University Professor John Kenneth Galbraith wrote in his influential book *The Affluent Society* (1958) that since the Second World War capitalism had worked "quite brilliantly."

Demand for reform at such a time seemed to some not only unnecessary but downright unpatriotic. The country was engaged in a moral struggle with communism, people believed, and during such a crusade one should support, not criticize, the government. The historian Henry Steele Commager regretted that he saw conformity everywhere—"the uncritical and unquestioning acceptance of America as it is." Many intellectuals who had flirted with radicalism in the 1930s, like Sidney Hook and Irving Kristol, became impassioned Cold War ideologues who believed that criticizing America gave comfort to the "enemy." They even took CIA subsidies to run their anti-Communist Congress for Cultural Freedom. College students shunned passionate political convictions, liking instead to be "cool." A weak minority on the left advocated checks on the political power of corporations, and a noisy minority on the right vilified the government for a supposed wishy-washy campaign against communism. But both liberal Democrats and moderate Republicans avoided extremism, satisfied to be occupying "the vital center."

Along with this attitude of conformity went trust

On July 4, 1961, patriotic residents of a Chicago neighborhood posed in front of their flag-draped homes. Patriotism was a prominent characteristic of the age of consensus. *National Archives.*

in and respect for established authority. In government, business, labor, the military, religion, and education, Americans let those at the top bargain on their behalf. And they chose to pursue economic goals more than moral ones, seeming to believe that the latter were not attainable. Like their leaders, Americans feared mass movements, even those with democratic goals like the civil rights movement, as threats to stability. People seemed to prefer to spend their time earning a living, raising a family, and contributing their tax dollars toward a stronger America rather than becoming involved in idealistic causes. "The fifties under Ike," Richard Lingeman of the *New York Times* observed, "represented a sort of national prefrontal lobotomy: tailfinned, we Sunday-drove down the superhighways of life while tensions that later bubbled up in the sixties seethed beneath the placid surface."

Scholars of the 1950s who subscribed to the consensus proclaimed the "end of ideology" in America. Since the early twentieth century, historians had told the American story as one of conflict—rich against poor, North against South,

▶ **Consensus Historiography** farmer against industrialist and banker. They focused on rebellions, strikes, moral crusades, and wars. The historians of the 1950s, on the other hand, wrote about stability, continuity, and cultural wholeness; they spoke of *the* American experience and *the* national character.

Important books were published on these themes, among them Daniel Boorstin's *The Americans: The Colonial Experience* (1958), Louis Hartz's *The Liberal Tradition in America* (1955), Richard Hofstadter's *The Age of Reform* (1955), and David Potter's *People of Plenty* (1954). Historians did not deny the existence of conflict in the American past, but they ascribed it less to flaws in society than to psychologically disturbed personalities. Among the people historians identified as maladjusted were abolitionists, feminists, Populists, and progressive reformers. The consensus interpretation thus shifted the emphasis away from society's faults—slavery, sexism, political corruption—and placed it on the critics who demanded reform. After analyzing his colleagues' consensus writings, the historian

John Higham observed that "a psychological approach to conflict enables historians to substitute a schism in the soul for a schism in society."

In this age of consensus, President Eisenhower approached his duties with a philosophy of "dynamic conservatism," meaning that he would be "conservative when it comes to money and liberal when it comes to human beings." Eisenhower's was "an Administration representing business and industry," admitted Interior Secretary Douglas McKay. One journalist referred to the cabinet as "eight millionaires and a plumber"—an accurate description until the plumber resigned within a year. Eisenhower and his appointees gave priority to reducing the federal budget, but they did not always succeed. Eisenhower officials recognized that they could not dismantle New Deal and Fair Deal programs, because doing so would have been politically impossible. They knew as well that most government expenditures consisted of fixed, built-in costs such as veterans' pensions, Social Security benefits, and interest payments on the national debt. Soon the Republican right wing complained that Ike was a "fifth-column Democrat" for not moving more forthrightly against the welfare state and slashing the budget more. In turn, Eisenhower grew impatient with those he privately scorned as "hidebound reactionaries." For the president, "progressive moderates" were more sensible.

> **"Dynamic Conservatism"**

True to the principles of the free marketplace and a balanced budget, Eisenhower tried in his first term to get the federal government out of agriculture. Since the 1930s the government had made payments to farmers based upon the difference between the market price and the higher parity price for farm goods. (The parity price was equivalent in value to the price farmers had enjoyed in the good year of 1909–1910.) After paying farmers this price support, the government took and stored their surplus products. Farmers received huge support payments, and government bins bulged with surplus wheat and other commodities. Meanwhile, farm production increased through the accelerated use of chemical fertilizers and machinery. Prices still fell, and farmers' purchasing power declined. Millions of farmers—most of them small landowners—abandoned farming altogether. Eisenhower

> **Farm Parity Payments and Surpluses**

officials concluded that lower, flexible price supports would discourage production. But the Agricultural Act of 1954 only lowered them to 75 to 90 percent of parity. Two years later the Soil Bank Act provided for federal payments to farmers who agreed to take cropland out of production. Another farm bill in 1958 reduced the price support for some crops to 65 percent of parity. None of these measures worked; the government spent more and the surpluses grew. President Eisenhower found all of this very distasteful. He remarked later that the federal farm program was a "national disgrace."

Eisenhower made more headway with other issues. In 1954 Congress passed legislation to begin the St. Lawrence Seaway project to construct a canal between Montreal and Lake Erie. This inland waterway was intended to spur the economic development of the Midwest by linking the Great Lakes to the Atlantic Ocean. The president also made a Cold War case for the joint Canadian-American project: it would strengthen the security of both nations. That year, too, Eisenhower revealed that he would not attempt to roll back New Deal programs when he signed into law amendments to the Social Security Act that raised benefits and added 7.5 million workers, largely self-employed farmers, to the program's coverage. The Housing Act of 1954, the first of many such measures during the decade, provided federal funds for the construction of houses for low-income families displaced by urban renewal's destruction of their neighborhoods. Congress also obliged the president in 1954 with tax reform that increased deductions and raised business depreciation allowances and with the Atomic Energy Act, which granted private companies the right to own reactors and nuclear materials for the production of electric power.

The Eisenhower administration presided over a dramatic change in the lives of Native Americans. During the 1940s, Indian programs had suffered budget cuts and sentiment had grown in Washington that the federal government should turn Native American affairs over to the states. In 1953, Congress adopted *termination*: the liquidation of Indian reservations and an end to federal services. Another act of that year made Indians subject to state laws. Native Americans were not asked if they approved of these departures from policies established a century before. Eisenhower officials ap-

> **Termination Policy for Native Americans**

Artist Wayne Thiebaud's "Interchange," a rendering of the massive interstate highway system that began in the 1950s. When the interstate highways entered urban areas, the multilane roads became a sometimes baffling network of ramps, overpasses, and interchanges that divided and encircled cities. *Collection of the Southland Corporation, Dallas, Texas.*

plauded the changes because they would reduce federal costs and serve states' rights. Critics—including most Indians—denounced termination as another white attempt to grab Indian lands and further exploit Native Americans.

Between 1954 and 1960, the federal government withdrew its benefits from sixty-one tribes. About one in eight Indians abandoned their reservations. Many found themselves joining the ranks of the urban poor in low-paying jobs. The government's efforts to provide assistance and vocational training, through relocation centers in Chicago, Denver, Los Angeles, and elsewhere, faltered. As under the Dawes Severalty Act of 1887 (see Chapter 16), land greed spurred termination and relocation. The Klamaths of Oregon, for example, lived on a reservation rich in ponderosa pine. Lumber interests coveted the timber. Enticed by cash payments, almost four-fifths of the Klamaths accepted termination and voted to sell their shares of the forest land.

A Senate committee reported in 1969 that since termination, the Klamaths had suffered "extreme social disorganization" and "many of them can be found in state mental and penal institutions." By the time termination was halted in the 1960s, so much human tragedy had struck Native Americans that observers compared their plight to the distress their forebears had endured in the late nineteenth century.

In the 1954 congressional elections, voters revealed that, although they still liked Ike, they remained loyal to the Democratic party. With a recession just winding down and the controversy over Joseph McCarthy as a backdrop, the voters gave the Democrats control of both houses of Congress. Lyndon B. Johnson became the new Senate majority leader. An energetic, pragmatic politician from Texas, he tried to work with the Republican White House to achieve legislation. A notable accomplishment was the Highway Act of 1956, which launched the largest public works program in

Interstate Highway System

American history. This law authorized the spending of $31 billion over the next thirteen years to build a 41,000-mile interstate highway system, intended to permit the military to move around the nation more easily and to assist commerce. The Highway Trust Fund, fed by new taxes on gasoline, would finance much of the construction. The interstate highways invigorated the tourist industry, further weakened the already ailing railroads, and spurred the growth of the suburbs, which were built farther and farther from the central cities (see Chapter 30).

Eisenhower suffered a heart attack in September 1955 but soon regained his strength and declared his intention to run again. The President wanted to

Election of 1956

dump Richard M. Nixon as vice president; but after Nixon refused to take a cabinet post, Eisenhower, who feared disrupting party unity if he forced Nixon out, reluctantly kept him on. The Democrats nominated Adlai E. Stevenson once more (see page 849). The campaigns lacked spirit, and the party platforms differed little. With recent crises over Hungary and Suez much on their minds, Americans decided to stick with an experienced military man and statesman at a time of world unrest. Eisenhower won a landslide victory in 1956: 35.6 million votes and 457 electoral votes to Stevenson's 26 million and 73. Still, his personal victory did not aid the Republicans in Congress, where the Democrats continued to dominate.

Eisenhower faced rising federal expenditures in his second term, in part because of the tremendous expense of America's global activities. In the first three years of his presidency he had managed to trim the budget, largely by controlling defense spending. But he discovered that he had to tolerate deficit spending to achieve his goals. In 1959 federal expenditures climbed to $92.1 billion, about half of that amount going to the military. This budget produced the largest peacetime deficit to that point in American history. In all, Eisenhower balanced only three of his eight budgets. Another reason for the administration's resort to deficit spending was the need to cushion the impact of three recessions—in the years 1953–1954, 1957–1958, and 1960–1961. A sluggish economy and unemployment (it peaked in 1958 at 7.6 percent) also reduced the tax dollars collected by the federal government. But most Americans remained employed, and the administration succeeded in keeping inflation down to about 1 percent through the 1950s.

A series of setbacks in 1958 marked the low point for the administration. Besides a lingering recession, scandal unsettled the White House. The

> **Setbacks of 1958**

president's chief aide, Sherman Adams, resigned in September under charges of influence-peddling. Then came large Republican losses in the 1958 congressional elections. The Democrats, helped by the Adams affair, economic slump, discontent among farmers, and their exaggerated claims that the administration had let the United States fall behind in the arms race, took the Senate 64 to 34 and the House 282 to 154. Some Republicans grumbled that Eisenhower had not given his party enough leadership; others realized that the Democrats were just too great in number to be beaten in the best of times. For the last two years of his presidency, then, Eisenhower had to confront what he called congressional "spenders" who proposed "every sort of foolish proposal" in the name of "national security and the 'poor' fellow." Often at odds with Congress, Eisenhower cast vetoes against bills he thought would plunge the nation into even greater debt, which stood at $286 billion by the end of 1960.

The Decline of McCarthyism

During Eisenhower's first term, one of the most vexing problems for the administration was the conduct of Senator Joseph R. McCarthy (see pages 842–844). The Wisconsin senator's no-holds-barred search for subversives in government turned up none, but it did affront political fair play, decency, and civil liberties. The president privately labeled

> **Eisenhower on McCarthy**

McCarthy a "pimple on the path of progress," but he avoided directly confronting him, saying he would not "get into the gutter with that guy." Eisenhower also feared that a showdown would splinter the Republican party. Instead, the president spoke against unnamed "demagogues thirsty for personal power" and hoped the media and Congress would bring McCarthy down. "You know," Eisenhower told his press secretary, "what we ought to do is get a word to put ahead of Republican. Something like 'new' or 'modern'" so that McCarthy and his ilk would bolt and form a third party.

While Eisenhower tried his quiet strategy to undermine the senator, his administration practiced its own brand of anticommunism. A new ex-

> **Administration Anti-Communist Activities**

ecutive order in 1953 broadened Truman's loyalty program (see pages 841–842). The administration periodically announced the number of "security risks," including State Department officials, it had dismissed from government jobs. One of Eisenhower's most controversial decisions came in June 1953 when he denied clemency to Julius and Ethel Rosenberg, who had been convicted of conspiracy to commit espionage and given a harsh sentence: death. They were executed at Sing Sing Prison as passionate pro- and anti-Rosenberg demonstrators waited outside and people around the world listened to radio reports of the Cold War event. Late that year, at the urging of the chairman of the Atomic Energy Commission, the president suspended the security clearance of J. Robert Oppenheimer, the celebrated physicist who had directed the atomic bomb project at Los Alamos

"Pussyfootprints on the sands of time" is the title of this 1954 Herblock cartoon. President Eisenhower and most senators disapproved Joseph McCarthy's disregard for the truth and his haranguing tactics, but they hesitated to confront him. By the time the Senate censured McCarthy in 1954, the nation had already been damaged by the abusive senator from Wisconsin and his stormy brand of anticommunism. *From* Herblock's Here and Now *(Simon & Schuster, 1955).*

during the Second World War. Oppenheimer's "crimes" were not that he was either disloyal to his nation or a risk to its security, but rather that he could not remember well the details of a 1943 conversation with a friend on Soviet interest in atomic secrets and that he had opposed the government's crash program to develop the hydrogen bomb.

In 1954 the Communist Control Act demonstrated that both liberals and conservatives shared the consensus on anticommunism. In effect making membership in the Communist party illegal, the measure passed the Senate unanimously and the House 265 to 2. The chief sponsor of the bill, liberal Democratic Senator Hubert H. Humphrey of Minnesota, told his colleagues just before he cast his vote: "We have closed all of the doors. These rats [Communists] will not get out of the trap." Years later Humphrey regretted his role in passing this

legislation: "It's not one of the things I'm proudest of."

As for Senator McCarthy, he finally undercut himself. He transgressed the limits of what the Senate and the public would tolerate. His crucial mistake was not merely taking on the United States Army, but doing so in front of millions of television viewers. At issue was the senator's wild accusation that the army was shielding and promoting Communists; he cited the case of one army dentist. The Army-McCarthy hearings, held by a Senate subcommittee in 1954, became a showcase for his abusive treatment of witnesses. At one general, whose loyalty was never in doubt, McCarthy shouted, "You are a disgrace to the uniform. You're shielding Communist conspirators. . . . You're not fit to be an officer. You're ignorant." McCarthy alternately ranted and, appearing drunk, slurred his words. Finally, after he had maligned a young lawyer who was not even involved in the hearings, Joseph Welch, counsel for the army, asked, "Have you no sense of decency, sir?" The gallery erupted in applause, and McCarthy's career as a witch-hunter plummeted. Republican Senator Ralph Flanders of Vermont, who courageously challenged McCarthy in the Senate, remarked that "were the junior Senator from Wisconsin in the pay of Communists, he could not have done a better job for them." In December 1954, in a 67-to-22 vote, the Senate condemned McCarthy, not for defiling the Bill of Rights but for sullying the dignity of the Senate with his contemptuous behavior. He remained a senator, but exhaustion and alcohol took their toll. He died in 1957 at the age of forty-eight.

President Eisenhower's reluctance publicly to discredit McCarthy gave the senator, other right-wing members of Congress, and some private and public institutions enough rein to divide and damage the nation and destroy the careers of many innocent people. The City University of New York, for example, fired eighteen professors—and did not apologize to them until 1980. Eisenhower's own government-sponsored McCarthyism demoralized and frightened federal workers, some of whom were driven from public service. The anti-Communist campaigns of the 1950s also discouraged people from freely expressing themselves and hence from debating critical issues of

Army-McCarthy Hearings

Chapter 29: An Age of Fragile Consensus, 1953–1961

the time. Fear and a contempt for the Bill of Rights, in short, helped sustain the consensus.

An Awakened Civil Rights Movement

If Eisenhower was pleased to be rid of McCarthy, he did not welcome the invigorated civil rights movement. Although the president completed the desegregation of the armed forces started under Truman and advanced the desegregation of the District of Columbia, he favored gradual change in race relations. But black leaders became increasingly more outspoken, insisting on significant federal action, and black people became less patient with their second-class citizenship and poverty in white America. The NAACP challenged segregation in the courts, and young blacks took direct action through boycotts, sit-ins, and demonstrations.

In May 1954 the NAACP won a historic victory that stunned the white South and energized blacks to challenge prejudice on several fronts. In *Brown*

> **Brown v. Board of Education of Topeka**

v. *Board of Education of Topeka* the Supreme Court grouped cases from several states under one hearing. Written by Chief Justice Earl Warren, the Court's unanimous decision concluded that "in the field of public education the doctrine of 'separate but equal' has no place. Separate educational facilities are inherently unequal." Such facilities, Warren wrote, produced in black children "a feeling of inferiority . . . that may affect their hearts and minds in a way unlikely ever to be undone." Because of segregation, the Court said, blacks were being "deprived of the equal protection of the laws guaranteed by the Fourteenth Amendment." But rather than demand immediate compliance, the Supreme Court waited a year before ordering the desegregation of schools "with all deliberate speed." This vague timetable encouraged the Southern states to resist.

Some border states quietly implemented the order, and Southern moderates, recognizing that "integration is as inevitable as the sunrise," in the words of the North Carolina school superintendent, advocated a gradual rollback of segregation. But the forces of resistance soon came to dominate, urging southern communities to defy the Court. Business and professional people created White Citizens' Councils for the express purpose of resisting the order. Known familiarly as "uptown Ku Klux Klans," the councils used their economic power against black civil rights activists, foreclosing on their mortgages and seeing to it that they were fired from their jobs or denied credit at local stores. Merchants withdrew their advertising from white-owned newspapers that did not editorialize on behalf of resistance. Attempting to exploit the anti-communism of the era, the councils charged that backers of integration had joined "a strategic campaign of the world communist movement." The Klan itself experienced another resurgence, and new groups, such as the National Association for the Advancement of White People, formed. One of the most effective resistance tactics was the enactment of state laws that paid tuition for white children who left public for private schools. In some cases, desegregated public schools were ordered closed.

Eisenhower, who had named Earl Warren chief justice in 1953, came to regret his appointment: "the biggest damn fool mistake I ever made." Al-

> **Eisenhower on Civil Rights**

though the president personally disapproved of segregation, he objected to "punitive or compulsory federal law" and he believed that improved race relations would develop "only if it starts locally." He also feared that the ugly public confrontations likely to follow rapid desegregation would jeopardize Republican inroads in the South. Eisenhower had even remarked to the chief justice before the *Brown* decision that white Southerners "are not bad people. All they are concerned about is to see that their sweet little girls are not required to sit in school alongside some big overgrown Negroes." Instead of stating forthrightly that the federal government would enforce the Court's decision as the nation's law—in short, instead of leading—Eisenhower spoke ambiguously and thereby encouraged massive resistance.

Dramatic events in Little Rock, Arkansas, forced the president to stop sidestepping the issue. In September 1957 Governor Orval E. Faubus intervened to halt a local plan for the gradual desegrega-

Escorted to school by federal marshals in Little Rock, Arkansas, in 1957, this black student and others had to endure racial slurs, spittings, and thrown objects—this three years after the Supreme Court's *Brown* decision against segregation in public schools. By the noted illustrator Norman Rockwell. *The Norman Rockwell Museum at the Old Corner House, Stockbridge, MA.*

> **Crisis in Little Rock, Arkansas**

tion of Little Rock's Central High School. Faubus mobilized the Arkansas National Guard to block the entry of black students. Eisenhower made no effort to impede Faubus's actions, and he seemed to agree with the sentiment behind them when he told a press conference that week, "You cannot change people's hearts merely by laws." Late that month, after bowing to a federal judge's order, Faubus withdrew the guardsmen. As hundreds of jeering whites threatened to storm the school, eight black children slipped inside Central High. The next day, fearing violence, Eisenhower federalized the Arkansas National Guard and dispatched paratroopers to Little Rock to ensure the children's safety. Troops patrolled the school for the rest of the year, but in response, the Little Rock officials closed all public high schools in 1958 and 1959 rather than desegregate them.

Elsewhere, blacks did not wait for Supreme Court or White House decisions to claim equal rights. In December 1955 Rosa Parks, a seamstress at a downtown department store in Montgomery, Alabama, and a NAACP member, refused to give up her seat to a white man on a public bus. Jim Crow practices required that blacks sit at the back of the bus and, when asked, surrender their seats to whites. Mrs. Parks was arrested. Local black leaders met and decided to boycott the city's bus system. They elected Martin Luther King, Jr., their leader. An overflow mass meeting at the Holt Street Baptist Church heard King launch the boycott with a moving speech that preached both militancy and restraint. Although blacks would no longer accept "oppression," they would confront "our white brothers" not with intimidation and violence but with the "deepest principles of our Christian faith." There could be no question who was right. "If we are wrong, the Constitution is wrong. If we are wrong, God Almighty is wrong. If we are wrong, Jesus of Nazareth was merely a utopian dreamer. . . . If we are wrong, justice is a lie."

> **Montgomery Bus Boycott**

For leading the movement to gain equality for blacks riding Montgomery, Alabama buses, Martin Luther King, Jr. (1929–1968) and other blacks, including twenty-three other ministers, were indicted by an all-white jury for violating an old law banning boycotts. In late March 1956 King was convicted and fined $500. A crowd of well-wishers cheered a smiling King (here with his wife Coretta) outside the courthouse, where King proudly declared, "The protest goes on!" King's arrest and conviction made the bus boycott front-page news across America. *UPI/Bettmann Archives.*

Martin Luther King, Jr., was an Atlanta-born, twenty-six-year-old Baptist minister who had recently earned a Ph.D. at Boston University. Disciplined and analytical, he insisted on nonviolent peaceful protest in the spirit of India's leader Gandhi. During the boycott, he received scores of hate letters and obscene telephone calls and he was jailed. A bomb blew the front from his home while his wife and child were inside. But King persisted. What the young minister-scholar gave to blacks was the "absence of fear," recalled black leader Bayard Rustin. In 1957, King became president of the Southern Christian Leadership Conference, organized to coordinate civil rights activities. But, remembered Ella Baker, another black leader, "the movement made Martin rather than Martin making the movement."

Martin Luther King, Jr.

In the year-long Montgomery bus boycott, blacks, young and old, walked or carpooled. "My feets is tired," remarked an elderly black woman, "but my soul is rested." With the bus company near bankruptcy and downtown merchants hurt by declining sales, city officials began harassing tactics to frighten blacks into abandoning the boycott. King urged perseverance. "This is not a war between the white and the Negro," he said, "but a conflict between justice and injustice." With the aid of a 1956 Supreme Court decision that declared unconstitutional Alabama's Jim Crow laws, Montgomery blacks triumphed. They and others across the nation won again in 1957 when Congress passed the Civil Rights Act, which created the U.S. Commission on Civil Rights to study, for example, voting discrimination. This measure, like a voting rights act passed three years later, proved ineffective. Critics claimed that Washington was more interested in quieting the civil rights question than in addressing it.

Blacks themselves tried new tactics. On February 1, 1960, four black students from North Carolina Agricultural and Technical College in Greensboro sat down at a department store lunch counter and ordered coffee. When told that "we do not serve Negroes," the students refused to budge. "I felt better that day than I had ever felt in my life," recalled one of the young men. "I felt as though I had gained my manhood." Thus began the sit-in movement, which spread from the South to the North, rolling back segregation in many public places. Inspired by the sit-ins, some activists met on Easter weekend in 1960 and organized the Student Nonviolent Coordinating Committee (SNCC). In the face of angry white mobs, SNCC members challenged the status quo, all the while singing the anthem of the civil rights movement, "We Shall Overcome," which includes the words, "We are not afraid."

> **The Sit-Ins**

Martin Luther King, Jr., joined the sit-in movement. In October 1960 he was arrested after trying to desegregate an Atlanta snack bar. Ultimately sent to a cold, cockroach-infested state penitentiary where he faced four months at hard labor, he became sick. As an apathetic Eisenhower White House looked on, the Baptist minister was rescued when Senator John F. Kennedy, running for the presidency, persuaded the sentencing judge to release King on bond. In November, grateful blacks cast their ballots for Kennedy and anticipated federal protection of their civil rights movement.

Eisenhower-Dulles Foreign Policy and the Cold War

Dwight D. Eisenhower had had more experience in foreign affairs than in domestic affairs before he became president. He had lived and traveled in Europe, Asia, and Latin America. During the Second World War General Eisenhower came to know Europe well, negotiated with world leaders, and made tough decisions of international conse-

quence. After the war he served as Army Chief of Staff and NATO Supreme Commander and learned the essentials of nuclear weapons development and secret intelligence operations. Like most Americans, Eisenhower accepted the Cold War consensus about the threat of communism and the need for a global watch by the United States. As president he controlled the making of foreign policy and enjoyed comfortable vote margins in Congress on key resolutions and programs.

The image of the bumbling, aging hero that partisan Democrats helped create was in part shaped by Eisenhower himself, because he deliberately counted heavily upon his secretary of state, the strong-willed John Foster Dulles. Polished and articulate, Dulles seemed to have lived his whole life in preparation for the nation's chief diplomatic post. He had studied at Princeton and trained in law at George Washington University before, at age thirty, assisting Woodrow Wilson at Versailles. As a senior partner in a prestigious Wall Street law firm Dulles had handled international cases, and as an officer of the Federal Council of Churches he had participated in programs on behalf of world peace. He had also helped the Truman administration negotiate a peace treaty with Japan. Dulles impressed people as arrogant, stubborn, and preachy—the "conscience and straightjacket of the free world," complained one European newspaper. The Eisenhower-Dulles relationship was mutually cooperative, for they agreed on basic policies, and the president delegated authority to Dulles with confidence.

> **John Foster Dulles**

Like his president, Dulles conceded much to the McCarthyites. He appointed one of Senator McCarthy's henchmen, Scott McLeod, as chief security officer of the State Department. McLeod went about trying to prove McCarthy's charge that the department was infested with Communists. Making few distinctions between New Dealers and Communists, he and Dulles forced many innocent, talented officers out of the Foreign Service. Unfortunately, they included Asian specialists whose expertise was thus later denied to American decision makers when they sent the United States to war in Indochina.

For the most part, Eisenhower and Dulles continued Truman's containment policy but introduced some memorable phrases to distinguish their administration from Truman's. Thinking con-

> **Eisenhower-Dulles Policies**

tainment too defensive a concept, Dulles invented *liberation*. (He did not, however, explain precisely how the countries of Eastern Europe could be freed from Soviet control.) *Massive retaliation* was the administration's phrase for the nuclear obliteration of the Soviet state or its assumed client, the People's Republic of China, if they took aggressive actions. Eisenhower said it "simply means the ability to blow hell out of them in a hurry if they start anything." The ability of the United States to make such a threat was thought to provide *deterrence,* or the prevention of hostile Soviet behavior.

Related to both massive retaliation and deterrence was the *New Look* of the American military. Eisenhower and Dulles emphasized air power and nuclear weaponry and de-emphasized conventional forces. The president's preference for heavy weapons stemmed in part from his desire to trim the federal budget ("more bang for the buck" in the words of the time). With this huge military arsenal, the United States in the 1950s practiced *brinkmanship:* not backing down in a crisis, even if it meant taking the nation to the brink of war. Eisenhower also popularized the *domino theory,* according to which small, weak nations would fall to communism like a row of dominoes if they were not propped up by the United States. Adopting a globalist perspective on wrenching changes in the Third World, the Eisenhower administration conducted a diplomacy of holding the line—against Soviet Russia, Communist China, neutralism, communism, socialism, nationalism, and revolution everywhere.

After the death of Stalin in 1953, Eisenhower hoped for a relaxation of Soviet-American relations but instead witnessed alternating thaws and freezes.

> **Nuclear Arms Race**

The nuclear arms race accelerated as the two superpowers developed new military technology and nuclear delivery systems. In November 1952 the United States detonated the first hydrogen bomb. In March 1954 the biggest bomb the United States has ever tested destroyed the Pacific island of Bikini. This fifteen-megaton H-bomb, packing the power of 15 million tons of TNT (or 750 times as powerful as the atomic bomb that leveled Hiroshima), produced a fallout of radioactive dust that showered a Japanese fishing boat in the area. The crew of the *Lucky Dragon*

Secretary of State John Foster Dulles (1888–1959) became a formidable debater in diplomatic negotiations. Many foreigners thought him too rigidly ideological and uncompromising. Although President Eisenhower admired him, he questioned Dulles's "practice of becoming a sort of international prosecuting attorney." Dulles seemed more eager to denounce the Soviets than to negotiate with them. The Reporter, *1956. Copyright 1956 by the Reporter Magazine Company, Inc.*

suffered nausea, fever, and blisters. International protest bombarded the United States after one of the sailors died, becoming the world's first victim of a hydrogen bomb.

The Soviets, who tested their first H-bomb in 1953, shocked Americans in October 1957 by propelling the first man-made satellite, *Sputnik,* into outer space. Just two months earlier, Soviet technicians had fired the first intercontinental ballistic missile (ICBM). Americans now felt vulnerable to air attack and inferior to the Russians in rocket technology. But the United States soon tested its own

"So Russia Launched a Satellite, but Has It Made Cars With Fins Yet?"

While American inventive genius was producing fancy consumer goods like the tail-finned automobiles of the 1950s, the Soviets were displaying technological feats such as the launching of the satellite *Sputnik*—or so Uncle Sam seems to be thinking in this Ross Lewis cartoon. *Milwaukee Public Library*.

ICBMs. It also enlarged its fleet of long-range bombers (the B-52s) and deployed intermediate-range missiles in Europe targeted against the Soviet Union. By the end of 1960 Americans had as well produced Polaris-missile-bearing submarines. To ensure future technological advancement, the National Aeronautics and Space Agency (NASA) was created in 1958. That same year Eisenhower signed the National Defense Education Act. This multi-million-dollar program loaned money to college students and provided funds for upgrading instruction in mathematics, the sciences, and foreign languages.

Through flights by the CIA's U-2 spy planes, American officials knew that the Soviets had deployed very few ICBMs. Yet critics charged that Eisenhower had allowed the United States to fall behind in the missile race. The much-publicized "missile gap" was actually a false notion inspired in part by political partisanship. "Everyone knows," Air Force General Nathan Twining privately told the president, "we already have a [nuclear] stockpile large enough to obliterate the Soviet Union." As the 1950s closed, the United States enjoyed overwhelming strategic dominance because of

its "triad" of long-range bombers, submarine-launched ballistic missiles (SLBMs), and ICBMs.

Still, President Eisenhower grew increasingly uneasy about the arms race. He feared nuclear war, and the cost of the new weapons made it difficult to balance the budget. In his 1953 Chance for Peace speech, the president had noted that "every gun that is made, every warship launched, every rocket fired signifies, in the final sense, a theft from those who hunger and are not fed. . . . The cost of one modern heavy bomber is this: a modern brick school in more than 30 cities." He also doubted the need for more and bigger nuclear weapons. How many times, he once asked, "could [you] kill the same man?" Spurred by such thoughts, by citizens' groups like the Committee for a Sane Nuclear Policy (founded in 1957 and popularly known as SANE), and by neutralist and Soviet appeals, the president cautiously initiated arms control proposals. But because he did not trust the Soviets, arms control talks never became a top priority. Indeed, he intended to preserve the American advantage and, in the propaganda duel with the Soviets, to put them on the defensive.

Eisenhower's 1953 "atoms for peace" initiative called upon the nuclear nations to contribute fissionable materials for use in industrial projects under the auspices of the United Nations. Two years later he issued his "open skies" proposal: aerial surveillance of both Soviet and American military sites to reduce the chances of surprise attacks. Despite numerous attempts at disarmament talks in Geneva, Switzerland, neither side could agree on suitable inspection systems to ensure compliance with arms control treaties or bans on nuclear testing. To satisfy world opinion about radioactive fallout, however, the two powers unilaterally suspended atmospheric testing from late 1958 to the fall of 1961, when the Soviets resumed it. The United States began testing again at the same time, but underground.

Failure of Arms Control

As the nuclear arms race accelerated, the Soviet Union and the United States waged the Cold War. The year 1955 provided a brief respite from the intensity of the competition. First, the superpowers agreed to end their ten-year joint occupation of Austria, making it an independent neutral state. Second, Eisenhower and Soviet leader Nikita

Khrushchev journeyed to Geneva for high-level talks. This first summit meeting in ten years produced no important resolutions, but the conferees "disagreed so nicely," as one reporter put it.

Events in Eastern Europe soon returned the Cold War to its accustomed acrimony. In 1956 Khrushchev called for "peaceful coexistence" between capitalists and Communists, denounced Stalin, and suggested that Moscow would tolerate different brands of communism. Soon revolts against Soviet power erupted in Poland and Hungary, testing this new permissiveness. When a new Hungarian government announced that Hungary was

> **Hungarian Uprising**

withdrawing from the Soviet-dominated alliance called the Warsaw Pact (formed in 1955), Moscow ordered troops into the upstart nation. In November, Soviet troops and tanks battled students and workers in the streets of Budapest and crushed the rebellion. The Eisenhower administration, on record as favoring the liberation of Eastern Europe, found itself unable to aid the rebels without igniting a third world war. All the United States could do was to welcome Hungarian immigrants in greater numbers than American quota laws allowed. The "West" could have reaped some propaganda advantage from this display of Soviet brute force had not British, French, and Israeli troops—American allies—invaded Egypt just before the Soviets smashed the Hungarian Revolution (see page 873).

Hardly had the turmoil in Eastern Europe subsided when the divided city of Berlin, in East Germany, once again became a Cold War flash point. The Soviets were angry about the placement in West Germany of American bombers capable of carrying nuclear warheads, and they were upset that West Berlin had become an escape route for disaffected East Germans. In 1958, Khrushchev boldly announced that the Soviet Union would recognize East German control of all of Berlin unless East and West began talks on German reunification and rearmament. The Americans, unwilling to give up their hold on West Berlin, sought to strengthen West German ties with NATO. The two sides talked of war; finally Khrushchev backed away from his ultimatum, resolving to discuss the issue at future conferences.

Berlin and Germany were on the agenda of a summit meeting planned for Paris in May 1960. But

> **U-2 Incident**

two weeks before the conference, an American U-2 spy plane carrying high-powered cameras crashed 1,200 miles inside the Soviet Union. Moscow announced that it had been shot down. At first Washington denied that its planes flew over Soviet territory, but Russian officials exposed that lie by displaying the captured CIA pilot, Francis Gary Powers, his aircraft, and the pictures he had been snapping of Soviet military installations. Moscow demanded an apology, Washington refused, and the Soviets walked out of the Paris summit.

While West and East sparred over Europe, both kept a wary eye on the People's Republic of China (PRC). Despite growing evidence of a Sino-Soviet

> **Tense Sino-American Relations**

split, most American officials continued to think of communism as a unified world movement. The United States refused to open diplomatic relations with the Chinese government and continued to give aid to Jiang Jieshi (Chiang Kai-shek) on Formosa, which the Chinese claimed as part of the PRC. Washington worried about PRC calls for anti-imperialist rebellions in the Third World and its support for revolutionaries in Indochina. In 1954 China and the United States negotiated face to face in Geneva over Indochina (see Chapter 31), but their relations were marked more by hostility than by conciliation.

In 1954 and 1955 a crisis brought the two nations to the brink of war. Just a few miles off the Chinese coast sat the tiny islands of Quemoy and Matsu. Jiang's forces used them as bases for commando raids against the PRC. In the fall of 1954 China bombarded the islands. Eisenhower decided to defend the outposts, and he let it be known that he was considering the use of nuclear weapons. Massive retaliation over such an insignificant issue? "Let's keep the Reds guessing," advised John Foster Dulles. But what if they guessed wrong? asked critics. Congress passed the Formosa Resolution (1955), which authorized the president to send troops to Formosa and adjoining islands. Two years later the United States installed on Formosa missiles capable of carrying nuclear warheads. Chinese and American diplomats talked in secret meetings in Geneva and Warsaw, but again in 1958 war loomed over Quemoy and Matsu. The crisis passed, but American defense of the islands became an issue in the election of 1960 at home.

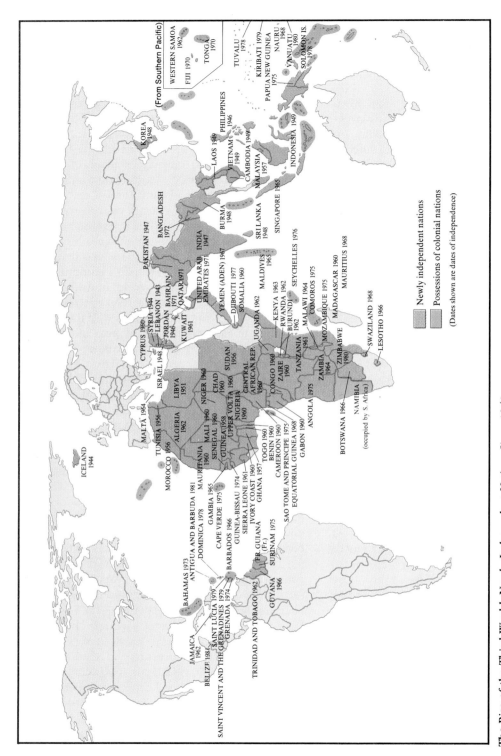

The Rise of the Third World: Newly Independent Nations Since 1943

Interventions in the Third World

Challenges from the Third World increasingly drew the Eisenhower administration's attention and resources. In the 1940s, as a result of changes wrought by the Second World War, a cavalcade of new nations began to alter the international community. From 1943 to 1989 no fewer than ninety-six countries cast off their colonial bonds. The march to independence was unrelenting: Lebanon (1943), Syria (1944), the Philippines (1946), India (1947), Indonesia (1949), Libya (1951), Morocco (1956), Ghana (1957). During the Eisenhower years twenty-four colonies became nations—eighteen in 1960 alone (see map).

These profound stirrings arose in what is now known as the Third World, a general term applied to the parts of the global community belonging to neither of the other two "worlds": the United States and its allies in the capitalist "West" and the Soviet Union and its allies in the Communist "East." Sometimes called developing countries, Third World nations on the whole are nonwhite, nonindustrialized, and located in the southern half of the globe—Asia, Africa, the Middle East, and Latin America. With Cold War lines drawn fairly tightly in Europe by the early 1950s, Soviet-American rivalry shifted increasingly to the Third World. Much was at stake. Third World nations possessed strategic raw materials such as manganese, oil, and tin. They also attracted foreign investment—in 1959 over one-third of America's private foreign investments were in Third World countries. Third World nations provided markets, especially for American products and technology. The great powers looked to these new states for support in the United Nations and for sites to be used as military and intelligence bases.

Many Third World states, like India, Ghana, Egypt, and Indonesia, did not wish to take sides in the contest between the great powers. To the dismay of both Washington and Moscow, they proudly declared themselves neutral, or nonaligned, in the Cold War. Nonalignment became an organized movement when twenty-nine Asian and African nations met in 1955 at the Bandung Conference in Indonesia. Dulles, alarmed that neutralist tendencies would deprive the United States of potential allies, declared neutralism immoral, a first step along the road to communism. Both he and Eisenhower argued that nations should take sides in the life-and-death Cold War struggle. Neutralism had to be contained.

> **Third World Neutralism**

If this negative view of neutralism inhibited United States efforts to strengthen relations with the Third World, so did America's domestic race relations. In August 1955, the ambassador from India, G. L. Mehta, sat down in a restaurant at the Houston International Airport. Texas law, however, required that whites and blacks be served in separate dining facilities. The dark-skinned diplomat, who had seated himself in a white-only area, was told to move. The insult stung deeply and was not soon forgotten. From Washington, Secretary Dulles telegraphed his apologies, fearing that the racial incident would injure relations with a nation whose allegiance the United States was seeking in the Cold War.

> **American Racism as Handicap**

Such embarrassments were not uncommon in the 1950s. Burma's minister of education was denied a meal in a Columbus, Ohio, restaurant; and the finance minister of Ghana was turned away from a Howard Johnson's just outside the nation's capital. Dulles complained that segregationist practices were becoming a "major international hazard," a threat to United States efforts to gain the friendship of Third World countries. Americans stood publicly condemned as a people who did not honor the ideal of equality. Thus when the attorney general appealed to the Supreme Court to strike down segregation in public schools, he noted the international implications. "It is in the context of the present world struggle between freedom and tyranny that the problem of racial discrimination must be viewed," he warned. The humiliation of dark-skinned diplomats in Washington, D.C., "the window through which the world looks into our house," was damaging to American interests. Racism "furnished grist for the Communist propaganda mills."

United States hostility toward revolution also obstructed the American quest for influence in the Third World. Despite its own history, the United States has been uncomfortable with and

American Intolerance of Revolution openly hostile toward significant twentieth-century revolutions—Mexican, Chinese, Russian, Cuban, Vietnamese, and Iranian. Although Americans in the 1950s paid lip service to the Spirit of '76, they were intolerant of revolutionary disorder—in part because Third World revolutions were directed against their Cold War allies, but also because such upheavals threatened American investments, markets, and military bases. Indeed, by midcentury the United States had become an established power in world affairs, eager for the stability and order that seemed to ensure American prosperity and security. During revolutionary crises, therefore, the United States usually threw its support to its European allies or to the conservative propertied classes in the Third World. In 1960, when forty-three African and Asian states sponsored a United Nations resolution appealing for decolonization, the United States abstained from the vote, signaling that it stood with the white imperialists.

Still another obstacle in America's relations with the rising Third World was the country's great wealth. Foreigners both envied and resented the "people of plenty," who had so much and wasted so much while poorer peoples went without. American movies offered enticing glimpses of middle-class materialism; American products drew attention at international trade fairs and were coveted items at native marketplaces. And Americans stationed overseas often flaunted their higher standard of living. The popular novel *The Ugly American* (1958) drew attention to the problem by describing the "golden ghettoes" of American diplomats, compounds separated from their poorer surroundings by high walls. Finally, many foreign peoples resented the ample profits that American corporations extracted from them. For all these reasons, the United States often found itself not the model of revolution but the target. Americans were blamed for the persistent poverty of the Third World, although the leaders of those nations made decisions that sometimes hindered their progress. Underfed India, for example, poured millions of dollars into the production of a nuclear bomb when it might have spent those funds improving agricultural production.

The Soviet Union enjoyed only a slight edge, if any, in the race to win friends in the Third World. It was true that Communist ideology encouraged anti-colonialism and that the Soviet Union was free of association with the long years of Western European imperialism. But though Moscow kept up a heavy drumbeat of propaganda, it could not easily explain away its subjugation of Eastern European countries. The Soviet invasion of Hungary in 1956 earned Russia international condemnation. Khrushchev toured India and Burma in the mid-1950s, but those nations refused to become Soviet clients. They were not about to replace one imperial master with another, and Soviet aid was minuscule compared with American offers. Even the People's Republic of China drifted away from Soviet influence, much as Yugoslavia had done in 1948. Like Americans, the Soviets ultimately concluded that Third World nations were playing the two superpowers against each other in order to garner larger amounts of aid and arms and that neutralism was anathema.

Obstacles to Soviet Influence

Americans nonetheless often interpreted Third World anti-imperialism, political instability, and attacks on foreign-owned property as Soviet inspired, rather than as profound expressions of nationalism or internal racial, class, religious, and ethnic divisiveness. American leaders either too simply labeled radicals, nationalists, reformers, and neutralists as Communists or assumed that they were susceptible to Communist influence. To thwart these presumed enemies, the United States resorted to alignments with undemocratic but friendly regimes and large programs of economic assistance (by 1961 over 90 percent of American foreign aid went to the Third World).

The United States also utilized the CIA to meet Third World challenges. President Eisenhower endorsed covert actions, even though espionage and the gathering of information had been defined as the CIA's primary functions at its birth in 1947. In the 1950s and later, the CIA bribed foreign politicians, subsidized foreign newspapers, hired mercenaries, conducted sabotage, sponsored labor unions, dispensed "disinformation" (circulation of false information), plotted the assassination of foreign leaders like Cuba's Fidel Castro, and staged coups. These and other spoiling operations were designed to influence foreign governments toward pro-American positions. The CIA helped overthrow the governments of Iran (1953) and Guatemala (1954) but failed in attempts to top-

CIA Covert Operations

"It seems the C.I.A. has not been inactive in this area."

Although the Central Intelligence Agency (CIA), created by the National Security Act of 1947, became famous both for its conspicuous and covert activities abroad, its clandestine agents seldom enjoyed the tremendous measure of success depicted in this cartoon. *Drawing by Dana Fradon; © 1970 The New York Magazine, Inc.*

ple regimes in Indonesia (1958) and Cuba (1961). The CIA and other parts of the American intelligence community followed the principle of "plausible deniability": covert operations should be conducted and the decisions that launched them concealed so that the president could deny any knowledge of them. Thus President Eisenhower denied the United States role in Guatemala, even though he ordered the operation; he also denied that he had ordered the CIA to assassinate Castro, whose government after 1959 became noisily anti-American (see pages 909–912).

In Latin America, long a United States sphere of influence, where poverty, overpopulation, illiteracy, economic sluggishness, and foreign exploitation fed discontent, anti-American feelings grew (see map, page 908). In 1951 the leftist Jacobo Arbenz Guzman was elected president of Guatemala, a poor country whose largest landowner was the American-owned United Fruit Company. United Fruit was a major force throughout Latin America. Its total assets in 1954 equaled $580 million; it owned three million acres of land and operated railroads, ports, ships, and telecommunications facilities. To fulfill his promise of land reform, Arbenz expropriated United Fruit's uncultivated land and offered compensation. United Fruit dismissed the offer and began an advertising campaign in the United States to rally official Washington against what the company called a Communist threat to Guatemala. Lacking evidence of actual Communist control of Arbenz's government, United States officials nevertheless cut off aid to

CIA in Guatemala Guatemala, and the CIA began a secret plot to subvert its government. When Arbenz learned that the CIA was working against him, he turned to Moscow, thus reinforcing American suspicions. The

Interventions in the Third World

Vice President Richard M. Nixon's "goodwill tour" of Latin America, in the spring of 1958, frequently aroused anti–United States demonstrations. In Caracas, Venezuela, protesters surrounded his automobile and threatened his life—providing yet another example of growing anti-Americanism in the Third World. *UPI/Bettmann Archives.*

CIA airlifted arms into Guatemala, dropping them at United Fruit facilities, and in June 1954 CIA-supported Guatemalans struck from Honduras. American planes bombed the capital; the invaders drove Arbenz from power; and the new pro-American regime returned United Fruit's land. Latin Americans wondered what had happened to the Good Neighbor policy (see page 769). Their growing hostility toward the United States surfaced in 1958, when rioters interrupted Vice President Richard M. Nixon's goodwill trip to South America. In Venezuela his limousine was stoned and his life threatened.

In the boiling Middle East the Eisenhower administration also confronted challenges to United States influence (see map, page 929). American stakes there included the survival of the Jewish state of Israel, carved out of the British mandate of Pales-

American Interests in the Middle East

tine in 1948, and extensive oil holdings (in the 1950s American companies produced about half the region's petroleum). Oil-rich Iran was a special friend, for the ruling shah had granted American oil companies a 40 percent interest in a new petroleum consortium in return for CIA help in the overthrow of his rival, Mohammed Mossadegh (1953). Mossadegh had attempted to nationalize foreign oil interests.

The major threat to American interests in the Middle East came from Egypt, where the Arab nationalist Gamal Abdul Nasser rose to power determined to push the British out of the Suez Canal Zone and the Israelis out of Palestine. The United States was caught in a double bind. It did not wish to anger the Arabs, for fear of losing its oil hold-

Chapter 29: An Age of Fragile Consensus, 1953–1961

ings. Nor did it wish to lose its ally Israel, which was supported at home by a vocal Jewish-American lobby. But when Nasser declared neutrality in the Cold War, Dulles lost patience with him. "Do nations which play both sides get better treatment than nations which are stalwart and work with us?" he asked angrily. Eisenhower doubted Nasser's neutrality. "If he was not a Communist," the president wrote later, "he certainly succeeded in making us suspicious of him." In July 1956 American officials withdrew their offer to help finance the Aswan Dam, a project to provide inexpensive electricity and water for thirsty Egyptian farmlands. Nasser quickly nationalized the British-owned Suez Canal, intending to use its profits to build the dam.

Western Europe received 75 percent of its oil from the Middle East, most of it transported through the Suez Canal. Fearing an interruption in this vital trade, the British and French conspired with Israel to bring down Nasser. On October 29, 1956, the Israelis invaded the Suez, joined two days later by Britain and France. Eisenhower fumed that his allies had not consulted him and that the attack had shifted attention from Soviet intervention in Hungary. He feared the move might cause Nasser to seek help from the Soviets, inviting the dread enemy into the Middle East. In early November Eisenhower bluntly told London, Paris, and Tel Aviv to pull out. The troops withdrew; Egypt paid $81 million for the canal; and the Soviets built the Aswan Dam.

In early 1957, in an effort to improve the deteriorating Western position in the Middle East and protect American interests there, the president proclaimed what became known

Eisenhower Doctrine
as the Eisenhower Doctrine. The United States would intervene in the Middle East, he said, if any government threatened by a Communist takeover asked for help. Fourteen thousand American troops scrambled ashore in Lebanon the next year to quell an internal political dispute that Washington feared might be exploited by pro-Nasser groups or Communists. Some critics protested that the United States was wrongfully acting as the world's policeman. Others complained that such a drastic resort to military intervention demonstrated that Eisenhower had failed miserably to thwart challenges to American power or win Cold War allies in the Third World.

As the Eisenhower presidency neared its end, accumulating foreign crises beleaguered Washington. In 1959 Eisenhower had had a friendly meeting with Khrushchev at the presidential retreat at Camp David, Maryland; but it was soon followed by renewed Soviet-American tensions, especially over the U-2 incident. In Laos and Vietnam inconclusive yet escalating American intervention threatened a wider war; and Cuba's Castro moved closer to the Soviets (see Chapter 31). The president also suffered the humiliating cancellation of his trip to Japan because of anti-American riots against the United States military presence there.

The Election of 1960 and the Eisenhower Record

The election of 1960 was one of the closest and most spirited in the twentieth century. Although Democratic candidate John F. Kennedy shared the

John F. Kennedy
two fundamental tenets of the 1950s consensus, he asserted that he could expand the benefits of economic progress and win foreign disputes through more vigorous leadership. People often contrasted his youth (forty-three years old) with Eisenhower's age (seventy years old). Handsome and intelligent, Kennedy was born to wealth, graduated from Harvard, and served as a congressman before joining the Senate in 1953. His running mate in 1960 was Senator Lyndon B. Johnson of Texas, who was added to the ticket to hold white southerners in the Democratic party as the civil rights issue heated up. Republican candidate Richard M. Nixon, the forty-seven-year-old vice president from California, and his running mate, Ambassador Henry Cabot Lodge of Massachusetts, expected a rugged campaign.

Kennedy, exploiting the media to great advantage, ran a risky, yet ultimately brilliant, race. Knowing his major liability was his Roman Catholicism,

How and Why Kennedy Beat Nixon
he addressed that issue head-on. He traveled to the Bible Belt to tell a group of Houston ministers that he respected the separation of church and state and would take

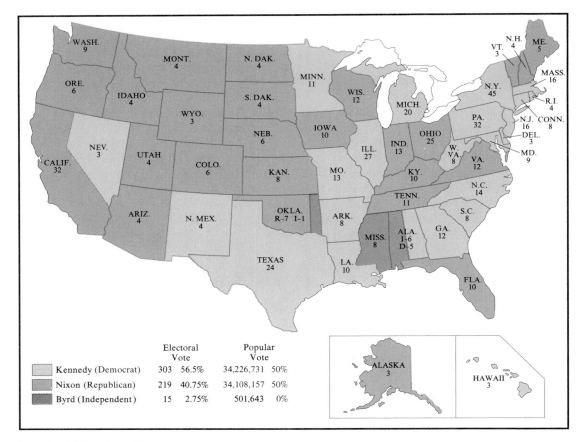

		Electoral Vote		Popular Vote	
	Kennedy (Democrat)	303	56.5%	34,226,731	50%
	Nixon (Republican)	219	40.75%	34,108,157	50%
	Byrd (Independent)	15	2.75%	501,643	0%

Presidential Election, 1960

his orders from the American people, not the pope. Seeing a major opportunity in the black vote, and calculating that Johnson could keep the white South loyal to the Democrats, Kennedy appealed to black voters. He promised to sign an executive order forbidding segregation in federally subsidized housing.

Foreign policy became a major issue. Nixon claimed that he knew how to deal with Communists, and he charged that because Kennedy lacked experience in foreign affairs he could not stand up to Khrushchev. Kennedy shot back, "I was not the Vice President of the United States who presided over the Communization of Cuba." Kennedy hit hard on Cuba, while Nixon played on the senator's statement that Quemoy and Matsu were not worth defending. Kennedy's most effective theme was that Eisenhower and Nixon had let American prestige and power slip. The Democratic candidate offered

Cold War victory instead of stalemate, and he vowed to secure Third World countries as allies of the United States.

As Kennedy gained momentum by stressing the anti-Communist theme, Nixon continued to suffer handicaps from the recession of 1960 and the U-2 incident. Nixon also presented an unsavory TV image; he came across as surly and heavy-jowled in televised debates with Kennedy. Perhaps worse, Eisenhower gave him only a tepid endorsement. Asked to list Nixon's significant decisions as vice president, the president replied: "If you give me a week, I might think of one."

In an election that saw the highest voter participation (62.8 percent) in half a century, Kennedy defeated Nixon by the razor-slim margin of 118,000 votes. The electoral college margin, 303 to 219, was much closer than the numbers suggest (see map). Slight shifts in the popular vote in Illinois and

Secretary of Defense Charles E. Wilson (1890–1961) left the presidency of General Motors to join Eisenhower's cabinet. A symbol of the military-industrial complex that the president came to criticize, Wilson once said that "what was good for our country was good for General Motors, and vice versa." Eisenhower often had to press Wilson to trim the Secretary's large defense budget requests. The outspoken Wilson resigned in 1956, much to the president's relief. Life *Magazine © 1970 Time, Inc.*

Texas, two states where electoral fraud may have helped produce narrow Democratic majorities, would have made Nixon president. Kennedy carried most of the large industrial states and most of the South. Black votes were important in providing him with triumphs in North Carolina, South Carolina, and Texas, and blacks in the inner cities turned out in large numbers for him. Although his Catholicism lost him votes, especially in the Midwest, it also gained him about 80 percent of Catholic voters. Religious bigotry did not decide the election, and Kennedy became the first Roman Catholic president.

Just before leaving office in early 1961, Eisenhower issued a warning to the nation. Because of the Cold War, he observed, the United States had

The "Military-Industrial Complex"

been "compelled to create a permanent industry of vast proportions," as well as a standing army of 3.5 million. "Now this conjunction of an immense military establishment and a large arms industry is new in the American experience." In it, he went on, resides the "potential for the disastrous rise of misplaced power." The demands of national security, he said, had created a powerful interest group that threatened the very existence of liberty. No doubt Eisenhower was thinking about a 1960 congressional report that showed that there were 1,400 retired military officers above the rank of major, including 261 generals and admirals, employed by the one hundred leading defense contractors.

Eisenhower urged Americans to guard against the "military-industrial complex." They did not.

Assessments of the Eisenhower administration used to emphasize its conservatism, passive style, limited achievements, and hesitancy to confront difficult issues. They pointed to Eisenhower's reluctance to take strong stands, keep abreast of events, or inspire needed reforms.

> **Eisenhower Presidency Assessed**

In recent years scholars have been researching in the now-declassified documents of the consensus era, and interpretations are changing. Many have begun to stress Eisenhower's influential style, command of policymaking, sensibly moderate approach to most problems, political savvy, and great popularity. Many historians now argue that he was not an aging bystander in the 1950s but a competent, pragmatic, compassionate leader who gave most Americans what they wanted at the time—a grandfatherly figure in the White House, economic comfort, and unrelenting anticommunism.

The record of Eisenhower's presidency is mixed. At home he failed to deal with problems that would wrack the country in the next decade: racism, poverty, urban decay. He dragged his feet on civil rights. He exacerbated the damage done by McCarthyism by refusing to come down hard on the reckless senator, and the president's own loyalty program was excessive. The economy suffered recessions and a growth rate of only 2.5 percent. Eisenhower never solved the farm problem, and he never moved his party to the moderate Republicanism that he championed. In foreign policy, he found no way to relax Cold War tensions, and in the end he accelerated the nuclear arms race that he so disliked. He unleashed the CIA upon the Third World and failed to adjust American diplomacy to the immense changes there.

On the other hand, in comparison with his successors, Eisenhower was cautious. He kept military budgets under control and managed crises so that the United States avoided major military ventures abroad. At home he curbed inflation, kept the nation prosperous (GNP rose from $365 billion in 1953 to $504 billion in 1961), and strengthened the infrastructure by building an interstate highway system and expanding Social Security coverage. He brought dignity to the presidency, and the American people respected him.

Suggestions for Further Reading

An Age of Fragile Consensus

Paul A. Carter, *Another Part of the Fifties* (1983); Howard Brick, *Daniel Bell and the Decline of Intellectual Radicalism* (1986); John Diggins, *The Proud Decades: 1941–1960* (1989); Ronald Lora, *Conservative Minds in America* (1971); Elaine T. May, *Homeward Bound: American Families in the Cold War Era* (1988); Douglas T. Miller and Marion Novak, *The Fifties* (1977); George H. Nash, *The Conservative Intellectual Movement in America* (1976); Loren J. Okroi, *Galbraith, Harrington, Heilbroner* (1988); William O'Neill, *American High* (1986); Richard H. Pells, *The Liberal Mind in a Conservative Age* (1985); Alan M. Wald, *The New York Intellectuals* (1987).

Eisenhower and the Politics of the 1950s

Charles C. Alexander, *Holding the Line* (1975); Stephen E. Ambrose, *Eisenhower: The President* (1984); Piers Brendon, *Ike* (1986); Robert F. Burk, *Dwight D. Eisenhower* (1986); Larry W. Burt, *Tribalism in Crisis: Federal Indian Policy, 1953–1961* (1982); Barbara B. Clowse, *Brainpower for the Cold War: The Sputnik Crisis and the National Defense Education Act of 1958* (1981); Donald L. Fixico, *Termination and Relocation: Federal Indian Policy, 1945–1970* (1986); David A. Frier, *Conflict of Interest in the Eisenhower Administration* (1969); Fred I. Greenstein, *The Hidden-Hand Presidency* (1982); Joann P. Krieg, ed., *Dwight D. Eisenhower* (1987); Peter Lyons, *Eisenhower* (1974); Herbert Parmet, *Eisenhower and the American Crusades* (1972); Nicol C. Rae, *The Decline and Fall of the Liberal Republicans* (1989); Gary W. Reichard, *Politics as Usual* (1988); Gary W. Reichard, *The Reaffirmation of Republicanism* (1975); David W. Reinhard, *The Republican Right Since 1945* (1983); Mark H. Rose, *Interstate: Express Highway Politics, 1941–1956* (1979). See also works cited in Chapter 28 on McCarthyism and in Chapter 30 on social and economic issues.

The Civil Rights Movement and Martin Luther King, Jr.

Numan V. Bartley, *The Rise of Massive Resistance* (1969); John Bloom, *Class, Race, & the Civil Rights Movement* (1987); Taylor Branch, *Parting the Waters: America in the King Years, 1954–1963* (1988); Robert F. Burk, *The Eisenhower Administration and Black Civil Rights* (1984); William H. Chafe, *Civilities and Civil Rights* (1980) (on the Greensboro sit-in); Charles W. Eagles, ed., *The Civil Rights Movement in America* (1986); David J. Garrow, *Bearing the Cross* (1986) (on King and SCLC); Elizabeth Huckaby, *Crisis at Central High, Little Rock, 1957–1958* (1980); Richard Kluger, *Simple Justice* (1975) (on the *Brown* decision); Robert J. Norrell,

Reaping the Whirlwind: The Civil Rights Movement in Tuskegee (1985); Stephen B. Oates, *Let the Trumpet Sound* (1982) (on King); Howell Raines, *My Soul Is Rested* (1977); Harvard Sitkoff, *The Struggle for Black Equality, 1954–1980* (1981).

Eisenhower-Dulles Foreign Policy

Stephen E. Ambrose, *Ike's Spies* (1981); Michael Beschloss, *MAYDAY* (1986) (on the U-2 crisis); Henry W. Brands, Jr., *Cold Warriors* (1988); Blanche W. Cook, *The Declassified Eisenhower* (1981); Robert A. Divine, *Eisenhower and the Cold War* (1981); Michael Guhin, *John Foster Dulles* (1972); Townsend Hoopes, *The Devil and John Foster Dulles* (1973); Burton I. Kaufman, *Trade and Aid* (1982); Richard A. Melanson and David A. Mayers, ed., *Reevaluating Eisenhower* (1986); Jack M. Schick, *The Berlin Crisis* (1971). Also see general works on foreign policy cited in Chapter 28.

Nuclear Arms Race

Howard Ball, *Justice Downwind: America's Nuclear Testing Program in the 1950s* (1986); Paul Boyer, *By the Bomb's Early Light* (1986); Robert A. Divine, *Blowing in the Wind: The Nuclear Test Ban Debate, 1954–1960* (1978); Lawrence Freedman, *The Evolution of Nuclear Strategy* (1981); Gregg Herken, *Counsels of War* (1985); Richard G. Hewlett and Jack M. Hall, *Atoms for Peace and War, 1953–1961* (1989); Jerome Kahan, *Security in the Nuclear Age* (1975); Fred Kaplan, *The Wizards of Armageddon* (1983); Walter A. McDougall, . . . *The Heavens and the Earth* (1985); Michael Mandelbaum, *The Nuclear Question* (1979); Richard Smoke, *National Security and the Nuclear Dilemma* (1988).

The United States and the Third World

Richard J. Barnet, *Intervention and Revolution,* rev. ed. (1972); Chester L. Cooper, *The Lion's Last Roar: Suez, 1956* (1978); Richard Immerman, *The CIA in Guatemala* (1982); Gabriel Kolko, *Confronting the Third World* (1988); Walter LaFeber, *Inevitable Revolutions* (1983); Gail E. Meyer, *Egypt and the United States* (1980); Stephen G. Rabe, *Eisenhower and Latin America* (1988); Robert W. Stookey, *America and the Arab States* (1975). Also see the works on Vietnam and Southeast Asia cited in Chapter 31.

WOT'LL IT BE

JOHN FALTER

"The remarkable thing," recalled Chuck Faust, "was that I had never expected to do anything other than follow in my father's footsteps as a farmer in central Kansas." But when Chuck was seventeen years old and a high school senior, a historic event changed his life forever: Pearl Harbor. The following spring, just days after the Salina High School class of 1942 had picked up its diplomas, Chuck enlisted in the army.

When Chuck Faust returned home in 1945, his mind was fixed not on farming but on college. While overseas, he had read about the GI Bill, which would pay living expenses and tuition for college-bound veterans. Soon after being discharged from the army, Chuck married his high school sweetheart, Annie Kempton, and the two moved to Lawrence, Kansas. For the next four years, the Fausts lived in a leftover Quonset hut near the University of Kansas campus. By graduation time, they were sharing it with their first-born, an early member of the postwar baby boom.

Like many Americans, Chuck and Annie Faust were determined to succeed, so their children could grow up in grassy suburban yards and attend good public schools. By the end of the 1950s the Fausts had added three more children to their family. Moreover, Chuck's income had enabled them to buy a comfortable home in a Kansas City suburb. The Fausts and their baby-boom children had joined the suburban middle class.

Material comfort was the hallmark of the postwar middle classes. Whether considered in terms of income levels or lifestyles, more Americans were better off than ever before—and most counted on their good fortune to continue. The baby boom was the most obvious expression of postwar optimism. From 1946 through 1964 births hit record highs. During this period 75.9 million babies were born in the United States, compared with only 44.4 million during the period of depression and war from 1929 through 1945. The peak baby-boom year was 1957, when 4.3 million babies were born. (By contrast, the number of births in the 1930s never exceeded 2.6 million per year.) The number of births began to decline after 1961, but it continued to exceed 4 million per year through 1964.

30

AMERICAN SOCIETY DURING THE BABY BOOM, 1945–1964

The Surprise by John Falter, for *The Saturday Evening Post,* April 18, 1953. *Reprinted with permission of* The Saturday Evening Post © *1953 The Curtis Publishing Company.*

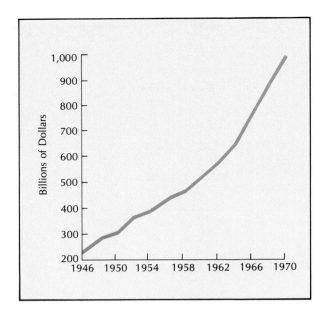

Gross National Product, 1946–1970 *Source: Adapted from U.S. Bureau of the Census,* Historical Statistics of the United States, Colonial Times to 1970, *Bicentennial Edition (Washington, D.C.: U.S. Government Printing Office, 1975), p. 224.*

Beginning with its vast size, this generation of newborns was different. For example, as parents were rearing these millions of children, "family togetherness" took on almost religious significance. Moreover, as this age group grew older, it had a successive impact on housing, elementary and secondary education, fads and popular music, higher education, and the adult job market. Landon Y. Jones, the author of a book on this generation, makes the analogy that "the baby-boom bulge" was like a "pig in a python."

Fueling Americans' postwar optimism was the twenty-five-year economic boom that began in 1946. Its cornerstones were the automobile, housing, and defense industries. As the gross national product grew, income levels rose and property ownership spread. Automobiles rolled from assembly lines; houses and schools sprang up throughout the country. More and more Americans, including many unionized blue-collar workers, bought homes in the suburbs.

To many people, it seemed that the American dream had come true. Even though the nation's economic progress was disrupted four times by recessions (1950, 1953, 1957, 1959–1960), most Americans enjoyed an increasingly comfortable standard of living throughout this period. Whatever the nation's shortcomings, economic or otherwise, Americans heralded it as the world's foremost land of opportunity. They boasted that they enjoyed political self-determination through the vote and social mobility through the melting pot. And public education guaranteed a better life to all who were willing to study and work hard.

The exceptions to the dream went unnoticed by most Americans. The lack of equal opportunities for women was concealed by an emphasis on femininity, piety, and family togetherness. Affluent families ignored evidence of poverty in society by indulging in their own pleasures and pursuing numerous ways to enjoy their leisure time. Yet in the early 1960s one of every four Americans was poor. Although poverty levels varied regionally, as well as among the cities, suburbs, small towns, and farms, it became clear by the early 1960s that the American poor were a much larger group than people in the complacent 1950s had imagined.

With the publication of Michael Harrington's *The Other America* in 1962, people became aware of this contradiction in their midst. America's poor, wrote Harrington, were "the strangest poor in the history of mankind": they "exist within the most powerful and rich society the world has ever known. Their misery has continued while the majority of the nation talked of itself as being 'affluent.'" Crowded into the cities or living in rural isolation, the poor had "dropped out of sight and out of mind," particularly to comfortable residents in the suburbs.

The Postwar Booms: Business and Babies

As Americans entered the postwar era, many wondered whether it would resemble another postwar epoch, the 1920s. In spring 1946 a *New York Times* writer predicted a return of the Roaring Twenties. Not everyone agreed. Reminding readers that the 1920s had culminated in economic depression and world war, another writer responded: "There are

1945	Demobilization of 12 million GIs
1946	Beginning of the baby boom Spock, *Baby and Child Care* Over 1 million GIs enroll in colleges 8,000 families own TVs
1947	Gross national product ($231.3 billion) begins postwar rise Levittown, New York, begun
1948	Kinsey, *Sexual Behavior in the Human Male*
1949	National Housing Act
1952	Peale, *The Power of Positive Thinking* Ellison, *Invisible Man*
1953	Kinsey, *Sexual Behavior in the Human Female*
1955	Salk polio vaccine approved for use AFL-CIO merger *Rebel Without a Cause*

1956	Highway Act Ginsberg, *Howl*
1957	Peak of baby boom (4.3 million births) Soviet Union launches *Sputnik* Kerouac, *On the Road*
1958	National Defense Education Act
1960	Gross national product reaches $503.7 billion
1962	Harrington, *The Other America*
1963	Friedan, *The Feminine Mystique*
1970	Gross national product reaches $977.1 billion Suburbs surpass central cities in population

too many people who, knowing the results which flowed from the attitudes of 1920, are going to see to it that history does not repeat itself." Indeed, most Americans expected a replay of the 1930s. After all, it was the war that had created jobs and prosperity; surely the end of war would bring a slump.

As it turned out, neither prediction was correct. The United States in 1945 entered one of its longest, steadiest periods of growth and prosperity. The keys to this success were increasing output and increasing demand. In the twenty-five years after 1945 the American economy grew at an average rate of 3.5 percent per year. Even with occasional recessions the gross national product seldom faltered, rising from just under $210 billion in 1946 to $285 billion in 1950, $504 billion in 1960, and close to $1 trillion in 1970 (see figure).

The United States was not alone in establishing new standards for economic growth and stability. Beginning in the 1950s, Japan and the nations of Western Europe were also booming. "In the 'Golden Age' of the 1950's and 1960's," stated Angus Maddison, a British economist, "economic growth in the advanced capitalist countries surpassed virtually all historical records."

When the economy produced more, Americans generally brought home bigger paychecks and had more money to spend. Between 1946 and 1950 per capita real income rose 5.9 percent—but that was only the beginning. In the

Increased Purchasing Power

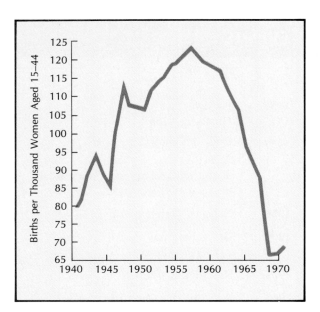

Birthrate, 1940–1970 *Source: Adapted from U.S. Bureau of the Census,* Historical Statistics of the United States, Colonial Times to 1970, *Bicentennial Edition (Washington, D.C.: U.S. Government Printing Office, 1975), p. 49.*

1950s it jumped another 15.2 percent; in the 1960s the increase was even greater—31.7 percent. Suddenly many Americans could afford goods and services that had been beyond their means in earlier decades. The result was a noticeable increase in the standard of living. To the vast majority of Americans, such prosperity was a vindication of the American system of free enterprise. Sociologist Seymour Martin Lipset went so far as to announce, "The fundamental problems of the industrial revolution have been solved."

At the end of the Second World War, just as the experts had tried to predict the nation's economic future, so too there was a debate over whether the postwar population would grow, flatten out, or even decline. As late as 1948, William F. Ogburn, a sociologist at the University of Chicago, wrote that the United States would have "a totally new experience" during the postwar era: "a cessation of population growth." Since there would be no baby boom, the "children of the next generation . . . should have room to move around and will not have to go hungry because of population pressures." Schools would not suffer from overcrowding, and there would be little pressure for the

construction of millions of tract homes in burgeoning suburbs. Ogburn was wrong.

The baby boom was both a cause and an effect of prosperity. In 1950, 3.5 million babies were born, a sizable jump from the 2.5 million born in 1940. It

▶ **Baby Boom** was natural for the birthrate to soar immediately following the Second World War. What was unusual was that it continued to do so throughout the late 1940s and 1950s. During the 1950s the annual total exceeded 4 million (see figure), reversing the downward trend in birthrates that had prevailed for 150 years. The baby-boom generation was the largest by far in the nation's history.

What the baby boom meant was that many women who gave birth to a first child in 1946 or 1947 had second, third, fourth, and even fifth children in the years ahead. According to the Census Bureau, 83 percent of the increase in births from 1940 to 1950 were first children. Of the increased births between 1950 and 1954, however, 84 percent occurred in families that already had at least one child. The popular belief that an only child was likely to grow up poorly adjusted had something to do with the continued increase. But *Business Week* was closer to the mark in crediting the boom to confidence in America's economic future. Professionals, white-collar workers, and college graduates contributed disproportionately to the baby boom. These were people who knew how to practice birth control and had done so in the past. (During the depression the birthrate had declined most sharply among the urban middle class.) And these were people who were now having children by choice.

The baby boom spelled business for builders, manufacturers, and school systems. "Take the 3,548,000 babies born in 1950," wrote Sylvia F. Porter in her syndicated newspaper column. "Bundle them into a batch, bounce them all over the bountiful land that is America. What do you get?" Porter's answer: "Boom. The biggest, boomiest boom ever known in history. Just imagine how much these extra people, these new markets, will absorb—in food, clothing, in gadgets, in housing, in services. Our factories must expand just to keep pace."

Of the three cornerstones of the postwar economic boom, two were related to the upsurge in

▶ **Auto Sales** births. The first was a construction boom to provide houses and schools for all these children.

Chapter 30: American Society During the Baby Boom, 1945–1964

Babies meant big business for companies that produced baby foods, toys, and clothing. "In its first year as a consumer," read the caption for this 1958 *Life* photo, "baby is a potential market for $800 worth of products." *Yale Joel,* Life *Magazine © 1958 Time, Inc.*

Office buildings, shopping centers, factories, airports, and stadiums also sprang up across the country. Much of this construction took place in suburbs (see pages 891–894). The postwar suburbanization of America would have been impossible without the second cornerstone, automobile manufacturing, for in the sprawling new communities a car was a necessity. Auto sales had plummeted during the Second World War, when manufacturers shifted to produce tanks and bombers; but from 1946 on, sales began to climb. In 1950 they hit 6.7 million, as Americans seized the chance to get back on the road again. The number of registered automobiles climbed from 25.8 million in 1945 to 89.3 million in 1970. Likewise, total automobile miles traveled more than quadrupled from 250 billion in 1945 to 1.1 trillion in 1970.

The third cornerstone of the postwar economic boom was military spending. When the Defense Department was established in 1949, the nation was spending just over $13 billion a year on defense. Beginning with the Korean War in the early 1950s, defense spending began to eclipse private domestic investment. By 1951, the Defense Department's budget was over $22 billion. Two years later it was over $50 billion. Except for a short dip from 1954 to 1956, it has been going up ever since. Some of the money spent on defense went into weapons research. From 1949 to 1960 funds spent on space research alone jumped from $49 million to $401 million; by 1966 the expenditures had zoomed to almost $6 billion.

Military Spending

Money spent on research stimulated the electronics industry. The invention of the transistor in 1948 inaugurated the computer revolution and stunning advances in electronics. Businesses and governments were so eager to buy electronic data-

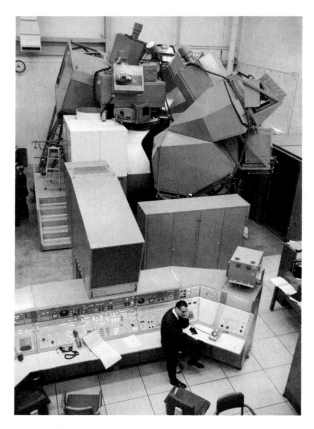

Prior to the advent of transistors and then microchip-based integrated circuits, computers were very large machines. The first postwar computer, powered by ten thousand vacuum tubes, weighed thirty tons and was as large as a railroad box car. *Cartier Bresson/Magnum Photos.*

processing machines that sales zoomed from $25 million in 1953 to $1 billion in 1960. By the early 1960s thousands of computers had been produced and sold, marking what economist Herbert A. Simon called "an advance in man's thinking processes as radical as the invention of writing."

The evolution of electronics was a trade-off for the American people. Computers brought about a rapid rise in productivity through the automation of numerous industries. But in doing so they stimulated technological unemployment: fewer workers were needed to accomplish the same amount of work. Computerized technology caused a decline in the demand for machinists; from 1950 to 1970 their numbers dropped from 535,000 to 390,000.

The spread of electronic technology also promoted the concentration of ownership in industry.

Sophisticated technology was expensive to develop or purchase. Often only large corporations could afford it; small corporations were shut out of the market. People who believed that competition was the lifeblood of the American economy saw this tendency toward bigness as a dangerous development.

As the need for large amounts of capital increased, companies that were already established in high-technology fields expanded into related industries. General Electric was one example of a large corporation that diversified after the war. Although GE had manufactured a variety of electrical products prior to the 1940s, during the Second World War and the Cold War it expanded further, undertaking the manufacture of jet engines, nuclear-powered generators, computers, and industrial automation systems.

Not all expansion was a matter of diversification into related fields. Beginning in the early 1950s a third great merger wave swept American business.

Conglomerate Mergers But unlike the first two waves in the 1890s and 1920s, which tended toward vertical and horizontal integration respectively (see pages 503–505, 696), the new wave was distinguished by conglomerate mergers. A *conglomerate* merged companies in totally unrelated fields as a hedge against instability in a particular market or industry. International Telephone and Telegraph, for instance, bought up companies in the fields of car rental (Avis), baking (Continental Baking), suburban development and home construction (Levitt and Sons), food sales (Canteen Corporation), hotels and motels (Sheraton Corporation), and insurance (Hartford Fire Insurance).

The new wave of mergers resulted in unprecedented concentration of industry. The Federal Trade Commission observed that in 1968 the two hundred largest manufacturing corporations held the same proportion of total manufacturing assets as had the one thousand largest in 1941. Reflecting the directions of America's postwar boom, the country's ten largest corporations at this time were in automobiles (GM, Ford, Chrysler), oil (Exxon, Mobil, Texaco), and electronics and communications (GE, IBM, IT&T, AT&T).

Even the labor movement experienced a merger. In 1955 the American Federation of Labor and the Congress of Industrial Organizations put aside their differences and established the AFL-CIO. Union membership remained fairly constant, however, increasing from just under 18 million at the time of the merger to only 20.7 million fifteen years later. Most new jobs were opening up not in the heavy industries that hired blue-collar workers but in the union-resistant white-collar service trades. Some observers complained that union leaders had become comfortable and lost the organizing zeal that had won over so many workers in the 1930s and 1940s. Revelations of corrupt union practices also tainted the labor movement. The nation's biggest union, the International Brotherhood of Teamsters, had ties to organized crime. When the Teamsters failed to clean their house, the AFL-CIO officially expelled the union in 1957. Two Teamsters' presidents, Dave Beck and James R. Hoffa, served federal prison sentences for offenses ranging from tax evasion to jury tampering.

The postwar economic boom was a good time for unionized blue-collar workers, many of whom not only benefited from real increases in wages, but

> **Union Workers' Benefits**

also enjoyed a middle-class lifestyle that heretofore had been the exclusive province of white-collar workers, businesspeople, and professionals. Because most union jobs paid well, these workers could obtain mortgages for suburban homes, especially if their spouses were also working. Many enjoyed job security, including a paid two-week vacation. With Social Security and union and company pension plans, they could look forward to retirement. They aspired to college educations for their children. They were more secure against inflation. In 1948 General Motors and the United Auto Workers agreed on automatic cost-of-living adjustments (COLAS) in workers' wages, a practice that spread to other industries.

The trend toward economic consolidation brought changes in agriculture as well as in business and labor. While new machines such as mechanical cotton-, tobacco-, and grape-pickers and crop-dusting planes revolutionized farming methods, the increased use of fertilizers and pesticides raised the total value of farm output from $28.8 billion in 1946 (in constant dollars) to $32.8 billion in 1950, $37.6 billion in 1960, and $54.2 billion in 1970. Meanwhile labor productivity tripled. The resulting improvement in profitability

drew large investors into agriculture. Average acreage per farm almost doubled from 1946 to 1970, rising from 193 in 1946 to 216 in 1950, 297 in 1960, and 373 in 1970. Simultaneously the value of farmland skyrocketed from $69 billion in 1945 to over $100 billion in 1950, $168 billion in 1960, and $266 billion in 1970. By the 1960s it took money—sometimes big money—to become a farmer. In many cases only banks, insurance companies, and other large businesses could afford the necessary land, machinery, and fertilizer.

By no means did all the effects of economic growth benefit the average American. In agriculture the movement toward consolidation threat-

> **Decline of the Family Farm**

ened the survival of the family farm. From 1945 to 1970 the nation's farm population declined from 24.4 million to just under 10 million, or from 17.5 percent of the population to 4.8 percent. When the harvesting of cotton in the South was mechanized in the 1940s and 1950s, more than 4 million people were displaced. One result was a shift of this poverty to the North and the cities. As one farmer lamented, "We lost country life when we moved to tractors." What was more, many of the people who stayed on did so not because they could still make a good living but because they were too old to leave their lifelong homes and follow their children and grandchildren to the cities. Living in relative isolation on limited incomes, the rural aged were among the hidden victims of mechanization.

The significant changes that postwar growth produced in industry and agriculture were matched by changes in Americans' buying habits and lifestyles. For many Americans the postwar economic boom brought what the economist John Kenneth Galbraith called the affluent society.

The Affluent Society

As America's productivity grew by leaps and bounds in the postwar years, so did its appetite for goods and services. During the depression and the Second World War, many Americans had dreamed

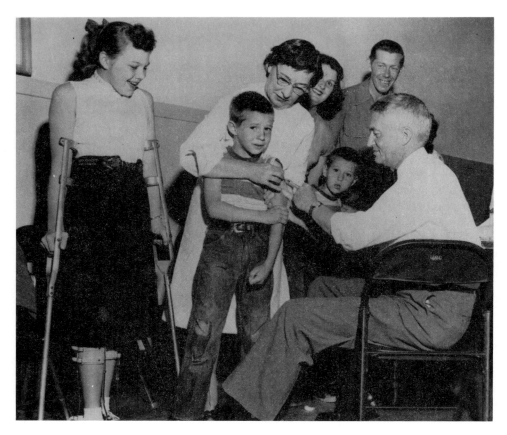

One of the most dreaded epidemics of the 1940s and early 1950s was infantile paralysis. But in 1955 the Salk polio vaccine was approved by the government for general use, and millions of children like this one received the vaccine. By 1962 the incidence of polio had dropped 97 percent. *UPI/Bettmann Archives.*

about buying a home or a car. In the affluent postwar years they could satisfy their deferred desires. Families purchased not one but sometimes two cars and equipped their new homes with the latest appliances and amusements—dishwashers, television sets, and stereophonic sound systems. When they lacked cash to buy what they wanted, they borrowed money. Credit to support the nation's shopping spree grew from over $8 billion worth of short- and intermediate-term loans in 1946 to $21 billion in 1950, $56 billion in 1960, and $127 billion in 1970. Here was the economic basis of the consumer culture.

As Americans consumed goods and services, they were using up the world's resources. Consumption of crude petroleum soared 118 percent from 1946 to 1970, but domestic production in-

creased only 97 percent. The extra oil had to be imported. Electricity use jumped too, from 270 billion kilowatt-hours to 1.6 trillion. By the mid-1960s the United States, with only 5 percent of the world's population, produced and consumed over one-third of the world's goods and services.

Advances in public health were a particularly happy effect of postwar prosperity. The average life span increased from 66.7 years in 1946 to 70.9 in 1970, due especially to a dramatic decline in the death rate among the young. (Racial differences, however, continued to be significant. In 1970, white men lived 6.7 years longer than black men, and white women lived 6.2 years longer than black women.) Affluent Americans could afford regular prenatal and

Improvements in Public Health

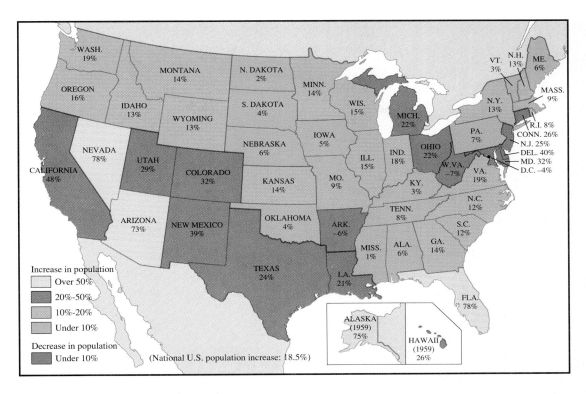

Rise of the Sunbelt, 1950–1960

pediatric care, and they benefited from increased federal funding for medical research. As a result the infant mortality rate dropped from 34 deaths per 1,000 live births in 1945 to 20 per 1,000 in 1970. (Here, too, the racial difference was great. Infant mortality for whites in 1970 was 17.8 per 1,000 live births; for blacks the figure was 30.9.) At the same time the discovery of wonder drugs such as streptomycin (1945) and aureomycin (1948) reduced deaths from influenza and postsurgical infection. The Salk polio vaccine, approved for public use in 1955, reduced the number of reported cases of polio 97 percent by 1962. Other diseases, like tuberculosis, whooping cough, and diphtheria, became little more than bad memories.

Millions of Americans began their search for the affluent society by migrating to the Sunbelt. This mass migration had started during the Second World War, when GIs and their families were ordered to new duty stations and war workers moved to the shipyards and aircraft factories of San

▶ **Growth of the Sunbelt**

Diego and other cities of the West and South. Soon the Sunbelt encompassed most of America's southern rim, the area running from southern California across the Southwest and South all the way to the Atlantic Coast. Between 1940 and 1950 Houston's population jumped from 385,000 to 596,000. Other Sunbelt cities that boomed in the 1940s were Baton Rouge, Long Beach, Miami, Mobile, and Phoenix.

The southward and westward migration continued to swell in the 1950s and 1960s (see map). Houston became a center not only of the aerospace industry but of oil and petrochemical production. Tucson, which had been scarcely more than a watering hole in the desert in 1950, grew to a city of 213,000 ten years later. California absorbed no less than one-fifth of the nation's entire population increase in the 1950s—enough, by 1963, to make the Golden State the most populous state in the union.

The economic bases of the Sunbelt's spectacular growth were easy to identify: agribusiness, the aerospace industry, the oil industry, real-estate development, recreation, and defense spending. Gov-

The Affluent Society

DISTRIBUTION OF TOTAL PERSONAL INCOME[a] AMONG VARIOUS SEGMENTS OF THE POPULATION, 1947–1970 (IN PERCENTAGES)

Year	Poorest Fifth	Second Poorest Fifth	Middle Fifth	Second Wealthiest Fifth	Wealthiest Fifth	Wealthiest 5 Percent
1947	3.5	10.6	16.7	23.6	45.6	18.7
1950	3.1	10.5	17.3	24.1	45.0	18.2
1960	3.2	10.6	17.6	24.7	44.0	17.0
1970	3.6	10.3	17.2	24.7	44.1	16.9

[a]Monetary income only.

Source: Adapted from U.S. Bureau of the Census, Historical Statistics of the United States, Colonial Times to 1970, Bicentennial Edition (Washington, D.C.: U.S. Government Printing Office, 1975), p. 292.

ernment policies—such as large tax breaks given to oil companies and decisions about where to build military bases and award defense and aerospace contracts—were crucial to the Sunbelt's development. Industry was also drawn to the southern rim by right-to-work laws, which outlawed the closed union shop, and by low taxes and low heating bills which reduced overhead expenses.

The millions of people who left the chilly industrial cities of the North and East for sunnier climes in the 1940s and 1950s strengthened the political clout of the Sunbelt. In a book published in the 1960s, Kevin Phillips, a conservative Republican, predicted an emerging Republican majority based on the votes of the South and West. Richard Nixon's triumph in the presidential election of 1968 seemed to support Phillips's thesis. So did the tendency of political parties to nominate Sunbelt candidates for national office. (The nation's four most recently elected presidents have hailed from the Sunbelt—one from Texas, two from California, and one from Georgia. And in 1980 the Census Bureau made it official: for the first time in the nation's history, voters in the South and West accounted for a majority of those eligible to cast ballots.

The economic boom that made for the political pre-eminence of the Sunbelt also brought increased security for whole classes of Americans. The expanding economy combined with federal welfare legislation to reduce poverty (see Chapter 32). But even with the reduction in poverty, there was little redistribution of income. The portions of total national income taken home by the rich, the middle classes, and the poor remained about the same from 1947 to 1960 and beyond to 1970 (see table).

The Other America

In the postwar age of abundance, most Americans found it especially hard to acknowledge the presence of poverty in their midst. But according to the Bureau of Labor Statistics, in 1962—even after fifteen years of economic boom—about 42.5 million Americans (nearly one out of every four people) were poor. These Americans earned less than $4,000 per year for a family of four, or $2,000 per year for a single person living alone. Age, race, sex, education, and marital status were all factors in their poverty. One-fourth of the poor were over age sixty-five; many lived alone on fixed incomes, their meager purchasing power continually reduced by inflation. More than one-third of the poor were under age eighteen. One-fifth were people of color, including almost half the nation's black population

Despite America's postwar economic boom, many people still lived in poverty. In 1945, these black farm workers in Belleglade, Florida, had little hope for the future. Fifteen years later, their plight was unchanged, as the historic television documentary "A Harvest of Shame" (1960) made clear. *National Archives.*

and more than half the Native American population. Two-thirds lived in households headed by a person with an eighth-grade education or less, and one-fourth lived in households headed by a single woman. For all these people, there was little reason for hope. The bureau constructed a budget to show what a poor family of four could afford: one book a year, a new car every twelve to eighteen years, no telephone, a movie once every three weeks. It is clear from this meager budget that no matter how much the economy might boom, there was a limit to the money that would trickle down to the poor.

In the years after 1945, while millions of Americans, most of them white, were settling in the suburbs, the poor were congregating in the inner cities. Starting with the wartime **Poor People** industrial boom of the early 1940s **in the** and continuing through the 1960s, **Inner Cities** almost 4.5 million blacks, many of whom were unskilled and illiter-

ate, trekked to the cities from the South. The black population, which had been 48.6 percent urban in 1940, shifted to 62.4 percent urban in 1950, 73.2 percent urban in 1960, and 81.3 percent urban in 1970. Joining African-Americans in the exodus to the cities were poor whites from the southern Appalachians, who moved to Cincinnati, Baltimore, St. Louis, Columbus, Detroit, and Chicago. Latin Americans were arriving in growing numbers from Mexico, Puerto Rico, the Dominican Republic, Colombia, Ecuador, and Cuba. New York City's Puerto Rican population spurted from 70,000 to over 600,000 in just twenty years.

Next to African-Americans, the largest group of urban newcomers were the Mexican-Americans, or Chicanos. Millions came during and after the war as farm workers, and increasingly they remained to make their lives in the United **Mexican-** States. Despite the initiation in **Americans** 1953 of Operation Wetback, a program to find and deport illegal aliens, Mexicans continued to enter the country in large numbers, many of them illegally. Many settled in cities. According to the 1960 census, over 500,000 Mexican-Americans had migrated to the *barrios* of the Los Angeles–Long Beach area since 1940. If estimates of uncounted illegal aliens were added to the census figure, the total was far higher. The same was true of the *barrios* of El Paso, Phoenix, and other southwestern cities, as well as Chicano communities in Denver, Kansas City, Chicago, Detroit, and other northern cities.

American Indians made up the country's poorest group with an average annual income that was half the amount of the poverty level. Indians moved to

> **American Indians**

the cities in the 1950s and 1960s, particularly after Congress in 1953 adopted the policy of termination, which ended the status of certain tribes as wards of the United States (see page 857). Accustomed to the rural, semicommunal life of the reservation, many had difficulty adjusting to the urban environment. The tragedy of many groups who migrated to cities was that, instead of finding a place to prosper, they found only a dumping ground for the poor.

Not all the poor, however, lived in cities. By 1960, 30 percent lived in small towns and 15 percent on farms. Tenant farmers and sharecroppers, both black and white, suffered economic hardship. Migratory farm workers lived in abject poverty. Elderly people tended to be poor regardless of where they lived.

These Americans were poor partially because they had been shortchanged by federal legislation. The Wagner Act and federal farm programs established during the New Deal chiefly helped unionized workers and landowning farmers (see pages 743 and 745). Neither Social Security nor the minimum wage covered hospital janitors and orderlies, bus boys, dishwashers, and other restaurant employees, or migratory farm workers. The programs available to the poor were generally designed to give them direct relief, not to better their chances of maintaining an independent income. Some states were stingy in the provision of poor relief. As calculated in 1960 by the Bureau of Labor Statistics, a "minimum comfort" budget for an urban family of four varied from $5,370 a year in Houston to $6,567 in Chicago. A widely accepted national average for the poverty line was $3,000,

but the five least-generous states defined subsistence as $1,600.

The number of people living in poverty fluctuated with the economy. During the postwar years, poverty was most widespread during the 1950 recession, when 36 percent of Americans were classified as poor. By 1962 poverty had fallen to about 25 percent; economic growth was clearly reducing the ranks of the poor. (President Lyndon B. Johnson's war on poverty cut the figure further, and it fell to 13 percent by 1969. See Chapter 32.)

A large share of the poor were women. Well-paying employment opportunities were limited, and there was extensive occupational segregation,

> **Women in Poverty**

with low-paying positions being labeled women's work and better-paying positions being reserved for men. In 1945 many women wanted to remain in the factories and shipyards, but they were pushed out to make way for returning veterans. Those who tried later to return to industrial work were discouraged. "Rosie [the Riveter] feels something like Typhoid Mary when she applies for a factory job," stated the *Detroit Free Press.* In 1960 the median annual earnings for full-time women workers stood at 60 percent of men's earnings. Moreover, many women's jobs were not covered by either the minimum wage or Social Security. Finally, if divorce, desertion, or death did rend a family, it was usually the woman who was left to bear responsibility for the health and welfare of children. Many ex-husbands did not make their child-support payments. And on welfare, or a salary that paid women sixty cents for each dollar a man got, many single mothers and their children slipped into poverty.

One of the least-known effects of economic hardship on the poor has been physical and emotional illness. A study done in the late 1950s in New Ha-

> **Poverty and Emotional Distress**

ven, Connecticut, found that the rate of treated psychiatric illness was three times as high for the lowest fifth of income earners as it was for the upper-middle and upper classes. Psychiatrists at Cornell University's Medical School described the "low social economic status individual" as "rigid, suspicious," and having "a fatalistic outlook on life. . . . They are prone to depression, have feelings of futility, lack of belongingness . . . and a lack of trust in others."

GEOGRAPHIC DISTRIBUTION OF U.S. POPULATION, 1930–1970 (IN PERCENTAGES)

Year	Central Cities	Suburbs	Rural Areas and Small Towns
1930	31.8	18.0	50.2
1940	31.6	19.5	48.9
1950	32.3	23.8	43.9
1960	32.6	30.7	36.7
1970	31.4	37.6	31.0

Source: Adapted from U.S. Bureau of the Census, Decennial Censuses, 1930–1970 (Washington, D.C.: U.S. Government Printing Office).

Graphic evidence of the emotional costs of poverty came during the economic recession of 1960, when the National Federation of Settlements and Neighborhood Centers assembled reports from around the country on the effects of the downturn. A social worker from Rochester, New York, bemoaned a sharp rise in "marital discord and desertions of families by the father, increased welfare dependency, increased crime, especially robberies, burglaries and muggings, and alcoholism." Ironically, all of this suffering was occurring in a nation that was being heralded as the affluent society.

The Growth of Suburbs

Suburban growth was closely associated with the affluent society. During the first six decades of the twentieth century, cityward migration steadily increased. But in the 1940s another migration—from the city to the suburbs—began to swell. By 1960 almost as many Americans resided in the suburbs as in the central cities, and by 1970 the suburbs had surpassed the central cities in total population (see table).

A combination of motives drew people to the suburbs. Many wanted to leave behind the sounds and smells of the city and be closer to nature. They also wanted homes with yards so that, as one suburbanite put it, "every kid [would have] an opportunity to grow up with grass stains on his pants." Or they wanted the privacy and quiet that detached homes provided, as well as family rooms, extra closets, and utility rooms. Many were also looking for a community of like-minded people, a place where they could have a measure of political influence. Big-city government was dense and impenetrable. In the suburbs, citizens could become involved in government and have an impact, particularly on the education their children received. "The American suburb," mused a Pittsburgh building executive in 1960, "is the last outpost of democracy, the only level on which the individual citizen can make his wishes felt, directly and immediately."

Judging from the massive numbers of three- and four-bedroom houses built in the suburbs, there was no question that suburbanites' major concern was their children. "This is a paradise for children," observed a newspaper writer in 1950, referring to the new suburb where he lived. "There are so many babies here," commented one of his neighbors, "you would think everybody would be blasé about them. Still, when a new one is coming, all the neighbors make a fuss over you."

Another allure of the suburbs was closeness in age and shared experience. In many suburbs most adults were young parents between the ages of twenty-five and thirty-five, and almost all the children were toddlers. In one suburb of nine thousand homes there were eight thousand children, only about one hundred of whom were old enough for high school; most of the rest were still

Age homogeneity distinguished suburban life during the height of the baby boom. Baby boomers, particularly those in strollers, abounded in this community. The trucks parked against the curb belonged to diaper services, which also enjoyed boom times. *Ralph Crane,* Life Magazine © *Time, Inc.*

war prosperity to produce a construction boom. In 1944 there had been only 142,000 housing starts, many of which represented temporary housing for soldiers and war workers. From 1945 to 1946 housing starts climbed from 326,000 to over 1 million, and in 1950 they approached 2 million. Never before had new starts exceeded 1 million; not until the early 1980s would they dip below that level.

To produce so much new housing so fast, contractors had to operate on a massive scale. In 1947 Arthur Levitt and Sons, a firm that built planned communities (Levittowns) in New York, New Jersey, and Pennsylvania, developed the pattern adopted by other companies: using interchangeable materials and designs. Levitt erected rows of nearly identical houses on uniform treeless lots. As suburbia spread, pasture lands yielded to whole neighborhoods with astounding rapidity. To supply the new communities, supermarkets, gas stations, shopping centers, and malls—all of them surrounded by vast parking lots—soon dotted the countryside.

At the same time highway construction opened up rural lands for the development of suburban communities. In 1947, Congress authorized the construction of a 37,000-mile chain of highways. In 1956, President Eisenhower signed the Highway Act, which launched a 41,000-mile nationwide network. Federal funds spent on highways swelled from $79 million in 1946 to $429 million in 1950, $2.9 billion in 1960, and $4.6 billion in 1970. State and local highway expenditures also mushroomed. The highways not only hastened suburbanization; they also strengthened common lifestyles and homogenized the landscape. Of special interest to the South, the highways carried the fast-moving trucks that accelerated the integration of this low-wage region into the national economy.

Highway Construction

By the mid-1960s most of the interstate system had been completed, and some towns along the way had prospered. Route I-70, for example, gave Junction City, Kansas, six new motels, several restaurants, and an economic boost. But the new road also siphoned traffic away from older roads. Small towns along two-lane highways withered as residents left to seek a better living in the city. The towns "didn't dry up and blow away," observed the editor of Junction City's daily newspaper, "but they

in playpens. "People could not outdo each other," one resident of this community reported, "because they almost all have the same income. . . . Nobody talks about the [Second World] war much, because they've all been in it. And most of the men have the same . . . commuting problem—which many have solved by car pools. All this helps to cement neighbors into friends."

Government funding and policies helped these new families to settle in the suburbs. Low-interest GI mortgages and Federal Housing Administration mortgage insurance made the difference for people who would otherwise have been unable to afford a home. Such easy credit combined with post-

Housing Boom

Levittown, Pennsylvania, one of the first housing developments built after the Second World War, provided a role model for other suburban builders to imitate. *Van Bucher/Photo Researchers.*

are much like the towns left off the railroad [lines] 100 years ago."

The spurt in highway construction combined with the mushrooming of suburbia to produce the *megalopolis,* a term first used by urban experts in the early 1960s to refer to the almost uninterrupted metropolitan complex stretching along the northeastern seaboard of the United States. Beginning in Boston and extending 600 miles south through New York, Philadelphia, Baltimore, and Washington, "Boswash" encompassed parts of eleven states and a population of 49 million people, all tied together by interstate highways. Although the suburbs within the megalopolis were politically independent, they were economically dependent on the cities and connecting highways. Other megalopolises that took shape following the Second World War were "Chipitts," a band of heavy

industry and dense population stretching from Chicago to Pittsburgh, and "San-San," the area from San Francisco to San Diego.

Middle-class whites benefited more than other Americans from the government-supported housing and highway boom. In 1948 the government cut mortgage subsidies for rental-unit construction and increased subsidies for privately owned single-family houses, a policy that worked against the poorest Americans. Moreover, the FHA refused to guarantee suburban home loans to the poor, people of color, Jews, and other "inharmonious racial and ethnic groups." Some federal programs actually worsened conditions for the poor. The National Housing Act of 1949, passed to make available "a decent home and a suitable living environment for every American family," failed in several respects. The primary features of the act were "urban rede-

The Growth of Suburbs

Dr. Benjamin Spock's *Baby and Child Care* (1946) encouraged the mothers of the baby boom to consider their children's needs first before considering their own needs. Although many mothers retained old-fashioned methods of discipline, in the postwar period there was a shift in child rearing to more permissive approaches. *The Saturday Evening Post © 1952 Curtis Publishing Company.*

velopment," or slum clearance; the construction of public housing for low-income people; and FHA mortgages for home buyers. Under the program, however, the slums were replaced not with low-income housing but with parking lots, shopping centers, luxury high-rise buildings, highways, and factories. The planned 810,000 housing units for the poor were constructed not in four years but in twenty.

Socially, the suburban emphasis on family togetherness tended to isolate families. Writing in 1957, sociologist David Riesman criticized "the decentralization of leisure in the **Critics of** suburbs . . . as the home itself, **Suburban** rather than the neighborhood, be-**Life** comes the chief gathering place for the family—either in the 'family room' with its games, its TV, its informality, or outdoors around the barbecue." The floor plan of

the ranch-style home, at whose center was the TV set enthroned on a swivel, was suited to the stay-at-home lifestyle. Even when families traveled, they were isolated in the family car.

Riesman was only one of many critics of suburban living. Other observers denounced the suburbs for breeding conformity. Some writers criticized suburbanites for trying to keep up with the Joneses by buying new cars and appliances. The word *suburbia,* Scott Donaldson wrote in *The Suburban Myth* (1969), had "unpleasant overtones, suggesting nothing so much as some kind of scruffy disease." The titles of magazine articles and books echoed his diagnosis: "Trouble in the Suburbs," "The Crabgrass Roots of Suburbia," *The Split Level Trap.* In Sloan Wilson's novel *The Man in the Gray Flannel Suit* (1955), the main character led a treadmill existence commuting to his white-collar job in the city. And C. Wright Mills, a sociologist, castigated white-collar suburbanites, who "sell not only their time and energy but their personalities as well. They sell . . . their smiles and their kindly gestures."

When all the pluses and minuses were tallied, however, most residents of suburbia seemed to prefer family togetherness to any other lifestyle of which they were aware. Of the college students interviewed by Riesman in the 1950s, the vast majority looked forward to living in the suburbs.

Ideals of Motherhood and the Family

In the early twentieth century, Sunday dinner had been an exasperating occasion for the youngest child in a large family, for the youngest was traditionally served last. If the dinner was chicken, the little one often got the back or the neck. "I was the youngest of five children," recalled one young father shortly after the Second World War, "and by the time I was served, all the white meat was gone. . . . I swore to myself that when I grew up I would eat all the white meat I could. So I'm grown up and a father—and my children get the first choice!" Times had changed, and so had the ways of the American family.

A good deal of the change was due to the publication in 1946 of Dr. Benjamin Spock's *Baby and*

Chapter 30: American Society During the Baby Boom, 1945–1964

Child Care. The book, which quickly became a bible for new parents, answered

Dr. Spock on Child Rearing ▶ many common questions about child rearing. Unlike earlier manuals, however, *Baby and Child Care* urged mothers (but not fathers, because Spock assigned them little formal role in child rearing) always to think of their children first. Dr. Spock's predecessors during the previous thirty years had advised mothers to consider their own needs as well as their children's. They had recommended early and strict toilet training; "putting away your children at six o'clock" in order to enjoy "the quiet comfort of a still household in the evening"; and ignoring a baby's crying except at feeding time. Now Dr. Spock urged the mother to be constantly available to feed and communicate with her baby, and to remember that "feeding is learning." Spock encouraged the baby's "self-realization," "self-discovery," and "self-motivated behavior."

Although no mother could be all things to her baby, women who embraced Dr. Spock's teachings tended to believe they had failed if they were not. Guilt was the inevitable result of the effort to be not only mother but teacher, psychologist, and buddy. The mother of an epileptic son wrote to Dr. Spock: "I try to give him a great deal of affection, although I am a working woman. . . . Sometimes it is so difficult to maintain my control that my hands shake. . . . Does he need the help or do I?" Another mother wrote, "We like to read and listen to music. Maybe we have neglected some aspects of A's development in our own selfishness."

At the same time Philip Wylie, author of the book *Generation of Vipers,* denounced such selfless behavior as Momism. In the guise of sacrificing for her children, Wylie wrote, Mom was pursuing "love of herself." She smothered her children with affection so they would become emotionally dependent on her and would not want to leave home. Some medical experts agreed. Army psychiatrists blamed recruits' nervous disorders on mothers who, as a psychiatric adviser to the secretary of war wrote, had "failed in the elementary mother function of weaning [their] offspring emotionally as well as physically."

But women were caught in a double bind, for if they pursued a life outside the home they were accused of being "imitation men" or "neurotic" feminists. Echoing the psychoanalyst Sigmund Freud, critics of working mothers contended that a woman could be happy and fulfilled only through domesticity. "Anatomy is destiny" was their catch phrase; a woman's gender determined her role in life. Reflecting on the contradictory expectations of women, anthropologist Margaret Mead wrote in 1946, "Choose any set of criteria you like, and the answer is the same: women—and men—are confused, uncertain, and discontented with the present definition of women's place in America."

A reason for women's dilemma was the conflicting roles she was expected to fulfill. On the one hand, the home was premised on a full-time house-

Women's Conflicting Roles ▶ wife who, with little regard for her own needs, provided her husband and children a haven from the outside world. In 1963 Betty Friedan gave this situation a name—*The Feminine Mystique.* On the other hand, women continued the wartime trend toward work outside the home. The female labor force rose from 16.8 million in 1946 to 18.4 million in 1950, 23.3 million in 1960, and 31.6 million in 1970. Many of the new women workers, however, found themselves segregated in low-paying work as clerks, secretaries, and nurses, while men commanded comfortable incomes as tradesmen, business managers, and doctors. These women had entered the labor force lacking the support of an organized women's movement, which was in decline during the hiatus between the "women's network" of the 1930s and the rebirth of feminism occurring in the later 1960s. Most women thus refrained from challenging sex-role stereotypes.

Many women were their families' sole source of income; they had to work. Still others took jobs not to challenge male dominance but to earn additional family income, enjoy adult company, or bolster their self-esteem. Despite the cult of motherhood, most new entrants to the job market were married, a trend that began during the Second World War (see figure, page 896), and most were mothers.

Immediately after the Second World War, many American families moved into abandoned military housing on college campuses. Accompanied by

GI Bill ▶ wives and babies, former GIs were getting an education. The legislation making it possible was the Servicemen's Readjustment Act of 1944, or GI Bill of Rights, which provided living allowances and tuition payments to college-bound veterans. Over 1

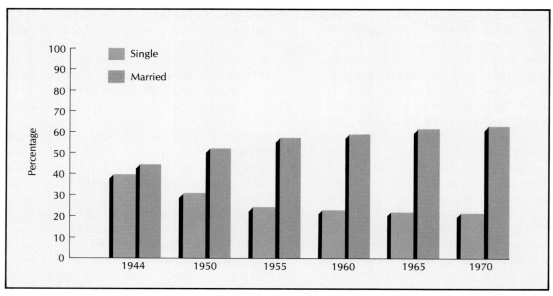

Marital Distribution of Female Labor Force, 1944–1970 *Source: Adapted from U.S. Bureau of the Census, Historical Statistics of the United States, Colonial Times to 1970, Bicentennial Edition (Washington, D.C.: U.S. Government Printing Office, 1975), p. 133.*

million enrolled in 1946—almost one out of every two students. Despite dire predictions to the contrary, the veterans succeeded as students. Benjamin Fine, education editor of the *New York Times,* called it "the most astonishing fact in the history of American higher education. . . . The G.I.'s are hogging the honor rolls and the Deans' lists. . . . Far from being an educational problem, the veteran has become an asset to higher education." But there was nothing astonishing about it. Veterans saw higher education as the key to upward mobility. (The downside of this success story was that colleges made places for male veterans by turning away qualified women.)

These veterans asserted their determination to provide economic security for their families. Men and women of their generation had been children and adolescents during the economic deprivation of the 1930s. They had experienced young adulthood during the Second World War, when many had been physically separated from their families and friends. Glen H. Elder, Jr., the sociologist, has written that men and women who had grown up in the 1930s "in Depression-marked homes were most likely to anchor their

> **Family Togetherness**

lives around family and children, perhaps reflecting the notion of home as a refuge in an unpredictable world." These men and women became parents of the baby boom and exponents of "family togetherness." Such togetherness included family TV-watching, outings to parks and beaches, and Little League games.

Popular periodicals echoed the importance that these parents attached to togetherness. "Ed and His Family Live Together and Love It" was the title of a typical article in a 1954 *McCall's.* "Caring for three lively children makes tremendous demands on Carol. . . . But Ed is a cheerful working partner to her, helps with the children and housework whenever he can, gives everything he has to make his family happy." In return, Ed's wife and children "give him all the love and affection a husband and father could hope for." Carol even took over some household tasks traditionally performed by men: "Paneling that extra room in the cellar used to be the man's job. But Ed and Carol do it together." Despite *McCall's* advocacy of shared tasks, the magazine stopped short of advocating complete equality. "For the sake of every member of the family, the family needs a head. This means Father, not Mother."

Most American families were preoccupied with education. As the baby boom became a grade-school boom, parents rushed to join the parent-teacher association so they would

Education of the Baby-Boom Generation have a voice in the educational process. They expressed concern that schools were overcrowded, understaffed, and aimless, or that teachers were using obsolete

methods. Educators encouraged their participation. "Just as war is 'too serious a matter to be left to the generals,' so, I think, the teaching of reading is too important to be left to the educators," wrote Dr. Rudolf Flesch in 1955 in his best-selling book *Why Johnny Can't Read.*

Two years later when the Russians launched *Sputnik,* the first earth-orbiting satellite, education became a matter of national security. The Russian success challenged American military and technological superiority, based ultimately on the nation's school system. James B. Conant, Hyman G. Rickover, and other critics argued that what the United States needed to regain its technological leadership was new emphasis on mathematics, foreign languages, and the sciences. In 1958, when Congress responded with the National Defense Education Act (NDEA), which funded elementary and high school programs in those disciplines and offered fellowships and loans to college students, parents were quick to endorse the new programs. After all, public education was "the engine of democracy," a guarantee of both upward social mobility and military superiority. One of the clearest indications of this belief was the surge in college enrollments, which jumped from 1.5 million in 1940 to 2.3 million in 1950, 3.6 million in 1960, and 7.4 million in 1970.

But even as college enrollments swelled, women lost ground in the postwar years. In an era in which the wife tended to subordinate her career goals to those of her husband, there was a decline in the percentage of women earning college degrees. The proportion of college graduates who were women dropped from 40 percent in 1940 to 25 percent in 1950. Fewer women earned postgraduate degrees. In 1960 only 10.7 percent of doctorates earned in the United States went to women, a drop from 1920 when the figure was 15.7 percent. The 1960s reversed this trend, and by 1970 the figure had again reached the 1920 level.

Families prayed together and vacationed together during the postwar years. After a troubled period of depression and world war, and faced with the threat of worldwide extinction through nuclear war, the parents of the baby boom took refuge in the security of the family and the home. *Wayne Miller/Magnum.*

Just as education became intertwined with national security, religion became synonymous with patriotism. As President Eisenhower put it, "Recognition of the Supreme Being is the first, the most basic expression of Americanism." After all, the United States was locked in mortal combat with an atheistic enemy. In America's Cold War with the godless Soviet Union, ministers, priests, and rabbis became foot soldiers in the battle for souls. Religious leaders emphasized family togetherness in their appeals for new converts. "The family that prays together stays together" was a famous slogan used during the 1950s and 1960s. The Bible topped the best-seller lists, and books with religious

Ideals of Motherhood and the Family

themes, such as Reverend Norman Vincent Peale's *The Power of Positive Thinking* (1952), sold in the millions. Evangelist Billy Graham exhorted television viewers and stadium audiences throughout the country. Membership in religious organizations nearly doubled in the twenty-five years after the Second World War, increasing from 74 million in 1946 to 87 million in 1950, 114 million in 1960, and 131 million in 1970.

Although Americans were eager to improve their minds and souls, they were not ready until the 1960s to liberate themselves sexually. When Dr. Alfred Kinsey, director of the Institute for Sex Research at Indiana University, published his pioneering book *Sexual Behavior in the Human Male* (1948), the American public was shocked. On the basis of interviews with numerous men, Kinsey estimated that 95 percent of American men had engaged in masturbation, premarital or extramarital intercourse, or homosexual behavior. Princeton's President Harold Dodds denounced the volume as "the work of small boys writing dirty words on fences." Five years later Kinsey caused even more of a disturbance with *Sexual Behavior in the Human Female,* which revealed that 62 percent of women masturbated and 50 percent had intercourse before marriage. Some angry Americans condemned the report as a slanderous attack not only on women but on motherhood and the family as well. A congressional representative from New York, who tried to bar the report from the mails, charged Kinsey with "hurling the insult of the century against our mothers, wives, daughters and sisters." Sex was nothing new, of course, but its existence was seldom acknowledged in polite conversation or respectable publications—and most Americans preferred that situation.

> **Sex in Postwar America**

Middle-Class America at Play

The prosperity that marked the postwar era was reflected in the materialistic values and pleasures of the period. Having satisfied their basic needs for food, clothing, and shelter, growing numbers of Americans turned their attention to luxury items. "More appliances make mom's work easier," read a typical advertisement. As families strove to acquire the latest conveniences, shopping became a form of recreation.

Of the new luxuries, television was the most revolutionary in its effects. One man who grew up in the postwar era recalled the purchase of the first family TV set in 1950. "And so the monumental change began in our lives and those of millions of other Americans. More than a year passed before we again visited a movie theater. Money which previously would have been spent for books was saved for the TV payments. Social evenings with friends became fewer and fewer still because we discovered we did not share the same TV program interests." By 1950 television had broken radio's grip on the American public. The number of households with TVs climbed from 8,000 in 1946 to 3.9 million in 1950, 46.3 million in 1960 (a 920 percent increase), and 60.6 million in 1970.

> **TV Enters the American Home**

Entertainment was TV's number one product. Situation comedies and action series were among the most popular shows. Topping these categories in the 1950s were "I Love Lucy," starring Lucille Ball, and "Dragnet," a detective series. Family togetherness was a theme of "Father Knows Best" and "Leave It to Beaver." There were programs for all age groups, ranging from "Ding Dong School," quiz shows, and westerns to the roller derby. As daily average TV viewing in the United States reached five hours in 1956 and continued to mount, the danger presented itself that television would become more than just entertainment. Some critics worried that with so much viewing, TV's distorted presentation of the world would significantly define people's sense of reality.

Advertising was the foundation of the television industry, as it had also been for radio. The first TV commercial, made by the Bulova Watch Company in 1941, was a one-minute effort that cost nine dollars. By the end of the decade, American families were spending several hours a day before the television set, and bargain rates had vanished; annual expenditures for TV advertising totaled $171 million in 1950 and $1.6 billion in 1960. By 1970 the figure had soared further to $3.6 billion.

Critics of the television industry have often wondered why American viewers put up with advertising. The answer is that, far from being an unwanted interruption, television advertising was a valuable service to consumers. Because keeping up with the Joneses was a goal of some suburbanites, television advertising provided visual evidence of just what the Joneses were buying. In the comfort of their living rooms Americans could study how to elevate their status through the purchase of a particular automobile, cigarette, or electric appliance. Indeed, it was not only commercials but programs themselves that tantalized viewers with glimpses of the sumptuous life. Situation comedies and dramas were nearly always set in well-furnished suburban homes; the characters dressed in the latest styles and drove the newest cars.

As television brought the world into their living rooms, Americans began to read newspapers and news magazines a little less carefully and to listen to radio a lot less frequently. But despite the lure of television, book readership went up. One reason for the increased consumption of literature was the mass marketing of the inexpensive paperbound book. Pocket Books hit the market in 1939; soon westerns, detective stories, and science fiction filled the newsstands, supermarkets, and drugstores. "The paperback democratized reading in America," Kenneth C. Davis has written in his history of "the paperbacking of America." The comic book, which had become popular in 1939 with the introduction of Superman, became another drugstore standard. Reprints of hardcover books and condensed books also did well. All in all, funds spent for books increased by 220 percent between 1946 and 1960 and by another 265 percent between 1960 and 1970.

One obvious casualty of the stay-at-home suburban culture was the motion picture. Americans continued to buy paperbacks and comic books in large numbers, but many of them stopped visiting movie theaters. Why fight traffic to go to a movie when you could watch TV in the comfort of your living room? Why pay a babysitter? From 1946 to 1948 Americans had attended movies at the rate of nearly 90 million a week. By 1950 the figure had dropped to 60 million a week; by 1960, 40 million. Thus the postwar years saw the steady closing of movie theaters—with the notable exception of the drive-in, which appealed to car-oriented suburban families as well as to teenagers.

Family togetherness was a theme of several successful television shows, including "Father Knows Best," starring Robert Young and Jane Wyatt. Described as "the classic wholesome family situation comedy," "Father Knows Best" was a popular series from 1954 to 1963. *Howard Frank Collection.*

There was one crucial exception to the downturn in moviegoing. By the late 1950s the first children of the postwar baby boom had become adolescents, and although their parents preferred to stay home and watch television, they themselves flocked to the theaters. No less than 72 percent of moviegoers during the 1950s were under age thirty. Hollywood responded to this youthful new audience with films portraying young people as sensitive and intelligent, adults as boorish and hostile. *Rebel Without a Cause,* starring James Dean, was one such movie. The cult of youth had been born.

Rise of the Youth Subculture

Soon the music industry was catering to teens with cheap 45 rpm records. Bored with the era's syrupy music, young Americans welcomed the driving energy and hard beat of rock 'n' roll. Bill Haley, the Everly Brothers, and Buddy Holly thrilled teenagers with their music. Elvis Presley horrified their parents with his suggestive gyra-

While Elvis Presley's performances upset parents, they thrilled the young people who cheered the gyrations of "Elvis the Pelvis." In this 1956 photo, Presley rocked wildly as he reached the climax of the song "Hillbilly Heartbreak." *UPI/Bettmann Archives.*

Although the roots of rock 'n' roll lay in black rhythm-and-blues, most white stars did not acknowledge the debt. Presley's hit tune "Hound Dog," for example, had originally been performed by the black singer Big Mama Thornton, but Thornton received little credit for her contribution. Among the black rock-'n'-roll stars of the 1950s were Chuck Berry and Little Richard. While white performers copied black rhythm-and-blues, serious black jazz artists like Charlie Parker and Dizzy Gillespie were experimenting with "bebop." In the 1950s jazz became increasingly fused with classical themes, compositions, and instrumentation. Intellectuals began to study this art form, which had once been looked down on as vulgar.

> **Black Roots of Rock 'n' Roll**

In other art forms, too, America's cultural influence grew worldwide in the 1950s and 1960s. In dance Martha Graham was lauded in international circles, and in painting Jackson Pollock became the pivotal figure of the abstract expressionist movement, which in the 1950s established New York City as the center of the art world. Rather than work with the traditional painter's easel, Pollock spread his canvas on the floor, where he was free to walk around it, "work from the four sides and literally be *in* the painting." He and other "action painters" worked with sticks, trowels, and knives, and they played with new materials like heavy impasto with "sand, broken glass and other foreign matter added." In the 1960s artists of the Pop Art movement satirized the consumer society, using commercial techniques to depict everyday objects. Andy Warhol painted Campbell soup cans; other artists did blowups of ice-cream sundaes, hamburgers, and comic-strip panels.

Consumerism was evident in Americans' postwar play and in the era's fads. Slinky, selling for a dollar, began loping down people's stairs in 1947; Silly Putty was introduced in 1950. The 1950s also had 3-D movies and Hula-Hoops. Within months of the Hula-Hoop's introduction in 1958, over 30 million had been sold. There were also signature items such as Hoppy watches, emblazoned with pictures of cowboy star Hopalong Cassidy. Although most crazes were short-lived, they created multi-million-dollar industries and effectively promoted dozens of movies and TV shows. Other postwar crazes are still with us—Scrabble, paint-by-number sets, and Barbie dolls, to name just a few. Between 1959 and

tions; but with the release of his first single ("Heartbreak Hotel") in 1956, he became the idol of millions of girls and boys. Before long, Presley's ducktail haircut and leather jacket had become the uniform for rebellious youth.

Parents worried. They feared that their children might become juvenile delinquents, and they blamed the influence not only of the new music but also of comic books, television, and the new youth films. Parental concerns reached panic proportions in 1955 when the Senate subcommittee to study juvenile delinquency heard experts testify about the evil influences of the mass media. The staff read into the record thousands of letters from angry fathers and mothers blaming the popular culture that their children so eagerly consumed. "Not even the Communist conspiracy," intoned one senator, "could devise a more effective way to demoralize, disrupt, confuse, and destroy our future citizens than apathy on the part of adult Americans to the scourge known as Juvenile Delinquency."

In this 1962 photo, Andy Warhol, one of the best-known figures in the Pop Art movement, held head-and-shoulder portraits of himself on either side of his face. In an age of anonymity—of nameless faces in the crowd—Warhol chose the mask as the image he showed to the world. *Ken Heyman.*

1980 more than 120 million Barbie and Barbie family dolls were sold. Frisbee-throwing has not only survived but has prevailed over similar outdoor games. Many of these toys and games succeeded because they were activities that brought the whole family together.

Some prewar activities flourished in the postwar years, notably golf and bowling. Americans still hunted and fished, but they no longer did so at the farm pond or in the woods down the road; they had to travel to get to the country. And travel they did. With more money and leisure time and a much-improved highway system, middle-class families took vacations that had formerly been restricted to the rich. They visited national monuments and parks, went camping, and even ventured abroad.

Needless to say, the consensus society of the 1950s and early 1960s was not receptive to social criticism. The filmgoing public preferred noncon-troversial doses of Doris Day and Rock Hudson and Dean Martin and Jerry Lewis. Readers bought novels and retreated into the criminal underworld, the wild West, or science-fiction fantasy. Even serious artists tended to ignore the country's social problems.

There were exceptions. Ralph Ellison's *Invisible Man* (1952) gave white Americans a glimpse of the psychic costs to black Americans of exclusion from the white American dream. Two films—*Gentleman's Agreement* (1947) and *Home of the Brave* (1949)—examined anti-Semitism and white racism. And in the 1950s, one group of writers repudiated the conventional world of the middle class and the suburbs. Rejecting the same social niceties that Kinsey had challenged, the writers of the Beat (for "beatific") Generation flaunted their freewheeling sexuality and consumption of

> **Beat Generation**

drugs. The Beats produced some memorable prose and poetry, including Allen Ginsberg's long poem *Howl* (1956) and Jack Kerouac's novel *On the Road* (1957), and they offered American youth an alternative to their parents' materialism and righteous self-congratulation. Although the Beats were mostly ignored during the 1950s, millions of young Americans discovered their writings and lifestyle in the 1960s.

One of the most influential books of the postwar years was the best-selling *The Affluent Society* (1958), by economist John Kenneth Galbraith. Galbraith's thesis dovetailed with the prevalent belief that economic growth would bring prosperity to everyone. Some would have more than others, of course, but in time everybody would have enough. "Production has eliminated the more acute tensions associated with [economic] inequality," Galbraith wrote. Not until Chapter 23 did the author mention poverty; when he did, he dismissed it as not "a universal or massive affliction," but "more nearly an afterthought."

Only in the 1960s would comfortable Americans of the middle class discover that millions of poor people lived in America (see Chapter 32). Politically and culturally, the 1960s would be vastly different from the consensus years that preceded them. Ironically, it would be the products of suburbia—the children of the baby boom—who formed the vanguard of the assault not only on poverty but on the whole value system of the American middle class.

Suggestions for Further Reading

The Baby Boom

Richard A. Easterlin, *Birth and Fortune* (1980); Landon Y. Jones, *Great Expectations: America and the Baby Boom Generation* (1980); Michael P. Nichols, *Turning Forty in the '80s* (1986).

The Affluent Society

Carl Abbott, *The New Urban America* (1987, rev. ed.); Richard M. Bernard and Bradley R. Rice, eds., *Sunbelt Cities* (1983); David P. Calleo, *The Imperious Economy* (1982); John Kenneth Galbraith, *The Affluent Society* (1958); John Kenneth Galbraith, *American Capitalism* (1952); David M. Potter, *People of Plenty* (1954); Kirkpatrick Sale, *Power Shift: The Rise of the Southern Rim and Its Challenge to the Eastern Establishment* (1975); Robert Sobel, *The Last Bull Market* (1980); Harold G. Vatter, *The U.S. Economy in the 1950s* (1963).

Farmers and Workers

Willard W. Cochrane and Mary E. Ryan, *American Farm Policy, 1948–1973* (1976); Gilbert C. Fite, *American Farmers* (1981); James R. Green, *The World of the Worker* (1980); John L. Shover, *First Majority—Last Minority: The Transforming of Rural Life in America* (1976); Philip Taft, *The A.F. of L. from the Death of Gompers to the Merger* (1959).

The Other America

Joseph H. Cash and Herbert T. Hoover, eds., *To Be an Indian: An Oral History* (1971); Harry M. Caudill, *Night Comes to the Cumberland* (1963); Richard B. Craig, *The Bracero Program* (1971); J. Wayne Flint, *Dixie's Forgotten People: The South's Poor Whites* (1979); Leo Grebler et al., *Mexican-American People* (1970); Michael Harrington, *The Other America*, rev. ed. (1981); August B. Hollingshead and Frederick C. Redlich, *Social Class and Mental Illness* (1958); Oscar Lewis, *La Vida* (1966); Herman P. Miller, *Rich Man, Poor Man* (1971); Dorothy K. Newman et al., *Politics and Prosperity: Black Americans and White Institutions, 1940–75* (1978); James T. Patterson, *America's Struggle Against Poverty, 1900–1985* (1986); David S. Walls and John B. Stephenson, eds., *Appalachia in the Sixties* (1972).

Suburbia

Bennett M. Berger, *Working-Class Suburb* (1960); Robert Fishman, *Bourgeois Utopias* (1987); Herbert J. Gans, *The Levittowners* (1967); Mark I. Gelfand, *A Nation of Cities* (1975); Dolores Hayden, *Redesigning the American Dream* (1984); Kenneth T. Jackson, *Crabgrass Frontier: The Suburbanization of the United States* (1985); Zane L. Miller, *Suburb* (1982); John B. Rae, *The American Automobile* (1965); William H. Whyte, *The Organization Man* (1956); Gwendolyn Wright, *Building the Dream: A Social History of Housing in America* (1981).

The Spread of Education

Keith W. Olson, *The GI Bill, the Veterans, and the Colleges* (1974); Diane Ravitch, *The Troubled Crusade: American Education, 1945–1980* (1983); Joel Spring, *The Sorting Machine: National Educational Policy Since 1945* (1976).

Motherhood, Work, and Family Togetherness

William H. Chafe, *The American Woman: Her Changing Social, Economic, and Political Role, 1920–1970* (1972); Ruth Schwartz Cowan, *More Work for Mother* (1983); Carl Degler, *At Odds: Woman and the Family in America from the Revolution to the Present* (1980); Barbara Ehrenreich, *The Hearts of Men: American Dreams and the Flight from Commitment* (1983); Benita Eisler, *Private Lives: Men and Women of the Fifties* (1986); Betty Friedan, *The Feminine Mystique* (1963); Cynthia Harrison, *On Account of Sex: The Politics of Women's Issues, 1945–1968* (1988); Susan M. Hartmann, *The Homefront and Beyond: American Women in the 1940s* (1982); Eugenia Kaledin, *Mothers and More: American Women in the 1950s* (1984); Susan Estabrook Kennedy, *If All We Did Was to Weep at Home: A History of White Working-Class Women in America* (1979); Glenna Matthews, *"Just a Housewife"* (1987); Elaine Tyler May, *Homeward Bound: American Families in the Cold War Era* (1988); Leila J. Rupp and Verta Taylor, *Survival in the Doldrums: The American Women Rights Movement, 1945 to the 1960s* (1987); Susan Strasser, *Never Done: A History of American Housework* (1982).

Popular Culture

Chuck Berry, *Chuck Berry* (1987); Peter Biskind, *Seeing Is Believing: How Hollywood Taught Us to Stop Worrying and Love the Fifties* (1983); Paul A. Carter, *Another Part of the Fifties* (1983); Kenneth C. Davis, *Two-Bit Culture: The Paperbacking of America* (1984); James Gilbert, *A Cycle of Outrage: America's Reaction to the Juvenile Delinquent* (1986); Charlie Gillett, *The Sound of the City: The Rise of Rock and Roll*, rev. ed. (1983); Serge Guilbaut, *How New York Stole the Idea of Modern Art* (1982); Douglas T. Miller and Marion Novak, *The Fifties* (1977); Gerald Nicosia, *Memory Babe: A Critical Biography of Jack Kerouac* (1983); Nora Sayre, *Running Time: Films of the Cold War* (1982); Jane and Michael Stern, *Elvis World* (1987); John Tytell, *Naked Angels: The Lives and Literature of the Beat Generation* (1976).

Television

Michael Arlen, *The Camera Age* (1981); Erik Barnouw, *Tube of Plenty*, rev. ed. (1982); George Comstock et al., *Television and Human Behavior* (1978); Todd Gitlin, *Inside Prime-Time* (1983); Frank Mankiewicz and Joel Swerdlow, *Remote Control: Television and the Manipulation of American Life* (1978).

The Joint Chiefs of Staff memorandum lay on the table. Its recommendation: add another 100,000 to the 80,000 American troops already in Vietnam, because the war was not going well. "Is there anyone here of the opinion we should not do what the memorandum says?" asked President Lyndon B. Johnson of his advisers, assembled for a tense meeting on the morning of July 21, 1965. Only Under Secretary of State George W. Ball spoke up: "Mr. President, I can foresee a perilous voyage, very dangerous." Johnson asked, "What other road can I go?"

Ball answered directly, "Take our losses, let their government fall apart, negotiate, discuss, knowing full well there will be a probable take-over by the Communists." The president, who had already made up his mind to escalate the American intervention in Vietnam but was willing to listen to Ball's oft-stated objections again so that he could always say he had carefully weighed all alternatives, did not like that answer. The hard-driving Texan recoiled from thoughts of losing. He simply could not accept that a small, primitive country like Vietnam could deny the United States victory.

31

VIETNAM AND THE COLD WAR: AMERICAN FOREIGN POLICY, 1961–1977

At an afternoon session, Ball again forthrightly argued a case he knew few of his colleagues endorsed. "The war will be long and protracted. The most we can hope for is a messy conclusion." Not only did dangers arise from possible Chinese intervention, negative world opinion, and domestic politics, but "the enemy cannot be seen in Vietnam. He is indigenous to the country." Ball seriously doubted that "an army of Westerners can successfully fight Orientals in an Asian jungle." He pressed on, "It is like giving cobalt treatment to a terminal cancer case." In the long run, then, the war "will disclose our weakness, not our strength." Johnson jumped in: "But George, wouldn't all these countries say that Uncle Sam was a paper tiger," with America losing its credibility? "No sir," Ball retorted. "The worse blow would be that the mightiest power on earth is unable to defeat a handful of guerrillas."

The next day Johnson huddled with the military brass. The generals told him that more men, more bombings, and more money were needed to keep America's South Vietnamese ally in

Tet offensive. Marine tank with wounded soldiers after the Battle of Hue, 1968. *John Olson,* Life *Magazine © 1968 Time Inc.*

power against the North Vietnamese and Vietcong. "But if we put in 100,000 men won't they put in an equal number, and then where will we be?" Johnson asked. He became excited, asking tough questions. When an admiral claimed that if the United States did not back the faltering South Vietnamese regime, allies around the world would lose faith in America's word, Johnson knew better: "We have few allies really helping us now." And have the bombing raids hurt the enemy? Not really, the generals answered, but if more sites were added to the target list, they would. Johnson grew worried: "Isn't this going off the diving board?" The secretary of defense argued that the United States had a "commitment" to South Vietnam. Johnson shot back, "But, if you make a commitment to jump off a building and you find out how high it is, you may want to withdraw that commitment."

In late July a troubled President Johnson nonetheless decided to keep that "commitment" by giving the Joint Chiefs of Staff what it wanted. A major decision of the Vietnam War, it meant that the United States was assuming, for the first time, primary responsibility for fighting the war. Fearing a national debate, Johnson muted the decision's importance when he announced it. By the end of 1965 nearly 200,000 American combat troops were at war in Vietnam. Yet Congress had not passed a declaration of war, and most of the American people remained ignorant of the government's massive venture in Southeast Asia. Ball later concluded that Johnson's July decision was "the greatest single error that America had made in its national history." Measured by the wrenching impact of the war on the United States, Ball was probably correct.

Vietnam, either because of the searing war experience itself or because of the lessons Americans later drew from that experience, bedeviled the Kennedy, Johnson, Nixon, and Ford presidencies. Other themes crowded the international agenda in the 1960s and 1970s: continued Soviet-American competition for global influence with dramatic swings from conciliation to confrontation in the Cold War; an accelerating nuclear arms race; turmoil in the Third World, much of it anti-American; eruptions in the Middle East; mean-spirited Cuban-American hostilities; and disorder in the world economy. But Vietnam, where Cold War and Third World issues seemed to merge, at least in American thinking, dominated United States foreign policy. Kennedy enlarged the United States presence in Southeast Asia; Johnson Americanized the war; Nixon struggled to pull American troops out of the war without losing it; and Ford and his successors had to deal with the aftermath of America's longest war. As he wound down the American combat role in Vietnam, Nixon also inched toward détente with the Soviet Union and China and intervened in Third World disputes to protect American interests he thought threatened.

Throughout the 1960s and 1970s Americans became uneasy not only about the troubled position of the United States in world affairs but also about the disorder wrought at home by foreign entanglements. Foreign policy and domestic developments had been traditionally interconnected, and foreign policy had always sprung from the domestic setting of the nation—its needs, wants, moods, and ideals. Yet the experience of the Vietnam War called into question those needs, wants, moods, and ideals, because a majority of Americans came to see the effects of the war as a threat to their economic well-being, social stability, moral standards, and political system (see Chapters 30 and 32). When the nation's longest war ended in 1975, Americans debated its meaning and its lessons, but they could not agree.

Kennedy's Quest for Cold War Victory

John F. Kennedy's diplomacy owed much to the past. He remembered the tragedy of appeasement in the 1930s as well as the triumph of containment in the 1940s. America had turned back nazism and had contained communism, Kennedy argued, and now in the 1960s communism would be routed. Kennedy's dynamic personal style suggested a new departure in foreign policy; actually it meant a bolder, more vigorous prosecution of the Cold War. An eloquent speaker, energetic worker, and fierce competitor, Kennedy was an "incandescent man. He was on fire, and he set people around him on fire," recalled Secretary of State Dean Rusk. As a diplomat, Kennedy was eager to prove his toughness. His administration kept box scores on the missile race, the arms race, the space race, and the race for influence in the Third World. When the young president prepared for his first meeting with

1960	Kennedy elected president	**1969**	543,400 U.S. troops in Vietnam
1961	Peace Corps founded		Nixon begins withdrawal of troops
	Alliance for Progress		Nixon Doctrine
	Bay of Pigs invasion		Détente policy announced
	Berlin crisis	**1970**	Invasion of Cambodia
	U.S. military build-up	**1971**	*Pentagon Papers* released
1962	Cuban missile crisis	**1972**	Nixon visits China
1963	Limited Test-Ban Treaty		SALT-I Treaty
	Diem assassinated in Vietnam		Nixon re-elected
	Kennedy assassinated; Johnson assumes presidency	**1973**	Vietnam cease-fire agreement
			Allende ousted in Chile
1964	Tonkin Gulf incident and resolution		Arab-Israeli War
	Johnson elected president		Arab oil embargo
1965	U.S. invasion of Dominican Republic		War Powers Resolution
	Johnson Americanizes Vietnam War	**1974**	Nixon resigns; Ford becomes president
1965–66	Antiwar teach-ins		New International Economic Order
1967	Peace rallies across the nation	**1975**	Egyptian-Israeli peace agreement
	Six-Day War in the Middle East		Vietnam War ends
1968	Tet offensive in Vietnam		Civil war in Angola
	My Lai massacre	**1976**	Carter elected president
	Vietnam peace talks open in Paris		
	Nixon elected president		

Russian Premier Nikita Khrushchev, he seemed poised for a contest rather than a talk: "I have to show him that we can be as tough as he is," remarked Kennedy. "I'll have to sit down with him and let him see who he's dealing with."

Kennedy appointed a staff of bright, often arrogant, people who were determined to score Cold War victories. Journalist Theodore White called them "action intellectuals." A disenchanted Under Secretary of State Chester Bowles complained later that the Kennedy team was "full of belligerence." And Adlai Stevenson told a friend

> **Kennedy as Cold War Activist**

privately that "they've got the damnedest bunch of boy commandos running around down there [in Washington] you ever saw." That there would be no halfway measures was apparent in Kennedy's inaugural address: "Let every nation know that we shall pay any price, bear any burden, meet any hardship, support any friend, oppose any foe to assure the survival and the success of liberty."

Khrushchev matched Kennedy's rhetoric with an endorsement of "wars of national liberation" in the Third World. And in the fall of 1961 the Soviet Union ended a moratorium on above-ground nuclear testing by exploding a giant 50-megaton

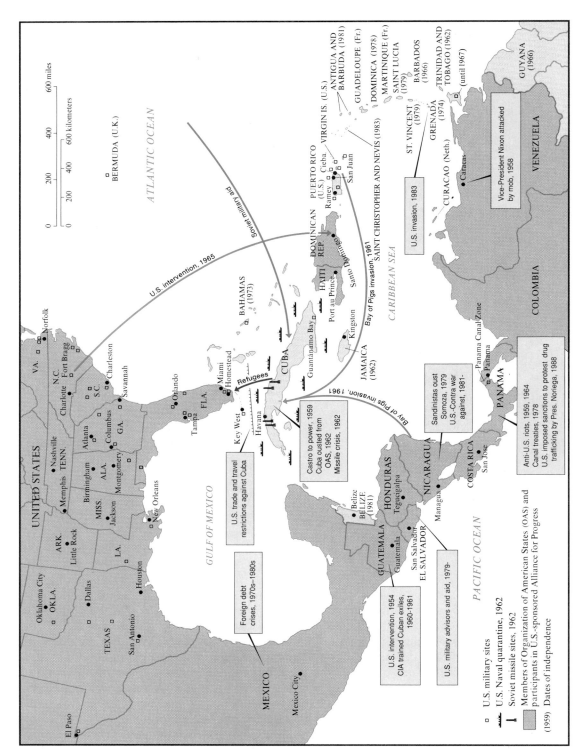

The United States in the Caribbean and Central America

600 miles

ATLANTIC OCEAN

600 kilometers

BERMUDA (U.K.)

ANTIGUA AND BARBUDA (1981)
GUADELOUPE (Fr.)
DOMINICA (1978)
MARTINIQUE (Fr.)
SAINT LUCIA (1979)
BARBADOS (1966)
TRINIDAD AND TOBAGO (1962)
(until 1967)
GUYANA (1966)

VIRGIN IS. (U.S.)
PUERTO RICO (U.S.)
Ceiba
Ramey
San Juan
SAINT CHRISTOPHER AND NEVIS (1983)
ST. VINCENT (1979)
GRENADA (1974)
CURAÇAO (Neth.)
Caracas

VENEZUELA

COLOMBIA

Vice-President Nixon attacked by mob, 1958

U.S. invasion, 1983

CARIBBEAN SEA

Soviet military aid

U.S. intervention, 1965

DOMINICAN REP.
HAITI
Port au Prince
Santo Domingo
Bay of Pigs invasion, 1961

BAHAMAS (1973)

Kingston
JAMAICA (1962)

Guantánamo Bay
CUBA
Havana
Key West
Refugees

Bay of Pigs invasion, 1961

Miami
Homestead

Norfolk
VA.
Fort Bragg
N.C.
Charlotte
Charleston
S.C.
Savannah
Orlando
FLA.
Tampa
Columbus
GA.
Atlanta
Nashville
TENN.
Montgomery
ALA.
Memphis
Birmingham
MISS.
Jackson
New Orleans
LA.
Little Rock
ARK.
Houston
Oklahoma City
OKLA.
Dallas
San Antonio
TEXAS
El Paso

UNITED STATES

GULF OF MEXICO

U.S. trade and travel restrictions against Cuba

Castro to power, 1959
Cuba ousted from OAS, 1962
Missile crisis, 1962

Foreign debt crises, 1970s–1980s

MEXICO
Mexico City

Belize
BELIZE (1981)
GUATEMALA
Guatemala
San Salvador
EL SALVADOR

HONDURAS
Tegucigalpa
NICARAGUA
Managua

COSTA RICA
San Jose

PANAMA
Panama
Panama Canal Zone

Sandinistas oust Somoza, 1979
U.S.-Contra war against, 1981–

Anti-U.S. riots, 1959, 1964
Canal treaties, 1978
U.S. imposed sanctions to protest drug trafficking by Pres. Noriega, 1988

U.S. intervention, 1954
CIA trained Cuban exiles, 1960-1961

U.S. military advisors and aid, 1979–

PACIFIC OCEAN

□ U.S. military sites
⌐ U.S. Naval quarantine, 1962
⌐ Soviet missile sites, 1962
▓ Members of Organization of American States (OAS) and participants in U.S.-sponsored Alliance for Progress
(1959) Dates of independence

908 ◄

When the Berlin Wall first went up in 1961 along the border between West and East Berlin, it was hastily constructed of barbed wire. Later the East German military added concrete blocks to the barricade, as they are doing here. President Kennedy drew criticism for not halting construction of the wall; but two years later West Berliners gave him a warm reception. *UPI/Bettmann Archives.*

bomb. Khrushchev also bragged about Russian ICBMs, raising American anxiety over Soviet capabilities. Intelligence data soon proved that there was no "missile gap"—except the one in America's favor. Kennedy nonetheless sought to fulfill his campaign commitment to a military build-up based on the principle of *flexible response*. Junking Eisenhower's concept of massive retaliation, which emphasized nuclear weapons, Kennedy sought ways to meet any kind of warfare, from guerrilla combat in the jungles to a nuclear showdown. In this way, he reasoned, he could contain both the Soviet Union and Third World revolutionary movements. In 1961 the military budget shot up 15 percent; ICBM arsenals swelled further; and plans were laid to increase NATO's nuclear firing power. The government even encouraged citizens to build fallout shelters in their backyards. By mid-1964, strategists measured a 150 percent increase in the number of American nuclear weapons. Kennedy could claim credit for the Arms Control and Disarmament Agency and the Limited Test Ban Treaty with Russia (1963), which banned nuclear testing in the atmosphere, in outer space, and under water; but his real legacy was an accelerated arms race.

During this time Berlin continued to claim headlines. The Russians again demanded negotiations to end the Western occupation of Berlin, which rested in East Germany. But Kennedy saw the historic city as "the great testing place of Western courage and will." Instead of negotiating, he asked Congress in 1961 for an additional $3.2 billion for defense and the authority to call up reservists. Events took an ugly turn in August 1961 when the Soviets erected the Berlin Wall, a concrete-and-barbed-wire barricade designed to halt the exodus of East Germans into the more prosperous and politically free West Berlin. Yet another example of Soviet repression, the wall inspired protests all over the non-Communist world. The crisis passed. When Kennedy visited the wall in 1963 he stirred a mass rally of West Berliners with the words "Ich bin ein Berliner" ("I am a Berliner").

Berlin Crisis

But it was over Cuba, a nation whose allegiance the United States had taken for granted since the turn of the century, that Kennedy had his most serious confrontation with the Soviet Union (see map). Cuba became an obsession of American policymakers in 1959, when Fidel Castro and rebels of his

26th of July Movement ousted America's long-time ally Fulgencio Batista, who had continued the practice of turning Havana into a pleasure capital of gambling and prostitution run by organized crime for American tourists. President Eisenhower had made a last-minute attempt in late 1958 to install a friendly military regime in order to deny the Cuban revolutionaries their hard-fought triumph. Since the early twentieth century, when the Platt Amendment was imposed on them, Cubans had resented such United States interventionism (see Chapters 22 and 26). In fact, anti-Americanism and the goal of reducing United States influence became patriotic features of the Cuban Revolution. From the start Castro also determined to break the economic power of American business, which owned 3 million acres of Cuba's land, controlled 40 percent of its sugar production and 90 percent of its telephone and electric service, and sold Cuba 70 percent of its imports. Indeed, American investments in the island at the time of Castro's victory totaled about $1 billion. The Castro government, which ruled with increasing authoritarianism, nationalized some American-owned property, suspended promised elections, indulged in a barrage of anti-American rhetoric, and in early 1960 signed a trade treaty with the Soviet Union.

> **The Cuban Revolution**

In mid-1960 President Eisenhower grew impatient with Castro and reduced American purchases of Cuban sugar. Castro's response was large-scale seizures of American-owned companies. Soon the Cuban premier began to appeal to the Soviet Union for support. Historians disagree on whether Castro was always a Communist or whether Washington's vehement opposition pushed him into Soviet arms. In any case, the Soviet Union gradually came to Cuba's assistance with loans and trade.

In March 1960, Eisenhower had ordered the CIA to train Cuban exiles for an invasion of their homeland. Just before he left office Eisenhower broke diplomatic relations with Castro and advised Kennedy to advance plans for the invasion. The picture sketched by the CIA appealed to Kennedy: Cuban exiles would land at the Bay of Pigs and secure a beachhead; the Cuban people would rise up against Castro; a Revolutionary Council organized in the United States would enter Havana in triumph. Kennedy was nonetheless uneasy over such a blatant attempt to topple a sovereign government; he ordered that no Americans be directly involved in the invasion so that the United States could maintain the fiction that the operation was solely a Cuban affair. The president never attempted to negotiate with Castro over Cuban-American troubles; Kennedy preferred victory over compromise.

The CIA-directed expedition departed Nicaragua in April 1961. Escorted by American warships, the fourteen hundred commandos scrambled ashore at the Bay of Pigs. Actually, the first man to hit the beaches was an American CIA operative. The Cuban people did not rise up against Castro, and within two days most of the commandos had been captured. Many of them later blamed Kennedy for the disaster, citing his refusal to permit an air strike at the time of the landing. But the operation, with or without more air support, had little chance of success. Boats went aground on coral reefs that the CIA had dismissed as seaweed. Equipment malfunctioned. The Bay of Pigs was Castro's favorite fishing spot, and he knew the details of its landscape. If the exiles of Brigade 2506 had managed to move inland, they would have encountered swamps; and the mountains that might have served as a sanctuary were eighty miles away. Before it was over, four Americans had died. "How could I have been so stupid to let them go ahead?" Kennedy asked himself about the entire operation.

> **Bay of Pigs**

Kennedy did not suffer defeat easily. Soon he and his advisers set about finding other means to unseat Castro. "My idea," Attorney General Robert Kennedy said, "is to stir things up on the island with espionage, sabotage, [and] general disorder." The president's brother instructed the CIA to let "no time, money, effort—or manpower—be spared" in a project that came to be known as Operation Mongoose. Government agents worked to disrupt the island's trade; they continued to aid anti-Castro groups in Miami; and they plotted with organized crime leaders to assassinate Castro. The United States also tightened its economic blockade of Cuba and engineered Cuba's eviction from the Organization of American States.

Cuba soon became the site of one of the scariest crises of the Cold War. Had there been no Bay of Pigs invasion, no Operation Mongoose, no assassination plots, and no program of diplomatic and economic isolation, there probably would have been no missile crisis, because Cuba would have had no urgent need for Soviet

> **Cuban Missile Crisis**

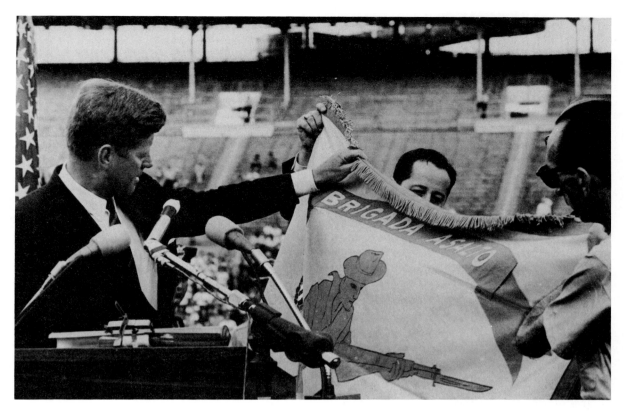

"This flag will be returned to this Brigade in a free Havana," President Kennedy promised CIA-trained commandos after their release from Cuban jails in December 1962. The men had been captured during the failed 1961 Bay of Pigs invasion. The president meant what he said; under Kennedy the United States government undertook a vast array of projects to undermine the Cuban Revolution and topple its charismatic leader Fidel Castro. *Wide World Photos.*

military assistance. For Castro, the relentless American hostility represented a real threat to Cuba's independence. And for the Soviets, American actions challenged the only pro-Communist regime in Latin America. "We had to think up some way of confronting America with more than words," recalled Premier Khrushchev, who also saw an opportunity to improve the Soviet position in the nuclear arms race. So Castro and Khrushchev devised a daring plan to deter any new American intervention, especially an invasion: installation of Soviet missiles and nuclear bombers at several sites in Cuba.

Although the Kennedy administration was aware of a military build-up on the island, it was not until October 14, 1962, that a U-2 plane photographed sites for medium-range missiles that could reach the United States. Whether the Soviets had acted to protect Cuba, to improve their own nuclear capability, to trigger negotiations over Berlin, or to force the United States to pull its missiles out of Turkey remains debatable. In any case, the president organized the "Executive Committee" and ordered it to find a way to remove the missiles from Cuba. Some members advised a surprise air strike, likely to kill both Soviet technicians and Cubans. Robert Kennedy scotched that idea; he wanted no Pearl Harbors on his brother's record. The Joint Chiefs of Staff recommended a full-scale military invasion, but that risked a prolonged war with Cuba, a Soviet attack against Berlin, or even nuclear holocaust. Soviet expert Charles Bohlen unsuccessfully urged quiet, direct negotiations with Soviet officials. Secretary of Defense Robert S. McNamara proposed the formula that the president found most acceptable: a naval quarantine of Cuba, to prevent further military shipments. Halfway between armed warfare and doing nothing, it left the administration free to attack or negotiate, depending on the Soviet response.

Over national television on October 22, Kennedy informed the Soviets of American policy and demanded their retreat. American warships headed for the Caribbean, B-52s loaded with nuclear bombs took to the skies, and American military forces around the globe went on alert. Khrushchev first replied that the missiles would be withdrawn if Washington pledged never to attack Cuba again. Then he demanded the removal of American Jupiter missiles from Turkey. Kennedy accepted the first condition but rejected the second. The days became tense, the advisers exhausted. On October 28 Khrushchev finally accepted the American pledge to respect Cuban sovereignty; in return he promised to ship the missiles back to the Soviet Union. The Soviet missiles in Cuba were dismantled, and Kennedy informally and privately promised to withdraw the Jupiters from Turkey, as was done. This was, said many, Kennedy's finest hour.

But critics then and now have raised questions. Would there have been such a frightening crisis in the first place if Kennedy had not been hell-bent on overthrowing the Castro regime and expunging the Cuban Revolution from the hemisphere? Was the crisis really necessary? Why did the president attempt to solve the crisis with public brinkmanship instead of private negotiations? Television addresses and public confrontations are the stuff not of statesmanship but of politics—and the congressional elections were just weeks away. Critics have noted too that Kennedy passed up a chance to protest the presence of the missiles when he met privately with Foreign Minister Andrei Gromyko in the White House on October 18. Finally, critics have claimed that the strategic balance of power was not seriously altered by the placement of Soviet missiles in Cuba; the United States still held a tremendous advantage over the Soviets in the nuclear arms race. Perhaps Kennedy risked doomsday when he did not need to?

In the Cuban missile crisis, the Soviets were forced to back down. Exposed as nuclear inferiors, the Soviets vowed to catch up—and they managed to do so by the late 1960s. The crisis did produce some relaxation in Soviet-American relations. The superpower leaders installed a Teletype "hot line" between Washington and Moscow staffed around the clock by translators and technicians, signed the Limited Test Ban Treaty, and refrained from further confrontation in Berlin.

In the Third World, which had bedeviled Eisenhower diplomacy, Kennedy called for "peaceful revolution" based on the concept of *nation building*. Drawing on the ideas of the economist Walt W. Rostow, who joined the Kennedy administration, the president determined to win favor in Third World countries by helping them through the infant stages of nationhood with programs aimed at improving agriculture, transportation, and communications. Kennedy thus created the multibillion-dollar Alliance for Progress in Latin America. Created for the same purpose, the Peace Corps, founded in 1961, sent teachers, agricultural specialists, and health workers into developing nations throughout the world. Within three years ten thousand idealistic young men and women volunteered for service. But the Peace Corps's humanitarian purpose competed with the administration's political needs. Periodic conflicts arose between corps members in the field, who identified with Third World peoples' desire for neutralism, and headquarters in Washington, where the goal was aligning those peoples with American foreign policy.

Peace Corps

Besides such development programs, Kennedy relied on *counterinsurgency:* the training of native troops and police forces by American military and technical advisers. The assumption was that American soldiers—especially the Special Forces units, or Green Berets—would help provide a protective shield against insurgents while American civilian personnel worked on economic projects.

The CIA continued to serve as one of the primary instruments of American foreign policy (see pages 870–871). In the Congo (now Zaire) in 1960–1961 the CIA plotted to poison Premier Patrice Lumumba through the lethal injection of a virus. Before that could be done, a CIA-backed Congolese political faction murdered Lumumba, who had turned to the Soviet Union for help after the Belgians and the United Nations sent troops to protect white Europeans during a civil war. In Brazil, the CIA spent $20 million to influence the 1962 elections against President Joao Goulart, who had earned American disapproval by expropriating the property of the American firm International Telephone and Telegraph and refusing to vote to oust Cuba from the Organization of American States. When Goulart's followers nonetheless won, the CIA then helped organize opposition groups.

CIA Interventions

Chapter 31: Vietnam and the Cold War: American Foreign Policy, 1961–1977

1861–87	French consolidate colonial rule in Indochina
1890	Ho Chi Minh born
1920	Ho Chi Minh joins Communist party
1940	Japan occupies Indochina
1941	Vietminh organized OSS cooperates with Vietminh
1945	Ho declares independence for Democratic Republic of Vietnam
1946	Anticolonial war against France begins
1950	U.S. recognizes government of Bao Dai U.S. sends military aid to French for war in Vietnam
1954	Dienbienphu crisis Geneva Conference and Accords Temporary partition of Vietnam U.S. backs government of Diem
1955	Diem, with U.S. support, rejects Geneva Accords
1956	Diem begins crackdown on opponents
1957	Anti-Diem insurgents begin terrorist attacks
1959	North Vietnam begins sending aid to Communists in the South
1960	National Liberation Front (Vietcong) organized in the South
1961	President Kennedy decides to increase U.S. military role in Vietnam

Note: For Vietnam events after 1961, see "Important Events," page 907.

In 1964, with United States complicity, the Brazilian military overthrew Goulart.

Nation building and its interventionist methods did not work. Americans assumed, as they had for much of the twentieth century in the Caribbean, that they could simply transfer their own model of capitalism and government to foreign cultures. But many foreigners resented American meddling in their affairs. And because monetary aid was usually funneled through a self-interested elite, it often did not reach the very poor. To people who preferred the relatively quick solutions of a managed economy, moreover, the American emphasis on private enterprise seemed inappropriate. "In the end," the presidential adviser and historian Arthur M. Schlesinger, Jr., later wrote, counterinsurgency proved "a ghastly illusion. Its primary consequence was to keep alive the American belief in their capacity and right to intervene in foreign lands."

Descent into the Longest War: Vietnam

The belief in the right to influence the internal affairs of other countries led to disaster in Southeast Asia. How Vietnam became the site of America's longest war (it lasted a quarter-century, from 1950 to 1975), how the world's most powerful nation failed to subdue a peasant people, how those people suffered enormous losses of life and property and yet persisted is one of the most remarkable and tragic stories of modern history.

The story begins with the French takeover of Vietnam during the late nineteenth century (see "Vietnam Chronology"). For decades the French exploited the colony for its rice, rubber, tin,

Ho Chi Minh (1890–1969), Vietnamese nationalist and communist, led his people's battle for independence against foreigners for decades. Defense Secretary Robert McNamara once called Ho a "tough old S.O.B. And he won't quit no matter how much bombing we do." *How-ard Sochurek,* Life *Magazine © 1955 Time Inc.*

French Imperialism in Vietnam

and tungsten, beating back peasant rebellions. All the while, Vietnamese nationalists grew in strength. They were led by Ho Chi Minh. Born in 1890, Ho moved to France before the First World War. At the close of the war he joined the French Communist party to use it as a vehicle for Vietnamese independence. For the next two decades, in China, the Soviet Union, and elsewhere, Ho planned and fought to free his nation from French colonialism.

Not until the Second World War, when the Japanese moved into Indochina, did French authority collapse. Seizing their chance, the Vietminh, an anti-imperialist coalition organized by Ho and other patriots, began guerrilla warfare in northern Vietnam. The Vietminh teamed up with American Office of Strategic Services (OSS) agents to harass the Japanese and their French collaborators. OSS

officers who worked with Ho in Vietnam were impressed by his determination to drive outsiders from his country and by his frequent references to the United States as a revolutionary model. When Ho declared Vietnam's independence on September 2, 1945, his words sounded familiar: "We hold these truths to be self-evident. That all men are created equal." Yet the Truman administration never answered Ho's appeals for support; instead it endorsed the restoration of French rule. With the help of the British, the French returned to Vietnam, but they were not welcomed.

U.S. Rejection of Vietnamese Independence

The United States did not recognize Vietnamese independence (and in fact attempted to undermine it) for several reasons. First, Americans wanted France's cooperation in the emerging Cold War. Second, Southeast Asia was an economic asset; its rice could feed America's soon-to-be ally Japan, and it was the world's largest producer of natural rubber and a rich source of other commodities. Third, the area seemed strategically vital to the defense of Japan and the Philippines. Finally, Ho Chi Minh was a Communist, who, it was assumed, would assist Soviet expansionism. Thus Vietnam became another test in the containment of communism—the Berlin of Asia. Overlooking the native roots of the nationalist rebellion against France, the history of Vietnamese resistance to foreign intruders, and the tenacity of a people fighting on and for their own land, American leaders from Truman through Ford took a globalist view of Vietnam, interpreting events through a Cold War lens.

American Support for the French

In the 1940s Vietnam was a French problem that few Americans watched with keen interest. More dramatic crises in Europe commanded their attention, even after the Vietminh and French went to war in late 1946. But when Jiang Jieshi (Chiang Kai-shek) went down to defeat in China less than three years later, the United States was aroused to action. The Truman administration made two crucial decisions in early 1950. First, it recognized the French puppet government of Bao Dai, a playboy and former emperor who had collaborated with the French and Japanese. Thus in Vietnamese eyes the United States became in essence a colonial power, an ally of the hated French. Second, the administration agreed to

This Vietnam refrain was expressed by presidents from Eisenhower to Ford, but victory proved elusive. Like their leaders, many Americans could not understand how the military giant of the world could not defeat the people of a small Southeast Asian country. © *1975 United Feature Syndicate, Inc.*

send weapons, and ultimately military advisers, to the French. By 1954 the United States had provided more than $2 billion in military assistance and was bearing three-fourths of the cost of the war.

Despite American aid, the French lost steadily to the Vietminh. Finally, in early 1954, Ho's forces surrounded the French fortress at Dienbienphu, in

Dienbienphu

northwest Vietnam. What would the United States do? Could the French be saved? President Eisenhower huddled with his advisers. Some considered the possibility of unleashing a massive American air strike against Vietminh positions, perhaps even using tactical atomic weapons. Eisenhower moved deliberately. Although Americans had been advising the French, they had not committed American forces to the war. If the president introduced American air power and it did not save the French, would American troops be required next? As one high-level doubter remarked, "One cannot go over Niagara Falls in a barrel only slightly." Army Chief of Staff Matthew Ridgway warned the president that air power could not guarantee victory and that American soldiers would have to fight in hostile terrain. American units, moreover, might have to be moved from elsewhere in Asia and Europe, a shift that could leave other regions vulnerable.

Eisenhower nonetheless worried aloud at the prospect of a Communist victory, comparing the weak nations of the world to a row of dominoes, all of which would topple if just one fell (this became known as the domino theory). Washington pressed the British to help, but they refused. At home, members of Congress who wanted "no more Koreas" and were uneasy about supporting colonialism warned the administration to avoid any commitment of the American military, especially in the absence of allied backing. On May 7 the weary French defenders at Dienbienphu surrendered.

To add to the administration's problems, the French wanted out of the war. They agreed to peace talks at Geneva, where France, the United States,

Geneva Accords

the Soviet Union, Britain, the People's Republic of China, Laos, and Cambodia joined the two competing Vietnamese regimes of Bao Dai and Ho Chi Minh. Dulles found the job unpleasant; he conducted himself, according to one biographer, like a "puritan in a house of ill repute." The 1954 Geneva Accords, signed by France and Ho's Democratic Republic of Vietnam, temporarily divided Vietnam at the 17th parallel, with Ho's government confined to the North. This parallel was supposed to serve as a military truce line, not a national boundary. National elections would be held in 1956, and the country would thereupon be unified. In the meantime, neither North nor South was to join a military alliance or permit foreign military bases on its soil. Asked at a press conference if he would meet with Chinese delegates before departing Geneva, Dulles replied: "Not unless our automobiles collide."

Certain that the Geneva agreements would ultimately mean Communist victory, the United States and Bao Dai refused to accept the accords and set about to sabotage them. Soon after the conference, a CIA team entered Vietnam and began secret operations against the North, including commando raids across the 17th parallel. In the South, the United States and Ngo Dinh Diem became allies. A Catholic in a Buddhist nation, Diem had many enemies and no mass support. But he was a

> **Ngo Dinh Diem** nationalist and an anti-Communist and with American aid he outmaneuvered his opponents, including Bao Dai. Diem staged a fraudulent election that gave him a remarkable 98 percent of the vote. When Ho called for national elections in keeping with the Geneva agreements, Diem and Eisenhower refused, fearing the charismatic Vietminh leader would win. In September 1954 the United States launched with Britain, France, Australia, New Zealand, the Philippines, Thailand, and Pakistan an anti-Communist pact called the Southeast Asia Treaty Organization (SEATO). Because the Geneva Accords prohibited southern Vietnam's membership in the alliance, SEATO allies signed a special protocol extending their protection against Communist aggression to southern Vietnam.

From 1955 to 1961 the Diem government received more than $1 billion worth of American aid, most of it military. American advisers organized and trained the South Vietnamese army. Michigan State University police experts helped to create a national guard. American agriculturalists worked to improve crops. American consumer products flowed into Vietnamese cities. Diem's Saigon regime became dependent on the United States for its very existence, and the culture of southern Vietnam began to be Americanized.

Meanwhile, Diem became bent on dictatorial leadership. He abolished village elections and appointed to public office people beholden to him. He threw dissenters into jail and shut down newspapers that criticized his regime. In the South non-

Communists and Communists alike began to strike back at Diem's corrupt and repressive government. Encouraged by Ho's regime in the northern capital of Hanoi, southern insurgents embarked on a program of terror, assassinating hundreds of Diem's village officials. In late 1960, southern Communists organized the National Liberation Front, or Vietcong. The Vietcong attracted other anti-Diem groups in the South. The war against imperialism had become a two-part Vietnamese civil war: Ho's North versus Diem's South, and Vietcong guerrillas versus the Diem government.

In the United States, newly elected President Kennedy decided to stand firm in Vietnam. He had suffered the humiliations of the Bay of Pigs and the

> **Kennedy's Escalation** Berlin Wall; he feared further criticism if the United States backed down in Asia (where he was already seeking negotiations to end civil war in Laos). But more important, he sought a Cold War victory. "How do we get moving?" he asked his advisers in his first meeting on Vietnam. Soon he ordered more military advisers and Special Forces units to South Vietnam and millions of dollars worth of additional aid. Yet Diem showed no signs of using the assistance effectively, and his opponents grew in number. Fearing Diem would drag the United States down to defeat, Kennedy pressed him to reform. Meanwhile, Project Beef-up was sending more Americans to South Vietnam; by late 1963, 16,700 American "advisers" were stationed there. That year, 489 Americans were killed, and an American project called the Strategic Hamlet Program actually strengthened resistance to Diem. That program, which aimed to isolate peasants from the Vietcong by uprooting them into barbed-wire compounds, simply alienated villagers. In major cities Buddhist priests began protests, charging Diem with religious persecution. Protesting monks poured gasoline over their robes and ignited themselves in the streets of Saigon. As yet more civil war spread across the south, a stunned Washington buzzed about what was going wrong in Vietnam.

American officials began to think that if Diem could not be reformed, he should be removed. "We could not sit still and be puppets of Diem's anti-Buddhist policies," recalled a high-ranking State Department officer. American leaders also grew alarmed that Diem, who knew that the United States was preparing to dump him, was apparently

In early 1966 Buddhist monks, ringed by barbed wire strung around them by South Vietnamese troops, demonstrated in the streets of Saigon (shown here) and elsewhere in South Vietnam. Buddhist protests had destabilized the Diem government in 1963; three years later Buddhists attempted to bring down an American-backed military regime. Nationalistic Buddhists appealed for peace talks with the Vietcong to halt the destruction of their country, an end to American interference (let Vietnamese decide their own fate), and free elections (which Buddhists thought they would win). The military regime answered by arresting Buddhist leaders and crushing their movement—one of many signs that the political stability the United States needed to win the war was absent. *Wide World Photos.*

trying to make peace with the North—"a possible basic incompatibility with U.S. objectives," worried General Maxwell Taylor. Through the CIA, the United States quietly encouraged disaffected South Vietnamese generals to stage a coup. With the ill-concealed backing of Ambassador Henry Cabot Lodge, the generals struck in early November 1963. Diem was captured and murdered—only a few weeks before Kennedy himself met death by an assassin's bullet.

With new governments in Saigon and Washington, some analysts thought it an appropriate time for reassessment. The Vietcong, United Nations General Secretary U Thant, France, and others called for a coalition government in South Vietnam. But the new American president, Lyndon B. Johnson, would have none of it. He declared that America's purpose was victory, for anything less "would only be another name for a Communist take-over."

Johnson and the War Without Victory

Lyndon B. Johnson was a Texan who liked to say that he lived by the lessons of the Alamo—fight to the end. An old New Dealer, he talked about building Tennessee Valley Authorities around the world. "I want to leave the footprints of America there [in Vietnam]. I want them to say, 'This is what Americans left—schools and hospitals and dams.'" The footprints America actually left were those of soldiers, bombs, and chemical defoliants.

Johnson saw the world in simple terms—them against us—and privately disparaged both his allies and his enemies. Vietnam was a "raggedy-ass fourth-rate country," his critics at home "rattle-brains" or "nervous nellies." Johnson sometimes lied or exaggerated, creating what became known as a credibility gap. His public speeches, larded with trite metaphors and delivered in a belabored drawl, led some to suggest that he was unintelligent. They were wrong, for Johnson had a quick mind; his limitation was that he held firmly to fixed ideas about American superiority, the menace of communism, and the necessity of global intervention. The problem, said Senator J. William Fulbright of Arkansas, chairman of the Foreign Relations Committee, was that both Johnson and the American people suffered from an "arrogance of power."

By early 1964 the Vietcong controlled nearly half of South Vietnam. Because the new Saigon government was shaky and seemed to be leaning toward neutralism, United States officials cooperated in a second coup. In neighboring Laos, American bombers hit supply routes connecting the Vietcong with the North Vietnamese. Laos, where the CIA had manipulated politics for years and where in 1962 non-Communists and Communists agreed to a neutralist government, was increasingly drawn into a wider Southeast Asian war. The bombings were kept secret from the American Congress and people; yet, as Ambassador William H. Sullivan admitted, "we ran Laos."

In August 1964 an incident in the Gulf of Tonkin, off the coast of North Vietnam, led to accelerated American war making (see map). On August 2, 1964, the U.S.S. *Maddox,* while participating in South Vietnamese commando raids against North Vietnam, came under attack from northern patrol boats, which suffered heavy damage. The unharmed *Maddox* sailed away. "If they do it again," said Secretary of State Dean Rusk, "they'll get another sting." On August 4, now joined by another destroyer, the *Maddox* moved again toward the North Vietnamese shore as if to bait the Communists. During bad weather, sonar technicians reported what they thought were enemy torpedoes; the two destroyers began firing ferociously. Yet when the captain of the *Maddox* asked his crew members what had happened, not one had seen or heard hostile gunfire.

> **Tonkin Gulf Incident**

President Johnson, although knowing that the evidence was very questionable and unwilling to acknowledge publicly that American ships were participating in covert raids against North Vietnam, announced on television that the United States was retaliating against an "unprovoked" attack. Ameri-

can planes, he said, would now bomb North Vietnam. On August 7, Congress gave him the Tonkin Gulf Resolution, passed 466 to 0 in the House and 88 to 2 in the Senate after brief debate. Only Wayne Morse of Oregon and Ernest Gruening of Alaska dissented from the resolution's sweeping language that authorized the president to "take all necessary measures to repel any armed attack against the forces of the United States and to prevent further aggression." The Tonkin Gulf Resolution, Johnson eventually argued, amounted to the declaration of war that Congress never voted. Members of Congress essentially surrendered their powers in the foreign policy process by giving the president wide latitude to conduct the war as he saw fit.

After winning the presidency in his own right in the fall 1964, Johnson directed the military to map plans for stepped-up bombing of North Vietnam and Laos. Under Secretary Ball urged caution: "Once on the tiger's back we cannot be sure of picking the place to dismount." Nonetheless, when a Vietcong attack on an American airfield at Pleiku took nine American lives in February 1965, Johnson ordered carrier-based jets to ravage the North. Soon Operation Rolling Thunder—a sustained bombing program above the 17th parallel—was under way. Before the longest war was over, more bombs would fall on Vietnam than American aircraft had dropped in the Second World War. But the North Vietnamese would not give up. They hid in shelters and rebuilt roads and bridges with a perseverance that frustrated and awed American decision makers.

The president, in his momentous decision of July 1965, also sent more troops to the South. By the end of 1965, 184,000 Americans were assigned to Vietnam; in 1966 the figure reached 385,000; in 1969 it peaked at 543,400. But Ho only increased the flow of arms and men to the rebels in the South; in this seemingly endless war of attrition, each American escalation begot a new Vietnamese escalation. "I feel like a hitchhiker caught in a hailstorm on a Texas highway," groaned Johnson. "I can't run, I can't hide, and I can't make it stop." He and his aides just could not believe that the Vietnamese could tangle successfully with the greatest power on the face of the earth—at least not for very long.

> **Americanization of the War**

The "Americanization" of the war in Vietnam under Johnson troubled growing numbers of

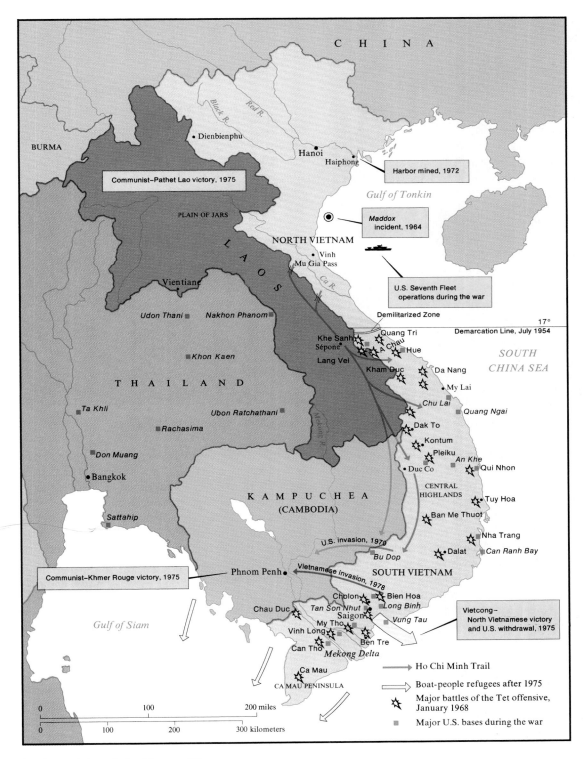

Southeast Asia and the Vietnam War

Wounded American soldiers after a battle in Vietnam. *Larry Burrows,* Life *Magazine © 1971 Time, Inc.*

Americans, especially as increased television coverage brought the ugliness of combat into their homes every night. The pictures and stories were not pretty. Innocent civilians were caught in the line of fire; refugees flooded "pacification" camps; villages considered friendly to the enemy were burned to the ground. To expose and destroy Vietcong hiding places, pilots whose motto was "Only You Can Prevent Forests" sprayed chemical defoliants like Agent Orange over the landscape to denude it. The Vietcong and North Vietnamese added to the carnage, but American guns, bombs, and chemicals took by far the greatest toll, and the Vietnamese people knew it. Indeed, America's search-and-destroy missions were counterproductive; rather than winning the war, they were molding an ever-growing population of anti-American peasants who gave secret aid to the Vietcong. An American official later admitted, "It was as if we were trying to build a house with a bulldozer and wrecking crane."

Stories of atrocities made their way home. Most gruesome was the My Lai massacre in March 1968 (not made public until twenty months later because of a military cover-up). An American unit, frustrated by its inability to pin down an elusive enemy and eager to revenge the loss of some buddies, shot to death more than 200 unarmed Vietnamese civilians, most of them women and children. Private Paul Meadlo, the father of two children himself, was there. "We huddled them up. We made them squat down. . . . I poured about four clips into the group. . . . The mothers was hugging their children. . . . Well, we kept right on firing. They was waving their arms and begging. . . . I still dream about it. About the women and children in my sleep. Some days . . . some nights, I can't even sleep."

Although many incidents of the deliberate shooting of civilians, torturing and killing of prisoners, taking of Vietnamese ears as trophies, and burning of villages have been recorded, most American soldiers were not committing atrocities. They were trying instead to save their young lives (their average age was only nineteen) and serve the United States mission by

American Soldiers in Vietnam

killing enemy troops, whom they usually called "gooks." Many of these Americans made up the rear-echelon forces that supported the "grunts" or "boonierats" in the field. Wherever they were, soldiers met an inhospitable environment, for no place in Vietnam was secure. Well-hidden booby traps blasted away parts of the body. The enemy was everywhere yet nowhere, often burrowed into elaborate underground tunnels or melded into the population, where every Vietnamese might be a Vietcong terrorist.

Infantrymen on maneuvers humped heavy rucksacks into thick jungle growth, their every step precarious. "In places the bamboo was over fifteen feet high," wrote the veteran John M. DelVecchio in his novel *The 13th Valley* (1982). "The point man felt as if he were breaking trail through knife blades of spring steel. His arms were soon slashed and bloody and his face had multiple tiny lacerations." Leeches sucked at weary bodies. Boots and human skin rotted from the rains, which alternated with withering suns. "It was as if the sun and the land itself were in league with the Vietcong," recalled the marine officer Philip Caputo in his book *A Rumor of War* (1977), "wearing us down, driving us mad, killing us." Wounded GIs shouted for a medic, who in turn might call in a "medevac" (medical evacuation helicopter), praying that it would not be shot down, knowing that a successful departure could carry the wounded within minutes to operating tables in MASH (Mobile Army Surgical Hospital) units or hospital ships like the U.S.S. *Sanctuary*. "What I saw were young men coming in, eighteen or nineteen years old . . . and they would be without a leg," remembered Gayle Smith, a nurse at the 3rd Surgical Hospital. "Vietnam was not John Wayne," remarked Ruth Sidisin of the Air Force Nurse Corps. "In Vietnam every day was disaster day."

Hundreds of thousands of the 2.8 million Vietnam veterans suffered post-traumatic stress disorder after returning home. This illness of nightmares and extreme nervousness was different from the shell shock of the First World War or the battle fatigue of the Second. Doctors reported that the disorder stemmed primarily from the fact that soldiers saw so many children, women, and elderly killed. Sometimes GIs themselves inadvertently killed these people, not always able to distinguish

Post-traumatic Stress Disorder

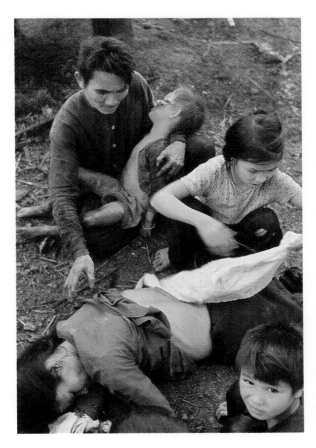

South Vietnamese villagers in 1967 after an American napalm attack. Released from flame throwers or fire bombs, napalm was a gel that stuck to its targets as it burned. *Dana Stone, Black Star.*

the innocent from the enemy; sometimes they vengefully killed them and later felt guilt. One saddened veteran remarked, "They were [Vietnamese] kids who did not know what Communism was any more than I did."

As the war ground on to no discernible conclusion, the army in Vietnam grew troubled and morale sagged. Desertions and absent-without-leave (AWOL) cases increased, especially in the early 1970s, when no GI wanted to be the last man killed in the war. Racial tensions intensified between whites and blacks. Drug abuse became serious. Many soldiers smoked plentiful, cheap marijuana; about one-third of the troops became addicted to opium and heroin, according to a 1971 official report.

"Fragging," the murder of an officer by soldiers using hand grenades or other weapons, also in-

The loud chopping sound of helicopter blades was familiar to all combatants in Vietnam. Here, in August 1967, helicopters of the U.S. Army's 199th Light Infantry Brigade lift off after landing South Vietnamese forces in the Mekong Delta near Saigon. *Wide World Photos.*

creased. "Grenades leave no fingerprints. Nobody's going to jail," recalled a helicopter pilot. The military elite in Washington grew alarmed too by numerous reports of disobedience—and by peace symbols scratched on helmets. At home, thousands of young men expressed their opposition to the war by fleeing the draft. By the end of 1972 more than 30,000 draft resisters were living in Canada, and thousands had gone into exile in Sweden and Mexico or lived under false identities in the United States. During the war half a million men committed draft violations, including a quarter-million who never registered and thousands who burned their draft cards in protest.

As American military engagement in Vietnam escalated, so did protest at home (see map, page 951). As early as April 1965, 25,000 people marched on the White House, and in October the National Committee to End the War in Vietnam mobilized more than 80,000 in nationwide demonstrations. In early 1966, Senator J. William Fulbright began public hearings on whether the national interest was being served by pursuing the war in Asia. What exactly was the threat? senators asked. To the surprise of some, the father of the containment doctrine, George F. Kennan, testified before television cameras that his theory was meant for Europe, not the volatile environment of Southeast Asia. In October 1967, 100,000 people marched on Washington, thousands of them reaching the steps of the Pentagon. Within the administration, too, disenchantment rose. Secretary of Defense Robert McNamara worked quietly to scale back the American military presence in Vietnam, but when he failed to persuade President Johnson, he resigned. "Ho Chi Minh is a tough old S.O.B.," McNamara told his aides. "And he won't quit no matter how much bombing we do." In a direct challenge to Johnson's policies, antiwar Senator Eugene McCarthy of Minnesota announced his candidacy for the Democratic presidential nomination.

Johnson dug in, snapping at his critics and vowing to continue the battle, cheered by opinion polls that showed Americans actually favoring escalation over withdrawal. "We are not going to shimmy," he insisted. At times he halted the bombing to encourage Ho Chi Minh to negotiate. Such pauses, however, were often accompanied by increases in American troop strength. And in some cases the United States resumed or accelerated the bombing just when a diplomatic breakthrough seemed imminent—such as in late 1966, when a Polish diplomat's efforts were inexplicably cut short by a resumption of the bombing. The North demanded a complete stop to the bombing raids before sitting down at the conference table. And Ho could not accept American terms: nonrecognition of the Vietcong; withdrawal of northern soldiers from the South; an end to North Vietnamese military aid to the Vietcong; in short, an abandonment of his lifelong dream of an independent, unified Vietnam.

Defeat, Withdrawal, and the Legacy of Vietnam

In January 1968, a shocking event forced Johnson to reappraise his position. During Tet, the Vietnamese lunar new year, Vietcong and North Vietnamese forces struck all across South Vietnam, hitting and

The agony of war. On the left is Marine Lance Corporal James Farley in Danang after a Vietcong ambush in which American troops died. On the right is President Lyndon B. Johnson (1908–1973) after the Tet offensive and his decision to end his political career by not running again for the presidency. *Left: Larry Burrows,* Life *Magazine, © 1965 Time, Inc.; right: Lyndon B. Johnson Library.*

Tet Offensive capturing provincial capitals. In Saigon, Vietcong raiders actually penetrated the American embassy compound. American and South Vietnamese units eventually regained much lost ground, inflicting heavy casualties on the enemy. But the destruction of the village of Ben Tre revealed the cost of driving the Vietcong out. "It became necessary to destroy the town to save it," reported a sober-faced American officer.

The Tet offensive jolted Americans. Although Tet ultimately was an American military victory, it was also an American psychological defeat. Hadn't the Vietcong and North Vietnamese demonstrated that they could strike when and where they wished? Didn't they have the advantage of fighting on home territory? Why did "their Vietnamese" fight harder than "our Vietnamese"? If all of America's firepower and dollars and half a million troops couldn't defeat the Vietcong once and for all, could anything? Had the American public been lied to? One television reporter asked, "Isn't there something Orwellian about it, that the more we kill, the stronger they get?"

The Tet offensive and its impact on public opinion hit the White House like a thunderclap. The new secretary of defense, Clark Clifford, told Johnson the war could not be won, even if the 206,000 more soldiers requested by the army were sent to Vietnam. The Cold Warrior of Cold Warriors, Dean Acheson, bluntly told a surprised president that the military brass did not know what they were talking about. Strained by exhausting sessions with advisers, realizing that further escalation would not bring victory, and faced with serious opposition within his own party, Johnson changed course. In a television appearance on March 31 he announced that he had stopped the bombing of most of North Vietnam and asked Hanoi to begin negotiations. Then he surprised the nation by dropping out of the presidential race.

The United States, knowing it could not win, would at least try not to lose. The war ground on as the diplomats talked without agreement in Paris. The administration demanded North Vietnamese concessions before completely halting the bombing, but Hanoi rejected reciprocity. Late in 1968 President-elect Richard M. Nixon met with Johnson and his key advisers to discuss the war. "The travail of the long war was etched on the faces around me," Nixon recalled. "They had no new approaches to recommend to me. I sensed that, despite the disappointment of defeat, they were relieved to be able to turn this morass over to someone else."

In July 1969 the new president announced the Nixon Doctrine: the United States would help those

Defeat, Withdrawal, and the Legacy of Vietnam

nations that helped themselves. This doctrine

> **Nixon Doctrine**

reflected official Washington's realization that it could no longer afford to sustain so many overseas commitments, as well as the growing assumption that the United States would have to rely more on allied regional powers (like Iran in the Middle East) to maintain an anti-Communist world order. In Southeast Asia the doctrine was implemented as "Vietnamization"—building up South Vietnamese forces to replace American troops. Nixon began a gradual withdrawal of American troops from Vietnam, decreasing their number to 139,000 by the end of 1971. But he also increased the bombing of the North, hoping to pound Hanoi into making concessions. Nixon's national security adviser, Henry A. Kissinger, called it jugular diplomacy. In October 1969, hundreds of thousands of people peacefully marched in cities across the nation to call for a moratorium on the war. On November 15, more than a quarter of a million marchers protested in Washington, D.C., alone. "Don't get rattled—don't waver—don't react," Nixon told himself.

On April 30, 1970, Nixon announced that South Vietnamese and American forces were invading Cambodia in search of arms depots and enemy

> **Cambodia and Antiwar Protest**

forces that used the neutral nation as a sanctuary. This escalation sparked demonstrations on college campuses, including Kent State University, where Ohio National Guardsmen fired upon protesting students, killing four (see page 958). Across the nation, students went on "strike" to protest the expanded violence in Indochina and America. Nixon belligerently called them "bums." In June the Senate joined the protest against Nixon's broadening of the war by terminating the Tonkin Gulf Resolution of 1964. In the Cooper-Church amendment, the Senate also forbade the expenditure of funds on the new war, but the House rejected this restriction, leaving Nixon free to continue the "secret" bombing of Cambodia.

Nixon's troubles at home mounted in mid-June 1971 when the *New York Times* began to publish the *Pentagon Papers,* a top-secret, official study of United States decisions in the Vietnam War. In 1967, Secretary McNamara had ordered preparation of the study to preserve the documentary record of the United States relationship with Vietnam. Daniel Ellsberg, a former Defense Department official working at the RAND Corporation (a think tank for analyzing defense policy), leaked the heavily documented report to the *Times.* Nixon secured an injunction to prevent publication, but the Supreme Court overturned the order. The *Pentagon Papers* revealed that American leaders had frequently lied to the American people. For example, whereas President Johnson repeatedly claimed in public that the United States only increased its forces in South Vietnam to respond to North Vietnamese infiltration, the secret Pentagon study showed that after mid-1967 the United States itself took the initiative in escalating the war because American officials believed that more troops would deliver victory.

Nixon and Kissinger continued to escalate the war, ordering "protective reaction strikes" against the North; acceleration of the CIA's Operation Phoenix (the assassination of thousands of enemy civilians in the South); the bombing of Cambodia; and the mining of Haiphong harbor in North Vietnam. In December 1972, a massive air strike called the Christmas bombing, or as one of Kissinger's aides put it, "calculated barbarism," hit the North. The air terror punished the Vietnamese; but twenty-six American planes, including fifteen B-52 bombers, were lost.

In Paris, meanwhile, the peace talks seemed to be going nowhere. The South Vietnamese delegate saw defeat coming and purposely stalled the negotiations.

> **Cease-Fire Agreement**

But Kissinger was meeting privately with Le Duc Tho, the chief delegate from North Vietnam. Eager to improve relations with the Soviet Union and China, win back the allegiance of America's allies, restore stability at home, and end a war that could not be won, Nixon decided to make concessions. On January 27, 1973, Kissinger and Le Duc Tho signed a cease-fire agreement. The United States promised to withdraw all of its troops within sixty days. Other troops would stay in place, and a coalition government that included the Vietcong would eventually be formed in the South. Pleased that a peace had been made, critics nonetheless noted that the terms of the agreement could have been accepted in 1969 and more than twenty thousand American lives could have been spared. To prevent a future Vietnam, Congress passed the War Powers Resolution in November 1973: the president could commit American troops abroad for no more than sixty

In Washington, D.C., the long, solemn walls of the Vietnam Veterans Memorial include the etched names of the more than 58,000 Americans who died in the war. *Susan Meiselas/Magnum Photos.*

days, and after that period he had to obtain congressional approval.

Leaving behind some advisers, the United States pulled its troops out of Vietnam and reduced but did not end its aid program. Both North and South soon violated the cease-fire, and full-scale war erupted once more. As many had predicted, the feeble South Vietnamese government, for so long an American puppet, could not hold out. Just before its surrender, hundreds of Americans, as well as Vietnamese who had worked for them, were hastily evacuated by helicopter from the roof of the American embassy in Saigon. But there was not enough space in the aircraft for many Vietnamese, and in those desperate last moments, American guards violently had to shove them back. On April 29, 1975, the South Vietnamese government collapsed. Shortly thereafter Saigon was renamed Ho Chi Minh City after the persevering national patriot, who had died in 1969.

After twenty-five years, American intervention in Southeast Asia came to this panicky end. The overall costs of the war were immense. More than 58,000 Americans and more than a million Asians died. In monetary terms the war cost the United States more than $150 billion, and billions more would be paid in future veterans' benefits. At home the war brought inflation, political schism, attacks on civil liberties, and retrenchment from reform programs (see Chapter 32). The war also had negative consequences internationally: delay in moving toward better relations with the Soviet Union and the People's Republic of China, friction with allies, and the alienation of Third World nations.

Meanwhile, in South Vietnam, Cambodia, and Laos, Communists assumed power and instituted repressive governments. Acute hunger afflicted the people of those devastated lands. Soon refugees were crowding aboard unsafe vessels in an attempt to escape their battered homelands. Many of these

Defeat, Withdrawal, and the Legacy of Vietnam

"boat people" emigrated to the United States, where Americans, reluctant to be reminded of their defeat in Asia, received them with mixed feelings. But thoughtful Americans realized that the United States, which had relentlessly bombed, burned, and defoliated once-rich agricultural lands, bore considerable responsibility for the plight of the Southeast Asian peoples.

This sad conclusion prompted an American ambassador to ask a central question about the American defeat: "How so many with so much could achieve so little for so long against so few"? General Maxwell Taylor summarized some of the reasons Americans could not win the Vietnam War when he said that "we didn't know our ally. Secondly, we knew even less about the enemy. And, the last, most inexcusable of our mistakes, was not knowing our own people."

When it was over, many Americans preferred to put the disaster out of mind. "Coming back to America," recalled a Vietnam veteran, "I was shocked . . . that no one even talked about it." But the veterans were unable to forget. One wrote,

> The longest war is over
> Or so they say
> Again
> But I can still hear the gunfire
> Every night
> From
> My bed.
>
> The longest nightmare
> Never seems to
> Ever
> Quite come
> To
> An end.[1]

Debate about the causes and consequences of the war gradually developed. Americans seemed both angry and confused. The historian William Appleman Williams observed that for the first time in their history Americans were suffering from a serious case of "empire shock."

The Lessons of Vietnam Debated

Hawkish leaders who debated the meaning of the war claimed that America's ignoble failure in Vietnam undermined the nation's credibility and tempted enemies to exploit opportunities at the expense of United States interests. They pointed to a Vietnam syndrome—a mood suspi-

cious of foreign entanglements—which would inhibit the United States from exercising its power. They advised that next time the military should be permitted to do its job, free from the constraints of whimsical public opinion, stab-in-the-back journalists, and meddlesome politicians. America lost in Vietnam, they asserted, because the American people lost their guts and will at home. "Remember," advised a former battalion commander, "we're watchdogs you unchain to eat up the burglar. Don't ask us to be mayors or sociologists worrying about hearts and minds. Let us eat up the burglar our own way and then put us back on the chain."

Others drew different lessons. Some people blamed the war on strong-willed presidents like Johnson and pusillanimous Congresses that had conceded too much power to the executive branch, as evident in the Tonkin Gulf Resolution. Trim the powers of the imperial presidency, they counseled, and America would become less interventionist. Others took a more hard-headed, even fatalistic, view: as long as the United States remained an industrial giant, with strong ideological, strategic, economic, and political needs that could be satisfied only through activism abroad, then the nation would continue to be expansionist and interventionist. The United States was destined, then, to intervene abroad, to sustain its role as the world's policeman, teacher, social worker, banker, and merchant. Still others found fault with the containment doctrine: it failed to make distinctions between areas peripheral and areas vital to the national security and relied too heavily upon military means. As well, containment could not work if there were no political stability and no effective and popular government in the country where it was being applied. Journalist Walter Lippmann endorsed "neo-isolationism." "Compared to people who thought they could run the universe," he wrote, "I *am* a neo-isolationist and proud of it."

Public discussion of the Vietnam War was also stimulated by veterans who called for better benefits to deal with post-traumatic stress disorder and the effects of Agent Orange and other chemicals with which they came into contact in Vietnam. Many returning veterans were also stung by the unsympathetic glances of Americans who did not want to be reminded of the unpleasant war or who blamed them for losing a war that could not be won. The veterans began to demand respect, arguing that the leaders who ordered them to Southeast

---

[1] From Jan Barry, "The Longest War." Reprinted by permission of the author.

Asia, not the GIs, should be held responsible for the negative results of the long war. Films like *Coming Home* (1978), *The Deer Hunter* (1978), and *Apocalypse Now* (1979), personal accounts like Philip Caputo's *A Rumor of War* (1977), and novels like James Webb's *Fields of Fire* (1978) focused attention on the soldier's Vietnam, raising questions about whether defeat was inevitable given the jungle conditions and elusive enemy.

Nixon, Kissinger, and Détente

For President Nixon, Vietnam was a "short-term problem"; for Kissinger it was a mere historical "footnote." Both considered the central question of international affairs to be the relationship between the United States and the Soviet Union. As a congressman, senator, and vice president, Nixon had been an ardent cold warrior. As one Soviet official commented, "We very well know with whom we have to deal." Kissinger was a German-born political scientist teaching at Harvard and a noted writer on diplomatic topics. Nixon appointed him national security adviser, a post he held until 1973, when he became secretary of state. Ambitious, witty, knowledgeable, and deliberate, Kissinger was a formidable negotiator. Critics, however, thought he adhered too callously to the principle that the end justifies the means. They cited his willingness to unseat foreign governments through secret operations, as in Chile (see page 930), and to sell massive amounts of arms to dictators like the shah of Iran. Kissinger had his own staff wiretapped.

Together Nixon and Kissinger pursued a grand strategy designed to promote a global balance of power, or "equilibrium." The first part of the strategy was *détente*, measured cooperation with the Soviets through negotiations within a general environment of rivalry. Détente's purpose, like that of the containment doctrine it resembled, was to check Soviet expansion and limit a Soviet arms build-up. The second part of the strategy was the curbing of revolution and radicalism in the Third World so as to resist threats to American interests. The grand design seemed attractive to its architects. The Cold War and limited wars like Vietnam were

Détente

Henry A. Kissinger (1923–), a German-born political scientist who taught at Harvard University, became President Richard M. Nixon's national security affairs adviser and secretary of state. Talented, witty, and arrogant, Kissinger vigorously prosecuted the Vietnam War, launched détente, and strove to create a world order dominated by the great powers. Instability in the Third World and in the international economy, much of it his own making, wrecked many of his plans. In 1973 he and Le Duc Tho won the Nobel Peace Prize for negotiating the cease-fire agreement in Vietnam. A disapproving *New York Times* editorial called it the "Nobel War Prize." *Gerald Ford Library.*

costing too much, and more trade with a friendlier Soviet Union might reduce the huge balance-of-payments deficit. Critics, even some who endorsed détente, faulted the Nixon-Kissinger posture for its arrogant assumption that the United States had the ability and the right to manipulate a disorderly world. They complained that the administration was wedded to archaic Cold War thinking and that it ignored the reality that instability in the Third World derived not from Soviet or Communist intrigue but from indigenous economic, political, religious, and ethnic differences. Rather than decreasing the need for intervention, said critics, the new design actually increased it.

Nixon and Kissinger pursued détente with extraordinary energy and fanfare. They expanded

STRATEGIC NUCLEAR FORCES AT THE TIME OF SALT-I, 1972		
	U.S.	U.S.S.R.
Intercontinental ballistic missiles (ICBMs)	1,054	1,607
Submarine-launched ballistic missiles (SLBMs)	656	740
Strategic bombers	450	200
Nuclear warheads	5,700	2,500

Source: U.S. Department of Defense; U.S. Department of State.

trade relations with the Soviet Union; a 1972 deal sent $1 billion worth of American grain to the Soviets at bargain prices. To slow the costly arms race, the Nixon administration initiated Strategic Arms Limitations Talks (SALT) with the Soviets. In 1972 the talks produced a SALT Treaty that limited antiballistic missile (ABM) systems. The defensive ABM systems made offensive missiles less vulnerable to attack—and hence encouraged the other side to build more missiles to overcome ABM protection. Limiting ABMs was thus a step toward halting a spiraling arms race. A second agreement placed a five-year freeze on the number of offensive nuclear missiles that each side could have. At the time of the agreement (see table) the Soviets held an advantage in total missiles, but the United States had more warheads per missile because of its MIRVs (multiple independently targeted re-entry vehicles). One missile loaded with MIRVs could send several nuclear warheads to different targets. In short, the United States had a 2-to-1 advantage in deliverable warheads. Because SALT did not restrict MIRVs, the nuclear arms build-up continued.

▷ **SALT Talks**

Nixon and Kissinger also cultivated détente with the People's Republic of China, ending almost three decades of Sino-American hostility. In February 1972 the president made a historic trip to what he used to call "Red" China. The Chinese Communists welcomed him because they sought to improve trade and they hoped friendlier Chinese-American relations would make the Soviets—a Chinese enemy—more cautious. Nixon reasoned the same way. The president visited the Great Wall, toured other famous sites, and exchanged 150-proof rice-liquor toasts with the ven-

▷ **Opening to China**

erable Chinese leaders Mao Zedong and Zhou Enlai. In the end, the conferees agreed to disagree on a number of issues, except one: the Soviet Union should not be permitted to make gains in Asia. The opening of this Sino-American dialogue ended one of the postwar era's longest and most bitter contests. Official diplomatic recognition and exchange of ambassadors came in 1979.

Turmoil in the Third World

Tortuous events in the Middle East revealed how fragile the Nixon-Kissinger grand strategy was. When Nixon took office in 1969 the Middle East was, in the president's words, a "powder keg." In the Six-Day War (1967) Israel had used American weapons to score victories against Egypt and Syria. The Israelis had seized the West Bank and the ancient city of Jerusalem from Jordan, the Golan Heights from Syria, and the Sinai peninsula from Egypt (see map). Soviet arms had backed the Arab nations that Israel fought. To further complicate matters, Palestinian Arabs, many of them expelled from their homes in 1948 when the nation of Israel was created, had organized the Palestine Liberation Organization (PLO) and pledged to destroy Israel. PLO sympathizers made hit-and-run raids on Jewish settlements, hijacked jetliners, and murdered Israeli athletes at the 1972 Olympic Games in Munich, West Germany. The Israelis retaliated by assassinating PLO figures abroad.

On October 6, 1973, Egypt and Syria attacked Israel. In spite of détente, Moscow, backing Egypt, and Washington, backing Israel, headed for a con-

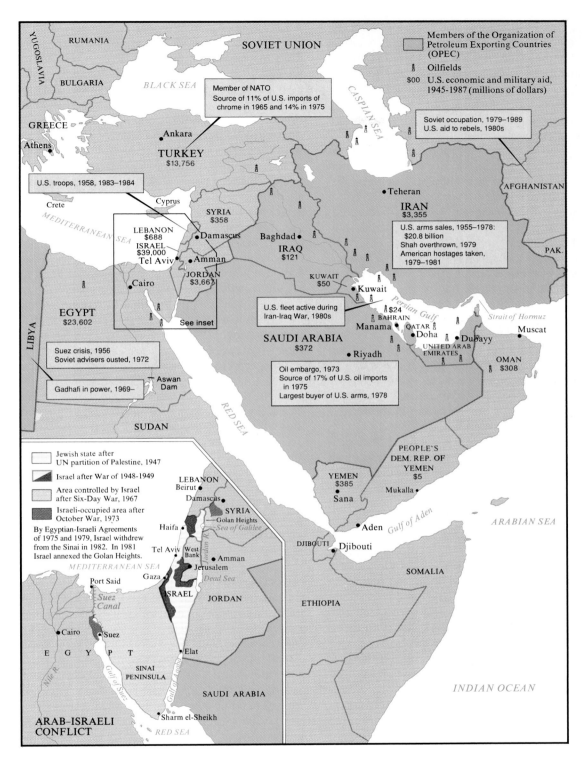

The Middle East

Map legend and labels:

Members of the Organization of Petroleum Exporting Countries (OPEC)

Oilfields

$00 U.S. economic and military aid, 1945–1987 (millions of dollars)

Member of NATO
Source of 11% of U.S. imports of chrome in 1965 and 14% in 1975

Soviet occupation, 1979–1989
U.S. aid to rebels, 1980s

U.S. troops, 1958, 1983–1984

U.S. arms sales, 1955–1978:
$20.8 billion
Shah overthrown, 1979
American hostages taken, 1979–1981

U.S. fleet active during Iran-Iraq War, 1980s

Suez crisis, 1956
Soviet advisers ousted, 1972

Gadhafi in power, 1969–

Oil embargo, 1973
Source of 17% of U.S. oil imports in 1975
Largest buyer of U.S. arms, 1978

YUGOSLAVIA
RUMANIA
SOVIET UNION
BULGARIA
BLACK SEA
CASPIAN SEA
GREECE
Athens
Ankara
TURKEY $13,756
AFGHANISTAN
Teheran
IRAN $3,355
PAK.
Crete
Cyprus
SYRIA $358
Baghdad
MEDITERRANEAN SEA
LEBANON $688
Damascus
IRAQ $121
ISRAEL $39,000
Tel Aviv
Amman
JORDAN $3,667
KUWAIT $50
Kuwait
Cairo
Persian Gulf
$24 BAHRAIN
Manama QATAR
Doha Dubayy
Strait of Hormuz
Muscat
LIBYA
EGYPT $23,602
See inset
SAUDI ARABIA $372
UNITED ARAB EMIRATES
OMAN $308
Riyadh
Aswan Dam
RED SEA
SUDAN
PEOPLE'S DEM. REP. OF YEMEN $5
YEMEN $385
Sana
Mukalla
ARABIAN SEA
Aden Gulf of Aden
DJIBOUTI Djibouti
SOMALIA
ETHIOPIA
INDIAN OCEAN

Inset map legend:

Jewish state after UN partition of Palestine, 1947

Israel after War of 1948-1949

Area controlled by Israel after Six-Day War, 1967

Israeli-occupied area after October War, 1973

By Egyptian-Israeli Agreements of 1975 and 1979, Israel withdrew from the Sinai in 1982. In 1981 Israel annexed the Golan Heights.

LEBANON
Beirut
Damascus
SYRIA
Golan Heights
Haifa
Sea of Galilee
Jordan R.
Tel Aviv West Bank
Amman
Jerusalem
Gaza
Dead Sea
MEDITERRANEAN SEA
ISRAEL
JORDAN
Port Said
Suez Canal
Cairo
Suez
EGYPT
Elat
SINAI PENINSULA
Gulf of Suez
Gulf of Aqaba
SAUDI ARABIA
Sharm el-Sheikh
RED SEA

ARAB–ISRAELI CONFLICT

Turmoil in the Third World

The 1973 War in the Middle East frontation; both superpowers put their armed forces—including nuclear forces—on alert. At the same time, in an attempt to pressure Americans into taking a pro-Arab stance, the Organization of Petroleum Exporting Countries (OPEC) imposed an embargo on shipments of oil to the United States.

Faced with an energy crisis at home from dramatically higher oil prices, the Nixon administration had to find a way to end Mideast hostilities. Kissinger arranged a cease-fire and undertook "shuttle diplomacy," flying back and forth repeatedly between Middle Eastern capitals in an exhausting search for a settlement. In March 1974, OPEC lifted the oil embargo. The next year Kissinger persuaded Egypt and Israel to accept a United Nations peace-keeping force in the Sinai. But other problems remained: the homeless Palestinian Arabs, Israeli occupation of Jerusalem and the West Bank, Israel's insistence on building settlements in occupied lands, and Arab threats to destroy the Jewish state. Furthermore, Soviet-American rivalry was still very much alive in the Middle East, especially after the exclusion of the Soviets from the peace negotiations and after Egypt moved closer to the United States, snubbing the Soviet Union.

In Latin America, Nixon continued President Johnson's interventionist policies. Johnson had dispatched 20,000 American troops to the Dominican Republic in 1965 to prevent a leftist government from coming to power. And in the Johnson Doctrine—the United States would prevent Communists from coming to power in Western Hemispheric nations—the president had reiterated the Roosevelt Corollary's insistence on United States policing powers in the region. In

Intervention in Chile 1970, when the people of Chile elected a Marxist president, Salvador Allende, Nixon did not send the marines to remove what he read as a Communist threat. Instead, he mobilized the CIA, which began secret operations to disrupt the Chilean economy, funneled money to newspapers critical of Allende, and apparently encouraged military officers to stage a coup. In 1973 a military junta ousted and killed Allende and installed an authoritarian regime in his place. Nixon and Kissinger privately pronounced their policy of "destabilization" successful, while publicly denying their role in the affair.

In Africa, Nixon-Kissinger maneuvers proved less successful. During the 1960s and early 1970s the CIA channeled funds to some of the groups fighting for the liberation of An-

Angola gola from Portuguese colonial rule—while Washington publicly supported Portugal. After Angola won its independence in 1975, civil war erupted. The United States, which stepped up covert aid, and South Africa, which sent troops, backed one faction while the Soviets helped another. When Congress learned about the secret aid, it voted to cut all funds. Kissinger complained that the Soviets would gain a foothold in Africa. But many members of Congress argued that Americans could not decide the outcome of an African civil war; that the United States should not be aligned with the white racist regime of South Africa; that Angola was unlikely to become a Soviet puppet; and that diplomacy should have been tried. After a leftist government came to power in Angola, Washington took a keener interest in the rest of Africa, building economic ties, sending arms to friendly black nations, and distancing the United States from the white minority governments in Rhodesia (now Zimbabwe) and South Africa. It was important, Kissinger said, to "prevent the radicalization of Africa."

If disputes in the Middle East, Latin America, and Africa bedeviled the Nixon-Kissinger grand design for world order, global economic issues also heightened political disorder.

International Economic Instability Kissinger explained that "international political stability requires international economic stability." But in the 1970s there was little economic stability; troubles could be seen everywhere. The worldwide recession in the early part of the decade was the worst since the 1930s. Inflation and high oil prices pinched rich and poor nations alike. Protectionist tendencies raised tariffs and impeded world trade. Economists coined the term "Fourth World" for poor, less-developed Third World countries that lacked profit-making raw materials, relied heavily upon food imports to combat famines, and built up large debts owed to governments and private banks. Third and Fourth World countries—often called the "South"—insisted that the wealthier, industrial "North" share economic resources. The gulf between rich and poor nations threatened world peace.

As a major participant in the world economy, the United States could not escape these problems. America's economic standing had declined since the olympian days of the 1940s and 1950s as other nations, such as Japan and West Germany, had recovered from the devastation of the Second World War and as Third World countries had gained more control over their raw materials. Nevertheless, Americans remained the richest people in the world. The United States produced about one-third of the world's goods and services. Many American companies, like Coca-Cola and Exxon, earned over half their profits abroad. One-fourth of agricultural sales came from exports; one out of every nine manufacturing jobs depended upon exports. The American economy also depended upon imports of strategic raw materials: three-fourths of the tin, over 95 percent of the manganese, and over half of the zinc consumed in the United States came from abroad. Such ties, as well as American investments abroad totaling more than $133 billion in the mid-1970s, explain in part why the United States was an interventionist power; threats to markets, investments, and raw materials were read as deadly stabs at the high American standard of living. American economic holdings did in fact become targets. Venezuela nationalized American oil properties in 1976, and terrorists around the world destroyed American facilities and kidnaped and sometimes murdered American business executives.

Multinational corporations became a symbol and a target of the conspicuous American economic position overseas. American-based multinationals

Multi-national Corporations like Exxon and General Motors actually enjoyed budgets and incomes larger than those of most countries. These giant firms brought home profits and exported American culture, but they aroused criticism. American workers protested that these global oligopolies stole their jobs when they moved factories abroad in search of cheaper labor. People of the "South" complained that multinationals exploited them, robbing their natural resources; that they corrupted politics, as when International Telephone and Telegraph tried to undermine President Allende in Chile and Lockheed Aircraft bribed foreign leaders to promote sales; that they sometimes provided "cover" for CIA agents; and that they evaded taxes by clever manipulations of their books.

Multinational officers and government officials defended these enterprises, pointing out that they invested in risky ventures that brought economic progress, including the transfer of technology. Multinationals, they insisted, helped rationalize a chaotic world economy, and privately owned multinationals made more rational economic choices—hence benefiting the consumer—than did government-owned companies. Nonetheless, many countries passed laws requiring a certain percentage of native ownership; India, for example, legislated that its nationals own a majority of voting shares in industrial firms. Other nations simply nationalized multinational properties.

Besides placing restraints on multinationals, the "South" pressed for lower prices on technology and manufactured goods, low-interest loans, and higher prices for raw materials. In 1974 the United Nations issued the "New International Economic Order" encompassing many of these points, but the "North" made few concessions. Food was another divisive issue in the "North-South" dialogue. Droughts, meager harvests, high birthrates, and swelling populations condemned millions to hunger. In Africa in the early 1970s famine killed 10,000 people a day. The United States sent food aid, especially to those nations considered political friends, but it preferred to sell its surplus food for profit, as evidenced by the large grain sales to the dollar-paying Soviets. Although total American foreign aid rose from $6.6 billion in 1970 to $7.8 billion in 1977, the aid dollars actually bought less because of rampant inflation.

Another question that pitted "North" against "South" was the Law of the Sea Treaty, patiently composed in the 1970s through extended negotiations. Developing nations argued that the rich seabed resources of petroleum and

Law of the Sea Treaty minerals should be shared among all nations as a "common heritage of mankind." The industrial states, alone having the capital and equipment to conduct the excavating and drilling, tended to prefer private enterprise or national exploitation, reaping the profits and raw materials for themselves. In the early 1980s the global community finally hammered out a compromise between international and national controls and rights, but the United States rejected the treaty in 1983. Angry Third World nations railed against what they perceived as selfish economic imperialism, whereas many American allies who supported the compromise predicted a chaotic future of competing claims of ownership, territorial disputes, and threats to freedom of navigation. Like other international economic issues, this one promised a future of political instability—and perhaps war.

Faced with so many international troubles, the Nixon administration clung to the now traditional globalist belief that the United States faced ubiquitous threats from Communists, radicals of all kinds, nationalists, and neutralists, and therefore that interventionism was a necessary burden. Thus in the mid-1970s some 686,000 American military personnel were stationed abroad; the United States had military links with ninety-two nations; American arms sales overseas climbed to $10 billion; and the CIA was active on every continent. These global activities were undertaken not only to impress Moscow with American might and will, but to serve as a counterrevolutionary force against nationalist stirrings that threatened American economic and strategic interests. Nixon, his successor Gerald Ford, and Kissinger stood in a long line of leaders who counterpoised American power against foreign peoples determined to decide their own fate—such as against the Vietnamese, who, in their dogged pursuit of independence and social revolution, collided so directly with Americans that the societies, politics, and economies of both Vietnam and the United States suffered terribly.

Suggestions for Further Reading

General and Soviet-American Relations

Stephen Ambrose, *Rise to Globalism,* 4th ed. (1985); Richard J. Barnet, *The Alliance* (1983); Barry M. Blechman and Stephen S. Kaplan et al., *Force Without War: U.S. Armed Forces as a Political Instrument* (1978); John L. Gaddis, *Strategies of Containment* (1982); Raymond L. Garthoff, *Détente and Confrontation: American-Soviet Relations from Nixon to Reagan* (1985); Alexander L. George and Richard Smoke, *Deterrence in American Foreign Policy* (1974); Robert C. Johansen, *The National Interest and the Human Interest* (1980); Gabriel Kolko, *Confronting the Third World* (1988); Walter LaFeber, *America, Russia, and the Cold War, 1945–1985,* 5th ed. (1985); Robert A. Packenham, *Liberal America and the Third World* (1973); Thomas G. Paterson, *Meeting the Communist Threat* (1988); Alvin Z. Rubenstein and Donald E. Smith, eds., *Anti-Americanism in the Third World* (1985); Adam B. Ulam, *Dangerous Relations* (1983). Also see works cited in Chapter 29.

Kennedy and Johnson Diplomacy

Warren I. Cohen, *Dean Rusk* (1980); Philip Geyelin, *Lyndon B. Johnson and the World* (1966); David Halberstam, *The Best and the Brightest* (1972); Jim Heath, *Decade of Disillusionment* (1975); Madeleine G. Kalb, *The Congo Cables* (1982); Doris Kearns, *Lyndon Johnson and the American Dream* (1976); Montague Kern et al., *The Kennedy Crises* (1984); Richard D. Mahoney, *JFK: Ordeal in Africa* (1983); Herbert S. Parmet, *JFK* (1983); Thomas G. Paterson, ed., *Kennedy's Quest for Victory* (1989); Gerald T. Rice, *The Bold Experiment: JFK's Peace Corps* (1985); Arthur M. Schlesinger, Jr., *Robert Kennedy and His Times* (1978); Arthur M. Schlesinger, Jr., *A Thousand Days* (1965); Thomas J. Schoenbaum, *Waging Peace and War* (1988); Richard Walton, *Cold War and Counterrevolution* (1972).

Latin America and Cuba

Graham Allison, *Essence of Decision: Explaining the Cuban Missile Crisis* (1971); Samuel Baily, *The United States and the Development of South America, 1945–1975* (1977); Cole Blasier, *Hovering Giant* (1974); Herbert Dinerstein, *The Making of a Missile Crisis* (1976); Jorge I. Domínguez, *To Make a World Safe for Revolution: Cuba's Foreign Policy* (1989); Trumbull Higgins, *The Perfect Failure* (1987) (on the Bay of Pigs invasion); Walter LaFeber, *Inevitable Revolutions* (1983) (on Central America); Walter LaFeber, *The Panama Canal* (1979); Morris Morley, *Imperial State and Revolution* (1987) (on Cuba); Louis A. Pérez, *Cuba* (1988); Stephen G. Rabe, *The Road to OPEC: United States Relations with Venezuela* (1982); Tad Szulc, *Fidel* (1986); Peter Wyden, *Bay of Pigs* (1979).

Middle East

Stephen Green, *Living by the Sword: America and Israel in the Middle East, 1968–87* (1988); George Lenczowski, *The Middle East in World Affairs,* 4th ed. (1980); William B. Quandt, *Decade of Decision: American Policy Toward the Arab-Israeli Conflict, 1967–1976* (1977); Bernard Reich, *Quest for Peace* (1977) (on Israel); Barry Rubin, *Paved with Good Intentions* (1980) (on Iran); Steven L. Spiegel, *The Other Arab-Israeli Conflict* (1985); Robert W. Stookey, *America and the Arab States* (1975).

The Vietnam War and Southeast Asia

Loren Baritz, *Backfire* (1985); Larry Berman, *Planning a Tragedy* (1982); Larry Berman, *Lyndon Johnson's War* (1989); William C. Berman, *William Fulbright and the Vietnam War* (1988); Melanie Billings-Yun, *Decision Against War: Eisenhower and Dien Bien Phu, 1954* (1988); Jeffrey J.

Clarke, *United States Army in Vietnam* (1989); Frances Fitz-Gerald, *Fire in the Lake* (1972); Lloyd C. Gardner, *Approaching Vietnam: From World War II Through Dienbienphu* (1988); Leslie H. Gelb and Richard K. Betts, *The Irony of Vietnam* (1979); William C. Gibbons, *The U.S. Government and the Vietnam War (1986–87)*; Daniel C. Hallin, *The "Uncensored War"* (1986); James P. Harrison, *The Endless War* (1989); George C. Herring, *America's Longest War*, 2nd ed. (1986); Gary Hess, *The United States' Emergence as a Southeast Asian Power* (1987); Arnold R. Isaacs, *Without Honor: Defeat in Vietnam and Cambodia* (1983); George McT. Kahin, *Intervention* (1986); Stanley Karnow, *Vietnam* (1983); Gabriel Kolko, *Anatomy of a War* (1986); Guenter Lewy, *America in Vietnam* (1978); Andrew Rotter, *The Path to Vietnam* (1987); Herbert Y. Schandler, *The Unmaking of a President: Lyndon Johnson and Vietnam* (1977); William Shawcross, *Sideshow* (1979) (on Cambodia); Ronald H. Spector, *United States Army in Vietnam* (1983); Nancy Zaroulis and Gerald Sullivan, *Who Spoke Up? American Protest Against the War in Vietnam, 1963–1975* (1984).

The Vietnam Legacy

Walter H. Capps, *The Unfinished War* (1982); Michael Charlton and Anthony Moncrieff, eds., *Many Reasons Why* (1978); John Hellman, *American Myth and the Legacy of Vietnam* (1986); Herbert Hendin and Ann P. Haas, *Wounds of War: The Psychological Aftermath of Combat in Vietnam* (1984); Myra MacPherson, *Long Time Passing: Vietnam and the Haunted Generation* (1984); Robert E. Osgood, *Limited War Revisited* (1979); Norman Podhoretz, *Why We Were in Vietnam* (1982); Earl C. Ravenal, *Never Again* (1978); Harrison E. Salisbury, ed., *Vietnam Reconsidered* (1984); Harry G. Summers, Jr., *On Strategy* (1982); W. Scott Thompson and Donaldson D. Frizzill, eds., *The Lessons of Vietnam* (1977).

Nixon, Kissinger, and Détente

Stephen Ambrose, *Nixon* (1987); Richard J. Barnet, *The Giants: Russia and America* (1977); Seymour M. Hersh, *The Price of Power* (1983); Stanley Hoffmann, *Primacy or World Order* (1978); Roger Morris, *Uncertain Greatness* (1977); Andrew J. Pierre, *The Global Politics of Arms Sales* (1982); Franz Schurmann, *The Foreign Politics of Richard Nixon* (1987); Richard Stevenson, *The Rise and Fall of Détente* (1985); John Stoessinger, *Henry Kissinger* (1976); Tad Szulc, *The Illusion of Peace* (1978).

The CIA and Counterinsurgency

Philip Agee, *Inside the Company* (1975); Douglas S. Blaufarb, *The Counterinsurgency Era* (1977); Ray Cline, *Secrets, Spies, and Scholars* (1976); Mark Lowenthal, *U.S. Intelligence* (1984); Victor Marchetti and John D. Marks, *The CIA and the Cult of Intelligence* (1974); Thomas Powers, *The Man Who Kept the Secrets* (1979); John Prados, *Presidents' Secret Wars* (1986); John Ranelagh, *The Agency* (1986); Harry H. Ransom, *The Intelligence Establishment* (1970); John Stockwell, *In Search of Enemies* (1978).

Nuclear Arms Race and SALT

Desmond Ball, *Politics and Force Levels: The Strategic Missile Program of the Kennedy Administration* (1980); John Newhouse, *Cold Dawn: The Story of SALT* (1973); Samuel B. Payne, Jr., *The Soviet Union and SALT* (1980); David N. Schwartz, *NATO's Nuclear Dilemmas* (1983); Glenn T. Seaborg, *Kennedy, Khrushchev, and the Test Ban* (1981); Stanford Arms Control Group, *International Arms Control,* 2nd ed. (1984). (See also works listed in Chapter 29 under "Nuclear Arms Race.")

The World Economy and "North-South" Issues

Richard J. Barnet, *The Lean Years* (1980); Richard J. Barnet and Ronald Müller, *Global Reach: The Power of the Multinational Corporations* (1974); David P. Calleo, *The Imperious Economy* (1982); Alfred E. Eckes, *The U.S. and Global Struggle for Minerals* (1979); Charles A. Jones, *The North-South Dialogue* (1983); Stephen D. Krasner, *Defending the National Interest* (1978); Robert K. Olson, *U.S. Foreign Policy and the New International Economic Order* (1981); William Paddock and Paul Paddock, *Time of Famines* (1976); Robert A. Pastor, *Congress and the Politics of U.S. Foreign Economic Policy, 1929–1976* (1980); Joan E. Spero, *The Politics of International Economic Relations,* 2nd ed. (1981); Herman Van Der Wee, *The Search for Prosperity: The World Economy, 1945–1980* (1986).

The first dreadful flash from Dallas clattered over newsroom Tele-type machines across the country at 1:34 P.M., Eastern Standard Time. Carried immediately over radio and television, the news was soon on the streets. People still remember precisely where they were and what they were doing when they heard that President John F. Kennedy had been shot and killed. For them, time stopped at that moment in what psychologists called flashbulb memory, the freeze-framing of an exceptionally emotional event down to the most incidental detail. For an earlier American generation, the indelible memory was of December 7, 1941, when radio reports of the Japanese attack at Pearl Harbor had stunned the nation into silence. But now, it was November 22, 1963, the day John Kennedy's promise was snuffed out.

32

REFORM AND CONFLICT: A TURBULENT ERA IN AMERICA, 1961–1973

In New York City that afternoon, a man braked his car to a halt in the middle of a busy intersection and ran over to a sidewalk luncheonette. "Is it true?" he asked. Without looking up, the counterman replied, "Yes, he's dead." The man returned to his car and slumped behind the wheel, oblivious to the impatient honking around him. Ken Kesey's play *One Flew over the Cuckoo's Nest* had just opened on Broadway, and Kesey and a couple of friends were driving triumphantly back to the West Coast. They were in Pennsylvania when they heard the news, and as "we stopped in at service stations and Howard Johnson's and little fast-food places across the United States, a really profound thing happened to us. We felt like we were seeing the real soul of America with its shirt torn open in grief."

For four days in late November 1963, Americans wept, prayed, and stared at their television sets, numbed by the unbelievable. Throughout the afternoon and night before the funeral, 250,000 people trod silently past the coffin in the Capitol Rotunda. Jacqueline Kennedy and her daughter, Caroline, paid a last visit to kneel and kiss the coffin. On the fourth day, a million people lined the streets of Washington and millions more watched on television as the president's body was borne by horse-drawn caisson to Arlington Cemetery. Throughout the country, people mourned.

Selma, 1965. *Dan Budnik/Woodfin Camp & Associated.*

Some of America's postwar confidence was riding on the caisson that carried Kennedy's body to the grave. "In retrospect," the journalist Godfrey Hodgson has written, "people looked back to Friday, November 22, 1963, as the end of a time of hope, the beginning of a time of troubles." What was ironic about America's outpouring of grief was that the Kennedy administration had failed in many of its goals. In the final months of his presidency Kennedy had been criticized for being ineffectual in domestic affairs and reckless in foreign affairs. But John Kennedy's assassination was a national tragedy. In their grief Americans remembered how handsome and eloquent he had been and how he had inspired their hopes for peace, prosperity, and social justice.

In the early 1960s, hope had run especially high among the nation's poor. Kennedy's presidency coincided with and was spurred by the modern African-American civil rights movement, and his call for a New Frontier had inspired liberal Democrats, idealists, and brave young activists to work to eliminate poverty, segregation, and voting rights abuses. Americans also supported Kennedy's desire to court the Third World and prevail in the Cold War. Lyndon B. Johnson, Kennedy's successor in the White House, presided over the Great Society, and Congress responded to his urgings with a flood of legislation. The 1960s saw more economic, political, and social reform than any period since the New Deal. But even during these years of liberal triumphs, anger occasionally flared into violence. Beginning with the assassination in 1963, ten years of events ensued—including bloody race riots, the murders of other political and civil rights leaders, and the war in Vietnam—that shattered the Kennedy and Johnson optimism.

In the cities, many blacks were angry that they still lived in poverty and segregation despite the civil rights movement and the passage of landmark civil rights laws. Their discontent exploded during the 1960s' "long hot summers." In July 1967, for example, twenty-six people were killed in Newark, New Jersey, in warfare between blacks, the police, and army troops. This event was followed a week later by the Detroit race riot, which led to the deaths of forty-three persons. The next year the National Advisory Commission on Civil Disorders, chaired by Governor Otto Kerner of Illinois, released its report identifying white racism as the cause of the race riots. "The nation is rapidly moving toward two increasingly separate Americas . . . a white society principally located in suburbs . . . and a Negro society largely concentrated within large central cities."

This social turbulence along with the growing movement opposing the Vietnam War brought down the presidency of Lyndon Johnson and gave rise to Black Power, the radical politics of the New Left, and a revived women's movement, not to mention the "hippie" counterculture. The New Left and the counterculture found their first homes in the early 1960s in Ann Arbor, Berkeley, and other university towns. But during the 1960s and early 1970s, practically every college community in the country witnessed antiwar protests and the appearance of alternative institutions based on drugs, rock music, and freely expressed sexuality. Lyndon Johnson's departure from office did not produce calm. And Richard Nixon, who was elected president in 1968, polarized the nation still further. Nixon's two immediate predecessors had been destroyed in office: both Dallas and Vietnam evoked those tragedies. A third place, Watergate, was to signify Richard Nixon's downfall. Battered by these events, by 1973 many Americans had ceased to believe in the American dream.

The Civil Rights Movement and Kennedy's New Frontier

He was, as Norman Mailer wrote of President John F. Kennedy, "our leading man." The handsome, vigorous new chief executive was young, the first president born in the twentieth century. Perceived by the public as an intellectual, he had a genuinely inquiring mind, and as a patron of the arts, he brought wit and sophistication to the White House. Kennedy was born to wealth and politics. His Irish-American grandfather had been mayor of Boston; his millionaire father, Joseph P. Kennedy, had served as ambassador to Great Britain. In 1946 the young Kennedy, home from the Second World War a hero, continued the family tradition by campaigning in Boston for a seat in the House of Representatives. He won easily.

1960	Kennedy elected president
1961	Freedom Rides
	Establishment of the first President's Commission on the Status of Women
1962	John Glenn orbits the globe
	SDS's Port Huron Statement
	Baker v. *Carr*
1963	Friedan, *The Feminine Mystique*
	March on Washington
	Birmingham, Alabama, Baptist church bombed
	Kennedy assassinated; Johnson assumes the presidency
1964	Economic Opportunity Act
	Civil Rights Act of 1964
	First of the "long hot summers"
	Free Speech Movement
	Johnson elected president
1965	Malcolm X assassinated
	Voting Rights Act of 1965
	Medicare
	Elementary and Secondary Education Act
	Watts race riot
1966	National Organization for Women (NOW) established
	Miranda v. *Arizona*
1967	Race riots in Newark, Detroit, and other cities
1968	U.S.S. *Pueblo* captured by North Korea
	Tet offensive
	Martin Luther King, Jr., assassinated
	Race riots in 168 cities and towns
	Civil Rights Act of 1968
	Antiwar protests escalate
	Robert F. Kennedy assassinated
	Violence at Democratic convention
	Nixon elected president
1969	Stonewall riot
	Apollo 11 moon landing
	Woodstock festival
	Moratorium Day
1970	U.S. invades Cambodia
	Students killed at Kent State University and Jackson State University
1971	*Pentagon Papers*
	Twenty-sixth Amendment ratified
	Attica prison revolt
	Swann v. *Charlotte-Mecklenberg*
1972	Nixon visits China and Russia
	Equal Rights Amendment (ERA) approved by Congress
	George Wallace shot
	Break-in at Watergate
	Revenue sharing adopted
	Nixon re-elected
1973	*Roe* v. *Wade*

As a Democratic politician, Kennedy inherited the New Deal commitment to America's welfare system. He generally cast liberal votes in line with the prolabor sentiments of his low-income, blue-collar constituents. But on issues of no direct concern to his district—flood control, farm price supports, the Tennessee Valley Authority—he cast his votes with some of the most conservative members of Congress. Kennedy avoided controversial issues such as civil rights and the censure of Joseph McCarthy. Although he won a Pulitzer Prize for a book *Profiles in Courage* (1956), a study of politicians who had acted on principle, some critics complained that he himself showed too much profile and not enough courage. And he shaded the truth when he claimed sole authorship of this book,

Caroline Kennedy kisses her father as her mother watches. President John F. Kennedy (1917–1963) and his wife, Jacqueline, symbolized youthful energy and idealism. Kennedy's New Frontier gave hope to people of color and the poor. *National Archives.*

which had been largely written by others. Kennedy nevertheless enjoyed an enthusiastic following, especially after his landslide re-election to the Senate in 1958.

Although he was elected president in 1960 by a razor-slim margin, Kennedy's vitality and style captured the imagination of many Americans. In a departure from the Eisenhower administration's staid, conservative image, the new president surrounded himself with young men of intellectual verve who proclaimed that they had fresh ideas for invigorating the nation. The writer David Halberstam called these men "the best and the brightest." (Kennedy appointed only one woman to a significant position; see page 955.) Secretary of Defense Robert McNamara, age forty-four, had been an assistant professor at Harvard at twenty-four and later the whiz-kid president of the Ford Motor Company. Kennedy's special assistant for national security affairs, McGeorge Bundy, age forty-one, had become a dean at Harvard at thirty-four with only a bachelor's degree. Kennedy himself was only forty-

> **"The Best and the Brightest"**

three, and his brother Robert, the attorney general, was thirty-five.

Kennedy's program, the New Frontier, was immensely ambitious and promised more than Kennedy could deliver: an end to racial discrimination, federal aid to farmers and to education, medical care for the elderly, and government action to halt the recession the country was suffering. Long-time members of Congress saw him and his administration as publicity hungry. Some feared the president would seek federal aid to parochial schools. The result was the defeat of federal aid to education and of a Kennedy-sponsored boost in the minimum wage. By August 1961, eight months into his first year, it was evident that Kennedy lacked the ability to move Congress, which was largely ruled by a conservative coalition of Republicans and southern Democrats.

Still struggling to work with these conservatives, the new president pursued civil rights with a lack of vigor. On the one hand, Kennedy established the President's Committee on Equal Employment Opportunity to eliminate racial discrimination in government hiring. But on the other hand, he waited until November 1962 before finally honoring a 1960 campaign pledge to issue an executive order forbidding segregation in federally subsidized housing. Meanwhile he appointed five die-hard segregationists to the federal bench in the Deep South. Although the struggle for black equality was the most important domestic issue of the time, Kennedy's performance disheartened civil rights advocates.

Despite the White House's lack of commitment, black civil rights activists continued their struggle through the tactic of nonviolent civil disobedience. Volunteers organized by the Southern Christian Leadership Conference (SCLC), headed by Martin Luther King, Jr., deliberately violated segregation laws by sitting in at white-only lunch counters, libraries, and bus stations in parts of the South. When arrested they went to jail as an act of conscience. The Congress of Racial Equality (CORE) initiated the Freedom Rides. In May 1961, the "Freedom Riders," an integrated group of thirteen persons, boarded buses and braved attacks by southern white mobs for daring to desegregate interstate transportation. Meanwhile, black students in the South were joining the Student Non-Violent Coordinating Committee

> **Civil Rights Movement**

A historic moment for the civil rights movement was the March on Washington of August 28, 1963. One-quarter million black people and white people stood together for racial equality. Waving to friends, the Reverend Martin Luther King, Jr., is about to begin delivering his "I Have a Dream" speech. *Francis Miller,* Life *Magazine © 1963 Time, Inc.*

(SNCC). More than any other volunteers, it was these field workers who walked the dusty back roads of Mississippi and Georgia, encouraging blacks to resist segregation and register to vote. Some SNCC volunteers were white, but most were black and many were from low-income families. These volunteers understood from experience how racism, powerlessness, and poverty intersected in the lives of African-Americans.

As the civil rights movement gained momentum, President Kennedy gradually made a commitment to first-class citizenship for blacks. In September 1962 he ordered United States marshals to protect and assist James Meredith, the first black student to attend the University of Mississippi. Under court order the following spring, federal officials ignored the defiant governor of Alabama, George C. Wallace, and forced desegregation of the University of Alabama. In June 1963 Kennedy finally requested legislation to outlaw segregation in public accommodations. When more than 250,000 people, black and white, gathered at the Lincoln Memorial for a March on Washington that August, they did so with

the knowledge that President Kennedy was at last on their side. The marchers also heard the civil rights movement's inspirational leader, Martin Luther King, Jr., speak. "I have a dream," he told the crowd, "that my four little children will one day live in a nation where they will not be judged by the color of their skin but by the content of their character."

Meanwhile, television news programs brought civil rights struggles into Americans' homes. The story was sometimes grisly. In 1963 Medgar Evers, director of the NAACP in Mississippi, was murdered in his own driveway. That same year police under the command of Sheriff "Bull" Connor of Birmingham, Alabama, attacked nonviolent civil rights demonstrators, including many children, with snarling dogs, fire hoses, and cattle prods. Then, while Kennedy's public accommodations bill was being held up by a Senate filibuster, two horrifying events helped to convince reluctant politicians that action on civil rights was long overdue. In September white terrorists exploded a bomb during Sunday-morning services at Birmingham's Sixteenth Street Baptist Church. Sunday school was in session, and four black girls were killed. A little more than two months later, on November 22, 1963, John Kennedy was assassinated in Dallas. If ever the civil rights movement had the moral force of most of the American people behind it, it was at this time of national tragedy and repugnance over violence.

Kennedy's murder still baffles many Americans. Was the accused assassin, Lee Harvey Oswald, acting alone or as part of a conspiracy? Was he the only gunman, or were there more? What was his motive? Whatever the answers, Kennedy's death traumatized the entire nation. Then two days later, in full view of millions of TV viewers, Oswald himself was shot dead by Jack Ruby, a nightclub owner and small-time Mafia figure. The same question was asked: what was Ruby's motive?

> **Assassination of President Kennedy**

Historians have wondered what John Kennedy would have accomplished had he lived. Although his legislative achievements were meager, he inspired idealism in Americans. When Kennedy said in his inaugural address, "Ask not what your country can do for you. Ask what you can do for your country," tens of thousands of Americans volunteered to spend two years of their lives in the Peace Corps. "We had such faith in what Kennedy was doing," recalled one volunteer, "and we all wanted to be a part of it." The new president created a sense of national purpose through his vigorous support of the space program. Americans beamed when on February 20, 1962, Marine Lieutenant Colonel John Glenn orbited the globe in a space capsule, and they embraced Kennedy's challenge to put a man on the moon by the end of the decade.

In recent years, however, some writers have described not Kennedy's idealism but his recklessness in world events, such as authorizing CIA assassination attempts on the life of Cuba's Premier Fidel Castro. It is clear, however, that Kennedy had begun to grow as president during his last few months in office. He made a moving appeal for racial equality, and he called for reductions in Cold War tensions. Then there was the Kennedy aura. James Reston of the *New York Times* called Kennedy "a story-book President," handsome, graceful, "with poetry on his tongue and a radiant young woman at his side." Jacqueline Kennedy said

> **Kennedy in Retrospect**

that for her the Kennedy era evoked the image of Camelot. Partly because of this aura, John Kennedy came to have a higher reputation in death than he enjoyed in life. And in a bizarre way he accomplished more in death than in life. In the post-assassination atmosphere of grief and remorse, Lyndon Johnson pushed through Congress practically the entire New Frontier agenda. Johnson had done, Walter Lippmann wrote, "what President Kennedy could not have done had he lived."

Johnson and the Great Society

The new president, Lyndon Johnson, was a big man and a passionate one. The Senate majority leader from 1954 to 1960, he knew how to manipulate people and power to achieve his ends. "This ponderous . . . Texan knows more about the sources of power in the political world of Washington than any President in this century," wrote columnists Rowland Evans and Robert Novak. "He can be gentle and solicitous as a nurse, but as ruthless and deceptive as a riverboat gambler." In the aftermath of the assassination, Johnson determined to unite the country behind the unfulfilled legislative program of the martyred president. But more than that, he wanted to realize Roosevelt's and Truman's unmet goals. He called his new program the Great Society.

Johnson made civil rights his top legislative priority. "No memorial oration or eulogy," he told a joint session of Congress five days after the assassination, "could more eloquently honor President Kennedy's memory than the earliest passage of the civil rights bill." It was fortunate for the civil rights movement that Johnson, a southerner, had become president. According to Clarence Mitchell, chief lobbyist for the NAACP, Johnson "made a greater contribution to giving a dignified and hopeful status to Negroes in the United States than any other president, including Lincoln, Roosevelt and Kennedy." Within months Johnson had signed into law the Civil Rights Act of 1964, which outlawed discrimination not only in public accommodations but also in employment on

> **Civil Rights Act of 1964**

Surrounded by an illustrious group of civil rights leaders, and members of Congress, President Lyndon B. Johnson signs the Civil Rights Act of 1964. Standing behind the president is the Reverend Martin Luther King, Jr. *Cecil Stoughton, Lyndon Baines Johnson Library.*

the basis of race, color, religion, sex, or national origin. An Equal Employment Opportunity Commission was established the same year to investigate and judge complaints of job discrimination. The act also authorized the government to withhold funds from public agencies that discriminated on the basis of race, and it gave the attorney general powers to guarantee voting rights and end school segregation.

Johnson enunciated another priority in January 1964, in his first State of the Union address: "The administration today, here and now, declares unconditional war on poverty." Eight months later, he signed into law the Economic Opportunity Act of 1964, which allocated almost $1 billion to fight poverty. The act, which became the opening salvo in Johnson's War on Poverty, promised to eliminate poverty "by opening to everyone the opportunity to live in decency and dignity."

In the year following Kennedy's death, Johnson sought to govern by consensus, appealing to the shared values and aspirations of the majority of the

Election of 1964

nation. Judging by his lopsided victory over his Republican opponent in 1964, Senator Barry Goldwater of Arizona, he succeeded. Johnson garnered 61 percent of the popular vote and the electoral votes of all but six states. Goldwater's narrowness certainly enhanced Johnson's appeal. The Republican candidate alienated voters by suggesting that Social Security be voluntary and the Tennessee Valley Authority be abolished, and he appeared reckless and provocative when he advocated using nuclear weapons in Vietnam. Republican leaders from the liberal eastern wing of the party either refused to support Goldwater or gave him half-hearted endorsements. He seemed to have solid support in only a few states in the Southwest and South.

Riding on Johnson's coattails, the Democrats won staggering majorities in both the House (295 to 140) and the Senate (68 to 32). Johnson knew that the moment for further reform had arrived. "Hurry, boys, hurry," he told his staff just after the election.

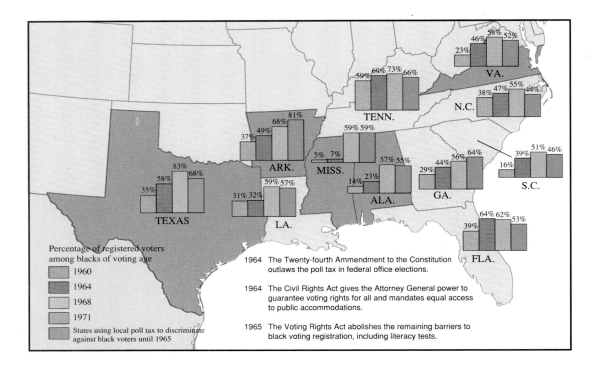

Black Voting Rights, 1960–1971 *Source: Harold W. Stanley,* Voter Mobilization and the Politics of Race: The South and Universal Suffrage, 1952–1984 *(Praeger Publishers, New York, a division of Greenwood Press, Inc., 1987), p. 97. Copyright © 1987 by Harold W. Stanley. Used with permission.*

"Get that legislation up to the Hill and out. Eighteen months from now ol' Landslide Lyndon will be Lame-Duck Lyndon." Congress responded in 1965 and 1966 with the most sweeping reform legislation since 1935. Skillfully guided by Johnson, the liberal Democratic majorities passed a remarkable 69 percent of the president's legislative proposals. The powerful conservative coalition of Republicans and southern Democrats, which had had its way on 74 percent of House roll-call votes in 1961 and 63 percent in 1963, was victorious on only 25 percent of the votes in 1965.

Three bills enacted in 1965 were legislative milestones. The Medicare program insured the elderly against medical and hospital bills. The Elementary and Secondary Education Act became the first general program of federal aid to education. The Voting Rights Act of 1965 empowered the attorney general to supervise voter registration in areas where fewer than half the minority residents of voting age were registered (see map). In 1960, only 29 percent of the South's black population was regis-

tered to vote; when Johnson left office in 1969, the proportion was approaching two-thirds. Even in the most resistant states, that trend continued. Only 6.7 percent of Mississippi's black citizens were registered to vote in 1964; in 1968 the figure was 59.4 percent.

Other accomplishments during Johnson's presidency included establishment of the Department of Housing and Urban Development and the National Endowments for the Arts and Humanities; water and air quality improvement acts; liberalization of immigration laws; and appropriations for the most ambitious federal housing program since 1949, including rent supplements to low-income families. In 1968, Johnson signed his third civil rights act, banning racial and religious discrimination in the sale and rental of housing. Another provision of this legislation, known as the Indian Bill of Rights, extended those constitutional protections to reservation Indians living under tribal self-government.

Even more ambitious was Johnson's War on Poverty. Because the gross national product had increased, Johnson and his advisers reasoned that the

> **War on Poverty** government could expect a "fiscal dividend" of several billion dollars in additional tax revenues. They decided to spend the extra money to wipe out poverty through education and job training programs. Beginning with the $1 billion appropriation in 1964, the War on Poverty evolved in 1965 and 1966 to include the Job Corps, to provide marketable skills, work experience, remedial education, and counseling for young people; Project Head Start, to prepare low-income preschoolers for grade school; and Upward Bound, for high school students from low-income families who aspired to a college education. Other antipoverty programs were Legal Services for the Poor; Volunteers in Service to America (VISTA); and the Model Cities program, which directed federal funds toward upgrading employment, housing, education, and health in targeted neighborhoods.

The War on Poverty was a mixed success. It was politically volatile; its "community action programs" aroused the ire of power-hungry mayors by encouraging the "maximum feasible participation" of the poor in decision making. Furthermore, confusion abounded in the ambitious program. Not even R. Sargent Shriver, who as head of the Office of Economic Opportunity (OEO) administered the War on Poverty, could deny this. "It's like we . . . launched a half dozen rockets at once," he later conceded. Another serious criticism was that the War on Poverty did little to reduce rural poverty or to check the South-to-North migration that worsened already overwhelming northern urban problems. In a Brookings Institution study, James Sundquist noted that "when it comes to the solution of the poverty problem, a good many of the urban poverty thinkers have written off the rural areas and have concluded that the only way to deal with rural poverty is to let the people move and then handle them in the cities." Another large group that remained poor despite the government's antipoverty efforts included the women and children living in female-headed families; they constituted 40 percent of the poor in the United States. The booming economy from 1963 to 1969 lifted 12 million people in male-headed families out of poverty. Left stranded in poverty were 11 million in families headed by women, the same number as in 1963 (see pages 956–957).

The War on Poverty lifted many people out of suffering. But this Harlem woman, photographed in 1966, has a bleak future, as do her children. She has dignity and strength but realizes that the odds are very high against her children ever escaping poverty themselves. *John Launois/Black Star.*

Still, the War on Poverty, in tandem with a rising gross national product, substantially alleviated hunger and suffering in the United States. For one

> **Successes in Reducing Poverty** thing, the War on Poverty directly attacked the debilitating housing, health, and nutritional conditions from which the poor suffered. For another, the tax cut and fresh infusions of federal funds for defense fueled the economy, and beginning in the mid-1960s, the social welfare budget soared. Between 1965 and 1970, federal spending for Social Security, health, welfare, and education more than doubled. During the same years, the GNP leaped from $685 billion to $977 billion. Not only did some of this prosperity trickle down to the poor, but also—and more important—millions of new jobs were created. The result was a startling reduction in the number of

poor people, from 25 percent of the population in 1962 to 11 percent in 1973. Particularly fortunate were the elderly, who benefited from large increases in Social Security benefits; poverty among the elderly dropped from about 40 percent in 1960 to 16 percent in 1974.

Despite the War on Poverty's successes, the period of liberal ascendancy it represented was short-lived; its legislative achievements occurred from 1964 to 1966. Disillusioned with America's deepening involvement in Vietnam (see Chapter 31), many of Johnson's allies began to reject both him and his liberal consensus. But one branch of government continued the liberal tradition—the Supreme Court.

The Warren Court

In the volatile 1960s, the Supreme Court was disposed by political sentiment and a belief in judicial activism to play a major role in the resurgence of liberalism. Its liberal majority included Chief Justice Earl Warren. After the 1954 and 1955 school desegregation cases (see page 860), the Warren Court did not disturb the political waters for the remainder of the 1950s. The next decade was to be markedly different. According to one constitutional historian, in the 1960s the United States "changed irrevocably," and the Warren Court was "midwife to that change—if not its sire."

In 1962 the Court began handing down a series of liberal decisions. In *Baker* v. *Carr* (1962) and subsequent rulings, it declared that the principle of "one person, one vote" must prevail at both state and national levels. This decision required the reapportionment of state legislatures so that each representative would serve the same number of constituents. Prior to this decision, some legislators from sparsely settled rural areas represented only half as many people as their counterparts from populous urban areas. In 1962 and 1963, the Court also outlawed required prayers and Bible readings in public schools, explaining that such practices placed an "indirect coercive pressure upon religious minorities." Some religious groups denounced these decisions, and a few communities, feeling they were losing their freedoms, announced their refusal to comply.

The Court also attacked the constitutional basis of McCarthyism, ruling in 1965 that a person need not register with the government as a member of a subversive organization, for to do so would violate constitutional safeguards against self-incrimination. It also ruled on birth control, holding in *Griswold* v. *Connecticut* (1965) that a state law prohibiting the use of contraceptives by married persons violated "a marital right of privacy" and was unconstitutional. The Court upheld the Civil Rights Act of 1964 and the Voting Rights Act of 1965. In *Jones* v. *Mayer* (1968) it decided that private discrimination in the rental or sale of housing was prohibited by the Civil Rights Act of 1866. In ruling the 1866 act constitutional under the Thirteenth Amendment, the Court opened new avenues for the pursuit of legal battles for equal rights. With its decisions on prayer and contraception, the Court had deeply affected people's personal lives. And in other rulings that particularly upset conservatives, the Court decreed that books, magazines, and films could not be banned as obscene unless they were "found to be utterly without redeeming social value."

> **Civil Rights Rulings**

Perhaps most controversial was the Court's transformation of the criminal justice system. Beginning with *Gideon* v. *Wainwright* (1963), the Court ruled that a poor person charged with a felony had the right to a state-appointed lawyer. In *Escobedo* v. *Illinois* (1964), it decreed that the accused had the right to counsel during interrogation and could remain silent. And in *Miranda* v. *Arizona* (1966), it added that police had to inform criminal suspects that they could see a lawyer and remain silent and that any statements they made could be used against them. Critics denounced the decisions as victories for criminals, and the John Birch Society, a right-wing organization, began a campaign to impeach Earl Warren.

Despite demands for Warren's removal, most constitutional historians judge him to have been perhaps the most influential chief justice in the nation's history. Whether or not one approved of the Warren Court, which ended with his retirement in 1969, there was no denying its impact on the American people. Bernard Schwartz, constitutional law professor at New York University, has made this appraisal: "In expanding civil liberties, broadening political freedom, extending the franchise, reinforcing freedoms of speech, assembly, and religion, limiting the power of the politicians in smoke-filled rooms, [and] defining the limits of police power, the Warren Court had no equal in American history."

Race Riots and the Movement Toward Black Power

Even as the civil rights movement registered legal and constitutional victories, some activists began to grumble that the federal government was not to be trusted. During the Mississippi Summer Project of 1964, hundreds of college-age volunteers from the North had joined SNCC and CORE field workers to establish "freedom schools" for black children. Many of these volunteers believed that the Federal Bureau of Investigation was hostile to the civil rights movement. They charged that FBI Director J. Edgar Hoover was a racist, and they were disturbed by rumors, later confirmed, that Hoover had wiretapped and bugged Martin Luther King, Jr.'s hotel rooms and planted allegations in the newspapers about his sexual improprieties. Why, activists asked themselves, had Johnson allowed Hoover to remain in office?

Indeed, some FBI informants had not only joined the Ku Klux Klan; they had reportedly become leaders of the terrorist group. One of them had organized several atrocities, including the bombing of Birmingham's Sixteenth Street Baptist Church in 1963. Small wonder that during the summer of 1964 there was an upsurge in racist violence in the South, particularly in Mississippi. White vigilantes bombed and burned two dozen black churches there, and three civil rights workers were murdered in Philadelphia, Mississippi, by a group that included sheriff's deputies.

Violent Attacks on Civil Rights Workers

Amid the terror, SNCC volunteers joined with black Mississippians to establish the Mississippi Freedom Democratic party (MFDP) and sent an opposition delegation to the Democratic national convention. Arguing that the MFDP supported civil rights while the state's regular Democratic organization was vehemently segregationist, the MFDP demanded that the convention honor its credentials. Fannie Lou Hamer, a leader of the MFDP, told the convention of her efforts to vote. "I was beaten until I was exhausted. I began to scream, and one white man . . . began to beat me on the head. . . . All of this on account we wanted to register, to become first class citizens." If the MFDP were not seated, Hamer said, "I question America." But President Johnson, fearful of alienating southern white politicians, resisted efforts to seat the delegation, thereby throwing into question the Democratic commitment to racial equality.

The year 1964 also brought the first of the "long hot summers" of race riots in northern cities. In Harlem and Rochester, New York, and in several New Jersey cities, black anger exploded. Brutal actions by white police officers sparked the riots. Blacks resented the unnecessary force that police sometimes used to keep the residents "in their place." To James Baldwin, the black writer, the white officers patrolling black neighborhoods represented "the force of the white world."

Explosion of Black Anger

Whites wondered why blacks were venting their frustration in violence at a time when real progress was being made in the civil rights struggle. Part of the reason was that the movement had been largely southern in focus, geared to abolishing Jim Crow and black disfranchisement. In the North blacks could vote, but many were still living in deep poverty. The black median income was little more than half that of whites: for every dollar the white worker took home in 1964, the black worker earned 54 cents. Black unemployment in the mid-1960s was twice that of whites, and for black males between eighteen and twenty-five it was five times as high. Many black families, particularly those headed solely by women, lived in perpetual poverty, and their numbers were increasing rapidly. One reason was that Aid to Families with Dependent Children (AFDC)—part of the 1935 Social Security Act that had been expanded in 1950 to include payments to the mothers as well as their dependent children—would provide payments only if there were no able-bodied man in the household. As a result, some unemployed men left home rather than make their families ineligible for AFDC. But more important, the payments themselves were inadequate to cover a family's rent, utility bills, and household expenses, let alone its food.

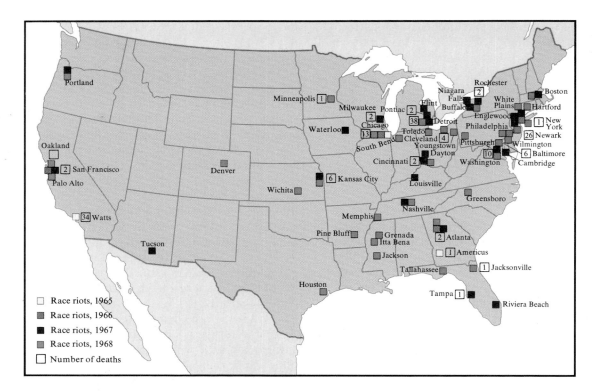

Race Riots, 1965–1968

On the basis of food budgets in 1970, it was estimated that over 60 percent of America's black children were being raised in poverty.

As northern blacks learned of the economic and civil rights gains of the 1960s, they wondered when they would benefit from the Great Society. Although blacks made up a smaller percentage of the overall population in the North than in the South, they tended to be concentrated in the inner cities. When blacks looked around the ghettos in which they lived, they knew their circumstances were deteriorating. Their neighborhoods were more segregated than ever, for whites had responded to the black migration from the South by fleeing to the suburbs. And as inner-city neighborhoods became all black, so did the neighborhood schools. As one writer commented, "It doesn't cost anything to move a few feet along a hamburger counter to make room for a Negro. But the cost—economic, social, psychological—of abolishing forever a Negro ghetto of half a million souls is only now becoming apparent."

If 1964 was fiery and violent, 1965 was even more so. In August, blacks gutted the Los Angeles neigh-

borhood of Watts; thirty-four people were killed (see map). Unlike the race riots of 1919 and 1943, white mobs did not provoke the violence; instead, blacks exploded in anger over their joblessness and lack of opportunity, looting white-owned stores, setting fires, and throwing rocks. "Get Whitey!" they screamed. "Burn, Baby, Burn!" "What white Americans have never fully understood," stated the Kerner Commission in its report several years later, "but what the Negro can never forget—is that white society is deeply implicated in the ghetto. White institutions created it, white institutions maintain it, and white society condones it."

> **Watts Race Riot**

Other cities exploded in riots between 1966 and 1968. It was obvious that many blacks, especially in the North, had begun to question whether the non-violent civil rights movement had ever addressed their needs. In 1963 Martin Luther King, Jr., had appealed to whites' humanitarian instincts in his "I have a dream" speech. But another voice was beginning to be heard, one that urged blacks to seize their freedom "by any means necessary." It was the

In 1965, unrest ran high in the sprawling Watts district of Los Angeles. The black residents openly despised the Los Angeles police whom they accused of brutality. The Watts riot erupted on the hot night of August 11, precipitated by the arrest of a drunk driver. While firemen bring water to this burning store, looters enter another store across the street. *Co Rentmeester,* Life *Magazine © 1965 Time, Inc.*

voice of Malcolm X, a one-time pimp and street hustler who, while in prison, had converted to the Nation of Islam religion, commonly known as the Black Muslims.

The Black Muslims, a small sect that espoused black pride along with separatism from white society, condemned the "white devil" as the chief source of evil in the world. They **Malcolm X** attempted to dissociate themselves from white society and exhorted blacks to lead sober lives and practice thrift. Unlike Martin Luther King, Jr., they advocated violence in self-defense. By the early 1960s Malcolm X had become their chief spokesperson, and his advice was straightforward: "If someone puts a hand on you, send him to the cemetery."

Malcolm X was murdered in a hail of bullets in February 1965; his assassins were Black Muslims who believed he had betrayed their cause. It was true that he had modified some of his ideas just before his death. He had met whites who were not devils, he said, and he had expressed cautious support for the nonviolent civil rights movement. Still, for both blacks and whites, Malcolm X symbolized black defiance and self-respect. A powerful figure in life, in death he would become even more of a hero to increasing numbers of black nationalists and proponents of Black Power.

Although Martin Luther King, Jr., continued to be the most admired leader of the civil rights movement, many younger blacks began to question not only his tactic of nonviolence but **Black** his dream of racial integration. In **Power** 1966 Stokely Carmichael, chairman of SNCC, called on blacks to assert Black Power. Carmichael believed that in order to be truly free from white oppression, blacks had to control their own institutions—businesses, politics, schools. They had to elect black candidates and teach black students in black schools. Soon organizations that had been committed to racial integration and nonviolence began to embrace Black Power. SNCC and CORE purged white members and repudiated integration, arguing that black people needed power, not white friendship.

The wellspring of this new militance was black nationalism, the concept that black peoples everywhere in the world shared a unique history and cultural heritage that set them apart from whites. College students pressed for black studies programs, and blacks began to call themselves black or Afro-American rather than Negro. More than at any time since the 1920s, African-Americans saw themselves as a nation within a nation.

To white America, one of the most fearsome of the new black groups was the Black Panther Party. Armed and wearing leather jackets, Panther leaders dedicated themselves to destroying capitalism. What worried white parents was that some of their own children agreed with the Panthers. This vocal minority of the baby-boom generation set out to "change the system." They began by denouncing the major political parties, big business and big labor, middle-class affluence and the suburban lifestyle, even the American dream itself.

The New Left and the Counterculture

"I'm tired of reading history," a philosophy student at the University of California complained in a letter to a friend in early 1964. "I want to make it." By autumn of that year, Mario Savio would realize his ambition as the leader of the Free Speech Movement, and Berkeley would become a synonym for the campus unrest of the 1960s. After teaching in SNCC's Mississippi Summer Project, Savio and other students had returned to Berkeley suspecting that the same power structure that dominated blacks' lives also controlled the bureaucratic machinery of the university. "Last summer I went to Mississippi to join the struggle there for civil rights. This fall I am engaged in another phase of the same struggle, this time in Berkeley. . . . The same rights are at stake in both places," Savio wrote.

In many ways the University of California in 1964 was a model university, with a worldwide reputa-
tion for excellence. Its chancellor, the economist Clark Kerr, had written *The Uses of the University,* in which he likened the university to a big business. But that was what bothered some students. Berkeley, a "multiversity" with tens of thousands of students, had become hopelessly impersonal. "I am a student," rang one lament of the Free Speech Movement. "Do not fold, spindle, or mutilate."

▶ **Free Speech Movement**

The struggle at Berkeley began in September 1964, when the university administration banned civil rights and antiwar recruitment in Sproul Plaza, the students' traditional gathering place. Militant students defied Kerr's ban; the administration suspended them or had them arrested. On October 1 several thousand students surrounded a police car in which a militant was being held, immobilizing it for thirty-two hours. Then in December the Free Speech Movement seized and occupied the main administration building. The governor dispatched state police to Berkeley, and over eight hundred people were arrested. Angry students shut down classes for several days in protest. By the end of the decade, the activism born at Berkeley would spread to hundreds of other campuses.

Over two years before the confrontation in Berkeley, another group of students had met in Port Huron, Michigan, for a national meeting of Students for a Democratic Society (SDS). Like their leaders, Tom Hayden and Al Haber, most SDS members were white college students, the children of middle-class Americans. In their platform, the Port Huron Statement, they condemned racism, poverty amid plenty, and "the enclosing fact of the Cold War," symbolized by the hydrogen bomb. Above all, SDS called upon America to practice its democratic ideals, not just pay them lip service. SDS sought nothing less than the revitalization of democracy through the return of power to the people.

▶ **Students for a Democratic Society (SDS)**

Inspired by the Free Speech Movement and SDS, a minority of students joined the New Left. Although the people in the New Left were united in their hatred of racism and the Vietnam War, they were divided in other ways. Indeed, the New Left was not a single organization or even a single movement. Some people were Marxists, others

▶ **New Left**

black nationalists, anarchists, or pacifists. Some believed in pursuing social change through negotiation; others were revolutionaries who regarded compromise as impossible.

In the wake of the New Left appeared a phenomenon that observers called the counterculture. Revolutionary figures like Mao Zedong and Fidel Castro became campus idols, **Counter-cultural Revolution** "Mao caps" a cult uniform, and "Right on" an all-purpose greeting. Following the advice of Timothy Leary, the LSD prophet, to "Turn on, tune in, drop out," millions of students experimented with marijuana, amphetamines, and hallucinogenic drugs. Young people tended to believe that they lived in a new era unconnected to the past. High school students ranked history the "most irrelevant" in a list of twenty-one standard subjects.

But it was music more than anything else that reflected the new attitudes. In 1962, the year the founders of SDS gathered at Port Huron, four young musicians from Liverpool, England, recorded "Love Me Do." Long before the Beatles sang "you say you want a revolution," it was evident that their music had inspired one. Soon music was the chief vehicle for the countercultural assault on the status quo. Bob Dylan promised revolutionary answers "blowin' in the wind," and young people cheered Jimi Hendrix, who sang of life in a drug-induced "purple haze," and Janis Joplin, who brought African-American blues to white Americans. Unlike their 1950s counterparts, the rock superstars of the 1960s acknowledged their roots in black rhythm-and-blues. Joplin, who moved crowds with her version of "Ball and Chain," was quick to credit its composer, Big Mama Thornton. Rock festivals became cultural happenings, the most famous of which was Woodstock (1969), an upstate New York festival that attracted 400,000 people. The huge crowd endured several days of rain and mud together, without shelter and without violence. Some among them began to dream of a peaceful "Woodstock nation" based on love, drugs, and rock music.

While some youths sought alternative experiences through drugs and music, others tried to construct alternative ways of life. Among the most conspicuous were the hippies. In the Haight-Ashbury section of San Francisco, "flower children" created an urban subculture as distinctive as

Beginning in 1964 with the Beatles' sensational television appearance on the *Ed Sullivan Show*, Beatlemania swept the nation. In addition to top-selling records, the Beatles made movies that delighted critics and audiences alike. These buttons, each depicting one of the Fab Four, promote the feature-length animated cartoon, *The Yellow Submarine* (1968), for which Paul McCartney and John Lennon wrote a number of songs. *The Nostalgia Factory.*

The New Left and the Counterculture

Hippies seemed drawn to buses. Ken Kesey and his Merry Pranksters traveled in a 1939 International Harvest school bus. This bus, named "The Road Hog," carries members of the New Buffalo Commune in the 1968 Fourth of July parade in El Rito, New Mexico. *Lisa Law/The Image Works.*

that of any Chinatown or Little Italy. "Hashbury" inspired numerous other communal living experiments. Throughout the country, hitchhikers hit the road in search of communes, America, and themselves.

Just as the New Left attracted a minority of students, so the counterculture represented only a small proportion of American youth. But to disconcerted middle-class parents, hippies seemed to be everywhere. Parents carped about long hair, love beads, and patched jeans. They complained that "acid rock" was loud, discordant, even savage. They feared their children would suffer lifelong damage from drugs. The "generation gap" was yawning wide, but most disturbing to parents were the casual sexual mores that young people were adopting. In 1960 the government approved the birth-control pill, and use of the pill accelerated in the 1960s, especially among young people. Americans formerly had linked sexuality to romance and reproduction. In the 1960s many

Drugs and Sex

young people viewed sexuality as a means of "self-expression" and as a gauge of personal happiness. For these people, living together no longer equaled living in sin; and as attitudes toward premarital sex changed, so did notions about pornography, homosexuality, sex roles, and familial relationships.

Also in the 1960s, examples of militancy—by blacks, feminists, and antiwar protesters—helped inspire the gay rights movement. Throughout the 1950s and much of the 1960s, many homosexuals had feared that disclosing their sexual preference would cause them to lose not only their jobs but even their friends and families. In June 1969 that attitude began to change. In New York City's Greenwich Village, a riot erupted between police and the patrons of the Stonewall Inn, a gay bar on Christopher Street. Police who raided the bar were not prepared for the volley of beer bottles that greeted them. Rioting continued into the night, and graffiti calling for "Gay Power" appeared along Christopher Street.

Gay Rights Movement

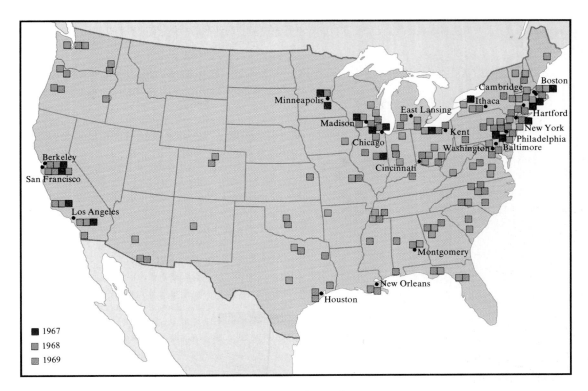

Disturbances on College and University Campuses, 1967–1969

As John D'Emilio, the historian, has written: "Stonewall thus marked a critical divide in the politics and consciousness of homosexuals and lesbians. A small, thinly spread reform effort suddenly grew into a large, grass-roots movement for liberation. The quality of gay life in America was permanently altered as a furtive subculture moved aggressively into the open."

For both cultural and political reasons, the slogan "Make Love, Not War" became popular in the 1960s. As the war in Vietnam escalated, the New Left and the counterculture discovered a common cause. Students held teach-ins on the war—open forums for discussion among students, professors, and guest speakers. Marches and demonstrations against the war became a popular protest tactic (see map and page 924). In addition to the young men who had fled the draft by moving to other countries, others protested, violently and nonviolently, at local draft board offices. Government officials expressed fears that the activities of the New Left and the counterculture threatened the nation's war-making powers.

By this time growing numbers of Americans,

young and old, had quit believing their elected leaders. President Johnson claimed the United States was fighting for honorable reasons, but people wondered what goal could justify the murder of Vietnamese women and children. As troop levels increased, many recalled ruefully that they had voted for Johnson as the more cautious of the two presidential candidates in 1964. By 1968 almost half a million American soldiers were stationed in Vietnam, and Johnson's credibility had vanished.

1968: A Year of Protest, Violence, and Loss

As stormy and violent as the years from 1963 through 1967 had been, many Americans were still trying to downplay the nation's distress in hopes it would go away. "We were in a kind of national sleepwalk," the novelist John Hersey wrote, "aware, on a dream level, of black rage; of the undertow of

Cesar Chavez provided charismatic leadership for the United Farm Workers Union and in doing so attracted the support of celebrities and political leaders, most notably Robert F. Kennedy. This poster advertises a 1968 benefit performance for the union to be held at New York City's Carnegie Hall. *Museum of American Political Life, University of Hartford. Photo by Sally Anderson-Bruce.*

Vietnam . . . of the way Lyndon Johnson's credibility gap was beginning to show." In 1968 the sleepers awoke to a series of violent quakes.

The first shock hit in late January 1968, when the U.S.S. *Pueblo,* a navy intelligence ship, was captured by the North Koreans near the port of Wonsan; not until Christmas of that year would the crew of eighty-two be released. On January 30 came the Tet offensive in Vietnam (see page 952). For the first time many Americans believed they might lose the war. Meanwhile, American casualties had been climbing. In fact, more Americans died in the first six months of 1968 than in all of 1967; on July 4, 1968, total American fatalities surpassed thirty thousand.

Controversy over the war deepened. Within the Democratic party two men rose to challenge Johnson for the 1968 presidential nomination. One of them, Senator Eugene McCarthy of Minnesota, entered the New Hampshire primary solely to contest Johnson's war policies. On March 12, McCarthy won 20 of 24 convention delegates. Soon after, another Democrat, Senator Robert F. Kennedy of New York, entered the fray.

On March 31, President Johnson went on national television and announced a scaling-down of the bombing in North Vietnam. Then he hurled a political thunderbolt—he would not be a candidate for re-election. Known to exaggerate and to wallow in self-pity, Johnson told reporters: "The only difference between the Kennedy assassination and mine is that I am alive and it has been more torturous."

Less than a week later a white assassin named James Earl Ray shot and killed Martin Luther King, Jr., in Memphis. People still wonder whether Ray

Assassination of Martin Luther King, Jr. was a deranged racist acting alone or a pawn in an organized conspiracy. Whatever his motive, his crime aroused instant rage in the nation's ghettos. Blacks rioted in 168 cities and towns, looting and burning white businesses and properties. Thirty-four blacks and five whites died in the violence. Tough talk flared from Maryland Governor Spiro Agnew, who denounced Baltimore's black leaders for not controlling "your people," and from Chicago's Mayor Richard Daley, who ordered police to shoot to kill arsonists. The terror provoked a white backlash against blacks, and hatred mounted on both sides. "When white America killed Dr. King last night, she declared war on us," charged Stokely Carmichael.

In April and May, Gallup polls reported Robert Kennedy the front-running presidential candidate among Democrats. In June he won the California

Assassination of Robert Kennedy primary. While celebrating his victory in a Los Angeles hotel, Kennedy decided to take a short cut through the kitchen to a press conference. Suddenly a young man stepped forward with a .22-caliber revolver and fired repeatedly. The assassin, it turned out, was an Arab nationalist named Sirhan Sirhan who despised Kennedy for his unwavering support of Israel.

Violence erupted in Chicago's Grant Park during the 1968 Democratic convention, as police and National Guardsmen used tear gas and clubs to stop twelve thousand protesters from marching to the convention hall. This woman finds her way blocked by National Guardsmen wearing gas masks and holding their rifles at the ready. *UPI/Bettmann Archives.*

The cumulative effect of so many assassinations made some Americans wonder and worry. Whenever a charismatic, progressive leader rose to prominence, it seemed, he was mowed down. The poor were especially grief-stricken by the assassination of Robert Kennedy because he had befriended blacks and Mexican-Americans. When Cesar Chavez led the United Farm Workers' strike against growers in 1965, Kennedy had traveled to California to stand with them. Many antiwar liberals also felt they had lost a friend in Kennedy.

Violence erupted again in August at the Democratic national convention in Chicago. The Democrats were divided, and adding to the dissension were the thousands of antiwar protesters and members of the Youth International Party ("Yippies") who had traveled to Chicago. The Chicago police force was still in the psychological grip of Mayor Daley's shoot-to-kill directive. Twelve

> **Violence at the Democratic Convention**

thousand police were assigned to twelve-hour shifts, and another twelve thousand army troops and National Guardsmen were on call with rifles, bazookas, and flame throwers. On Michigan Avenue, in front of the Conrad Hilton Hotel, they attacked, wading into ranks of demonstrators, reporters, and TV camera operators. Throughout the nation, viewers watched as club-swinging police beat protesters to the ground. When onlookers rushed to shield the injured, they too were clubbed. Inside the convention hall, Senator Abraham Ribicoff of Connecticut put aside his prepared speech to denounce "those Gestapo tactics in the streets of Chicago."

The Democratic convention nominated Vice President Hubert Humphrey (Lyndon Johnson's candidate) for president and Senator Edmund Muskie of Maine for vice president. Like Johnson and Kennedy before him, Humphrey was a political descendant of the New Deal, committed to the welfare system and supported by a coalition of northern

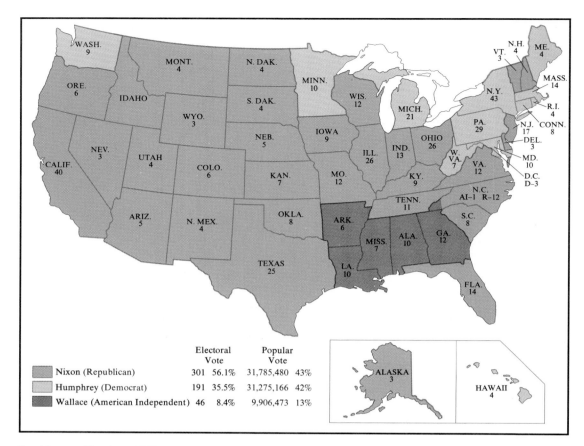

	Electoral Vote		Popular Vote	
Nixon (Republican)	301	56.1%	31,785,480	43%
Humphrey (Democrat)	191	35.5%	31,275,166	42%
Wallace (American Independent)	46	8.4%	9,906,473	13%

Presidential Election, 1968

liberals, big-city bosses, blacks, and union members. First elected to the Senate from Minnesota in 1948, Humphrey was known not just as a champion of civil rights but as a supporter of the Cold War doctrine of containment that had led to Vietnam. Humphrey's unstinting public support of the war angered some and saddened others, who repudiated him as the candidate of Johnson, Daley, and the war.

The Republicans selected Richard M. Nixon as their presidential nominee. After his defeat by John Kennedy in 1960 and his loss in the California gubernatorial race in 1962, Nixon's political career seemed to be over. But he spent much of the decade campaigning for fellow Republicans and built up credits with party regulars and office-holders around the country. In 1968 Nixon cashed in his credits and defeated Governor Nelson Rockefeller of New York and Governor Ronald Reagan of California for the nomination. For his running mate, Nixon chose Governor Spiro Agnew of Maryland.

There was little voter enthusiasm for either Humphrey or Nixon. A Gallup poll taken at the time of the convention showed that 66 percent of Americans believed the United States

> **Election of 1968**

should turn over more of the fighting to the South Vietnamese and begin withdrawing American troops. Yet both major candidates endorsed the continuation of the war while negotiations stalled in Paris. In 1968, the nation was deeply divided between the "hawks" (who favored escalation of the war) and the "doves" (who favored immediate withdrawal). The Gallup poll reported that 41 percent of the people described themselves as hawks and 41 percent as doves, with 18 percent holding no opinion.

The candidate with the most appeal for conservatives was Governor George C. Wallace of Alabama. The nominee of the American Independent party, Wallace exhorted citizens to "stand up for America," and he argued that the United States should bomb North Vietnam to rubble with nuclear weapons. He also appealed to people concerned about "law and order," code words for the suppression of protest. If a civil rights protester ever lay down in front of his car, Wallace declared, he would drive over the person.

When the votes were tabulated, Nixon emerged the winner. Just four years after the Goldwater debacle, the Republicans had captured the White House, though by the slimmest of margins. Wallace collected almost 10 million votes, or 13.5 percent of the total, the best performance by a third party since 1924. His strong showing made Nixon a minority president, elected with only 43.4 percent of the popular vote (see map). Moreover, the Democrats maintained control of the House (243 to 192) and the Senate (58 to 42).

Still, the election had been a triumph for conservatism, as the combined vote for Nixon and Wallace was 57 percent. The war had hurt the Democrats' appeal, but even more politically damaging was the party's identification with the cause of racial justice. In 1968, while Humphrey received 97 percent of the black vote, he gained only 35 percent of the white vote. Among the defectors from the New Deal coalition were northern, blue-collar, ethnic voters. "In city after city," one observer noted, "racial conflicts had destroyed the old alliance. The New Deal had unraveled block by block." Soon there would be a new president and a new decade, but Americans doubted whether they could heal the wounds of war, poverty, racism, sexism, black rage, youthful disaffection, and the shattered promise of the American dream.

The Rebirth of Feminism

During the turbulence of the 1960s, another liberation movement gained momentum, at first quietly and then on the picket line. Following the adoption of the Nineteenth Amendment in 1920, the women's rights movement had languished. But in the 1960s feminism was reborn.

The Feminine Mystique

Many women were dissatisifed with their lives, and in 1963, with the publication of *The Feminine Mystique,* they found a voice. Betty Friedan, the book's author, wrote that women across the country were deeply troubled by "the problem that has no name." Most women believed that "all they had to do was devote their lives from earliest girlhood to finding a husband and bearing children." The problem was that "this mystique of feminine fulfillment" left many wives and mothers feeling "empty" or "incomplete." Such feelings were at odds with the images conveyed by the TV advertisers, magazine writers, beauticians, and psychiatrists who had conspired to create the image of a woman "gaily content in a world of bedroom, kitchen, sex, babies and home." Any woman who was dissatisfied with such surroundings was considered neurotic. But as Friedan pointed out, the woman who spent her life in a world of children sacrificed her adult frame of reference and sometimes her very identity. Friedan quoted a young mother: "I've tried everything women are supposed to do—hobbies, gardening, pickling, canning, and being very social with my neighbors. . . . I love the kids and Bob and my home. . . . But I'm desperate. I begin to feel that I have no personality. . . . Who am I?"

Although President Kennedy had appointed only one woman to a policymaking post in his administration, she was an effective advocate of women's equal rights. Esther Peterson, assistant secretary of labor, urged Kennedy in 1961 to establish the first President's Commission on the Status of Women in the nation's history. Eleanor Roosevelt served as the commission's first chairperson. Its report, *American Women,* issued in 1963, argued that every obstacle to women's full participation in society must be removed. Interest in women's issues spread; by 1967, all fifty states had established commissions to promote women's equality. Still, little federal action had followed the release of *American Women,* and it was clear that the government was failing to enforce the gender equality provisions of the Civil Rights Act of 1964. The need for action inspired the founding in 1966 of the National Organization for Women (NOW). A reform organization, NOW battled for "equal rights in partnership with men" by lobbying for legislation and testing laws in the courts.

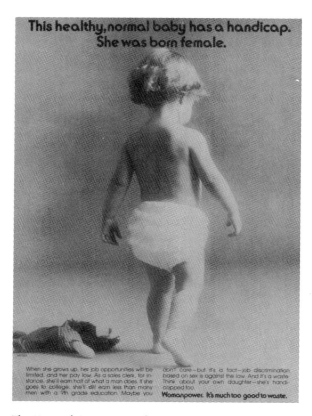

This healthy, normal baby has a handicap. She was born female.

When she grows up, her job opportunities will be limited, and her pay low. As a sales clerk, for instance, she'll earn half of what a man does. If she goes to college, she'll still earn less than many men with a 9th grade education. Maybe you don't care—but it's a fact—job discrimination based on sex is against the law. And it's a waste. Think about your own daughter—she's handicapped too.

Womanpower. It's much too good to waste.

The National Organization for Women (NOW), founded in 1966, went from one thousand members in 1967 to forty thousand members in 1974. NOW's advertisements about sexual inequality were simple and to the point. This one became a classic. *NOW Legal Defense and Education Fund, Inc.*

Not long after NOW's formation, a new generation of radical feminists emerged—once again, the baby boom was making an impact on American life. Most were white and well

Radical Feminism educated; many were the daughters of working mothers. Most had been raised in the era of sexual liberation, in which birth-control pills and other contraceptives were taken for granted. The intellectual ferment of their movement produced a new feminist literature. Feminists challenged everything from women's economic, political, and legal inequality to sexual double standards and sex-role stereotypes. And unlike the members of NOW, the radical feminists practiced direct action, as when they picketed the 1968 Miss America contest in Atlantic City. One woman auctioned off an effigy of

Miss America: "Gentlemen, I offer you the 1969 model. . . . She walks. She talks. She smiles on cue. *And* she does the housework." Into the "freedom trash can" the pickets dumped false eyelashes, curlers, girdles, and *Playboy*. These feminists were protesting the view of women as servants and sex objects. They were also practicing "personal politics." "There is no private domain of a person's life that is not political," explained Charlotte Bunch, a feminist, "and there is no political issue that is not ultimately personal."

Many radical feminists had struggled earlier for black civil rights and against the Vietnam War, but they had discovered they were second-class citizens even in movements dedicated to equality. Instead of making policy, they were expected to make coffee, take minutes, and even provide sexual favors. Radicalized but wanting to put their political energies into antisexist causes, these feminists joined in consciousness-raising groups where they discussed sensitive issues such as homosexuality and abortion. The issue of homosexuality caused a split in the women's movement, and in 1969 and 1970 NOW forced lesbians to resign from membership and offices in the organization. This rift was healed in 1971, largely because homosexuals had begun to fight back (see page 950).

For working women in the 1960s, the major problems were sex discrimination in employment, lack of professional opportunities, unequal pay for

Occupational Segregation equal work, lack of adequate day care for children, and prohibitions against abortion. In 1963 the average woman earned 63 cents for every dollar a man earned. Ten years later the figure had fallen to 57 cents. What this gender-based discrimination meant for many women was less food on the table and no new shoes for the children. An underlying cause of this pay disparity was "occupational segregation." Throughout the labor force, work was broken down into men's jobs and women's jobs, and women were concentrated in the low-paying positions. In the 1960s, the situation became even more pronounced as women flooded entry-level jobs in female-dominated fields like secretarial and clerical work. The number of women workers jumped from 23.2 million in 1960 to 31.5 million in 1970 and 34.1 million in 1972, but "men's jobs" still paid higher wages. Many women with college educations earned less than men with eighth-grade educations.

It was thus natural that two feminist goals of the 1960s were equal job opportunity and equal pay for equal work. Another goal was childcare, but here, too, opposition was widespread and intense. In December 1971 President Nixon vetoed a bill that would have set up a national system of day-care facilities for the children of working mothers. The bill, Nixon asserted, would have committed government to "communal approaches to child-rearing over against the family-centered approach," thus imperiling "the keystone of our civilization," the American family.

Despite such opposition, women made impressive gains. They entered professional schools in record numbers: from 1969 to 1973, the numbers of women law students almost quadrupled and of women medical students more than doubled. Under Title IX of the Educational Amendments of 1972, female college athletes gained the right to the same financial support as male athletes. In the same year Congress approved the Equal Rights Amendment (ERA) and sent it to the states for ratification. (The ERA stated, "Equality of rights under the law shall not be denied or abridged by the United States or by any State on account of sex.")

During these years, the Supreme Court ruled on issues essential to women. In 1973, the Court struck down state laws that made abortion a crime (*Roe* v.

Legal Advances for Women

Wade). Ruling that such laws violated a woman's right of privacy, it held that the Constitution protected a woman's decision about whether to end her pregnancy. Only in the last three months of pregnancy could a state absolutely bar abortion; otherwise, the state's power to regulate abortion was either nonexistent or subordinate to the issue of maternal health. Also the Court attacked sex discrimination. In a 1971 ruling (*Reed* v. *Reed*), it held that legislation differentiating between the sexes "must be reasonable, not arbitary," and in 1973 (*Frontiero* v. *Richardson*), several justices went a step further in declaring that "classifications based on sex," like those based on race, were "inherently suspect." As a result of these victories the women's movement gained new confidence in the 1970s. "If the 1960s belonged to the blacks, the next ten years are ours," remarked one feminist.

On July 20, 1969, four days after the Apollo 11 space mission took off for the moon, the American astronauts Neil Armstrong and Edwin Aldrin walked on the lunar surface. After a day on the moon, the pair lifted off in their module and rejoined the orbiting command ship flown by Michael Collins. All three men were welcomed home as heroes. *The Nostalgia Factory*.

Nixon and the Persistence of Chaos

Richard Nixon's presidency was born in chaos. In 1969 a hundred black students armed with rifles and shotguns seized the student union at Cornell University and occupied the building for thirty-six hours. Harvard students took over the president's office before being evicted by police. Bloody confrontations occurred at Berkeley, San Francisco State, Wisconsin, and scores of other colleges and universities. In October 1969, three hundred Weathermen, members of an SDS splinter group, raced through Chicago's downtown district, smashing windows and attacking police officers in an attempt to incite armed class struggle. A month later half a million people assembled peacefully at the Washington Monument on Moratorium Day to call for an end to the Vietnam War.

One bright spot for President Nixon in 1969 was the flight of *Apollo 11,* a manned spaceship, to the

In May 1970, at Kent State University in Ohio, National Guardsmen confront student protesters against the war. Soon afterward, with no provocation, soldiers opened fire into a group of fleeing students. Four were killed, including two women who had been walking to class. *Wide World Photos.*

moon. After separating in space from the *Apollo* craft, the lunar module reached its destination in mid-July, and on July 20 astronaut Neil Armstrong made history by taking the first step onto the moon's surface. After taking rock and soil samples, Armstrong and his flightmate Edwin Aldrin successfully rendezvoused with the *Apollo* command ship, docked, and returned to earth, splashing down 950 miles southwest of Hawaii on July 24. Led by the president, the nation cheered this accomplishment.

> **Moon Landing**

If 1969 had proved to be bloody and turbulent, 1970 would be even more so. On April 30, President Nixon appeared on television to announce that the United States had launched an "incursion" into Cambodia (see page 924), a neutral country. Protest against the war escalated at home. On May 4, national guardsmen in Ohio killed four students at

> **Kent State and Jackson State**

Kent State University. Ten days later, police and state highway patrolmen armed with automatic weapons blasted a women's dormitory at Jackson State, an all-black university in Mississippi, killing two students and wounding nine others. No evidence of student sniping could be found; the police fired no tear gas or warning shots.

While police and soldiers waged official violence in 1970, revolutionaries conducted an unofficial campaign of terror. They bombed the New York offices of Mobil Oil, IBM, General Telephone and Electronics, and various banks. In March a bomb factory exploded in Greenwich Village, blowing up at least three young revolutionaries. There were scores of politically motivated skyjackings.

Worst of all, as far as many Americans were concerned, was street crime. "Fortress America: A nation behind locked doors," proclaimed the heading of a *Newsweek* article on crime. Sales of pistols, burglar alarms, and bulletproof vests soared, as

> **Fear of Crime**

◀ Chapter 32: Reform and Conflict: A Turbulent Era in America, 1961–1973 did the demand for private guards and special police. Conservatives accused liberals of causing the crime wave by coddling criminals. "You know what a conservative is?" asked Frank Rizzo, the hard-line police-chief-turned-mayor of Philadelphia. "That's a liberal who got mugged the night before."

In the tense atmosphere, government officials sometimes overreacted. Governor Nelson Rockefeller of New York did so in September 1971 when more than a thousand inmates of the Attica State Correctional Facility seized thirty-eight guards and took over a cellblock. Rather than give in to the prisoners' demand that he visit Attica to negotiate, Rockefeller ordered state troopers, sheriff's deputies, and guards to storm the prison. Under a pall of tear gas Rockefeller's army regained control, but at a horrifying cost: twenty-nine inmates and ten hostages dead.

In the wake of this new wave of riots and violent crime, Nixon became convinced that the nation was plunging into anarchy. He worried, as had Lyndon Johnson before him, that the antiwar movement was Communist-inspired. In June 1970 he ordered the FBI, the CIA, the National Security Agency, and the Defense Intelligence Agency to formulate a coordinated attack on "internal threats." "Everything is valid," a Nixon aide told the group, "everything is possible." Had it not been for FBI Director J. Edgar Hoover's refusal to cooperate in the illegal plot, the group would have had free rein to open mail, tap telephones, and break into citizens' homes and offices.

The administration also worked to put the Democratic party on the defensive. Vice President Agnew took to the road in September to warn the country of threats to its internal **Politics of Divisiveness** security posed "by a disruptive, radical, and militant minority." The same month Jeb Stuart Magruder, a White House assistant, defined the theme of the upcoming congressional elections in a memorandum. "The Democrats should be portrayed as being on the fringes: radical liberals who . . . excuse disorder, tolerate crime, apologize for our wealth, and undercut the President's foreign policy," Magruder wrote. But Republican attempts to discredit the Democrats failed. In the election the Democrats gained nine seats in the House and dropped only two in the Senate. The Republicans lost eleven state governorships.

Nixon's fortunes declined further in 1971. On June 13 the *New York Times* began to publish the *Pentagon Papers,* a top-secret Defense Department study of the Vietnam War (see **Stagflation** page 924). Nixon also had to contend with inflation, a problem not entirely of his making. Rather, it was Lyndon Johnson's policy of guns and butter—massive deficit financing to support both the Vietnam War and the Great Society—that had fueled inflation. Not until 1967 had Johnson proposed tax increases to reduce the government deficit and dampen inflation, and not until June 1968 had Congress responded with a 10 percent tax surcharge. Johnson had also trimmed federal spending by $6 billion, but the cut was too little too late. Nixon's policies, including a $2.5 billion tax cut in late 1969, only boosted rising prices. By January 1971 the United States was suffering from a 5.3 percent inflation rate and a 6 percent unemployment rate. Soon after this period the word *stagflation* would be coined to describe this coexistence of economic recession (stagnation) and inflation.

That January, Nixon shocked both critics and allies by declaring, "I am now a Keynesian." Like his Democratic predecessors, he would try to stimulate the economy through government spending. The budget for fiscal 1971 would have a built-in deficit of $23 billion, just slightly under the all-time high of $25 billion (1968 to 1969). Then in August, in an effort to correct the nation's balance-of-payments deficit, Nixon announced he would devalue the dollar by allowing it to "float" in international money markets. Finally, to curb inflation, the president froze prices, wages, and rents for ninety days, then set limits on their increase. Nixon's commitment to the controversial wage and price controls buckled the next year under pressure from businesses and unions. Although some economists, businesspeople, and politicians argued that the controls were bound to fail, others contended that they would have been successful had they been allowed more time to work.

The wage and price controls were just one sign of what surprised observers called Nixon's "great turnabout." Another was his announcement in July 1971 that he would travel to the People's Republic of China, an enemy Nixon had denounced for years. It was clear that the president was preparing for the 1972 presidential election.

The Southern Strategy and the Election of 1972

Political observers believed that Nixon would have a hard time running for re-election on his first-term record. Having urged Americans to use "cool" words and "lower our voices," he had ordered Vice President Agnew to denounce the press and student protesters. Having espoused unity, he had practiced the politics of polarization. Having campaigned as a fiscal conservative, he had authorized near-record budget deficits. And having promised peace, he had widened the war in Southeast Asia.

Moreover, congressional accomplishments had been made more in spite of Nixon than because of him. The Democrats dominated both houses of

> **Democratic Legislative Victories**

Congress during his first term, and they continued to follow a liberal agenda. The Twenty-sixth Amendment gave eighteen-year-olds the vote; Social Security payments and food-stamp funding were increased; and the Occupational Safety and Health Administration was established. Congress responded to the growing environmental movement by passing the Clean Air Act, the Water Quality Improvement Act, and the Resource Recovery Act.

One Nixon innovation that bore fruit in 1972 was revenue sharing, a program that returned federal funds to the states to use as they saw fit. Nixon's effort to shift responsibility to state and local governments was known as the New Federalism. A less-popular program was the Family Assistance Plan, under which a family of four would receive a guaranteed income of $1,600 per year plus $860 in food stamps. (Welfare payments fell below that level in twenty states.) Michael Harrington, the author of *The Other America,* called the plan "the most radical idea since the New Deal"; most conservatives denounced it. But a handful of conservatives supported the Family Assistance Plan, arguing that simple cash payments to the poor would do away with the mammoth welfare bureaucracy. The program did not pass Congress, in part because Democrats considered the benefit payments too low.

In his campaign for re-election, Nixon was less interested in running on his record than in employing a "southern strategy" of political conserva-

> **Nixon's Southern Strategy**

tism. A product of the Sunbelt himself, Nixon was attuned to the growing political power of that conservative region. Thus he appealed to "the silent majority," the white suburbanites, blue-collar workers, Catholics, and ethnic groups of "middle America." As in the 1970 congressional elections, Nixon equated the Republican party with law and order and the Democratic party with permissiveness, crime, drugs, pornography, the hippie lifestyle, student radicalism, black militancy, feminism, homosexuality, and the dissolution of the family.

Actually, Nixon had been pursuing a southern strategy all along. A furor had arisen in February 1970 when the press published a memorandum written by Daniel Moynihan, Nixon's adviser on urban affairs and social welfare. While insisting that blacks should continue to make progress, Moynihan had recommended that "the issue of race could benefit from a period of benign neglect." Moreover, Attorney General John Mitchell had courted southern white voters by trying to delay school desegregation in Mississippi and to prevent extension of the 1965 Voting Rights Act. Mitchell sought vigorous prosecution of antiwar activists as well.

The southern strategy had also guided Nixon's nomination of Supreme Court justices. After appointing Warren Burger, a conservative federal judge, to succeed Earl Warren as chief justice, Nixon had selected two southerners to serve as associate justices. One of them was a segregationist. When the Senate declined to confirm either nominee, Nixon protested angrily, "I understand the bitter feelings of millions of Americans who live in the South." By 1972, however, the president had managed to appoint three more conservatives to the Supreme Court. Ironically, the new appointees did not always vote as Nixon would have wished. The Court's decisions on abortion, publication of the *Pentagon Papers,* the death sentence, wiretapping, and busing for school desegregation all ran counter to Nixon's politics.

The Court was at the center of one of the most emotional issues of the 1972 election: busing. In 1971, in *Swann* v. *Charlotte-Mecklenburg,* the justices had upheld a desegregation plan that required a school system in North Carolina to work toward racial integration through massive crosstown busing. The decision generated widespread protest. In

March 1972, Governor George Wallace of Alabama won the Democratic primary in Florida after taking a strong antibusing stand. Three days later Nixon proposed that Congress pass a busing moratorium, and he appeared on television to denounce busing as a reckless and extreme remedy for segregation. Although Nixon's response to busing was a well-planned part of his southern strategy, his stand clearly appealed to northern whites as well.

Besides Wallace, Democratic candidates for the 1972 presidential nomination included Senators Hubert Humphrey, Edward Kennedy, George McGovern, and Edmund Muskie.

> **Election of 1972** After his defeat by Nixon in 1968, Humphrey inspired little enthusiasm. For many Americans, Kennedy had ceased to be a contender in 1969, when he left the scene of an accident at Chappaquiddick, near Martha's Vineyard, in which a woman passenger in his car drowned. Senator Muskie fell victim to a dirty trick, a forged letter published during the New Hampshire primary that accused the senator of laughing at disparaging remarks about Canadian-Americans. When the letter and other slurs brought Muskie to the point of tears in public, he too ceased to be a serious candidate. Governor Wallace was shot and paralyzed by a disturbed young man and began a long convalescence. After his shooting the right-wing law-and-order vote had no place to turn but to Nixon. Meanwhile, Senator McGovern won several primaries and arrived at the Democratic convention with enough votes for the nomination.

Nixon campaigned by assuming the elevated role of world statesman: in February 1972 he traveled to China and in May to the Soviet Union. Both trips were elaborately staged and televised for maximum political effect. But it was the campaign waged by George McGovern that handed victory to the Republicans. When McGovern committed himself to a $30 billion cut in the defense budget, people began to fear he was a neo-isolationist who would reduce the United States to a second-rate power. McGovern's proposals split the Democrats between his supporters—blacks, feminists, antiwar activists, young militants—and old-guard urban bosses, labor and ethnic leaders, and white southerners.

Much to Nixon's advantage was the rumor that the Vietnam War was near its end. Troops were being pulled out; by September 1972 the death rate was almost zero. Then in late October, less than two weeks before the election, Henry Kissinger an-

During the 1972 presidential election, thousands of college students and antiwar activists campaigned for Senator George McGovern. These volunteers in "McGovern's army" helped the senator to win important primary elections in several states. These supporters came to Miami, site of the 1972 Democratic National Convention. *Burt Glinn/Magnum.*

nounced a breakthrough in the peace negotiations. "Peace is at hand," he proclaimed. The announcement proved inaccurate but helped persuade some people to vote for Nixon.

Nixon's victory in November was overwhelming. He polled 47 million votes, 60.7 percent of the votes cast. McGovern received only 29 million and

> **Nixon's Landslide Victory** won in just one state, Massachusetts, and the District of Columbia. Nixon's southern strategy was supremely successful: he carried all of the Deep South, which had once been solidly Democratic. He also gained a majority of the urban vote, winning over such long-time Democrats as blue-collar workers, Catholics, and ethnics. Only blacks, Jews, and low-income voters stuck by the Democrats. Remarkably, the Democrats retained control of both houses of Congress and won two additional seats in the Senate. Democratic voters were becoming independent,

resorting to ticket-splitting when they perceived a Democratic candidate to be unacceptable.

Americans' outlook was different in 1973 from what it had been in 1961. "Americans," the journalist Godfrey Hodgson explained, "had gone into the age of Kennedy and Nixon convinced that their government's action . . . could make over the world, at home and abroad. Now they had been burned." They had learned that it was much harder to change the world than their leaders had told them it would be. They had learned too "that there was moral ambiguity where they had once thought the issues of right and wrong were clearest . . . and that there seemed little that political action could achieve, however idealistic its intentions, without evoking unforeseen and unwanted reaction."

When John F. Kennedy delivered his inaugural address in 1961, he had challenged Americans to "pay any price, bear any burden, meet any hardship" to defend freedom and inspire the world. Twelve years later, Richard M. Nixon echoed that rhetoric: "Let us pledge to make these four years the best four years in America's history, so that on its 200th birthday America will be as young and vital as when it began, and as bright a beacon of hope for all the world." Largely because of the president's own actions, however, the next four years would be among the most dismal in the nation's history. As for Nixon, he would resign the presidency before the nation celebrated its bicentennial in 1976.

Suggestions for Further Reading

The 1960s

William H. Chafe, *The Unfinished Journey: America Since World War II* (1986); Richard N. Goodwin, *Remembering America* (1988); Godfrey Hodgson, *America in Our Time* (1976); Allen J. Matusow, *The Unraveling of America: A History of Liberalism in the 1960s* (1984); Charles R. Morris, *A Time of Passion: America, 1960–1980* (1984); Geoffrey O'Brien, *Dream Time* (1988); William O'Neill, *Coming Apart* (1971); Tom Shachtman, *Decade of Shocks: Dallas to Watergate, 1963–1974* (1983); Milton Viorst, *Fire in the Streets* (1979); Theodore H. White, *America in Search of Itself: The Making of the President, 1954–1980* (1982).

The Kennedy Administration

Thomas Brown, *JFK: History of an Image* (1988); David Burner, *John F. Kennedy and a New Generation* (1988); Henry Fairlie, *The Kennedy Promise* (1973); David Halberstam, *The Best and the Brightest* (1972); Jim F. Heath, *Decade of Disillusionment: The Kennedy-Johnson Years* (1975); Bruce Miroff, *Pragmatic Illusions: The Presidential Politics of John F. Kennedy* (1976); Herbert S. Parmet, *J.F.K.—The Presidency of John F. Kennedy* (1983); Arthur M. Schlesinger, Jr., *Robert Kennedy and His Times* (1978); Arthur M. Schlesinger, Jr., *A Thousand Days: John F. Kennedy in the White House* (1965); Theodore C. Sorenson, *Kennedy* (1965); Gary Wills, *The Kennedy Imprisonment* (1982).

The Kennedy Assassination

Edward Jay Epstein, *Legend: The Secret World of Lee Harvey Oswald* (1978); Henry Hurt, *Reasonable Doubt* (1985); Michael L. Kurtz, *Crime of the Century* (1982); Anthony Summers, *Conspiracy* (1980).

Lyndon Johnson and the Great Society

Vaughn D. Bornet, *The Presidency of Lyndon B. Johnson* (1983); Paul K. Conkin, *Big Daddy from the Pedernales: Lyndon Baines Johnson* (1986); Ronnie Dugger, *The Politician* (1982); Lyndon B. Johnson, *The Vantage Point* (1971); Doris Kearns, *Lyndon Johnson and the American Dream* (1976); Sar A. Levitan and Robert Taggart, *The Promise of Greatness* (1976); Charles Murray, *Losing Ground: American Social Policy, 1950–1980* (1983); James T. Patterson, *America's Struggle Against Poverty, 1900–1985* (1986); John E. Schwarz, *America's Hidden Success: A Reassessment of Twenty Years of Public Policy* (1983); Carl Solberg, *Hubert Humphrey* (1984).

Civil Rights and Black Power

Carl M. Brauer, *John F. Kennedy and the Second Reconstruction* (1977); Clayborne Carson, *In Struggle: SNCC and the Black Awakening of the 1960s* (1981); William H. Chafe, *Civilities and Civil Rights: Greensboro, North Carolina, and the Black Struggle for Freedom* (1980); Charles E. Fager, *Selma 1965*, rev. ed. (1985); David J. Garrow, *Bearing the Cross: Martin Luther King, Jr., and the Southern Christian Leadership Conference* (1986); Doug McAdam, *Freedom Summer* (1988); Malcolm X and Alex Haley, *The Autobiography of Malcolm X* (1965); August Meier and Elliott Rudwick, *CORE* (1973); Robert J. Norrell, *Reaping the Whirlwind: The Civil Rights Movement in Tuskegee* (1985); Stephen B. Oates, *Let the Trumpet Sound: The Life of Martin Luther King, Jr.* (1982); Howell Raines, *My Soul Is Rested* (1977); Harvard Sitkoff, *The Struggle for Black Equality, 1954–1980* (1981).

Warren Court

Alexander M. Bickel, *The Supreme Court and the Idea of Progress* (1970); Gerald Dunne, *Hugo Black and the Judicial Revolution* (1977); G. Theodore Mitau, *Decade of Decision: The Supreme Court and the Constitutional Revolution, 1954–1964* (1967); Bernard Schwartz, *Super Chief: Earl Warren and His Supreme Court* (1983); G. Edward White, *Earl Warren* (1982).

The New Left and the Antiwar Movement

Wini Breines, *The Great Refusal: Community and Organization in the New Left* (1983); Todd Gitlin, *The Sixties: Years of Hope, Days of Rage* (1987); Todd Gitlin, *The Whole World Is Watching: Mass Media in the Making and Unmaking of the New Left* (1980); James Miller, *"Democracy Is in the Streets": From Port Huron to the Siege of Chicago* (1987); Thomas Powers, *Vietnam, the War at Home* (1984); W. J. Rorabaugh, *Berkeley at War* (1989); Kirkpatrick Sale, *SDS* (1973); Sohnya Sayres et al., eds., *The 60s, Without Apology* (1984); Nancy Zaroulis and Gerald Sullivan, *Who Spoke Up? American Protest Against the War in Vietnam, 1963–1975* (1984).

The Counterculture

Stanley Booth, *Dance with the Devil: The Rolling Stones and Their Times* (1984); Morris Dickstein, *Gates of Eden: American Culture in the Sixties* (1977); Michael Medved and David Wallechinsky, *What Really Happened to the Class of '65?* (1976); Philip Norman, *Shout! The Beatles in Their Generation* (1981); Charles Perry, *The Haight-Ashbury* (1984); Charles Reich, *The Greening of America* (1970); Theodore Roszak, *The Making of a Counter Culture* (1969); Philip Slater, *The Pursuit of Loneliness,* rev. ed. (1976); Jon Weiner, *Come Together: John Lennon in His time* (1984); Tom Wolfe, *The Electric Kool-Aid Acid Test* (1968).

The Rebirth of Feminism

William H. Chafe, *The American Woman: Her Changing Social, Economic, and Political Role, 1920–1970* (1972); Sara Evans, *Personal Politics* (1978); Marian Faux, *Roe v. Wade* (1988); Shulamith Firestone, *The Dialectic of Sex* (1970); Jo Freeman, *The Politics of Women's Liberation* (1975); Betty Friedan, *The Feminine Mystique* (1963); Judith Hole and Ellen Levine, *Rebirth of Feminism* (1971); Alice Kessler-Harris, *Out to Work: A History of Wage-Earning Women in the United States* (1982); Kate Millett, *Sexual Politics* (1970); Robin Morgan, ed., *Sisterhood Is Powerful* (1970); Sheila M. Rothman, *Women's Proper Place* (1978); Gayle Graham Yates, *What Women Want: The Ideas of the Movement* (1975).

Year of Shocks: 1968

David Caute, *The Year of the Barricades* (1988); Lewis Chester et al., *An American Melodrama: The Presidential Campaign of 1968* (1969); David Farber, *Chicago '68* (1988); Ronald Fraser et al., *1968: A Student Generation in Revolt* (1988); Charles Kaiser, *1968 in America* (1988); George Katsiaficas, *The Imagination of the New Left: A Global Analysis of 1968* (1987); Hans Koning, *Nineteen Sixty-Eight* (1987); Theodore H. White, *The Making of the President, 1968* (1969).

The Nixon Administration

Daniel P. Moynihan, *The Politics of a Guaranteed Income* (1973); Richard M. Nixon, *RN: The Memoirs of Richard Nixon* (1978); Leon E. Panetta and Peter Gall, *Bring Us Together: The Nixon Team and the Civil Rights Retreat* (1971); Kevin Phillips, *The Emerging Republican Majority* (1969); Raymond Price, *With Nixon* (1977); James A. Reichley, *Conservatives in an Era of Change: The Nixon and Ford Administrations* (1981); Jonathan Schell, *The Time of Illusion* (1975); Leonard Silk, *Nixonomics* (1972); Herbert Stein, *Presidential Economics* (1984); Garry Wills, *Nixon Agonistes* (1970).